WEBSTER'S NEW SPANISH-ENGLISH ENGLISH-SPANISH DICTIONARY

Published by
The Popular Group, LLC
1700 Broadway
New York, NY 10019

Publishing Consultant: Charles M. Levine
Design and Composition: Charlotte Staub

Published by arrangement with K DICTIONARIES LTD
http://kdictionaries.com

FOR K DICTIONARIES
Project Manager: Ilan J. Kernerman
Editor: Juan José García Pañero
Database Administrator: Vladimír Benko

ISBN: 1-59027-079-7

Printed in the United States of America

9 8 7 6 5 4 3 2

SPANISH-ENGLISH DICTIONARY

A

a *prep.* **1.** to **2.** into **3.** in **4.** at **5.** on **6.** with
abad *noun m.* abbot
abadesa *noun f.* abbess
abadía *noun f.* abbey
abajo *adv.* **1.** down **2.** downstairs **3.** below **4.** under **5.** beneath
—**cuesta abajo** downhill
—**hacia abajo** downward
abajo *interj.* down with!
abalanzarse *verb.* to rush forward
abandonado, -da *adj.* **1.** abandoned, deserted **2.** derelict **3.** neglected
abandonar *verb.* **1.** to abandon **2.** desert **3.** leave **4.** neglect **5.** give up **6.** renounce
—**abandonarse a** to abandon oneself to
abandono *noun m.* **1.** abandonment **2.** neglect **3.** withdrawal, resignation
abanicar *verb.* to fan
abanico *noun m.* fan
abaratar *verb.* to lower the price of
abarcar *verb.* **1.** to cover **2.** include
abarrotado, -da *adj.* **1.** packed **2.** crowded
abarrotar *verb.* to pack
abastecer *verb.* **1.** to supply **2.** provide **3.** stock
abastecimiento *noun m.* **1.** supply, provision **2.** supplying
abatido, -da *adj.* depressed
abatir *verb.* **1.** to knock down, demolish **2.** depress
abdicar *verb.* to abdicate
abdomen *noun m.* abdomen
abdominal *adj.* abdominal
abecé *noun m.* ABC
abecedario *noun m.* alphabet
abeja *noun f.* bee
abertura *noun f.* **1.** opening **2.** hole
abiertamente *adv.* openly
abierto, -ta *adj.* open
abofetear *verb.* to slap
abogado, -da *noun.* lawyer, attorney
abolición *noun f.* abolition
abolir *verb.* to abolish
abolladura *noun f.* dent
abonar *verb.* **1.** to pay **2.** fertilize
—**abonarse** to subscribe
abono *noun m.* **1.** payment, installment **2.** fertilizer, manure **3.** subscription, season ticket
abordar *verb.* **1.** to tackle **2.** deal with
aborrecer *verb.* to loathe, hate
abortar *verb.* **1.** to abort, foil, frustrate **2.** have an abortion, have a miscarriage
aborto *noun m.* **1.** abortion **2.** miscarriage
abrazadera *noun f.* brace, clamp
abrazar *verb.* **1.** to embrace, hug **2.** adopt
abrazo *noun m.* embrace, hug
abreviatura *noun f.* abbreviation
abrigar *verb.* **1.** to shelter, protect **2.** keep warm **3.** cherish, harbor
—**abrigarse 1.** to take shelter **2.** wrap oneself up
abrigo *noun m.* **1.** coat **2.** shelter
abril *noun m.* April
abrillantar *verb.* to polish
abrir *verb.* **1.** to open **2.** unlock **3.** undo
abrochar *verb.* to button, fasten
—**abrocharse** to button, tie up
abrumador, -dora *adj.* devastating, overwhelming, crushing
abrumar *verb.* **1.** to overwhelm **2.** oppress
abrupto, -ta *adj.* abrupt
absolutamente *adv.* absolutely
absoluto, -ta *adj.* absolute
—**en absoluto** not at all
absolver *verb.* **1.** to absolve **2.** acquit, clear

absorber *verb.* to absorb, soak up
absorción *noun f.* absorption
absorto, -ta *adj.* absorb
abstracto, -ta *adj.* abstract
absurdo, -da *adj.* absurd
abuela *noun f.* grandmother
abuelo *noun m.* grandfather
—**abuelos** grandparents
abultar *verb.* to bulge
abundancia *noun f.* abundance
abundante *adj.* abundant, plentiful
abundar *verb.* to abound, be plentiful
aburrido, -da *adj.* **1.** boring, tedious **2.** bored, fed up
aburrimiento *noun m.* boredom, tedium
aburrir *verb.* to bore
—**aburrirse** to be bored, get bored
abusar (de) *verb.* **1.** to abuse **2.** take advantage of
abuso *noun m.* abuse
acá *adv.* here, over here
acabado *noun m.* finish
acabado, -da *adj.* finished, done, complete, over
acabar *verb.* to finish, complete, end
—**acabarse 1.** to finish, come to an end **2.** run out
—**acabar de** to just have
academia *noun f.* academy
académico, -ca *noun.* academic, academician
académico, -ca *adj.* academic
acallar *verb.* to quiet, silence
acalorado, -da *adj.* heated
acalorarse *verb.* **1.** to get hot **2.** get worked up, get excited
acampar *verb.* to camp
acantilado *noun m.* cliff
acariciar *verb.* to caress, stroke, pet
acarrear *verb.* **1.** to carry, haul **2.** bring, give rise to
acaso *adv.* perhaps
—**por si acaso** just in case
acceder *verb.* **1.** to agree **2.** access, gain access to
accesible *adj.* accessible, attainable
acceso *noun m.* **1.** access, entry **2.** admittance, entrance
accesorio *noun m.* accessory
accidentado, -da *adj.* **1.** rough, uneven **2.** troubled, eventful
accidental *adj.* accidental
accidente *noun m.* accident
acción *noun m.* **1.** action **2.** act, deed **3.** share, stock
accionista *noun mf.* shareholder, stockholder
ace *noun m.* ace
acebo *noun m.* holly
aceite *noun m.* oil
aceituna *noun f.* olive
aceleración *noun f.* acceleration
acelerado, -da *adj.* intensive, accelerated
acelerar *verb.* **1.** to accelerate, speed up **2.** hasten **3.** hurry
acento *noun m.* **1.** accent **2.** stress, emphasis
acentuar *verb.* **1.** to accent **2.** stress, emphasize
aceptable *adj.* acceptable
aceptación *noun f.* acceptance
aceptar *verb.* **1.** to accept **2.** approve
acera *noun f.* sidewalk
acerca de *prep.* about
acercamiento *noun m.* **1.** approach **2.** rapprochement
acercar *verb.* **1.** to bring closer **2.** take
—**acercarse** to approach, get closer
acero *noun m.* steel
acertado, -da *adj.* correct, accurate
achaque *noun m.* ailment, malady
ácido *noun m.* acid
ácido, -da *adj.* sour, acid
acierto *noun m.* **1.** correct answer **2.** good hit
aclamación *noun f.* acclaim, acclamation
aclamar *verb.* to acclaim, cheer
aclaración *noun f.* clarification, explanation
aclarar *verb.* **1.** to clarify, explain **2.** lighten **3.** rinse
—**aclararse 1.** to become clear **2.** clear up
acogedor, -dora *adj.* cozy, friendly
acoger *verb.* **1.** to take in, receive, welcome **2.** host
—**acogerse** to take refuge

acogida *noun f.* **1.** reception, welcome **2.** refuge, shelter
acolchar *verb.* to pad
acometer *verb.* **1.** to undertake, tackle **2.** attack
acomodado, -da *adj.* **1.** suitable, appropriate **2.** well-off, well-to-do
acomodar *verb.* to accommodate, make room for
—**acomodarse** to adapt to
acompañamiento *noun m.* accompaniment
acompañante *noun mf.* **1.** companion **2.** accompanist
acompañar *verb.* **1.** to accompany **2.** go with
acondicionador *noun m.* conditioner
acondicionar *verb.* to arrange
aconsejable *adj.* advisable
aconsejar *verb.* to advise, counsel
acontecer *verb.* to occur, happen
acontecimiento *noun m.* event
acoplar *verb.* to connect, couple
acordar *verb.* to agree, resolve
—**acordarse** to remember
acorde *noun m.* chord
acorralar *verb.* **1.** to corner **2.** corral
acortar *verb.* to shorten, reduce
—**acortarse** to get shorter
acosar *verb.* to harass, hound
acoso *noun m.* harassment
acostarse *verb.* **1.** to go to bed **2.** lie down
acostumbrado, -da *adj.* **1.** accustomed **2.** usual, customary
acostumbrar *verb.* to accustom
—**acostumbrarse** to get accustomed, get used
acrecentar *verb.* to increase
acreedor, -dora *noun.* creditor
acribillar *verb.* to pepper
acta *noun f.* **1.** certificate **2.** minutes **3.** proceedings
actitud *noun f.* **1.** attitude **2.** posture
activamente *adv.* actively
activar *verb.* **1.** to activate **2.** stimulate
actividad *noun f.* **1.** activity **2.** work
activo, -va *adj.* active
acto *noun m.* act, deed
actor *noun m.* actor
actriz *noun f.* actress
actuación *noun f.* performance
actual *adj.* **1.** current, present **2.** topical **3.** up-to-date
actualidad *noun f.* **1.** present time **2.** current affairs, news
—**en la actualidad** nowadays, currently, at present
actualizado, -da *adj.* up-to-date
actualizar *verb.* **1.** to update, to bring up to date **2.** upgrade
actualmente *adv.* **1.** currently **2.** nowadays **3.** presently
actuar *verb.* to act, perform
acuario *noun m.* aquarium
acuartelar *verb.* to quarter
acuchillar *verb.* to knife, stab
acudir *verb.* to go, come
—**acudir a** to turn to
acuerdo *noun m.* agreement, deal, understanding
—**de acuerdo** OK, all right
—**de acuerdo con** in accordance to
—**estar de acuerdo** to agree
acumulación *noun f.* accumulation
acumular *verb.* to accumulate, amass, gather
—**acumularse** to pile up
acumulativo, -va *adj.* cumulative
acunar *verb.* to cradle, rock
acuñar *verb.* to coin, mint
acusación *noun f.* **1.** accusation, charge **2.** prosecution
acusado, -da *noun.* defendant
acusado, -da *adj.* marked, pronounced
acusador, -dora *noun.* **1.** accuser **2.** prosecutor
acusar *verb.* to accuse, charge
acusica *noun mf.* sneak, tattler
acústica *noun f.* acoustics
adaptación *noun f.* adaptation
adaptar *verb.* **1.** to adapt **2.** adjust
—**adaptarse** to conform, adapt
adecuadamente *adv.* appropriately
adecuado, -da *adj.* appropriate
adecuar *verb.* to adapt
adelantado, -da *adj.* **1.** advanced **2.** fast
—**por adelantado** in advance

adelantar *verb.* **1.** to advance **2.** move forward **3.** pass
—**adelantarse a** to anticipate
adelante *adv.* forward
—**más adelante** further on, later on
adelanto *noun m.* **1.** advance, progress **2.** advance payment
adelgazar *verb.* **1.** to lose weight **2.** thin
ademán *noun m.* gesture
además *adv.* also, besides, furthermore, moreover
—**además de** besides, as well as
adentro *adv.* inside, within
aderezar *verb.* to season, dress
adherir *verb.* to adhere, stick
—**adherirse a** to join
adicción *noun f.* addiction
adición *noun f.* addition
adicional *adj.* additional
adicto, -ta *noun.* addict
adiós *noun m.* goodbye, farewell
¡adiós! *interj.* goodbye!
adivinanza *noun f.* riddle
adivinar *verb.* **1.** to guess **2.** foretell, predict
adjetivo *noun m.* adjective
adjudicar *verb.* to award
adjuntar *verb.* to attach, enclose
adjunto, -ta *noun.* assistant, deputy
adjunto, -ta *adj.* attached, enclosed
administración *noun f.* **1.** administration **2.** management
—**administración pública** public administration
administrador, -dora *noun.* administrator, manager
administrar *verb.* **1.** to manage, run **2.** administer
administrativo, -va *adj.* administrative
admirable *adj.* admirable
admiración *noun f.* admiration
admirador, -dora *noun.* admirer
admirar *verb.* to admire
admisible *adj.* acceptable
admisión *noun f.* admission
admitir *verb.* **1.** to admit **2.** acknowledge, concede **3.** allow, permit
adolescente *noun mf.* adolescent, teenager
adolescente *adj.* adolescent, teenage
adonde *adv.* where
—**adónde** where?
adondequiera *adv.* wherever, anywhere
adopción *noun f.* adoption
adoptar *verb.* **1.** to adopt **2.** take
adoptivo, -va *adj.* **1.** adopted (son) **2.** adoptive (parents)
adoquín *noun m.* paving stone, cobblestone
adoquinar *verb.* to pave, cobble
adoración *noun f.* adoration, worship
adorar *verb.* to adore, worship
adornar *verb.* **1.** to adorn, decorate **2.** trim
adorno *noun m.* ornament
adquirir *verb.* **1.** to acquire, gain **2.** purchase
adquisición *noun f.* **1.** acquisition **2.** purchase
aduana *noun f.* customs, customs office
adular *verb.* to flatter
adulterar *verb.* to adulterate
adulterio *noun m.* adultery
adulto, -ta *noun. adj.* adult
advenimiento *noun m.* advent
adverbio *noun m.* adverb
adversario, -ria *noun.* adversary, opponent
adverso, -sa *adj.* adverse, unfavorable
advertencia *noun f.* warning, caution
advertir *verb.* **1.** to warn, caution **2.** notice
adyacente *adj.* adjacent
aéreo, -rea *adj.* aerial, air
aeronáutica *noun f.* aeronautics
aeronave *noun f.* aircraft
aeropuerto *noun m.* airport
afable *adj.* affable
afán *noun m.* eagerness, desire
afectación *noun f.* affectation, pose
afectado, -da *adj.* **1.** affected **2.** afflicted
afectar *verb.* **1.** to affect **2.** feign
afecto *noun m.* affection
afectuoso, -sa *adj.* affectionate
afeitado *noun m.* shave
afeitar *verb.* to shave
—**afeitarse** to shave, have a shave

aferrarse *verb.* to cling
afición *noun f.* **1.** fondness, liking, taste **2.** hobby, pastime
—**la afición** the fans
aficionado, -da *noun.* **1.** lover, enthusiast **2.** amateur **3.** fan, supporter
aficionado, -da *adj.* **1.** enthusiastic, keen **2.** amateur
afilado, -da *adj.* sharp
afiliación *noun f.* membership, affiliation
afiliado, -da *noun.* member
afiliarse *verb.* to join, affiliate
afinar *verb.* to tune
afinidad *noun f.* affinity, similarity
afirmación *noun f.* affirmation, assertion
afirmar *verb.* to affirm, assert
afirmativo, -va *adj.* affirmative
aflicción *noun f.* affliction, grief, sorrow
afligido, -da *adj.* grief-stricken, sorrowful
afligir *verb.* **1.** to afflict **2.** distress
aflojar *verb.* to loosen, slacken
aforo *noun m.* capacity
afortunadamente *adv.* fortunately, luckily
afortunado, -da *adj.* fortunate, lucky
África *noun f.* Africa
africano, -na *noun. adj.* African
afrontar *verb.* to confront, face up to
afuera *adv.* **1.** out **2.** outside
afueras *noun f. plural.* outskirts
agachar *verb.* to lower, bend
—**agacharse** to crouch, squat, bend down
agalla *noun f.* gill
agarrar *verb.* **1.** to hold, seize, grab, grasp **2.** catch
—**agarrarse 1.** to hold on, cling **2.** have a fight
agarre *noun m.* grip
agazaparse *verb.* **1.** to crouch **2.** hide
agencia *noun f.* agency, bureau
agenda *noun f.* **1.** agenda **2.** address book
agente *noun mf.* agent
—**agente de bolsa** stockbroker
—**agente inmobiliario** estate agent
ágil *adj.* agile, nimble
agitación *noun f.* agitation
agitado, -da *adj.* agitated, excited
agitar *verb.* **1.** to shake, agitate **2.** wave, flap
—**agitarse 1.** to stir **2.** toss
aglomeración *noun f.* **1.** agglomeration **2.** crowd
agobiante *adj.* overwhelming
agobiar *verb.* to overwhelm
agolparse *verb.* to crowd together
agonía *noun f.* agony, death throes
agosto *noun m.* August
agotado, -da *adj.* **1.** tired **2.** exhausted **3.** sold out
agotador, -dora *adj.* exhausting
agotamiento *noun m.* exhaustion
agotar *verb.* **1.** to tire out, wear out **2.** exhaust
—**agotarse 1.** to get exhausted, tire oneself out, wear oneself out **2.** sell out
agradable *adj.* agreeable, pleasant
agradar *verb.* to be pleasing, please, like
agradecer *verb.* **1.** to thank **2.** be grateful for
agradecido, -da *adj.* grateful
agradecimiento *noun m.* gratitude
agraviar *verb.* to offend, insult
agravio *noun m.* **1.** offense, insult **2.** grievance
agredir *verb.* **1.** to assault **2.** attack
agregar *verb.* to add
agresión *noun f.* **1.** aggression **2.** assault, attack
agresividad *noun f.* aggressiveness
agresivo, -va *adj.* aggressive
agresor, -sora *noun.* **1.** aggressor **2.** assailant, attacker
agreste *adj.* wild
agriar *verb.* to sour
—**agriarse** to turn sour
agrícola *adj.* agricultural
agricultor, -ora *noun.* farmer
agricultura *noun f.* agriculture, farming
agrietado, -da *adj.* cracked
agrietar *verb.* to crack
agrio, -gria *adj.* sour
agrupación *noun f.* group, association
agrupar *verb.* to group
—**agruparse** to gather together

agua *noun f.* water
—**agua corriente** running water
—**agua dulce** fresh water
—**agua mineral** mineral water
—**agua oxigenada** hydrogen peroxide
—**aguas residuales** sewage
aguado, -da *adj.* watered down, diluted
aguafiestas *noun mf.* killjoy, spoilsport
aguantar *verb.* **1.** to bear, endure, withstand **2.** hold
—**aguantarse** to restrain oneself
aguante *noun m.* **1.** tolerance, patience **2.** endurance
aguardar *verb.* to wait for, await
aguardiente *noun m.* brandy
agudeza *noun f.* **1.** sharpness, acuteness **2.** wit, wittiness
agudizarse *verb.* to intensify, sharpen
agudo, -da *adj.* **1.** sharp, acute **2.** high, high-pitched **3.** clever, witty
aguijón *noun m.* **1.** sting **2.** goad
águila *noun f.* eagle
aguja *noun f.* needle
agujerear *verb.* to pierce, make holes in
agujero *noun m.* hole
ah *interj.* ah!, oh!
ahí *adv.* there
ahogar *verb.* **1.** to drown **2.** choke
ahora *adv.* **1.** now **2.** presently
—**ahora mismo** right now
—**hasta ahora** so far
ahorcar *verb.* to hang
ahorita *adv.* right now
ahorrador, -dora *adj.* thrifty
ahorrar *verb.* to save
ahorro *noun m.* saving
ahumado, -da *adj.* smoked
ahumar *verb.* to smoke
ahuyentar *verb.* to chase away
aire *noun m.* air
—**aire acondicionado** air conditioning
airear *verb.* to air
aislado, -da *adj.* isolated
aislamiento *noun m.* **1.** isolation **2.** insulation
ajardinar *verb.* to landscape
ajedrez *noun m.* chess
ajeno, -na *adj.* **1.** alien **2.** of another, of others
—**ajeno a** alien to, foreign to
ajo *noun m.* garlic
ajustado, -da *adj.* **1.** tight, tight-fitting **2.** close
ajustar *verb.* **1.** to adjust **2.** fit, tighten
—**ajustarse** **1.** to adjust, fit **2.** conform
ajuste *noun m.* adjustment
al *cont.* (See a. Contraction of a and el)
ala *noun f.* wing
alabanza *noun f.* praise
alabar *verb.* to praise
alambre *noun m.* wire
alarde *noun m.* display, show
alardear *verb.* to boast, brag
alargar *verb.* **1.** to lengthen, stretch **2.** prolong, extend
alarido *noun m.* howl, yell, scream
alarma *noun f.* alarm
alarmante *adj.* alarming
alarmar *verb.* to alarm
alba *noun f.* dawn
albañil *noun mf.* mason, construction worker
albedrío *noun m.* will
albergue *noun m.* **1.** lodging, hostel **2.** shelter, refuge
alboroto *noun m.* **1.** disturbance **2.** riot
álbum *noun m.* album
alcalde, -desa *noun.* mayor
alcance *noun m.* **1.** reach, scope **2.** range **3.** extent
alcanzar *verb.* **1.** to reach **2.** catch up with **3.** achieve, attain **4.** suffice, be enough
alcoba *noun f.* bedroom
alcohol *noun m.* alcohol
alcohólico, -ca *noun. adj.* alcoholic
aldeano, -na *noun.* villager
aleatorio, -ria *adj.* random
alegación *noun f.* allegation
alegar *verb.* **1.** to allege **2.** plead **3.** argue
alegato *noun m.* **1.** plea **2.** argument, dispute
alegrar *verb.* **1.** to cheer up, make happy **2.** liven up
—**alegrarse** to be glad, be happy
alegre *adj.* **1.** glad, cheerful, happy **2.** bright **3.** lively **4.** merry

alegremente *adv.* cheerfully, happily
alegría *noun f.* happiness, joy
alejado, -da *adj.* remote, distant
alejar *verb.* to move away
—**alejarse** to go away, move away
alemán, -mana *noun. adj.* German
Alemania *noun f.* Germany
alentador, -dora *adj.* encouraging
alentar *verb.* to encourage
alergia *noun f.* allergy
alerta *noun f.* alert
alerta *adj.* alert, watchful
alertar *verb.* to alert
aleta *noun f.* fin
alevín *noun m.* **1.** youngster, novice **2.** fry, young fish
alfabeto *noun m.* alphabet
alfarería *noun f.* pottery
alfarero, -ra *noun.* potter
alférez *noun mf.* second lieutenant
alfil *noun m.* bishop
alfiler *noun m.* **1.** pin **2.** brooch
alfombra *noun f.* carpet
alfombrilla *noun f.* rug, mat
alga *noun f.* alga
algo *adv.* somewhat, rather
algo *pron.* something, anything
—**algo de** some, a little
algodón *noun m.* cotton
alguacil *noun mf.* sheriff, constable
alguien *pron.* **1.** somebody, someone **2.** anybody, anyone
algún *adj.* (see alguno. Used before masculine singular nouns)
alguno, -na *adj.* **1.** some, any **2.** not any, not at all (in negative sentences)
—**algunas veces** sometimes
alguno, -na *pron.* someone, somebody
—**alguno que otro** a few
—**algunos, -nas** some
alhaja *noun f.* jewel
aliado, -da *noun.* ally
aliado, -da *adj.* allied
alianza *noun f.* **1.** alliance **2.** covenant
aliarse *verb.* to form an alliance, to ally oneself (with)
aliciente *noun m.* incentive
aliento *noun m.* **1.** breath **2.** courage, strength
aligerar *verb.* **1.** to lighten **2.** hurry
alimentación *noun f.* nutrition
alimentar *verb.* **1.** to feed **2.** be nutritious
—**alimentarse 1.** to eat **2.** feed
alimento *noun m.* food
alinear *verb.* to line up
aliñar *verb.* to season, dress
aliño *noun m.* seasoning, dressing
alisar *verb.* to smooth
aliviado, -da *adj.* relieved
aliviar *verb.* **1.** to relieve, ease **2.** soothe
alivio *noun m.* relief
allá *adv.* there, over there
—**más allá** farther away
—**más allá de** beyond
allí *adv.* there, over there
alma *noun f.* soul
almacén *noun m.* **1.** store **2.** warehouse
almacenamiento *noun m.* storage
almacenar *verb.* to store
almeja *noun f.* clam
almendra *noun f.* almond
almendro *noun m.* almond tree
almirante *noun mf.* admiral
almirez *noun m.* mortar
almohada *noun f.* pillow
almohadilla *noun f.* cushion
almorzar *verb.* **1.** to have lunch **2.** have for lunch
almuerzo *verb.* lunch
alocado, -da *adj.* **1.** crazy **2.** wild
alocución *noun f.* speech, address
alojamiento *noun m.* accommodation , rooms, lodgings
alojar *verb.* to accommodate
—**alojarse** to lodge, stay
alpinista *noun mf.* climber
alquilar *verb.* to let, rent
alquiler *noun m.* rent, rental
alrededor *adv.* around
—**alrededor de** around, about, approximately
alrededores *noun m. plural.* **1.** surroundings **2.** outskirts
alta *noun f.* **1.** discharge **2.** membership, entry
—**dar de alta** to discharge
—**darse de alta** to join

altanero, -ra *adj.* arrogant
altar *noun m.* altar
altavoz *noun m.* loudspeaker
alteración *noun f.* **1.** alteration, change **2.** disturbance
alterado, -da *adj.* upset
alterar *verb.* **1.** to alter, modify **2.** disturb
—**alterarse** to get excited, get upset
altercado *noun m.* altercation, dispute
alternar *verb.* **1.** to alternate **2.** socialize
alternativa *noun f.* alternative, choice, option
alternativamente *adv.* alternatively
alternativo, -va *adj.* **1.** alternative **2.** alternating
alterno, -na *adj.* **1.** alternate **2.** alternating
altiplano *noun m.* high plateau
altitud *noun f.* altitude
alto *noun m.* **1.** height **2.** halt, stop
alto, -ta *adj.* **1.** tall **2.** high **3.** loud
alto *adv.* **1.** high **2.** loudly
altura *noun f.* **1.** height **2.** altitude **3.** level **4.** loftiness
alumbramiento *noun m.* birth
alumbrar *verb.* **1.** to light, give light **2.** give birth
aluminio *noun m.* aluminum
alumno, -na *noun.* **1.** student **2.** pupil, schoolboy, schoolgirl
alusión *noun f.* allusion, reference
alza *noun f.* rise
alzamiento *noun m.* uprising
alzar *verb.* to lift, raise
—**alzarse** to rise
ama *noun f.* (see amo)
amabilidad *noun f.* kindness
amable *adj.* kind, nice
amablemente *adv.* kindly
amado, -da *noun. adj.* beloved
amamantar *verb.* to suckle, nurse
amanecer *noun m.* dawn, daybreak
amanecer *verb.* to dawn
amante *noun mf.* lover
amante *adj.* loving, fond
amañado, -da *adj.* fixed
amañar *verb.* to fix
amar *verb.* to love
amargado, -da *adj.* bitter, embittered
amargamente *adv.* bitterly
amargo, -da *adj.* bitter
amargura *noun f.* bitterness
amarillear *verb.* to yellow, turn yellow
amarillo *noun m.* yellow
amarillo, -lla *adj.* yellow
amarrar *verb.* to tie up, fasten
amasar *verb.* **1.** to amass **2.** mix, prepare
amateur *noun mf. adj.* amateur
ámbar *noun m.* amber
ambición *noun f.* ambition
ambicioso, -sa *adj.* ambitious
ambiental *adj.* environmental
ambiente *noun m.* **1.** atmosphere **2.** environment
ambigüedad *noun f.* ambiguity
ambiguo, -gua *adj.* ambiguous
ambos, -bas *adj. pron.* both
ambulancia *noun f.* ambulance
amenaza *noun f.* menace, threat
amenazador, -dora *adj.* menacing, threatening
amenazar *verb.* to threaten
América *noun f.* America
americano, -na *noun. adj.* American
amigable *adj.* amicable, friendly
amigo, -ga *noun.* **1.** friend **2.** boyfriend or girlfriend
amigo, -ga *adj.* friendly
amistad *noun f.* friendship
amnistía *noun f.* amnesty
amo, -ma *noun.* **1.** master or mistress **2.** owner
—**ama de casa** housewife
—**ama de llaves** housekeeper
amoldar *verb.* to adapt, adjust
—**amoldarse** to adapt oneself, adjust oneself
amontonar *verb.* **1.** to pile up, heap up **2.** hoard
—**amontonarse** to pile up, accumulate
amor *noun m.* **1.** love **2.** beloved
—**amor propio** pride, self-esteem
—**hacer el amor** make love
amoral *adj.* amoral
amorío *noun m.* love affair, romance
amortiguador *noun m.* shock absorber

amortiguar *verb.* **1.** to absorb, cushion **2.** alleviate
amotinarse *verb.* to riot
amparar *verb.* to safeguard, protect —**ampararse** to shelter
amparo *noun m.* protection, refuge, shelter
amperio *noun m.* ampère
ampliación *noun f.* **1.** extension, expansion **2.** enlargement
ampliamente *adv.* widely, extensively
ampliar *verb.* **1.** to expand, extend **2.** enlarge **3.** widen
amplio, -plia *adj.* ample, wide, spacious
amplitud *noun f.* extent, wideness, spaciousness
amueblado, -da *adj.* furnished
amueblar *verb.* furnish
amuleto *noun m.* amulet, charm
amurallar *verb.* to wall, fortify
analfabetismo *noun m.* illiteracy
analfabeto, -ta *noun. adj.* illiterate
análisis *noun m.* **1.** analysis **2.** test
analista *noun mf.* analyst
analítico, -ca *adj.* analytical
analizar *verb.* to analyze
analogía *noun f.* analogy, similarity
análogo, -ga *adj.* analogous, similar
anatomía *noun f.* anatomy
ancho *noun m.* breadth, width
ancho, -cha *adj.* **1.** broad, wide **2.** loose
anchura *noun f.* breadth, width
anciano, -na *noun.* elderly person, old person
anciano, -na *adj.* aged, elderly, old
ancla *noun f.* anchor
anclar *verb.* to anchor
andador *noun m.* **1.** walker **2.** baby walker, reins
andar *noun m.* walk
andar *verb.* **1.** to walk **2.** function, work, run —**andar tras** to follow, go after
andén *noun m.* platform
andrajos *noun m. plural.* rags
andrajoso, -sa *adj.* ragged
anegar *verb.* to flood
anestesia *noun f.* anesthesia
anexar *verb.* to annex, attach
anexión *noun f.* annexation
anexionar *verb.* to annex
anexo *noun m.* annex
anexo, -xa *adj.* attached, enclosed
anfibio *noun m.* amphibian
anfiteatro *noun m.* amphitheater
anfitrión, -triona *noun.* host or hostess
ángel *noun m.* angel
anglicano, -na *noun. adj.* Anglican
anguila *noun f.* eel
ángulo *noun m.* angle
angustia *noun f.* **1.** anguish, distress **2.** anxiety
angustiado, -da *adj.* **1.** anguished, distressed **2.** anxious
angustiar *verb.* **1.** to anguish, distress **2.** make anxious
angustioso, -sa *adj.* **1.** anguished, distressed **2.** distressing
anhelar *verb.* to long for, yearn for
anhelo *noun m.* longing, yearning
anidar *verb.* to nest
anillo *noun m.* ring
animación *noun f.* **1.** life, activity **2.** animation
animado, -da *adj.* cheerful, alive
animal *noun m.* animal —**animal de compañía** pet
animar *verb.* **1.** to cheer up, brighten up **2.** enliven, liven up **3.** encourage —**animarse** *verb.* **1.** to cheer up, brighten up **2.** liven up
ánimo *noun m.* **1.** spirits **2.** encouragement **3.** intention
aniquilamiento *noun m.* annihilation
aniquilar *verb.* to annihilate
aniversario *noun m.* anniversary
anoche *adv.* last night, yesterday evening
anochecer *verb.* to get dark
anonimato *noun m.* anonymity
anónimo, -ma *adj.* anonymous
anormal *adj.* abnormal
anotación *noun f.* **1.** note, annotation **2.** scoring
anotar *verb.* **1.** to note down, write down **2.** annotate **3.** score
ansiar *verb.* to long for, yearn for
ansiedad *noun f.* anxiety
ansiosamente *adv.* anxiously

ansioso, -sa *adj.* **1.** anxious, worried **2.** eager
ante *noun m.* **1.** elk, moose **2.** suede
ante *prep.* **1.** before **2.** considering, faced with
—**ante todo** above all, first and foremost
anteanoche, antes de anoche *adv.* the night before last
anteayer, antes de ayer *adv.* the day before yesterday
antecedente *noun m.* **1.** antecedent **2.** precedent
—**antecedentes 1.** record **2.** background
—**antecedentes penales** criminal record
anteceder *verb.* to precede
antecesor, -sora *noun.* **1.** predecessor **2.** ancestor, forebear
antena *noun f.* **1.** antenna **2.** aerial
anteojos *noun m. plural.* glasses, eyeglasses
antepasado, -da *noun.* ancestor, forebear
antepenúltimo, -ma *adj.* antepenultimate, third from last
anterior *adj.* **1.** previous, former **2.** front
anteriormente *adv.* previously
antes *adv.* **1.** before, earlier **2.** rather, sooner **3.** formerly, previously
—**antes bien** on the contrary
—**antes de anoche** the night before last
—**antes de ayer** the day before yesterday
—**antes de Cristo** before Christ, BC
—**antes (de) que** before
—**cuanto antes** as soon as possible
antibiótico *noun m.* antibiotic
anticipación *noun f.* anticipation
—**con anticipación** in advance
anticipado, -da *adj.* early
—**por anticipado** in advance
anticipar *verb.* **1.** to anticipate **2.** foresee **3.** pay in advance
—**anticiparse 1.** to anticipate **2.** act in advance of **3.** be ahead of
anticipo *noun m.* **1.** advance **2.** foretaste, preview
anticuado, -da *adj.* old-fashioned, outdated
antigüedad *noun f.* **1.** antiquity **2.** seniority **3.** antique
antiguamente *adv.* formerly
antiguo, -gua *adj.* **1.** old **2.** ancient **3.** former
antillano, -na *noun. adj.* West Indian
antinatural *adj.* unnatural
antipatía *noun f.* antipathy, dislike
antipático, -ca *adj.* unpleasant
antorcha *noun f.* torch
antropología *noun f.* anthropology
anual *adj.* annual, yearly
anualmente *adv.* annually, yearly
anuario *noun m.* annual, yearbook
anudar *verb.* to knot, tie
anulación *noun f.* cancellation, annulment
anular *verb.* **1.** to cancel, annul, rescind **2.** declare null and void
anunciante *noun mf.* advertiser
anunciar *verb.* **1.** to advertise **2.** announce
anuncio *noun m.* **1.** advertisement, ad, commercial **2.** announcement
anzuelo *noun m.* **1.** fishhook **2.** bait, lure
añadir *verb.* to add
año *noun m.* **1.** year **2.** grade
—**año bisiesto** leap year
—**Año Nuevo** New Year
—**tener (cinco) años** to be (five) years old
añoranza *noun f.* longing, yearning
añorar *verb.* **1.** to long for, yearn for **2.** miss
apabullante *adj.* overwhelming
apabullar *verb.* to overwhelm
apacible *adj.* calm, gentle, mild
apaciguar *verb.* to appease, pacify
—**apaciguar** to calm down
apagado, -da *adj.* **1.** off, out **2.** dull, subdued
apagar *verb.* **1.** to turn off, switch off **2.** put out, blow out
—**apagarse 1.** to go out, blow out **2.** die away
apagón *noun m.* blackout

apalear *verb.* to beat, thrash
aparato *noun m.* **1.** machine **2.** apparatus **3.** appliance, set **4.** system
aparcamiento *noun m.* **1.** parking **2.** parking lot
aparcar *verb.* to park
aparear *verb.* to mate
aparecer *verb.* **1.** to appear, turn up **2.** come out
aparejar *verb.* **1.** to prepare, get ready **2.** saddle, harness
aparejo *noun m.* **1.** equipment, gear **2.** saddle, harness **3.** rig
aparentar *verb.* **1.** to look, seem **2.** feign, pretend
aparente *adj.* apparent
aparentemente *adv.* apparently, seemingly
aparición *noun f.* **1.** appearance **2.** publication, release
apariencia *noun f.* appearance, look
—**en apariencia** apparently, seemingly
apartado *noun m.* section
—**apartado de correos, apartado postal** Pox Office Box, P.O. Box
apartado, -da *adj.* **1.** remote, isolated **2.** solitary
apartamento *noun m.* apartment
apartar *verb.* **1.** to separate, put aside, set aside **2.** move away
—**apartarse** to move away
aparte *noun m.* aside (theater)
aparte *adj.* separate, special
aparte *adv.* **1.** aside, apart **2.** separately **3.** besides
—**aparte de** apart from, besides
apasionado, -da *adj.* passionate
apasionante *adj.* fascinating, exciting
apasionar *verb.* to excite, love
—**apasionarse** to get excited, enthuse
apeadero *noun m.* halt
apearse *verb.* **1.** to get off **2.** dismount
apedrear *verb.* to stone, throw stones at
apegado, -da *adj.* attached, close
apego *noun m.* attachment, fondness
apelación *noun f.* appeal
apelar *verb.* to appeal
apellido *noun m.* last name, surname
apenar *verb.* to sadden
—**apenarse 1.** to become sad **2.** to become embarrassed
apenas *adv.* **1.** barely **2.** hardly, scarcely
apenas *conj.* as soon as
apéndice *noun m.* appendix
apertura *noun f.* **1.** opening **2.** start, beginning
apestar *verb.* to stink
apetecer *verb.* to feel like
apetecible *adj.* desirable, attractive
apetito *noun m.* appetite
apilar *verb.* to heap up, pile up
apiñar *verb.* to pack
—**apiñarse** to crowd together
apisonar *verb.* to roll
aplanar *verb.* to level
aplastante *adj.* overwhelming, crushing, sweeping
aplastar *verb.* **1.** to crush, squash **2.** overwhelm
aplaudir *verb.* to applaud, clap
aplauso *noun m.* applause, clapping
aplazamiento *noun m.* **1.** postponement **2.** deferment
aplazar *verb.* **1.** to postpone **2.** defer
aplicable *adj.* applicable
aplicación *noun f.* **1.** application **2.** diligence, dedication
aplicar *verb.* to apply
—**aplicarse** to work harder
apodar *verb.* to dub, nickname
apoderado, -da *noun.* agent, manager
apoderar *verb.* to authorize, empower
—**apoderarse de** *verb.* seize
apodo *noun m.* nickname
apología *noun f.* defense
apogeo *noun m.* height, peak
aporrear *verb.* to beat, club
aportación *noun f.* contribution
aportar *verb.* **1.** to contribute **2.** provide
apósito *noun m.* dressing
apostar *verb.* **1.** to bet, gamble **2.** station
apoyar *verb.* **1.** to support, back **2.** rest, lean
—**apoyarse 1.** to rely on, lean on **2.** lean against

apoyo *noun m.* support
apreciación *noun f.* appreciation
apreciar *verb.* to appreciate, be fond of, value, esteem
—**apreciarse** to increase in value
aprecio *noun m.* esteem
apremiante *adj.* urgent, pressing
apremiar *verb.* **1.** to urge, press **2.** be urgent
aprender *verb.* to learn
aprendiz, -diza *noun.* **1.** apprentice **2.** trainee
aprendizaje *noun m.* apprenticeship
aprensión *noun f.* apprehension
apresamiento *noun m.* seizure, capture
apresuradamente *adv.* hastily, hurriedly
apresurado, -da *adj.* hasty, hurried
apresurar *verb.* to hurry, quicken, speed up
—**apresurarse** to hurry
apretado, -da *adj.* tight
apretar *verb.* **1.** to press **2.** tighten **3.** squeeze **4.** pinch, be too tight
apretón *noun m.* squeeze
—**apretón de manos** handshake
aprieto *noun m.* predicament
aprobación *noun f.* approval, endorsement
aprobado *noun m.* pass certificate
aprobar *verb.* **1.** to approve, endorse **2.** pass **3.** approve of
apropiadamente *adv.* appropriately, suitably
apropiado, -da *adj.* appropriate, suitable
apropiarse de *verb.* to appropriate, take possession of
aprovechado, -da *noun.* opportunist
aprovechado, -da *adj.* opportunistic
—**bien aprovechado** well-used, well-spent, well-exploited
—**mal aprovechado** wasted, badly-exploited
aprovechar *verb.* **1.** to use **2.** make (good) use of
—**aprovecharse** to take advantage, exploit
aprovisionamiento *noun m.* supplies
aprovisionar *verb.* to supply
aproximación *noun f.* **1.** approach, rapprochement **2.** approximation
aproximadamente *adv.* approximately
aproximado, -da *adj.* approximate, rough
aproximar *verb.* to bring nearer
—**aproximarse** to approach
aptitud *noun f.* aptitude
apto, -ta *adj.* fit, suitable
apuesta *noun f.* bet
apuntador, -dora *noun.* prompter
apuntar *verb.* **1.** to aim **2.** point **3.** note down **4.** prompt **5.** suggest, hint
—**apuntarse 1.** to enroll, register, join **2.** score
apunte *noun m.* **1.** note **2.** sketch
apuñalar *verb.* to stab
apurar *verb.* **1.** to exhaust, drain **2.** eat up, drink up **3.** hurry
—**apurarse 1.** to hurry up **2.** worry
apuro *noun m.* **1.** predicament **2.** hurry **3.** embarrassment
aquel, aquella *adj.* that
—**aquellos, aquellas** those
aquél, aquélla *pron.* **1.** that, that one **2.** the former
—**aquéllos, aquéllas 1.** those, those one **2.** the former
aquello *pron.* that, that matter
aquí *adv.* here
—**de aquí en adelante** from now on
aquietar *verb.* to calm
árabe *noun mf.* **1.** Arab **2.** Arabic (language)
árabe *adj.* Arab, Arabian
Arabia *noun f.* Arabia
arábigo, -ga *adj.* Arabian
—**números arábigos** Arabic numerals
arado *noun m.* plow
arancel *noun m.* tariff, duty
araña *noun f.* spider
arañar *verb.* to scratch
arañazo *noun m.* scratch
arar *verb.* to plow
arbitraje *noun m.* **1.** arbitration **2.** refereeing
arbitrar *verb.* **1.** to arbitrate **2.** referee
arbitrario, -ria *adj.* arbitrary

árbitro, -tra *noun.* **1.** arbitrator, arbiter **2.** referee
árbol *noun m.* tree
—**árbol genealógico** family tree
—**árboles maderables** timber
arbusto *noun m.* bush, shrub
arca *noun f.* **1.** chest, coffer **2.** ark
archivar *verb.* **1.** to file **2.** save **3.** shelve
archivo *noun m.* **1.** file **2.** archive **3.** record
arcilla *noun f.* clay
arco *noun m.* **1.** arc **2.** arch **3.** bow
—**arco iris** rainbow
arder *verb.* **1.** to burn **2.** smart, sting
ardiente *adj.* **1.** ardent, passionate **2.** burning
ardilla *noun f.* squirrel
ardor *noun m.* ardor
área *noun f.* area
arena *noun f.* **1.** sand **2.** arena
arenoso, -sa *adj.* sandy
argamasa *noun f.* mortar
Argentina *noun f.* Argentina
argentino, -na *noun. adj.* Argentinean
argüir *verb.* **1.** to argue **2.** claim
argolla *noun f.* ring
argumentar *verb.* to argue
argumento *noun m.* **1.** argument, reasoning **2.** plot
ariete *noun m.* ram
aria *noun f.* aria
aridez *noun f.* aridity, dryness
árido, -da *adj.* arid, dry
arista *noun f.* edge
aristocracia *noun f.* aristocracy
aristócrata *noun mf.* aristocrat
aristocrático, -ca *adj.* aristocratic
aritmética *noun f.* arithmetic
arma *noun f.* weapon
—**arma de fuego** firearm
armada *noun f.* fleet, navy
armado, -da *adj.* **1.** armed **2.** assembled
armadura *noun f.* armor
armar *verb.* **1.** to arm **2.** assemble, put together
—**armar un escándalo** to kick up a storm
armario *noun m.* **1.** closet **2.** cupboard
armazón *noun mf.* **1.** frame **2.** framework **3.** skeleton
armisticio *noun m.* armistice
armonía *noun f.* harmony
arnés *noun m.* harness
aro *noun m.* ring, hoop
aroma *noun m.* aroma, scent
arpa *noun f.* harp
arquear *verb.* to arch, bend
arqueología *noun f.* archaeology
arqueológico, -ca *adj.* archaeological
arquitecto, -ta *noun.* architect
arquitectónico, -ca *adj.* architectural
arquitectura *noun f.* architecture
arraigar *verb.* to take root
arrancar *verb.* **1.** to pull out, tear out **2.** pluck **3.** snatch **4.** start
arranque *noun m.* **1.** starting mechanism **2.** outburst, fit
arrasar *verb.* **1.** to level **2.** raze **3.** sweep the board, be a runaway success
arrastrar *verb.* **1.** to drag, pull **2.** sweep away **3.** attract
—**arrastrarse 1.** to crawl **2.** grovel
arrebatar *verb.* **1.** to snatch away, take **2.** captivate
arrebato *noun m.* outburst, fit
arrecife *noun m.* reef
arreglado, -da *adj.* **1.** repaired, fixed **2.** settled, sorted out **3.** neat, tidy **4.** smart, trim
arreglar *verb.* **1.** to repair, fix, mend **2.** settle, sort out, solve, work out **3.** tidy up
—**arreglarse** to get oneself ready
arreglo *noun m.* **1.** repair **2.** agreement **3.** arrangement
arremeter *verb.* to attack, charge
arrendador, -dora *noun.* landlord or landlady
arrendar *verb.* to rent, lease
arrendatario, -ria *noun.* tenant, renter
arreos *noun m. plural.* harness
arrepentido, -da *adj.* repentant, sorry
arrepentimiento *noun m.* **1.** regret **2.** repentance
arrepentirse *verb.* **1.** to regret, be sorry **2.** repent
arrestar *verb.* to arrest, detain

arresto *noun m.* arrest
arriate *noun m.* border
arriba *adv.* **1.** above **2.** up, upward **3.** upstairs
—**cuesta arriba** uphill
—**de arriba abajo** from head to foot, from top to bottom
—**hacia arriba** upward
arriba *interj.* long live!
arribista *noun mf.* upstart, social climber
arriesgado, -da *adj.* risky
arriesgar *verb.* to risk, venture
—**arriesgarse** to take a risk
arrinconar *verb.* **1.** to corner **2.** lay aside
arrodillarse *verb.* to kneel (down)
arrogancia *noun f.* arrogance
arrogante *adj.* arrogant
arrojar *verb.* **1.** to throw, hurl, cast **2.** produce, yield **3.** spew, vomit
—**arrojarse** to throw oneself
arrollador, -dora *adj.* sweeping
arrostrar *verb.* to brave, face up
arroyo *noun m.* brook, stream
arroz *noun m.* rice
arruga *noun f.* **1.** wrinkle, line **2.** crease
arrugado, -da *adj.* **1.** wrinkled, lined **2.** creased
arruinado, -da *adj.* broke, ruined
arruinar *verb.* **1.** to ruin **2.** wreck, destroy
—**arruinarse** to go bankrupt
arsenal *noun m.* arsenal
arte *noun mf.* **1.** art **2.** skill
arteria *noun f.* artery
artesanal *adj.* handmade
artesanía *noun f.* **1.** craftsmanship **2.** crafts, handicrafts
artesano, -na *noun.* craftsman or craftswoman , artisan
ártico, -ca *adj.* Arctic
articulación *noun f.* **1.** articulation **2.** joint
articular *verb.* **1.** to articulate **2.** join together
artículo *noun m.* **1.** article **2.** commodity **3.** item
—**artículos alimenticios** foodstuffs
—**artículos de consumo** consumer goods
—**artículos de primera necesidad** essentials
artificial *adj.* artificial
artillería *noun f.* artillery
artista *noun mf.* artist
artístico, -ca *adj.* artistic
arzobispo *noun m.* archbishop
as *noun m.* ace
asa *noun f.* handle
asado *noun m.* **1.** roast **2.** barbecue
asado, -da *adj.* roasted, broiled
asador *noun m.* spit
asalariado, -da *noun.* wage-earner
asalariado, -da *adj.* wage-earning
asaltar *verb.* **1.** to assault **2.** mug, rob **3.** storm
asalto *noun m.* **1.** assault **2.** mugging, robbery **3.** round
asamblea *noun f.* assembly
asar *verb.* to roast, broil
ascendencia *noun f.* descent, ancestry, origin
ascendente *adj.* upward
ascender *verb.* **1.** to ascend, rise **2.** promote **3.** be promoted **4.** amount, reach, total
ascensión *noun f.* ascent, rise
—**la Ascensión** the Ascension
ascenso *noun m.* **1.** ascent, rise **2.** promotion
ascensor *noun m.* elevator
asco *noun m.* disgust
—**dar asco** to disgust
aseado, -da *adj.* clean, neat, tidy, trim
asediar *verb.* to besiege
asegurador, -dora *noun.* insurer
aseguradora *noun m.* insurance company
asegurar *verb.* **1.** to assure, ensure **2.** secure **3.** insure
—**asegurarse** **1.** to make sure **2.** insure oneself
asentar *verb.* **1.** to place, set up **2.** lay down
—**asentarse** **1.** to stand, be situated **2.** settle
asentir *verb.* **1.** to assent, agree **2.** nod
aseo *noun m.* **1.** toilet **2.** cleanliness
—**aseos** rest room

aserción *noun f.* assertion
aserto *noun m.* assertion
asesinar *verb.* **1.** to murder **2.** assassinate
asesinato *noun m.* **1.** murder, homicide **2.** assassination
asesino, -na *noun.* **1.** killer, murderer or murderess **2.** assassin
asesor, -sora *noun.* consultant, advisor
asesor, -sora *adj.* advisory
asesorar *verb.* to advice, counsel
—**asesorarse** to take advice, consult
aseverar *verb.* to assert, state
asfaltar *verb.* to asphalt
asfalto *noun m.* asphalt
asfixia *noun f.* asphyxia, suffocation
asfixiar *verb.* to suffocate
así *adj.* such
así *adv.* **1.** like this, like that **2.** so, thus, in this way
—**así así** so-so
—**así como 1.** as well as **2.** whereas, while
—**no así** unlike
así *conj.* even if
Asia *noun f.* Asia
asiático, -ca *noun. adj.* Asian
asiento *noun m.* **1.** seat, place **2.** contract **3.** bottom
asignación *noun f.* **1.** allocation **2.** allowance
asignar *verb.* **1.** to assign **2.** allocate
asignatura *noun f.* subject
asilo *noun m.* **1.** asylum **2.** shelter
asimilar *verb.* to assimilate
asimismo *adv.* **1.** similarly, likewise **2.** also, as well
asir *verb.* to seize, grab, grasp
asistencia *noun f.* **1.** assistance, help **2.** attendance
—**asistencia médica/sanitaria** medical or health care
—**asistencia social** welfare
asistente, -ta *noun mf.* **1.** assistant **2.** orderly
—**asistenta doméstica** housemaid
—**asistente social** social worker
—**los asistentes** those present
asistir *verb.* **1.** to attend, go **2.** witness **3.** help, assist
—**asistir un parto** to deliver a baby
asma *noun f.* asthma
asno *noun m.* ass, donkey
asociación *noun f.* **1.** association **2.** society
asociado, -da *noun.* **1.** associate, partner **2.** member
asociado, -da *adj.* associate, associated
asociar *verb.* **1.** to associate **2.** connect
—**asociarse 1.** to join **2.** become partners, form a partnership
asolar *verb.* to raze, destroy
asomar *verb.* to show
—**asomarse 1.** to come out, appear **2.** lean out, look out
asombrar *verb.* to amaze, astonish
—**asombrarse** to marvel, be amazed, be astonished
asombro *noun m.* amazement, astonishment
asombroso, -sa *adj.* amazing, astonishing
asomo *noun m.* **1.** appearance **2.** sign, trace
—**ni por asomo** by no means
aspa *noun f.* blade
aspaviento *noun m.* fuss
aspecto *noun m.* **1.** aspect **2.** look
ásperamente *adv.* roughly
áspero, -ra *adj.* **1.** rough **2.** coarse **3.** harsh
aspiración *noun f.* **1.** breathing in, inhalation **2.** aspiration
aspiradora *noun f.* vacuum cleaner
aspirante *noun mf.* **1.** applicant, candidate **2.** challenger
aspirar *verb.* to breathe in, inhale
—**aspirar a** to aspire to
aspirina *noun f.* aspirin
asquear *verb.* to disgust
asqueroso, -sa *adj.* **1.** disgusting **2.** filthy
asta *noun f.* **1.** horn **2.** flagpole
astillero *noun m.* dockyard, shipyard
astrónomo, -ma *noun.* astronomer
astucia *noun f.* **1.** astuteness, shrewdness **2.** cunning, guile
astuto, -ta *adj.* **1.** astute, shrewd **2.** crafty
asumir *verb.* to assume

asunto *noun m.* affair, business, issue, matter
asustado, -da *adj.* **1.** frightened, scared, afraid **2.** scared
asustar *verb.* to frighten, scare
—**asustarse** to be frightened, get scared
atacante *noun mf.* assailant, attacker
atacar *verb.* to attack
ataque *noun m.* attack
—**ataque al corazón** heart attack
—**ataque de nervios** nervous breakdown
atar *verb.* to tie, tie up
atardecer *noun m.* evening, dusk
atasco *noun m.* **1.** traffic jam **2.** obstruction, blockage
ataúd *noun m.* coffin
atavío *noun m.* attire, dress
atemorizado, -da *adj.* frightened, scared
atemorizar *verb.* to frighten, scare
atención *noun f.* attention
—**llamar la atención** to attract somebody's attention
—**prestar atención** to pay attention
atender *verb.* **1.** to take care of, look after **2.** attend **3.** pay attention **4.** wait on
atentado *noun m.* attack, attempt
atentamente *adv.* **1.** attentively **2.** sincerely yours
atentar *verb.* **1.** to make an attempt (on somebody's life) **2.** break (the law)
atento, -ta *adj.* attentive
atenuar *verb.* **1.** to attenuate **2.** dim, tone down
ateo, -tea *noun.* atheist
ateo, -tea *adj.* atheistic
aterrador, -dora *adj.* frightening, terrifying
aterrar *verb.* to terrify
aterrizaje *noun m.* landing
aterrizar *verb.* to land
aterrorizado, -da *adj.* terrified
aterrorizar *verb.* **1.** to terrify **2.** terrorize
atesorar *verb.* **1.** to hoard **2.** treasure
atestado, -da *adj.* crowded, packed
atestar *verb.* **1.** to crowd, pack, stuff **2.** attest, testify
atestiguar *verb.* to attest, testify
atiborrar *verb.* to stuff
ático *noun m.* **1.** penthouse **2.** attic
atisbo *noun m.* indication
atizar *verb.* **1.** to poke, stir **2.** fan **3.** give
atlántico, -ca *adj.* Atlantic
atleta *noun mf.* athlete
atlético, -ca *adj.* athletic
atletismo *noun m.* athletics
atmósfera *noun f.* atmosphere
atmosférico, -ca *adj.* atmospheric
atómico, -ca *adj.* atomic
átomo *noun m.* atom
atontado, -da *adj.* stupid
atormentar *verb.* **1.** to torture **2.** torment
—**atormentarse** to torture oneself
atornillar *verb.* to screw
atracar *verb.* **1.** to dock **2.** mug, rob
atracción *noun f.* attraction
—**atracción turística** sight
atractivo *noun m.* attraction, appeal
atractivo, -va *adj.* attractive
atraer *verb.* **1.** to attract **2.** draw
atrancar *verb.* to bar, block
atrapar *verb.* **1.** to trap, capture **2.** catch
atrás *adv.* **1.** back, behind **2.** ago
—**atrás de** behind
—**hacia/para atrás** backwards
atrasado, -da *adj.* **1.** backward **2.** late **3.** overdue **4.** slow
atraso *noun m.* **1.** backwardness **2.** delay
—**atrasos** arrears
atravesar *verb.* **1.** to cross **2.** put across **3.** pierce **4.** go through
atrayente *adj.* attractive
atreverse *verb.* to dare
atrevido, -da *adj.* daring, bold
atrevimiento *noun m.* daring, boldness
atribución *noun f.* attribution
atribuir *verb.* **1.** to attribute **2.** assign **3.** confer
—**atribuirse** to claim something for oneself
atributo *noun m.* attribute
atrocidad *noun f.* atrocity
atropellar *verb.* **1.** to run over **2.** disregard, violate

atroz *adj.* atrocious
atún *noun m.* tuna fish, tuna
aturdir *verb.* to stun
audaz *adj.* bold, audacious
audiencia *noun f.* **1.** audience **2.** court
auditar *verb.* to audit
auditor, -tora *noun.* auditor
auditoría *noun f.* audit
auge *noun m.* **1.** boom **2.** height, peak
augusto, -ta *adj.* august
aullar *verb.* to howl
aullido *noun m.* howl
aumentar *verb.* **1.** to increase **2.** raise
aumento *noun m.* **1.** increase **2.** raise
aun *adv.* even
aún *adv.* still, yet
aunque *conj.* although, though, even though, even if
auricular *noun m.* receiver
auscultar *verb.* sound
ausencia *noun f.* absence
ausentarse *verb.* to absent oneself
ausente *noun mf.* absentee
ausente *adj.* absent
austero, -ra *adj.* austere
Australia *noun f.* Australia
australiano, -na *noun. adj.* Australian
Austria *noun f.* Austria
austríaco, -ca *noun. adj.* Austrian
auténticamente *adv.* genuinely
auténtico, -ca *adj.* **1.** authentic **2.** genuine
auto *noun m.* **1.** automobile, car **2.** sentence, decision
auto- *prefix* self-
autobiografía *noun f.* autobiography
autobús *noun m.* bus
autorización *noun f.* permission
automáticamente *adv.* automatically
automático, -ca *adj.* automatic
automóvil *noun m.* automobile
automovilista *noun mf.* motorist
autonomía *noun f.* autonomy
autónomo, -ma *adj.* autonomous
autopista *noun f.* highway, freeway
—**autopista de peaje** turnpike
autor, -tora *noun.* author
autoridad *noun f.* authority
autoritario, -ria *adj.* authoritarian
autorización *noun f.* authorization
autorizar *verb.* **1.** to authorize, sanction **2.** approve
auxiliar *noun mf.* assistant, helper
auxiliar *adj.* assistant, auxiliary
auxiliar *verb.* to aid, help, assist
auxilio *noun m.* aid, help, assistance
—**primeros auxilios** first aid
avalancha *noun f.* **1.** avalanche **2.** flood
avance *noun m.* **1.** advance **2.** preview
avanzado, -da *adj.* advanced
avanzar *verb.* **1.** to advance, move forward **2.** progress
avaricia *noun f.* greed, avarice
avaricioso, -sa *adj.* greedy, avaricious
ave *noun f.* bird
—**aves de corral** poultry
avellano *noun m.* hazel
avenida *noun f.* avenue
aventajar *verb.* **1.** to surpass, excel **2.** lead
aventura *noun f.* **1.** adventure **2.** risk, venture
aventurar *verb.* to risk, venture
avergonzado, -da *adj.* ashamed
avergonzar *verb.* **1.** to shame, put shame **2.** embarrass
—**avergonzarse 1.** to be ashamed **2.** be embarrassed
avería *noun f.* **1.** breakdown **2.** damage
averiado, -da *adj.* **1.** broken down **2.** damaged
averiar *verb.* **1.** to cause a breakdown **2.** damage
—**averiarse 1.** to break down **2.** get damaged
averiguar *verb.* to find out
aversión *noun f.* dislike
aviación *noun f.* aviation
ávido, -da *adj.* eager, avid
avión *noun m.* airplane
—**avión a reacción** jet
—**avión de combate** fighter
avisar *verb.* **1.** to notify, inform **2.** warn **3.** call
aviso *noun m.* **1.** notice **2.** warning **3.** advertisement
avivar *verb.* **1.** to enliven, brighten **2.** arouse, excite

ay *interj.* oh!, ow!
ayer *adv.* yesterday
ayuda *noun f.* help, assistance, aid
ayudante *noun mf.* assistant, helper
ayudar *verb.* to help, aid, assist
ayunar *verb.* to fast
ayuno *noun m.* fast
ayuntamiento *noun m.* **1.** city council, town council **2.** city hall, town hall
azabache *noun m. adj.* jet
azotar *verb.* to whip, lash
azote *noun m.* whip, lash
azúcar *noun mf.* sugar
azucarado, -da *adj.* sweet
azucarar *verb.* to add sugar
azucena *noun f.* lily
azufre *noun m.* sulfur
azul *noun m. adj.* blue
—**azul marino** navy blue
azulejo *noun m.* tile

B

babor *noun m.* port
bache *noun m.* **1.** pothole **2.** bad period
bacteria *noun f.* bacteria
báculo *noun m.* **1.** stick, staff **2.** crook
bahía *noun f.* bay
bailar *verb.* to dance
bailarín, -rina *noun.* dancer
baile *noun m.* **1.** dance **2.** dancing **3.** ball
baja *noun f.* **1.** casualty **2.** fall, drop, slump **3.** discharge **4.** dismissal
—**dar de baja** to discharge, dismiss
—**darse de baja** to leave
—**estar de baja** to be on sick leave
bajada *noun f.* **1.** descent **2.** fall, drop **3.** slope
bajar *verb.* **1.** to lower **2.** descend **3.** fall **4.** reduce **5.** take down
—**bajarse (de)** to get off, get out of
bajo *noun m.* **1.** bass **2.** first floor
bajo, -ja *adj.* **1.** low **2.** short **3.** lower **4.** soft **5.** base, vile
bajo *adv.* **1.** low **2.** softly, quietly
bajo *prep.* **1.** under **2.** beneath **3.** below
bajón *noun m.* slump
bala *noun f.* **1.** bullet **2.** bale
balancear *verb.* to balance, swing, sway
—**balancearse** to swing, rock, sway
balanceo *noun m.* sway, rocking
balanza *noun f.* **1.** balance **2.** scales
balbucir *verb.* **1.** to stammer **2.** babble
balcón *noun m.* balcony
baldear *verb.* bale
baldosa *noun f.* tile
ballena *noun f.* whale
ballet *noun m.* ballet
balón *noun m.* ball
baloncesto *noun m.* basketball
bamboleo *noun m.* sway
banal *adj.* banal, trivial
banana *noun f.* banana
banca *noun f.* **1.** banking **2.** bench
bancal *noun m.* terrace
banco *noun m.* **1.** bank **2.** bench, stool **3.** school
banda *noun f.* **1.** band **2.** gang **3.** strip
—**banda ancha** broadband
bandada *noun f.* flock
bandeja *noun f.* tray
bandera *noun f.* flag, banner
bando *noun m.* **1.** edict **2.** side, faction
banquero, -ra *noun.* banker
banquete *noun m.* banquet, feast
banquetear *verb.* to feast
banquillo *noun m.* **1.** bench **2.** dock
bañar *verb.* **1.** to bathe, wash **2.** dip, coat
—**bañarse** **1.** to have a bathe, take a bath **2.** swim
bañera *noun f.* bathtub
baño *noun m.* **1.** bath, swim **2.** bathtub **3.** bathroom
bar *noun m.* bar
baraja *noun f.* deck
barajar *verb.* **1.** to shuffle **2.** consider
barato, -ta *adj.* cheap

barba *noun f.* beard
bárbaro, -ra *noun m.* barbarian
bárbaro, -ra *adj.* **1.** barbarian, uncivilized **2.** fantastic
barbilla *noun f.* chin
barca *noun f.* boat
barcaza *noun f.* barge
barco *noun m.* **1.** boat **2.** ship
barman *noun m.* bartender
barómetro *noun m.* barometer
barón *noun m.* baron
baronesa *noun f.* baroness
barra *noun f.* **1.** bar **2.** rail **3.** rod
barrer *verb.* to sweep
barrera *noun f.* barrier
barricada *noun f.* barricade
barrido *noun m.* sweep
barriga *noun f.* belly
barril *noun m.* barrel
barrio *noun m.* **1.** neighborhood **2.** quarter
barro *noun m.* **1.** clay **2.** mud
barroco, -ca *adj.* baroque
barrote *noun m.* bar
bártulos *noun m. plural.* things, belongings
basar *verb.* to base
—**basarse en** to be based on
base *noun f.* **1.** base **2.** basis
—**base de datos** database
básicamente *adv.* basically
básico, -ca *adj.* basic
bastante *adj.* **1.** enough, sufficient **2.** quite a lot of **3.** quite a few
bastante *adv.* **1.** enough, sufficiently **2.** quite, rather
bastante *pron.* enough
bastar *verb.* to suffice, be enough
bastardo, -da *noun. adj.* bastard
bastidor *noun m.* **1.** frame **2.** wings
basto, -ta *adj.* coarse
bastón *noun m.* stick, cane
basura *noun f.* **1.** garbage **2.** trash can
bata *noun f.* **1.** bathrobe, housecoat **2.** lab coat
batalla *noun f.* battle
batallón *noun m.* battalion
bate *noun m.* bat
batería *noun f.* **1.** battery **2.** drums
—**batería de cocina** set of kitchen utensils
batida *noun f.* **1.** beating **2.** search
batido *noun m.* shake
batidora *noun f.* mixer, blender, whisk
batir *verb.* **1.** to beat **2.** mix, whisk, whip
baúl *noun m.* trunk
baya *noun f.* berry
bebé *noun m.* baby
beber *verb.* to drink
—**beber a sorbos** to sip
—**beber a tragos** to gulp
bebida *noun f.* drink, beverage
—**bebida no alcohólica** soft drink
beca *noun f.* **1.** grant **2.** scholarship
becario, -ria *noun.* **1.** grant holder **2.** scholar holder
béisbol *noun m.* baseball
belga *noun mf. adj.* Belgian
Bélgica *noun f.* Belgium
belleza *noun f.* beauty
bello, -lla *adj.* **1.** beautiful **2.** lovely
bemol *noun m.* flat
bendecir *verb.* **1.** to bless **2.** praise
bendición *noun f.* blessing
bendito, -ta *adj.* blessed, holy
beneficiario, -ria *noun.* beneficiary
beneficiar *verb.* to benefit
—**beneficiarse** to profit, benefit
beneficio *noun m.* **1.** benefit **2.** gain, profit
beneficioso, -sa *adj.* beneficial
benéfico, -ca *adj.* charitable
benigno, -na *adj.* benign, mild
bermejo, -ja *adj.* ginger, reddish
berrear *verb.* **1.** to bellow **2.** howl
besar *verb.* to kiss
beso *noun m.* kiss
bestia *noun f.* beast
besuquearse *verb.* to neck
betún *noun m.* shoe polish
Biblia *noun f.* Bible
bíblico, -ca *adj.* biblical
biblioteca *noun f.* library
bibliotecario, -ria *noun.* librarian
bicho *noun m.* bug, small animal
bicicleta *noun f.* bicycle
bidón *noun m.* drum, can
bien *noun m.* good

—**bienes** goods, property
—**bienes de consumo** consumer goods
—**bienes de equipo** capital goods
—**bienes raíces** real state
bien *adj.* well-to-do
bien *adv.* **1.** well **2.** correctly, properly **3.** all right **4.** easily
—**más bien** rather
—**si bien** although
bien *interj.* good
bienestar *noun m.* **1.** comfort **2.** welfare, well-being
bienvenida *noun f.* welcome
—**dar la bienvenida** to welcome
bienvenido, -da *adj.* welcome
bifurcación *noun f.* fork
bifurcarse *verb.* to fork
bigote *noun m.* moustache
bilateral *adj.* bilateral
bilis *noun f.* bile
billar *noun m.* **1.** pool, billiards **2.** snooker
billete *noun m.* **1.** bill **2.** ticket
—**billete de ida y vuelta** round-trip ticket
—**billete sencillo** one-way ticket
billón *noun m.* trillion
binario, -ria *adj.* binary
biografía *noun f.* biography
biología *noun f.* biology
biológico, -ca *adj.* biological
biombo *noun m.* screen
birlar *verb.* to pinch
Birmania *noun f.* Burma
birmano, -na *noun. adj.* Burmese
bit *noun m.* bit
bizcocho *noun m.* **1.** biscuit **2.** sponge cake
blanco *noun m.* **1.** white **2.** blank **3.** target
blanco, -ca *adj.* white
blandir *verb.* to brandish, flourish
blando, -da *adj.* **1.** soft, tender **2.** weak
blandura *noun f.* softness, tenderness
blasfemar *verb.* **1.** to blaspheme **2.** curse, swear
blindado, -da *adj.* armored
blindaje *noun m.* armor
bloc *noun m.* pad
bloque *noun m.* **1.** block **2.** bloc
bloquear *verb.* **1.** to block **2.** blockade **3.** jam
bloqueo *noun m.* blockade
blusa *noun f.* blouse
bobada *noun f.* nonsense
bobina *noun f.* reel
bobo, -ba *noun.* fool, simpleton
bobo, -ba *adj.* silly, stupid
boca *noun f.* mouth
—**boca abajo** face down, prone
—**boca arriba** face up
bocadillo *noun m.* sandwich
bocado *noun m.* **1.** bite **2.** mouthful
boceto *noun m.* sketch, outline
bocha *noun f.* bowl
bochorno *noun m.* **1.** sultry weather **2.** shame, embarrassment
bochornoso, -sa *adj.* **1.** close **2.** shameful, embarrassing
bocina *noun f.* horn
boda *noun f.* wedding, marriage
bodega *noun f.* cellar
bofetada *noun f.* slap
—**dar bofetadas a alguien** to slap somebody
bofetón *noun m.* slap
boicot *noun m.* boycott
boicotear *verb.* to boycott
bol *noun m.* bowl
bola *noun f.* **1.** ball **2.** lie, fib
boletín *noun m.* **1.** bulletin **2.** journal, review
boleto *noun m.* **1.** ticket **2.** coupon
—**boleto de ida y vuelta** round-trip ticket
—**boleto sencillo** one-way ticket
boliche *noun m.* bowling
bolígrafo *noun m.* ballpoint pen, pen
bollo *noun m.* bread roll, bun
bolo *noun m.* tenpin
—**bolos** bowling
bolsa *noun f.* **1.** bag **2.** pocket
—**la Bolsa** the Stock Exchange, the Stock Market
bolsillo *noun m.* pocket
bolso *noun m.* bag, handbag, purse
bomba *noun f.* **1.** bomb **2.** pump
—**bomba atómica** A-bomb

bombardear *verb.* **1.** to bomb, shell **2.** bombard
bombardeo *noun m.* **1.** bombing, shelling **2.** bombardment
bombardero *noun m.* bomber
bombear *verb.* to pump
bombilla *noun f.* bulb, light bulb
bombón *noun m.* bonbon, chocolate
bondad *noun f.* goodness, kindness
bondadoso, -sa *adj.* kind, kindly
bonito, -ta *adj.* nice, pretty
bono *noun m.* **1.** voucher **2.** bond
boom *noun m.* boom
boqueada *noun f.* gasp
boquilla *noun f.* mouthpiece
borde *noun m.* border, edge, brink
—**al borde de** on the brink of, on the verge of
bordear *verb.* **1.** to border, skirt **2.** border on
bordillo *noun m.* curb
borne *noun m.* terminal
borracho, -cha *noun.* drunk, drunkard
borracho, -cha *adj.* drunk
borrador *noun m.* **1.** draft **2.** sketch
borrar *verb.* to erase
borrascoso, -sa *adj.* stormy
bosque *noun m.* forest, wood
bota *noun f.* boot
botar *verb.* **1.** to bounce **2.** throw out, throw away **3.** fire, sack **4.** launch
bote *noun m.* **1.** bounce **2.** can, tin, jar, container **3.** boat
—**bote salvavidas** lifeboat
botella *noun f.* bottle
botín *noun m.* **1.** booty, loot **2.** ankle boot
botón *noun m.* button
botones *noun m.* bellhop
bóveda *noun f.* vault, arch
boxeador, -dora *noun.* boxer
boxear *verb.* to box
boxeo *noun m.* boxing
boya *noun f.* **1.** float **2.** buoy
bragas *noun f. plural.* pants, underwear
bragueta *noun f.* zipper, fly
bramar *verb.* **1.** to roar **2.** howl
bramido *noun m.* roar
branquia *noun f.* gill
Brasil *noun m.* Brazil
brasileño, -ña *noun. adj.* Brazilian
bravo, -va *adj.* **1.** ferocious, fierce **2.** great, excellent **3.** angry
brazada *noun f.* stroke
brazo *noun m.* arm
brea *noun f.* pitch
brecha *noun f.* **1.** breach, gap **2.** gash, wound
breve *adj.* brief, short
brevemente *adv.* briefly
brezo *noun m.* heather
brigada *noun f.* brigade
brillante *noun m.* diamond
brillante *adj.* bright, brilliant, shiny
brillantemente *adv.* brightly, brilliantly
brillar *verb.* **1.** to shine **2.** sparkle **3.** glitter
brillo *noun m.* **1.** shine **2.** glitter
brincar *verb.* to jump around
brinco *noun m.* jump, leap
brindar *verb.* **1.** to toast **2.** offer
brindis *noun m.* toast
brisa *noun f.* breeze
británico, -ca *noun. adj.* British
brizna *noun f.* **1.** blade **2.** piece, scrap
broma *noun f.* joke
bromear *verb.* to fool, joke, kid
bromista *noun mf.* joker
bronca *noun f.* fight, quarrel, row
bronce *noun m.* bronze
bronceado *noun m.* tan, suntan
bronceado, -da *adj.* tanned, brown
broncearse *verb.* to get a suntan
brotar *verb.* **1.** to bud, sprout **2.** spring up **3.** break out
brote *noun m.* **1.** bud, sprout **2.** outbreak
bruja *noun f.* witch
brujo *noun m.* wizard, sorcerer
brújula *noun f.* compass
brusco, -ca *adj.* **1.** sudden, abrupt **2.** brusque, rough
brutal *adj.* brutal
bruto, -ta *noun.* brute, beast
bruto, -ta *adj.* **1.** gross, raw **2.** brutish, stupid
buche *noun m.* crop

budín *noun m.* pudding
buen *adj.* (see bueno. Used before masculine singular nouns and infinitives used as nouns)
bueno, -na *adj.* **1.** good **2.** kind, nice **3.** large, considerable **4.** healthy, well
bufanda *noun f.* scarf
bufé *noun m.* buffet
bufete *noun m.* law firm
buhardilla *noun f.* attic
búho *noun m.* owl
bulbo *noun m.* **1.** bulb **2.** stir
bullir *verb.* to boil
bulto *noun m.* **1.** bulge **2.** pack, bundle **3.** shape **4.** lump
bungalow *noun m.* bungalow
búnker *noun m.* bunker
buque *noun m.* ship, vessel
burbuja *noun f.* bubble
burbujear *verb.* to bubble
burgués, -guesa *noun. adj.* bourgeois
burguesía *noun f.* bourgeoisie
burla *noun f.* mockery
burlar *verb.* to deceive
—**burlarse** to mock
burocracia *noun f.* bureaucracy
burocrático, -ca *adj.* bureaucratic
burro, -rra *noun.* ass, donkey
busca *noun f.* **1.** search **2.** quest
buscar *verb.* **1.** to look for, seek **2.** search
búsqueda *noun f.* **1.** search **2.** quest
busto *noun m.* bust
butaca *noun f.* **1.** armchair **2.** seat

C

caballería *noun f.* **1.** cavalry **2.** knighthood, chivalry
caballero *noun m.* **1.** gentleman **2.** knight
caballeroso, -sa *adj.* **1.** gentlemanly **2.** chivalrous
caballete *noun m.* **1.** easel **2.** ridge **3.** bridge (of the nose)
caballo *noun m.* **1.** horse **2.** knight (in chess)
cabaña *noun f.* cabin, hut
cabecear *verb.* **1.** to head **2.** nod **3.** pitch
cabecera *noun f.* **1.** top, heading, titlepage **2.** bedside **3.** head
cabello *noun m.* hair
caber *verb.* **1.** to fit **2.** be possible
cabeza *noun f.* head
—**cabeza de familia** head of the household
—**cabeza de serie** seed
—**cabeza de turco** scapegoat
—**cabeza dura** stubborn person
cabezazo *noun m.* **1.** butt **2.** header
cabezota *noun mf.* stubborn person
cabina *noun f.* **1.** booth **2.** cab **3.** cabin **4.** cockpit
cable *noun m.* **1.** cable **2.** wire
cablegrafiar *verb.* to cable, wire
cablegrama *noun m.* cable
cabo *noun m.* **1.** cape **2.** corporal **3.** thread
—**al cabo de** after
—**al fin y al cabo** after all
—**llevar a cabo** to carry out
cabra *noun f.* goat
cabrito *noun m.* kid
cacao *noun m.* cacao, cocoa
cacería *noun f.* hunting
cacerola *noun f.* pan, saucepan
cacharro *noun m.* object, piece of junk
—**cacharros de cocina** pots and pans
cachear *verb.* to search, frisk
cacheo *noun m.* searching, frisking
cachete *noun m.* cheek, slap
cachivache *noun m.* junk
cacho *noun m.* piece
cachorro *noun m.* **1.** cub **2.** pup
cada *adj.* **1.** each **2.** every
—**cada vez más** more and more
—**cada vez mejor** better and better
cadáver *noun m.* body, corpse
cadena *noun f.* **1.** chain **2.** channel **3.** range

—**cadena perpetua** life
cadera *noun f.* hip
caducar *verb.* to expire
caduco, -ca *adj.* **1.** out of date, expired **2.** deciduous **3.** outdated, outmoded
caer *verb.* **1.** to fall **2.** drop **3.** hang
—**caerse** to fall (down)
—**caer bien** to like
—**caer mal** to dislike
café *noun m.* **1.** coffee **2.** coffee shop
cagar *verb.* to shit
caída *noun f.* **1.** fall **2.** drop **3.** collapse **4.** loss
caja *noun f.* **1.** box **2.** checkout counter **3.** case
—**caja de caudales** safe
cajetilla *noun f.* pack
cajón *noun m.* **1.** drawer **2.** box, crate
cal *noun f.* lime
calada *noun f.* puff
calado *noun m.* **1.** draft **2.** openwork
calado, -da *adj.* soaked
calavera *noun f.* skull
calcar *verb.* **1.** to trace **2.** copy, imitate
calcetín *noun m.* sock
calcio *noun m.* calcium
calcomanía *noun f.* transfer
calculadora *noun f.* calculator
calcular *verb.* **1.** to calculate **2.** reckon, estimate
cálculo *noun m.* **1.** calculation **2.** reckoning, estimate **3.** stone
caldera *noun f.* **1.** boiler **2.** cauldron
calderilla *noun f.* small change
caldo *noun m.* stock, broth
calefacción *noun f.* heating
calendario *noun m.* **1.** calendar **2.** schedule
calentador *noun m.* heater
calentar *verb.* to warm, heat
—**calentarse** to warm oneself, warm up, heat up
calibrador *noun m.* gauge
calibrar *verb.* **1.** to calibrate **2.** gage
calibre *noun m.* caliber
calidad *noun f.* **1.** quality, grade **2.** position, status
cálidamente *adv.* warmly
cálido, -da *adj.* **1.** warm **2.** hot
caliente *adj.* **1.** hot **2.** warm
calificar *verb.* **1.** to describe **2.** grade
caligrafía *noun f.* handwriting
caliza *noun f.* limestone
callado, -da *adj.* quiet, silent
calle *noun f.* street, road
callejero, -ra *adj.* **1.** street **2.** stray
callejón *noun m.* alley
callejuela *noun f.* alley
callo *noun m.* corn, callus
calma *noun f.* calm, quiet
calmado, -da *adj.* calm
calmar *verb.* to calm, soothe
—**calmarse** to calm down
calor *noun m.* **1.** heat **2.** warmth
caloría *noun f.* calorie
calumnia *noun f.* libel
calurosamente *adv.* warmly
caluroso, -sa *adj.* **1.** hot **2.** warm
calvo, -va *noun.* bald person
calvo, -va *adj.* bald
calzada *noun f.* road
calzado *noun m.* footwear
calzoncillos *noun m. plural.* underpants, briefs, shorts
cama *noun f.* bed
camada *noun f.* litter
cámara *noun f.* **1.** camera **2.** chamber **3.** house
—**cámara de video** video camera
—**cámara fotográfica** camera
camarada *noun mf.* **1.** comrade **2.** colleague
camarero, -ra *noun.* **1.** waiter or waitress **2.** steward or stewardess
camarote *noun m.* cabin
cambiante *adj.* **1.** changing **2.** changeable **3.** moody
cambiar *verb.* **1.** to change **2.** exchange, swap **3.** move
cambio *noun m.* **1.** change **2.** alteration **3.** exchange, swap
—**a cambio** in return, in exchange
—**en cambio** whereas
caminar *verb.* to walk
caminata *noun f.* hike, walk
camino *noun m.* **1.** road, path, track **2.** way **3.** journey **4.** course
camión *noun m.* truck

camioneta *noun f.* van
camisa *noun f.* shirt
camiseta *noun f.* **1.** undershirt **2.** T-shirt
campamento *noun m.* camp
campana *noun f.* bell
campanada *noun f.* stroke
campanilla *noun f.* bell
campaña *noun f.* **1.** campaign **2.** country
campeón, -peona *noun.* champion
campeonato *noun m.* championship
campesinado *noun m.* peasantry
campesino, -na *noun.* peasant, farmer
campo *noun m.* **1.** country, countryside **2.** field
campus *noun m.* campus
Canadá *noun m.* Canada
canadiense *noun mf. adj.* Canadian
canal *noun m.* **1.** canal **2.** channel
canalizar *verb.* to channel
canalla *noun mf.* swine, rat
canapé *noun m.* **1.** couch **2.** canapé
canasta *noun f.* basket
cancelación *noun f.* cancellation
cancelar *verb.* **1.** to cancel **2.** pay off
cáncer *noun m.* cancer
cancha *noun f.* court, field
canciller *noun m.* chancellor
canción *noun f.* song
candente *adj.* live
candidato, -ta *noun.* **1.** applicant **2.** candidate **3.** nominee
candidatura *noun f.* candidature, candidacy
cándido, -da *adj.* **1.** naïve, naive **2.** simple
canica *noun f.* marble
canje *noun m.* exchange, swap
cano, -na *adj.* gray
canon *noun m.* canon
canónigo *noun m.* canon
cansado, -da *adj.* **1.** tired, weary **2.** tiring
cansancio *noun m.* weariness, fatigue
cansar *verb.* **1.** to tire **2.** be tiring
cansarse *verb.* to get tired
cantante *noun mf.* singer
cantar *verb.* to sing
cantera *noun f.* quarry
cántico *noun m.* chant, canticle
cantidad *noun f.* **1.** quantity, amount **2.** sum
cantimplora *noun f.* canteen, water bottle
cantina *noun f.* canteen, cafeteria
canto *noun m.* **1.** singing **2.** song **3.** chant **4.** edge
caña *noun f.* **1.** cane **2.** reed
—**caña de pescar** fishing rod
cañería *noun f.* **1.** pipe **2.** pipes
cañón *noun m.* **1.** cannon **2.** barrel **3.** canyon
caoba *noun f.* mahogany
caos *noun m.* chaos
capa *noun f.* **1.** cape, cloak **2.** coat **3.** layer
capacidad *noun f.* **1.** capacity **2.** ability, capability
capacitado, -da *adj.* qualified
capacitar *verb.* **1.** to qualify **2.** train, prepare
capataz *noun mf.* foreman or forewoman
capaz *adj.* able, capable
capilla *noun f.* chapel
capirotazo *noun m.* flip
capital *noun f.* capital
—**capital humano** human resources
capital *adj.* **1.** main, chief, key **2.** capital
capitalismo *noun m.* capitalism
capitalista *noun mf. adj.* capitalist
capitán, -tana *noun.* captain
capitanear *verb.* **1.** to captain **2.** command
capitel *noun m.* capital
capítulo *noun m.* chapter
capó *noun m.* hood
capricho *noun m.* **1.** whim, fancy **2.** caprice
captar *verb.* **1.** to catch, grasp **2.** win, attract
captura *noun f.* **1.** capture **2.** seizure **3.** catch
capturar *verb.* **1.** to capture **2.** seize
capucha *noun f.* hood
capuchón *noun m.* cap
cara *noun f.* **1.** face **2.** side **3.** look, appearance **4.** nerve, cheek
caracol *noun m.* snail
carácter *noun m.* **1.** character **2.** nature
característica *noun f.* characteristic, feature, trait
característico, -ca *adj.* characteristic

caracterizar *verb.* to characterize
carajo *interj.* damn!
caramelo *noun m.* **1.** candy **2.** caramel
carátula *noun f.* **1.** cover **2.** mask
caravana *noun f.* **1.** convoy **2.** caravan **3.** trailer
carbohidrato *noun m.* carbohydrate
carbón *noun m.* **1.** coal **2.** charcoal
carbono *noun m.* carbon
carcajada *noun f.* laughter
cárcel *noun f.* jail, prison
cardenal *noun m.* **1.** cardinal **2.** bruise
cardinal *adj.* cardinal
carecer (de) *verb.* to lack
carencia *noun f.* **1.** lack **2.** shortage
careta *noun f.* mask
carga *noun f.* **1.** load, freight, cargo **2.** burden **3.** charge
cargado, -da *adj.* **1.** loaded **2.** charged **3.** strong
cargador *noun m.* **1.** loader, longshoreman **2.** battery charger
cargamento *noun m.* cargo, load
cargar *verb.* **1.** to load **2.** carry **3.** charge
cargo *noun m.* **1.** load, burden **2.** charge **3.** post, office
cariarse *verb.* to decay
caricatura *noun f.* **1.** caricature **2.** cartoon
caricia *noun f.* **1.** caress **2.** pat, stroke
caridad *noun f.* charity
caries *noun f.* decay
cariño *noun m.* **1.** affection, love **2.** honey, darling, sweet
cariñoso, -sa *adj.* affectionate, loving
caritativo, -va *adj.* charitable
carnada *noun f.* bait
carnaval *noun m.* carnival
carnaza *noun f.* bait
carne *noun f.* **1.** meat **2.** flesh
carnero *noun m.* **1.** ram **2.** mutton
carnicería *noun f.* **1.** butcher shop **2.** slaughter
carnicero, -ra *noun.* butcher
caro, -ra *adj.* **1.** expensive **2.** dear
carpa *noun f.* **1.** carp **2.** tent **3.** big top
carpeta *noun f.* **1.** file, folder **2.** portfolio
carrera *noun f.* **1.** run **2.** race **3.** course **4.** career
carreta *noun f.* cart
carrete *noun m.* **1.** film **2.** reel
carretera *noun f.* road, highway
carretilla *noun f.* wheelbarrow
carril *noun m.* **1.** lane **2.** rail
carrito *noun m.* cart
carro *noun m.* **1.** car **2.** cart **3.** wagon
carruaje *noun m.* carriage
carta *noun f.* **1.** letter **2.** card **3.** charter **4.** map **5.** menu
cartearse con *verb.* correspond
cartel *noun m.* cartel
cartera *noun f.* **1.** wallet, billfold **2.** portfolio
cartón *noun m.* **1.** cardboard **2.** card
cartucho *noun m.* cartridge
casa *noun f.* **1.** house **2.** home **3.** household **4.** firm, company
casado, -da *adj.* married
casamiento *noun m.* **1.** wedding **2.** marriage
casar *verb.* **1.** to marry **2.** match up
—**casarse** to get marry
—**casarse con** to marry
cascar *verb.* to crack
cáscara *noun f.* **1.** skin, peel **2.** shell
casco *noun m.* **1.** helmet **2.** hull **3.** empty bottle **4.** headphones
—**casco antiguo** old quarter
casero, -ra *noun.* landlord or landlady
casero, -ra *adj.* home, homemade
casete *noun mf.* cassette
casi *adv.* **1.** almost, nearly **2.** hardly (in negative sentences)
casino *noun m.* casino
caso *noun m.* **1.** case **2.** affair
—**hacer caso de** to notice, pay attention to
casta *noun f.* **1.** caste **2.** lineage, stock
castigar *verb.* to punish
castigo *noun m.* **1.** punishment **2.** penalty
castillo *noun m.* castle
casual *adj.* **1.** chance **2.** fortuitous
casualidad *noun f.* **1.** chance **2.** coincidence
—**por casualidad** by chance
casualmente *adv.* by chance
catalogar *verb.* to catalog, classify

catálogo *noun m.* catalog
catar *verb.* to taste
catarata *noun f.* **1.** waterfall **2.** cataract
catástrofe *noun f.* catastrophe
cátedra *noun f.* chair
catedral *noun f.* cathedral
catedrático, -ca *noun.* professor
categoría *noun f.* **1.** category **2.** grade, rank
catering *noun m.* catering
católico, -ca *noun. adj.* Catholic
catorce *noun m. adj.* **1.** fourteen **2.** fourteenth
caucho *noun m.* rubber
causa *noun f.* cause
—**por causa de** because of
causar *verb.* **1.** to cause **2.** make
cautela *noun f.* caution
cauteloso, -sa *adj.* cautious
cautivador, -dora *adj.* captivating
cautivar *verb.* to captivate
cautivo, -va *noun. adj.* captive
cauto, -ta *adj.* cautious
cavar *verb.* to dig
caverna *noun f.* cave
cavidad *noun f.* cavity
cayado *noun m.* crook
caza *noun f.* **1.** hunting **2.** game
caza *noun m.* fighter plane
cazador, -dora *noun m.* hunter
cazar *verb.* **1.** to hunt **2.** catch **3.** land
cazo *noun m.* **1.** saucepan **2.** ladle
cazuela *noun f.* **1.** pan **2.** casserole
CD *noun m.* CD, compact disk
cebada *noun f.* barley
cebar *verb.* **1.** to bait **2.** fatten
cebo *noun m.* bait
cebolla *noun f.* onion
ceder *verb.* **1.** to cede, hand over **2.** give in, yield **3.** diminish, abate
cegar *verb.* **1.** to blind **2.** block
ceja *noun f.* eyebrow
celda *noun f.* cell
celebración *noun f.* celebration
celebrar *verb.* **1.** to celebrate **2.** hold **3.** perform
célebre *adj.* celebrated, noted
celebridad *noun f.* **1.** celebrity **2.** fame, renown
celoso, -sa *adj.* jealous
Celsius *adj.* Celsius
celta *adj.* Celtic
célula *noun f.* cell
celular *adj.* cellular
cementerio *noun m.* cemetery
cemento *noun m.* cement
cena *noun f.* dinner, supper
cenar *verb.* **1.** to have dinner, have supper, dine **2.** have for dinner, have for supper
cenicero *noun m.* ashtray
ceniza *noun f.* ash
censo *noun m.* census
censura *noun f.* **1.** censorship **2.** censure, criticism
censurar *verb.* **1.** to censor **2.** censure, criticize
centavo *noun m.* cent
centellear *verb.* to sparkle
centelleo *noun m.* sparkle
centena *noun f.* hundred
centenario *noun m.* centennial
centenario, -ria *adj.* centenarian
centeno *noun m.* rye
centígrado *adj.* centigrade
centímetro *noun m.* centimeter
céntimo *noun m.* cent
central *noun f.* **1.** head office, headquarters **2.** plant, station
—**central eléctrica** power station
central *adj.* **1.** central **2.** main
centrar *verb.* **1.** to center **2.** focus
—**centrarse en** to focus on, center on
céntrico, -ca *adj.* central
centro *noun m.* **1.** center **2.** downtown
ceño *noun m.* frown
cepa *noun f.* **1.** stock **2.** stump
cepillado *noun m.* brushing
cepillar *verb.* **1.** to brush **2.** plane
cepillo *noun m.* **1.** brush **2.** plane
cera *noun f.* **1.** polish **2.** wax
cerámica *noun f.* **1.** ceramics **2.** pottery
ceramista *noun mf.* potter
cerca *noun f.* **1.** fence **2.** wall
cerca *adv.* close, near, nearby
—**cerca de** nearly, almost
cercado *noun m.* enclosure
cercanía *noun f.* proximity

—**cercanías** 1. neighborhood 2. outskirts, suburbs
cercano, -na *adj.* close, near, nearby
cercar *verb.* **1.** to enclose, fence **2.** surround
cerco *noun m.* **1.** enclosure **2.** fence **3.** siege
cerdo, -da *noun.* pig, hog
—**carne de cerdo** pork
cereal *noun m.* **1.** cereal **2.** grain
cerebral *adj.* cerebral
cerebro *noun m.* brain
ceremonia *noun f.* ceremony
cerilla *noun f.* match
cero *noun m.* zero
cerrado, -da *adj.* **1.** closed, shut **2.** thick **3.** reserved
cerradura *noun f.* lock
cerrar *verb.* **1.** to close, shut **2.** lock **3.** turn off **4.** seal
—**cerrarse** **1.** to close, shut **2.** end
certamen *noun m.* contest
certeza *noun f.* certainty
certificado *noun m.* certificate
certificado, -da *adj.* registered
certificar *verb.* **1.** to certify **2.** register
cervecería *noun f.* beer hall, bar
cerveza *noun f.* beer
cesar *verb.* **1.** to cease, stop **2.** dismiss
césped *noun m.* **1.** grass **2.** lawn
cesta *noun f.* basket
chal *noun m.* shawl
chalado, -da *adj.* nutty, crazy
chaleco *noun m.* vest
chalet *noun m.* villa
champán, champaña *noun m.* champagne
champiñón *noun m.* mushroom
chanza *noun m.* joke
chaparrón *noun m.* downpour, shower
chapotear *verb.* to splash
chapoteo *noun m.* splash
chapuzón *noun m.* dip
chaqueta *noun f.* jacket
charco *noun m.* pool, puddle
charla *noun f.* chat, talk
charlar *verb.* to chat, talk
charlatán, -tana *noun.* chatterbox
chasquear *verb.* **1.** to clip **2.** crack **3.** snap
chasquido *noun m.* **1.** clip **2.** crack **3.** snap
chatarra *noun f.* scrap
chaval, -vala *noun.* kid, lad
chavo, -va *noun.* kid, lad
checo, -ca *noun. adj.* Czech
chelín *noun m.* shilling
cheque *noun m.* check
chichón *noun m.* bump
chicle *noun m.* chewing gum
chico, -ca *noun.* boy or girl
chico, -ca *adj.* **1.** little, small **2.** young
chiflado, -da *adj.* nutty, crazy
chile *noun m.* chili
Chile *noun m.* Chile
chileno, -na *noun. adj.* Chilean
chillar *verb.* to scream
chillido *noun m.* scream
chillón, -llona *adj.* **1.** shrill **2.** loud
chimenea *noun f.* **1.** chimney **2.** fireplace
China *noun f.* China
chinche *noun m.* bedbug
chino, -na *noun. adj.* Chinese
chip *noun m.* chip
Chipre *noun m.* Cyprus
chipriota *noun mf. adj.* Cypriot
chirriar *verb.* to creak, squeak
chirrido *noun m.* squeak
chisme *noun m.* **1.** gossip **2.** stuff
chismorrear *verb.* to gossip
chismorreo *noun m.* gossip
chismoso, -sa *adj.* gossiping
chispa *noun f.* spark
chispeante *adj.* sparkling
chispear *verb.* **1.** to throw out sparks **2.** sparkle
chiste *noun m.* joke
chistoso, -sa *noun.* wit
chivar *verb.* to rat, squeal
chivato, -ta *noun.* **1.** informer **2.** sneak
chivo, -va *noun.* young goat
chocar *verb.* **1.** to collide, crash **2.** clash **3.** shock **4.** shake **5.** clink
chocolate *noun m.* **1.** chocolate **2.** cocoa
choque *noun m.* **1.** collision, crash **2.** clash **3.** shock
chorrear *verb.* **1.** to drip **2.** pour

chorro *noun m.* jet, stream
chubasco *noun m.* downpour
chuchería *noun f.* candy
chuleta *noun f.* chop, cutlet
chupada *noun f.* **1.** suck **2.** puff
chupar *verb.* **1.** to suck **2.** puff on **3.** absorb
chusma *noun f.* rabble
chutar *verb.* to shoot
cicatriz *noun f.* scar
ciclo *noun m.* cycle
ciego, -ga *noun.* blind person
ciego, -ga *adj.* blind
—**a ciegas** blindly
cielo *noun m.* **1.** sky **2.** heaven
cien *noun m.* one hundred
cien *adj.* hundred, a hundred
ciénaga *noun f.* bog, swamp
ciencia *noun f.* science
científico, -ca *noun.* scientist
científico, -ca *adj.* scientific
cierre *noun m.* **1.** closure, closing **2.** clasp, fastener
cierto, -ta *adj.* **1.** certain **2.** true **3.** one, some
—**por cierto** by the way
ciervo, -va *noun.* deer, stag
cifra *noun f.* **1.** figure **2.** number
cifrar *verb.* **1.** to code, encode **2.** pin, place
—**cifrarse** to calculate
cigarro *noun m.* cigarette
cilindro *noun m.* cylinder
cima *noun f.* top, height, summit
cimiento *noun m.* base, foundation
cinc *noun m.* zinc
cinco *noun m. adj.* **1.** five **2.** fifth
cincuenta *noun m. adj.* fifty
cine *noun m.* **1.** cinema **2.** movie theater
cínico, -ca *noun.* cynic
cínico, -ca *adj.* cynical
cinta *noun f.* **1.** ribbon **2.** tape
cintura *noun f.* waist
cinturón *noun m.* belt
circo *noun m.* circus
circuito *noun m.* circuit
circulación *noun f.* circulation
circular *noun f. adj.* circular
circular *verb.* **1.** to circulate **2.** run **3.** walk **4.** flow
círculo *noun m.* circle
circundar *verb.* to surround
circunscripción *noun f.* constituency
circunstancia *noun f.* circumstance
ciruela *noun f.* plum
—**ciruela pasa** prune
cirugía *noun f.* surgery
cirujano, -na *noun.* surgeon
cisne *noun m.* swan
cisterna *noun f.* **1.** tank **2.** flush
cita *noun f.* **1.** appointment, date **2.** quotation
citación *noun f.* **1.** summons **2.** quotation
citar *verb.* **1.** to quote **2.** make an appointment **3.** summon
ciudad *noun f.* city, town
ciudadanía *noun f.* citizenship
ciudadano, -na *noun.* citizen
cívico, -ca *adj.* civic
civil *adj.* **1.** civil **2.** civilian
civilización *noun f.* civilization
clan *noun m.* clan
clara *noun f.* egg white
claramente *adv.* clearly
claridad *noun f.* clarity
claro *noun m.* clearing
—**claro de luna** moonlight
claro, -ra *adj.* **1.** clear **2.** evident **3.** bright **4.** fair, light **5.** weak, thin **6.** frank
claro *adv.* **1.** clearly **2.** sure **3.** frankly **4.** of course
clase *noun f.* **1.** class **2.** sort, type
clásico *noun m.* classic
clásico, -ca *adj.* **1.** classic **2.** classical
clasificación *noun f.* **1.** classification **2.** rating
clasificar *verb.* **1.** to classify **2.** sort **3.** rank
—**clasificarse** to qualify
cláusula *noun f.* clause
clavar *verb.* **1.** to hammer **2.** nail **3.** plunge **4.** fix
clave *noun f.* **1.** key **2.** code **3.** clef
clave *adj.* key
clavija *noun f.* **1.** peg **2.** plug
clavo *noun m.* **1.** nail **2.** clove
claxon *noun m.* horn
clemencia *noun f.* mercy

clerical *adj.* clerical
clérigo *noun m.* clergyman, priest
clero *noun m.* clergy
clic *noun m.* click
cliente, -ta *noun.* client, customer
clientela *noun f.* **1.** customers **2.** practice
clima *noun m.* climate
clímax *noun m.* climax
clínica *noun f.* clinic
clínico, -ca *adj.* clinical
clip *noun m.* clip
club *noun m.* club
coalición *noun f.* coalition
cobertizo *noun m.* shed
cobertor *noun m.* bedspread
cobertura *noun f.* coverage
cobrador, -dora *noun.* **1.** collector **2.** conductor
cobrar *verb.* **1.** to charge **2.** collect **3.** get, earn **4.** draw
cobre *noun m.* copper
cocaína *noun f.* cocaine
cocer *verb.* **1.** to boil **2.** cook
coche *noun m.* car
cochera *noun f.* garage
cocido *noun m.* stew
cocina *noun f.* **1.** kitchen **2.** cuisine
cocinar *verb.* to cook
cocinero, -ra *noun.* **1.** chef **2.** cook
cóctel *noun m.* cocktail
codicia *noun f.* lust, greed
codicioso, -sa *adj.* greedy
codificar *verb.* **1.** to codify **2.** code
código *noun m.* code
—**código postal** zip code
codo *noun m.* elbow
cofia *noun f.* cap
coger *verb.* **1.** to take **2.** seize **3.** catch **4.** gather **5.** pick
coherencia *noun f.* coherence
coherente *adj.* coherent
cohete *noun m.* rocket
coincidencia *noun f.* coincidence
coincidir *verb.* to coincide
cojear *verb.* to limp
cojera *noun f.* limp
cojín *noun m.* cushion
cojinete *noun m.* bearing
cola *noun f.* **1.** tail **2.** line **3.** glue
colaboración *noun f.* collaboration
colaborador, -dora *noun.* **1.** contributor **2.** collaborator
colada *noun f.* washing
colapso *noun m.* collapse
colar *verb.* to strain
colcha *noun f.* bedspread
colección *noun f.* collection
coleccionista *noun mf.* collector
colectividad *noun f.* community
colectivo *noun m.* collective
colectivo, -va *adj.* collective
colega *noun mf.* **1.** colleague **2.** counterpart
colegio *noun m.* **1.** school **2.** college
cólera *noun f.* anger
cólera *noun m.* cholera
colérico, -ca *adj.* **1.** angry **2.** irritable
colgado, -da *adj.* hanging, hanged, hung
colgar *verb.* to hang
colina *noun f.* hill
colisión *noun f.* collision, crash
colisionar *verb.* to collide, crash
collar *noun m.* **1.** necklace **2.** collar
colmar *verb.* to heap
colmo *noun m.* height, extreme
colocar *verb.* **1.** to place, put **2.** arrange —**colocarse 1.** to get a job **2.** position oneself
colon *noun m.* colon
colonia *noun f.* **1.** colony, settlement **2.** cologne
colonial *adj.* colonial
colonizador, -dora *noun.* colonizer, settler
colono, -na *noun.* **1.** colonizer, settler **2.** tenant farmer
color *noun m.* color
colorante *noun m.* coloring
colorear *verb.* to color
columna *noun f.* column
—**columna vertebral** spine
columnista *noun mf.* columnist
columpio *noun m.* swing
comandante *noun mf.* **1.** commander **2.** major
combate *noun m.* **1.** combat **2.** fight

combatiente *noun mf.* fighter
combatir *verb.* to combat, fight
combatividad *noun f.* fighting spirit
combinación *noun f.* combination
combinar *verb.* **1.** to combine **2.** match
—**combinarse** to get together, join together
combustible *noun m.* fuel
comedia *noun f.* comedy
comedido, -da *adj.* restrained
comedor *noun m.* dining-room
comentar *verb.* **1.** to comment **2.** remark
comentario *noun m.* **1.** comment, remark **2.** commentary
comentarista *noun mf.* commentator
comenzar *verb.* to begin, start
comer *verb.* to eat
—**dar de comer** to feed
comercial *adj.* commercial
comerciante *noun mf.* **1.** dealer **2.** merchant **3.** trader
—**comerciante al por menor** retailer
comerciar *verb.* **1.** to deal, trade **2.** do business (with)
comercio *noun m.* **1.** commerce, trade **2.** store
cometa *noun f.* **1.** comet **2.** kite
cometer *verb.* **1.** to commit **2.** make
cometido *noun m.* assignment
cómic *noun m.* comic
comicidad *noun m.* humor
cómico, -ca *noun.* comedian or comedienne
cómico, -ca *adj.* comic, comical
comida *noun f.* **1.** food **2.** dinner **3.** meal
comienzo *noun m.* start, beginning
comisaría *noun f.* police station
comisario, -ria *noun.* commissioner
comisión *noun f.* **1.** commission **2.** committee
comité *noun m.* committee
como *conj.* **1.** as **2.** like **3.** if **4.** since, given that
como *prep.* as, like
cómo *adv.* how
cómo *interj.* what?
cómoda *noun f.* bureau
cómodamente *adv.* **1.** comfortably **2.** conveniently
comodidad *noun f.* **1.** comfort **2.** convenience
cómodo, -da *adj.* **1.** comfortable **2.** convenient
compacto, -ta *adj.* compact
compadecer *verb.* **1.** to feel sorry, pity **2.** sympathize with
compañerismo *noun m.* fellowship, comradeship
compañero, -ra *noun.* companion, fellow
compañía *noun f.* company
comparable *adj.* comparable
comparación *noun f.* comparison
comparar *verb.* to compare
comparativo, -va *adj.* comparative
comparecencia *noun f.* appearance
comparecer *verb.* to appear
compartimiento *noun m.* compartment
compartir *verb.* to share
compás *noun m.* **1.** compass **2.** measure **3.** rhythm
compasión *noun f.* **1.** compassion **2.** pity
compasivo, -va *adj.* compassionate
compatibilidad *noun f.* compatibility
compatible *adj.* compatible
compeler *verb.* to compel
compensar *verb.* **1.** to compensate (for) **2.** make up (for)
competencia *noun f.* **1.** competence **2.** competition
competente *adj.* able, capable, competent
competición *noun f.* **1.** competition **2.** contest
competidor, -dora *noun.* competitor
competir *verb.* to compete
competitivo, -va *adj.* competitive
compilar *verb.* to compile
complacer *verb.* **1.** to please **2.** indulge
complaciente *adj.* obliging
complejidad *noun f.* complexity
complejo *noun m.* complex
complejo, -ja *adj.* complex
complementar *verb.* to complement, supplement
—**complementarse** to complement each other
complementario, -ria *adj.* complementary

complemento *noun m.* **1.** complement **2.** object
—complementos accessories
completamente *adv.* completely
completar *verb.* to complete, finish
completo, -ta *adj.* **1.** complete **2.** full
complexión *noun f.* constitution, build
complicación *noun f.* complication
complicado, -da *adj.* complicated
complicar *verb.* **1.** to complicate **2.** involve
cómplice *noun mf.* accomplice
complot *noun m.* plot
componente *noun m.* component, constituent
componer *verb.* **1.** to compose, write **2.** make up **3.** fix, repair
—componerse de to consist of
comportamiento *noun m.* behavior, conduct
comportar *verb.* to involve, carry
—comportarse to behave
composición *noun f.* composition
compositor, -tora *noun.* composer
compra *noun f.* purchase, buying
comprador, -dora *noun.* purchaser, buyer
comprar *verb.* to buy, purchase
comprender *verb.* **1.** to understand, realize **2.** comprise, cover
comprensible *adj.* understandable
comprensión *noun f.* **1.** understanding, comprehension **2.** sympathy
comprensivo, -va *adj.* understanding
compresión *noun f.* compression
comprimido *noun m.* tablet
comprimir *verb.* to compress
comprobante *noun m.* **1.** proof **2.** voucher
comprobar *verb.* **1.** to check **2.** verify, probe
comprometer *verb.* **1.** to compromise **2.** commit **3.** jeopardize
—comprometerse to commit oneself
—comprometerse con to get engaged to
comprometido, -da *adj.* **1.** committed **2.** compromising
compromiso *noun m.* **1.** commitment **2.** engagement
compuesto *noun m.* compound
compuesto, -ta *adj.* **1.** compound **2.** composed
computadora *noun f.* computer
computar *verb.* to compute
computerizar *verb.* to computerize
común *adj.* common
comunal *adj.* communal
comunicación *noun f.* communication
comunicado *noun m.* statement
—comunicado de prensa press release
comunicar *verb.* **1.** to announce, inform **2.** connect
—comunicarse to communicate
comunicativo, -va *adj.* communicative
comunidad *noun f.* community
comunión *noun f.* communion
comunismo *noun m.* communism
comunista *noun mf. adj.* communist
comunitario, -ria *adj.* communal
con *prep.* **1.** with **2.** to, towards **3.** although
—con tal que provided that
concebir *verb.* **1.** to conceive, devise **2.** imagine
conceder *verb.* **1.** to award, grant **2.** concede, admit
concejal, -jala *noun.* councilor, councilman or councilwoman
concentración *noun f.* concentration
concentrar *verb.* to concentrate
—concentrarse **1.** to focus, concentrate **2.** gather
concepción *noun f.* conception
concepto *noun m.* concept
concernir *verb.* to concern
concesión *noun f.* **1.** concession **2.** franchise, license
concha *noun f.* shell
conciencia *noun f.* **1.** conscience **2.** consciousness
concienzudo, -da *adj.* thorough
concierto *noun m.* concert
conciliar *verb.* to reconcile
concluir *verb.* **1.** to conclude **2.** end
conclusión *noun f.* conclusion, end
concluyente *adj.* conclusive
concordar *verb.* **1.** to agree **2.** bring to agreement

concreto, -ta *adj.* **1.** concrete **2.** specific
concurrido, -da *adj.* busy, crowded
concurso *noun m.* **1.** contest **2.** competition
condado *noun m.* county
conde, -desa *noun.* count or countess, earl
condecoración *noun f.* decoration, honor
condecorar *verb.* to decorate, honor
condena *noun f.* **1.** condemnation **2.** conviction
condenado, -da *noun.* convict
condenado, -da *adj.* **1.** convicted **2.** damned **3.** doomed
condenar *verb.* **1.** to condemn **2.** sentence, convict **3.** damn
condición *noun f.* **1.** condition **2.** position
condicional *adj.* conditional
condicionar *verb.* to condition
condimentar *verb.* to flavor, spice
condimento *noun m.* seasoning, flavoring
condón *noun m.* condom
conducir *verb.* **1.** to drive **2.** conduct **3.** lead
conductor, -tora *noun.* driver
conectar *verb.* **1.** to connect **2.** link
conejo, -ja *noun.* rabbit
conexión *noun f.* connection
confección *noun f.* **1.** preparation **2.** dressmaking
confeccionar *verb.* **1.** to prepare **2.** make
confederación *noun f.* confederation
conferencia *noun f.* **1.** conference **2.** lecture
conferenciante *noun mf.* lecturer
confesar *verb.* to confess
confesión *noun f.* confession
confiado, -da *adj.* **1.** confident **2.** trusting
confianza *noun f.* **1.** trust **2.** confidence
confiar *verb.* **1.** to trust **2.** confide
—**confiarse** to be over-confident
confidencial *adj.* confidential
confidencialidad *noun f.* confidentiality
confinar *verb.* to confine
confirmación *noun f.* confirmation
confirmar *verb.* to confirm
confitura *noun f.* **1.** jam **2.** preserve
conflictivo, -va *adj.* **1.** controversial **2.** troubled
conflicto *noun m.* conflict
confluir *verb.* to gather
conforme *adj.* satisfied
—**conforme a** in accordance with
conforme *conj.* as
conformidad *noun f.* agreement, consent
confort *noun m.* comfort
confundido, -da *adj.* **1.** confused **2.** mistaken, wrong
confundir *verb.* to confuse
—**confundirse** to make a mistake
confusión *noun f.* confusion
confuso, -sa *adj.* confused
congelar *verb.* to freeze
congregación *noun f.* congregation
congregar *verb.* to bring together
—**congregarse** to gather
congresista *noun mf.* congressman or congresswoman
congreso *noun m.* **1.** congress **2.** conference
conjetura *noun f.* guess
conjunción *noun f.* conjunction
conjuntamente *adv.* jointly
conjunto *noun m.* **1.** group **2.** ensemble **3.** set
—**en conjunto** as a whole, altogether
conjunto, -ta *adj.* joint
conmemorar *verb.* to commemorate
conmigo *pron.* with me
conmoción *noun f.* shock
conmocionar *verb.* to shock, shake
conmovedor, -dora *adj.* moving, touching
conmover *verb.* to move, touch
—**conmoverse** to be moved, be touched
conmutador *noun m.* switch
conocedor, -dora *noun.* connoisseur
conocer *verb.* **1.** to know **2.** meet
—**conocerse** **1.** to know oneself **2.** know each other **3.** meet

conocido, -da *noun.* acquaintance
conocido, -da *adj.* **1.** familiar **2.** well-known
conocimiento *noun m.* **1.** knowledge **2.** consciousness
conquista *noun f.* conquest
conquistar *verb.* to conquer
consagración *noun f.* consecration, dedication
consagrar *verb.* **1.** to consecrate, dedicate **2.** devote
consciencia *noun f.* (see conciencia)
consciente *adj.* aware, conscious
conscientemente *adv.* consciously
consecuencia *noun f.* consequence
consecuente *adj.* consistent
consecutivo, -va *adj.* consecutive
conseguir *verb.* **1.** to achieve, attain **2.** get **3.** manage (to)
consejero, -ra *noun.* adviser, counselor
consejo *noun m.* **1.** advice, counsel **2.** council
consenso *noun m.* consensus
consentimiento *noun m.* consent
consentir *verb.* **1.** to allow, consent **2.** spoil
conservación *noun f.* **1.** conservation **2.** preservation
conservador, -dora *noun.* **1.** conservative **2.** curator
conservador, -dora *adj.* conservative
conservadurismo *noun m.* conservatism
conservar *verb.* **1.** to keep, conserve **2.** preserve
considerable *adj.* considerable
consideración *noun f.* **1.** consideration **2.** regard
considerado, -da *adj.* **1.** thoughtful **2.** respected
considerar *verb.* **1.** to consider **2.** deem
consignar *verb.* **1.** to consign **2.** assign **3.** record
consigo *adv.* with you, with him, with her, with them, with one
consistencia *noun f.* consistency
consistente *adj.* **1.** consistent **2.** strong, sound
consolación *noun f.* consolation
consolar *verb.* to console
consolidación *noun f.* consolidation
consolidar *verb.* to consolidate
consonante *noun f.* consonant
consorcio *noun m.* consortium
conspiración *noun f.* conspiracy
conspirar *verb.* to plot, conspire
constancia *noun f.* **1.** record **2.** proof **3.** perseverance
constante *adj.* constant
constar *verb.* to be clear
—**constar de** to consist of
constelación *noun f.* constellation
consternación *noun f.* dismay
consternar *verb.* to dismay
constitución *noun f.* constitution
constitucional *adj.* constitutional
constituir *verb.* **1.** to constitute **2.** set up
constitutivo, -va *adj.* constituent
constituyente *adj.* constituent
construcción *noun f.* **1.** building **2.** construction
constructivo, -va *adj.* constructive
constructor, -tora *noun.* builder
construir *verb.* to build, construct
consuelo *noun m.* consolation
consulta *noun f.* consultation
consultar *verb.* to consult
consultor, -tora *noun.* consultant
consultorio *noun m.* office
consumado, -da *adj.* consummate, accomplished
consumidor, -dora *noun.* consumer
consumir *verb.* to consume
consumo *noun m.* consumption
contabilidad *noun f.* **1.** accountancy **2.** accounting
contactar *verb.* to contact
contacto *noun m.* contact
contador *noun m.* meter
contagiar *verb.* **1.** to infect **2.** transmit
—**contagiarse 1.** to become infected **2.** be contagious
contagioso, -sa *adj.* catching, contagious
contaminación *noun f.* contamination, pollution
contaminar *verb.* to contaminate, pollute

contar *verb.* **1.** to count **2.** tell
—**contar con** to rely on, count on
contemplar *verb.* **1.** to contemplate **2.** look at
contemporáneo, -nea *noun. adj.* contemporary
contencioso, -sa *adj.* contentious
contendiente *noun mf.* contender
contenedor *noun m.* container
contener *verb.* **1.** to contain **2.** hold
—**contenerse** to restrain oneself
contenido *noun m.* content
contentar *verb.* to please
contento, -ta *adj.* glad, happy, pleased
contestación *noun f.* answer
contestador *noun m.* answering machine
contestar *verb.* to answer
contexto *noun m.* context
contigo *pron.* with you
continental *adj.* continental
continente *noun m.* continent
contingencia *noun f.* contingency
contingente *noun m.* contingent
continuación *noun f.* continuation
—**a continuación** next
continuar *verb.* to continue, go on
continuidad *noun f.* continuity
continuo, -nua *adj.* continuous, constant
contorno *noun m.* outline
contra *prep.* against
contracción *noun f.* contraction
contradicción *noun f.* contradiction
contradictorio, -ria *adj.* contradictory
contraer *verb.* **1.** to contract **2.** catch
—**contraer matrimonio** to get married
contrariar *verb.* **1.** to contradict **2.** oppose **3.** annoy
contrario, -ria *adj.* contrary, opposite
—**al contrario** on the contrary
contrastar *verb.* to contrast
contraste *noun m.* contrast
contratar *verb.* to hire
contratista *noun mf.* contractor
contrato *noun m.* contract
contribución *noun f.* contribution
contribuir *verb.* **1.** to contribute **2.** pay
contribuyente *noun mf.* taxpayer
contrincante *noun mf.* opponent, challenger
control *noun m.* **1.** control **2.** check
controlador, -dora *noun.* controller
controlar *verb.* **1.** to control **2.** monitor
controversia *noun f.* controversy
controvertido, -da *adj.* controversial
convencer *verb.* to convince, persuade
convencido, -da *adj.* **1.** sure **2.** convinced
convención *noun f.* convention
convencional *adj.* conventional
convenido, -da *adj.* appointed
conveniencia *noun f.* convenience
conveniente *adj.* **1.** appropriate **2.** convenient **3.** suitable
convenio *noun m.* **1.** agreement, pact **2.** covenant
convenir *verb.* **1.** to suit **2.** agree
convento *noun m.* convent
convergencia *noun f.* convergence
conversación *noun f.* conversation, talk
conversar *verb.* to converse, talk
conversión *noun f.* conversion
converso, -sa *noun.* convert
convertible *adj.* convertible
convertir *verb.* to convert
—**convertirse en** to turn into
convicción *noun f.* conviction
convidar *verb.* to invite
convincente *adj.* convincing
convocar *verb.* to call, convene, summon
convoy *noun m.* convoy
conyugal *adj.* conjugal, marital
coñac *noun m.* brandy
cooperación *noun f.* cooperation
cooperativa *noun f.* cooperative
cooperativo, -va *adj.* cooperative
coordinación *noun f.* coordination
coordinar *verb.* to coordinate
copa *noun f.* **1.** cup **2.** drink **3.** glass
copia *noun f.* **1.** copy **2.** imitation
copiar *verb.* to copy
coque *noun m.* coke
coraje *noun m.* courage
coral *noun f.* chorale
coral *noun m.* coral
corazón *noun m.* **1.** heart **2.** core

corbata *noun f.* tie
corchete *noun m.* bracket
corcho *noun m.* cork
cordel *noun m.* cord, string
cordero *noun m.* lamb
cordillera *noun f.* range
cordón *noun m.* **1.** lace, cord **2.** cordon
Corea *noun f.* Korea
coreano, -na *noun. adj.* Korean
corear *verb.* to chant, chorus
cornear *verb.* to gore
coro *noun m.* **1.** choir **2.** chorus
corona *noun f.* crown
coronación *noun f.* coronation
coronar *verb.* to crown
coronel *noun mf.* colonel
coronilla *noun f.* crown
corporación *noun f.* corporation
corporal *adj.* bodily, corporal
corpulento, -ta *adj.* stout
corral *noun m.* farmyard, corral
correa *noun f.* belt, strap
corrección *noun f.* correction
correcto, -ta *adj.* correct, right
corredor *noun m.* corridor
corredor, -dora *noun.* **1.** runner **2.** broker
corregir *verb.* **1.** to correct **2.** grade
correo *noun m.* mail, post
correr *verb.* **1.** to run, **2.** rush **3.** flow
correspondencia *noun f.* **1.** correspondence, mail **2.** equivalence
corresponder *verb.* **1.** to correspond **2.** belong **3.** return
correspondiente *adj.* corresponding
corresponsal *noun mf.* correspondent
corriente *noun f.* **1.** current **2.** draft **3.** tendency, trend
corriente *adj.* **1.** common **2.** ordinary
corroborar *verb.* to corroborate
corroer *verb.* **1.** to corrode **2.** erode
corromper *verb.* **1.** to corrupt **2.** rot
corrosivo, -va *adj.* corrosive
corrupción *noun f.* corruption
corrupto, -ta *adj.* corrupt
cortante *adj.* cutting, sharp
cortar *verb.* **1.** to cut **2.** slice **3.** chop **4.** trim **5.** interrupt **6.** block
—**cortarse 1.** to cut oneself **2.** go off
corte *noun f.* court
corte *noun m.* cut
cortejar *verb.* to court, woo
cortés *adj.* courteous, polite
cortesía *noun f.* courtesy, politeness
corteza *noun f.* **1.** bark **2.** crust **3.** peel
cortina *noun f.* curtain
corto, -ta *adj.* **1.** short **2.** shy, timid **3.** scarce
cosa *noun f.* **1.** thing, object, stuff **2.** matter, affair
cosecha *noun f.* crop, harvest
cosechar *verb.* **1.** to harvest **2.** win, earn
coser *verb.* **1.** to sew **2.** stitch
cosmético *noun m.* cosmetic
cosmético, -ca *adj.* cosmetic
costa *noun f.* coast, shore
—**a toda costa** at all costs
costado *noun m.* **1.** flank **2.** side
costar *verb.* to cost
costero, -ra *adj.* coastal
costilla *noun f.* rib
costo *noun m.* cost, price
costoso, -sa *adj.* costly
costra *noun f.* crust
costumbre *noun f.* **1.** custom **2.** habit
costura *noun f.* **1.** seam **2.** sewing
cotidiano, -na *adj.* everyday, daily
cotilla *noun mf.* gossip
cotillear *verb.* to gossip
cotilleo *noun m.* gossip
cotización *noun f.* quotation
cotizar *verb.* **1.** to value **2.** pay contributions
—**cotizarse** to be valued
coto *noun m.* preserve, reserve
craso, -sa *adj.* gross
creación *noun f.* creation
creador, -dora *noun.* creator
crear *verb.* **1.** to create **2.** originate
creatividad *noun f.* creativity
creativo, -va *adj.* creative
crecer *verb.* **1.** to grow **2.** expand **3.** increase
creciente *adj.* growing, increasing
crecimiento *noun m.* growth
credibilidad *noun f.* credibility
crédito *noun m.* credit
credo *noun m.* creed
creencia *noun f.* belief

creer *verb.* **1.** to believe **2.** think
creíble *adj.* credible, believable
crema *noun f.* cream
crepúsculo *noun m.* dusk, twilight
cresta *noun f.* **1.** crest **2.** comb
cría *noun f.* **1.** rearing, breeding **2.** baby, cub, pup, young
criado, -da *noun.* servant, maid
crianza *noun f.* upbringing, rearing
criar *verb.* **1.** to raise, bring up **2.** breed
criatura *noun f.* **1.** creature **2.** baby
crimen *noun m.* crime
criminal *noun mf. adj.* criminal
crisis *noun f.* crisis
—**crisis nerviosa** nervous breakdown
cristal *noun m.* crystal
cristalino *noun m.* lens
cristianismo *noun m.* Christianity
cristiano, -tiana *noun. adj.* Christian
Cristo *noun m.* Christ
criterio *noun m.* criterion
crítica *noun f.* **1.** criticism **2.** review
criticar *verb.* to criticize
crítico *noun mf.* critic
crítico, -ca *adj.* critical
crónica *noun f.* chronicle
crónico, -ca *adj.* chronic
cronometrar *verb.* to clock, time
croquis *noun m.* sketch
cruce *noun m.* **1.** cross, crossing **2.** crossroads
crucero *noun m.* cruise
crucial *adj.* crucial
crudo, -da *adj.* **1.** crude **2.** raw
cruel *adj.* cruel
crueldad *noun f.* cruelty
crujido *noun m.* crunch
crujiente *adj.* crunchy, crisp
crujir *verb.* to crunch
cruz *noun f.* cross
cruzada *noun f.* crusade
cruzar *verb.* **1.** to cross **2.** exchange
—**cruzarse** to intersect
cuaderno *noun m.* notebook
cuadragésimo, -ma *noun. adj.* fortieth
cuadrícula *noun f.* grid
cuadrilátero *noun m.* **1.** quadrilateral **2.** ring
cuadrilla *noun f.* gang
cuadro *noun m.* **1.** square **2.** picture, painting
cual *pron.* **1.** which **2.** who, whom
cuál *pron.* what (one), which (one)
cualidad *noun f.* quality
cualificado, -da *adj.* **1.** qualified **2.** skilled
cualquier *adj.* (see cualquiera. Used before nouns)
cualquiera *adj.* **1.** any **2.** everyday, ordinary
cualquiera *pron.* **1.** anybody, anyone, whoever **2.** whichever, whatever
cuán *adv.* how
cuando *conj.* **1.** when **2.** if
cuando *prep.* **1.** during **2.** if
cuándo *adv.* when
cuanto, -ta *adj.* as many
—**cuanto más** the more
—**cuanto menos** the less
cuanto *adv.* as much as
—**cuanto antes** as soon as possible
cuanto, -ta *pron.* all what, everything
—**unos cuantos** a few
cuánto, -ta *adj. pron.* how much, how many
cuánto *adv.* **1.** how much **2.** how far
cuarenta *noun m. adj.* forty
Cuaresma *noun f.* Lent
cuartear *verb.* to quarter
cuartel *noun m.* barracks
—**cuartel general** headquarters
cuarteto *noun m.* quartet
cuarto *noun m.* **1.** room **2.** quarter, fourth
cuarto, -ta *noun. adj.* fourth
cuatro *noun m. adj.* four
cuba *noun f.* barrel
Cuba *noun f.* Cuba
cubano, -na *noun. adj.* Cuban
cubierta *noun f.* **1.** cover **2.** deck
cubierto *noun m.* **1.** cover, shelter **2.** utensil **3.** table setting
cubo *noun m.* **1.** bucket **2.** cube
—**cubo de la basura** trash can
cubrir *verb.* to cover
cuchara *noun f.* spoon
cucharada *noun f.* spoonful
cucharilla *noun f.* teaspoon
cucharón *noun m.* ladle
cuchichear *verb.* to whisper

cuchillo *noun m.* knife
cuello *noun m.* **1.** neck **2.** collar
cuenca *noun f.* basin
cuenco *noun m.* basin, bowl
cuenta *noun f.* **1.** account **2.** bill, check **3.** count
cuento *noun m.* story, tale
cuerda *noun f.* cord, rope, string
cuerno *noun m.* horn
cuero *noun m.* **1.** leather **2.** hide
cuerpo *noun m.* **1.** body **2.** corps
cuesta *noun f.* slope
cuestión *noun f.* matter
cuestionable *adj.* questionable
cuestionar *verb.* to question
cuestionario *noun m.* **1.** questionnaire **2.** quiz
cueva *noun f.* cave
cuidado *noun m.* **1.** care **2.** worry, concern
—**tener cuidado** to be careful
cuidado, -da *adj.* trim
cuidadoso, -sa *adj.* careful
cuidar *verb.* **1.** to take care of, look after **2.** pay attention to, watch
culo *noun m.* **1.** bottom **2.** ass
culpa *noun f.* blame, fault
culpabilidad *noun f.* guilt
culpable *adj.* guilty
culpar *verb.* to blame
cultivado, -da *adj.* cultivated
cultivador, -dora *noun.* cultivator
cultivar *verb.* **1.** to cultivate **2.** farm **3.** raise, grow
cultivo *noun m.* **1.** crop **2.** cultivation, farming
culto *noun m.* cult
culto, -ta *adj.* cultivated, educated
cultura *noun f.* culture
cultural *adj.* cultural
cumbre *noun f.* height, peak, summit, top
cumpleaños *noun m.* birthday
cumplido *noun m.* compliment
cumplimiento *noun m.* **1.** fulfillment **2.** performance
cumplir *verb.* **1.** to accomplish, carry out **2.** fulfill, comply with **3.** expire
—**cumplirse 1.** to be fulfilled **2.** expire
cuna *noun f.* **1.** cradle **2.** birthplace
cuña *noun f.* wedge
cuota *noun f.* **1.** share **2.** quota **3.** subscription, fee **4.** installment, payment
cupón *noun m.* coupon
cúpula *noun f.* dome
cura *noun f.* cure, treatment
cura *noun m.* priest
curar *verb.* **1.** to cure **2.** heal
curiosidad *noun f.* curiosity
curioso, -sa *adj.* **1.** curious **2.** peculiar, unusual
currículum *noun m.* curriculum
curry *noun m.* curry
curso *noun m.* **1.** course **2.** school year
curtir *verb.* to tan
curva *noun f.* curve, bend
curvar *verb.* to bend
curvo, -va *adj.* curved, bent
cúspide *noun f.* height, peak, summit
custodia *noun f.* custody
cuyo, -ya *pron.* whose

D

dado *noun m.* dice
dado, -da *adj.* given
dama *noun f.* lady
danés, -nesa *noun. adj.* Danish
danza *noun f.* **1.** dance **2.** dancing
dañar *verb.* **1.** to damage **2.** harm, hurt
dañino, -na *adj.* harmful
daño *noun m.* **1.** damage **2.** harm
dar *verb.* **1.** to give **2.** hit, strike **3.** hand over, deliver **4.** produce, yield **5.** be enough
—**dar a** to overlook
—**dar con** to find
—**dar contra** to hit
—**dar por** to consider
—**darse a** to take to

—**darse de sí** to stretch
—**dárselas de** to boast about
dardo *noun m.* dart
datar (de) *verb.* to date (from)
dátil *noun m.* date
dato *noun m.* fact, piece of information
—**datos** data
de *prep.* **1.** of **2.** from **3.** in, at **4.** than **5.** by
deambular *verb.* to wander
debajo *adv.* underneath
—**debajo de** under, beneath
—**por debajo** below
debate *noun m.* debate
debatir *verb.* to debate
deber *noun m.* duty
deber *verb.* **1.** must **2.** ought to, should **3.** to owe
debidamente *adv.* duly, properly
debido, -da *adj.* due, proper
débil *adj.* **1.** weak **2.** faint **3.** feeble
debilidad *noun f.* weakness, feebleness
debilitar *verb.* to weaken
debut *noun m.* debut
década *noun f.* decade
decadencia *noun f.* **1.** decadence **2.** decline
decaer *verb.* **1.** to decline, decay **2.** weaken
decano, -na *noun.* **1.** dean **2.** senior member
decencia *noun f.* decency
decente *adj.* decent
decepción *noun f.* disappointment
decepcionado, -da *adj.* disappointed
decepcionante *adj.* disappointing
decepcionar *verb.* to disappoint, let down
decidido, -da *adj.* **1.** decisive **2.** determined
decidir *verb.* **1.** to decide **2.** determine **3.** settle
—**decidirse** to make up one's mind
décimo, -ma *noun. adj.* tenth
decimoctavo, -va *noun. adj.* eighteenth
decimocuarto, -ta *noun. adj.* fourteenth
decimonoveno, -na *noun. adj.* nineteenth
decimoquinto, -ta *noun. adj.* fifteenth
decimoséptimo, -ma *noun. adj.* seventeenth
decimosexto, -ta *noun. adj.* sixteenth
decimotercero, -ra *noun. adj.* thirteenth
decir *verb.* **1.** to say **2.** tell **3.** speak
—**decirse** to be said
decisión *noun f.* decision, choice
decisivo, -va *adj.* decisive
declaración *noun f.* **1.** declaration, statement **2.** testimony
declarar *verb.* **1.** to declare, state **2.** testify
—**declararse 1.** to plead **2.** confess one's love
declive *noun m.* **1.** decline **2.** slope
decoración *noun f.* decoration
decorado *noun m.* scenery, stage set
decorar *verb.* to decorate
decorativo, -va *adj.* decorative
decoro *noun m.* decorum
decretar *verb.* to decree
decreto *noun m.* decree
dedicación *noun f.* **1.** dedication **2.** devotion
dedicado, -da *adj.* **1.** dedicated **2.** devoted
dedicar *verb.* **1.** to dedicate **2.** devote
—**dedicarse a** to devote oneself to
dedicatoria *noun f.* dedication
dedo *noun m.* **1.** finger (hand) **2.** toe (foot)
deducción *noun f.* deduction
deducir *verb.* **1.** to deduce **2.** deduct
defecto *noun m.* **1.** defect **2.** flaw
defectuoso, -sa *adj.* **1.** defective **2.** faulty
defender *verb.* to defend
—**defenderse 1.** to protect oneself, defend oneself **2.** get by
defensa *noun f.* defense
defensivo, -va *adj.* defensive
defensor, -sora *noun.* **1.** advocate **2.** champion **3.** defender
deficiencia *noun f.* deficiency
deficiente *noun mf.* handicapped person
déficit *noun m.* deficit
definición *noun f.* definition

definido, -da *adj.* definite
definir *verb.* to define
definitivo, -va *adj.* definitive
—**en definitiva** all in all
deformación *noun f.* **1.** deformation **2.** distortion
deformar *verb.* **1.** to deform **2.** distort
defraudar *verb.* **1.** to disappoint **2.** defraud
degustación *noun f.* tasting, sampling
degustar *verb.* to taste
dejadez *noun f.* **1.** laziness **2.** slovenliness
dejar *verb.* **1.** to leave **2.** abandon **3.** give up **4.** let **5.** allow, permit
—**dejar de** to stop, quit
—**dejarse 1.** to leave **2.** forget **3.** grow **4.** let oneself go
delantal *noun m.* apron
delante *adv.* ahead
—**delante de** before
delantera *noun f.* **1.** front **2.** forward line
delantero, -ra *noun m.* forward
delantero, -ra *adj.* **1.** front, fore **2.** forward
delatar *verb.* **1.** to betray **2.** inform against, denounce
delegación *noun f.* **1.** delegation **2.** mission
delegado, -da *noun.* delegate
delegar *verb.* to delegate
deleitar *verb.* to delight
deleite *noun m.* delight
deletrear *verb.* to spell
delfín *noun m.* dolphin
delgado, -da *adj.* **1.** thin, skinny **2.** slender, slim
deliberado, -da *adj.* deliberate
delicadeza *noun f.* **1.** delicacy **2.** tact, discretion
delicado, -da *adj.* **1.** delicate **2.** fine **3.** ill **4.** sensitive **5.** tactful
delicioso, -sa *adj.* **1.** delicious **2.** delightful
delictivo, -va *adj.* criminal
delincuente *noun mf.* delinquent
delirar *verb.* **1.** to rave **2.** be delirious
delirio *noun m.* **1.** delirium **2.** nonsense, ravings
delito *noun m.* **1.** crime **2.** offence
delta *noun m.* delta
demacrado, -da *adj.* drawn
demanda *noun f.* **1.** demand **2.** lawsuit **3.** request
demandado, -da *noun.* defendant
demandante *noun mf.* plaintiff
demandar *verb.* **1.** to sue **2.** sue, file a lawsuit **3.** call for
demás *adj.* rest, remaining
—**lo demás** the rest, everything else
—**los demás, las demás** the rest, everything else, the others, everyone else
—**por lo demás 1.** otherwise **2.** apart from that
—**y demás** and so on
demasiado, -da *adj.* too much, too many
demasiado *adv.* too, too much
demente *adj.* insane
democracia *noun f.* democracy
demócrata *noun mf.* democrat
demócrata *adj.* democratic
democrático, -ca *adj.* democratic
demoler *verb.* to demolish
demolición *noun f.* demolition
demonio *noun m.* demon, devil
demora *noun f.* delay
demorar *verb.* to delay
—**demorarse** to take a long time
demostración *noun f.* **1.** demonstration **2.** show, display
demostrar *verb.* **1.** to demonstrate **2.** show
denegación *noun f.* denial, refusal
denominar *verb.* to designate, name
densidad *noun f.* density, thickness
denso, -sa *adj.* dense, thick
dentadura *noun f.* teeth
—**dentadura postiza** dentures
dental *adj.* dental
dentista *noun mf.* dentist
dentro *adv.* **1.** inside **2.** indoors
—**dentro de 1.** in, inside **2.** within
—**dentro de poco** shortly, soon
—**por dentro** inside
denuncia *noun f.* denunciation
denunciar *verb.* **1.** to denounce **2.** report

departamento *noun m.* department
dependencia *noun f.* dependence
depender (de) *verb.* to depend (on)
dependiente, -ta *noun m.* salesperson, clerk
dependiente *adj.* dependent
deportar *verb.* to deport
deporte *noun m.* sport
deportivo, -va *adj.* **1.** sporting **2.** sports
depositar *verb.* **1.** to deposit, place **2.** store
depósito *noun m.* **1.** deposit **2.** storehouse, warehouse
depredador, -dora *noun.* predator
depresión *noun f.* **1.** depression **2.** slump, recession
deprimente *adj.* depressing
deprimido, -da *adj.* depressed, blue
deprisa *adv.* quick
derecha *noun f.* right
derecho *noun m.* **1.** law **2.** right
—**derechos civiles** civil rights
—**derechos de autor** **1.** copyright **2.** royalties
derecho, -cha *adj.* **1.** right **2.** straight **3.** upright
derivación *noun f.* derivation
derivar *verb.* to drift
—**derivar de** to come from, derive from
—**derivar en** to result in
derramar *verb.* **1.** to spill **2.** pour **3.** shed
derretir *verb.* to melt
derribar *verb.* **1.** to demolish **2.** shoot down
derrocar *verb.* to overthrow
derrota *noun f.* defeat
derrotar *verb.* to defeat
derrumbar *verb.* to topple
—**derrumbarse** to collapse
desabrido, -da *adj.* bland, tasteless
desacato *noun m.* contempt
desacreditar *verb.* to discredit
desacuerdo *noun m.* disagreement
desafiante *adj.* defiant
desafiar *verb.* **1.** to defy **2.** challenge
desafilado, -da *adj.* blunt
desafinado, -da *adj.* out-of-tune
desafío *noun m.* **1.** challenge **2.** defiance
desafortunadamente *adv.* unfortunately
desafortunado, -da *adj.* unfortunate, unlucky
desagradable *adj.* unpleasant, disagreeable
desahogado, -da *adj.* comfortable, well-off
desalentar *verb.* to discourage
desalojar *verb.* **1.** to remove, clear **2.** evacuate **3.** evict
desamparado, -da *adj.* helpless
desanimar *verb.* to discourage
desaparecer *verb.* to disappear, vanish
desaparecido, -da *adj.* **1.** missing **2.** deceased
desaparición *noun f.* disappearance
desaprobación *noun f.* disapproval
desaprovechar *verb.* to waste, misuse
desarmar *verb.* to disarm
desarrollar *verb.* to develop
—**desarrollarse** to take place
desarrollo *noun m.* development
desastre *noun m.* disaster
desastroso, -sa *adj.* disastrous
desatar *verb.* **1.** to untie, undo **2.** trigger
desatender *verb.* **1.** to disregard **2.** neglect
desayunar *verb.* to have breakfast
desayuno *noun m.* breakfast
desbancar *verb.* to oust
descansar *verb.* to rest
descansillo *noun m.* landing
descanso *noun m.* **1.** rest **2.** break
descarga *noun f.* discharge
descargar *verb.* **1.** to discharge **2.** unload
descaro *noun m.* cheek, nerve
descartar *verb.* to rule out, reject
descendente *adj.* downward, descending
descender *verb.* **1.** to descend **2.** go down **3.** fall, drop
—**descender de** to be a descendant of
descenso *noun m.* **1.** descent **2.** drop, fall
descifrar *verb.* to decipher, decode
descomponer *verb.* **1.** to rot **2.** break
—**descomponerse** **1.** to break down **2.** decompose
descomposición *noun f.* **1.** breakdown **2.** decay

descomunal *adj.* **1.** enormous, giant, huge **2.** extraordinary
desconcertado, -da *adj.* confused
desconcertar *verb.* to disconcert, confuse
desconectar *verb.* to disconnect, switch off
desconfiado, -da *adj.* suspicious, distrustful
desconfiar *verb.* to suspect, distrust
desconocido, -da *noun.* stranger
desconocido, -da *adj.* **1.** unfamiliar **2.** unknown
descontar *verb.* to discount, deduct
descontento *noun m.* discontent
descontento, -ta *adj.* discontented
descorrer *verb.* to draw
descrédito *noun m.* discredit
describir *verb.* to describe
descripción *noun f.* description
descubierto, -ta *adj.* **1.** exposed, revealed **2.** naked
descubrimiento *noun m.* discovery
descubrir *verb.* **1.** to discover, find out **2.** uncover **3.** unveil
descuento *noun m.* discount
descuidado, -da *adj.* careless
descuidar *verb.* to neglect
—**descuidarse** to drop one's guard
descuido *noun m.* **1.** carelessness **2.** negligence
desde *prep.* **1.** since **2.** from
—**desde ahora** from now on
—**desde entonces** since then
—**desde luego** of course
desdén *noun m.* disdain, contempt
desdicha *noun f.* misery
deseable *adj.* desirable
desear *verb.* **1.** to wish **2.** want **3.** desire
desechar *verb.* to discard
desecho *noun m.* waste
—**desechos** garbage
desembarcadero *noun m.* landing
desembarcar *verb.* land
desembarco *noun m.* to disembark
desembocadura *noun f.* mouth
desempeñar *verb.* **1.** to play, fulfill **2.** redeem
desempeño *noun m.* performance, fulfillment
desempleado, -da *noun.* unemployed person
desempleado, -da *adj.* unemployed
desempleo *noun m.* unemployment
desencadenar *verb.* to trigger
desentonar *verb.* **1.** to clash **2.** be out of tune
deseo *noun m.* desire, wish
deseoso, -sa *adj.* **1.** eager **2.** anxious
desertar *verb.* to defect, desert
desesperación *noun f.* despair, desperation
desesperado, -da *adj.* desperate, hopeless
desesperar *verb.* **1.** to despair **2.** exasperate
desestimar *verb.* to reject
desfasado, -da *adj.* dated
desfavorable *adj.* unfavorable, adverse
desfilar *verb.* to parade
desfile *noun m.* **1.** parade **2.** procession
desgarrar *verb.* to tear, rip
desgarrón *noun m.* tear, rip
desgastar *verb.* to wear out, wear down
desgaste *noun m.* wear
desgracia *noun f.* **1.** disgrace **2.** misfortune
—**por desgracia** unfortunately
desgraciadamente *adv.* unfortunately
desgraciado, -da *adj.* unfortunate
deshacer *verb.* **1.** to destroy **2.** dissolve, melt **3.** break
—**deshacerse** to fall apart
—**deshacerse de** to get rid of
deshecho, -cha *adj.* **1.** destroyed **2.** broken
deshonra *noun f.* dishonor, disgrace, shame
deshonrar *verb.* to dishonor, disgrace
deshuesar *verb.* **1.** to bone **2.** pit
desierto *noun m.* desert
desierto, -ta *adj.* **1.** deserted **2.** empty
designar *verb.* to designate, appoint
desigual *adj.* **1.** unequal **2.** uneven
desigualdad *noun f.* **1.** inequality **2.** unevenness
desintegrar *verb.* to disintegrate
desleal *adj.* disloyal
desliz *noun m.* **1.** mistake **2.** slip

deslizar *verb.* to slide, slip
deslumbrante *adj.* dazzling
deslumbrar *verb.* to dazzle
desmayarse *verb.* to faint
desmayo *noun m.* faint
desmentir *verb.* to deny
desmenuzar *verb.* to crumble
desmigajar *verb.* to crumble
desmontar *verb.* **1.** to dismantle **2.** dismount
desnudar *verb.* to undress, strip
desnudo, -da *adj.* bare, naked
desocupado, -da *adj.* **1.** vacant, empty **2.** free **3.** unemployed
desorden *noun m.* **1.** disorder, mess **2.** disturbance
despachar *verb.* to dispatch
despacho *noun m.* **1.** office **2.** dispatch
despacio *adv.* slow, slowly
desparramar *verb.* **1.** to spill **2.** spread, scatter
despedazar *verb.* to cut to pieces
despedida *noun f.* farewell, good-bye
despedir *verb.* **1.** to dismiss, fire **2.** give, emit **3.** see out
—**despedirse** to say good-bye
despejado, -da *adj.* clear
despejar *verb.* clear
despejar *verb.* to clear
despellejar *verb.* to skin
desperdiciar *verb.* **1.** to waste **2.** miss
desperdicio *noun m.* waste
despertar *verb.* **1.** to arouse **2.** awaken, wake
—**despertarse** to wake up
despiadado, -da *adj.* ruthless
despido *noun m.* dismissal
despierto, -ta *adj.* **1.** alert **2.** awake **3.** smart **4.** vivid
desplazar *verb.* **1.** to displace **2.** move, shift
desplegar *verb.* **1.** to unfold **2.** deploy
desplomarse *verb.* **1.** to fall **2.** collapse
despojar *verb.* to strip
—**despojarse (de)** to remove
desportilladura *noun f.* chip
desportillar *verb.* to chip
despreciable *adj.* **1.** despicable **2.** negligible
desprecio *noun m.* disdain, contempt
desprender *verb.* **1.** to detach, loosen **2.** give, emit
—**desprenderse (de) 1.** to come off **2.** get rid of
despreocupado, -da *adj.* careless
desprestigio *noun m.* discredit
después *adv.* **1.** afterwards **2.** next, then
—**después de** after
—**después de todo** after all
despuntado, -da *adj.* blunt
despuntar *verb.* **1.** to blunt **2.** excel, stand out
desquitarse *verb.* to retaliate
destacado, -da *adj.* outstanding, prominent
destacamento *noun m.* detachment
destacar *verb.* **1.** to highlight, emphasize **2.** stand out
destapar *verb.* **1.** to open **2.** reveal, unveil
destellar *verb.* to flash, sparkle
destello *noun m.* flash, sparkle
desteñir *verb.* to fade
destinar *verb.* **1.** to appoint, assign **2.** allocate, earmark
destinatario, -ria *noun.* recipient
destino *noun m.* **1.** destination **2.** destiny, fate **3.** assignment
destitución *noun f.* dismissal
destituir *verb.* to dismiss
destreza *noun f.* skill
destrucción *noun f.* destruction
destructivo, -va *adj.* destructive
destruir *verb.* to destroy
desvalido, -da *adj.* helpless
desvalijar *verb.* to ransack, rob
desvalorizar *verb.* to devalue
desván *noun f.* attic
desvanecer *verb.* **1.** to dispel **2.** fade
—**desvanecerse 1.** to vanish **2.** fade **3.** faint
desvanecimiento *noun m.* **1.** fade **2.** faint
desventaja *noun f.* **1.** disadvantage **2.** handicap
desventurado, -da *adj.* unfortunate
desvergonzado, -da *adj.* shameless

desviación *noun f.* **1.** deviation **2.** diversion, detour
desviar *verb.* **1.** to divert **2.** turn away
—**desviarse 1.** to turn aside, turn away **2.** make a detour
desvío *noun m.* **1.** deviation **2.** diversion, detour
detallado, -da *adj.* detailed
detalle *noun m.* detail
detallista *noun mf.* **1.** retailer **2.** perfectionist
detectar *verb.* to detect
detective *noun mf.* detective
detención *noun f.* **1.** arrest, detention **2.** stop, halt
detener *verb.* **1.** to arrest, detain **2.** stop, halt
—**detenerse 1.** to stop **2.** delay
detenidamente *adv.* at length
deteriorado, -da *adj.* **1.** damaged **2.** worn
deteriorar *verb.* to damage
—**deteriorarse 1.** to deteriorate **2.** get damaged
deterioro *noun m.* **1.** worsening, decline **2.** deterioration, wear
determinación *noun f.* determination, purpose, resolve
determinado, -da *adj.* **1.** determined **2.** certain, particular
determinar *verb.* **1.** to determine **2.** bring out
—**determinarse** to make up one's mind
detestar *verb.* to detest
detonación *noun f.* detonation, blast
detonar *verb.* to detonate, explode
detrás *adv.* behind
—**detrás de 1.** behind **2.** after
deuda *noun f.* debt
deudor, -dora *noun.* debtor
devaluación *noun f.* devaluation
devaluar *verb.* to devalue
—**devaluarse** to depreciate
devastador, -dora *adj.* devastating
devoción *noun f.* devotion
devolver *verb.* **1.** to return, give back **2.** refund **3.** vomit
día *noun m.* **1.** day **2.** daytime
—**al día** up-to-date
—**día festivo** holiday
diabetes *noun f.* diabetes
diabético, -ca *noun. adj.* diabetic
diablo *noun m.* devil, demon
diagnosticar *verb.* to diagnose
diagnóstico *noun m.* diagnosis
diagrama *noun m.* **1.** diagram **2.** figure
dialecto *noun m.* dialect
dialogar *verb.* to dialogue
diálogo *noun m.* dialogue
diamante *noun m.* diamond
diámetro *noun m.* diameter
diana *noun f.* target, bull's eye
diapositiva *noun f.* slide
diariamente *adv.* daily
diario *noun m.* **1.** diary **2.** newspaper
diario, -ria *adj.* daily
diarrea *noun f.* diarrhea
dibujar *verb.* **1.** to draw **2.** portray
dibujo *noun m.* **1.** design **2.** drawing
—**dibujos animados** cartoon
diccionario *noun m.* dictionary
dicha *noun f.* happiness
dicho *noun m.* saying
dichoso, -sa *adj.* happy
diciembre *noun m.* December
dictador, -dora *noun.* dictator
dictadura *noun f.* dictatorship
dictar *verb.* **1.** to dictate **2.** give
diecinueve *noun m. adj.* nineteen
dieciocho *noun m. adj.* eighteen
dieciséis *noun m. adj.* sixteen
diecisiete *noun m. adj.* seventeen
diente *noun m.* tooth
dieta *noun f.* diet
diez *noun m. adj.* ten
difamación *noun f.* libel, slander
difamar *verb.* to libel, slander
diferencia *noun f.* difference
—**a diferencia de** in contrast to, unlike
diferenciación *noun f.* differentiation
diferenciar *verb.* **1.** to differentiate **2.** distinguish
diferente *adj.* different
difícil *adj.* difficult, hard
difícilmente *adv.* hardly
dificultad *noun f.* difficulty
difundir *verb.* **1.** to broadcast **2.** spread out

difunto, -ta *noun.* deceased
difunto, -ta *adj.* **1.** deceased **2.** late
digerir *verb.* to digest
digestión *noun f.* digestion
digital *adj.* digital
dignidad *noun f.* dignity
dignatario, -ria *noun.* dignitary
digno, -na *adj.* worthy
dilatar *verb.* to dilate, expand
dilema *noun m.* dilemma
diligencia *noun f.* **1.** diligence, industry **2.** promptness, speed
diluir *verb.* to dilute
dimensión *noun f.* dimension
diminuto, -ta *adj.* minute, tiny
dimisión *noun f.* resignation
dimitir *verb.* to resign
Dinamarca *noun m.* Denmark
dinámica *noun f.* dynamics
dinámico, -ca *adj.* dynamic
dinastía *noun f.* dynasty
dinero *noun m.* money
dinosaurio *noun m.* dinosaur
diócesis *noun f.* diocese
dios, diosa *noun.* god or goddess
Dios *noun m.* God
diploma *noun m.* diploma
diplomacia *noun f.* diplomacy
diplomado, -da *noun.* graduate
diplomarse *verb.* to graduate
diplomático, -ca *noun.* diplomat
diplomático, -ca *adj.* diplomatic
diputado, -da *noun.* representative
dique *noun m.* dike
dirección *noun f.* **1.** address **2.** direction, way **3.** management **4.** steering
directiva *noun f.* directive
directivo, -va *noun.* director, executive
directivo, -va *adj.* managerial, executive
directriz *noun f.* guideline
directo, -ta *adj.* **1.** direct **2.** immediate
—**en directo** live
director, -tora *noun.* director, manager, head, headmaster
—**director de orquesta** conductor
dirigente *noun m.* leader, ruler
dirigente *adj.* leading, ruling
dirigir *verb.* **1.** to direct, lead **2.** conduct **3.** address
dirigirse a *verb.* **1.** to address, speak to **2.** head for, go towards
discapacidad *noun f.* **1.** disability **2.** handicap
discapacitado, -da *adj.* **1.** disabled **2.** handicapped
disciplina *noun f.* discipline
disciplinar *verb.* to discipline
discjockey *noun mf.* disc jockey
disco *noun m.* **1.** disc, disk **2.** discus **3.** record
—**disco compacto** compact disc
—**disco sencillo** single
disconformidad *noun f.* disagreement
discontinuo, -nua *adj.* discontinuous
discoteca *noun f.* disco, discotheque
discreción *noun f.* discretion
discrepar *verb.* **1.** to disagree **2.** dissent
discreto, -ta *adj.* discreet
discriminación *noun f.* discrimination
disculpa *noun f.* **1.** apology **2.** excuse
disculpar *verb.* to excuse, pardon
—**disculparse** to apologize
discurso *noun m.* **1.** discourse **2.** speech, address
discusión *noun f.* **1.** argument **2.** discussion **3.** dispute
discutir *verb.* **1.** to argue **2.** discuss **3.** dispute **4.** quarrel
disecar *verb.* **1.** to stuff **2.** dissect
diseminar *verb.* to disseminate, disperse
disentir *verb.* to dissent, disagree
diseñador, -dora *noun.* designer
diseñar *verb.* to design
diseño *noun m.* **1.** design **2.** designing
disfraz *noun m.* **1.** costume **2.** disguise
disfrazar *verb.* **1.** to disguise **2.** conceal
—**disfrazarse** *verb.* to be in disguise
disfrutar *verb.* to enjoy
disidente *noun mf. adj.* dissident
disimular *verb.* to conceal
disminución *noun f.* decrease, drop, fall
disminuir *verb.* **1.** to decrease **2.** drop, fall
disolución *noun f.* dissolution
disolver *verb.* to dissolve
disparar *verb.* **1.** to fire **2.** shoot
—**dispararse** to rocket
disparatado, -da *adj.* absurd

disparate *noun m.* nonsense
disparo *noun m.* shot
dispensar *verb.* **1.** to dispense **2.** excuse
dispersar *verb.* to scatter, disperse
disperso, -sa *adj.* scattered, dispersed
disponer *verb.* **1.** to arrange **2.** set out **3.** order **4.** prepare
disponer a hacer algo *verb.* to be about to
disponibilidad *noun f.* availability
disponible *adj.* available
disposición *noun f.* **1.** arrangement **2.** disposition **3.** provision **4.** willingness
dispuesto, -ta *adj.* ready, prepared
disputa *noun f.* dispute
distancia *noun f.* distance
distante *adj.* distant
distinción *noun f.* **1.** distinction **2.** honor
distinguido, -da *adj.* distinguished
distinguir *verb.* **1.** to differentiate, distinguish **2.** honor
distintivo, -va *adj.* distinctive
distinto, -ta *adj.* **1.** different **2.** distinct
distorsión *noun f.* distortion
distorsionar *verb.* to distort
distracción *noun f.* **1.** distraction **2.** entertainment, amusement
distraer *verb.* **1.** to distract **2.** entertain
distraído, -da *adj.* **1.** distracted **2.** absent-minded **3.** entertained, amused
distribución *noun f.* distribution
distribuir *verb.* to distribute
distrito *noun m.* district
disturbio *noun m.* disturbance
disuadir *verb.* to dissuade, deter
disuasión *noun f.* dissuasion
diversidad *noun f.* diversity
diversificar *verb.* to diversify
diversión *noun f.* amusement, diversion
diverso, -sa *adj.* diverse, various
divertido, -da *adj.* **1.** amusing, funny **2.** entertaining
divertir *verb.* to amuse, entertain
—divertirse to have a good time, have fun
dividendo *noun m.* dividend
dividir *verb.* to divide, split
divino, -na *adj.* divine
divisar *verb.* to discern
división *noun f.* division
divisor *noun m.* divisor
divorciar *verb.* to divorce
—divorciarse to get divorced
divorcio *noun m.* divorce
divulgar *verb.* **1.** to divulge **2.** spread **3.** broadcast
doblar *verb.* **1.** to double **2.** fold **3.** dub **4.** toll **5.** turn
doble *noun mf. adj.* double
doblegar *verb.* to break, vanquish
—doblegarse to give in
doce *noun m. adj.* twelve
docena *noun f.* dozen
docente *noun mf.* teacher
docente *adj.* educational
doctor, -tora *noun.* doctor
doctorado *noun m.* doctorate, PhD
doctrina *noun f.* doctrine
documentación *noun f.* documentation
documental *noun m. adj.* documentary
documento *noun m.* document
—documentos papers
dólar *noun m.* dollar
dolencia *noun f.* ailment
doler *verb.* **1.** to hurt, ache **2.** grieve
—dolerse to complain
dolor *noun m.* **1.** ache, pain **2.** grief, sorrow
dolorido *adj.* **1.** aching, painful, sore **2.** hurt
dolorosamente *adv.* painfully
doloroso, -sa *adj.* **1.** painful **2.** distressing
doméstico, -ca *adj.* domestic
dominación *noun f.* domination
dominante *adj.* dominant
dominar *verb.* **1.** to dominate **2.** master **3.** prevail
—dominarse to control oneself
domingo *noun m.* Sunday
dominio *noun m.* **1.** domain **2.** dominance, domination **3.** mastery
don *noun m.* gift
donación *noun f.* **1.** donation **2.** contribution
donante *noun mf.* **1.** donor **2.** contributor
donar *verb.* to donate

doncella *noun f.* maiden
donde *adv.* **1.** where **2.** wherever
dónde *adv.* where
dondequiera *adv.* wherever, anywhere
dorado *noun m.* gilt
dorado, -da *adj.* golden
dormido, -da *adj.* asleep
dormir *verb.* to sleep
—**dormirse** to fall asleep
dormitorio *noun m.* bedroom
dos *noun m. adj.* two
dosis *noun f.* **1.** dose **2.** amount
dotación *noun f.* **1.** endowment **2.** staff
dotar *verb.* **1.** to endow **2.** provide, equip
dragón *noun m.* dragon
drama *noun m.* drama
dramático, -ca *adj.* dramatic
dramaturgo, -ga *noun.* playwright, dramatist
drástico, -ca *adj.* drastic
drenaje *noun m.* drainage
drenar *verb.* to drain
droga *noun f.* drug
drogar *verb.* to drug
—**drogarse** to take drugs
ducha *noun f.* shower
ducharse *verb.* to take a shower
duda *noun f.* **1.** doubt **2.** hesitation
dudar *verb.* **1.** to doubt **2.** hesitate
dudoso, -sa *adj.* **1.** doubtful **2.** dubious **3.** questionable
duende *noun m.* elf
dueño, -ña *noun.* **1.** landlord or landlady **2.** master or mistress **3.** owner
dulce *noun m.* candy, sweet
dulce *adj.* **1.** sweet **2.** gentle
duodécimo, -ma *noun. adj.* twelfth
duplicar *verb.* **1.** to double **2.** duplicate, copy
duque, -sa *noun.* duke or duchess
duración *noun f.* duration, length
duradero, -ra *adj.* durable, lasting
durante *prep.* during, for
durar *verb.* **1.** to last **2.** endure
duro, -ra *adj.* **1.** hard **2.** harsh **3.** rough
duro *adv.* hard

E

echar *verb.* **1.** to throw, throw out **2.** fire, dismiss **3.** put forth **4.** add **5.** launch **6.** put
—**echar a perder** to spoil
—**echar de menos** to miss
—**echarse** to lie down
eclesiástico *noun m.* cleric, clergyman
eclesiástico, -ca *adj.* ecclesiastic, ecclesiastical
eco *noun m.* echo
ecografía *noun f.* scan
ecología *noun f.* ecology
ecológico, -ca *adj.* ecological
ecologista *noun mf.* ecologist, environmentalist
economía *noun f.* **1.** economy **2.** economics
económico, -ca *adj.* **1.** economic **2.** economical
economista *noun mf.* economist
economizar *verb.* to save
ecuación *noun f.* equation
edad *noun f.* age
edición *noun f.* **1.** edition **2.** publishing
edificar *verb.* **1.** to edify **2.** build, construct
edificio *noun m.* building
editar *verb.* **1.** to edit **2.** publish
editor, -tora *noun.* **1.** editor **2.** publisher
editorial *noun f.* editorial
editorial *adj.* **1.** editorial **2.** publishing
educación *noun f.* education
educado, -da *adj.* polite
educar *verb.* **1.** to educate **2.** raise, bring up **3.** train
educativo, -va *adj.* educational
efectivamente *adv.* **1.** indeed **2.** really
efectivo *noun m.* cash
efectivo, -va *adj.* **1.** effective **2.** real, actual

efecto *noun m.* effect
—**efectos personales** goods, property
—**en efecto** in fact, actually
efectuar *verb.* to carry out
eficacia *noun f.* **1.** efficacy **2.** efficiency
eficaz *adj.* **1.** effective **2.** efficient
eficiencia *noun f.* efficiency
eficiente *adj.* efficient
efímero, -ra *adj.* ephemeral, short-lived
egipcio, -cia *noun. adj.* Egyptian
Egipto *noun m.* Egypt
ego *noun m.* ego
egoísta *adj.* selfish
eje *noun m.* **1.** axis **2.** shaft
ejecución *noun f.* **1.** execution **2.** performance
ejecutar *verb.* **1.** to execute **2.** perform
ejecutivo, -va *noun. adj.* executive
ejemplar *noun m.* **1.** copy **2.** specimen
ejemplo *noun m.* example
—**por ejemplo** for example
ejercer *verb.* **1.** to exercise **2.** exert **3.** practice
ejercicio *noun m.* **1.** exercise **2.** practice
ejercitar *verb.* **1.** to exercise **2.** train
ejército *noun m.* army
el *art.* the
el *pron.* the one
—**el que** he who, whoever, the one that
él *pron.* **1.** he **2.** him, it **3.** his, its
elaboración *noun f.* **1.** production **2.** preparation
elaborar *verb.* **1.** to produce **2.** make **3.** prepare
elasticidad *noun f.* elasticity
elástico *noun m.* elastic
elástico, -ca *adj.* elastic
elección *noun f.* **1.** election **2.** choice, selection
electo, -ta *adj.* elect
elector, -tora *noun.* elector, voter
electorado *noun m.* electorate
electoral *adj.* electoral
electricidad *noun f.* electricity
eléctrico, -ca *adj.* electric, electrical
electrificar *verb.* to electrify
electrodoméstico *noun m.* appliance
electrón *noun m.* electron
electrónica *noun f.* electronics
electrónico, -ca *adj.* electronic
elefante, -ta *noun.* elephant
elegancia *noun f.* elegance
elegante *adj.* elegant, smart
elegir *verb.* **1.** to elect **2.** choose, select
elemental *adj.* **1.** basic, elementary **2.** essential
elemento *noun m.* element
elepé *noun m.* long-playing record
elevación *noun f.* elevation, height
elevado, -da *adj.* **1.** high **2.** elevated
elevador *noun m.* elevator
elevar *verb.* **1.** to raise, lift **2.** increase **3.** promote
—**elevarse** to rise
—**elevarse a** to amount to, total
eliminación *noun f.* **1.** elimination **2.** removal
eliminar *verb.* **1.** to eliminate **2.** remove **3.** kill
ella *pron.* **1.** she **2.** it **3.** her **4.** hers, its
ello *pron.* it
ellos, ellas *pron.* **1.** they **2.** them
—**de ellos, de ellas** theirs
elocuente *adj.* eloquent
elogiar *verb.* to praise
elogio *noun m.* praise
emancipación *noun f.* emancipation
embajada *noun f.* embassy
embajador, -dora *noun.* ambassador
embalaje *noun m.* packing, packaging
embaldosar *verb.* to tile
embalsar *verb.* to dam
embalse *noun m.* dam, reservoir
embarazada *adj.* pregnant
embarazo *noun m.* pregnancy
embarazoso, -sa *adj.* embarrassing
embarcación *noun f.* boat, craft
embarcadero *noun m.* pier, wharf
embarcar *verb.* to embark
embargar *verb.* **1.** to seize, impound **2.** overwhelm
embargo *noun m.* **1.** embargo **2.** seizure
embarque *noun m.* shipment
embestir *verb.* to charge
embolsar *verb.* to pocket
emboscada *noun f.* ambush
embotellamiento *noun m.* traffic jam
embotellar *verb.* to bottle

embrague *noun m.* clutch
embrión *noun m.* embryo
embrionario, -ria *adj.* embryonic
embrujar *verb.* to bewitch
embutir *verb.* to jam, stuff
emergencia *noun f.* emergency
emerger *verb.* to emerge
emigrante *noun mf. adj.* emigrant
emigrar *verb.* **1.** to emigrate **2.** migrate
eminente *adj.* eminent
emisión *noun f.* **1.** emission **2.** broadcast **3.** issue
emitir *verb.* **1.** to emit **2.** broadcast **3.** issue
emoción *noun f.* emotion, excitement
emocionado, -da *adj.* excited
emocional *adj.* emotional
emocionante *adj.* exciting
emocionar *verb.* **1.** to excite, thrill **2.** move, touch
emotivo, -va *adj.* emotional, moving, touching
empalme *noun m.* **1.** connection, link **2.** junction
empanada *noun f.* pie
empañar *verb.* **1.** to steam up **2.** tarnish
empapado, -da *adj.* soaked
empaparse *verb.* to soak
empapelar *verb.* to wallpaper
empaquetar *verb.* to pack, package
emparejar *verb.* **1.** to pair, match **2.** make even
—**emparejarse** to match
emparentado, -da *adj.* related
empastar *verb.* **1.** to fill **2.** bind
empaste *noun m.* filling
empatar *verb.* to draw, tie
empate *noun m.* draw, tie
empedernido, -da *adj.* **1.** inveterate **2.** heavy
empedrar *verb.* to pave
empeñar *verb.* to pawn, pledge
—**empeñarse** **1.** to insist (on) **2.** get into debt
empeño *noun m.* **1.** pledge **2.** pawning **3.** insistence
empeorar *verb.* to worsen
emperador, -dora *noun.* emperor or empress
empezar *verb.* to begin, start
empleado, -da *noun.* employee, employee
empleado, -da *adj.* employed
emplear *verb.* **1.** to employ **2.** use
empleo *noun m.* **1.** employment **2.** use, usage
empollar *verb.* to incubate
empolvar *verb.* to powder
emprendedor, -dora *adj.* enterprising, go-ahead
emprender *verb.* to undertake
empresa *noun f.* **1.** company, corporation, firm, business **2.** undertaking, venture
empresario, -ria *noun.* **1.** businessman or businesswoman **2.** impresario, manager
empréstito *noun m.* loan
empujar *verb.* **1.** to push **2.** shove
empuje *noun m.* drive, push
empujón *noun m.* push, shove
empuñar *verb.* to grasp
en *prep.* **1.** in **2.** on **3.** at **4.** by **5.** inside **6.** into
enamorado, -da *noun.* lover
enamorado, -da *adj.* in love
enano, -na *noun.* dwarf
enardecer *verb.* **1.** to arouse **2.** stir up
encabezamiento *noun m.* heading
encabezar *verb.* **1.** to head, lead **2.** put a heading
encadenar *verb.* **1.** to chain **2.** link
encajar *verb.* **1.** to fit **2.** stick **3.** take
encaje *noun m.* lace
encaminar *verb.* to direct
—**encaminarse hacia** to head for
encanecer *verb.* to gray
encantado, -da *adj.* **1.** delighted **2.** charmed **3.** haunted
encantador, -dora *adj.* **1.** delightful **2.** charming
encantar *verb.* **1.** to delight, charm **2.** enchant, bewitch **3.** love
encanto *noun m.* **1.** charm **2.** spell
encarcelamiento *noun m.* imprisonment
encarcelar *verb.* to imprison, jail
encargado, -da *noun.* person in charge

encargar *verb.* to order
—**encargarse de** to take charge of
encargo *noun m.* **1.** order **2.** errand **3.** commission, job
encarnar *verb.* to embody
encarnizado, -da *adj.* bloody, bitter
encendedor *noun m.* lighter
encender *verb.* **1.** to light **2.** switch on **3.** start **4.** arouse
encenderse *verb.* to blush
encerar *verb.* **1.** to wax **2.** polish
encerrar *verb.* **1.** to lock up, shut up **2.** contain
enchufe *noun m.* **1.** plug, socket **2.** contact, patronage
encía *noun f.* gum
encierro *noun m.* **1.** enclosure **2.** confinement
encima *adv.* **1.** above, on top **2.** upon **3.** on top of that
—**encima de 1.** above, on top, over **2.** over **3.** as well, besides
encinta *adj.* pregnant
encoger *verb.* to shrink
—**encogerse de hombros** to shrug
encontrar *verb.* **1.** to find **2.** meet **3.** encounter
—**encontrarse 1.** to meet **2.** be, feel **3.** clash
encorvar *verb.* to bend, curve
encrucijada *noun f.* crossroads
encuadernación *noun f.* binding
encuadernar *verb.* to bind
encuadrar *verb.* **1.** to frame **2.** fit, place
encuentro *noun m.* **1.** meeting, encounter **2.** match
encuesta *noun f.* survey, poll
enderezar *verb.* to straighten
endosar *verb.* to endorse
endulzar *verb.* to sweeten
endurecer *verb.* to harden
enemigo, -ga *noun. adj.* enemy
energía *noun f.* energy
enérgico, -ca *adj.* energetic
enero *noun m.* January
enfadado, -da *adj.* angry
enfadar *verb.* to annoy, make angry
—**enfadarse** *verb.* to get annoyed, get angry
énfasis *noun m.* emphasis
enfatizar *verb.* emphasize, stress
enfermedad *noun f.* **1.** disease **2.** illness, sickness
enfermería *noun f.* infirmary
enfermero, -ra *noun.* nurse
enfermo, -ma *noun.* sick person, patient
enfermo, -ma *adj.* ill, sick
enfocar *verb.* to focus
enfrentamiento *noun m.* clash, confrontation
enfrentar *verb.* to face, confront
enfriar *verb.* to cool, chill
—**enfriarse 1.** to cool down **2.** catch a cold
enfurecer *verb.* to enrage
—**enfurecerse** to fly into a rage
enganchar *verb.* to hook
engañar *verb.* **1.** to cheat **2.** deceive
engaño *noun m.* **1.** deception **2.** trick
engañoso, -sa *adj.* **1.** misleading **2.** deceitful
engastado, -da *adj.* set
engastar *verb.* to set
engendrar *verb.* **1.** to beget, father **2.** engender
engranaje *noun m.* gear
engranar *verb.* to engage
engrasar *verb.* to grease
engullir *verb.* to gulp, swallow
enigma *noun f.* enigma
enjabonar *verb.* to soap
enjaular *verb.* to cage
enjuagar *verb.* to rinse
enjuague *noun m.* rinse
enjugar *verb.* to wipe away
enjuiciar *verb.* **1.** to prosecute **2.** try
enlace *noun m.* **1.** link, connection **2.** liaison
enlatar *verb.* to can
enlazar *verb.* to join, link, connect
enlucido *noun m.* plaster
enlucir *verb.* to plaster
enmarañar *verb.* to tangle
enmarcar *verb.* to frame
enmendar *verb.* **1.** to amend **2.** correct
ennegrecer *verb.* to blacken
enojado, -da *adj.* angry
enorgullecerse *verb.* to pride oneself

enorme *adj.* enormous
enredar *verb.* **1.** to confuse **2.** tangle
enredo *noun m.* **1.** mess **2.** tangle
enriquecerse *verb.* to get rich
enrollar *verb.* to roll up
enroscar *verb.* **1.** to screw **2.** coil
ensalada *noun f.* salad
ensamblaje *noun m.* assembly
ensamblar *verb.* **1.** to assemble **2.** join
ensanchar *verb.* **1.** to widen **2.** expand
ensangrentado, -da *adj.* bloody
ensartar *verb.* to thread, string
ensayo *noun m.* **1.** essay **2.** rehearsal **3.** test **4.** trial
enseña *noun f.* **1.** emblem, banner **2.** colors
enseñanza *noun f.* teaching
enseñar *verb.* **1.** to teach **2.** show
ensillar *verb.* to saddle
ensuciar *verb.* to dirty, soil
entablar *verb.* to engage, enter into
entender *verb.* **1.** to understand **2.** think, believe
—**entender de** to know about
entendido, -da *noun.* expert
entendimiento *noun m.* understanding
enteramente *adv.* entirely, fully
enterar *verb.* to inform
—**enterarse** to learn, find out
entero, -ra *adj.* **1.** entire **2.** full **3.** intact **4.** whole
enterrar *verb.* to bury
entierro *noun m.* burial
entonces *adv.* then
entorno *noun m.* **1.** environment **2.** surroundings
entrada *noun f.* **1.** ticket **2.** access **3.** doorway **4.** entrance, entry
entraña *noun f.* heart
—**entrañas** bowels, entrails
entrar *verb.* **1.** to enter, go in **2.** access
entre *prep.* **1.** between **2.** among
entrega *noun f.* **1.** delivery **2.** handing over **3.** submission **4.** dedication, devotion
entregado, -da *adj.* dedicated, devoted
entregar *verb.* **1.** to deliver **2.** hand over **3.** present
—**entregarse** **1.** to surrender **2.** indulge, give in **3.** devote oneself
entrelazar *verb.* to intertwine, interweave
entrenador, -dora *noun.* coach, trainer, instructor
entrenamiento *noun m.* training, practice
entrenar *verb.* **1.** to train **2.** practice
entretanto *adv.* meanwhile
entretener *verb.* **1.** to entertain, amuse **2.** distract
—**entretenerse** to dally
entretenido, -da *adj.* entertaining, amusing
entretenimiento *noun m.* amusement, entertainment
entrever *verb.* **1.** to glimpse **2.** make out
entrevista *noun f.* interview
entrevistador, -dora *noun.* interviewer
entrevistar *verb.* to interview
entristecer *verb.* to sadden
entrometerse *verb.* to interfere, meddle
entusiasmar *verb.* to excite
entusiasmo *noun m.* enthusiasm
entusiasta *noun mf.* enthusiast
entusiasta *adj.* enthusiastic
envasar *verb.* **1.** to pack **2.** bottle **3.** can
envase *noun m.* **1.** container **2.** empty **3.** can
envejecer *verb.* to age, grow old
envenenar *verb.* to poison
enviado, -da *noun.* envoy
enviar *verb.* **1.** to send **2.** dispatch **3.** ship
envidia *noun f.* envy, jealousy
envidiar *verb.* to envy
envidioso, -sa *adj.* envious, jealous
envío *noun m.* **1.** dispatch **2.** shipment
enviudar *verb.* to be widowed, become a widow or widower
envoltorio *noun m.* package, bundle
envolver *verb.* **1.** to wrap **2.** surround
enyesar *verb.* to plaster
epidemia *noun f.* epidemic
episodio *noun m.* episode
época *noun f.* age, epoch, time, period
epopeya *noun f.* epic poem
equidad *noun f.* equity

equilibrado, -da *adj.* well-balanced
equilibrar *verb.* to balance
equilibrio *noun m.* balance, equilibrium
equipaje *noun m.* baggage, luggage
equipamiento *noun m.* equipment
equipar *verb.* to equip
equiparar *verb.* **1.** to compare **2.** put on a same level
equipo *noun m.* **1.** crew **2.** team **3.** gear, equipment **4.** kit
equitativo, -va *adj.* equitable, fair
equivalente *noun m.* **1.** equivalent **2.** counterpart
equivalente *adj.* equivalent
equivaler *verb.* **1.** to be equal to, be equivalent to **2.** correspond
equivocación *noun f.* mistake
equivocar *verb.* to mistake
—**equivocarse** to make a mistake, be wrong
era *noun f.* era
erecto, -ta *adj.* erect
erguido, -da *adj.* erect
erguir *verb.* to raise
erigir *verb.* **1.** to erect, build **2.** establish, found
erigirse *verb.* to set oneself up as
erosión *noun f.* erosion
erosionar *verb.* to erode
erótico, -ca *adj.* erotic
errar *verb.* **1.** to miss **2.** wander **3.** be mistaken
erróneo, -nea *adj.* erroneous, wrong
error *noun m.* error, mistake
erudición *noun f.* learning, scholarship
erudito, -ta *noun.* scholar
erudito, -ta *adj.* learned
erupción *noun f.* **1.** eruption **2.** rash
esbelto, -ta *adj.* slender, slim
esbozar *verb.* **1.** to outline **2.** sketch
esbozo *noun m.* **1.** outline **2.** draft **3.** sketch
escabullirse *verb.* to slip away
escala *noun f.* **1.** range **2.** scale
escalada *noun f.* climb
escalador, -dora *noun.* climber
escalar *verb.* **1.** to climb, scale **2.** escalate
escalera *noun f.* **1.** stairs **2.** ladder
escalofrío *noun m.* shiver, chill
escalón *noun m.* echelon
escama *noun f.* **1.** scale **2.** flake
escandalizar *verb.* to shock, scandalize
—**escandalizarse** to be shocked
escándalo *noun m.* scandal
escandaloso, -sa *adj.* **1.** shocking, scandalous **2.** outrageous **3.** noisy
escanear *verb.* to scan
escáner *noun m.* scanner
escapar *verb.* to escape, run away
escape *noun m.* **1.** escape **2.** leak
escarcha *noun f.* frost
escarchar *verb.* to frost
escarlata *noun f. adj.* scarlet
escarpado, -da *adj.* steep, sheer
escasez *noun f.* **1.** scarcity, lack, shortage **2.** want
escaso, -sa *adj.* scarce, scant
—**escaso de** short of
escatimar *verb.* to spare
escayola *noun f.* plaster, plaster cast
escena *noun f.* scene
escenario *noun m.* **1.** stage **2.** scene, setting
escepticismo *noun m.* skepticism
escéptico, -ca *adj.* skeptical
esclarecer *verb.* to clarify
esclavo, -va *noun.* slave
esclusa *noun f.* lock
escocer *verb.* to smart, sting
escocés *noun m.* Scots (language)
escocés, -cesa *noun.* Scot
escocés, -cesa *adj.* Scots, Scottish, Scotch
Escocia *noun f.* Scotland
escoger *verb.* to choose, pick, select
escolta *noun mf.* escort
escoltar *verb.* to escort
escombro *noun m.* debris
esconder *verb.* to hide, conceal
escondido, -da *adj.* hidden
escondite *noun m.* hiding place
escondrijo *noun m.* hiding place
escorar *verb.* to heel, list
escoria *noun m.* scum
escribir *verb.* to write
—**escribir a máquina** to type
escrito *noun m.* **1.** written document **2.** writings

escritor, -tora *noun.* writer
escritorio *noun m.* desk
escritura *noun f.* **1.** writing, handwriting **2.** deed
escrutinio *noun m.* scrutiny
escuadrón *noun m.* squadron
escuchar *verb.* **1.** to listen (to) **2.** hear
escudo *noun m.* shield
escuela *noun f.* school
escueto, -ta *adj.* plain, simple, concise
esculpir *verb.* **1.** to sculpt **2.** carve
escultura *noun f.* sculpture
escupir *verb.* to spit
escurrir *verb.* to drain
—**escurrirse** to slip away
ese, esa *adj.* that
—**esos** those
ése, ésa *pron.* that one
—**ésos** those ones
esencia *noun f.* essence
esencial *adj.* essential
esfera *noun f.* **1.** sphere **2.** dial
esforzarse *verb.* to strive, make an effort
esfuerzo *noun m.* effort
esguince *noun m.* strain
eslabón *noun m.* link
eslogan *noun m.* **1.** chant **2.** slogan
eso *pron.* that
espacio *noun m.* **1.** space **2.** room **3.** period, length
espacioso, -sa *adj.* spacious
espada *noun f.* sword
espalda *noun f.* back
espanto *noun m.* fright, fear
espantoso, -sa *adj.* **1.** frightening **2.** dreadful
España *noun f.* Spain
español, -ñola *noun. adj.* Spanish
esparadrapo *noun m.* adhesive bandage
esparcir *verb.* **1.** to scatter **2.** spread
—**esparcirse 1.** to spread out **2.** have fun
especia *noun f.* spice
especial *adj.* special
especialidad *noun f.* specialty
especialista *noun mf.* specialist
especializarse *verb.* to specialize
especie *noun f.* **1.** species **2.** type, kind
específicamente *adv.* specifically
especificar *verb.* to specify
específico, -ca *adj.* specific
espécimen *noun m.* specimen
espectacular *adj.* spectacular
espectáculo *noun m.* **1.** spectacle **2.** show
espectador, -dora *noun.* spectator
espectro *noun m.* spectrum
especulación *noun f.* speculation
especular *verb.* to speculate
espejo *noun m.* mirror
espera *noun f.* wait
esperanza *noun f.* hope, expectation
esperar *verb.* **1.** to wait for, await **2.** expect **3.** hope
—**esperarse 1.** to expect **2.** hold on, hang on
esperma *noun m.* sperm
espeso, -sa *adj.* dense, thick
espesor *noun m.* density, thickness
espía *noun mf.* spy
espiar *verb.* to spy
espiga *noun f.* ear
espina *noun f.* **1.** spine **2.** thorn **3.** fish bone
espinoso, -sa *adj.* **1.** thorny **2.** difficult
espiral *noun f. adj.* spiral
espíritu *noun m.* **1.** spirit **2.** state of mind
espiritual *adj.* spiritual
espléndido, -da *adj.* **1.** splendid, great **2.** generous
esplendor *noun m.* splendor, glory
espliego *noun m.* lavender
esponja *noun f.* sponge
espontáneo, -nea *adj.* spontaneous
esposo, -sa *noun.* husband or wife
espuma *noun f.* **1.** foam **2.** scum
esqueje *noun m.* cutting
esqueleto *noun m.* **1.** skeleton **2.** framework
esquema *noun m.* sketch
esquí *noun m.* ski
esquiar *verb.* to ski
esquina *noun f.* corner
esquivar *verb.* **1.** to dodge **2.** avoid
esquivo, -va *adj.* **1.** elusive **2.** aloof
estable *adj.* stable, steady

establecer *verb.* to establish, set up, found
—**establecerse 1.** to settle **2.** establish oneself
establecimiento *noun m.* **1.** establishment **2.** institution **3.** premises
estaca *noun f.* stake
estación *noun f.* season
estacionar *verb.* **1.** to station, place **2.** park
estado *noun m.* **1.** state **2.** status **3.** condition
Estados Unidos de América *noun m. plural.* America, United States of America
estadounidense *noun mf. adj.* American
estafa *noun f.* swindle
estafar *verb.* to swindle
estafeta *noun f.* courier
estallar *verb.* **1.** to explode **2.** burst **3.** break out
estallido *noun m.* **1.** explosion **2.** burst **3.** outbreak
estampar *verb.* **1.** to stamp **2.** print
estancia *noun f.* **1.** stay, residence **2.** farm
estandarte *noun m.* banner, standard
estanque *noun m.* pond
estante *noun m.* shelf
estaño *noun m.* tin
estar *verb.* to be
—**estar en contra** to oppose
—**estarse** to stay, remain
estatuto *noun m.* **1.** statute **2.** charter
este *noun m.* east
este *adj.* east, eastern
este, esta *adj.* this
—**estos** these
éste, ésta *pron.* **1.** this one **2.** the latter
—**éstos** these ones
estela *noun f.* **1.** trail **2.** wake
estera *noun f.* mat
estigmatizar *verb.* to stigmatize, brand
estilo *noun m.* **1.** style **2.** fashion, manner
estima *noun f.* esteem, regard
estimación *noun f.* **1.** esteem, regard **2.** estimate
estimar *verb.* **1.** to esteem **2.** estimate **3.** consider, regard
estimulación *noun f.* stimulation
estimulante *noun m.* stimulant
estimulante *adj.* stimulating
estimular *verb.* **1.** to stimulate **2.** encourage
estímulo *noun m.* **1.** stimulus **2.** encouragement
estirado, -da *adj.* **1.** stretched **2.** stiff
estiramiento *noun m.* stretching
estirar *verb.* to stretch
estirón *noun m.* tug
esto *pron.* this
—**a todo esto** meanwhile
—**en esto** at this point
estómago *noun m.* stomach
estorbar *verb.* **1.** to hinder **2.** obstruct
estorbo *noun m.* **1.** hindrance **2.** obstacle
estratagema *noun f.* stratagem, device
estrategia *noun f.* strategy
estratégico, -ca *adj.* strategic
estrechar *verb.* **1.** to narrow **2.** tighten **3.** hug
—**estrechar la mano** to shake hands (with)
estrecho *adj.* **1.** narrow, tight **2.** close
estrella *noun f.* **1.** star **2.** fate, fortune
estrellar *verb.* to smash, crash
—**estrellarse** to crash
estremecerse *verb.* to shiver
estremecimiento *noun m.* shivering
estrenar *verb.* **1.** to use for the first time **2.** inaugurate, open
estreno *noun m.* premiere
estrés *noun m.* stress
estribillo *noun m.* chorus
estricto, -ta *adj.* strict
estrofa *noun f.* stanza, verse
estropear *verb.* **1.** to spoil, ruin **2.** damage
—**estropearse** to spoil
estructura *noun f.* **1.** structure **2.** framework
estructural *adj.* structural
estructurar *verb.* to structure
estrujar *verb.* **1.** to squeeze **2.** press
estuario *noun m.* estuary

estuche *noun m.* case, kit
estudiante *noun mf.* student
estudiar *verb.* to study
estudio *noun m.* **1.** study **2.** studio **3.** den
estudioso, -sa *adj.* studious
estufa *noun f.* stove
estupendo, -da *adj.* stupendous, wonderful
estupidez *noun f.* stupidity
estúpido, -da *noun f.* idiot
estúpido, -da *adj.* stupid
etapa *noun f.* stage
eterno, -na *adj.* eternal
ética *noun f.* ethics
ético, -ca *adj.* ethical
etiqueta *noun f.* **1.** label, tag **2.** etiquette
etiquetar *verb.* to label
étnico, -ca *adj.* ethnic
euro *noun m.* euro
Europa *noun f.* Europe
europeo, -pea *noun. adj.* European
evacuar *verb.* **1.** to evacuate **2.** vacate
evaluación *noun f.* evaluation, assessment
evaluar *verb.* to evaluate, assess
evangelio *noun m.* gospel
evasiva *noun f.* excuse, pretext
evento *noun m.* event
eventual *adj.* **1.** temporary **2.** possible
evidente *adj.* evident, obvious
evitar *verb.* **1.** to avoid **2.** prevent
evocador, -dora *adj.* evocative
evocar *verb.* to evoke
evolución *noun f.* evolution
evolucionar *verb.* **1.** to evolve **2.** develop
evolutivo, -va *adj.* evolutionary
exactamente *adv.* exactly
exactitud *noun f.* accuracy, exactitude
exacto, -ta *adj.* accurate, exact
exagerar *verb.* to exaggerate
examen *noun m.* **1.** examination, exam **2.** investigation
examinar *verb.* **1.** to examine **2.** inspect
—**examinarse** *verb.* to take an exam
excavación *noun f.* excavation
excavar *verb.* to excavate
excedente *noun m. adj.* excess, surplus
exceder *verb.* to exceed, surpass
excelencia *noun f.* excellence
excelente *adj.* excellent
excéntrico, -ca *noun. adj.* eccentric
excepción *noun f.* exception
excepcional *adj.* exceptional, outstanding
excepto *prep.* except, save
exceptuar *verb.* to except
excesivo, -va *adj.* excessive
exceso *noun m.* excess
excitar *verb.* to excite
exclamar *verb.* to exclaim
excluir *verb.* to exclude, leave out
exclusión *noun f.* exclusion
exclusivamente *adv.* exclusively
exclusivo, -va *adj.* **1.** exclusive **2.** sole
excremento *noun m.* excrement
excursión *noun f.* **1.** excursion, trip **2.** hike
excursionista *noun mf.* **1.** excursionist **2.** hiker
excusa *noun f.* excuse
excusar *verb.* to excuse
—**excusarse** to apologize
exención *noun f.* exemption
exento, -ta *adj.* exempt, free
exhibición *noun f.* **1.** exhibition, show **2.** display
exhibir *verb.* **1.** to exhibit, show **2.** display
exhortar *verb.* to exhort
exigencia *noun f.* demand, requirement
exigente *adj.* demanding, exacting
exigir *verb.* **1.** to demand, require **2.** exact
exiliado, -da *noun m.* exile
exiliado, -da *adj.* exiled
exiliar *verb.* to exile
—**exiliarse** to go into exile
exilio *noun m.* exile
eximir *verb.* to exempt
existencia *noun f.* existence
—**existencias** stock
existir *verb.* to exist
éxito *noun m.* success, hit
—**tener éxito** to be successful
exitoso, -sa *adj.* successful

exótico, -ca *adj.* exotic
expansión *noun f.* expansion
expectación *noun f.* expectation, anticipation
expectativa *noun f.* **1.** expectancy **2.** expectation
expedición *noun f.* expedition
expediente *noun m.* **1.** expedient **2.** brief, file, record
experiencia *noun f.* experience
experimentado, -da *adj.* experienced
experimental *adj.* experimental
experimentar *verb.* **1.** to experiment **2.** experience
experimento *noun m.* experiment
experto, -ta *noun. adj.* expert
expirar *verb.* **1.** to expire **2.** die, pass away
explicación *noun f.* explanation
explicar *verb.* to explain
explicativo, -va *adj.* explanatory
explícitamente *adv.* explicitly
explícito, -va *adj.* explicit
exploración *noun f.* exploration
explorador, -dora *noun.* explorer, scout
explorar *verb.* to explore
explosión *noun f.* **1.** explosion **2.** outbreak, outburst
explosivo *noun m.* explosive
explosivo, -va *adj.* explosive
explotación *noun f.* exploitation, development
explotar *verb.* **1.** to exploit **2.** to run, operate
exponer *verb.* **1.** to exhibit, show **2.** display **3.** expose **4.** explain
exportación *noun f.* export
exportar *verb.* to export
exposición *noun f.* **1.** exhibition, show **2.** display **3.** exposure
expresamente *adv.* expressly
expresar *verb.* to express
expresión *noun f.* expression
expresivo, -va *adj.* expressive
expreso *noun m.* express train
expreso, -sa *adj.* express
exprimir *verb.* to squeeze
expulsar *verb.* **1.** to expel, eject **2.** dismiss
expulsión *noun f.* expulsion
exquisito, -ta *adj.* exquisite
éxtasis *noun m.* ecstasy
extender *verb.* **1.** to extend **2.** stretch **3.** spread **4.** write out
—**extenderse 1.** to stretch **2.** spread
extendido, -da *adj.* **1.** outstretched **2.** widespread
extensión *noun f.* **1.** extension **2.** length **3.** extent
extenso, -sa *adj.* **1.** extensive **2.** vast
exterior *noun m.* **1.** exterior **2.** outside
exterior *adj.* **1.** exterior **2.** foreign
externo, -na *adj.* external
extinción *noun f.* extinction
extirpación *noun f.* removal
extirpar *verb.* to extirpate, eradicate, excise
extra *noun m.* extra, bonus
extra *noun mf.* extra (in movies)
extra *adj.* **1.** extra **2.** superior
extracción *noun f.* extraction
extracto *noun m.* **1.** extract **2.** abstract, summary
extraditar *verb.* to extradite
extraer *verb.* to extract
extranjero, -ra *noun.* **1.** foreigner **2.** foreign country, abroad, overseas
extranjero, -ra *adj.* foreign, alien
extrañar *verb.* to miss
—**extrañarse** to be amazed
extraño, -ña *noun.* stranger
extraño, -ña *adj.* **1.** strange, odd **2.** alien, foreign
extraordinario, -ria *adj.* extraordinary, outstanding
extraterrestre *noun mf. adj.* alien
extraviar *verb.* **1.** to mislead **2.** lose
—**extraviarse** to get lost
extremadamente *adv.* extremely
extremado, -da *adj.* extreme
extremidad *noun f.* extremity
extremista *noun mf. adj.* extremist
extremo *noun m.* end, extreme
extremo, -ma *adj.* extreme, utmost
extrovertido, -da *adj.* outgoing

F

fábrica *noun f.* **1.** factory **2.** plant
fabricación *noun f.* **1.** making **2.** manufacture
fabricante *noun mf.* manufacturer, maker
fabricar *verb.* **1.** to make **2.** manufacture
fabuloso, -sa *adj.* **1.** fabulous, terrific **2.** fabled
facción *noun f.* **1.** faction **2.** feature
facial *adj.* facial
fácil *adj.* **1.** easy **2.** likely
facilidad *noun f.* ease, facility
facilitar *verb.* **1.** to provide **2.** facilitate
fácilmente *adv.* easily, readily
factibilidad *noun f.* feasibility
factible *adj.* feasible, practicable
factor *noun m.* factor
factual *adj.* factual
factura *noun f.* **1.** invoice, bill **2.** workmanship
facturación *noun f.* **1.** turnover **2.** check-in
facturar *verb.* **1.** to invoice, bill **2.** check in
facultad *noun f.* **1.** faculty **2.** authority, power **3.** school
faja *noun f.* **1.** strip **2.** belt **3.** girdle
falda *noun f.* **1.** skirt **2.** side
faldón *noun m.* flap
falla *noun f.* fault
fallar *verb.* **1.** to fail **2.** miss **3.** rule
fallo *noun m.* **1.** fault, mistake **2.** sentence, verdict
falsedad *noun f.* **1.** falseness **2.** lie
falsificación *noun f.* fake, forgery, falsification
falsificar *verb.* to fake, forge, falsify
falso, -sa *adj.* **1.** false, untrue **2.** fake
falta *noun f.* **1.** lack, want **2.** fault, error **3.** foul
faltar *verb.* **1.** to be lacking **2.** be absent **3.** be unfaithful, break **4.** remain
fama *noun f.* **1.** fame **2.** name
familia *noun f.* family
familiar *adj.* **1.** familiar **2.** informal
familiaridad *noun f.* **1.** familiarity **2.** informality
famoso, -sa *noun.* celebrity
famoso, -sa *adj.* famous, well-known
fanático, -ca *noun. adj.* fanatic
fanfarronear *verb.* to boast
fantasía *noun f.* **1.** fantasy **2.** fancy, imagination
fantasma *noun m.* ghost
fantástico, -ca *adj.* **1.** fantastic **2.** great, terrific
fardo *noun m.* **1.** bundle **2.** package
farmacéutico, -ca *noun.* pharmacist
farmacéutico, -ca *adj.* pharmaceutical
farmacia *noun f.* drugstore, pharmacy
fascinación *noun f.* fascination
fascinante *adj.* fascinating
fascinar *verb.* to fascinate
fascismo *noun m.* Fascism
fascista *noun mf. adj.* fascist
fase *noun f.* phase, period
fastidiar *verb.* to annoy, bother
fastidio *noun m.* annoyance, nuisance
fatal *adj.* fatal
fatiga *noun f.* fatigue
fatigado, -da *adj.* tired, weary
fatigar *verb.* to fatigue, tire
—**fatigarse** to wear oneself out
fauna *noun f.* fauna
favor *noun m.* favor
—**por favor** please
favorable *adj.* favorable
favorecedor, -dora *adj.* becoming
favorecer *verb.* **1.** to favor **2.** suit
favorito, -ta *noun. adj.* favorite
fax *noun m.* fax
faxear *verb.* to fax
fe *noun f.* **1.** faith **2.** belief **3.** testimony
febrero *noun m.* February
fecha *noun f.* date
—**fecha de caducidad** expiration date
—**fecha límite** deadline
fechar *verb.* to date
federación *noun f.* federation
federal *adj.* federal
felicidad *noun f.* happiness
felicitar *verb.* to congratulate
felino, -na *noun. adj.* feline
feliz *adj.* happy

femenino, -na *adj.* feminine
feminismo *noun m.* feminism
feminista *noun mf. adj.* feminist
fénix *noun m.* phoenix
fenómeno *noun m.* phenomenon
feo, fea *adj.* **1.** ugly **2.** nasty
feria *noun f.* **1.** fair **2.** market **3.** festival
feroz *adj.* fierce, ferocious
ferretería *noun f.* **1.** hardware **2.** hardware store
ferrocarril *noun m.* railway, railroad
ferry *noun m.* ferry
fértil *adj.* **1.** fertile **2.** productive
fertilidad *noun f.* fertility
fertilizante *noun m.* fertilizer
festejar *verb.* **1.** to feast **2.** celebrate
festejo *noun m.* **1.** feast **2.** celebration
festín *noun m.* feast
festival *noun m.* festival
fétido, -da *adj.* fetid, foul
feudal *adj.* feudal
fiabilidad *noun f.* reliability
fiable *adj.* reliable
fianza *noun f.* **1.** bail **2.** deposit
fiar *verb.* **1.** to sell on credit **2.** confide
—**fiarse de** to place trust in
fibra *noun f.* fiber
ficción *noun f.* fiction
ficha *noun f.* **1.** file, record **2.** chip, counter **3.** token
fichar *verb.* **1.** to record on a file **2.** punch in or out **3.** sign up
ficticio, -cia *adj.* fictitious, fictional
fidelidad *noun f.* fidelity
fideo *noun m.* noodle
fiebre *noun f.* **1.** fever **2.** temperature
fiel *adj.* **1.** faithful **2.** accurate
fieltro *noun m.* felt
fiesta *noun f.* **1.** party **2.** holiday
figura *noun f.* **1.** figure **2.** shape
figurar *verb.* **1.** to figure **2.** be among **3.** stand out
—**figurarse** to fancy, imagine
fijar *verb.* **1.** to fix **2.** establish, set up **3.** appoint **4.** fasten
—**fijarse** to settle
—**fijarse en** to notice
fijo, -ja *adj.* **1.** fixed **2.** firm **3.** permanent
fila *noun f.* **1.** file, line **2.** queue **3.** rank, row
filial *noun f.* subsidiary
filial *adj.* filial
filmar *verb.* to film
filo *noun m.* **1.** blade **2.** edge
filosofía *noun f.* philosophy
filosófico, -ca *adj.* philosophical, philosophic
filósofo, -fa *noun.* philosopher
filtración *noun f.* leaking
filtrar *verb.* **1.** to filter **2.** leak
filtro *noun m.* filter
fin *noun m.* **1.** end **2.** aim, purpose
—**fin de semana** weekend
—**por fin** at last
final *noun m.* end, final
final *adj.* final
finalidad *noun f.* goal, finality, end
finalización *noun f.* completion
finalizar *verb.* to finish, end
financiar *verb.* to finance
financiero, -ra *adj.* financial
finanzas *noun f. plural.* finance, finances
finca *noun f.* **1.** land, real state **2.** farm, ranch
fingido, -da *adj.* feigned
fingir *verb.* to feign, pretend
finito, -ta *adj.* finite
finlandés, -desa *noun. adj.* Finnish
Finlandia *noun f.* Finland
fino, -na *adj.* **1.** fine **2.** delicate **3.** slender, slim, thin **4.** refined
firma *noun f.* **1.** signature **2.** company, firm
firmar *verb.* to sign
firme *adj.* **1.** firm **2.** secure **3.** steady
firmemente *adv.* firmly
física *noun f.* physics
físico *noun m.* physique
físico, -ca *noun.* physicist
físico, -ca *adj.* physical
fláccido, -da *adj.* **1.** flaccid **2.** limp
flaco, -ca *adj.* **1.** thin, skinny **2.** feeble, weak
flanco *noun m.* flank
flanquear *verb.* to flank
flaquear *verb.* to flag, weaken
flauta *noun f.* flute
flautista *noun mf.* flutist
flecha *noun f.* arrow

fleco *noun m.* fringe
fletar *verb.* to charter
flete *noun m.* freight
flexibilidad *noun f.* flexibility
flexible *adj.* flexible
flojo, -ja *adj.* **1.** loose **2.** weak **3.** limp **4.** lazy
flor *noun f.* flower
flora *noun f.* flora
floración *noun f.* flowering
florecer *verb.* **1.** to bloom, blossom, flower **2.** flourish
floreciente *adj.* **1.** flowering **2.** flourishing
florero *noun m.* vase
flota *noun f.* fleet
flotar *verb.* to float
fluctuar *verb.* to fluctuate
fluido *noun m.* fluid
fluido, -da *adj.* **1.** fluid **2.** fluent
fluir *verb.* **1.** to flow **2.** roll
flujo *noun m.* flow
foca *noun f.* seal
focal *adj.* focal
foco *noun m.* **1.** focus **2.** spotlight **3.** center
folclore *noun m.* folklore
folclórico, -ca *adj.* folk
follaje *noun m.* foliage
follar *verb.* to fuck
folleto *noun m.* leaflet, brochure
fomentar *verb.* **1.** to foster, promote **2.** foment
fomento *noun m.* promotion
fonda *noun f.* inn
fondo *noun m.* **1.** bottom **2.** back, rear **3.** background **4.** fund
foráneo, -nea *adj.* foreign
forastero, -ra *noun m.* outsider, stranger
forcejear *verb.* to struggle
forense *adj.* forensic
forja *noun f.* forge
forjar *verb.* **1.** to forge **2.** create
forma *noun f.* **1.** form, shape **2.** manner, way
—**estar en forma** to be fit, be in shape
formación *noun f.* **1.** formation **2.** training
formal *adj.* **1.** formal **2.** serious **3.** reliable
formalidad *noun f.* **1.** formality **2.** seriousness **3.** reliability
formalmente *adv.* formally
formar *verb.* **1.** to form **2.** educate, train **3.** constitute
—**formarse** to develop, grow
formatear *verb.* to format
formato *noun m.* format
formidable *adj.* **1.** formidable **2.** huge
fórmula *noun f.* formula
formular *verb.* to formulate
formulario *noun m.* form
foro *noun m.* forum
forrar *verb.* **1.** to line **2.** cover
forro *noun m.* **1.** lining **2.** cover
fortalecer *verb.* to fortify, strengthen
fortaleza *noun f.* **1.** fortress **2.** strength
fortuito, -ta *adj.* fortuitous
fortuna *noun f.* **1.** fortune **2.** wealth
forzar *verb.* **1.** to force, compel **2.** strain
forzoso, -sa *adj.* **1.** forced, compulsory **2.** unavoidable, inevitable
fosa *noun f.* **1.** pit, ditch **2.** grave **3.** cavity
fósforo *noun m.* **1.** match **2.** phosphorus
fósil *noun m.* fossil
foso *noun m.* pit, ditch
foto *noun f.* photo, picture
fotografía *noun f.* **1.** photograph **2.** photography
fotografiar *verb.* to photograph
fotógrafo, -fa *noun.* photographer
fracasado, -da *noun.* failure
fracasado, -da *adj.* **1.** unsuccessful, failed **2.** would-be
fracasar *verb.* **1.** to fail **2.** collapse
fracaso *noun m.* failure
fracción *noun f.* fraction
fractura *noun f.* fracture
fracturar *verb.* to fracture
fragancia *noun f.* fragrance
frágil *adj.* **1.** frail, delicate **2.** fragile
fragmentar *verb.* to fragment
fragmento *noun m.* **1.** fragment **2.** excerpt
fragor *noun m.* roar, noise
francamente *adv.* **1.** frankly **2.** really
francés, -cesa *noun. adj.* French
Francia *noun f.* France

franco, -ca *adj.* **1.** frank **2.** clear **3.** exempt
franja *noun f.* **1.** band, stripe **2.** fringe
franquear *verb.* **1.** to cross **2.** exempt
franquicia *noun f.* **1.** franchise **2.** exemption
frase *noun f.* **1.** phrase **2.** sentence
fraude *noun m.* fraud
frecuencia *noun f.* frequency
frecuentar *verb.* to frequent, haunt
frecuente *adj.* frequent
fregadero *noun m.* sink
fregado *noun m.* scrubbing
fregar *verb.* **1.** to scrub **2.** wash
freír *verb.* to fry
frenar *verb.* **1.** to brake **2.** check
frenético, -ca *adj.* frantic
freno *noun m.* **1.** brake **2.** check **3.** restraint
frente *noun f.* **1.** front **2.** brow, forehead
fresa *noun f.* strawberry
fresco *noun m.* coolness
fresco, -ca *adj.* **1.** cool **2.** fresh
frescura *noun f.* **1.** coolness **2.** freshness
fricción *noun f.* friction
frigorífico *noun m.* refrigerator
frío *noun m.* **1.** cold **2.** coldness, indifference
frío, fría *adj.* **1.** cold **2.** indifferent, distant
frívolo, -la *adj.* frivolous
frontal *adj.* frontal, head-on
frontera *noun f.* border, frontier, boundary
frotar *verb.* to rub
fruncir *verb.* to gather
—**fruncir el ceño** to frown
frustración *noun f.* frustration
frustrado, -da *adj.* **1.** frustrated, would-be **2.** failed, unsuccessful
frustrar *verb.* to frustrate
fruta *noun f.* fruit
fruto *noun m.* **1.** fruit **2.** product, result
fuego *noun m.* **1.** fire **2.** light **3.** burner
fuente *noun f.* **1.** fountain **2.** spring **3.** source, origin
fuera *adv.* **1.** outside, out **2.** away **3.** abroad
—**fuera de** besides
fuerte *noun m.* fort
fuerte *adj.* **1.** strong **2.** loud
fuerte *adv.* **1.** hard **2.** loudly
fuerza *noun f.* **1.** strength **2.** force **3.** might **4.** power
—**fuerzas armadas** armed forces
fuga *noun f.* **1.** flight, escape **2.** leak **3.** fugue
fugarse *verb.* **1.** to escape **2.** run away
fugitivo, -va *noun. adj.* fugitive
fumar *verb.* to smoke
función *noun f.* **1.** function **2.** duty **3.** performance
funcional *adj.* functional
funcionamiento *noun m.* functioning
—**en funcionamiento** in operation
funcionar *verb.* **1.** to function **2.** run, work
funcionario, -ria *noun.* official, civil servant
funda *noun f.* case, cover
fundación *noun f.* foundation
fundador, -dora *noun.* founder
fundamental *adj.* basic, fundamental
fundamento *noun m.* basis, foundation
fundar *verb.* **1.** to found, establish **2.** base
funeral *noun m.* funeral
furgoneta *noun f.* van
furia *noun f.* **1.** fury **2.** rage
furioso, -sa *adj.* furious
furor *noun m.* **1.** fury **2.** rage
furúnculo *noun m.* boil
fusilar *verb.* to shoot
fusión *noun f.* **1.** fusion **2.** merger
fusionar *verb.* to merge
fusta *noun f.* crop
fustigar *verb.* to whip
fútbol *noun m.* soccer
—**fútbol americano** football
futuro *noun m.* future
futuro, -ra *adj.* future

G

gabarra *noun f.* barge
gabinete *noun m.* **1.** cabinet **2.** office
gafas *noun f. plural.* glasses, spectacles
gaita *noun f.* bagpipe
galaxia *noun f.* galaxy
galería *noun f.* gallery
galés *noun m.* Welsh (language)
galés, -lesa *noun. adj.* Welsh
galleta *noun f.* biscuit, cookie
gallina *noun f.* hen
gallinero *noun m.* **1.** coop **2.** gallery
gallo *noun m.* cock
galón *noun m.* **1.** gallon **2.** stripe
gama *noun f.* range, spectrum
gana *noun f.* desire, wish
—**tener ganas de** to feel like
ganadería *noun f.* cattle raising
ganadero, -ra *noun.* cattle raiser
ganado *noun m.* cattle, livestock
ganador, -dora *noun.* winner
ganador, -dora *adj.* winning
ganancia *noun f.* profit, gain
ganar *verb.* **1.** to win **2.** earn **3.** gain **4.** profit **5.** make
gancho *noun m.* hook
ganga *noun f.* bargain
ganso, -sa *noun.* goose
garaje *noun m.* garage
garantía *noun f.* **1.** guarantee **2.** security
garantizar *verb.* to guarantee, assure
garganta *noun f.* **1.** throat **2.** neck **3.** defile
garra *noun f.* **1.** claw **2.** paw
gas *noun m.* gas
gaseosa *noun f.* soda
gasolina *noun f.* gasoline, gas, petrol
gasolinera *noun f.* gas station, service station
gastar *verb.* **1.** to spend **2.** use
gasto *noun m.* expense, expenditure
gatear *verb.* to crawl
gatillo *noun m.* trigger
gato, -ta *noun.* **1.** cat **2.** jack
gay *adj.* gay
gemelo, -la *noun. adj.* twin
—**gemelos** **1.** cuff links **2.** binoculars
gemido *noun m.* groan, moan
gemir *verb.* to groan, moan
gen *noun m.* gene
generación *noun f.* generation
generador *noun m.* generator
general *noun mf. adj.* general
—**en general/por lo general** generally, in general
generalizado, -da *adj.* widespread
generalmente *adv.* usually, generally
generar *verb.* to generate
genérico, -ca *adj.* generic
género *noun m.* **1.** gender **2.** genre **3.** kind, sort
generosidad *noun f.* generosity
generoso, -sa *adj.* generous
genética *noun f.* genetics
genético, -ca *adj.* genetic
genio *noun m.* **1.** genius **2.** temper
gente *noun f.* people
genuino, -na *adj.* genuine
geografía *noun f.* geography
geográfico, -ca *adj.* geographic, geographical
geología *noun f.* geology
geológico, -ca *adj.* geological
gerente *noun mf.* manager
gestión *noun f.* **1.** management **2.** procedure
gesto *noun m.* **1.** gesture **2.** facial expression **3.** sign
gigante, -ta *noun.* giant
gigante *adj.* giant
gigantesco, -ca *adj.* giant
gimnasia *noun f.* gymnastics
gimnasio *noun m.* gym, gymnasium
ginebra *noun f.* gin
girar *verb.* **1.** to turn around **2.** rotate **3.** swing around
giro *noun m.* **1.** turn **2.** revolution
—**giro postal** postal order
gitano, -na *noun. adj.* gypsy
glacial *adj.* glacial, icy
glamour *noun m.* glamour
glándula *noun f.* gland
global *adj.* global

globo *noun m.* **1.** balloon **2.** globe
gloria *noun f.* **1.** glory **2.** fame
glorieta *noun f.* traffic circle
glorioso, -sa *adj.* glorious
glucosa *noun f.* glucose
gobernador, -dora *noun.* governor
gobernanta *noun f.* housekeeper
gobernante *noun mf.* ruler
gobernante *adj.* ruling
gobernar *verb.* to govern, rule
gobierno *noun m.* government
goce *noun m.* enjoyment
gol *noun m.* goal
golf *noun m.* golf
golfista *noun mf.* golfer
golfo *noun m.* gulf
golondrina *noun f.* swallow
golosina *noun f.* candy, sweet
golpe *noun m.* **1.** blow **2.** knock **3.** stroke
—**de golpe** suddenly
—**golpe de estado** coup d'etat
golpear *verb.* **1.** to beat, hit **2.** knock **3.** strike
goma *noun f.* **1.** gum **2.** rubber
gordo, -da *adj.* **1.** fat **2.** thick **3.** greasy, oily
gorra *noun f.* **1.** bonnet **2.** cap
gorro *noun m.* cap
gota *noun f.* **1.** drop **2.** gout
gotear *verb.* **1.** to drip **2.** leak
goteo *noun m.* drip, dripping
gozar *verb.* to enjoy
grabación *noun f.* recording
grabado *noun m.* engraving
grabadora *noun f.* tape recorder
grabar *verb.* **1.** to engrave **2.** tape, record
gracia *noun f.* **1.** grace **2.** humor, wit **3.** favor
—**gracias** thanks, thank you
gracioso, -sa *adj.* funny, witty
grado *noun m.* **1.** degree **2.** grade **3.** extent
graduación *noun f.* **1.** graduation **2.** rank
gradual *adj.* gradual
graduar *verb.* **1.** to regulate **2.** gauge
—**graduarse** to graduate
gráfica *noun f.* **1.** graph, chart **2.** graphic
gráfico *noun m.* **1.** graph, chart **2.** graphic
gráfico, -ca *adj.* graphic
gramática *noun f.* grammar
gramatical *adj.* grammatical
gran *adj.* (see grande. Used before singular nouns)
Gran Bretaña *noun f.* Great Britain
grande *adj.* **1.** big **2.** large **3.** great
grandeza *noun f.* **1.** greatness **2.** generosity **3.** magnificence
granero *noun m.* barn
granito *noun m.* granite
granizar *verb.* to hail
granizo *noun m.* hail
granja *noun f.* **1.** farm **2.** farmhouse
granjero, -ra *noun.* farmer
grano *noun m.* grain
grapa *noun f.* **1.** clamp **2.** staple
grasa *noun f.* **1.** fat **2.** grease
graso, -sa *adj.* **1.** fatty **2.** greasy
gratis *adj.* free
gratitud *noun f.* gratitude
grato, -ta *adj.* pleasant, agreeable
gratuito, -ta *adj.* free
grava *noun f.* gravel
gravar *verb.* **1.** to tax **2.** burden
grave *adj.* **1.** grave **2.** acute **3.** serious
gravedad *noun f.* **1.** gravity **2.** seriousness
Grecia *noun f.* Greece
griego, -ga *noun. adj.* Greek
grieta *noun f.* crack
grifo *noun m.* **1.** tap **2.** cock, faucet
grillo *noun m.* cricket
gripe *noun f.* flu
gris *adj.* gray
gritar *verb.* to shout, cry, scream
grito *noun m.* shout, cry, scream
grosero, -ra *adj.* **1.** coarse **2.** rude
grúa *noun f.* crane
grueso, -sa *adj.* **1.** stout **2.** thick **3.** coarse
grumo *noun m.* lump
gruñido *noun m.* growl
gruñir *verb.* to growl
grupo *noun m.* **1.** group **2.** band
—**grupo de presión** lobby
guante *noun m.* glove

guapo, -pa *adj.* handsome, good-looking
guarda *noun mf.* **1.** guard **2.** keeper **3.** warden
guardaespaldas *noun mf.* bodyguard
guardar *verb.* **1.** to guard **2.** keep **3.** preserve **4.** maintain **5.** observe
—**guardarse de** to refrain from
guardarropa *noun m.* wardrobe
guardia *noun mf.* **1.** guard **2.** policeman or policewoman
guardián, -diana *noun.* **1.** guardian **2.** keeper
guarida *noun f.* den
guarnecer *verb.* **1.** to adorn, decorate **2.** garrison
guarnición *noun f.* **1.** garrison **2.** garnish
guarro, -rra *noun.* pig
gubernamental *adj.* governmental
guerra *noun f.* **1.** war **2.** warfare
guerrero, -ra *noun.* warrior, fighter
guerrero, -ra *adj.* war, fighting
gueto *noun m.* ghetto
guía *noun f.* **1.** directory, guidebook **2.** guidance
guía *noun mf.* guide
guiar *verb.* **1.** to guide **2.** conduct, lead **3.** pilot
guión *noun m.* **1.** script **2.** dash
guisante *noun m.* pea
guisar *verb.* **1.** to stew **2.** cook
guiso *noun m.* stew
guitarra *noun f.* guitar
guitarrista *noun mf.* guitarist
gula *noun f.* greed
gusano *noun m.* **1.** worm **2.** maggot
gustar *verb.* **1.** to like **2.** be pleasing
gusto *noun m.* **1.** taste **2.** liking
—**a gusto** comfortable, at ease

H

haber *verb.* to have
—**haber de 1.** to be necessary **2.** must
—**hay** there is, there are
habichuela *noun f.* bean
hábil *adj.* **1.** clever, able, skillful **2.** working
habilidad *noun f.* ability, skill
habitación *noun f.* **1.** room **2.** bedroom **3.** habitation, dwelling
habitante *noun mf.* inhabitant, resident
habitar *verb.* **1.** to inhabit **2.** reside
hábitat *noun m.* habitat
hábito *noun m.* habit
habitual *adj.* usual, habitual
habla *noun f.* **1.** speech **2.** language, dialect
—**de habla** speaking
hablado, -da *adj.* spoken
hablador, -dora *adj.* talkative
hablar *verb.* **1.** to speak **2.** talk
hacer *verb.* **1.** to make **2.** do **3.** be
—**hace dos años** two years ago
—**hacer falta** to be neccessary
—**hacerse 1.** to become **2.** get **3.** pretend, play
hacha *noun f.* ax, hatchet
hacia *prep.* **1.** towards, toward **2.** near, about
—**hacia abajo** downward
—**hacia adelante** forward
—**hacia arriba** upward
—**hacia atrás** backward
—**hacia dentro** inward
hacienda *noun f.* **1.** estate, ranch **2.** tax office
hacinar *verb.* to stack
hada *noun f.* fairy
halago *noun m.* flattery, compliment
halcón *noun m.* hawk
hallar *verb.* **1.** to find **2.** discover
hallazgo *noun m.* **1.** discovery **2.** find
hambre *noun f.* **1.** famine **2.** hunger
—**tener hambre** to be hungry
hambriento, -ta *adj.* hungry
hambruna *noun f.* famine
handicap *noun m.* handicap
harapiento, -ta *adj.* ragged
hardware *noun m.* hardware
harina *noun f.* flour

harto, -ta *adj.* **1.** full **2.** fed up
hasta *prep.* **1.** until, till **2.** as far as
hazaña *noun f.* exploit, feat
hebra *noun f.* strand, thread
hechizar *verb.* **1.** to bewitch **2.** charm
hechizo *noun m.* **1.** spell **2.** charm
hecho *noun m.* **1.** fact **2.** deed **3.** event
hecho, -cha *adj.* **1.** done, made **2.** finished
hectárea *noun f.* hectare
hedor *noun m.* stink
helada *noun f.* frost
helado *noun m.* ice cream
helado, -da *adj.* freezing, icy
helar *verb.* to freeze
helicóptero *noun m.* helicopter
hembra *noun f.* female
hembra *adj.* **1.** female **2.** she
hemisferio *noun m.* hemisphere
hendidura *noun f.* crack
heno *noun m.* hay
heraldo *noun m.* herald
heredar *verb.* to inherit
heredero, -ra *noun.* heir or heiress
hereditario, -ria *adj.* hereditary
herencia *noun f.* **1.** heritage **2.** inheritance **3.** legacy
herida *noun f.* injury, wound
herido, -da *noun.* injured person
herido, -da *adj.* **1.** injured, wounded **2.** hurt
herir *verb.* **1.** to injure, wound **2.** hurt
hermano, -na *noun.* sibling, brother or sister
hermoso, -sa *adj.* **1.** beautiful **2.** lovely
héroe *noun m.* hero
heroico, -ca *adj.* heroic
heroína *noun f.* **1.** heroin **2.** heroine
herradura *noun f.* horseshoe
herramienta *noun f.* tool
herrero, -ra *noun.* smith
hervir *verb.* to boil
hidrógeno *noun m.* hydrogen
hiedra *noun f.* ivy
hiel *noun f.* **1.** bile **2.** gall
hielo *noun m.* ice
hierba *noun f.* **1.** grass **2.** herb
hierro *noun m.* iron
hígado *noun m.* liver
higiene *noun f.* hygiene
higo *noun f.* fig
hijo, -ja *noun.* **1.** son or daughter **2.** child
—**hijos** children
hilar *verb.* to spin
hilera *noun f.* line, row
hilo *noun m.* **1.** thread **2.** wire **3.** linen
hincar *verb.* **1.** to sink **2.** stick
—**hincarse de rodillas** to kneel
hinchado, -da *adj.* swollen
hinchar *verb.* to inflate
—**hincharse** to swell
hinchazón *noun f.* swelling
hindú *noun mf. adj.* Hindu
hipoteca *noun f.* mortgage
hipotecar *verb.* to mortgage
hipótesis *noun f.* hypothesis
hipotético, -ca *adj.* hypothetical
hispano, -na *noun. adj.* Hispanic
historia *noun f.* **1.** history **2.** story **3.** tale
historiador, -dora *noun.* historian
historial *noun m.* **1.** record **2.** background
histórico, -ca *adj.* **1.** historic **2.** historical
hito *noun m.* landmark
hockey *noun m.* hockey
hogar *noun m.* home
hoja *noun f.* **1.** sheet, page **2.** leaf **3.** blade
hojalata *noun f.* tinplate
hola *interj.* hello!, hi!
Holanda *noun f.* Holland
holandés, -desa *noun. adj.* Dutch
holgazán, -zana *noun.* idler
holgazanear *verb.* to idle
hollar *verb.* to tread
hombre *noun m.* man
hombro *noun m.* shoulder
homenaje *noun m.* homage, tribute
homicidio *noun m.* murder
homogéneo, -nea *adj.* homogeneous
homólogo, -ga *noun.* counterpart
homólogo, -ga *adj.* homologous
homosexual *noun mf. adj.* homosexual, gay
homosexualidad *noun f.* homosexuality
hondonada *noun f.* hollow
honestidad *noun f.* honesty

honesto, -ta *adj.* honest
hongo *noun m.* **1.** mushroom **2.** fungus
honor *noun m.* honor
honorable *adj.* honorable
honorario, -ria *adj.* honorary
honorarios *noun m. plural.* fees
honorífico, -ca *adj.* honorary
honradez *noun f.* honesty
honrado, -da *adj.* honest
honrar *verb.* to honor
hora *noun f.* **1.** hour **2.** time **3.** appointment
horario *noun m.* timetable, schedule
horizontal *adj.* horizontal
horizonte *noun m.* horizon
hormiga *noun f.* ant
hormigón *noun m.* concrete
hormona *noun f.* hormone
hornada *noun f.* batch
horno *noun m.* **1.** oven **2.** kiln
horrible *adj.* horrible
horror *noun m.* horror
horrorizar *verb.* to horrify
horroroso, -sa *adj.* horrible, horrifying
hortaliza *noun f.* vegetable
hospedar *verb.* to lodge
hospital *noun m.* hospital
hospitalidad *noun f.* hospitality
hostigar *verb.* to harass
hostil *adj.* hostile
hostilidad *noun f.* hostility
hotel *noun m.* hotel
hoy *adv.* today
—**hoy en día** nowadays, today
hoyo *noun m.* hole
hueco *noun m.* **1.** hole, hollow **2.** space
hueco, -ca *adj.* hollow
huelga *noun f.* strike
—**hacer huelga** to strike
huelguista *noun mf.* striker
huella *noun f.* **1.** footprint **2.** fingerprint **3.** track
huerto *noun m.* **1.** garden **2.** orchard
hueso *noun m.* **1.** bone **2.** pit, stone
huésped, -peda *noun.* **1.** guest **2.** host
huevo *noun m.* egg
huida *noun f.* flight
huir *verb.* **1.** to flee **2.** fly
humanidad *noun f.* **1.** humanity **2.** mankind
humano *noun m.* human being
humano, -na *adj.* human
humedad *noun f.* **1.** humidity **2.** dampness, moistness
húmedo, -da *adj.* **1.** humid **2.** damp, moist
humilde *adj.* humble
humillación *noun f.* humiliation
humillar *verb.* to humiliate
—**humillarse** to humble oneself
humo *noun m.* smoke
humor *noun m.* **1.** humor **2.** mood **3.** temper
hundir *verb.* to sink
húngaro, -ra *noun. adj.* Hungarian
Hungría *noun f.* Hungary
huracán *noun m.* hurricane
hurtar *verb.* to steal
hurto *noun m.* theft
husmear *verb.* to sniff out

I

ida *noun f.* **1.** going **2.** departure
idea *noun f.* **1.** idea **2.** notion
ideal *noun m. adj.* ideal
idear *verb.* to devise
idéntico, -ca *adj.* identical
identidad *noun f.* identity
identificación *noun f.* identification
identificar *verb.* to identify
idioma *noun m.* language
idiota *noun mf.* idiot
idiota *adj.* stupid, idiotic
idóneo, -nea *adj.* suitable, competent
iglesia *noun f.* church
ignorancia *noun f.* ignorance
ignorante *noun mf.* ignorant person
ignorante *adj.* ignorant
ignorar *verb.* **1.** to ignore **2.** be unaware of

igual *noun mf.* equal
igual *adj.* **1.** equal **2.** alike **3.** same
igualado, -da *adj.* **1.** even **2.** close
igualar *verb.* **1.** to equal **2.** level **3.** tie
igualdad *noun f.* equality
igualmente *adv.* **1.** equally **2.** likewise
ilegal *adj.* illegal
iluminación *noun f.* **1.** illumination **2.** lighting
iluminar *verb.* to illuminate, light
ilusión *noun f.* illusion
ilustración *noun f.* illustration
ilustrado, -da *adj.* illustrated
ilustrar *verb.* to illustrate
imagen *noun f.* image
imaginación *noun f.* imagination
imaginar *verb.* to imagine
imaginario, -ria *adj.* imaginary
imaginativo, -va *adj.* imaginative
imbécil *noun mf.* **1.** imbecile **2.** idiot, fool
imbécil *adj.* stupid
imitación *noun f.* imitation
imitar *verb.* to imitate, copy
impaciente *adj.* impatient
impacto *noun m.* **1.** impact **2.** shock
impar *adj.* odd
imparcial *adj.* impartial
imparcialidad *noun f.* impartiality
impedir *verb.* **1.** to impede **2.** prevent **3.** block
imperante *adj.* prevailing
imperativo *noun m.* imperative
imperativo, -va *adj.* imperative
imperial *adj.* imperial
imperio *noun m.* empire
ímpetu *noun m.* **1.** impetus **2.** momentum
impetuoso, -sa *adj.* impetuous
implacable *adj.* relentless
implicar *verb.* **1.** to involve **2.** imply
implícito, -ta *adj.* implicit
imponente *adj.* imposing
imponer *verb.* **1.** to impose **2.** exact —**imponerse** to prevail
impopular *adj.* unpopular
importación *noun f.* import
importancia *noun f.* importance
importante *adj.* important
importar *verb.* **1.** to import **2.** matter, mind **3.** be important
imposible *adj.* impossible
imposición *noun f.* **1.** imposition **2.** tax
imprescindible *adj.* essential, indispensable
impresión *noun f.* **1.** feeling, impression **2.** printing
impresionante *adj.* impressive
impresionar *verb.* to impress
impresor, -sora *noun.* printer
impresora *noun f.* printer
imprimir *verb.* to print
improbable *adj.* unlikely
imprudente *adj.* imprudent, rash
impuesto *noun m.* tax, duty
impulsar *verb.* **1.** to impel **2.** drive
impulso *noun m.* **1.** impulse **2.** drive
impuro, -ra *adj.* impure
inactivo, -va *adj.* inactive, idle
inadecuado, -da *adj.* **1.** inadequate **2.** inappropriate
inalterable *adj.* unalterable
inapropiado, -da *adj.* inappropriate
inauguración *noun f.* inauguration, opening
incapacidad *noun f.* **1.** inability **2.** disability
incapaz *adj.* **1.** incapable, unable **2.** incompetent
incautar *verb.* to seize
incendio *noun m.* fire
incentivo *noun m.* incentive
incidente *noun m.* incident
incierto, -ta *adj.* **1.** uncertain **2.** unknown
incitar *verb.* **1.** to incite **2.** urge, encourage
inclinación *noun f.* **1.** inclination **2.** slope **3.** propensity
inclinar *verb.* **1.** to incline **2.** tilt —**inclinarse** to lean
incluir *verb.* to include
inclusión *noun f.* inclusion
incomodidad *noun f.* **1.** inconvenience, bother **2.** discomfort
incómodo, -da *adj.* uncomfortable
incompatible *adj.* incompatible
incompleto, -ta *adj.* incomplete
incondicional *adj.* unconditional
inconsciente *adj.* unaware, unconscious

inconsecuente *adj.* inconsistent
inconsistente *adj.* inconsistent, weak
incontable *adj.* countless
incorporar *verb.* **1.** to incorporate **2.** include
—**incorporarse a** to join
incorrecto, -ta *adj.* incorrect, wrong
increíble *adj.* incredible, unbelievable
incriminar *verb.* to incriminate
incubar *verb.* **1.** to incubate **2.** hatch
incumplimiento *noun m.* nonfulfillment, breach
incurrir (en) *verb.* to incur
incursión *noun f.* incursion, raid
indagación *noun f.* inquiry
indagar *verb.* to inquire
indebido, -da *adj.* undue, improper
indecente *adj.* indecent
indecisión *noun f.* hesitation, indecision
indeciso, -sa *adj.* **1.** undecided **2.** hesitant
indefenso, -sa *adj.* defenseless, helpless
indemnización *noun f.* indemnification, compensation
indemnizar *verb.* to indemnify, compensate
independencia *noun f.* independence
independiente *adj.* independent
indeseable *adj.* undesirable
India *noun f.* India
indicación *noun f.* **1.** indication **2.** hint **3.** sign, signal
indicador *noun m.* **1.** gauge **2.** indicator
indicar *verb.* **1.** to indicate **2.** point out **3.** show
indicativo *noun m.* indicative
indicativo, -va *adj.* indicative
índice *noun m.* index
indicio *noun m.* **1.** indication **2.** evidence **3.** trace
indiferencia *noun f.* indifference
indiferente *adj.* indifferent
indígena *noun mf.* native
indígena *adj.* indigenous, native
indio, -dia *noun. adj.* Indian
indirecta *noun f.* hint
—**echar indirectas** to drop hints
indirecto, -ta *adj.* indirect
indiscreto, -ta *adj.* indiscreet
individual *adj.* **1.** individual **2.** single
individuo *noun m.* individual, guy, person
Indonesia *noun f.* Indonesia
indonesio, -sia *noun. adj.* Indonesian
indudable *adj.* unquestionable, indubitable
indultar *verb.* to pardon
indulto *noun m.* pardon
industria *noun f.* industry
industrial *adj.* industrial
ineficaz *adj.* **1.** ineffective **2.** inefficient
inesperado, -da *adj.* unexpected
inestabilidad *noun f.* instability
inestable *adj.* unstable
inestimable *adj.* invaluable, inestimable
inevitable *adj.* inevitable, unavoidable
inexperto, -ta *adj.* inexperienced, unskilled
infantería *noun f.* infantry
infantil *adj.* childish, infantile
infarto *noun m.* heart attack
infección *noun f.* infection
infeccioso, -sa *adj.* infectious
infectar *verb.* to infect
infeliz *adj.* **1.** unhappy **2.** unfortunate
inferencia *noun f.* inference
inferior *noun mf. adj.* inferior
infierno *noun m.* hell
infinitivo *noun m.* infinitive
infinito, -ta *adj.* infinite
inflación *noun f.* inflation
inflar *verb.* to inflate
—**inflarse** to swell
infligir *verb.* to inflict
influencia *noun f.* influence
influenciar *verb.* **1.** to influence **2.** sway
influir *verb.* **1.** to influence **2.** sway
influyente *adj.* influential
información *noun f.* information
informal *adj.* informal, casual
informar *verb.* **1.** to inform **2.** report
informativo, -va *adj.* informative
informatizar *verb.* to computerize
informe *noun m.* report
infracción *noun f.* infraction, offence
infractor, -tora *noun.* offender
infringir *verb.* to infringe, break
infundir *verb.* to infuse, instill
ingeniería *noun f.* engineering

ingeniero, -ra *noun.* engineer
ingenio *noun m.* **1.** wit **2.** device
ingenioso, -sa *adj.* witty, clever
ingenuo, -nua *adj.* naive
Inglaterra *noun f.* England
inglés, -glesa *noun. adj.* English
ingrediente *noun m.* ingredient
ingresar *verb.* to deposit
—**ingresar en** to join
ingreso *noun m.* entrance, entry
—**ingresos** earnings, revenue
inhabitual *adj.* unusual
inherente *adj.* inherent
inhibición *noun f.* inhibition
inhumano, -na *adj.* inhumane, inhuman
iniciado, -da *noun.* initiate
inicial *noun f. adj.* initial
iniciar *verb.* to initiate
iniciativa *noun f.* initiative
injuriar *verb.* to insult, abuse
injusticia *noun f.* injustice
injusto, -ta *adj.* unfair, unjust
inmaculado, -da *adj.* immaculate
inmediatamente *adv.* immediately
inmediato, -ta *adj.* **1.** immediate **2.** adjoining, nearby
inmenso, -sa *adj.* immense, vast
inmigración *noun f.* immigration
inmigrante *noun mf. adj.* immigrant
inminente *adj.* imminent
inmobiliario, -ria *adj.* real estate
inmóvil *adj.* still
inmovilizar *verb.* to immobilize
inmune *adj.* immune
inmunidad *noun f.* immunity
innato, -ta *adj.* innate
innecesario, -ria *adj.* unnecessary
innecesario *adv.* needless
innovación *noun f.* innovation
innumerable *adj.* countless
inocencia *noun f.* innocence
inocente *adj.* innocent
inocuo, -cua *adj.* harmless
inofensivo, -va *adj.* harmless, inoffensive
inquietar *verb.* to disturb, worry, trouble
inquieto, -ta *adj.* **1.** restless **2.** troubled, uneasy
inquietud *noun f.* **1.** restlessness **2.** concern, uneasiness
inquilino, -na *noun.* tenant
insatisfacción *noun f.* dissatisfaction
insatisfactorio, -ria *adj.* unsatisfactory
inscribir *verb.* **1.** to inscribe **2.** register **3.** enter
inscripción *noun f.* **1.** inscription **2.** registration
insecto *noun m.* insect
inseguro, -ra *adj.* **1.** insecure **2.** unsafe
insertar *verb.* to insert
insignia *noun f.* badge, insignia
insignificante *adj.* insignificant
insinuación *noun f.* hint,insinuation
insinuar *verb.* to hint, insinuate
insípido, -da *adj.* bland, insipid
insistencia *noun f.* insistence
insistir *verb.* to insist
insolvencia *noun f.* insolvency, bankruptcy
insolvente *adj.* insolvent, bankrupt
insoportable *adj.* unbearable
inspección *noun f.* **1.** inspection **2.** check
inspeccionar *verb.* **1.** to inspect **2.** check
inspector, -tora *noun.* inspector
inspiración *noun f.* **1.** inspiration **2.** inhalation
inspirar *verb.* **1.** to inspire **2.** inhale
instalación *noun f.* installation
instalar *verb.* to install
—**instalarse** to settle
instancia *noun f.* petition
instantáneo, -nea *adj.* instant
instante *noun m.* instant
—**al instante** immediately, at once
instintivo *adj.* instinctive
instinto *noun m.* instinct
institución *noun f.* institution
institucional *adj.* institutional
instituto *noun m.* institute
instrucción *noun f.* instruction
instructor, -tora *noun.* instructor
instruir *verb.* **1.** to instruct **2.** train
instrumental *adj.* instrumental
instrumento *noun m.* **1.** instrument **2.** tool, implement
insuficiente *adj.* insufficient, inadequate
insulina *noun f.* insulin

insultante *adj.* offensive
insultar *verb.* to insult
insulto *noun m.* insult
intacto, -ta *adj.* intact
integración *noun f.* integration
integrar *verb.* to integrate
integridad *noun f.* integrity
íntegro, -gra *adj.* **1.** whole **2.** honest
intelectual *noun mf. adj.* intellectual
inteligencia *noun f.* intelligence
inteligente *adj.* intelligent
intención *noun f.* intention
intencionado, -da *adj.* deliberate
intensidad *noun f.* intensity
intensificar *verb.* to intensify
intensivo, -va *adj.* intensive
intenso, -sa *adj.* intense
intentar *verb.* to try, attempt
intento *noun m.* **1.** try, attempt **2.** effort
interacción *noun f.* interaction
interactivo, -va *adj.* interactive
intercambiar *verb.* to exchange
intercambio *noun m.* exchange
interés *noun m.* interest
interesado, -da *adj.* **1.** interested **2.** selfish
interesante *adj.* interesting
interesar *verb.* **1.** to interest **2.** be of interest
interferencia *noun f.* interference
interferir *verb.* to interfere
interior *noun m.* **1.** inside **2.** interior **3.** inland
interior *adj.* **1.** interior **2.** inner **3.** internal **4.** indoor
interlocutor, -tora *noun.* speaker, interlocutor
intermediario, -ria *noun. adj.* intermediary, go-between
intermedio *noun m.* intermission
intermedio, -dia *adj.* intermediate
interminable *adj.* endless
internacional *adj.* international
internar *verb.* to confine, commit —**internarse** **1.** to penetrate **2.** go (into the interior)
interno, -na *noun.* inmate
interno, -na *adj.* internal
interpretación *noun f.* interpretation
interpretar *verb.* **1.** to interpret **2.** perform
intérprete *noun mf.* **1.** interpreter **2.** performer
interrogar *verb.* to question
interrogatorio *noun m.* questioning, interrogation
interrumpir *verb.* to interrupt
interrupción *noun f.* interruption
interruptor *noun m.* switch
intervalo *noun m.* interval
intervención *noun f.* **1.** intervention **2.** operation
intervenir *verb.* **1.** to intervene **2.** take part **3.** operate
intestinal *adj.* intestinal
intestino *noun m.* intestine
intimidad *noun f.* **1.** intimacy **2.** privacy
intimidar *verb.* to intimidate
íntimo, -ma *adj.* **1.** intimate **2.** private
intolerable *adj.* intolerable
intrincado, -da *adj.* intricate
introducción *noun f.* introduction
introducir *verb.* **1.** to introduce **2.** insert **3.** input, insert
introductorio, -ria *adj.* introductory
inundación *noun f.* flood
inundar *verb.* to flood, inundate
inútil *adj.* useless
invadir *verb.* to invade
invalidez *noun f.* **1.** invalidity **2.** disability
inválido, -da *noun. adj.* invalid
invasión *noun f.* invasion
invención *noun f.* **1.** invention **2.** lie
inventar *verb.* **1.** to invent **2.** devise
inventario *noun m.* inventory
invento *noun m.* invention
invernadero *noun m.* greenhouse
inversión *noun f.* **1.** inversion, reversal **2.** investment
inversor, -sora *noun.* investor
invertir *verb.* **1.** to invert, reverse **2.** invest
investigación *noun f.* **1.** investigation, inquiry **2.** research
investigador, -dora *noun.* **1.** investigator **2.** researcher
investigar *verb.* **1.** to investigate, inquire **2.** research

invierno *noun m.* winter
invisible *adj.* invisible
invitación *noun f.* invitation
invitado, -da *noun.* guest
invitar *verb.* to invite
invocar *verb.* to invoke
inyección *noun f.* injection, shot
inyectar *verb.* to inject
ir *verb.* **1.** to go **2.** get on **3.** extend
—**ir a** to be going to
—**ir a pie** to walk
—**irse 1.** to go **2.** leave
ira *noun f.* wrath
Irak *noun m.* Iraq
Irán *noun m.* Iran
iraní *noun mf. adj.* Iranian
Iraq *noun m.* Iraq
iraquí *noun mf. adj.* Iraqi
iris *noun m.* iris
Irlanda *noun f.* Ireland
irlandés, -desa *noun. adj.* Irish
ironía *noun f.* irony
irrazonable *adj.* unreasonable
irregular *adj.* irregular
irrelevante *adj.* irrelevant
irresistible *adj.* irresistible
irritación *noun f.* **1.** irritation **2.** exasperation
irritar *verb.* **1.** to irritate **2.** exasperate
irrumpir *verb.* to burst into, break in
isla *noun f.* **1.** island **2.** isle
Islam *noun m.* Islam
Islámico, -ca *adj.* Islamic
islandés, -desa *noun. adj.* Icelandic
Israel *noun m.* Israel
israelí *noun mf. adj.* Israeli
Italia *noun f.* Italy
italiano, -na *noun. adj.* Italian
itinerario *noun m.* route, itinerary
izquierda *noun f.* left
izquierdista *noun mf. adj.* leftist
izquierdo, -da *adj.* left

J

jabón *noun m.* soap
jactarse *verb.* to boast
jadear *verb.* to gasp
jadeo *noun m.* gasp
jaguar *noun m.* jaguar
jalea *noun f.* jelly
Jamaica *noun f.* Jamaica
jamaicano, -na *noun. adj.* Jamaican
jamón *noun m.* ham
Japón *noun m.* Japan
japonés, -nesa *noun. adj.* Japanese
jaque *noun m.* check
jardín *noun m.* garden
jardinería *noun f.* gardening
jardinero, -ra *noun.* gardener
jarra *noun f.* **1.** jug **2.** mug
jarro *noun m.* **1.** jug **2.** mug
jarrón *noun m.* vase
jaula *noun f.* cage
jazz *noun m.* jazz
jefe, -fa *noun.* **1.** boss **2.** head **3.** chief
jengibre *noun m.* ginger
jerarquía *noun f.* hierarchy
jerárquico, -ca *adj.* hierarchical
jerez *noun m.* sherry
jerga *noun f.* jargon
jersey *noun m.* **1.** jersey **2.** sweater
jinete *noun mf.* rider, horseman or horsewoman
jira *noun f.* picnic
jirón *noun m.* shred
jockey *noun m.* jockey
joder *verb.* **1.** to fuck **2.** screw
jornada *noun f.* day's journey
jornalero, -ra *noun f.* day laborer
joven *noun mf.* **1.** young person **2.** youngster
joven *adj.* **1.** young **2.** youthful
joya *noun f.* jewel
joyería *noun f.* **1.** jewelry **2.** jewelry store
jubilación *noun f.* **1.** retirement **2.** pension
jubilado, -da *noun.* retired person

jubilado, -da *adj.* retired
jubilar *verb.* to retire
jubileo *noun m.* jubilee
júbilo *noun m.* joy
judía *noun f.* bean
judicial *adj.* judicial
judío, -día *noun.* Jew
judío, -día *adj.* Jewish
juego *noun m.* **1.** play **2.** gambling **3.** game **4.** match **5.** set
—**Juegos Olímpicos** Olympic Games
jueves *noun m.* Thursday
juez *noun mf.* judge
jueza *noun f.* judge
jugada *noun f.* **1.** move **2.** trick
jugador, -dora *noun.* **1.** player **2.** gambler
jugar *verb.* **1.** to play **2.** gamble
jugo *noun m.* juice
juguete *noun m.* toy
juicio *noun m.* **1.** trial **2.** sense, reason **3.** opinion
juicioso, -sa *adj.* **1.** reasonable **2.** wise
julio *noun m.* July
junco *noun m.* **1.** junk **2.** reed, rush
junio *noun m.* June
junta *noun f.* **1.** board **2.** meeting, assembly **3.** joint
juntar *verb.* **1.** to unite **2.** assemble, collect **3.** gather **4.** pool
—**juntarse** to join
—**juntarse con** to frequent the company of
junto, -ta *adj.* **1.** united **2.** together
—**junto a** by, next to
juntura *noun f.* joint
jurado *noun m.* jury
juramento *noun m.* oath
jurar *verb.* **1.** to swear **2.** take an oath
jurídico, -ca *adj.* legal
jurisdicción *noun f.* jurisdiction
justamente *adv.* **1.** exactly, precisely **2.** fairly
justicia *noun f.* **1.** justice **2.** fairness
justificación *noun f.* justification
justificadamente *adv.* rightly
justificar *verb.* to justify
justo, -ta *adj.* **1.** fair **2.** just **3.** exact
justo *adv.* **1.** justly **2.** exactly
juvenil *adj.* **1.** juvenile **2.** youthful
juventud *noun f.* **1.** young people **2.** youth
juzgado *noun m.* court
juzgar *verb.* **1.** to judge, try **2.** deem

K

kilogramo *noun m.* kilogram
kilómetro *noun m.* kilometer
kit *noun m.* kit
Kuwait *noun m.* Kuwait
kuwaití *noun mf. adj.* Kuwaiti

L

la *art.* the
la *pron.* **1.** her, it **2.** the one
labio *noun m.* lip
laboratorio *noun m.* laboratory
labor *noun f.* labor, work
labrador, -dora *noun.* peasant, farmer
ladear *verb.* to tilt, tip
—**ladearse** to bend over
ladera *noun f.* hillside, slope
lado *noun m.* side
—**al lado** next (to)
ladrar *verb.* to bark
ladrido *noun m.* bark
ladrillo *noun m.* brick

ladrón, -drona *noun.* thief, robber
lady *noun m.* lady
lagarto *noun f.* lizard
lago *noun m.* lake
lágrima *noun f.* tear
laico, -ca *adj.* lay
lamentar *verb.* **1.** to be sorry **2.** regret **3.** lament
—**lamentarse** to bemoan
lamer *verb.* to lick
lámina *noun f.* plate
lámpara *noun f.* **1.** lamp **2.** light
lana *noun f.* wool
lanzadera *noun f.* shuttle
lanzamiento *noun m.* **1.** throw **2.** launch **3.** pitch
lanzar *verb.* **1.** to throw, hurl **2.** launch **3.** pitch
—**lanzarse 1.** to undertake **2.** throw oneself
lápida *noun f.* tombstone
lápiz *noun m.* pencil
—**lápiz de labios** lipstick
largo *noun m.* length
largo, -ga *adj.* long
—**a la larga** in the long run
—**a lo largo 1.** lengthwise **2.** along
largometraje *noun m.* feature film
láser *noun m.* laser
lástima *noun f.* **1.** pity **2.** shame
lastimar *verb.* **1.** to hurt, harm, injure **2.** wound
lata *noun f.* **1.** can **2.** nuisance
—**dar la lata** to annoy
latente *adj.* latent
lateral *adj.* lateral
latido *noun m.* beat
latigazo *noun m.* lash
látigo *noun m.* whip, lash
latín *noun m.* Latin
latino, -na *noun. adj.* Latin
latinoamericano, -na *noun. adj.* Latin American
latir *verb.* to beat
latón *noun m.* brass
laurel *noun m.* **1.** laurel **2.** bay
lavabo *noun m.* **1.** sink **2.** lavatory, toilet
lavado *noun m.* wash, cleaning
lavanda *noun f.* lavender
lavandería *noun f.* laundry
lavar *verb.* to wash, clean
lazo *noun m.* **1.** bond **2.** link **3.** bow
le *pron.* **1.** to him, to her, to it **2.** for him, for her, for it **3.** from him, from her, from it **4.** to you, for you
leal *adj.* faithful, loyal
lealtad *noun f.* allegiance, loyalty
lección *noun f.* lesson
leche *noun f.* milk
lechería *noun f.* dairy store
lecho *noun m.* bed
lechuza *noun f.* owl
lector, -tora *noun.* **1.** reader **2.** scanner
lectura *noun f.* reading
leer *verb.* to read
legal *adj.* legal, lawful
legendario, -ria *adj.* legendary
legión *noun f.* legion
legislación *noun f.* legislation
legislativo, -va *adj.* legislative
legitimidad *noun f.* legitimacy
legítimo, -ma *adj.* legitimate
lego, -ga *adj.* lay
legua *noun f.* league
lejano, -na *adj.* distant, far, remote
lejos *adv.* distant, far away
—**lejos de** far from
lema *noun m.* slogan, motto
lengua *noun f.* **1.** tongue **2.** language
lenguado *noun m.* sole
lenguaje *noun m.* **1.** language **2.** speech
lentamente *adv.* slowly
lente *noun f.* lens
lento, -ta *adj.* **1.** slow **2.** dull
leña *noun f.* firewood
leño *noun m.* log
león, -ona *noun.* lion
les *pron.* **1.** to them **2.** for them **3.** from them **4.** to you
lesión *noun f.* injury, lesion
lesionado, -da *adj.* injured
letal *adj.* lethal
letra *noun f.* **1.** letter **2.** lyrics **3.** type
letrero *noun m.* sign
leucemia *noun f.* leukemia
levantar *verb.* **1.** to lift, raise **2.** erect **3.** arouse
—**levantarse 1.** to get up **2.** stand up **3.** rise

leve *adj.* light, mild
léxico *noun m.* lexicon
ley *noun f.* **1.** law **2.** purity
leyenda *noun f.* **1.** legend **2.** caption
liar *verb.* **1.** to roll **2.** tie up **3.** confuse
liberación *noun f.* **1.** liberation **2.** release
liberal *adj.* liberal
liberar *verb.* **1.** to free **2.** liberate **3.** release
libertad *noun f.* freedom, liberty
—**libertad bajo fianza** bail
—**libertad provisional** parole
libra *noun f.* pound
librar *verb.* **1.** to deliver **2.** wage **3.** issue
—**librarse de 1.** to get rid of **2.** escape
libre *adj.* **1.** free **2.** vacant
librería *noun f.* bookstore
libreta *noun f.* notebook
libro *noun m.* book
licencia *noun f.* **1.** permission **2.** franchise **3.** license **4.** permit
licenciado, -da *noun.* graduate
licenciar *verb.* **1.** to license, permit **2.** discharge **3.** dismiss **4.** confer a university degree
—**licenciarse** to graduate
licenciatura *noun f.* college degree
lícito, -ta *adj.* licit, lawful
licor *noun m.* liquor
líder *noun mf.* leader
líder *adj.* leading
liderar *verb.* to lead
liderato *noun m.* leadership
liderazgo *noun m.* leadership
lienzo *noun m.* **1.** canvas **2.** linen
liga *noun f.* league
ligeramente *adv.* **1.** slightly **2.** lightly
ligero, -ra *adj.* **1.** slight **2.** light, lightweight **3.** quick, agile
lijar *verb.* to sand
lima *noun f.* **1.** file **2.** lime
limar *verb.* to file
limitación *noun f.* **1.** limitation **2.** restriction
limitado, -da *adj.* **1.** limited **2.** restricted **3.** dull
limitar *verb.* to restrict, limit
límite *noun m.* **1.** limit **2.** border, boundary
limón *noun m.* lemon
limonada *noun f.* lemonade
limpiador, -dora *noun.* cleaner
limpiar *verb.* to clean
limpio, -pia *adj.* **1.** clean **2.** free **3.** clear
—**juego limpio** fair game
linaje *noun m.* lineage
lindar (con) *verb.* to border
lindo, -da *adj.* **1.** cute **2.** lovely **3.** pretty
lindo *adv.* beautifully
línea *noun f.* line
lineal *adj.* linear
lingüística *noun f.* linguistics
lingüístico, -ca *adj.* linguistic
lino *noun m.* **1.** linen **2.** flax
linterna *noun f.* lantern
lío *noun m.* **1.** mess **2.** trouble **3.** affair, liaison
líquido *noun m.* **1.** liquid, fluid **2.** liquid assets, ready cash
líquido, -da *adj.* **1.** liquid, fluid **2.** net
lírico, -ca *adj.* lyric, lyrical
lirio *noun m.* **1.** iris **2.** lily
lisiado, -da *noun.* cripple, disabled person
lisiado, -da *adj.* cripple
liso, -sa *adj.* **1.** smooth **2.** even **3.** flat **4.** plain **5.** straight
lista *noun f.* **1.** list **2.** roll **3.** stripe
listo, -ta *adj.* **1.** ready **2.** clever, smart
literal *adj.* literal
literario, -ria *adj.* literary
literatura *noun f.* literature
litigio *noun m.* litigation
litro *noun m.* liter
llaga *noun f.* sore
llama *noun f.* **1.** flame **2.** llama
llamada *noun f.* call
llamar *verb.* **1.** to call **2.** knock **3.** name
—**llamar por teléfono** to phone
—**llamarse** to be called, be named
llamativo, -va *adj.* showy, striking
llamear *verb.* to blaze, throw out flames
llano *noun m.* plain
llano, -na *adj.* **1.** even, flat **2.** plain, simple
llanta *noun f.* **1.** tire **2.** rim
llanura *noun f.* plain

llave *noun f.* **1.** key **2.** switch **3.** faucet
llegada *noun f.* **1.** arrival **2.** advent
llegar *verb.* **1.** to arrive **2.** appear **3.** come **4.** suffice
—**llegar a ser** to become
llenar *verb.* **1.** to fill **2.** fulfill, please
—**llenarse** to fill up
lleno, -na *adj.* full, filled
—**de lleno** completely
llevar *verb.* **1.** to carry **2.** take, take away **3.** wear **4.** endure, bear
—**llevar a cabo** to carry out, accomplish
—**llevarse 1.** to take away **2.** get along
llorar *verb.* to cry, weep
llover *verb.* to rain
lluvia *noun f.* **1.** rain **2.** shower
lo *art.* **1.** the **2.** how
lo *pron.* **1.** him, it **2.** you
—**lo que** what
lobo, -ba *noun.* wolf
lóbrego, -ga *adj.* gloomy
local *noun m.* premises
local *adj.* **1.** local **2.** home
localidad *noun f.* locality
localizar *verb.* **1.** to locate **2.** localize
loco, -ca *noun.* crazy person
loco, -ca *adj.* crazy, mad
—**volverse loco** to go crazy
locomotora *noun f.* locomotive
locura *noun f.* **1.** folly **2.** madness
lodo *noun m.* mud
lógica *noun f.* logic
lógico, -ca *adj.* logical
lograr *verb.* **1.** to achieve **2.** attain **3.** get **4.** succeed in
logro *noun m.* achievement
loma *noun f.* hill
lombriz *noun f.* worm
lomo *noun m.* **1.** back **2.** loin **3.** spine
lona *noun f.* canvas
longitud *noun f.* length
lord *noun m.* lord
los *pron.* **1.** them **2.** you
—**los que** those who
losa *noun f.* slab
lote *noun m.* lot, batch
lotería *noun f.* lottery
loto *noun m.* lotus
lubina *noun f.* bass
lubricar *verb.* to lubricate, oil
lucha *noun f.* **1.** fight **2.** struggle **3.** wrestling
luchador, -dora *noun.* **1.** fighter **2.** wrestler
luchar *verb.* **1.** to fight **2.** struggle **3.** wrestle
lucir *verb.* to shine
—**lucirse 1.** to excel **2.** wear
lucrativo, -va *adj.* lucrative, profitable
lucro *noun m.* profit
luego *adv.* **1.** later **2.** then
—**desde luego** of course
—**hasta luego** see you later
luego *conj.* therefore
lugar *noun m.* **1.** place **2.** position **3.** space
—**en lugar de** instead of
—**tener lugar** to take place
lujo *noun m.* luxury
lujoso, -sa *adj.* luxurious
lujuria *noun f.* lust
luminoso, -sa *adj.* luminous, bright
luna *noun f.* moon
—**luna de miel** honeymoon
lunar *noun m.* mole
lunes *noun m.* Monday
lustrar *verb.* to shine
lustre *noun m.* shine
lustroso, -sa *adj.* shiny
luz *noun f.* **1.** light **2.** electricity **3.** span
—**dar a luz** to give birth

M

macanudo, -da *adj.* great, fantastic
maceta *noun f.* pot
macho *noun m.* male
macho *adj.* **1.** male **2.** he
macizo, -za *adj.* **1.** solid **2.** strong
madera *noun f.* **1.** wood **2.** timber
madre *noun f.* mother
madriguera *noun f.* den
madrugador, -dora *noun.* early riser
madurar *verb.* **1.** to mature **2.** ripen
madurez *noun f.* **1.** maturity **2.** ripeness
maduro, -ra *adj.* **1.** mature **2.** ripe
maestro, -tra *noun.* **1.** master **2.** teacher
maestro, -tra *adj.* masterly
magia *noun f.* magic
mágico, -ca *adj.* magic, magical
magistrado, -da *noun.* magistrate, judge
magnate *noun mf.* tycoon, magnate
magnético, -ca *adj.* magnetic
magnífico, -ca *adj.* magnificent, superb
magnitud *noun f.* magnitude
magro, -gra *adj.* **1.** lean **2.** meager
magulladura *noun f.* bruise
magullar *verb.* to bruise
maíz *noun m.* maize, corn
majestad *noun f.* majesty
mal *noun m.* **1.** evil **2.** wrong **3.** harm **4.** misfortune **5.** illness, disease
mal *adj.* (see malo. Used before masculine singular nouns)
mal *adv.* **1.** badly, poorly **2.** hardly **3.** wrong
Malasia *noun f.* Malaysia
malayo, -ya *noun. adj.* Malaysian
maldad *noun f.* evil
maldecir *verb.* to curse, damn
maldición *noun f.* curse
maldito, -ta *adj.* cursed, damned
maleante *noun mf.* crook
maleducado, -ta *adj.* rude, ill-mannered
malentendido *noun m.* misunderstanding
malestar *noun m.* **1.** discontent **2.** discomfort **3.** indisposition, illness
maleta *noun f.* suitcase
maletero *noun m.* **1.** trunk **2.** porter
malgastar *verb.* **1.** to waste **2.** squander
malhumorado, -da *adj.* ill-humored
malicia *noun f.* **1.** malice, wickedness **2.** cunning
malintencionado *adj.* malicious
malla *noun f.* **1.** tights **2.** mesh **3.** net
malo, -la *noun.* villain, bad person
malo, -la *adj.* **1.** bad **2.** evil **3.** harmful **4.** ill **5.** poor, cheap **6.** rotten
maltratar *verb.* to abuse
maltrato *noun m.* abuse
malvado, -da *adj.* evil, wicked
mamá *noun f.* mamma, mama, mum, mummy
mamar *verb.* to suckle, suck
—**dar de mamar** to breast-feed
mamífero *noun m.* mammal
manada *noun f.* herd, pack
manar *verb.* to flow, stream
mancha *noun f.* mark, stain, spot
manchar *verb.* to stain, soil
mandar *verb.* **1.** to order **2.** command **3.** send
mandíbula *noun f.* jaw
mandil *noun m.* apron
mando *noun m.* **1.** command **2.** control
—**mando a distancia** remote control
manecilla *noun f.* hand
manejar *verb.* **1.** to handle **2.** manage **3.** manipulate
manera *noun f.* way, manner
—**de manera que** so that
—**de ninguna manera** by no means
—**de todas maneras** anyway
manga *noun f.* sleeve
mango *noun m.* **1.** handle **2.** mango
manicomio *noun m.* asylum
manifestación *noun f.* **1.** demonstration **2.** manifestation
manifestante *noun mf.* demonstrator
manifestar *verb.* **1.** to demonstrate **2.** exhibit, display
—**manifestarse** **1.** to demonstrate **2.** state one's position
manifiesto *noun m.* manifesto

manifiesto, -ta *adj.* manifest, overt
manilla *noun f.* handle
maniobra *noun f.* maneuver
maniobrar *verb.* to maneuver
manipulación *noun f.* manipulation
manipular *verb.* **1.** to manipulate **2.** handle
maniquí *noun mf.* model
mano *noun f.* **1.** hand **2.** coat
—**de primera mano** firsthand
—**mano de obra** manpower, workforce
manojo *noun m.* bunch
manosear *verb.* **1.** to finger **2.** touch repeatedly
mansión *noun f.* mansion
manta *noun f.* blanket
manteca *noun f.* lard, fat
mantener *verb.* **1.** to keep **2.** maintain **3.** hold **4.** support **5.** sustain
mantenimiento *noun m.* **1.** maintenance **2.** preservation
mantequilla *noun f.* butter
manual *noun m.* handbook, manual
manual *adj.* manual
manuscrito *noun m.* manuscript
manzana *noun f.* **1.** apple **2.** block
mañana *noun f.* **1.** morning **2.** tomorrow
mañoso, -sa *adj.* skillful
mapa *noun m.* map
maqueta *noun f.* model
maquillaje *noun m.* make-up
máquina *noun f.* **1.** machine **2.** engine
maquinar *verb.* to plot, scheme
maquinaria *noun f.* **1.** machinery **2.** mechanism
mar *noun mf.* sea
maraña *noun f.* tangle
maratón *noun f.* marathon
maravilla *noun f.* marvel, wonder
maravilloso, -sa *adj.* marvelous, wonderful
marca *noun f.* **1.** mark, sign **2.** brand **3.** trademark **4.** record
marcador *noun m.* **1.** marker **2.** scoreboard
marcar *verb.* **1.** to mark **2.** brand **3.** score **4.** indicate **5.** dial
marcha *noun f.* **1.** march **2.** departure **3.** speed **4.** progress, course **5.** gear
marchar *verb.* **1.** to march **2.** work **3.** go
—**marcharse 1.** to depart **2.** leave
marcial *adj.* martial
marco *noun m.* **1.** frame, framework **2.** mark
marea *noun f.* tide
mareado, -da *adj.* **1.** dizzy **2.** sick
mareo *noun m.* **1.** faint **2.** sickness
marfil *noun m.* ivory
margarita *noun f.* daisy
margen *noun m.* **1.** margin **2.** border, edge
marginal *adj.* marginal
marido *noun m.* husband
marina *noun f.* navy
marinero *noun m.* sailor
marino *noun m.* sailor
marino, -na *adj.* marine
mariposa *noun f.* butterfly
marítimo, -ma *adj.* maritime
marketing *noun m.* marketing
mármol *noun m.* marble
marrano, -na *noun.* **1.** pig, hog **2.** Marrano
marrano, -na *adj.* filthy
marrón *noun m. adj.* brown
martes *noun m.* Tuesday
martillar *verb.* to hammer
martillo *noun m.* hammer
marzo *noun m.* March
mas *conj.* but
más *noun m.* plus sign
más *adj.* **1.** more **2.** most **3.** else
más *adv.* **1.** more **2.** most **3.** further **4.** longer **5.** rather
—**más bien** rather
—**más vale** better
más *prep.* plus
—**más allá de** beyond
más *pron.* more
—**por más que** no matter how much
masa *noun f.* **1.** mass **2.** dough
masacrar *verb.* to massacre, butcher
masacre *noun f.* massacre
masaje *noun m.* massage
masajear *verb.* to massage
mascar *verb.* to chew
máscara *noun f.* mask
mascarilla *noun f.* mask

mascota *noun f.* pet
masculino, -na *adj.* masculine
masivo, -va *adj.* mass
matadero *noun m.* abattoir, slaughterhouse
matanza *noun f.* slaughter
matar *verb.* **1.** to kill **2.** butcher, slaughter **3.** pass, waste
mate *noun m.* **1.** mate **2.** smash
matemáticas *noun f. plural.* mathematics
matemático, -ca *noun.* mathematician
matemático, -ca *adj.* mathematical
materia *noun f.* **1.** material **2.** matter
material *noun m.* **1.** material **2.** stuff
material *adj.* material
maternal *adj.* maternal
maternidad *noun f.* maternity
materno, -na *adj.* maternal
matiz *noun m.* **1.** hue **2.** shade
matón *noun m.* bully
matrícula *noun f.* **1.** registration **2.** register
matricular *verb.* **1.** to register **2.** matriculate
matrimonio *noun m.* **1.** marriage **2.** married couple
máxima *noun f.* maxim
máximo *noun m.* maximum
—**al máximo** to the utmost
—**como máximo** at the most, at the latest
máximo, -ma *adj.* maximum
mayo *noun m.* May
mayor *noun mf.* adult
mayor *adj.* **1.** main, major **2.** bigger, biggest **3.** larger, largest **4.** greater, greatest **5.** elder, oldest
—**al por mayor** wholesale
mayoría *noun f.* majority
mayorista *noun mf.* wholesaler
mayúscula *noun f.* capital letter
me *pron.* **1.** me **2.** to me, for me, from me **3.** myself
mecánica *noun f.* mechanics
mecánico, -ca *noun.* mechanic
mecánico, -ca *adj.* mechanical
mecanismo *noun m.* mechanism, device
mecanografía *noun f.* typing, typewriting
mecanografiar *verb.* to type
mecenas *noun mf.* patron
mecenazgo *noun m.* patronage
mecer *verb.* **1.** to rock **2.** sway
mechón *noun m.* lock
medalla *noun f.* medal
media *noun f.* **1.** average **2.** stocking
mediano, -na *adj.* medium
medianoche *noun f.* midnight
mediar *verb.* **1.** to mediate **2.** intervene **3.** reach the middle
medicamento *noun m.* medicine, drug
medicina *noun f.* medicine
medicar *verb.* to medicate
medición *noun f.* measurement, measuring
médico *noun mf.* doctor, physician
médico, -ca *adj.* medical
medida *noun f.* **1.** measure, measurement **2.** step **3.** extent
medieval *adj.* medieval
medio *noun m.* **1.** middle **2.** element **3.** medium **4.** means
—**medio ambiente** environment
medio, -dia *adj.* **1.** middle **2.** half **3.** average **4.** medium
medio *adv.* **1.** half **2.** rather
mediocre *adj.* mediocre, ordinary
mediodía *noun m.* midday, noon
medir *verb.* **1.** to measure **2.** gauge **3.** weigh
meditación *noun f.* meditation
meditar *verb.* **1.** to meditate **2.** ponder
médium *noun mf.* medium
mejilla *noun f.* cheek
mejor *adj.* **1.** better **2.** best
mejor *adv.* **1.** better **2.** best **3.** rather
—**a lo mejor** probably, maybe
mejora *noun f.* **1.** improvement **2.** upgrade
mejorar *verb.* **1.** to improve **2.** make better
melancolía *noun f.* melancholy, sadness
melancólico, -ca *adj.* melancholy, sad, blue
melocotón *noun m.* peach
melodía *noun f.* melody, tune
membrana *noun f.* membrane
memorable *adj.* memorable
memorándum *noun m.* memorandum, memo
memoria *noun f.* **1.** memory **2.** report
—**memorias** memoirs
mena *noun f.* ore

mención *noun f.* mention
mencionar *verb.* to mention
menor *noun mf.* minor
menor *adj.* **1.** minor **2.** smaller, smallest **3.** lesser, least **4.** younger, youngest
—**al por menor** retail
menos *noun m.* minus sign
menos *adj.* **1.** less, least **2.** fewer, fewest
menos *adv.* **1.** less **2.** least
—**a menos que** unless
—**por lo menos** at least
menos *prep.* **1.** except **2.** minus
menos *pron.* less, fewer
mensaje *noun m.* message
mensajero, -ra *noun.* messenger
mensual *adj.* monthly
menta *noun f.* mint
mental *adj.* mental
mente *noun f.* mind
mentir *verb.* to lie
mentira *noun f.* lie
mentón *noun m.* chin
menú *noun m.* menu
mercadería *noun f.* merchandise
mercado *noun m.* **1.** market **2.** fair
mercancía *noun f.* merchandise, goods
mercurio *noun m.* mercury
merecedor, -dora *adj.* worthy
merecer *verb.* to deserve, be worthy of
merecido *noun m.* due
merecido, -da *adj.* just, due
merecimiento *noun m.* merit
meridional *adj.* southern
mérito *noun m.* merit
merma *noun f.* **1.** decrease, drop **2.** loss, waste
mermelada *noun f.* marmalade, jam
mero, -ra *adj.* mere, simple, plain
mes *noun m.* month
mesa *noun f.* table
meseta *noun f.* plateau
meta *noun f.* aim, goal
metáfora *noun f.* metaphor
metal *noun m.* **1.** metal **2.** brass
metálico, -ca *adj.* metallic
meter *verb.* **1.** to put (in) **2.** insert, introduce **3.** place **4.** cause **5.** make
—**meter prisa** to hurry
—**meterse** **1.** to enter, get into **2.** meddle
—**meterse a** to become
—**meterse con** to tease
método *noun m.* method
metro *noun m.* **1.** meter **2.** subway **3.** underground
metropolitano, -na *adj.* metropolitan
mexicano, -na *noun. adj.* Mexican
México *noun m.* Mexico
mezcla *noun f.* mix, mixture, blend
mezclar *verb.* **1.** to mix, blend **2.** involve
—**mezclarse** to socialize, mingle
mezquino, -na *adj.* mean, petty
mezquita *noun f.* mosque
mi *adj.* my
mí *pron.* me
microbio *noun m.* microbe
micrófono *noun m.* microphone
microondas *noun m.* microwave
microscopio *noun m.* microscope
miedo *noun m.* fear
—**dar miedo** to frighten
—**tener miedo** to be afraid
miel *noun f.* honey
miembro *noun m.* **1.** member **2.** limb
mientras *conj.* **1.** while, as **2.** as long as
—**mientras que** while, whereas
—**mientras tanto** meanwhile, in the meantime
miércoles *noun m.* Wednesday
mierda *noun f.* shit
migración *noun f.* migration
migrar *verb.* to migrate
mil *noun m.* a thousand, one thousand
mil *adj.* thousand
milagro *noun m.* **1.** miracle **2.** wonder
mililitro *noun m.* milliliter
milímetro *noun m.* millimeter
militante *noun mf. adj.* militant, activist
militar *noun mf.* soldier
militar *adj.* military
milla *noun f.* mile
millar *noun m.* thousand
millardo *noun m.* billion
millón *noun m.* million
millonario, -ria *noun.* millionaire
millonésimo *noun m.* millionth
millonésimo, -ma *adj.* millionth
mimar *verb.* to spoil
mina *noun f.* **1.** mine **2.** lead

minar *verb.* **1.** to mine **2.** undermine
mineral *noun m. adj.* mineral
minería *noun f.* mining
minero, -ra *noun.* miner
minero, -ra *adj.* mining
miniatura *noun f.* miniature
minifalda *noun f.* miniskirt
minimizar *verb.* to minimize
mínimo *noun m.* minimum
mínimo, -ma *adj.* **1.** least, smallest **2.** minimum
ministerial *adj.* ministerial
ministerio *noun m.* department, ministry
ministro, -tra *noun.* secretary, minister
minoría *noun f.* minority
minuciosamente *adv.* thoroughly
minucioso, -sa *adj.* **1.** minute **2.** detailed **3.** thorough
minúsculo, -la *adj.* minute, tiny
minusvalía *noun f.* disability, handicap
minusválido, -da *noun.* handicapped person
minusválido, -da *adj.* disabled, handicapped
minuto *noun m.* minute
mío, mía *adj.* my, mine
mío, mía *pron.* mine
mirada *noun f.* look, glance, glare, gaze
mirar *verb.* **1.** to look, look at **2.** watch **3.** consider
—**mirarse** **1.** to look at oneself **2.** look at each other
misa *noun f.* mass
miserable *adj.* **1.** miserable, wretched **2.** despicable
miseria *noun f.* **1.** misery **2.** poverty
misil *noun m.* missile
misión *noun f.* mission
misionero, -ra *noun.* missionary
mismo, -ma *adj.* **1.** same **2.** very **3.** oneself
misterio *noun m.* mystery
misterioso, -sa *adj.* mysterious
mitad *noun f.* **1.** half **2.** middle
mito *noun m.* myth
mixto, -ta *adj.* mixed
mobiliario *noun m.* furniture
moción *noun f.* motion
moda *noun f.* **1.** fashion **2.** style
—**a la moda** fashionable
modales *noun m. plural.* manners
modelar *verb.* to model, mold, shape
modelo *noun m.* example, model, pattern
modelo *noun mf.* model
módem *noun m.* modem
moderado, -da *noun. adj.* moderate
moderar *verb.* to moderate
modernizar *verb.* to modernize
moderno, -na *adj.* **1.** modern **2.** up-to-date
modesto, -ta *adj.* **1.** modest **2.** humble
modificación *noun f.* modification, alteration
modificar *verb.* to modify, alter
modo *noun m.* **1.** way, manner **2.** mode **3.** mood
—**de cualquier modo** anyway
—**de modo que** so
—**de todos modos** anyway
módulo *noun m.* module
mojado, -da *adj.* wet
mojar *verb.* to wet
molde *noun m.* **1.** mold **2.** cast
moldear *verb.* **1.** to mold **2.** cast
molécula *noun f.* molecule
molecular *adj.* molecular
moler *verb.* to grind
molestar *verb.* **1.** to annoy, bother **2.** disturb **3.** trouble
—**molestarse en** to take the trouble, bother
molestia *noun f.* **1.** annoyance, bother, nuisance **2.** trouble
molesto, -ta *adj.* **1.** annoyed, bothered **2.** annoying, bothersome
molinero, -ra *noun.* miller
molino *noun m.* mill
momento *noun m.* **1.** moment **2.** time
—**al momento** immediately
momia *noun f.* mummy
monarca *noun mf.* monarch
monarquía *noun f.* monarchy
monasterio *noun m.* monastery
moneda *noun f.* **1.** coin **2.** currency
monedero *noun m.* purse
monetario, -ria *adj.* monetary
monitor *noun m.* **1.** instructor **2.** monitor

monja *noun f.* sister
monje *noun m.* monk
mono, -na *noun.* monkey
mono, -na *adj.* pretty, funny
monopolio *noun m.* monopoly
monstruo *noun m.* monster
montacargas *noun m.* elevator
montaje *noun m.* assembly
montaña *noun f.* mountain
montar *verb.* **1.** to mount **2.** assemble **3.** establish, set up **4.** stage **5.** whip
—**montar a caballo** to ride a horse
—**montar en bicicleta** to ride a bicycle
monte *noun m.* mountain, mount
montículo *noun m.* mound
montón *noun m.* heap, pile
—**montones de** loads of, tons of, plenty of
montura *noun f.* **1.** frame **2.** setting **3.** mount
monumento *noun m.* monument
morada *noun f.* dwelling
morado *noun m.* purple
morado, -da *adj.* purple
moral *noun f.* **1.** morale **2.** morality
moral *adj.* moral
moraleja *noun f.* moral
mordaz *adj.* sarcastic, biting
morder *verb.* to bite
mordisco *noun m.* bite
moreno, -na *adj.* dark-skinned, brown
morir *verb.* to die
mortal *noun. adj.* mortal
mortalidad *noun f.* mortality
mortero *noun m.* mortar
mosaico *noun m.* mosaic
mosca *noun f.* fly
mostaza *noun f.* mustard
mostrador *noun m.* counter
mostrar *verb.* **1.** to show **2.** display **3.** manifest
moteado, -da *adj.* spotted
motín *noun m.* riot
motivación *noun f.* motivation
motivar *verb.* **1.** to motivate **2.** cause
motivo *noun m.* **1.** motive **2.** cause
motor *noun m.* **1.** motor, engine **2.** cause
mover *verb.* **1.** to move **2.** shift **3.** shake **4.** prompt **5.** stir
móvil *adj.* mobile
movilidad *noun f.* mobility
movilizar *verb.* to mobilize
movimiento *noun m.* **1.** movement **2.** motion
mozo, -za *adj.* young
muchacha *noun f.* **1.** girl **2.** maid
muchacho *noun m.* boy
muchedumbre *noun f.* multitude, crowd
mucho, -cha *adj.* many, much, a lot of, plenty of
mucho *adv.* much, a lot
—**como mucho** at most
—**con mucho** by far
—**mucho tiempo** long
mucho, -cha *pron.* many, much, a lot
mudanza *noun f.* **1.** move **2.** change
mudar *verb.* **1.** to change **2.** shed
—**mudarse** **1.** to move **2.** change
mudo, -da *adj.* **1.** dumb **2.** mute
muebles *noun m. plural.* furniture
muelle *noun m.* **1.** dock, wharf **2.** spring
muerte *noun f.* death
muerto, -ta *noun.* dead person
muerto, -ta *adj.* dead
muesca *noun f.* nick
muestra *noun f.* **1.** sample **2.** show
mujer *noun f.* **1.** woman **2.** wife
multa *noun f.* fine
multar *verb.* to fine
múltiple *adj.* multiple
multiplicar *verb.* to multiply
múltiplo *noun m.* multiple
multitud *noun f.* multitude, crowd
mundial *adj.* world, worldwide
mundo *noun m.* world
—**todo el mundo** everyone, everybody
munición *noun f.* ammunition
municipal *adj.* municipal
municipio *noun m.* municipality
muñeca *noun f.* **1.** doll **2.** wrist
muñón *noun m.* stump
muralla *noun f.* wall
murciélago *noun m.* bat
murmullo *noun m.* murmur
murmurar *verb.* to murmur, mutter, whisper
muro *noun m.* wall

muscular *adj.* muscular
músculo *noun m.* muscle
musculoso, -sa *adj.* muscular
museo *noun m.* museum
musgo *noun m.* moss
música *noun f.* music
musical *noun m. adj.* musical
músico, -ca *noun.* musician
muslo *noun m.* thigh
musulmán, -mana *noun. adj.* Muslim
mutuo, -tua *adj.* **1.** mutual **2.** reciprocal
muy *adv.* **1.** very **2.** quite

N

nacer *verb.* **1.** to be born **2.** rise
nacimiento *noun m.* **1.** birth **2.** source
nación *noun f.* **1.** nation **2.** country
nacional *noun mf.* citizen
nacional *adj.* **1.** national **2.** domestic
nacionalidad *noun f.* nationality
nacionalismo *noun m.* nationalism
nacionalista *noun mf.* nationalist
nada *noun f.* **1.** nothingness **2.** naught
nada *adv.* not at all
—**casi nada** very little
—**de nada** you are welcome
nada *pron.* nothing, anything
nadar *verb.* to swim
nadie *pron.* **1.** nobody **2.** no one
naranja *noun f.* orange (fruit)
naranja *noun m. adj.* orange (color)
nariz *noun f.* nose
narración *noun f.* narration
narrar *verb.* to narrate, relate, tell
narrativa *noun f.* narrative
nata *noun f.* cream
natal *adj.* native
nativo, -va *noun. adj.* native
natural *adj.* **1.** natural **2.** native
naturaleza *noun f.* nature
naturalmente *adv.* **1.** naturally **2.** of course
naufragio *noun m.* shipwreck
naval *adj.* naval
nave *noun f.* **1.** ship **2.** nave
navegación *noun f.* navigation
navegar *verb.* to sail
Navidad *noun f.* Christmas
necesario, -ria *adj.* necessary
necesidad *noun f.* **1.** need, necessity **2.** poverty, want
necesitar *verb.* **1.** to need **2.** require
necrología *noun f.* obituary
neerlandés, -desa *noun. adj.* Dutch
negar *verb.* **1.** to deny **2.** refuse
negativa *noun f.* **1.** denial **2.** refusal
negativo *noun m.* negative
negativo, -va *adj.* negative, adverse
negligencia *noun f.* negligence
negociación *noun f.* negotiation
negociador, -dora *noun.* negotiator
negociar *verb.* **1.** to negotiate **2.** deal
negocio *noun m.* **1.** business **2.** trade
—**hombre/mujer de negocios** businessman or businesswoman
negro, -gra *noun.* black person
negro, -gra *adj.* **1.** black **2.** disastrous, awful
nervio *noun m.* **1.** nerve **2.** vein **3.** energy, vigor
nervioso, -sa *adj.* nervous
neto, -ta *adj.* **1.** net **2.** clean, clear
neumático *noun m.* tire
neutral *adj.* neutral
neutralidad *noun f.* neutrality
neutro, -tra *adj.* **1.** neuter **2.** neutral
nevar *verb.* to snow
nevera *noun f.* refrigerator
ni *conj.* neither, nor
—**ni siquiera** not even
nido *noun m.* nest
niebla *noun f.* fog
nieto, -ta *noun.* grandson or granddaughter
—**nietos** grandchildren
nieve *noun f.* snow
ningún *adj.* (see ninguno. Used before masculine singular nouns)
ninguno, -na *adj.* no, none

ninguno, -na *pron.* **1.** none **2.** neither **3.** no one, no other
niñero, -ra *noun.* nanny, baby-sitter
niño, -ña *noun.* child, boy or girl
nítido, -da *adj.* clear, sharp
nitrógeno *noun m.* nitrogen
nivel *noun m.* **1.** level **2.** standard **3.** grade
nivelar *verb.* to level
no *adv.* **1.** no, not **2.** non
noble *noun mf.* nobleman or noblewoman
noble *adj.* noble
nobleza *noun f.* nobility
noche *noun f.* **1.** night **2.** evening
—**esta noche** tonight
noción *noun f.* notion, conception
nocivo, -va *adj.* harmful
nombramiento *noun m.* appointment, nomination
nombrar *verb.* **1.** to appoint **2.** name
nombre *noun m.* **1.** name **2.** noun
nominación *noun f.* nomination
nominal *adj.* nominal
nono, -na *adj.* ninth
norma *noun f.* **1.** rule **2.** norm
normal *adj.* **1.** normal **2.** usual **3.** standard
normalmente *adv.* usually, normally
norte *noun m.* north
norte *adj.* northern
norteamericano, -ca *noun. adj.* **1.** North American **2.** American
norteño, -ña *adj.* northern
Noruega *noun f.* Norway
noruego, -ga *noun. adj.* Norwegian
nos *pron.* **1.** us **2.** ourselves **3.** to us, for us, from us **4.** each other
nosotros, nosotras *pron.* **1.** we **2.** us
—**nosotros mismos, nosotras mismas** ourselves
nostalgia *noun f.* nostalgia
nota *noun f.* **1.** note **2.** grade, mark **3.** announcement **4.** touch
notable *adj.* notable, remarkable
notación *noun f.* notation
notar *verb.* to notice
noticia *noun f.* piece of news
—**noticias** news
novato, -ta *noun.* novice
novedad *noun f.* novelty
novedoso, -sa *adj.* novel
novela *noun f.* novel
novelista *noun mf.* novelist
noveno, -na *noun. adj.* ninth
noventa *noun m. adj.* ninety
novicio, -cia *noun.* novice
noviembre *noun m.* November
novio, -via *noun.* **1.** boyfriend or girlfriend **2.** fiancé or bride
nube *noun f.* cloud
nublar *verb.* to cloud
nuclear *adj.* nuclear
núcleo *noun m.* **1.** core **2.** nucleus
nudo *noun m.* **1.** knot **2.** node
nuestro, nuestra *adj.* our
nuestro, nuestra *pron.* ours
nueve *noun m. adj.* nine
nuevo, -va *adj.* new
—**de nuevo** again
nuez *noun f.* nut
nulo, -la *adj.* **1.** null **2.** null and void **3.** inept
numerar *verb.* to number
numérico, -ca *adj.* numerical
número *noun m.* **1.** number **2.** issue **3.** figure **4.** size
nunca *adv.* never, ever
nutrición *noun f.* nutrition
nutriente *noun m.* nutrient

O

o *conj.* **1.** or **2.** either
obedecer *verb.* to obey
obediencia *noun f.* obedience
obispo *noun m.* bishop
obituario *noun m.* obituary
objeción *noun f.* objection
objetar *verb.* to object
objetividad *noun f.* objectivity

objetivo *noun m.* **1.** objective, aim, goal **2.** lens
objetivo, -va *adj.* objective
objeto *noun m.* **1.** object **2.** objective
obligación *noun f.* obligation, duty
obligar *verb.* to force, compel, oblige
obligatorio, -ria *adj.* compulsory
obra *noun f.* **1.** work **2.** play
—**obra maestra** masterpiece
obrero, -ra *noun.* worker, laborer
obrero, -ra *adj.* working
obsceno, -na *adj.* obscene
obsequio *noun m.* gift, present
observación *noun f.* **1.** observation **2.** remark
observador, -dora *noun.* observer
observador, -dora *adj.* observant
observar *verb.* **1.** to observe **2.** notice **3.** watch
obsesión *noun f.* obsession
obsesionar *verb.* **1.** to obsess **2.** haunt
obstáculo *noun m.* obstacle
obstrucción *noun f.* obstruction
obstruir *verb.* to obstruct, block
obtener *verb.* **1.** to obtain, get **2.** attain
obvio, -via *adj.* obvious
ocasión *noun f.* **1.** occasion **2.** chance **3.** opportunity
ocasional *adj.* **1.** occasional **2.** fortuitous
ocasionar *verb.* to cause
occidental *adj.* western, occidental
occidente *noun m.* **1.** west **2.** the West
océano *noun m.* ocean
ochenta *noun m. adj.* eighty
ocho *noun m. adj.* eight
ocio *noun m.* leisure
octavo, -va *noun. adj.* eighth
octogésimo, -ma *noun. adj.* eightieth
octubre *noun m.* October
ocultar *verb.* to conceal, hide
oculto, -ta *adj.* concealed, hidden
ocupación *noun f.* occupation
ocupado, -da *adj.* **1.** busy **2.** occupied
ocupar *verb.* **1.** to occupy **2.** employ **3.** inhabit **4.** hold
—**ocuparse de** to attend, take care of
ocurrir *verb.* to happen, occur
—**ocurrirse** to have an idea, strike
odiar *verb.* to hate
odio *noun m.* hate, hatred
odontólogo, -ga *noun.* dentist
oeste *noun m.* west
oeste *adj.* west, western
ofender *verb.* to offend
ofensa *noun f.* offence
ofensiva *noun f.* offensive
ofensivo, -va *adj.* offensive
oferta *noun f.* **1.** offer **2.** bid, bidding
—**oferta y demanda** supply and demand
oficial *noun mf.* officer
oficial *adj.* official
oficina *noun f.* office
oficio *noun m.* **1.** occupation, trade **2.** craft
ofrecer *verb.* **1.** to offer **2.** present
—**ofrecerse** to volunteer
ofrecimiento *noun m.* offer
ofrenda *noun f.* offering
oído *noun m.* **1.** ear **2.** hearing
oír *verb.* **1.** to hear **2.** listen to
ojalá *interj.* I hope, I wish, hopefully
ojeada *noun f.* glance
ojera *noun f.* shadow
ojo *noun m.* eye
ola *noun f.* wave
óleo *noun m.* **1.** oil **2.** oil painting
oleoducto *noun m.* pipeline
oler *verb.* to smell
—**olerse** to suspect
olfatear *verb.* to sniff
olfato *noun m.* sense of smell
oliva *noun f.* olive
olivo *noun m.* olive tree
olor *noun m.* odor, smell
olvidar *verb.* **1.** to forget **2.** leave behind
olvido *noun m.* oblivion
omisión *noun f.* omission
omitir *verb.* to omit
once *noun m. adj.* eleven
onda *noun f.* wave
ondear *verb.* to wave
ondular *verb.* to wave
onza *noun f.* ounce
opción *noun f.* option, choice
opcional *adj.* optional
ópera *noun f.* opera

operación *noun f.* **1.** operation **2.** transaction
operar *verb.* to operate
—**operarse** to have an operation
operario, -ria *noun.* worker
operativo, -va *adj.* operational
opinar *verb.* to think
opinión *noun f.* opinion
oponente *noun mf.* opponent
oponer *verb.* to oppose
oportunidad *noun f.* opportunity
oportuno, -na *adj.* opportune, timely
oposición *noun f.* **1.** opposition **2.** competitive exam
opresión *noun f.* oppression
oprimir *verb.* to oppress
optar (por) *verb.* to opt (for)
óptico, -ca *adj.* optical
optimismo *noun m.* optimism
optimista *noun mf.* optimist
optimista *adj.* optimistic
opuesto, -ta *adj.* **1.** opposite **2.** opposed
oración *noun f.* **1.** prayer **2.** sentence, clause
oráculo *noun m.* oracle
oral *adj.* **1.** oral **2.** spoken
orar *verb.* to pray
órbita *noun f.* orbit
orden *noun f.* order, command
—**orden judicial** warrant
orden *noun m.* order
—**orden del día** agenda
ordenado, -da *adj.* orderly
ordenador *noun m.* computer
ordenar *verb.* **1.** to order **2.** arrange
ordeñar *verb.* to milk
ordinario, -ria *adj.* **1.** ordinary **2.** common
oreja *noun f.* ear
orgánico, -ca *adj.* organic
organismo *noun m.* **1.** organism **2.** organization
organización *noun f.* organization
organizador, -dora *noun.* organizer
organizar *verb.* to organize, arrange
órgano *noun m.* organ
orgullo *noun m.* pride
orgulloso, -sa *adj.* proud
orientación *noun f.* **1.** orientation **2.** direction **3.** guidance
oriental *adj.* **1.** oriental **2.** eastern
orientar *verb.* **1.** to guide **2.** orient
oriente *adj.* **1.** east **2.** the East, the Orient
—**Oriente Medio** Middle East
origen *noun m.* **1.** origin **2.** source
—**orígenes** background
original *noun m. adj.* original
originar *verb.* to originate
originario, -ria *adj.* native
orilla *noun f.* **1.** shore **2.** bank
orina *noun f.* urine
oro *noun m.* gold
orquesta *noun f.* orchestra
ortodoxo, -xa *adj.* orthodox
ortografía *noun f.* spelling
os *pron.* **1.** you, to you **2.** each other
osadía *noun f.* daring
osar *verb.* to dare
oscurecer *verb.* **1.** to darken **2.** obscure
oscuridad *noun f.* **1.** darkness **2.** obscurity
oscuro, -ra *adj.* **1.** dark **2.** obscure
oso, -sa *noun.* bear
—**oso de peluche** teddy bear
ostentación *noun f.* display
otoño *noun m.* autumn, fall
otorgar *verb.* to award, grant
otro, otra *adj.* **1.** other **2.** another
—**otra vez** again
otro, otra *pron.* **1.** other one **2.** another one
oval *adj.* oval
ovalado, -da *adj.* oval
óvalo *noun m.* oval
oveja *noun f.* sheep
ovillo *noun m.* ball
óvulo *noun m.* egg
oxígeno *noun m.* oxygen
ozono *noun m.* ozone

P

pabellón *noun m.* pavilion
pacer *verb.* to graze
paciencia *noun f.* patience
paciente *noun mf. adj.* patient
pacto *noun m.* **1.** pact, agreement **2.** covenant
padecer *verb.* to suffer
padre *noun m.* father
—**padres** parents
paga *noun f.* **1.** allowance **2.** pay
pagadero, -ra *adj.* payable
pagano, -na *noun. adj.* pagan
pagar *verb.* to pay
página *noun f.* page
pago *noun m.* payment
país *noun m.* **1.** country **2.** region
paisaje *noun m.* **1.** landscape **2.** scenery
Países Bajos *noun m. plural.* Netherlands
paja *noun f.* straw
pajarera *noun f.* aviary
pájaro *noun m.* bird
paje *noun m.* page
pala *noun f.* shovel
palabra *noun f.* **1.** word **2.** faith
palacio *noun m.* **1.** palace **2.** court
palanca *noun f.* lever
palangana *noun f.* basin
palco *noun m.* box
Palestina *noun f.* Palestine
palestino, -na *noun. adj.* Palestinian
palidecer *verb.* to turn pale
pálido, -da *adj.* pale
paliza *noun f.* beating
—**dar una paliza** to thrash
palma *noun f.* palm
palmada *noun f.* **1.** slap **2.** pat, tap
palmera *noun f.* palm
palmo *noun m.* span
palo *noun m.* stick
paloma *noun f.* pigeon, dove
palpar *verb.* to touch, feel
pan *noun m.* bread
pana *noun f.* corduroy
panadería *noun f.* bakery
panadero, -ra *noun.* baker
pancarta *noun f.* placard
pandilla *noun f.* **1.** group **2.** gang
panecillo *noun m.* roll
panel *noun m.* panel
pánico *noun m.* panic, scare
panorama *noun m.* **1.** panorama **2.** prospect **3.** scene
pantalla *noun f.* **1.** screen **2.** monitor
pantalones *noun m. plural.* pants, trousers
pantano *noun m.* swamp, marsh
pantorrilla *noun f.* calf
pañal *noun m.* diaper
paño *noun m.* cloth
pañuelo *noun m.* handkerchief
—**pañuelo de papel** tissue
papa *noun f.* potato
—**papas fritas** french fries
Papa *noun m.* pope
papá *noun m.* dad, daddy
papal *adj.* papal
papel *noun m.* **1.** paper **2.** part, role
papelera *noun f.* bin
paquete *noun m.* **1.** package **2.** packet **3.** parcel
par *noun m.* **1.** pair, couple **2.** par **3.** peer
par *adj.* even
para *prep.* **1.** for **2.** to **3.** towards **4.** by
—**para adelante** forwards
—**para detrás** backwards
—**para que** so that, in order to
paracaídas *noun m.* parachute
parachoques *noun m.* bumper
parada *noun f.* **1.** stop, halt **2.** catch, save
paradero *noun m.* whereabouts
parado, -da *noun.* unemployed person
parado, -da *adj.* **1.** motionless **2.** still **3.** unemployed
paradoja *noun f.* paradox
paraguas *noun m.* umbrella
paraíso *noun m.* **1.** paradise, heaven **2.** balcony
paralelo *noun m.* parallel
paralelo, -la *adj.* parallel

parar *verb.* **1.** to stop **2.** halt
parcela *noun f.* parcel
parche *noun m.* patch
parcial *adj.* partial
parcialidad *noun f.* bias
parecer *noun m.* **1.** opinion, view **2.** appearance
parecer *verb.* **1.** to seem **2.** look **3.** appear **4.** think
—**parecerse** to resemble, look alike
parecido *noun m.* **1.** similarity **2.** resemblance
parecido, -da *adj.* **1.** alike **2.** similar
pared *noun f.* wall
pareja *noun f.* **1.** couple **2.** pair **3.** partner
parentesco *noun m.* kinship
paréntesis *noun m.* parenthesis
pariente *noun mf.* relative
parir *verb.* to give birth, bear
parking *noun m.* parking
parlamentario, -ria *noun.* member of parliament
parlamentario, -ria *adj.* parliamentary
parlamento *noun m.* parliament
paro *noun m.* **1.** stoppage **2.** unemployment
parpadear *verb.* to blink
parpadeo *noun m.* blink
párpado *noun m.* eyelid
parque *noun m.* park
parra *noun f.* vine
párrafo *noun m.* paragraph
parrilla *noun f.* grill
párroco *noun m.* parson, parish priest
parroquia *noun f.* parish
parroquiano, -na *noun.* patron, customer
parte *noun f.* **1.** part **2.** share **3.** side, party **4.** place **5.** role
—**en parte** partly
—**parte delantera** front
—**parte trasera** back
parte *noun m.* report, dispatch
participación *noun f.* **1.** participation **2.** share
participante *noun mf.* **1.** participant **2.** competitor
participar *verb.* **1.** to take part, participate **2.** share, have a share **3.** announce
partícula *noun f.* particle
particular *noun m.* private individual
—**particulares** details
particular *adj.* **1.** particular **2.** private **3.** special, peculiar
particularmente *adv.* specially
partida *noun f.* **1.** departure **2.** game **3.** certificate **4.** item
partidario, -ria *noun.* supporter
partido *noun m.* **1.** party **2.** game, match **3.** play **4.** tie
—**sacar partido** to profit
partir *verb.* **1.** to cut, halve, split **2.** break, crack **3.** divide **4.** depart, leave
—**a partir de** from
—**partir de** to start from
partitura *noun f.* score
parto *noun m.* birth, delivery, labor
pasada *noun f.* passing
pasado *noun m.* past
pasado, -da *adj.* **1.** past **2.** out-of-date, old-fashioned **3.** bad, spoiled
pasaje *noun m.* **1.** passage **2.** ticket
pasajero, -ra *noun.* passenger
pasajero, -ra *adj.* passing
pasaporte *noun m.* passport
pasar *verb.* **1.** to happen **2.** pass **3.** come in, enter **4.** surpass **5.** cross **6.** give **7.** undergo, suffer **8.** omit
—**pasar de largo** to go by without stopping
—**pasar por alto** to omit, overlook
—**pasarlo bien** to have a good time
—**pasarlo mal** to have a bad time
—**pasarse** to go too far
pasatiempo *noun m.* hobby
Pascua *noun f.* **1.** Easter **2.** Passover **3.** Christmas
pase *noun m.* **1.** pass **2.** permit
paseante *noun mf.* stroller
pasear *verb.* to take a walk, stroll
paseo *noun m.* **1.** walk, stroll **2.** ride
pasillo *noun m.* corridor, aisle
pasión *noun f.* passion
pasivo, -va *adj.* passive
pasmar *verb.* to stun, amaze
paso *noun m.* **1.** passage **2.** footstep **3.** pace **4.** way
pasta *noun f.* **1.** paste **2.** pasta

pastar *verb.* to graze
pastel *noun m.* **1.** cake **2.** pie
pastelería *noun f.* pastry shop
pastilla *noun f.* **1.** pill **2.** tablet **3.** cake
pasto *noun m.* pasture
pastor, -tora *noun.* **1.** shepherd or shepherdess **2.** minister
pastoral *noun f. adj.* pastoral
pastoril *adj.* pastoral
pata *noun f.* **1.** paw **2.** leg **3.** foot
patada *noun f.* kick
patata *noun f.* potato
patentar *verb.* to patent
patente *noun f.* patent
paterno, -na *adj.* parental
patético, -ca *adj.* pathetic
patín *noun m.* skate
patinar *verb.* to skate
patio *noun m.* courtyard
—**patio de recreo** playground
pato, -ta *noun.* duck
patoso, -sa *adj.* awkward
patria *noun f.* homeland
patrimonio *noun m.* patrimony
patriota *noun mf.* patriot
patriota *adj.* patriotic
patrocinador, -dora *noun.* sponsor
patrocinar *verb.* to sponsor
patrocinio *noun m.* **1.** sponsorship **2.** patronage
patrón *noun m.* **1.** model, pattern **2.** standard
patrón, -trona *noun.* **1.** employer **2.** patron saint
patrulla *noun f.* patrol
patrullar *verb.* to patrol
pausa *noun f.* break, pause
pausado, -da *adj.* deliberate, slow
pavimentar *verb.* to pave
pavimento *noun m.* pavement
pavo, -va *noun.* turkey
pavor *noun m.* terror
paz *noun f.* peace
peaje *noun m.* toll
peatón, -tona *noun.* pedestrian
pecado *noun m.* sin
pecar *verb.* to sin
pecho *noun m.* **1.** chest **2.** breast
pechuga *noun f.* breast
peculiar *adj.* peculiar
pedazo *noun m.* **1.** bit **2.** piece
pedestre *adj.* pedestrian
pedido *noun m.* order
pedir *verb.* **1.** to ask for, request **2.** order
pegamento *noun m.* glue
pegar *verb.* **1.** to hit, strike **2.** glue, stick **3.** paste **4.** attach
—**pegarse** to be contagious
peinar *verb.* to comb
peine *noun m.* comb
pelado, -da *adj.* **1.** bald **2.** bare
pelaje *noun m.* coat, fur
pelar *verb.* to peel
—**pelarse** to have a haircut
pelea *noun f.* **1.** fight **2.** quarrel **3.** row
pelear *verb.* **1.** to fight **2.** quarrel
película *noun f.* **1.** film **2.** movie
peligro *noun m.* **1.** danger **2.** hazard **3.** menace
peligroso, -sa *adj.* **1.** dangerous **2.** hazardous
pelirrojo, -ja *adj.* red-haired
pellejo *noun m.* hide, skin
pellizcar *verb.* to pinch
pellizco *noun m.* pinch
pelmazo, -za *noun.* bore
pelo *noun m.* **1.** hair **2.** fur **3.** pile
pelota *noun f.* ball
—**en pelotas** naked
peluca *noun f.* wig
pena *noun f.* **1.** pity **2.** sorrow **3.** penalty, punishment **4.** difficulty, trouble **5.** shame
—**valer la pena** to be worthwhile
pender *verb.* to hang
pendiente *noun f.* slope
pendiente *noun m.* earring
pendiente *adj.* pending
pene *noun m.* penis
penetración *noun f.* penetration
penetrante *adj.* sharp, acute
penetrar *verb.* **1.** to penetrate **2.** enter
península *noun f.* peninsula
pensamiento *noun m.* thought
pensar *verb.* **1.** to think **2.** intend
pensativo, -va *adj.* thoughtful
pensión *noun f.* **1.** pension **2.** boarding house

pensionista *noun mf.* pensioner
pentágono *noun m.* pentagon
peña *noun f.* rock
peor *adj.* **1.** worse **2.** worst
peor *adv.* **1.** worse **2.** worst
pequeño, -ña *adj.* **1.** small **2.** little **3.** young **4.** short
pera *noun f.* pear
percepción *noun f.* perception
percha *noun f.* **1.** hanger **2.** perch
percibir *verb.* **1.** to perceive **2.** earn
perdedor, -dora *noun.* loser
perder *verb.* **1.** to lose **2.** miss **3.** waste
—**perderse** **1.** to get lost **2.** miss
pérdida *noun f.* **1.** loss **2.** waste
perdido, -da *adj.* **1.** lost **2.** inveterate
perdón *noun m.* pardon, forgiveness
perdón *interj.* sorry!, excuse me!
perdonar *verb.* **1.** to forgive, pardon **2.** excuse **3.** spare
perdurar *verb.* **1.** to last **2.** linger
peregrinación *noun f.* pilgrimage
peregrino, -na *noun.* pilgrim
perejil *noun m.* parsley
perenne *adj.* perennial
pereza *noun f.* laziness
perezoso, -sa *adj.* lazy
perfección *noun f.* perfection
perfeccionar *verb.* to perfect
perfecto, -ta *adj.* perfect
perfil *noun m.* profile
—**de perfil** sideways
perfilar *verb.* to outline
perforar *verb.* **1.** to perforate **2.** pierce **3.** drill
perfumar *verb.* to perfume, scent
perfume *noun m.* perfume, scent, fragrance
periférico, -ca *adj.* peripheral
periódico *noun m.* newspaper
periódico, -ca *adj.* periodic
periodismo *noun m.* journalism
periodista *noun mf.* journalist
período *noun m.* period
perjudicar *verb.* to harm
perjudicial *adj.* harmful
perjuicio *noun m.* harm, damage
perla *noun f.* pearl
permanecer *verb.* to remain
permanente *adj.* permanent
permiso *noun m.* **1.** permission **2.** leave **3.** licence, permit **4.** pass
—**con permiso** excuse me!
permitir *verb.* to allow, permit
—**permitirse el lujo de** to afford
pernera *noun f.* leg
pero *noun m.* fault, objection
pero *conj.* but, yet
perpetuo, -tua *adj.* perpetual
perro, -rra *noun.* dog
persecución *noun f.* **1.** persecution **2.** pursuit
perseguir *verb.* **1.** to persecute **2.** pursue **3.** worry, torment
persiana *noun f.* blind
persistencia *noun f.* persistence
persistente *adj.* persistent
persistir *verb.* **1.** to persist **2.** linger
persona *noun f.* person
personaje *noun m.* **1.** character **2.** personage
personal *noun m.* staff, personnel
personal *adj.* personal
personalidad *noun f.* personality
personalmente *adv.* personally
personificar *verb.* to embody
perspectiva *noun f.* **1.** perspective **2.** prospect, outlook
persuadir *verb.* to persuade
persuasión *noun f.* persuasion
persuasivo, -va *adj.* persuasive
pertenecer *verb.* to belong
pertinencia *noun f.* relevance
pertinente *adj.* relevant
pertrechos *noun m. plural.* equipment
perturbar *verb.* to disturb
Perú *noun m.* Peru
peruano, -na *noun. adj.* Peruvian
pesa *noun f.* weight
pesadilla *noun f.* nightmare
pesado, -da *noun.* bore, pest
pesado, -da *adj.* **1.** heavy **2.** difficult **3.** boring
pesar *noun m.* grief, sorrow
—**a pesar de** despite, in spite of
pesar *verb.* **1.** to weigh **2.** be important **3.** grieve, cause regret
pescado *noun m.* fish

pescador, -dora *noun.* fisherman or fisherwoman
pescar *verb.* **1.** to fish **2.** catch
pesimismo *noun m.* pessimism
pesimista *noun mf.* pessimist
pesimista *adj.* pessimistic
pésimo, -ma *adj.* terrible, very bad
peso *noun m.* **1.** weight **2.** burden **3.** importance
pesquisa *noun f.* inquiry
pestaña *noun f.* eyelash
pestañear *verb.* to blink
pestañeo *noun m.* blink
peste *noun f.* **1.** plague **2.** stink
pesticida *noun m.* pesticide
pestillo *noun m.* bolt
petición *noun f.* petition, request
petróleo *noun m.* oil, petroleum
petrolero *noun m.* oil tanker
pez *noun m.* fish
piano *noun m.* piano
picadura *noun f.* sting, bite
picante *adj.* hot, spicy
picar *verb.* **1.** to sting, bite **2.** itch **3.** punch **4.** grind
picnic *noun m.* picnic
pico *noun m.* **1.** peak **2.** beak, bill **3.** pick
pie *noun m.* **1.** foot **2.** cue
piedra *noun f.* **1.** stone **2.** flint
piel *noun f.* **1.** skin **2.** leather, hide **3.** fur **4.** peel
pierna *noun f.* leg
pieza *noun f.* **1.** piece **2.** component, part
—**pieza de recambio/repuesto** spare part
pila *noun f.* **1.** battery **2.** pile **3.** sink
pilar *noun m.* pillar
píldora *noun f.* pill
pillar *verb.* **1.** to catch **2.** get
pilotar *verb.* to pilot, drive
piloto *noun mf.* pilot, driver
pimienta *noun f.* pepper
pimiento *noun m.* pepper
pinchadiscos *noun mf.* disc jockey
pinchar *verb.* **1.** to puncture **2.** prick
—**pincharse** to get an injection
pinchazo *noun m.* **1.** puncture **2.** prick **3.** shot
pingüino *noun m.* penguin
pino *noun m.* pine, pine tree
pinta *noun f.* **1.** aspect **2.** pint
pintar *verb.* **1.** to paint **2.** draw **3.** depict
pintor, -tora *noun.* painter
pintoresco, -ca *adj.* picturesque
pintura *noun f.* **1.** paint **2.** painting
pinza *noun f.* clothespin
pionero, -ra *noun.* pioneer
pionero, -ra *adj.* pioneering
pipa *noun f.* pipe
pirámide *noun f.* pyramid
pirata *noun mf.* pirate
pisada *noun f.* footstep
pisar *verb.* to tread, trample
piscina *noun f.* pool
piso *noun m.* **1.** floor **2.** apartment
pisotear *verb.* to tread, trample
pista *noun f.* **1.** track **2.** trail **3.** clue **4.** ring, court
—**pista de aterrizaje** runway
pistola *noun f.* pistol, gun
pistolero *noun m.* gunman
pitar *verb.* **1.** to whistle **2.** boo
pitido *noun m.* whistle
pito *noun m.* whistle
pizarra *noun f.* **1.** slate **2.** blackboard
pizca *noun f.* **1.** pinch **2.** trace
pizza *noun f.* pizza
placa *noun f.* **1.** plate **2.** plaque
placer *noun m.* pleasure, delight
placer *verb.* to please, give pleasure
plaga *noun f.* plague
plan *noun m.* **1.** plan **2.** scheme
plancha *noun f.* **1.** iron **2.** grill
planchar *verb.* to iron
planear *verb.* **1.** to plan **2.** glide
planeta *noun m.* planet
planificación *noun f.* planning
planificador, -dora *noun.* planner
planificar *verb.* to plan
plano *noun m.* **1.** plan, map **2.** flat **3.** plane
plano, -na *adj.* flat, level
planta *noun f.* **1.** plant **2.** floor **3.** sole
plantación *noun f.* plantation
plantar *verb.* **1.** to plant **2.** sow
—**plantarse** **1.** to quit **2.** stand firm
plantear *verb.* **1.** to pose **2.** raise

—**plantearse** to think about
plasma *noun m.* plasma
plástico *noun m.* plastic
plástico, -ca *adj.* plastic
plata *noun f.* **1.** silver **2.** money
plataforma *noun f.* **1.** platform **2.** shelf
—**plataforma petrolífera** oil rig
plátano *noun m.* banana
plato *noun m.* **1.** dish **2.** plate **3.** course
plausible *adj.* plausible
playa *noun f.* **1.** beach **2.** shore
plaza *noun f.* **1.** square **2.** marketplace **3.** place, seat
plazo *noun m.* **1.** term, period **2.** installment
—**pagar a plazos** to pay in installments
plegable *adj.* folding
plegar *verb.* to fold
—**plegarse** to give in
pleito *noun m.* lawsuit
plenamente *adv.* fully, completely
pleno, -na *adj.* full, complete
pliegue *noun m.* fold
plomo *noun m.* lead
pluma *noun f.* **1.** feather **2.** pen
plumón *noun m.* down
plus *noun m.* bonus
plusmarca *noun f.* record
población *noun f.* **1.** population **2.** city, town, village
poblado *noun m.* settlement
poblado, -da *adj.* populated
poblar *verb.* to populate, settle
pobre *adj.* **1.** poor **2.** weak
pobreza *noun f.* **1.** poverty **2.** want
poco, -ca *adj.* little, few, not much
poco *adv.* little, few
—**poco a poco** little by little
—**por poco** almost, nearly
poco, -ca *pron.* little, few
podar *verb.* to prune
poder *noun m.* **1.** power **2.** control **3.** possession **4.** strength, force
poder *verb.* **1.** can **2.** to be able **3.** may
poderoso, -sa *adj.* **1.** powerful **2.** mighty
podrido, -da *adj.* rotten
poema *noun m.* poem
poesía *noun f.* **1.** poetry **2.** poem
poeta *noun mf.* poet
poético, -ca *adj.* poetic
polaco, -ca *noun. adj.* Polish
polar *adj.* polar
polémica *noun f.* polemics, controversy
polémico, -ca *adj.* polemical, controversial
policía *noun f.* police
policía *noun mf.* policeman or policewoman
polifacético, -ca *adj.* versatile, many-sided
politécnico *noun m.* polytechnic
política *noun f.* **1.** policy **2.** politics
político, -ca *noun.* politician
político, -ca *adj.* **1.** political **2.** in-law, by marriage
póliza *noun f.* policy
polla *noun f.* cock
pollo *noun m.* chicken
polo *noun m.* **1.** pole **2.** polo
Polonia *noun f.* Poland
polvera *noun f.* compact
polvo *noun m.* **1.** dust **2.** powder **3.** fuck
pólvora *noun f.* powder
polvoriento, -ta *adj.* dusty
pomo *noun m.* handle
ponche *noun m.* punch
poner *verb.* **1.** to put **2.** place **3.** set **4.** set up, establish **5.** add **6.** switch on, put on **7.** lay **8.** install
—**poner al día** to update
—**ponerse 1.** to wear, put on **2.** become **3.** set (sun) **4.** move
póney *noun m.* pony
popular *adj.* **1.** popular **2.** folk
popularidad *noun f.* popularity
por *prep.* **1.** for **2.** during **3.** by **4.** through **5.** along **6.** around **7.** per **8.** from **9.** because of **10.** instead of
—**¿por qué?** why?
—**por si acaso** in case
porcelana *noun f.* porcelain, china
porcentaje *noun m.* percentage
porche *noun m.* porch
porción *noun f.* **1.** portion **2.** serving
pormenor *noun m.* detail
pormenorizado, -da *adj.* detailed
porque *conj.* because

porqué *noun m.* reason, cause
porra *noun f.* club
porrazo *noun m.* bash, blow
portal *noun m.* **1.** portal **2.** doorway
portátil *noun m.* laptop
portátil *adj.* portable
portavoz *noun mf.* spokesperson, spokesman or spokeswoman
portazo *noun m.* slam
porte *noun m.* **1.** bearing **2.** carriage
portería *noun f.* **1.** caretaker's office **2.** goal
portero, -ra *noun.* **1.** doorman, caretaker **2.** goalkeeper
pórtico *noun m.* portico
Portugal *noun m.* Portugal
portugués, -guesa *noun. adj.* Portuguese
posada *noun f.* inn
posar *verb.* **1.** to pose **2.** place —**posarse** **1.** to perch **2.** settle
pose *noun f.* pose
poseer *verb.* to possess, have, hold, own
posesión *noun f.* possession
posibilidad *noun f.* possibility
posible *adj.* possible
posición *noun f.* **1.** position **2.** attitude **3.** status **4.** rating
positivo, -va *adj.* positive
poso *noun m.* grounds
posponer *verb.* to postpone
postal *noun f.* postcard
postal *adj.* postal
poste *noun m.* **1.** pole **2.** post
póster *noun m.* poster
posterior *adj.* **1.** back **2.** subsequent, later
posteriormente *adv.* afterwards, subsequently
postizo, -za *adj.* false
postre *noun m.* dessert
postura *noun f.* **1.** position **2.** posture
pote *noun m.* pot
potencia *noun f.* **1.** power **2.** potency
potencial *noun m. adj.* potential
potente *adj.* **1.** powerful, mighty **2.** potent
pozo *noun m.* **1.** well **2.** pool **3.** shaft
práctica *noun f.* practice
practicable *adj.* practicable
prácticamente *adv.* practically, virtually
practicar *verb.* **1.** to practice **2.** exercise
práctico, -ca *adj.* practical
prado *noun m.* meadow
precaución *noun f.* **1.** caution **2.** precaution
precedente *noun m.* precedent
precedente *adj.* preceding, previous
preceder *verb.* to precede
precio *noun m.* **1.** price, value **2.** cost
precioso, -sa *adj.* **1.** beautiful **2.** precious
precipitado, -da *adj.* **1.** hasty **2.** rash
precipitarse *verb.* **1.** to rush **2.** rash **3.** throw oneself
precisamente *adv.* precisely
precisar *verb.* **1.** to require, need **2.** specify
precisión *noun f.* accuracy, precision
preciso, -sa *adj.* **1.** necessary **2.** accurate, precise **3.** exact
precursor, -sora *noun.* forerunner, pioneer
predador, -dora *noun.* predator
predecesor, -sora *noun.* predecessor
predecible *adj.* predictable
predecir *verb.* to predict
predicar *verb.* to preach
predicción *noun f.* prediction
predisponer *verb.* **1.** to predispose **2.** bias, prejudice
predisposición *noun f.* **1.** predisposition **2.** bias, prejudice
predominancia *noun f.* prevalence
predominante *adj.* **1.** prevailing **2.** prevalent
predominar *verb.* to prevail
preestreno *noun m.* preview
prefacio *noun m.* preface, introduction
preferencia *noun f.* preference
preferible *adj.* preferable
preferido, -da *noun. adj.* favorite
preferir *verb.* to prefer
pregunta *noun f.* question
preguntar *verb.* **1.** to ask, question **2.** inquire —**preguntarse** to wonder

prejuicio *noun m.* bias, prejudice
preliminar *noun m. adj.* preliminary
prematuro, -ra *adj.* premature
premiado, -da *adj.* winning
premiar *verb.* **1.** to reward **2.** award
premio *noun m.* **1.** award **2.** prize
prenda *noun f.* **1.** garment **2.** pledge
prender *verb.* **1.** to pin **2.** catch **3.** seize —**prender fuego** to catch fire
prensa *noun f.* **1.** press **2.** printing-press
prensar *verb.* to press
preocupación *noun f.* concern, preoccupation, worry
preocupado, -da *adj.* worried
preocupar *verb.* to concern, trouble, worry
preparación *noun f.* preparation
preparado *noun m.* mixture
preparado, -da *adj.* **1.** ready, prepared **2.** trained
preparar *verb.* **1.** to prepare **2.** coach, train
preparativo *noun m.* preparation —**preparativos** arrangements
presa *noun f.* **1.** catch **2.** prey **3.** seizure **4.** dam
prescindir de *verb.* to do without
prescribir *verb.* to prescribe
prescripción *verb.* prescription
presencia *noun f.* presence
presenciar *verb.* to witness
presentación *noun f.* **1.** presentation **2.** debut **3.** introduction
presentador, -dora *noun.* newscaster
presentar *verb.* **1.** to present **2.** introduce **3.** submit **4.** make a gift —**presentarse 1.** to introduce oneself **2.** appear
presente *noun m.* **1.** present **2.** gift
presente *adj.* present
presentir *verb.* to sense
presidencia *noun f.* **1.** presidency **2.** chairmanship
presidencial *adj.* presidential
presidente, -ta *noun.* **1.** president **2.** chairperson, chairman or chairwoman
presidiario, -ria *noun.* convict
presidir *verb.* to preside, chair
presión *noun f.* pressure
presionar *verb.* **1.** to press, push **2.** pressure
preso, -sa *noun.* prisoner
preso, -sa *adj.* imprisoned
préstamo *noun m.* loan
prestar *verb.* **1.** to lend, loan **2.** render —**prestar atención** to pay attention
prestigio *noun m.* prestige
presumido, -da *adj.* vain
presumir *verb.* to presume
presunción *noun f.* presumption
presunto, -ta *adj.* alleged
presupuestar *verb.* to budget
presupuesto *noun m.* budget
pretender *verb.* **1.** to attempt **2.** seek **3.** claim **4.** intend
pretexto *noun m.* pretext, excuse
prevalecer *verb.* to prevail
prevención *noun f.* prevention
prevenir *verb.* **1.** to prevent **2.** warn
prever *verb.* anticipate, envisage, foresee
previamente *adv.* previously
previo, -via *adj.* **1.** previous, prior **2.** upon, after
previsible *adj.* predictable
previsión *noun f.* forecast
prima *noun f.* bonus
primario, -ria *adj.* primary
primavera *noun f.* spring
primer *adj.* (see primero. Used before masculine singular nouns)
primero, -ra *noun.* first
primero, -ra *adj.* **1.** first **2.** former **3.** prime
primero *adv.* first
primicia *noun f.* scoop
primitivo, -va *adj.* primitive
primo, -ma *noun.* cousin
princesa *noun f.* princess
principal *adj.* **1.** principal **2.** main **3.** foremost **4.** major
príncipe *noun m.* prince —**príncipe heredero** crown prince
principiante *noun mf.* beginner, novice
principio *noun m.* **1.** beginning, outset **2.** principle
prior, priora *noun.* prior or prioress
prioridad *noun f.* priority

prisa *noun f.* hurry, rush
—**darse prisa** to hurry
—**tener prisa** to be in a hurry
prisión *noun f.* **1.** jail, prison **2.** imprisonment
prisionero, -ra *noun.* prisoner
prismáticos *noun m. plural.* binoculars
privacidad *noun f.* privacy
privación *noun f.* **1.** deprivation **2.** hardship
privado, -da *adj.* private
privar *verb.* to deprive
privilegiado, -da *adj.* privileged
privilegio *noun m.* privilege
proa *noun f.* bow
probabilidad *noun f.* probability, likelihood
probable *adj.* probable, likely
probar *verb.* **1.** to try **2.** prove **3.** taste **4.** test **5.** demonstrate
problema *noun m.* problem
problemático, -ca *adj.* problematic
proceder *verb.* **1.** to proceed **2.** behave
—**proceder de** to come from
procedimiento *noun m.* procedure
procesado, -da *noun.* defendant
procesar *verb.* **1.** to process **2.** prosecute, try
procesión *noun f.* procession
proceso *noun m.* **1.** process **2.** prosecution, trial
proclamar *verb.* to proclaim
procurador, -dora *noun.* attorney
procurar *verb.* **1.** to try **2.** get
prodigar *verb.* to lavish
pródigo, -ga *adj.* **1.** lavish **2.** prodigal
producción *noun f.* production, output
producir *verb.* **1.** to produce, yield **2.** cause
productividad *noun f.* productivity
productivo, -va *adj.* productive
producto *noun m.* product
productor, -tora *noun.* producer
proeza *noun f.* feat
profesión *noun f.* profession
profesional *noun mf. adj.* professional
profesor, -sora *noun.* **1.** teacher **2.** professor
profundidad *noun f.* depth
profundizar *verb.* **1.** to deepen **2.** study in depth
profundo, -da *adj.* **1.** deep **2.** profound
programa *noun m.* program
—**programa de estudios** syllabus
programar *verb.* **1.** to program **2.** schedule
progresar *verb.* to progress
progresivo, -va *adj.* progressive
progreso *noun m.* progress
prohibición *noun f.* ban, prohibition
prohibido, -da *adj.* forbidden
prohibir *verb.* to ban, forbid, prohibit
proletariado *noun m.* working class
proletario, -ria *noun. adj.* proletarian
promedio *noun m.* average
promesa *noun f.* **1.** promise **2.** vow
prometedor, -dora *adj.* promising
prometer *verb.* to promise
prometido, -da *noun.* fiancé or fiancée
prometido, -da *adj.* engaged
prominencia *noun f.* prominence
prominente *adj.* prominent
promoción *noun f.* promotion
promotor, -tora *noun.* promoter
promover *verb.* **1.** to promote **2.** foster **3.** further
promulgar *verb.* to enact
pronombre *noun m.* pronoun
pronosticar *verb.* to forecast, predict
pronóstico *noun m.* **1.** forecast, prediction **2.** prognosis
pronto, -ta *adj.* **1.** quick **2.** ready
pronto *adv.* **1.** quickly **2.** soon
—**de pronto** suddenly
pronunciación *noun f.* pronunciation
pronunciado, -da *adj.* **1.** pronounced **2.** marked
pronunciar *verb.* **1.** to pronounce **2.** deliver
—**pronunciarse** to declare oneself
propaganda *noun f.* propaganda
propensión *noun f.* inclination
propenso, -sa *adj.* prone
propicio, -cia *adj.* favorable, propitious
propiedad *noun f.* **1.** property **2.** ownership
propietario, -ria *noun.* owner, proprietor
propina *noun f.* tip

propio, -pia *adj.* **1.** own **2.** typical **3.** self
proponer *verb.* to propose, suggest
—**proponerse** to intend
proporción *noun f.* **1.** proportion **2.** ratio
—**proporciones** size, proportions
proporcional *adj.* proportional
proporcionar *verb.* to provide, supply
proposición *noun f.* proposal, proposition
propósito *noun m.* purpose, intention, aim
—**a propósito** **1.** by the way **2.** on purpose, intentionally
propuesta *noun f.* proposal
prosa *noun f.* prose
proseguir *verb.* to continue, go on
prosperar *verb.* to prosper, thrive
prosperidad *noun f.* prosperity
próspero, -ra *adj.* prosperous, thriving
prostituto, -ta *noun.* prostitute
protagonista *noun mf.* protagonist, main character, hero or heroine
protección *noun f.* protection
protector, -tora *noun.* **1.** protector **2.** patron
protector, -tora *adj.* protective
proteger *verb.* **1.** to protect **2.** preserve
proteína *noun f.* protein
protesta *noun f.* protest
protestante *noun mf. adj.* Protestant
protestar *verb.* to protest
prototipo *noun m.* prototype
provecho *noun m.* gain, profit
proveer *verb.* to provide, supply
—**proveerse de** to supply oneself with
provenir de *verb.* to come from
provincia *noun f.* province
provincial *adj.* provincial
provisión *noun f.* provision
provisional *adj.* provisional
provocador, -dora *noun.* instigator
provocar *verb.* to provoke
proximidad *noun f.* proximity
próximo, -ma *adj.* **1.** next, forthcoming **2.** near
proyección *noun f.* projection
proyectar *verb.* **1.** to plan **2.** project **3.** screen
proyectil *noun m.* projectile
proyecto *noun m.* project, plan, scheme
prudencia *noun f.* prudence
prudente *adj.* prudent
prueba *noun f.* **1.** proof **2.** evidence **3.** event **4.** test, trial **5.** token
psicoanálisis *noun m.* psychoanalysis
psicoanalista *noun mf.* psychoanalyst
psicología *noun f.* psychology
psicológico, -ca *adj.* psychological
psicólogo, -ga *noun.* psychologist
psiquiatra *noun mf.* psychiatrist
psiquiátrico *noun m.* mental hospital
psiquiátrico, -ca *adj.* psychiatric
publicación *noun f.* publication
publicar *verb.* **1.** to publish **2.** reveal
publicidad *noun f.* publicity
público *noun m.* audience
público, -ca *adj.* public
puchero *noun m.* pot
pudín *noun m.* pudding
pudrirse *verb.* to rot
pueblo *noun m.* **1.** village, town **2.** people **3.** common people
puente *noun m.* bridge
puerco, -ca *noun.* pig, hog
puerco, -ca *adj.* filthy
puerta *noun f.* **1.** door **2.** gate
puerto *noun m.* **1.** port, harbor **2.** mountain pass
Puerto Rico *noun m.* Puerto Rico
puertorriqueño, -ña *noun. adj.* Puerto Rican
pues *conj.* since, because, as
pues *interj.* well, then
puesta *noun f.* setting
—**puesta de sol** sunset
puesto *noun m.* **1.** place **2.** position **3.** post **4.** booth, stall
—**puesto que** since
puja *noun f.* bidding
pujar *verb.* to bid
pulcro, -cra *adj.* neat
pulgada *noun f.* inch
pulgar *noun m.* thumb
pulir *verb.* to polish
pulmón *noun m.* lung
pulpa *noun f.* pulp, flesh
pulsar *verb.* **1.** to press **2.** beat
pulso *noun m.* pulse

punta *noun f.* **1.** point, head **2.** end, tip
puntada *noun f.* stitch
puntal *noun m.* prop
puntapié *noun m.* kick
puntería *noun f.* aim
puntiagudo, -da *adj.* pointed, sharp
punto *noun m.* **1.** point **2.** dot **3.** period **4.** stitch
—**dos puntos** colon
—**punto final** full stop
—**punto y coma** semicolon
puntual *adj.* prompt, punctual
punzada *noun f.* stitch
puñado *noun m.* handful
puñal *noun m.* dagger
puñetazo *noun m.* punch
puño *noun m.* **1.** fist **2.** cuff
pupila *noun f.* pupil (eye)
pupilo, -la *noun.* **1.** ward **2.** pupil, student
pupitre *noun m.* desk
pureza *noun f.* purity
puro, -ra *adj.* **1.** pure **2.** sheer, simple
púrpura *noun f.* purple

Q

que *conj.* **1.** that, than **2.** let
que *pron.* **1.** that **2.** who **3.** which **4.** whom
qué *adj.* what, which
qué *adv.* how, what
qué *pron.* what
quebradizo, -za *adj.* breakable
quebrantar *verb.* to break
quebrar *verb.* **1.** to break **2.** go bankrupt
quedar *verb.* **1.** to remain **2.** fit, suit **3.** be left **4.** suit
—**quedar en** to agree
—**quedarse 1.** to stay **2.** linger
queja *noun f.* **1.** complaint **2.** protest
quejarse *verb.* to complain
quemadura *noun f.* burn
quemar *verb.* to burn
querellante *noun mf.* plaintiff
querer *verb.* **1.** to want **2.** love **3.** like
—**querer decir** to mean
querido, -da *noun.* dear, honey
querido, -da *adj.* dear, beloved
queso *noun m.* cheese
quiebra *noun f.* **1.** bankruptcy **2.** break
quien *pron.* **1.** who, whom **2.** whoever, whomever
quién *pron.* who, whom
—**de quién** whose
quienquiera *pron.* whoever, whomever
quieto, -ta *adj.* **1.** still **2.** quiet
química *noun f.* chemistry
químico, -ca *noun.* chemist
químico, -ca *adj.* chemical
quince *noun m. adj.* fifteen
quincena *noun f.* fortnight
quincuagésimo, -ma *noun. adj.* fiftieth
quinta *noun f.* villa
quinto, -ta *noun. adj.* fifth
quirófano *noun m.* operating-room
quirúrgico, -ca *adj.* surgical
quitar *verb.* **1.** to remove **2.** take off **3.** clear **4.** rob
—**quitarse 1.** to leave **2.** take off
—**quitarse a alguien/algo de encima** to get rid of
quizá, quizás *adv.* maybe, perhaps

R

rabia *noun f.* rage
rabiar *verb.* to rage
rabo *noun m.* tail
racha *noun f.* **1.** run, streak **2.** gust
racial *adj.* racial
racimo *noun m.* bunch, cluster
ración *noun f.* helping, portion, serving
racional *adj.* rational
racionalidad *noun f.* rationality
racismo *noun m.* racism
racista *noun mf. adj.* racist
radar *noun m.* radar
radiación *noun f.* radiation
radiador *noun m.* radiator
radical *noun mf.* radical
radical *adj.* radical, drastic
radio *noun f.* radio
radio *noun m.* **1.** radium **2.** radius
radioactivo, -va *adj.* radioactive
radiografía *noun f.* X-ray
radionovela *noun f.* serial
ráfaga *noun f.* blast, gust
raíl *noun m.* rail
raíz *noun f.* root
raja *noun f.* crack, split
rajar *verb.* to crack, split
ralentizar *verb.* to slow
rallar *verb.* to grate
rally *noun m.* rally
ralo, -la *adj.* thin
rama *noun f.* branch
ramificarse *verb.* to branch
ramo *noun m.* **1.** branch **2.** division **3.** bunch
rampa *noun f.* ramp
rana *noun f.* frog
rango *noun m.* rank
ranura *noun f.* groove, slot
rapidez *noun f.* speed
rápido, -da *adj.* fast, quick, swift
rápido *adv.* quick
raptar *verb.* to kidnap
raqueta *noun f.* racket
raro, -ra *adj.* **1.** rare, uncommon, unusual, funny **2.** bizarre, weird **3.** odd
—**rara vez** seldom
rasar *verb.* to level
rascar *verb.* **1.** to scrape **2.** scratch
rasgadura *noun f.* tear, rip
rasgar *verb.* to tear, rip
rasgo *noun m.* trait
—**rasgos** features
rasgón *noun m.* tear, rip
rasguño *noun m.* scratch
raspadura *noun f.* scraping, scratching
raspar *verb.* to scrape
rastrear *verb.* to track
rastro *noun m.* **1.** trace **2.** track, trail
rata *noun f.* rat
ratificar *verb.* to ratify
rato *noun m.* while
ratón, -tona *noun.* mouse
raya *noun f.* **1.** stripe **2.** skate **3.** streak **4.** parting
rayar *verb.* **1.** to scratch **2.** streak
—**rayar en** to verge on, border on
rayo *noun m.* **1.** ray, beam **2.** bolt, lightning
raza *noun f.* **1.** race **2.** breed, strain
razón *noun f.* **1.** reason **2.** reasoning **3.** right
—**tener razón** to be right
razonable *adj.* reasonable
razonamiento *noun m.* reasoning
razonar *verb.* to reason
reacción *noun f.* reaction
reaccionar *verb.* to react, respond
reacio, -cia *adj.* reluctant
reactor *noun m.* **1.** reactor **2.** jet
real *adj.* **1.** teal **2.** true **3.** royal
realeza *noun f.* royalty
realidad *noun f.* reality, fact
realismo *noun m.* realism
realista *noun mf.* **1.** realist **2.** royalist
realista *adj.* **1.** realistic **2.** royalist
realizable *adj.* practicable
realización *noun f.* realization, fulfilment
realizado, -da *adj.* fulfilled
realizar *verb.* **1.** to execute, perform, carry out **2.** fulfill **3.** realize
—**realizarse** to come true
realmente *adv.* really

realzar *verb.* to enhance
reanimación *noun f.* revival
reanimar *verb.* to revive
—**reanimarse** to recover
reanudar *verb.* to resume
rebaja *noun f.* **1.** reduction **2.** discount
—**rebajas** sales
rebajar *verb.* to reduce, lower
—**rebajarse** to humble oneself
rebaño *noun m.* **1.** flock **2.** herd
rebelarse *verb.* to rebel
rebelde *noun mf.* rebel
rebelión *noun f.* rebellion
rebotar *verb.* to bounce
recado *noun m.* message
recalcar *verb.* to stress
recatado, -da *adj.* modest
recaudación *noun f.* collection
recaudar *verb.* to collect, levy
recepción *noun f.* reception
receptor, -tora *noun.* recipient
recesión *noun f.* **1.** recession **2.** slump
receta *noun f.* **1.** recipe **2.** prescription
recetar *verb.* to prescribe
rechazar *verb.* **1.** to reject, decline **2.** refuse
rechazo *noun m.* rejection, refusal
rechoncho, -cha *adj.* plump, chubby
recibir *verb.* **1.** to receive **2.** get **3.** welcome **4.** entertain
recibo *noun m.* receipt
reciclar *verb.* to recycle
recién *adv.* newly, recently
reciente *adj.* recent
recinto *noun m.* compound
recipiente *noun m.* **1.** container **2.** vessel
reclamación *noun f.* **1.** claim **2.** complaint
reclamar *verb.* **1.** to demand **2.** claim **3.** complain
recluir *verb.* to confine
recluso, -sa *noun.* convict, inmate, prisoner
recluta *noun mf.* recruit
reclutamiento *noun m.* draft, recruitment
reclutar *verb.* to draft, recruit
recobrar *verb.* to recover, regain, retrieve
recodo *noun m.* loop, turn
recoger *verb.* to collect, gather
recogida *noun f.* collection
recolectar *verb.* **1.** to collect, gather **2.** harvest
recomendación *noun f.* recommendation
recomendar *verb.* **1.** to recommend **2.** advocate
recompensa *noun f.* reward
recompensar *verb.* to reward
reconciliación *noun f.* reconciliation
reconciliarse *verb.* to reconcile
reconfortante *adj.* comforting
reconocer *verb.* **1.** to recognize **2.** acknowledge **3.** admit **4.** examine
reconocimiento *noun m.* **1.** recognition **2.** acknowledgment **3.** admission **4.** examination
reconstrucción *noun f.* reconstruction
recopilar *verb.* to compile, collect
récord *noun m.* record
recordar *verb.* **1.** to remember, recall **2.** remind
recordatorio *noun m.* reminder
recorrer *verb.* **1.** to travel through **2.** cover
recorrido *noun m.* **1.** journey **2.** route
recortar *verb.* **1.** to cut, reduce **2.** trim
recorte *noun m.* cut, reduction
recreación *noun f.* recreation
recreativo, -va *adj.* recreational
rectangular *adj.* rectangular
recto, -ta *adj.* **1.** straight **2.** upright
recto *adv.* straight
rector, -tora *noun.* rector
recubrir *verb.* to cover
recuento *noun m.* **1.** recount **2.** scrutiny
recuerdo *noun m.* **1.** memory **2.** souvenir
—**recuerdos** regards
recuperación *noun f.* **1.** recovery **2.** retrieval
recuperar *verb.* **1.** to recover **2.** retrieve
recurrencia *noun f.* recurrence
recurrente *adj.* recurrent
recurrir *verb.* to appeal
—**recurrir a 1.** to resort to **2.** appeal to, turn to
recurso *noun m.* **1.** appeal **2.** resort **3.** resource
—**recursos** means, resources
red *noun f.* **1.** net **2.** network

redacción *noun f.* **1.** writing, composition **2.** editorial board
redactar *verb.* **1.** to write **2.** edit
redactor, -tora *noun.* editor
redada *noun f.* haul
redención *noun f.* redemption
redil *noun m.* fold
redondo, -da *adj.* **1.** round **2.** great, excellent
reducción *noun f.* reduction
reducir *verb.* **1.** to reduce, cut **2.** decrease **3.** subdue
reelegir *verb.* to re-elect
reembolsar *verb.* to refund
reembolso *noun m.* refund
reemplazar *verb.* to replace
reestreno *noun m.* revival
referencia *noun f.* reference
referéndum *noun m.* referendum
referente (a) *prep.* concerning
referir *verb.* **1.** to refer **2.** tell, relate
—**referirse a** to refer to
refinado, -da *adj.* refined
reflector *adj.* reflecting
reflejar *verb.* to reflect
reflejo *noun m.* reflection
reflexión *noun f.* reflection, thought
reflexionar *verb.* to reflect, think
reforma *noun f.* reform
reformador, -dora *noun.* reformer
reformar *verb.* **1.** to reform **2.** renovate, repair
—**reformarse** to mend one's ways
reforzar *verb.* to reinforce, bolster
refrenado, -da *adj.* restrained
refrenar *verb.* to restrain, curb
refrendar *verb.* to endorse
refrescante *adj.* refreshing
refrescar *verb.* to refresh
refresco *noun m.* **1.** refreshment **2.** soft drink
refuerzo *noun m.* **1.** reinforcement **2.** brace
refugiado, -da *noun.* refugee
refugiar *verb.* to shelter
—**refugiarse** to take refuge
refugio *noun m.* haven, refuge, shelter
refutar *verb.* to refute
regalar *verb.* to present, give
regalo *noun m.* **1.** gift, present **2.** comfort
regar *verb.* to water
regatear *verb.* bargain
regazo *noun m.* lap
régimen *noun m.* **1.** regime **2.** diet
regimiento *noun m.* regiment
región *noun f.* region
regional *adj.* regional
regir *verb.* **1.** to rule **2.** govern **3.** be in force
registrador, -dora *noun.* registrar
registrar *verb.* **1.** to register **2.** record **3.** search
—**registrarse** **1.** to register **2.** happen
registro *noun m.* **1.** register **2.** registry **3.** record **4.** search
regla *noun f.* **1.** regulation, rule **2.** ruler **3.** menstruation
reglamentar *verb.* to regulate
reglamento *noun m.* rule, regulation, ordinance
regordete, -ta *adj.* plump, chubby
regresar *verb.* to return
regreso *noun m.* return
reguero *noun m.* trail
regulación *noun f.* regulation
regulador *noun m.* regulator
regular *adj.* **1.** regular **2.** fair
regular *verb.* to regulate
rehabilitación *noun f.* rehabilitation
rehabilitar *verb.* to rehabilitate
rehén *noun mf.* hostage
rehusar *verb.* to decline, refuse
reina *noun f.* queen
reinado *noun m.* reign
reinar *verb.* **1.** to reign **2.** prevail
reino *noun m.* kingdom, realm
reír *verb.* to laugh
reivindicación *noun f.* **1.** vindication **2.** claim
reivindicar *verb.* **1.** to vindicate **2.** claim
reja *noun f.* **1.** bar **2.** grating
rejilla *noun f.* grid, grating
relación *noun f.* **1.** relation **2.** relationship **3.** account **4.** connection **5.** liaison
—**relaciones públicas** public relations
—**relación sexual** sexual intercourse
relacionar *verb.* to relate
—**relacionarse** to interact, socialize

relajación *noun f.* relaxation
relajado, -da *adj.* relaxed, quiet
relajar *verb.* to relax
relámpago *noun m.* lightning
relatar *verb.* to relate, report
relativo, -va *adj.* **1.** relative **2.** comparative
relato *noun m.* **1.** account **2.** narration, story, tale
relegación *noun f.* relegation
relegar *verb.* to relegate
relevancia *noun f.* relevance
relevante *adj.* relevant
relevar *verb.* to relieve
relevo *noun m.* **1.** relief **2.** relay
relieve *noun m.* **1.** relief **2.** prominence
religión *noun f.* religion
religioso, -sa *adj.* religious
rellano *noun m.* landing
rellenar *verb.* **1.** to fill **2.** stuff
relleno *noun m.* filling, stuffing
reloj *noun m.* **1.** clock **2.** watch
reluciente *adj.* **1.** glittering, shining **2.** shiny
relucir *verb.* to glitter, gleam, shine
—**sacar a relucir** to bring up
reluctante *adj.* unwilling
remar *verb.* to row
rematar *verb.* **1.** to finish off **2.** end, finish **3.** shoot
remediar *verb.* to remedy
remedio *noun m.* **1.** remedy, cure **2.** option
remendar *verb.* to patch
remiendo *noun m.* patch
remitir *verb.* **1.** to dispatch, send **2.** refer
remojar *verb.* to soak
remolcador *noun m.* tug
remolcar *verb.* to tow
remolque *noun m.* **1.** tow **2.** trailer
remontar *verb.* to soar
—**remontarse a** to date from
remordimiento *noun m.* remorse
remoto, -ta *adj.* remote
remover *verb.* **1.** to stir **2.** remove
remuneración *noun f.* pay, remuneration
remunerar *verb.* to pay, remunerate
renacimiento *noun m.* **1.** Renaissance **2.** revival
rendición *noun f.* surrender, fall
rendija *noun f.* crack
rendimiento *noun m.* **1.** yield **2.** efficiency
rendir *verb.* **1.** to yield **2.** render **3.** cause to surrender **4.** tire
—**rendirse** to surrender
renovación *noun f.* **1.** renewal **2.** renovation
renovar *verb.* **1.** to renew **2.** renovate
rentable *adj.* profitable
renuencia *noun f.* reluctance
renuente *adj.* reluctant
renuncia *noun f.* **1.** renunciation **2.** resignation
renunciar *verb.* **1.** to renounce **2.** resign
reñir *verb.* to quarrel
reorganización *noun f.* reorganization
reorganizar *verb.* to reorganize
reparación *noun f.* **1.** repair **2.** reparation
reparar *verb.* to repair, fix
—**reparar en** to notice
repartidor, -dora *noun.* distributor
repartir *verb.* **1.** to deliver **2.** distribute **3.** divide, share **4.** deal
reparto *noun m.* **1.** delivery **2.** distribution **3.** deal **4.** cast
repentino, -na *adj.* sudden
repertorio *noun m.* repertory
repetición *noun f.* **1.** repeat **2.** repetition
repetidamente *adv.* repeatedly
repetido, -da *adj.* repeated
repetir *verb.* to repeat
réplica *noun f.* **1.** retort, reply **2.** replica
replicar *verb.* to retort, reply
repollo *noun m.* cabbage
reportaje *noun m.* report
reportar *verb.* **1.** to yield, bring **2.** report **3.** restrain
—**reportarse** to control oneself
reportero, -ra *noun.* reporter
reposar *verb.* **1.** to rest **2.** lie
reposo *noun m.* rest
representación *noun f.* **1.** performance **2.** representation
—**en representación de** on behalf of
representante *noun mf.* representative

representar *verb.* **1.** to represent **2.** perform **3.** portray
—**representarse** to imagine, picture oneself
representativo, -va *adj.* representative
represión *noun f.* repression
reprimir *verb.* **1.** to repress **2.** suppress
reprochar *verb.* to reproach, blame
reproducción *noun f.* reproduction
reproducir *verb.* to reproduce
—**reproducirse** to breed, reproduce
reproductor, -tora *adj.* reproductive
reptar *verb.* to crawl, creep
república *noun f.* republic
republicano, -na *noun. adj.* republican
repugnancia *noun f.* repugnance, disgust
repugnante *adj.* repugnant, disgusting
repugnar *verb.* to disgust, hate
reputación *noun f.* reputation, name
resaltar *verb.* **1.** to stand out **2.** stress
resbalar *verb.* to slip
resbalón *noun m.* slip
rescatar *verb.* to rescue, save
rescate *noun m.* **1.** rescue **2.** ransom
resentimiento *noun m.* resentment
resentirse *verb.* **1.** to suffer **2.** be hurt
reserva *noun f.* **1.** reservation **2.** booking **3.** confidentiality **4.** reserve
reservado, -da *adj.* reserved
reservar *verb.* **1.** to reserve **2.** book
resfriado *noun m.* cold
resguardar *verb.* to protect
resguardo *noun m.* receipt, voucher
residencia *noun f.* **1.** residence **2.** boarding house
residencial *adj.* residential
residente *adj.* resident
residir *verb.* **1.** to live, reside **2.** lie
residual *adj.* residual
residuo *noun m.* residue
—**residuos** waste
resignación *noun f.* resignation
resignar *verb.* to resign
—**resignarse a** to reconcile oneself to
resistencia *noun f.* resistance
resistente *adj.* **1.** resistant **2.** tough
resistir *verb.* **1.** to resist **2.** endure **3.** hold
resolución *noun f.* **1.** resolution **2.** resolve **3.** decision
resolver *verb.* **1.** to solve **2.** resolve **3.** decision
resonar *verb.* to resound, echo, ring
respaldar *verb.* to back, support
respectivamente *adv.* respectively
respectivo, -va *adj.* respective
respecto *prep.* regard, reference
—**con respecto a** regarding, in regard to
respetable *adj.* respectable
respetar *verb.* to respect, observe
respeto *noun m.* respect
respiración *noun f.* breath
respirar *verb.* to breathe
respiratorio, -ria *adj.* respiratory
resplandecer *verb.* to shine, glow
resplandeciente *adj.* shining, glowing
resplandor *noun m.* blaze, glitter, radiance
responder *verb.* to answer, reply, respond
responsabilidad *noun f.* responsibility
responsable *adj.* responsible
respuesta *noun f.* answer, reply, response
resquebrajarse *verb.* to crack, split
resquicio *noun m.* **1.** crack, slit **2.** chance
resta *noun f.* subtraction
restablecer *verb.* to restore, reestablish
—**restablecerse** to recover
restablecimiento *noun m.* **1.** reestablishment **2.** recovery
restar *verb.* **1.** to deduct **2.** remain
—**restar importancia** to minimize, play down
restauración *noun f.* **1.** restoration **2.** catering
restaurante *noun m.* restaurant
restaurar *verb.* to restore
resto *noun m.* remainder
—**restos** remains, leftovers
restregar *verb.* **1.** to rub **2.** scrub
restricción *noun f.* restriction
restrictivo, -va *adj.* restrictive
restringido, -da *adj.* limited, restricted
restringir *verb.* to limit, restrict

resucitar *verb.* **1.** to resuscitate **2.** raise
resuelto, -ta *adj.* **1.** determined, resolved **2.** solved
resultado *noun m.* **1.** outcome, result **2.** score
resultar *verb.* **1.** to result **2.** prove **3.** work
resumen *noun m.* summary
resumir *verb.* to summarize
resurgimiento *noun m.* revival
resurgir *verb.* to revive
resurrección *noun f.* resurrection
retar *verb.* to challenge
retazo *noun m.* **1.** scrap **2.** excerpt, fragment
retención *noun f.* retention
retener *verb.* **1.** to retain, keep **2.** detain **3.** hold
retirada *noun f.* **1.** retreat **2.** withdrawal
retirar *verb.* **1.** to take away, remove **2.** withdraw
—retirarse 1. to retreat **2.** retire
retiro *noun m.* **1.** retreat **2.** retirement
reto *noun m.* challenge, dare
retoño *noun m.* shoot
retoque *noun m.* finishing touch
retorcer *verb.* to twist
retornar *verb.* to return
retorno *noun m.* return, comeback
retraído, -da *adj.* retiring
retransmisión *noun f.* broadcast
retransmitir *verb.* to broadcast
retrasado, -da *adj.* **1.** retarded **2.** backward **3.** behind
retrasar *verb.* **1.** to delay **2.** postpone
—retrasarse 1. be late **2.** lag
retraso *noun m.* **1.** delay **2.** lag
retratar *verb.* **1.** to portray **2.** photograph **3.** depict
retrato *noun m.* **1.** portrait **2.** photograph **3.** depiction
retribuir *verb.* to pay
retroceder *verb.* **1.** to move back **2.** shrink
retumbar *verb.* **1.** to resound **2.** roar **3.** roll
retumbo *noun m.* **1.** reverberation **2.** roll **3.** roar
reunión *noun f.* meeting, gathering, rally, reunion
reunir *verb.* **1.** to gather, collect **2.** raise **3.** join **4.** unite **5.** have
—reunirse to meet
revelación *noun f.* revelation
revelador, -dora *adj.* revealing
revelar *verb.* **1.** to reveal, disclose, unfold **2.** develop
reventar *verb.* to burst
reventón *noun m.* burst
reverencia *noun f.* bow, curtsy
reverendo, -da *noun. adj.* reverend
reverso *noun m.* **1.** back **2.** reverse
revés *noun m.* **1.** back **2.** reversal **3.** backhand
—al revés the other way, inside out, upside down
revestimiento *noun m.* covering, lining
revestir *verb.* **1.** to cover, line **2.** to take on
revisar *verb.* **1.** to check, inspect **2.** revise
revisión *noun f.* **1.** check, inspection **2.** revision
revista *noun f.* journal, magazine
revocar *verb.* to revoke
revolución *noun f.* revolution
revolucionario, -ria *noun. adj.* revolutionary
revolver *verb.* **1.** to stir **2.** turn upside down
revuelta *noun f.* revolt
rey *noun m.* king
rezar *verb.* to pray
rezo *noun m.* prayer
riachuelo *noun m.* brook, stream
ribera *noun f.* bank
ribetear *verb.* to edge
rico, -ca *adj.* **1.** rich **2.** wealthy **3.** delicious
ridículo, -la *adj.* ridiculous
rienda *noun f.* rein
riesgo *noun m.* risk
rifa *noun f.* raffle
rifar *verb.* to raffle
rifle *noun m.* rifle
rígido, -da *adj.* rigid, stiff
riguroso, -sa *adj.* rigorous, strict
rincón *noun m.* corner
ring *noun m.* ring
riña *noun f.* quarrel

riñón *noun m.* kidney
río *noun m.* river
riqueza *noun f.* wealth
risa *noun f.* laugh, laughter
risueño, -ña *adj.* cheerful
rítmico, -ca *adj.* rhythmic, rhythmical
ritmo *noun m.* **1.** rhythm **2.** pace
rito *noun m.* rite
ritual *noun. adj.* ritual
rival *noun. adj.* rival
rivalidad *noun f.* rivalry
rivalizar *verb.* to compete, rival
rizado, -da *adj.* curly
rizar *verb.* to curl
rizo *noun m.* curl
róbalo *noun m.* bass
robar *verb.* **1.** to rob, steal **2.** abduct
roble *noun m.* oak
robo *noun m.* burglary, robbery, theft
robusto, -ta *adj.* robust, stout, sturdy
roca *noun f.* rock
roce *noun m.* **1.** brush, graze **2.** friction
rock *noun m.* rock
rocoso, -sa *adj.* rocky
rodar *verb.* **1.** to roll **2.** film, shoot
rodear *verb.* **1.** to go around **2.** surround, encircle
rodilla *noun f.* knee
rodillo *noun m.* roller
rogar *verb.* **1.** to beg **2.** pray
rojo *noun m.* red
rojo, -ja *adj.* red
rollo *noun m.* **1.** roll **2.** bore
romance *noun m.* romance
romano, -na *noun. adj.* Roman
romántico, -ca *adj.* romantic
rompecabezas *noun m.* puzzle
romper *verb.* **1.** to break **2.** smash, shatter **3.** rip, tear
—**romper a** to begin to
ronda *noun f.* **1.** round **2.** beat, patrol
rondar *verb.* **1.** to patrol, police **2.** haunt **3.** be approximately
ronzar *verb.* to crunch
ropa *noun f.* clothing, clothes
—**ropa blanca** linen
—**ropa sucia** laundry
ropero *noun m.* wardrobe
rosa *noun f.* **1.** rose **2.** pink
rosa *adj.* pink
rosado, -da *adj.* pink
rosca *noun f.* thread
rostro *noun m.* face
rotación *noun f.* rotation
rotar *verb.* **1.** to rotate **2.** spin
roto, -ta *adj.* **1.** broken **2.** ripped, torn
rotulador *noun m.* marker
rotura *noun f.* break, tear
rozar *verb.* **1.** to graze **2.** scrape **3.** touch
rubio, -bia *adj.* blond
rublo *noun m.* ruble
rubor *noun m.* flush, blush
ruborizarse *verb.* to blush
rudimentario, -ria *adj.* rudimentary
rudimentos *noun m. plural.* basics
rudo, -da *adj.* rough
rueda *noun f.* wheel
rugby *noun m.* rugby
rugido *noun m.* roar
rugir *verb.* to roar
ruido *noun m.* noise, sound
ruidoso, -sa *adj.* noisy
ruina *noun f.* **1.** ruin **2.** downfall, collapse
rulo *noun m.* roller
Rumania *noun f.* Romania
rumano, -na *noun. adj.* Romanian
rumbo *noun m.* course, direction, route
rumor *noun m.* rumor
rural *adj.* rural
Rusia *noun f.* Russia
ruso, -sa *noun. adj.* Russian
ruta *noun f.* route
rutina *noun f.* routine
rutinario, -ria *adj.* routine

S

sábado *noun m.* Saturday
sábana *noun f.* sheet
saber *noun m.* knowledge
saber *verb.* **1.** to know **2.** can **3.** learn
—**a saber** namely
—**saber a** to taste like
sabiduría *noun f.* wisdom
sabio, -bia *noun.* wise person, learned person
sabio, -bia *adj.* wise, learned
sabor *noun m.* flavor, taste
saborear *verb.* **1.** to taste, savor **2.** relish
sacar *verb.* **1.** to take out **2.** get, obtain **3.** get out **4.** produce, invent **5.** introduce **6.** take (a photo) **7.** release (a book, a disc, a film) **8.** make (a copy) **9.** stick out (one's tongue)
sacerdocio *noun m.* priesthood
sacerdote, -tisa *noun.* priest or priestess
saco *noun m.* **1.** sack **2.** coat
sacrificar *verb.* to sacrifice
sacrificio *noun m.* sacrifice
sacudida *noun f.* **1.** shaking **2.** jerk
sacudir *verb.* **1.** to shake **2.** jerk
—**sacudirse** to shake off
safari *noun m.* safari
sagrado, -da *adj.* sacred, holy
sainete *noun m.* comedy sketch
sal *noun f.* salt
sala *noun f.* **1.** hall, room **2.** living room
salado, -da *adj.* salty
salar *verb.* to salt
salario *noun m.* salary, wage
salchicha *noun f.* sausage
saldar *verb.* to settle
saldo *noun m.* balance
salida *noun f.* **1.** exit **2.** departure **3.** way out **4.** witty remark
—**salida del sol** sunrise
saliente *adj.* **1.** outgoing **2.** salient, prominent
salir *verb.* **1.** to go out, get out **2.** depart, leave **3.** come out, appear **4.** turn out **5**. become, be elected
—**salir a** to resemble
saliva *noun f.* saliva
salmón *noun m.* salmon
salón *noun m.* **1.** lounge **2.** parlor, sitting-room **3.** salon
salpicadura *noun f.* splash
salpicar *verb.* to splash
salsa *noun f.* **1.** sauce **2.** salsa
saltar *verb.* **1.** to jump, leap **2.** burst, explode **3.** pop out
—**saltarse** to skip
salto *noun m.* **1.** jump, leap, skip **2.** gap **3.** dive
salud *noun f.* health
saludable *adj.* healthy
saludar *verb.* **1.** to greet **2.** salute
saludo *noun m.* **1.** greeting **2.** salute
—**saludos** regards
salvación *noun f.* salvation
salvaguardar *verb.* to safeguard
salvaguardia *noun f.* safeguard
salvaje *noun mf.* savage
salvaje *adj.* **1.** savage **2.** wild
salvar *verb.* **1.** to save **2.** overcome **3.** cover
—**salvarse** **1.** to escape **2.** save one's soul
salve *interj.* hail!
salvedad *noun f.* qualification, reservation
salvo, -va *adj.* safe
salvo *prep.* except, save
—**salvo que** unless
sanción *noun f.* sanction
sancionar *verb.* to sanction
sándwich *noun m.* sandwich
sangrar *verb.* to bleed
sangre *noun f.* blood
sangría *noun f.* **1.** drain **2.** sangria
sangriento, -ta *adj.* bloody
sano, -na *adj.* **1.** healthy **2.** unhurt, unharmed
santo, -ta *noun.* saint
santo, -ta *adj.* **1.** holy **2.** saint
santuario *noun m.* sanctuary, shrine
saque *noun m.* service
saquear *verb.* to sack, loot
sarcástico, -ca *adj.* sarcastic

sargento *noun mf.* sergeant
sarpullido *noun m.* rash
sarta *noun f.* string
sartén *noun f.* frying pan
sastre, -tra *noun.* tailor
satélite *noun m.* satellite
satisfacción *noun f.* satisfaction
satisfacer *verb.* **1.** to satisfy **2.** fulfill, meet **3.** settle
satisfactorio, -ria *adj.* **1.** satisfactory **2.** satisfying
satisfecho, -cha *adj.* content, pleased, satisfied
sazonar *verb.* to season, spice
se *pron.* **1.** to him, to her, to you, to them **2.** himself, herself, itself, yourself, yourselves, themselves **3.** each other
secar *verb.* to dry
sección *noun f.* **1.** department **2.** section
seco, -ca *adj.* **1.** dry **2.** dried **3.** sharp **4.** barren, arid **5.** curt, brusque
secreción *noun f.* secretion
secretario, -ria *noun.* secretary
secreto *noun m.* **1.** secret **2.** secrecy
secreto, -ta *adj.* secret
sector *noun m.* sector
secuela *noun f.* sequel
—**secuelas** aftermath
secuencia *noun f.* sequence
secuestrar *verb.* **1.** to kidnap **2.** hijack
secular *adj.* secular
secundar *verb.* to second, support
secundario, -ria *adj.* secondary
sed *noun f.* thirst
—**tener sed** to be thirsty
seda *noun f.* silk
sedal *noun m.* fishing line
sede *noun f.* **1.** seat **2.** see
—**sede central** headquarters
sedimento *noun m.* sediment
seducir *verb.* to seduce
seglar *adj.* secular
segmento *noun m.* segment
seguido, -da *adj.* **1.** consecutive **2.** straight
—**en seguida** immediately
seguido *adv.* straight
seguidor, -dora *noun.* follower
seguimiento *noun m.* follow-up
seguir *verb.* **1.** to follow **2.** keep on **3.** pursue **4.** remain
según *verb.* **1.** according to **2.** depending on
segundo *noun m.* second
segundo, -da *noun. adj.* second
seguramente *adv.* **1.** probably **2.** surely
seguridad *noun f.* **1.** security **2.** assurance, certainty **3.** confidence
seguro *noun m.* **1.** insurance **2.** fastener, clasp
seguro, -ra *adj.* **1.** safe, secure **2.** sure **3.** reliable **4.** self-assured, confident **5.** firm, fixed
seguro *adv.* certainly
seis *noun m. adj.* six
selección *noun f.* selection
seleccionar *verb.* to select
selectivo, -va *adj.* selective
selecto, -ta *adj.* **1.** exclusive **2.** select
sellar *verb.* **1.** to seal **2.** stamp
sello *noun m.* **1.** seal **2.** stamp
selva *noun f.* **1.** jungle **2.** forest
semana *noun f.* week
semanal *adj.* weekly
semanalmente *adv.* weekly
semanario *noun m.* weekly
sembrar *verb.* to sow, plant
semejante *adj.* **1.** similar **2.** such
semejanza *noun f.* resemblance, similarity
semestre *noun m.* semester
semifinal *noun f.* semi-final
semilla *noun f.* seed
senado *noun m.* senate
senador, -dora *noun.* senator
sencillez *noun f.* simplicity
sencillo, -lla *adj.* **1.** simple, easy **2.** plain **3.** single **4.** straightforward
senda *noun f.* path
sendero *noun m.* path
sendos, -das *adj.* each
seno *noun m.* breast
sensación *noun f.* **1.** feeling **2.** sensation
sensatez *noun f.* good sense
sensato, -ta *adj.* reasonable, sensible, sound, wise
sensibilidad *noun f.* **1.** feeling **2.** sensitivity

sensible *adj.* sensitive
sentar *verb.* **1.** to sit, seat **2.** set, establish
—**sentar bien 1.** to suit **2.** agree with
—**sentarse** to sit down
sentencia *noun f.* sentence
sentenciar *verb.* to sentence
sentido *noun m.* **1.** sense **2.** meaning **3.** direction, way **4.** consciousness
sentimental *adj.* sentimental
sentimiento *noun m.* **1.** sentiment, emotion, feeling **2.** sorrow, grief
sentir *verb.* **1.** to feel **2.** feel sorry, regret **3.** sense
—**sentirse** to feel
seña *noun f.* sign
—**señas** domicile, address
señal *noun f.* **1.** signal **2.** sign **3.** deposit **4.** mark **5.** token
señalar *verb.* **1.** to indicate, show **2.** mark **3.** point out
señor *noun m.* **1.** gentleman **2.** sir **3.** owner, master **4.** mister **5.** lord
señora *noun f.* **1.** lady **2.** madam **3.** mistress **4.** wife
señoría *noun f.* lordship
señorita *noun f.* **1.** young woman **2.** Miss
separación *noun f.* **1.** separation **2.** division **3.** gap
separado, -da *adj.* separate
separar *verb.* **1.** to separate **2.** divide
—**separarse** to divorce
separatista *noun mf.* separatist
septiembre *noun m.* September
séptimo, -ma *noun. adj.* seventh
septuagésimo, -ma *noun. adj.* seventieth
sequía *noun f.* drought
ser *noun m.* being
ser *verb.* to be
—**ser de** to belong to
seriado, -da *adj.* serial
serie *noun f.* **1.** series **2.** serial
seriedad *noun f.* seriousness
serio, -ria *adj.* **1.** serious, earnest **2.** important
sermón *noun m.* **1.** sermon **2.** lecture
sermonear *verb.* to lecture
serpentear *verb.* to twist, wind
serpiente *noun f.* snake
serrar *verb.* to saw
servicial *adj.* helpful
servicio *noun m.* **1.** service **2.** serve
—**servicios** restroom, toilet
servir *verb.* **1.** to serve **2.** be of use **3.** work
—**servirse** to help oneself
—**servirse de** to make use of
sesenta *noun m. adj.* sixty
sesión *noun f.* session
set *noun m.* set
seta *noun f.* mushroom
setenta *noun m. adj.* seventy
seto *noun m.* **1.** fence **2.** hedge
severidad *noun f.* severity
severo, -ra *adj.* **1.** severe **2.** strict
sexagésimo, -ma *noun. adj.* sixtieth
sexo *noun m.* sex
sexto, -ta *noun. adj.* sixth
sexual *adj.* sexual
shock *noun m.* shock
si *conj.* **1.** if **2.** whether
—**si bien** although
—**si no** otherwise
sí *interj.* yes
sida *noun m.* AIDS
sidra *noun f.* cider
siempre *adv.* always
—**para siempre** forever
—**siempre que 1.** whenever, every time **2.** provided that
sien *noun f.* temple
sierra *noun f.* **1.** mountain range **2.** saw
siete *noun m. adj.* seven
siglo *noun m.* **1.** century **2.** age
significado *noun m.* **1.** meaning, sense **2.** significance, importance
significar *verb.* to mean
significativo, -va *adj.* significant
signo *noun m.* **1.** sign **2.** mark
siguiente *adj.* following, next
sílaba *noun f.* syllable
silbar *verb.* to whistle
silbato *noun m.* whistle
silbido *noun m.* whistle, whistling
silenciar *verb.* to silence
silencio *noun m.* silence
silencioso, -sa *adj.* quiet, silent
silla *noun f.* chair

—**silla de montar** saddle
—**silla de ruedas** wheelchair
sillón *noun m.* armchair
silvicultura *noun f.* forestry
simbólico, -ca *adj.* symbolic
símbolo *noun m.* symbol
simetría *noun f.* symmetry
simétrico, -ca *adj.* symmetrical, symmetric
similar *adj.* similar
similitud *noun f.* similarity
simpático, -ca *adj.* nice, friendly
simple *adj.* **1.** mere **2.** simple
simplificar *verb.* to simplify
simulación *noun f.* simulation
simular *verb.* to feign, pretend
simultáneo, -nea *adj.* simultaneous
sin *prep.* without
—**sin embargo** nevertheless, however
sinceridad *noun f.* sincerity
sincero, -ra *adj.* sincere
sindicato *noun m.* union, trade union
sinfonía *noun f.* symphony
singular *noun m.* singular
siniestro, -tra *adj.* **1.** sinister **2.** left
sino *noun m.* fate, destiny
sino *conj.* **1.** but **2.** except
sintaxis *noun f.* syntax
síntesis *noun f.* synthesis
sintético, -ca *adj.* synthetic
síntoma *noun m.* symptom
sintonizar *verb.* to tune in
Siria *noun f.* Syria
sirio, -ria *noun. adj.* Syrian
sirviente, -ta *noun.* **1.** servant **2.** maid (f.)
sistema *noun m.* system
sistemático, -ca *adj.* systematic
sitiar *verb.* to besiege
sitio *noun m.* **1.** place **2.** site, spot **3.** room, space **4.** siege
situación *noun f.* situation
situado, -da *adj.* situated, placed
situar *verb.* to situate, locate, place
soberano, -na *noun. adj.* sovereign
soberbia *noun f.* **1.** pride **2.** magnificence
soberbio, -bia *adj.* **1.** proud **2.** superb, magnificent
sobornar *verb.* to bribe
soborno *noun m.* **1.** bribe **2.** bribery
sobra *noun f.* excess, surplus
—**de sobra 1.** in excess **2.** extra
—**sobras** scraps, leftovers
sobre *noun m.* **1.** envelope **2.** packet
sobre *prep.* **1.** on, upon, on top of **2.** over **3.** about
—**sobre todo 1.** especially **2.** above all
sobrepasar *verb.* to surpass, exceed
sobresaliente *adj.* **1.** projecting, protruding **2.** outstanding
sobresalir *verb.* **1.** to project, protrude **2.** stand out
sobresaltar *verb.* to frighten
sobrevivir *verb.* to survive
sobrino, -na *noun.* nephew/niece
sobrio, -bria *adj.* sober
sociable *adj.* sociable
social *adj.* social
socialismo *noun m.* socialism
socialista *noun mf. adj.* socialist
sociedad *noun f.* **1.** society **2.** company
—**sociedad anónima** incorporated company
socio, -cia *noun.* **1.** member **2.** partner
socorrer *verb.* to aid, assist
socorro *noun m.* aid, help
sodio *noun m.* sodium
sofá *noun m.* couch, sofa
sofisticación *noun f.* sophistication
sofisticado, -da *adj.* sophisticated
software *noun m.* software
sol *noun m.* sun
solamente *adv.* just, only
solapa *noun f.* **1.** flap **2.** lapel
solaparse *verb.* to overlap
solar *noun m.* lot, plot
solar *adj.* solar
soldado *noun mf.* soldier
—**soldado raso** private
soleado, -da *adj.* sunny
soledad *noun f.* loneliness
solemne *adj.* solemn
soicitante *noun mf.* applicant
solicitar *verb.* **1.** to apply for **2.** request
solicitud *noun f.* **1.** application **2.** request
solidaridad *noun f.* solidarity

sólido *noun m.* solid
sólido, -da *adj.* **1.** solid **2.** firm **3.** sound
solitario *noun m.* solitaire
solitario, -ria *noun.* loner
solitario, -ria *adj.* **1.** lone **2.** lonely **3.** deserted
solo, -la *adj.* **1.** alone **2.** only, unique, sole, single
sólo *adv.* **1.** just, only **2.** solely
soltar *verb.* **1.** to release **2.** loosen
soltero, -ra *noun.* bachelor, single man or woman
soltero, -ra *adj.* single
soltura *noun f.* **1.** ease **2.** looseness **3.** fluency
solución *noun f.* **1.** solution **2.** answer
solucionar *verb.* to solve
solvente *adj.* **1.** solvent **2.** reliable
sombra *noun f.* **1.** shade **2.** shadow
sombrear *verb.* to shade
sombrero *noun m.* hat
sombrío, -bría *adj.* somber, gloomy
someter *verb.* **1.** to subjugate **2.** subject
—**someterse** to submit
—**someterse a** to undergo
sonajero *noun m.* rattle
sonar *verb.* **1.** to sound **2.** ring
sondeo *noun m.* survey, poll
sonido *noun m.* sound
sonoro, -ra *adj.* **1.** loud **2.** voiced
sonreír *verb.* to smile
sonriente *adj.* smiling
sonrisa *noun f.* smile
sonrojarse *verb.* to blush, flush
soñar *verb.* to dream
sopa *noun f.* soup
soplar *verb.* to blow
soplón, -plona *noun.* sneak
soportar *verb.* **1.** to bear, endure **2.** carry **3.** support
soporte *noun m.* bracket, support
sorber *verb.* to sip
sorbo *noun m.* sip
sordo, -da *adj.* deaf
sorprendente *adj.* surprising
sorprender *verb.* to surprise
sorpresa *noun f.* surprise
sorteo *noun m.* drawing
sosegado, -da *adj.* calm
sosiego *noun m.* calm
soso, -sa *adj.* **1.** flavorless, saltless **2.** dull
sospecha *noun f.* suspicion
sospechar *verb.* to suspect
sospechoso, -sa *noun.* suspect
sospechoso, -sa *adj.* suspect, suspicious
sostener *verb.* **1.** to support **2.** hold **3.** defend, uphold **4.** maintain, sustain
—**sostenerse** to stand
sostenido, -da *adj.* **1.** sustained **2.** sharp
sótano *noun m.* basement
sotavento *noun m.* lee
soviético, -ca *adj.* soviet
su *adj.* **1.** his, her, its, their **2.** your
suave *adj.* **1.** soft **2.** smooth **3.** delicate **4.** gentle, mild
suavizar *verb.* to soften
subasta *noun f.* auction
subastar *verb.* to auction
súbdito, -ta *noun.* subject
subestimar *verb.* to underestimate
subida *noun f.* **1.** rise **2.** ascent, climb
subir *verb.* **1.** to increase, rise **2.** raise **3.** climb
—**subir a** to get on
súbitamente *adv.* suddenly
súbito, -ta *adj.* sudden
subjetivo, -va *adj.* subjective
sublevación *noun f.* uprising
submarino *noun m.* submarine
submarino, -na *adj.* submarine
subordinado, -da *noun. adj.* subordinate
subrayar *verb.* **1.** to underline **2.** emphasize, stress
subsidio *noun m.* subsidy
subsiguiente *adj.* subsequent
subsistir *verb.* **1.** to subsist **2.** endure, last
subterráneo, -nea *adj.* underground
subvención *noun f.* grant, subsidy
subvencionar *verb.* to subsidize
subyugar *verb.* to subjugate
suceder *verb.* **1.** to happen, occur **2.** succeed, follow, come after
sucesión *noun f.* **1.** succession **2.** sequence

sucesivo, -va *adj.* successive
suceso *noun m.* **1.** event, occurrence **2.** incident
sucesor, -sora *noun.* successor
suciedad *noun f.* dirt
sucio, -cia *adj.* dirty, filthy, messy
sucumbir *verb.* to succumb
sucursal *noun f.* branch
sudar *verb.* to sweat
sudor *noun m.* sweat
Suecia *noun f.* Sweden
sueco, -ca *noun. adj.* Swedish
suela *noun f.* sole
sueldo *noun m.* salary, wage
suelo *noun m.* **1.** floor **2.** ground **3.** soil
suelto, -ta *adj.* **1.** loose **2.** odd
sueño *noun m.* **1.** dream **2.** sleep
suero *noun m.* serum
suerte *noun f.* **1.** luck, fortune, chance **2.** fate, lot **3.** kind, sort
suéter *noun m.* sweater
suficiente *adj.* enough, sufficient
sufragio *noun m.* suffrage
sufrido, -da *adj.* patient
sufrimiento *noun m.* suffering
sufrir *verb.* **1.** to suffer **2.** endure, bear
sugerencia *noun f.* suggestion
sugerir *verb.* to suggest
suicida *noun mf.* suicide
suicida *adj.* suicidal
suicidio *noun m.* suicide
suite *noun f.* suite
Suiza *noun f.* Switzerland
suizo, -za *noun. adj.* Swiss
sujetar *verb.* **1.** to hold **2.** attach, fasten, secure **3.** subdue
sujeto *noun m.* **1.** subject **2.** individual
sujeto, -ta *adj.* fastened, secure
—**sujeto a** subject to
suma *noun f.* **1.** sum, amount **2.** addition
sumar *verb.* **1.** to add **2.** total
suministrar *verb.* to supply, provide
suministro *noun m.* supply, provision
sumisión *noun f.* submission
suntuoso, -sa *adj.* sumptuous
superar *verb.* **1.** to surpass **2.** overcome
superficial *adj.* superficial
superficie *noun f.* **1.** surface **2.** area
superintendente *noun mf.* superintendent
superior *noun m.* superior
superior *adj.* **1.** superior **2.** higher **3.** upper
superioridad *noun f.* superiority
supermercado *noun m.* supermarket
supervisar *verb.* to supervise, oversee
supervisión *noun f.* supervision
supervisor, -sora *noun.* supervisor
supervivencia *noun f.* survival
superviviente *noun mf.* survivor
superviviente *adj.* surviving
suplementario, -ria *adj.* supplementary
suplemento *noun m.* supplement
suplente *noun mf.* **1.** substitute **2.** deputy
súplica *noun f.* plea
suplicar *verb.* to beg, plead
suponer *verb.* **1.** to suppose, presume **2.** assume **3.** involve
suposición *noun f.* supposition, presumption
supremo, -ma *adj.* supreme, high
supresión *noun f.* suppression
suprimir *verb.* to suppress
supuesto *noun m.* supposition
supuesto, -ta *adj.* supposed
—**por supuesto** of course
sur *noun m.* south
sur *adj.* south, southern
sureño, -ña *adj.* southern
surgir *verb.* to arise, emerge
surtido *noun m.* assortment, variety
susceptible *adj.* **1.** sensitive **2.** susceptible
suscitar *verb.* to provoke, arise
suscripción *noun f.* subscription
suspender *verb.* **1.** to suspend **2.** fail
suspensión *noun f.* suspension
suspenso *noun m.* failure
suspirar *verb.* to sigh
suspiro *noun m.* sigh
sustancia *noun f.* substance
sustancial *adj.* substantial
sustantivo *noun m.* noun
sustentar *verb.* **1.** to sustain **2.** maintain
sustento *noun m.* **1.** sustenance **2.** livelihood
sustitución *noun f.* substitution, replacement

sustituir *verb.* to substitute, replace
sustituto, -ta *noun.* substitute
susto *noun m.* scare
sustraer *verb.* **1.** to take away **2.** rob, steal **3.** subtract
susurrar *verb.* **1.** to whisper **2.** murmur
susurro *noun m.* **1.** whisper **2.** murmur
sutil *adj.* **1.** subtle **2.** fine
suturar *verb.* to suture
suyo, suya *adj.* **1.** his, her, its, theirs **2.** yours
suyo, suya *pron.* **1.** his, her, theirs **2.** yours

T

tabaco *noun m.* tobacco
tabla *noun f.* **1.** table **2.** board, plank
—**tablas 1.** boards, stage **2.** draw
tablero *noun m.* board
tableta *noun f.* **1.** tablet **2.** bar
tabloide *noun m.* tabloid
tablón *noun m.* **1.** plank **2.** board
taburete *noun m.* stool
tacaño, -ña *adj.* stingy
tachar *verb.* to cross out, delete
—**tachar de** to accuse of
tachuela *noun f.* tack
taco *noun m.* **1.** plug, stopper **2.** pad **3.** cue
tacón *noun m.* heel
táctica *noun f.* tactics
táctico, -ca *adj.* tactical
tacto *noun m.* **1.** touch **2.** tact
tailandés, -desa *noun. adj.* Thai
Tailandia *noun f.* Thailand
tajada *noun f.* hack, slash
tajar *verb.* to hack, slash
tajo *noun m.* hack, slash
tal *adj.* **1.** such **2.** said
—**tal vez** perhaps, maybe
tal *adv.* so, thus
—**con tal que** provided that
—**¿qué tal?** how are you?, what's new?
tal *pron.* **1.** such a one **2.** such a thing
tala *noun f.* felling
taladrar *verb.* to drill
taladro *noun m.* drill
talar *verb.* to fell
talento *noun m.* talent, gift
talentoso, -sa *adj.* talented, gifted
talla *noun f.* **1.** carving **2.** cutting **3.** height **4.** stature **5.** size
tallar *verb.* **1.** to carve **2.** cut **3.** measure (height)
talle *noun m.* **1.** waist **2.** figure, shape
taller *noun m.* **1.** workshop **2.** studio
talón *noun m.* heel
tamaño *noun m.* size
también *adv.* **1.** also, likewise, too **2.** so
tambor *noun m.* drum
tamborilear *verb.* to drum
tampoco *adv.* neither, not either
tan *adv.* **1.** so **2.** as
—**tan sólo** only
tangible *adj.* tangible
tanque *noun m.* tank
tanteo *noun m.* **1.** score **2.** estimate
tanto *noun m.* **1.** point, goal **2.** certain amount **3.** rate
—**tanto por ciento** percentage, rate
tanto, -ta *adj.* **1.** so many, so much, such **2.** as many, as much
tanto *adv.* **1.** so much **2.** so long
—**al tanto** aware
—**entre tanto** meanwhile
—**por lo tanto** therefore
—**un tanto** rather, somewhat
tanto, -ta *pron.* so many, so much
tañer *verb.* to toll
tapa *noun f.* cover, lid
tapadera *noun f.* cover, top
tapar *verb.* **1.** to cover **2.** block **3.** hide, keep secret
tapete *noun m.* rug
tapia *noun f.* wall
tapón *noun m.* **1.** cap **2.** cork **3.** plug
taquilla *verb.* box office
tara *noun f.* fault
tararear *verb.* to hum
tarde *noun f.* **1.** afternoon **2.** evening

tarde *adv.* late
tarea *noun f.* job, task, work
tarifa *noun f.* **1.** fare **2.** rate **3.** duty
tarjeta *noun f.* card
—**tarjeta de crédito** credit card
tarro *noun m.* jar, pot
tarta *noun f.* cake
tasa *noun f.* rate
tasar *verb.* **1.** to set the price **2.** value
taxi *noun m.* taxi
taxímetro *noun m.* taximeter
taza *noun f.* **1.** cup **2.** bowl
tazón *noun m.* mug
te *pron.* **1.** you **2.** for you, from you, to you **3.** yourself
té *noun m.* tea
teatral *adj.* theatrical
teatro *noun m.* theatre
tebeo *noun m.* comic
techar *verb.* to roof
techo *noun m.* **1.** ceiling **2.** roof
tecla *noun f.* key
teclado *noun m.* keyboard
técnica *noun f.* skill, technique
técnico, -ca *noun.* technician, engineer
técnico, -ca *adj.* technical
tecnología *noun f.* technology
tecnológico, -ca *adj.* technological
tedioso, -sa *adj.* tedious
teja *noun f.* tile
tejado *noun m.* roof
tejer *verb.* **1.** to knit **2.** weave
tejido *noun m.* **1.** tissue **2.** fabric **3.** texture
tela *noun f.* cloth, fabric, material, stuff
telar *noun m.* loom
tele *noun f.* TV, television
telecomunicación *noun f.* telecommunication
telefonear *verb.* to call, phone, telephone
telefonista *noun mf.* telephone operator
teléfono *noun m.* phone, telephone
—**teléfono móvil** mobile phone
telegrafiar *verb.* to telegraph, wire
telégrafo *noun m.* telegraph, wire
telegrama *noun m.* cable, wire
telenovela *noun f.* serial
telescopio *noun m.* telescope
televisar *verb.* to televise
televisión *noun f.* television
televisor *noun m.* television
tema *noun m.* theme, topic
temblar *verb.* to shiver, tremble
temblor *noun m.* tremble
temer *verb.* to fear, dread
temerario, -ria *adj.* reckless
temeroso, -sa *adj.* fearful
temible *adj.* fearsome, dreadful
temor *noun m.* fear, dread
temperamento *noun m.* temperament
temperatura *noun f.* temperature
templado, -da *adj.* **1.** warm **2.** mild **3.** moderate
templar *verb.* **1.** to warm up **2.** temper **3.** moderate
templo *noun m.* temple
tempo *noun m.* tempo
temporada *noun f.* season
temporal *adj.* **1.** temporal **2.** temporary
temprano, -na *adj. adv.* early
tendencia *noun f.* **1.** tendency **2.** trend
tender *verb.* **1.** to spread out **2.** hang out **3.** lay
—**tender a** to tend to
—**tender una emboscada** to ambush
—**tenderse** to lie down
tendero, -ra *noun.* storekeeper
tenebroso, -sa *adj.* gloomy
tenedor *noun m.* fork
tener *verb.* **1.** to have **2.** hold **3.** own, possess **4.** feel
—**tener en cuenta** to bear in mind
—**tener que** **1.** to have to **2.** must
—**tenerse por** to consider oneself
teniente *noun mf.* lieutenant
tenis *noun m.* tennis
tensar *verb.* **1.** to tense **2.** tighten
tensión *noun f.* **1.** tension **2.** strain, stress
—**tensión arterial** blood pressure
tenso, -sa *adj.* tense
tentación *noun f.* temptation
tentador, -dora *adj.* tempting, inviting
tentar *verb.* **1.** to tempt **2.** touch, feel
tentativa *noun f.* attempt, try
tentempié *noun m.* snack
tenue *adj.* **1.** tenuous **2.** faint, dim **3.** delicate, slender

teñir *verb.* to dye
teología *noun f.* theology
teológico, -ca *adj.* theological
teoría *noun f.* theory
teórico, -ca *noun.* theorist
teórico, -ca *adj.* theoretical
tepe *noun m.* turf
terapeuta *noun mf.* therapist
terapéutico, -ca *adj.* therapeutic
terapia *noun f.* therapy
tercero, -ra *noun. adj.* third
tercio *noun m.* third
terciopelo *noun m.* velvet
terco, -ca *adj.* stubborn
termal *adj.* thermal
térmico, -ca *adj.* thermal
terminal *noun f. adj.* terminal
terminar *verb.* **1.** to end **2.** conclude **3.** complete **4.** finish **5.** expire
término *noun m.* **1.** term **2.** end
terminología *noun f.* terminology
ternera *noun f.* veal
ternero, -ra *noun.* calf
terraplén *noun m.* embankment
terrateniente *noun mf.* landowner
terraza *noun f.* terrace
terremoto *noun m.* earthquake
terreno *noun m.* **1.** terrain **2.** ground, land **3.** plot
terrible *adj.* terrible, horrible
territorial *adj.* territorial
territorio *noun m.* territory
terrón *noun m.* lump
terror *noun m.* terror
terrorismo *noun m.* terrorism
terrorista *noun mf. adj.* terrorist
tesis *noun f.* thesis
tesorero, -ra *noun.* treasurer
tesoro *noun m.* treasure
test *noun m.* test
testamento *noun m.* testament, will
testigo *noun mf.* witness
testimonio *noun m.* testimony
tetera *noun f.* kettle
textil *noun m. adj.* textile
texto *noun m.* text
textura *noun f.* texture
tez *noun f.* coloring, skin
ti *pron.* you
tía *noun f.* (see tío)
tiempo *noun m.* **1.** time **2.** period, epoch, age **3.** weather **4.** tense **5.** tempo
tienda *noun f.* store, shop
—**tienda de campaña** tent
tierno, -na *adj.* **1.** tender **2.** soft **3.** affectionate
tierra *noun f.* **1.** earth **2.** land **3.** soil **4.** homeland
—**tierra firme** mainland
tieso, -sa *adj.* stiff
tiesto *noun m.* pot
tigre, -gresa *noun.* **1.** tiger or tigress **2.** jaguar
tijeras *noun f. plural.* scissors
tilde *noun f.* accent mark
timar *verb.* to cheat, con, swindle
timbre *noun m.* **1.** bell **2.** tone
tímido, -da *adj.* shy
timo *noun m.* con, swindle
timonel *noun m.* coxswain
tímpano *noun m.* eardrum
tina *noun f.* bathtub
tinaja *noun f.* vat
tinta *noun f.* ink
tinte *noun m.* **1.** dye **2.** overtone
tintinear *verb.* to jingle, tinkle
tintineo *noun m.* jingle, tinkle
tío, tía *noun.* **1.** uncle or aunt **2.** guy or gal
típico, -ca *adj.* typical
tipo *noun m.* **1.** type **2.** kind, sort **3.** style
—**tipo de interés** interest rate
tipo, -pa *noun.* guy or gal
tipografía *noun f.* typography, printing
tira *noun f.* band, strip
—**tira cómica** comic strip
tirada *noun f.* **1.** throw **2.** edition, issue **3.** circulation
tirador *noun m.* handle, knob
tirante *adj.* tense
tirantes *noun m. plural.* suspenders
tirar *verb.* **1.** to throw, hurl, toss **2.** throw away **3.** shoot, fire **4.** pull, draw **5.** attract **6.** print
—**ir tirando** to get by, manage
—**tirar a** to be rather
—**tirar de la cadena** to flush
—**tirar para** to turn to
tiritar *verb.* to shiver

tiro *noun m.* shot
 —a tiro within range
tirón *noun m.* pull, tug
titubear *verb.* **1.** to stammer **2.** hesitate
titular *noun m.* headline
titular *noun mf.* holder, owner
titular *verb.* to entitle
 —titularse 1. to be entitled, be called **2.** obtain a degree
título *noun m.* **1.** title **2.** degree, qualification **3.** diploma, certificate **4.** bond
tiza *noun f.* chalk
toalla *noun f.* towel
tobillo *noun m.* ankle
tobogán *noun m.* slide
tocar *verb.* **1.** to touch **2.** feel **3.** play **4.** ring, knock **5.** concern, affect
 —tocarle a to be one's turn
tocino *noun m.* bacon
tocón *noun m.* stump
todavía *adv.* **1.** still, yet **2.** even
todo *noun m.* whole
todo, -da *adj.* **1.** every, each **2.** all, whole, entire
 —todo el mundo everybody, everyone
todo *adv.* wholly, entirely
 —a todo esto in the meanwhile
 —ante todo in the first place
 —con todo nevertheless
todo, -da *pron.* all, everything
 —todos, todas everybody, everyone
toga *noun f.* gown
tolerancia *noun f.* tolerance
tolerante *adj.* tolerant
tolerar *verb.* to tolerate
toma *noun f.* **1.** taking **2.** intake **3.** dose **4.** capture, seizure
tomar *verb.* **1.** to take **2.** drink, have **3.** capture, seize
 —tomar por to go in the direction of
 —tomarse 1. to take **2.** have, drink, eat
tomate *noun m.* tomato
tonelada *noun f.* ton
tónica *noun f.* **1.** tonic **2.** trend
tónico *noun m.* tonic
tónico, -ca *adj.* tonic
tono *noun m.* **1.** tone **2.** key, pitch **3.** shade
tontear *verb.* to fool around
tontería *noun f.* foolishness, stupidity
tonto, -ta *noun.* fool
tonto, -ta *adj.* foolish, stupid
toparse (con) *verb.* to come across
tope *noun m.* **1.** limit, end **2.** stop
topo *noun m.* mole
toque *noun m.* touch
 —toque de queda curfew
torcedura *noun f.* **1.** twisting **2.** sprain
torcer *verb.* **1.** to turn **2.** bend, twist **3.** sprain, strain
torcido, -da *adj.* twisted
tormenta *noun f.* storm
tormento *noun m.* torment
torneo *noun m.* tournament
tornillo *noun m.* bolt, screw
toro *noun m.* bull
torpe *adj.* **1.** awkward, clumsy **2.** dull
torre *noun f.* **1.** tower **2.** rook
torrente *noun m.* torrent
torsión *noun f.* twisting, torsion
torta *noun f.* cake
tortuoso, -sa *adj.* tortuous, winding
tortura *noun f.* torture
torturar *verb.* to torture
tos *noun f.* cough
toser *verb.* to cough
tostada *noun f.* toast
tostado, -da *adj.* brown, tanned
tostar *verb.* **1.** to roast **2.** toast **3.** tan
total *noun m. adj.* total
totalidad *noun f.* whole, totality
tóxico *noun m.* toxic substance
tóxico, -ca *adj.* toxic
trabajador, -dora *noun.* laborer, worker
trabajador, -dora *adj.* hard-working
trabajar *verb.* **1.** to work **2.** labor
trabajo *noun m.* **1.** work, job **2.** labor **3.** effort
tractor *noun m.* tractor
tradición *noun f.* tradition
tradicional *adj.* traditional
traducción *noun f.* translation
traducir *verb.* to translate
traductor, -tora *noun.* translator
traer *verb.* **1.** to bring, fetch **2.** cause **3.** have **4.** wear
 —traer consigo to entail, involve
traficar *verb.* to trade, deal

tráfico *noun m.* traffic
tragar *verb.* to swallow
tragedia *noun f.* tragedy
trágico, -ca *adj.* tragic
trago *noun m.* **1.** swallow **2.** draft
traición *noun f.* betrayal
traicionar *verb.* to betray
tráiler *noun m.* trailer
traje *noun m.* **1.** costume, outfit **2.** dress, apparel **3.** suit
trama *noun f.* **1.** plot **2.** weave
tramar *verb.* **1.** to plot, devise **2.** weave
tramo *noun m.* **1.** stretch **2.** flight
trampa *noun f.* **1.** trap **2.** trick
tramposo, -sa *noun.* cheat, swindler
tranca *noun m.* bar
tranquilidad *noun f.* tranquility, quietness
tranquilizador, -dora *adj.* **1.** soothing **2.** reassuring
tranquilizante *noun m.* tranquilizer
tranquilizar *verb.* to calm down, soothe
tranquilo, -la *adj.* calm, quiet
transacción *noun f.* transaction, deal
transatlántico *noun m.* liner
transbordador *noun m.* ferry
transcripción *noun f.* transcript
transcurrir *verb.* to elapse, pass
transferir *verb.* **1.** to transfer **2.** convey
transformación *noun f.* conversion, transformation
transformar *verb.* **1.** to convert **2.** transform, change
transición *noun f.* transition
transigir *verb.* to give in
—**transigir con** to put up with
transitable *adj.* passable, traversable
tránsito *noun m.* **1.** transit **2.** traffic
transitorio, -ria *adj.* transitory
transmisión *noun f.* transmission
transmitir *verb.* **1.** to transmit, broadcast **2.** pass on
transparente *adj.* transparent
transportar *verb.* **1.** to carry **2.** transport
transporte *noun m.* carriage, transport, transportation
trapo *noun m.* cloth, rag
tras *prep.* **1.** after **2.** behind
trasero *noun m.* buttocks
trasero, -ra *adj.* back, rear
trasladar *verb.* to move, transfer
—**trasladarse** to relocate, move
traslado *noun m.* move, transfer
traspasar *verb.* **1.** to pierce **2.** cross **3.** go too far **4.** convey
traspié *noun m.* slip
trasplantar *verb.* to transplant
trasplante *noun m.* transplant
trastornar *verb.* to disrupt, upset
trastorno *noun m.* **1.** disorder **2.** disruption, upset
trastos *noun m. plural.* **1.** utensils **2.** junk, stuff
tratado *noun m.* treaty
tratamiento *noun m.* treatment
tratar *verb.* **1.** to treat **2.** handle
—**tratar con** to deal with, have contact with
—**tratar de 1.** to try to, attempt **2.** be about **3.** address as
trato *noun m.* **1.** deal **2.** treatment
travesía *noun f.* crossing, voyage
travieso, -sa *adj.* naughty
trayecto *noun m.* **1.** route **2.** journey
trayectoria *noun f.* trajectory
trazado *noun m.* plan, design
trazar *verb.* **1.** to trace **2.** plan, design
trébol *noun m.* **1.** clover **2.** clubs
trece *noun m. adj.* thirteen
trecho *noun m.* **1.** stretch **2.** distance
tregua *noun f.* truce
treinta *noun m. adj.* thirty
tremendo, -da *adj.* **1.** tremendous **2.** terrible
tren *noun m.* train
trepar *verb.* **1.** to climb **2.** creep
tres *noun m. adj.* three
triángulo *noun m.* triangle
tribal *adj.* tribal
tribu *noun f.* tribe
tribuna *noun f.* **1.** platform **2.** gallery
tribunal *noun m.* court, tribunal
tributo *noun m.* **1.** tribute **2.** tax
tridimensional *adj.* three-dimensional
trigésimo, -ma *noun. adj.* thirtieth
trigo *noun m.* wheat
trimestral *adj.* quarterly
trimestre *noun m.* quarter

trinchar *verb.* to carve
trinchera *noun f.* trench
trío *noun m.* trio
tripa *noun f.* gut
triple *noun m. adj.* triple
triplicar *verb.* to treble, triple
tripulación *noun f.* crew
tripular *verb.* to man
triste *adj.* **1.** sad, blue, gloomy **2.** sorry
tristeza *noun f.* sadness
triturar *verb.* to grind
triunfante *adj.* triumphant
triunfar *verb.* to triumph
triunfo *noun m.* triumph
trivial *adj.* trivial
triza *noun f.* shred
—**hacer trizas** to tear into shreds
trofeo *noun m.* trophy
trompa *noun f.* **1.** horn **2.** tube **3.** trunk
trompeta *noun f.* trumpet
tronar *verb.* **1.** to thunder **2.** be furious
tronco *noun m.* **1.** torso **2.** trunk **3.** log
trono *noun m.* throne
tropa *noun f.* troop
tropezar *verb.* to stumble
—**tropezarse con** to bump into, chance upon
tropezón *noun m.* stumble
tropical *adj.* tropical
trópico *noun m.* tropic
tropiezo *noun m.* setback
troquel *noun m.* die
trozo *noun m.* **1.** piece, bit, chunk **2.** fragment
trucha *noun f.* trout
truco *noun m.* trick
trueno *noun m.* thunder
trueque *noun m.* barter
trust *noun m.* trust
tu *adj.* your
tú *pron.* you
tubería *noun f.* pipes, tubing
tubo *noun m.* **1.** tube **2.** pipe **3.** canal
—**tubo de escape** exhaust pipe
tuerca *noun f.* nut
tumba *noun f.* **1.** grave **2.** tomb
tumbar *verb.* to knock down
—**tumbarse** to lie down
tumbo *noun m.* tumble
tumor *noun m.* tumor
túnel *noun m.* tunnel
turbulento, -ta *adj.* turbulent
turco, -ca *noun.* Turk
turco, -ca *adj.* Turkish
turismo *noun m.* tourism
turista *noun mf.* tourist
turístico, -ca *adj.* tourist
turno *noun m.* **1.** turn **2.** shift
Turquía *noun f.* Turkey
tutor, -tora *noun.* **1.** guardian **2.** tutor

U

ubicación *noun f.* **1.** location **2.** situation
ubicar *verb.* to locate
úlcera *noun f.* **1.** sore **2.** ulcer
últimamente *adv.* lately
tuyo, tuya *adj.* yours, of yours
tuyo, tuya *pron.* yours
u *conj.* or
último, -ma *adj.* **1.** last **2.** final **3.** latter
—**por último** finally
ultrajar *verb.* to outrage, insult
ultraje *noun m.* outrage, insult
umbral *noun m.* doorstep, threshold
un *adj.* one
un, una *art.* a, an
—**una vez** once
—**unos, unas 1.** some, a few **2.** about
unánime *adj.* unanimous
undécimo, -ma *noun. adj.* eleventh
único, -ca *noun.* only one
único, -ca *adj.* **1.** only, single, sole **2.** unique
unidad *noun f.* **1.** unit **2.** unity
unido, -da *adj.* joined, united
unificación *noun f.* unification
unificar *verb.* to unify
uniforme *noun m. adj.* uniform
unión *noun f.* **1.** union **2.** joint

unir *verb.* to unite, join, link
—**unirse** to join together
—**unirse a** to join
universal *adj.* **1.** universal **2.** worldwide
universidad *noun f.* university
universo *noun m.* universe
uno *noun m.* one, number one
uno, -na *adj.* one
uno, una *pron.* one
—**uno y otro** both
—**unos, unas** some, some people
—**unos y otros** all of them
untar *verb.* **1.** to smear **2.** bribe
uña *noun f.* nail
uranio *noun m.* uranium
urbanización *noun f.* residential area
urbano, -na *adj.* urban
urgencia *noun f.* urgency
urgente *adj.* urgent
usado, -da *adj.* **1.** used **2.** worn
usar *verb.* **1.** to use **2.** wear
uso *noun m.* **1.** use **2.** wear **3.** custom, usage
usted *pron.* you
—**ustedes** you
usual *adj.* usual
usuario, -ria *noun.* user
útil *adj.* useful, helpful
utilidad *noun f.* utility, usefulness
utilización *noun f.* use
utilizar *verb.* to use, utilize
uva *noun f.* grape

V

vaca *noun f.* cow
vacación *noun f.* vacation, holiday
vacante *noun f.* vacancy
vaciar *verb.* to drain, empty
vacilación *noun f.* hesitation
vacilar *verb.* to hesitate
vacío *noun m.* **1.** emptiness, void **2.** gap **3.** vacuum
vacío, -cía *adj.* **1.** empty **2.** vacant
vacuna *noun f.* vaccine
vacuno, -na *adj.* bovine
vadear *verb.* to ford
vado *noun m.* ford
vagabundo, -da *noun.* rover, vagabond
vagar *verb.* to wander
vago, -ga *noun.* idler
vago, -ga *adj.* **1.** idle, lazy **2.** vague
vagón *noun m.* car
vaivén *noun m.* **1.** swing **2.** change, instability
vajilla *noun f.* dishes
vale *noun m.* voucher
valentía *noun f.* courage
valer *verb.* **1.** to cost **2.** be worth **3.** be valid
—**valerse de** to make use of
valeroso, -sa *adj.* brave
válido, -da *adj.* valid
valiente *adj.* bold, brave
valioso, -sa *adj.* valuable
valla *noun f.* **1.** fence **2.** hurdle
valle *noun m.* vale, valley
valor *noun m.* **1.** value, worth **2.** courage, heart, nerve
—**valores 1.** values **2.** bonds, securities
valoración *noun f.* assessment, valuation
valorar *verb.* **1.** to assess, evaluate **2.** value
válvula *noun f.* valve
vanagloriarse *verb.* to boast
vanguardia *noun f.* vanguard
—**a la vanguardia** in the forefront
vanidad *noun f.* vanity
vanidoso, -sa *adj.* vain
vano, -na *adj.* vain
vapor *noun m.* vapor, steam
vaquero, -ra *noun.* cowboy or cowgirl
vaquero, -ra *adj.* cowboy or cowgirl
—**vaqueros** jeans
vara *noun f.* rod, stick
varar *verb.* to beach
variable *noun f. adj.* variable
variación *noun f.* variation
variado, -da *adj.* diverse, mixed, varied
variante *noun f.* variant
variar *verb.* **1.** to vary **2.** change

variedad *noun f.* variety, diversity
varilla *noun f.* **1.** rod, bar **2.** rib
vario, -ria *adj.* diverse
—**varios, -rias** several, various
varón *noun m.* man, male
vaso *noun m.* glass
vasto, -ta *adj.* vast
vatio *noun m.* watt
vecindad *noun f.* neighborhood, vicinity
vecino, -na *noun.* **1.** neighbor **2.** resident, inhabitant
vecino, -na *adj.* neighboring
veda *noun f.* **1.** prohibition **2.** closed season
vedar *verb.* to ban, prohibit
vegetación *noun f.* vegetation
vegetal *noun m.* vegetable
vegetariano, -na *noun. adj.* vegetarian
vehículo *noun m.* vehicle
veinte *noun m. adj.* twenty
veintena *noun f.* group of twenty, score
vejiga *noun f.* bladder
vela *noun f.* **1.** candle **2.** sail
velar *verb.* to veil
velo *noun m.* veil
velocidad *noun f.* speed, velocity
veloz *adj.* swift, fast
vena *noun f.* **1.** vein **2.** strain
venado *noun m.* deer
vencedor, -dora *noun.* winner, victor
vencedor, -dora *adj.* winning
vencejo *noun m.* swift
vencer *verb.* **1.** to win **2.** defeat **3.** overcome **4.** expire
vendaje *noun m.* bandage, dressing
vendar *verb.* to bandage
vendedor, -dora *noun.* salesperson, salesman or saleswoman
vender *verb.* to sell
veneno *noun m.* poison
venezolano, -na *noun. adj.* Venezuelan
Venezuela *noun f.* Venezuela
venganza *noun f.* revenge, vengeance
vengar *verb.* to avenge
—**vengarse** to take revenge
venidero, -ra *adj.* coming, forthcoming, future
venir *verb.* **1.** to come **2.** arrive **3.** fit **4.** follow, come after
—**venirse abajo** to fall, collapse
venta *noun f.* sale
ventaja *noun f.* **1.** advantage **2.** lead
ventajoso, -sa *adj.* **1.** advantageous **2.** profitable
ventana *noun f.* window
ventanilla *noun f.* **1.** box office **2.** window
ventilación *noun f.* ventilation
ventilador *noun m.* **1.** ventilator **2.** fan
ventilar *verb.* **1.** to ventilate **2.** air
ventoso, -sa *adj.* windy
ver *verb.* **1.** to see **2.** understand **3.** examine **4.** visit **5.** witness
verano *noun m.* summer
verbal *adj.* verbal
verbo *noun m.* verb
verdad *noun f.* truth
—**¿de verdad?** really?
verdadero, -ra *adj.* real, true
verde *noun m. adj.* green
verdura *noun f.* vegetables, greens
veredicto *noun m.* verdict
vergonzoso, -sa *adj.* **1.** shameful **2.** shy
vergüenza *noun f.* **1.** shame, disgrace **2.** embarrassment **3.** shyness
verificar *verb.* **1.** to verify **2.** check
verja *noun f.* gate
versátil *adj.* versatile
versículo *noun m.* verse
versión *noun f.* version
verso *noun m.* verse
versus *prep.* against, versus
vertedero *noun m.* garbage dump
verter *verb.* **1.** to pour **2.** empty out **3.** pour
vertical *adj.* vertical, upright
vertiente *noun f.* **1.** slope **2.** side
vestíbulo *noun m.* hall, lobby
vestido *noun m.* **1.** dress **2.** clothes
vestigio *noun m.* trace
vestimenta *noun f.* clothes
vestir *verb.* to dress
vestuario *noun m.* **1.** wardrobe **2.** locker room
veta *noun f.* **1.** grain **2.** streak
vetar *verb.* to veto
veterano, -na *noun. adj.* veteran
veterinario, -ria *noun.* veterinarian

veterinario, -ria *adj.* veterinary
veto *noun m.* veto
vez *noun f.* **1.** time **2.** occasion
—**en vez de** instead of
vía *noun f.* **1.** way **2.** road, railway, track **3.** means
—**por vía** by
vía *prep.* via
viajante *noun mf.* commercial traveler, traveling salesman or saleswoman
viajar *verb.* to travel
viaje *noun m.* **1.** journey, trip **2.** voyage
viajero, -ra *noun.* **1.** traveler **2.** passenger
vicio *noun m.* vice
víctima *noun f.* **1.** victim **2.** casualty
victoria *noun f.* victory
vid *noun f.* vine
vida *noun f.* **1.** life **2.** lifetime
vídeo *noun m.* video
vidrio *noun m.* glass
viejo, -ja *noun.* old man or woman
viejo, -ja *adj.* **1.** old **2.** worn
viento *noun m.* wind
vientre *noun m.* belly, abdomen
viernes *noun m.* Friday
viga *noun f.* beam
vigente *adj.* valid, in force
vigésimo, -ma *noun. adj.* twentieth
vigía *noun mf.* watch
vigilancia *noun f.* vigilance
vigilante *noun mf.* watchman, guard
vigilante *adj.* alert, vigilant
vigilar *verb.* **1.** to watch, guard **2.** police **3.** look after
vigor *noun m.* vigor
—**en vigor** valid, in force
vigoroso, -sa *adj.* vigorous
vil *adj.* vile
villa *noun f.* **1.** village, town **2.** villa
villancico *noun m.* carol
vinagre *noun m.* vinegar
vínculo *noun m.* bond, link, tie
vino *noun m.* wine
viña *noun f.* vineyard
viñedo *noun m.* vineyard
violación *noun f.* **1.** violation **2.** rape
violar *verb.* **1.** to violate **2.** rape
violencia *noun f.* violence
violento, -ta *adj.* **1.** violent **2.** embarrassing
violeta *noun f.* violet (flower)
violeta *noun m. adj.* violet
violín *noun m.* violin
viraje *noun m.* turn
virar *verb.* to turn, tack
virgen *noun mf. adj.* virgin
vírico, -ca *adj.* viral
virtual *adj.* virtual
virtud *noun f.* virtue
virus *noun m.* virus
visa *noun f.* visa
visibilidad *noun f.* visibility
visible *adj.* visible
visión *noun f.* **1.** vision **2.** view
visita *noun f.* **1.** call, visit **2.** visitor
visitante *noun mf.* visitor
visitante *adj.* visiting
visitar *verb.* to visit
vislumbrar *verb.* **1.** to distinguish **2.** glimpse
vislumbre *noun m.* glimpse
víspera *noun f.* eve
vista *noun f.* **1.** vision, eyesight **2.** view, sight **3.** glance, look **4.** hearing
vistazo *noun m.* glance, look
vistoso, -sa *adj.* colorful
visual *adj.* visual
vital *adj.* vital
vitalidad *noun f.* vitality
vitamina *noun f.* vitamin
vitorear *verb.* cheer
vitrina *noun f.* **1.** cabinet **2.** case
viudo, -da *noun.* widower or widow
vivero *noun m.* nursery
viveza *noun f.* **1.** liveliness **2.** vividness
vivienda *noun f.* **1.** housing **2.** dwelling
vivir *verb.* **1.** to live **2.** be alive **3.** reside **4.** go through
vivo, -va *adj.* **1.** alive **2.** lively **3.** vivid
vocabulario *noun m.* vocabulary
vocación *noun f.* calling, vocation
vocal *noun f.* vowel
vocal *noun mf.* voting member
vocal *adj.* vocal
vociferar *verb.* to shout
volante *noun m.* wheel
volar *verb.* **1.** to fly **2.** hurry **3.** disappear **4.** burst, explode
volcán *noun m.* volcano

volcánico, -ca *adj.* volcanic
volcar *verb.* **1.** to overturn **2.** topple **3.** upset
voltaje *noun m.* voltage
voltear *verb.* **1.** to turn over **2.** roll over **3.** tumble
voltereta *noun f.* tumble
voltio *noun m.* volt
volumen *noun m.* **1.** volume **2.** amount **3.** size
voluntad *noun f.* **1.** will **2.** intention
voluntario, -ria *noun.* volunteer
voluntario, -ria *adj.* voluntary
volver *verb.* **1.** to return **2.** go back, come back **3.** revert **4.** cause, drive, make **5.** turn over
—**volver a** to do again
—**volverse 1.** to become **2.** turn around
vomitar *verb.* to vomit
vómito *noun m.* **1.** vomit **2.** vomiting
vos *pron.* you
vosotros, vosotras *pron.* you
votación *noun f.* voting
votante *noun mf.* voter
votar *verb.* to vote
voto *noun m.* **1.** vote **2.** vow
voz *noun f.* **1.** voice **2.** word
vuelo *noun m.* **1.** flight **2.** fullness
vuelta *noun f.* **1.** turn **2.** revolution **3.** return **4.** round **5.** stroll, walk, ride **6.** bend, curve **7.** change **8.** back
vuestro, vuestra *adj.* your, of yours
vuestro, vuestra *pron.* yours
vulgar *adj.* **1.** common **2.** vulgar
vulnerabilidad *noun f.* vulnerability
vulnerable *adj.* vulnerable

W, X, Y, Z

western *noun m.* western
whisky *noun m.* whiskey
xenofobia *noun f.* xenophobia
xenófobo, -ba *noun.* xenophobe
xenófobo, -ba *adj.* xenophobic
y *conj.* and
ya *adv.* **1.** already **2.** now **3.** anymore, no longer **4.** later, soon
—**ya que** since
yacimiento *noun m.* deposit, field
yarda *noun f.* yard
yate *noun m.* yacht
yegua *noun f.* mare
yen *noun m.* yen
yermo *noun m.* wasteland
yeso *noun m.* plaster
yo *pron.* **1.** I **2.** me
zalamero, -ra *noun.* flatterer
zalamero, -ra *adj.* flattering
zambullida *noun f.* dive, plunge
zambullirse *verb.* to dive, plunge
zanahoria *noun f.* carrot
zancada *noun f.* stride
zanja *noun f.* ditch
zapato *noun m.* shoe
zarcillo *noun m.* earring
zarpar *verb.* to set sail
zigzaguear *verb.* to zigzag
zona *noun f.* area, district, zone
zoo *noun m.* zoo
zorra *noun f.* bitch
zorro *noun m.* fox or vixen
zumbar *verb.* **1.** to buzz, hum **2.** thrash
zumbido *noun m.* buzzing, humming
zumo *noun m.* juice
zurdo, -da *noun.* left-handed person
zurdo, -da *adj.* left-handed

ENGLISH-SPANISH DICTIONARY

A

a, an *indef. art.* **1.** un, una **2.** por, al, a la
abacus *noun.* ábaco
abandon *verb.* **1.** abandonar, dejar **2.** suspender
abandoned *adj.* **1.** abandonado **2.** inmoral, desvergonzado
abandonment *noun.* abandono
abbey *noun.* abadía
abbot *noun.* abad
ABC *noun.* **1.** abecedario **2.** abecé
abdominal *adj.* abdominal
ability *noun.* capacidad, habilidad
able *adj.* **1.** capaz **2.** competente
abnormal *adj.* anormal
aboard *adv. prep.* a bordo
abolish *verb.* abolir
abolition *noun.* abolición
abortion *noun.* aborto
about *prep. adv.* **1.** alrededor de, aproximadamente **2.** casi **3.** cerca, por aquí, por ahí
about *prep.* de, sobre, acerca de
above *prep.* **1.** (por) encima de **2.** sobre **3.** superior
above *adv.* **1.** arriba **2.** mayor
abroad *adv.* en el extranjero, fuera
abrupt *adj.* **1.** brusco, repentino **2.** abrupto
abruptly *adv.* bruscamente
absence *noun.* ausencia
absent *verb.* ausentarse
absent *adj.* ausente
absolute *adj.* absoluto
absolutely *adv.* absolutamente
absorb *verb.* absorber
absorption *noun.* absorción
abstract *noun.* resumen
abstract *adj.* abstracto
absurd *adj.* absurdo
abundance *noun.* abundancia
abundant *adj.* abundante
abuse *noun.* **1.** abuso **2.** insulto, injuria
abuse *verb.* **1.** abusar de **2.** insultar, injuriar
academic *noun.* profesor de universidad
academic *adj.* académico
academy *noun.* **1.** academia **2.** colegio
accelerate *verb.* acelerar
acceleration *noun.* aceleración
accent *noun.* **1.** acento, tilde **2.** énfasis
accent *verb.* acentuar
accept *verb.* aceptar
acceptable *adj.* **1.** aceptable **2.** grato
acceptance *noun.* aceptación
accepted *adj.* reconocido
access *noun.* acceso, entrada
accessible *adj.* accesible
accession *noun.* **1.** ascensión, subida **2.** adquisición, adición **3.** accesión, adhesión
accessory *noun.* **1.** complemento, accesorio **2.** cómplice
accident *noun.* **1.** accidente **2.** casualidad
accidental *adj.* accidental, fortuito
accidentally *adv.* **1.** por casualidad, accidentalmente **2.** sin querer
acclaim *noun.* aclamación
acclaim *verb.* **1.** aclamar, vitorear **2.** proclamar
accommodate *verb.* **1.** acomodar **2.** complacer **3.** proveer **4.** hospedar, alojar
accommodation *noun.* **1.** acomodación, acomodamiento **2.** alojamiento, sitio
accompany *verb.* acompañar
accomplish *verb.* realizar, lograr
accomplished *adj.* consumado, experto
accord *noun.* acuerdo
accord with *verb.* **1.** concordar (con) **2.** conceder

accordance *noun.* acuerdo, conformidad
—**in accordance with** de acuerdo con, conforme a
according to *prep.* según, conforme, por
accordingly *adv.* **1.** en consecuencia **2.** por consiguiente
account *noun.* **1.** cuenta **2.** factura **3.** relato, versión
—**by all accounts** a decir de todos
—**on account of** a causa de
accountancy *noun.* contabilidad
accountant *noun.* contable
accumulate *verb.* acumular, acumularse
accumulation *noun.* acumulación
accuracy *noun.* precisión, exactitud, fidelidad
accurate *adj.* **1.** exacto, preciso, fiel **2.** certero
accurately *adv.* **1.** con exactitud, fielmente **2.** certeramente
accusation *noun.* acusación
accuse of *verb.* acusar
accustomed *adj.* acostumbrado, usual
ace *noun.* **1.** as **2.** ace
ache *noun.* dolor
ache *verb.* **1.** doler **2.** ansiar, desear
achieve *verb.* conseguir, lograr, realizar
achievement *noun.* logro, hazaña
acid *noun.* ácido
acid *adj.* **1.** ácido **2.** mordaz, sarcástico
acknowledge *verb.* **1.** reconocer, admitir, confesar **2.** agradecer **3.** acusar recibo de
acoustic *adj.* acústico
acquaintance *noun.* conocido
—**acquaintance with** conocimiento de
acquire *verb.* adquirir
acquisition *noun.* adquisición
across *prep.* **1.** a través de **2.** al otro lado de
across *adv.* **1.** a través, de través, transversalmente **2.** al otro lado
act *noun.* **1.** acto, acción **2.** función
—**act (of law)** *noun.* ley
act *verb.* **1.** actuar **2.** comportarse **3.** representar, fingir
acting *adj.* en funciones
action *noun.* **1.** acción, actuación **2.** proceso **3.** combate, batalla
activate *verb.* activar
active *adj.* **1.** activo **2.** en vigor **3.** en actividad
actively *adv.* activamente
activity *noun.* actividad
actor *noun.* actor
actual *adj.* real
actually *adv.* **1.** en realidad, realmente **2.** de hecho
acute *adj.* **1.** agudo, perspicaz, fino **2.** grave
ad *noun.* anuncio
AD *abbr.* d.C., después de Cristo
Adam's apple *noun.* nuez
adapt *verb.* adaptar
adaptation *noun.* adaptación
add *verb.* **1.** sumar **2.** añadir, agregar
addict *noun.* adicto
addiction *noun.* adicción
addition *noun.* **1.** suma **2.** adición
additional *adj.* adicional
address *noun.* **1.** dirección, señas **2.** discurso, alocución
address *verb.* **1.** poner la dirección, dirigir **2.** dirigirse a, pronunciar
adequate *adj.* suficiente, adecuado
adequately *adv.* suficientemente
adjacent (to) *adj.* adyacente
adjective *noun.* adjetivo
adjust (to) *verb.* **1.** amoldarse **2.** ajustar
adjustment *noun.* ajuste
administer *verb.* **1.** administrar **2.** aplicar
administration *noun.* administración
administrative *adj.* administrativo
administrator *noun.* administrador
admirable *adj.* admirable
admiral *noun.* almirante
admiration *noun.* admiración
admire *verb.* admirar
admission *noun.* **1.** admisión **2.** confesión, reconocimiento
admit *verb.* **1.** admitir, dejar entrar **2.** reconocer
admittedly *adv.* sin duda, ciertamente
adolescent *noun. adj.* adolescente
adopt *verb.* adoptar
adoption *noun.* adopción
adult *noun. adj.* adulto
advance *noun.* **1.** avance, progreso, mejora **2.** anticipo, adelanto

—**advances** insinuaciones, requerimientos
advance *verb.* **1.** avanzar, proceder **2.** adelantar
advance *adj.* **1.** por adelantado, anticipado **2.** avanzadilla
advanced *adj.* avanzado
advantage *noun.* ventaja
advent *noun.* advenimiento, llegada
adventure *noun.* aventura
adverse *adj.* adverso, desfavorable, negativo
advert *noun.* anuncio
advertise *verb.* anunciar, hacer publicidad
advertisement, ad *noun.* anuncio
advice *noun.* consejo
advisable *adj.* aconsejable, conveniente
advise *verb.* aconsejar
—**advise of** avisar, informar
adviser, advisor *noun.* consejero
advisory *adj.* asesor, consultivo
advocate *noun.* abogado, defensor
advocate *verb.* defender, abogar, recomendar
aerial *adj.* aéreo
affair *noun.* **1.** caso **2.** cosa **3.** amorío, relación
—**affairs** asuntos
affect *verb.* afectar
affection *noun.* afecto, cariño
affirm *verb.* afirmar
afford *verb.* permitirse, darse el gusto de
afraid *adj.* temeroso, con miedo
—**be afraid that** sentir, lamentar, temer
Africa *noun.* África
African *noun. adj.* africano
after *conj.* después de que
after *prep.* **1.** después (de) **2.** detrás (de), tras **3.** según, al estilo de
after *adv.* después
aftermath *noun.* secuelas, consecuencias
afternoon *noun.* tarde
afterwards *adv.* después, posteriormente, a continuación
again *adv.* otra vez, de nuevo
against *prep.* contra, en contra de
age *noun.* **1.** edad **2.** época, período
—**ages** años, siglos, mucho tiempo
age *verb.* envejecer
aged *adj.* **1.** viejo, anciano **2.** de la edad de
agency *noun.* agencia
agenda *noun.* orden del día
agent *noun.* agente
aggregate *noun.* total
aggression *noun.* agresión
aggressive *adj.* agresivo
agitation *noun.* agitación
ago *adv.* hace
agony *noun.* agonía
agree *verb.* **1.** estar de acuerdo con **2.** acordar, consentir, aceptar **3.** concordar, llevarse bien
—**agree with** sentar bien
agreement *noun.* **1.** acuerdo, pacto, contrato **2.** contrato
agricultural *adj.* agrícola
agriculture *noun.* agricultura
ahead (of) *adv.* delante
aid *noun.* ayuda, auxilio
aid *verb.* ayudar, auxiliar
AIDS *abbr.* sida
aim *noun.* **1.** puntería **2.** objetivo, meta, intención
aim *verb.* apuntar
—**aim to/at** tener intención de, proponerse
air *noun.* aire
air *verb.* airear, ventilar
air force *noun.* **1.** fuerzas aérea **2.** flota aérea
aircraft *noun.* aeronave, avión
airfield *noun.* campo de aviación
airlift *noun.* puente aéreo
airline *noun.* línea aérea, compañía aérea
airplane *noun.* avión
airport *noun.* aeropuerto
airway *noun.* ruta aérea
alarm *noun.* **1.** alarma, sobresalto **2.** toque de alarma
alarm *verb.* alarmar, asustar
alarming *adj.* alarmante
album *noun.* álbum
alcohol *noun.* alcohol

alcoholic *noun.* alcohólico
alcoholic *adj.* alcohólico
ale *noun.* cerveza
alert *noun.* alerta
alert *verb.* alertar
alert *adj.* despierto, espabilado, alerta
algae *noun plural.* algas
alien *noun.* **1.** extranjero **2.** extraterrestre
alien *adj.* **1.** extraño, extranjero, ajeno **2.** extraterrestre
alienate *verb.* **1.** enajenar, alienar **2.** malquistar
alike *adj.* parecido
alike *adv.* igual, del mismo modo
alive *adj.* **1.** vivo **2.** animado, activo
all *adj. pron.* **1.** todo **2.** todos
—**all the better** tanto mejor
all *adv.* completamente, totalmente
—**not at all** en absoluto
allegation *noun.* alegación
allege *verb.* alegar
allegiance *noun.* lealtad
allergy *noun.* alergia
alley *noun.* **1.** callejón, callejuela **2.** pista (de bolos)
alliance *noun.* alianza
allied *adj.* aliado
—**allied to** emparentado, afín, relacionado
—**allied with** junto con
allocate *verb.* **1.** asignar, designar, destinar **2.** distribuir, repartir
allocation *noun.* **1.** asignación **2.** distribución, reparto
allow *verb.* **1.** permitir, dejar **2.** dar, asignar **3.** admitir
—**allow for** tener en cuenta, calcular
allowance *noun.* **1.** asignación, subsidio, prestación **2.** dinero de bolsillo, plus **3.** margen **4.** ración **5.** concesión
ally *noun.* aliado
ally *verb.* aliarse (con)
almost *adv.* casi
alone *adj.* solo
alone *adv.* sólo, solamente
along *prep.* por, a lo largo de
along *adv.* **1.** adelante **2.** con (una persona) **3.** aquí, allí
—**along with** junto con, en compañía de
alongside *prep. adv.* al lado de
aloud *adv.* en voz alta
alpine *adj.* alpino
already *adv.* ya
also *adv.* también
altar *noun.* altar
alter *verb.* cambiar, modificar, alterar
alteration *noun.* cambio, modificación, alteración
alternate *verb.* alternar
alternate *adj.* **1.** alterno **2.** uno sí y otro no
alternative *noun.* alternativa
alternative *adj.* alternativo
alternatively *adv.* o bien, alternativamente, si no
although *conj.* aunque
altitude *noun.* altitud
altogether *adv.* **1.** del todo, totalmente **2.** en conjunto
aluminum *noun. adj.* aluminio
always *adv.* siempre
a.m., A.M. *abbr.* de la mañana
amateur *noun.* aficionado
amateur *adj.* aficionado, amateur
amaze *verb.* asombrar, pasmar
amazement *noun.* asombro, pasmo, sorpresa
amazing *adj.* **1.** asombroso **2.** extraordinario
ambassador *noun.* embajador
amber *noun. adj.* ámbar
ambiguity *noun.* ambigüedad
ambiguous *adj.* ambiguo
ambition *noun.* ambición
ambitious *adj.* ambicioso
ambulance *noun.* ambulancia
ambush *noun.* emboscada
ambush *verb.* tender una emboscada, agarrar por sorpresa
amend *verb.* enmendar, corregir
America *noun.* **1.** Estados Unidos de América **2.** América
American *noun. adj.* **1.** estadounidense, norteamericano **2.** americano
amid, amidst *prep.* en medio de, entre
amiss *adj.* **1.** mal **2.** inoportuno

ammunition *noun.* munición
amnesty *noun.* amnistía
among *prep.* entre
amount *noun.* cantidad, suma, importe
amount to *verb.* **1.** sumar, ascender a **2.** equivaler, venir a ser lo mismo
ample *adj.* **1.** bastante, de sobra **2.** amplio, generoso
ampère *noun.* amperio
amuse *verb.* **1.** divertir, entretener **2.** divertirse
amusement *noun.* distracción, diversión, entretenimiento
amusing *adj.* divertido
an, a *indef. art.* **1.** un, una **2.** por, al, a la
analysis *noun.* **1.** análisis **2.** psicoanálisis
analyst *noun.* **1.** analista **2.** psicoanalista
analytical *adj.* analítico
analyze *verb.* analizar
anatomy *noun.* anatomía
ancestor *noun.* antepasado
anchor *noun.* ancla
anchor *verb.* anclar
ancient *adj.* **1.** antiguo **2.** viejo
and *conj.* y, e (before i-, hi, but not hie-)
angel *noun.* ángel
anger *noun.* enojo, ira
anger *verb.* enojar, enfadar
angle *noun.* **1.** ángulo **2.** punto de vista **3.** esquina, rincón
angle *verb.* pescar con caña
angler *noun.* pescador de caña
Anglican *noun. adj.* anglicano
angrily *adv.* enojado, con ira
angry *adj.* **1.** enojado, enfadado **2.** inflamado
anguish *noun.* angustia
animal *noun.* animal
ankle *noun.* tobillo
anniversary *noun.* aniversario
announce *verb.* **1.** anunciar **2.** declarar **3.** presentar
announcement *noun.* **1.** anuncio **2.** declaración
annoy *verb.* fastidiar, molestar
annoyed *adj.* enojado, molesto
annual *noun.* **1.** anuario **2.** planta anual
annual *adj.* anual
annually *adv.* anualmente
anonymous *adj.* anónimo
another *adj. pron.* otro
answer *noun.* **1.** respuesta, contestación **2.** solución
answer *verb.* **1.** responder, contestar **2.** abrir, atender (la puerta) **3.** coger (el teléfono)
—**answer for** ser responsable de
answering machine *noun.* contestador
ant *noun.* hormiga
Antarctic *adj.* antártico
antenna *noun.* antena
anthropology *noun.* antropología
antibiotic *noun.* antibiótico
anticipate *verb.* **1.** esperar, contar con **2.** prever **3.** anticiparse
anticipation *noun.* **1.** espera **2.** expectación, esperanza **3.** anticipación, previsión
antique *noun.* antigüedad
antique *adj.* **1.** antiguo, de época **2.** anticuado
anxiety *noun.* ansiedad
anxious *adj.* **1.** inquieto, preocupado **2.** angustioso **3.** ansioso, deseoso
anxiously *adv.* **1.** con inquietud **2.** impacientemente **3.** ansiosamente
any *adv.* **1.** para nada **2.** algo
any *pron. adj.* **1.** cualquier, cualquiera **2.** algún **3.** ningún
anybody *pron.* **1.** alguien **2.** nadie (in negative sentences) **3.** cualquiera
anyhow *adv.* **1.** en cualquier caso, de todas formas **2.** de cualquier manera
anyone *pron.* **1.** alguien **2.** nadie (in negative sentences) **3.** cualquiera
anything *pron.* **1.** algo **2.** nada (in negative sentences) **3.** cualquier cosa, lo que
anyway *adv.* de todas formas, de todos modos
anywhere *adv.* **1.** en alguna parte **2.** en ninguna parte (in negative sentences) **3.** en cualquier parte
apart *adv.* **1.** aparte **2.** separado **3.** en pedazos, en piezas
apartment *noun.* apartamento, departamento, piso
apologize *verb.* disculparse, pedir perdón

apology *noun.* disculpa
appall *verb.* horrorizar
appalling *adj.* horrible
apparatus *noun.* aparato, equipo
apparent *adj.* **1.** evidente, claro **2.** aparente
apparently *adv.* **1.** por lo visto, al parecer **2.** aparentemente
appeal *noun.* **1.** solicitud, súplica, petición, llamado **2.** apelación **3.** atractivo, encanto
appeal *verb.* **1.** suplicar, rogar **2.** apelar, recurrir
—**appeal to** gustar, agradar, atraer
appealing *adj.* **1.** atrayente, encantador **2.** suplicante
appear *verb.* **1.** aparecer, salir **2.** comparecer **3.** parecer
appearance *noun.* **1.** apariencia, imagen, aspecto **2.** aparición, comparecencia **3.** publicación
appendix *noun.* apéndice
appetite *noun.* apetito
applaud *verb.* aplaudir
applause *noun.* aplauso
apple *noun.* manzana
appliance *noun.* aparato, electrodoméstico
applicable *adj.* aplicable
applicant *noun.* solicitante, candidato, aspirante
application *noun.* **1.** solicitud, petición **2.** aplicación
apply *verb.* **1.** aplicar **2.** emplear **3.** ser válido, estar en vigor
—**apply for** solicitar
—**apply to** aplicarse
appoint *verb.* **1.** nombrar, designar **2.** convenir, fijar
appointed *adj.* convenido, fijado
appointment *noun.* **1.** cita, hora **2.** nombramiento, puesto, empleo
appreciate *verb.* **1.** agradecer **2.** valorar, apreciar **3.** comprender, hacerse cargo de **4.** revalorizarse, aumentar en valor
appreciation *noun.* **1.** agradecimiento, gratitud, reconocimiento **2.** apreciación **3.** comprensión **4.** revaloración, aumento en valor **5.** crítica, informe
apprehension *noun.* **1.** aprensión, temor **2.** comprensión, percepción
apprentice *noun.* aprendiz
apprentice *verb.* poner de aprendiz
apprenticeship *noun.* aprendizaje
approach *noun.* **1.** aproximación, acercamiento **2.** acceso **3.** propuesta, proposición
approach *verb.* **1.** acercarse, aproximarse, dirigirse a **2.** abordar
approaching *adj.* **1.** venidero **2.** que viene en dirección contraria
appropriate *adj.* apropiado, adecuado, conveniente
appropriately *adv.* apropiadamente, adecuadamente
approval *noun.* aprobación
approve *verb.* **1.** aprobar, tener un buen concepto de **2.** aceptar
approximate *adj.* aproximado
approximately *adv.* aproximadamente
April *noun.* abril
apron *noun.* delantal, mandil
apt *adj.* **1.** propenso, inclinado **2.** apropiado, oportuno **3.** listo, talentoso
aquarium *noun.* acuario
Arab *noun. adj.* árabe
Arabia *noun.* Arabia
Arabian *adj.* árabe, arábigo
Arabic *noun.* árabe
arbitrary *adj.* arbitrario
arbitration *noun.* arbitraje
arc *noun.* arco
arch *noun.* **1.** arco **2.** empeine
arch *verb.* arquear
archaeological *adj.* arqueológico
archaeology *noun.* arqueología
archbishop *noun.* arzobispo
architect *noun.* arquitecto
architectural *adj.* arquitectónico
architecture *noun.* arquitectura
archives *noun plural.* archivo
Arctic *adj.* **1.** ártico **2.** glacial, gélido
area *noun.* **1.** área, superficie **2.** zona
arena *noun.* arena
Argentina *noun.* Argentina
Argentinean *noun. adj.* argentino

argue *verb.* **1.** discutir **2.** sostener
—**argue for/against** argüir, argumentar
argument *noun.* **1.** discusión **2.** argumento
arise *verb.* **1.** surgir, presentarse **2.** levantarse, alzarse
aristocracy *noun.* aristocracia
aristocratic *adj.* aristocrático
arithmetic *noun.* aritmética
arm *noun.* **1.** brazo **2.** arma
—**coat of arms** escudo, blasón
arm *verb.* **1.** armar **2.** armarse
armchair *noun.* sillón, butaca
armed *adj.* armado
armor *noun.* **1.** armadura **2.** blindaje
armored *adj.* blindado
army *noun.* **1.** ejército **2.** multitud, bandada
around *adv.* **1.** alrededor **2.** aproximadamente, más o menos **3.** por ahí
around *prep.* **1.** alrededor de **2.** cerca de **3.** a la vuelta de
arouse *verb.* despertar, provocar
arrange *verb.* **1.** ordenar, disponer **2.** organizar, planear **3.** arreglar, adaptar
arrangement *noun.* **1.** disposición **2.** arreglo
—**arrangements** preparativos
array *noun.* **1.** serie, conjunto, colección **2.** atavío
array *verb.* **1.** alinear, disponer **2.** engalanarse
arrears *noun plural.* atrasos
arrest *noun.* **1.** detención, arresto, captura **2.** paro
arrest *verb.* **1.** detener, arrestar, capturar **2.** parar
arrival *noun.* **1.** llegada **2.** recién nacido, recién llegado
arrive *verb.* llegar
arrogance *noun.* arrogancia
arrogant *adj.* arrogante
arrow *noun.* flecha
arsenal *noun.* arsenal
art *noun.* arte
—**Arts** Letras, Filosofía y Letras
—**fine arts** bellas artes
artery *noun.* arteria
article *noun.* artículo
articulate *verb.* articular
articulate *adj.* que se expresa bien
artificial *adj.* artificial
artillery *noun.* artillería
artist *noun.* artista
artistic *adj.* artístico
as *conj.* **1.** cuando, mientras **2.** como, igual que **3.** aunque, por mucho que (with subjunctive verb) **4.** al igual que
as *prep.* **1.** como **2.** en tanto que
as *adv.* tan, tanto
ascent *noun.* **1.** ascensión **2.** cuesta, pendiente
ascertain *verb.* esclarecer, descubrir
ash *noun.* ceniza
ashamed *adj.* avergonzado
ashore *adv.* a/en tierra firme
ashtray *noun.* cenicero
Asia *noun.* Asia
Asian *noun. adj.* asiático
aside *noun.* aparte
aside *adv.* aparte, a un lado
ask *verb.* **1.** preguntar **2.** pedir, preguntar por **3.** invitar
asleep *adj.* dormido
aspect *noun.* **1.** aspecto **2.** orientación **3.** pinta
aspiration *noun.* aspiración
ass *noun.* **1.** asno, burro **2.** imbécil
assassinate *verb.* asesinar
assassination *noun.* asesinato
assault *noun.* **1.** asalto, ataque **2.** agresión sexual, intento de violación
assault *verb.* **1.** asaltar **2.** agredir sexualmente
assemble *verb.* **1.** reunirse **2.** reunir **3.** montar
assembly *noun.* **1.** asamblea **2.** montaje, ensamblaje
assert *verb.* **1.** aseverar, afirmar, sostener **2.** defender, hacer valer
assertion *noun.* aserción, aserto, afirmación
assess *verb.* **1.** evaluar **2.** calcular
assessment *noun.* evaluación
asset *noun.* ventaja, factor positivo
—**assets** bienes, haberes
assign *verb.* **1.** asignar, atribuir **2.** destinar

assignment *noun.* cometido, tarea
assist *verb.* ayudar
assistance *noun.* ayuda, asistencia
assistant *noun.* **1.** ayudante **2.** dependiente
associate *noun.* socio
associate *verb.* asociar
—**associate with** encontrarse, relacionarse
associate *adj.* **1.** adjunto **2.** asociado
association *noun.* asociación
assume *verb.* **1.** suponer **2.** asumir **3.** adquirir, adoptar
assumed *adj.* presunto, falso
assumption *noun.* supuesto
assurance *noun.* **1.** seguridad **2.** garantía, promesa, palabra de honor **3.** seguro
assure *verb.* **1.** asegurar **2.** garantizar
assured *adj.* seguro
asthma *noun.* asma
astonishing *adj.* asombroso, sorprendente
astonishment *noun.* asombro, sorpresa
astronomer *noun.* astrónomo
asylum *noun.* **1.** asilo **2.** manicomio
at *prep.* **1.** en **2.** a, hacia
athlete *noun.* atleta
athletic *adj.* atlético
athletics *noun singular.* atletismo
Atlantic *noun.* Atlántico
atmosphere *noun.* **1.** atmósfera **2.** ambiente
atmospheric *adj.* atmosférico
atom *noun.* **1.** átomo **2.** ápice, pizca, gota
atomic *adj.* atómico
atrocity *noun.* atrocidad
attach *verb.* atar, sujetar, adjuntar
attached (to) *adj.* apegado
attachment *noun.* accesorio
—**attachment for/to** cariño, apego
attack *noun.* ataque
attack *verb.* **1.** atacar **2.** lanzarse (a)
attain *verb.* conseguir, alcanzar, lograr
attempt *noun.* **1.** tentativa, intento **2.** atentado
attempt *verb.* intentar, tratar de
attend *verb.* **1.** asistir **2.** atender, ocuparse de
attendance *noun.* asistencia
attendant *noun.* encargado
attention *noun.* **1.** atención **2.** cuidado **3.** posición de firmes
attic *noun.* ático, desván, buhardilla
attitude *noun.* **1.** actitud (hacia), postura **2.** posición
attorney *noun.* **1.** apoderado **2.** abogado
attract *verb.* atraer
attraction *noun.* atracción
attractive *adj.* **1.** atractivo **2.** atrayente, interesante
attribute *noun.* atributo
attribute *verb.* **1.** atribuir **2.** acusar
auction *noun.* subasta
auction *verb.* subastar
audience *noun.* **1.** público **2.** audiencia
audit *noun.* auditoría
audit *verb.* auditar, revisar las cuentas
auditor *noun.* auditor, revisor de cuentas
august *adj.* augusto
August *noun.* agosto
aunt *noun.* tía
auntie, aunty *noun.* tita
Australia *noun.* Australia
Australian *noun. adj.* australiano
Austria *noun.* Austria
Austrian *noun. adj.* austríaco
authentic *adj.* auténtico
author *noun.* autor
authoritarian *adj.* autoritario
authoritative *adj.* autorizado, acreditado
authority *noun.* autoridad
authorize *verb.* autorizar
auto *noun.* carro, coche, automóvil
autobiography *noun.* autobiografía
automatic *noun.* arma automática
automatic *adj.* automático
automatically *adv.* automáticamente
automobile *noun.* automóvil
autonomous *adj.* autónomo
autonomy *noun.* autonomía
availability *noun.* disponibilidad
available *adj.* disponible
avenue *noun.* avenida
average *noun.* media
average *verb.* hacer un promedio de

average *adj.* **1.** medio, promedio **2.** corriente, común
avert *verb.* **1.** desviar, apartar **2.** prevenir, impedir
aviary *noun.* pajarera
aviation *noun.* **1.** aviación **2.** aeronáutica
avoid *verb.* evitar
avoidance *noun.* evitación
await *verb.* esperar, aguardar
awake *verb.* **1.** despertar **2.** despertarse
awake *adj.* despierto
award *noun.* premio
award *verb.* **1.** conceder, otorgar **2.** adjudicar
aware *adj.* informado, consciente
awareness *noun.* consciencia
away *adv.* **1.** a, lejos **2.** hacia el otro lado, para otra parte **3.** por completo **4.** sin pausa **5.** fuera, en otro sitio
awe *noun.* temor, respeto
awe *verb.* infundir temor/respeto, atemorizar
awful *adj.* **1.** enorme, imponente, terrible, tremendo **2.** horrible, horroroso
awkward *adj.* **1.** patoso, desgarbado, torpe **2.** difícil, delicado, peliagudo
ax, axe *noun.* hacha
axis *noun.* eje

B

BA, B.A. *abbr.* **1.** licenciatura en Letras **2.** licenciado en Letras
baby *noun.* **1.** bebé **2.** cría
back *noun.* **1.** espalda (of a person) **2.** lomo (of an animal) **3.** parte trasera, fondo, dorso, reverso, respaldo **4.** defensa (in sports)
back *verb.* **1.** dar marcha atrás, mover hacia atrás **2.** apoyar **3.** apostar por
back *adj.* de detrás, trasero
back *adv.* **1.** atrás **2.** hacia atrás, para atrás **3.** de vuelta
background *noun.* **1.** fondo **2.** antecedentes **3.** orígenes, formación, educación
backward *adj.* **1.** hacia atrás **2.** atrasado, retrasado
backward *adv.* **1.** hacia atrás **2.** de espaldas **3.** al revés
bacon *noun.* tocino
bacterium *noun plural.* bacteria
bad *adj.* **1.** malo, mal **2.** perverso **3.** podrido, pasado, picado **4.** perjudicial, nocivo, pernicioso **5.** grave, fuerte **6.** incobrable
badge *noun.* insignia, distintivo
badly *adv.* **1.** mal **2.** gravemente, desesperadamente
bag *noun.* **1.** saco, bolsa, bolso, maleta **2.** caza
bag *verb.* **1.** ensacar, meter en una bolsa/en bolsas **2.** cazar
bail *noun.* **1.** fianza **2.** fiador
bait *noun.* cebo, anzuelo
bait *verb.* cebar
bake *verb.* **1.** cocer al horno **2.** endurecer
baker *noun.* panadero, pastelero
bakery *noun.* panadería, pastelería
balance *noun.* **1.** balanza **2.** equilibrio **3.** saldo **4.** contrapeso
balance *verb.* **1.** equilibrar, nivelar **2.** cuadrar **3.** sopesar, comparar **4.** mantener(se) en equilibrio
balcony *noun.* **1.** balcón **2.** galería, anfiteatro
bald *adj.* **1.** calvo **2.** pelado, desnudo **3.** escueto, sencillo
ball *noun.* **1.** bola, esfera, globo **2.** pelota, balón **3.** ovillo **4.** bala **5.** yema **6.** huevo, cojón **7.** baile
ballet *noun.* ballet
balloon *noun.* globo
ballot *noun.* **1.** votación **2.** papeleta para votar
ban *noun.* prohibición

ban *verb.* prohibir
banana *noun.* plátano, banana
band *noun.* **1.** banda, tira, faja **2.** franja, lista **3.** orquesta, conjunto **4.** grupo, pandilla
band *verb.* unirse, asociarse
bang *noun.* **1.** estallido, detonación, portazo **2.** golpe
bang *verb.* **1.** estallar, detonar **2.** dar un portazo **3.** golpear, golpearse, darse
bank *noun.* **1.** banco **2.** ribera, terraplén, loma **3.** hilera
bank *verb.* **1.** depositar/ingresar en el banco **2.** amontonar, apilar **3.** ladearse
banker *noun.* banquero
bankrupt *noun.* quebrado, insolvente
—**to be bankrupt** estar en quiebra
—**to go bankrupt** quebrar, declararse en quiebra
bankrupt *adj.* en bancarrota, en quiebra
bankruptcy *noun.* quiebra, insolvencia
banner *noun.* bandera, estandarte
bar *prep.* excepto, con excepción de
bar *noun.* **1.** barra, tableta, pastilla **2.** barrote, reja **3.** tranca **4.** palanca **5.** bar, cantina **6.** mostrador **7.** compás **8.** impedimento, obstáculo, prohibición **9.** abogacía **10.** tribunal
bar *verb.* **1.** atrancar **2.** obstruir, impedir **3.** excluir, prohibir
bare *verb.* descubrir, desnudar, revelar
bare *adj.* **1.** desnudo, descubierto, descalzo **2.** vacío **3.** mero, escaso, escueto **4.** pelado, árido **5.** raído
barely *adv.* apenas
bargain *noun.* **1.** ganga **2.** trato, negocio
bargain *verb.* **1.** regatear **2.** negociar
barge *noun.* barcaza, gabarra
barge *verb.* **1.** moverse torpemente **2.** chocar contra, dar contra
—**barge in** irrumpir con rudeza
bark *noun.* **1.** corteza **2.** ladrido
bark *verb.* **1.** ladrar **2.** berrear, vociferar **3.** raspar
barley *noun.* cebada
barn *noun.* **1.** granero **2.** cuadra, establo
baron *noun.* **1.** barón **2.** magnate
barracks *noun.* cuartel
barrel *noun.* **1.** barril, tonel **2.** cañón
barricade *noun.* barricada
barricade *verb.* obstruir, cerrar con barricadas
barrier *noun.* **1.** barrera **2.** obstáculo
barrow *noun.* **1.** carretilla, carretón **2.** túmulo
base *noun.* **1.** base, sede **2.** pie
base *adj.* bajo, vil
base (on) *verb.* basar, fundar
baseball *noun.* béisbol
basement *noun.* sótano
bash *noun.* porrazo
bash (in) *verb.* golpear, aporrear
basic *adj.* **1.** básico, fundamental **2.** elemental
basically *adv.* básicamente, en el fondo
basin *noun.* **1.** palangana, jofaina **2.** cuenco, bol **3.** cuenca **4.** dársena
basis *noun.* base, cimientos, piedra angular
basket *noun.* cesta, capazo
basketball *noun.* baloncesto
bass *noun.* **1.** bajo **2.** róbalo, lubina
bastard *noun. adj.* bastardo
bat *noun.* **1.** bate, pala, raqueta **2.** murciélago
bat *verb.* apalear, golpear
batch *noun.* hornada, lote
bath *noun.* **1.** bañera, tina **2.** baño
bathe *verb.* bañar, bañarse, lavar
bathroom *noun.* servicio, baño
battalion *noun.* batallón
batter *noun.* mezcla para rebozar
batter *verb.* moler a palos, apalear
battered *adj.* maltratado
battery *noun.* **1.** pila, batería **2.** criadero **3.** retahíla
battle *noun.* batalla
battle *verb.* luchar, batirse, combatir
battlefield *noun.* campo de batalla
bay *noun.* **1.** bahía **2.** crujía
bay *verb.* aullar
bay *adj.* bayo
bay (tree) *noun.* laurel
BC *abbr.* a.C., antes de Cristo
be *verb.* **1.** estar + gerundio **2.** ir a + infinitivo **3.** ser **4.** deber + infinitivo, tener como propósito
—**be about** estar a punto de

BE, B.E. *abbr.* licenciatura en Ingeniería
beach *noun.* playa
beach *verb.* varar
beam *noun.* **1.** viga **2.** rayo **3.** manga
beam *verb.* **1.** sonreír de oreja a oreja **2.** emitir
bean *noun.* **1.** frijol, judía, habichuela **2.** grano
bear *noun.* oso
bear *verb.* **1.** aguantar, soportar **2.** dar a luz, parir **3.** cargar, llevar **4.** llevar **5.** desviarse
beard *noun.* **1.** barba **2.** arista
bearing *noun.* **1.** comportamiento, modales **2.** cojinete
beast *noun.* **1.** bestia **2.** bruto, animal **3.** descortés, rudo
beat *noun.* **1.** compás, ritmo **2.** ronda
beat *verb.* **1.** batir, golpear, percutir **2.** derrotar **3.** latir, pulsar **4.** marcar, llevar (el compás)
beaten *adj.* **1.** derrotado **2.** batido
beating *noun.* golpeo, latido, batida
beautiful *adj.* bello, hermoso, guapo, lindo
beautifully *adv.* **1.** bellamente **2.** maravillosamente, perfectamente
beauty *noun.* **1.** belleza **2.** monada, guapada
because *conj.* porque
beck *noun.* **to be at someone's beck and call** estar a disposición de
become *verb.* **1.** volverse, ponerse, convertirse **2.** hacerse, llegar a ser **3.** sentar bien, quedar bien
—**become of** ser de
becoming *adj.* favorecedor
bed *noun.* **1.** cama **2.** lecho **3.** macizo, cuadro **4.** capa, estrato
B.Ed. *abbr.* licenciatura en Magisterio
bedroom *noun.* dormitorio
bedside *noun.* cabecera
bee *noun.* **1.** abeja **2.** trabajo colectivo
beef *noun.* carne de vaca
beer *noun.* cerveza
before *conj.* antes (de que)
before *prep.* **1.** antes (de) **2.** delante (de), antes (de/que) **3.** antes que
before *adv.* antes
beforehand *adv.* de antemano, previamente
beg *verb.* **1.** pedir **2.** suplicar
begin *verb.* empezar, comenzar
beginner *noun.* principiante
behalf *noun.* favor, beneficio
—**on behalf of (someone)** en nombre de, en beneficio de
behave *verb.* comportarse
behavior *noun.* comportamiento
behind *prep.* **1.** detrás de **2.** tras **3.** con
behind *noun.* trasero
behind *adv.* **1.** detrás, atrás **2.** atrasado, retrasado
being *noun.* **1.** existencia **2.** ser
Belgian *noun. adj.* belga
Belgium *noun.* Bélgica
belief(s) *noun.* **1.** confianza, fe **2.** creencia
believe *verb.* creer (que), pensar (que)
bell *noun.* **1.** campana **2.** timbre, campanilla
belly *noun.* **1.** barriga, vientre **2.** estómago
belong (to) *verb.* **1.** pertenecer, ser propiedad (de) **2.** ser miembro, formar parte de
—**belong with** ir con
beloved *noun.* amado, amor
beloved *adj.* adorado
below *prep.* debajo (de), por debajo
below *adv.* de abajo
belt *noun.* **1.** cinturón **2.** correa **3.** faja
belt *verb.* **1.** ponerse el cinturón **2.** dar una paliza
bench *noun.* **1.** banco **2.** banco de trabajo, banco de carpintero
bend *noun.* curva
bend *verb.* **1.** doblar(se), curvar **2.** doblegar, compeler, obligar
beneath *adv.* de abajo
beneath *prep.* bajo, debajo (de)
beneficial *adj.* beneficioso
beneficiary *noun.* beneficiario
benefit *noun.* beneficio
benefit from, benefit by *verb.* **1.** aprovecharse, beneficiarse **2.** hacer bien (a)
benign *adj.* benigno, bondadoso
bent *noun.* inclinación

berry *noun.* baya
beside *prep.* junto a, al lado de
besides *prep.* aparte de, además de
besides *adv.* además
besiege *verb.* sitiar, asediar
—**besiege with** asediar
best *verb.* vencer
best *adj. pron. adv.* mejor
bet *noun.* apuesta
bet (on) *verb.* apostar
betray *verb.* **1.** traicionar **2.** revelar, delatar
betrayal *noun.* traición
better *verb.* mejorar
better *adj.* **1.** mejor **2.** mejorado, recuperado **3.** más vale
better *adv.* mejor
between *prep.* entre
beware (of) *verb.* tener cuidado
beyond *prep.* **1.** más allá de **2.** fuera de **3.** más de, algo más de
bias *noun.* **1.** parcialidad, prejuicio **2.** desviación
bias *verb.* influenciar, predisponer
Bible *noun.* Biblia
biblical, Biblical *adj.* bíblico
bicycle, cycle *verb.* ir/montar en bicicleta
bicycle *noun.* bicicleta
bid *noun.* **1.** oferta **2.** intento/tentativa (de conseguir)
bid *verb.* **1.** pujar, hacer una oferta **2.** pedir, rogar **3.** dar
—**bid for** hacer una oferta de adquisición, hacer una licitación
bidding *noun.* puja, oferta, orden
big *adj.* **1.** grande **2.** importante
bike *noun.* bicicleta
bilateral *adj.* bilateral
bile *noun.* **1.** bilis, hiel **2.** mal genio
bill *noun.* **1.** pico **2.** factura, cuenta **3.** billete **4.** cartel
bill *verb.* facturar
billion *noun. adj.* millardo, mil millones
bin *noun.* cubo
binary *adj.* binario
bind *verb.* **1.** atar, amarrar **2.** encuadernar
binding *noun.* encuadernación
binoculars *noun plural.* prismáticos
biography *noun.* biografía
biological *adj.* biológico
biology *noun.* biología
bird *noun.* ave, pájaro
birth *noun.* **1.** nacimiento **2.** comienzo, inicio
birthday *noun.* cumpleaños
bishop *noun.* **1.** obispo **2.** alfil
bit *noun.* freno, bocado
bit *noun.* **1.** pedazo, trozo **2.** pequeño **3.** un poco, un poquito, un segundo **4.** bit, unidad de información
bitch *noun.* **1.** perra, loba, zorra **2.** zorra, lagarta
bite *noun.* **1.** mordisco, picadura **2.** picada
bite *verb.* morder, picar
biting *adj.* **1.** penetrante, cortante **2.** mordaz, incisivo
bitter *adj.* **1.** amargo **2.** hostil, encarnizado **3.** helado
bitterly *adv.* amargamente
bitterness *noun.* amargura
bizarre *adj.* extraño, raro
black *noun.* negro
black *verb.* ennegrecer, volver negro
black *adj.* **1.** negro **2.** oscuro **3.** solo
bladder *noun.* vejiga
blade *noun.* **1.** hoja, filo **2.** brizna **3.** pala
blame *noun.* culpa, responsabilidad
blame *verb.* **1.** culpar, responsabilizar, echar la culpa **2.** reprochar (algo a alguien)
bland *adj.* **1.** de sabor imperceptible, insípido **2.** inexpresivo, insulso, desabrido
blank *noun.* **1.** espacio en blanco **2.** cartucho sin bala
blank *adj.* **1.** en blanco **2.** vacío, inexpresivo **3.** liso
blanket *noun.* **1.** manta **2.** manto
blanket *verb.* cubrir de, envolver en
blanket *adj.* general
blast *noun.* **1.** ráfaga **2.** toque **3.** explosión, detonación
blast *verb.* volar
—**blast out** emitir a todo volumen, prorrumpir

blaze *noun.* **1.** llamarada, incendio, resplandor **2.** arranque, explosión **3.** fulgor
blaze *verb.* fulgurar, resplandecer
—**blaze a trail** abrir (el) camino, dar los primeros pasos
blazing *adj.* **1.** fulgurante, resplandeciente **2.** violento, encolerizado
bleak *adj.* **1.** inhóspito, desolado **2.** desesperanzador, nada prometedor
bleed *verb.* sangrar
bleeding *adj.* sangrante, sangriento
blend *noun.* mezcla
blend *verb.* mezclar, combinar
bless *verb.* bendecir
blessed *adj.* bendito
blessing *noun.* **1.** bendición **2.** merced, gracia
blind *noun.* **1.** persiana **2.** pretexto, evasiva, subterfugio
blind *verb.* cegar, volver ciego
blind *adj.* **1.** ciego **2.** sin visibilidad **3.** para invidentes/ciegos
—**blind to** ciego, que no se da cuenta de algo
blink *noun.* parpadeo, pestañeo
blink *verb.* parpadear, pestañear
bloc *noun.* bloque
block *noun.* **1.** bloque **2.** zoquete, tarugo **3.** barrera, control policial **4.** manzana
block *verb.* bloquear, obstruir
blockade *noun.* bloqueo
blockade *verb.* bloquear
blocked *adj.* taponado, congestionado
blonde *noun.* rubia
blood *noun.* sangre
—**blood pressure** presión sanguínea, tensión arterial
bloody *adj.* **1.** ensangrentado **2.** que sangra **3.** sangriento **4.** maldito
bloom *noun.* **1.** flor **2.** floración, en flor **3.** estar en la flor de (la vida), lozanía, frescura
bloom *verb.* florecer
blossom *noun.* flor
blossom *verb.* **1.** florecer **2.** transformarse en, convertirse en
blouse *noun.* blusa
blow *noun.* **1.** golpe **2.** golpe (duro)
blow *verb.* **1.** soplar **2.** llevarse **3.** salir volando/despedido, moverse con el aire, viento, etc. **4.** tocar, hacer sonar
blue *noun.* **1.** azul **2.** cielo **3.** mar
blue *adj.* **1.** azul **2.** triste, deprimido, melancólico
blunt *verb.* desafilar, despuntar
blunt *adj.* **1.** desafilado, despuntado **2.** abrupto, brusco, directo
blur *noun.* imagen borrosa/imprecisa
blur *verb.* empañar, hacer borroso
board *noun.* **1.** tabla, plancha **2.** tablón, tablero **3.** pensión, comida **4.** consejo, junta
board *verb.* **1.** subir a **2.** alojarse en, estar hospedado en
boast *noun.* objeto de orgullo, alarde
boast *verb.* vanagloriarse, jactarse de, fanfarronear
boat *noun.* **1.** barco, barca, embarcación, navío, buque **2.** salsera
boat *verb.* navegar
bob *verb.* fluctuar
bodily *adj.* corporal, físico
bodily *adv.* en peso
body *noun.* **1.** cuerpo **2.** cadáver **3.** parte principal **4.** conjunto, colección
bodyguard *noun.* guardaespaldas
bog *noun.* pantano, ciénaga
boil *noun.* furúnculo
boil *verb.* hervir, bullir, cocer
boiler *noun.* caldera
bold *adj.* **1.** valiente, audaz, atrevido **2.** nítido, vivo **3.** en negrita
bolster *noun.* travesaño
bolster (up) *verb.* apoyar, reforzar
bolt *noun.* **1.** pestillo **2.** tornillo **3.** rayo **4.** rollo
bolt *verb.* **1.** echar el cerrojo **2.** engullir, tragar **3.** escaparse, huir
bomb *noun.* bomba
—**A-bomb** bomba atómica
bomb *verb.* **1.** bombardear **2.** fracasar
bomber *noun.* **1.** bombardero **2.** persona que pone bombas
bond *noun.* **1.** lazo **2.** vínculo
bone *noun.* hueso
bone *verb.* deshuesar

bonus *noun.* **1.** plus, prima **2.** regalo, bendición
book *noun.* **1.** cuaderno **2.** libro **3.** talonario
book *verb.* reservar
booking *noun.* registro, reserva
booklet *noun.* folleto
bookstore *noun.* librería
boom *noun.* **1.** boom, auge **2.** estruendo
boom *verb.* **1.** estar en auge **2.** retumbar
boomerang *noun.* bumerang
boost *noun.* impulso
boost *verb.* aumentar
boot *noun.* **1.** bota **2.** maletero
boot *verb.* dar una patada
booth *noun.* **1.** puesto **2.** cabina
border *noun.* **1.** borde **2.** frontera **3.** arriate
border on *verb.* lindar con
bore *noun.* **1.** pelmazo, pesado **2.** taladro
bore *verb.* **1.** perforar **2.** aburrir
boredom *noun.* aburrimiento
boring *adj.* aburrido
borough *noun.* municipio
borrow *verb.* tomar prestado
borrower *noun.* persona que toma algo prestado
borrowing *noun.* préstamo
boss *noun.* jefe
boss (about/around) *verb.* mandar
bossy *adj.* mandón
botanist *noun.* botánico, botanista
both *adj. pron.* ambos
bother *noun.* **1.** molestia **2.** incomodidad
bother *verb.* **1.** molestar **2.** molestarse
bottle *noun.* botella
bottle *verb.* embotellar
bottleneck *noun.* **1.** atasco, embotellamiento **2.** obstáculo
bottom *noun.* **1.** fondo **2.** trasero, culo
bough *noun.* rama
bounce *noun.* **1.** bote **2.** vitalidad
bounce *verb.* **1.** hacer botar, botar, rebotar **2.** ser rechazado por el banco
bound *noun.* **1.** salto **2.** límite
bound *verb.* dar saltos, brincar
boundary *noun.* **1.** frontera **2.** punto
bounty *noun.* **1.** generosidad **2.** recompensa
bout *noun.* **1.** ataque (of illness), tanda **2.** asalto, lucha, combate
bow *noun.* **1.** arco **2.** lazo **3.** proa **4.** inclinación, reverencia
bow *verb.* inclinar(se), hacer una reverencia
—**bow to** ceder ante, transigir con
bowed (down) *adj.* inclinado, arqueado
bowel *noun.* **1.** intestino **2.** (**bowels**) entrañas
bowl *noun.* **1.** bol, cuenco **2.** cazoleta
—**bowls** bolos
bowl *verb.* **1.** jugar a los bolos **2.** lanzar la pelota **3.** dejar fuera de juego
bowler *noun.* lanzador, jugador de bochas
bowling *noun.* bolos, boliche
box *noun.* **1.** caja, cajón, estuche **2.** palco **3.** cachete
—**box office** *noun.* taquilla
box *verb.* **1.** boxear **2.** poner/meter en una caja
boxer *noun.* boxeador
boxing *noun.* boxeo
boy *noun.* niño, muchacho, chico
boycott *noun.* boicot
boycott *verb.* boicotear
boyfriend *noun.* novio, amigo
brace *noun.* refuerzo, abrazadera
brace *verb.* fortalecer, prepararse
bracket *noun.* soporte, repisa
bracket *verb.* agrupar, poner juntos
brain *noun.* **1.** cerebro **2.** seso
brake *noun.* freno
brake *verb.* frenar
branch *noun.* **1.** rama, ramo, sección **2.** sucursal
branch *verb.* ramificarse
brand *noun.* marca
brand *verb.* **1.** marcar **2.** grabar, registrar **3.** estigmatizar
brand-new *adj.* completamente nuevo, recién comprado
brandy *noun.* coñac
brass *noun.* **1.** latón **2.** metales (music)
brave *noun.* guerrero indio
brave *verb.* desafiar, arrostrar

brave *adj.* valiente, valeroso
Brazil *noun.* Brasil
Brazilian *noun. adj.* brasileño
breach *noun.* **1.** infracción, violación **2.** brecha
breach *verb.* abrir brecha en
bread *noun.* pan
breadth *noun.* **1.** anchura, ancho **2.** amplitud
break *noun.* **1.** rotura, ruptura, abertura **2.** interrupción, pausa **3.** cambio **4.** oportunidad
break *verb.* **1.** romper, quebrar **2.** quebrantar, infringir **3.** batir **4.** interrumpir **5.** comunicar, hacer público **6.** mudar, cambiar **7.** amortiguar **8.** estallar, desatarse
—**break away/off** partir, romper
—**break down 1.** frustrarse, malograrse **2.** averiarse
—**break into** abrir, forzar
—**break out 1.** aparecer, salir **2.** estallar **3.** escaparse
—**break up 1.** romperse **2.** separarse 3. disolverse
—**break through** penetrar, abrirse paso
breakdown *noun.* **1.** colapso, crisis nerviosa **2.** avería
breakfast *noun.* desayuno
breakfast *verb.* desayunar, tomar el desayuno
breakthrough *noun.* avance, descubrimiento
breast *noun.* **1.** pecho, seno **2.** pechuga
breast *verb.* **1.** enfrentarse a, arrostrar **2.** subir a la cumbre, coronar la cumbre
breath *noun.* aliento, respiración
breathe *verb.* **1.** respirar **2.** soplar, revelar
breathless *adj.* sin aliento, sofocado
bred *adj.* **1.** educado, criado **2.** de raza
breed *noun.* raza
breed *verb.* criar, reproducirse
breeding *noun.* educación, modales
breeze *noun.* brisa
brew *verb.* **1.** elaborar bebidas fermentadas **2.** preparar **3.** avecinarse, prepararse
brewery *noun.* cervecería
bribe *noun.* soborno
bribe *verb.* sobornar
brick *noun.* ladrillo
bride *noun.* novia
bridge *noun.* **1.** puente **2.** puente de mando **3.** caballete
bridge *verb.* **1.** construir/tender un puente **2.** llenar, salvar
brief *noun.* informe, expediente
brief *verb.* dar instrucciones
brief *adj.* breve
briefing *noun.* instrucciones, sesión informativa
briefly *adv.* brevemente, en pocas palabras
brigade *noun.* **1.** brigada **2.** cuerpo
bright *adj.* **1.** luminoso, resplandeciente, brillante **2.** vivo **3.** radiante, alegre **4.** inteligente
brightly *adv.* **1.** brillantemente **2.** alegremente **3.** inteligentemente
brilliant *adj.* **1.** brillante, luminoso **2.** genial, sobresaliente
brilliantly *adv.* **1.** brillantemente **2.** genialmente
bring *verb.* **1.** traer, llevar, conducir **2.** ocasionar, producir, dar, causar
—**bring about** ocasionar, provocar
—**bring out** sacar, publicar
—**bring up 1.** mencionar, sacar a relucir **2.** criar
brink *noun.* borde
brisk *adj.* activo, movido, rápido
Britain, Great Britain *noun.* Gran Bretaña
British *noun. adj.* británico
Briton *noun.* británico
broad *adj.* **1.** ancho, amplio, extenso **2.** general
broadcast *noun.* retransmisión, emisión
broadcast *verb.* **1.** retransmitir, radiar **2.** difundir, divulgar
broadcaster *noun.* locutor, presentador
broadcasting *noun.* retransmisión, emisión
broadly *adv.* en general
brochure *noun.* folleto
broke *adj.* arruinado, sin blanca

broken *adj.* **1.** roto, quebrado, fracturado **2.** estropeado, averiado **3.** entrecortado, interrumpido **4.** deshecho, quebrantado, destrozado
broker *noun.* agente, corredor de bolsa
bronze *noun. adj.* **1.** bronce **2.** color bronce **3.** objeto de bronce
brook *noun.* arroyo
brook *verb.* aguantar, tolerar, permitir
brother *noun.* **1.** hermano **2.** compañero
brow *noun.* **1.** ceja **2.** frente **3.** cresta
brown *noun.* marrón, color café, castaño
brown *verb.* broncearse, ponerse moreno
brown *adj.* **1.** marrón, color café, castaño **2.** moreno, bronceado
bruise *noun.* moretón, cardenal, magulladura
bruise *verb.* amorotonar, magullar
brush *noun.* **1.** cepillo **2.** hopo **3.** roce
brush *verb.* **1.** cepillar, barrer **2.** rozar
brutal *adj.* brutal
bubble *noun.* burbuja
bubble *verb.* burbujear
buck *noun.* macho
buck *verb.* corcovear
bucket *noun.* cubo
bud *noun.* brote, capullo
bud *verb.* brotar
budget *noun.* presupuesto
budget *verb.* hacer un presupuesto
—**budget for** asignar
buffer *noun.* amortiguador
buffet *noun.* **1.** bar, cantina **2.** bufé **3.** bofetada
buffet *verb.* **1.** golpear **2.** zarandear
buffet *adj.* bufé
bug *noun.* **1.** chinche **2.** bicho **3.** microbio **4.** micrófono oculto **5.** entusiasta
bug *verb.* **1.** pinchar, intervenir **2.** molestar
buggy *noun.* cochecito de bebé
build *noun.* constitución, complexión
build *verb.* construir, edificar
builder *noun.* constructor
building *noun.* **1.** construcción **2.** edificio
built-in *adj.* incorporado
bulb *noun.* **1.** bulbo **2.** bombilla, bombillo **3.** cubeta
bulk *noun.* **1.** la mayor parte, la mayoría **2.** masa, bulto
bulk *adj.* a granel, en grandes cantidades
bull *noun.* **1.** toro **2.** macho **3.** diana
bullet *noun.* bala
bulletin *noun.* boletín
bully *noun.* matón
bully *verb.* intimidar
bum *noun.* vago
bum *adj.* inútil, que no vale
bump *noun.* **1.** golpe **2.** chichón, bollo, bache
bump *verb.* dar(se) un golpe, chocar
bumper *noun.* parachoques
bunch *noun.* manojo, ramo, racimo
bunch *verb.* apretujarse
bundle *noun.* fardo
bundle *verb.* **1.** empaquetar, liar **2.** echar, despachar
bungalow *noun.* bungalow
bunker *noun.* búnker
burden *noun.* carga, peso
burden *verb.* cargar (con)
bureau *noun.* **1.** cómoda **2.** agencia, departamento
bureaucracy *noun.* burocracia
bureaucratic *adj.* burocrático
burglary *noun.* robo
burial *noun.* entierro
Burma *noun.* Birmania
Burmese *noun. adj.* birmano
burn *noun.* quemadura
burn *verb.* **1.** quemar, incendiar **2.** arder
burst *noun.* **1.** reventón **2.** estallido
burst *verb.* **1.** reventar, estallar **2.** desbordarse, salirse de madre
—**burst in/into/through** entrar precipitadamente
bury *verb.* **1.** enterrar, sepultar **2.** esconder
bus *noun.* autobús, camión (México)
bus *verb.* transportar en autobús
bush *noun.* arbusto
business *noun.* **1.** negocio, empresa **2.** asunto

businessman *noun.* hombre de negocios, empresario
bust *noun.* **1.** busto **2.** pecho
bust *verb.* (*slang*) **1.** agarrar, trincar **2.** destrozar
bust *adj.* estropeado
busy *adj.* **1.** ocupado **2.** concurrido
busy (with) *verb.* ocuparse
but *conj.* pero
but *prep.* excepto, menos, salvo
butcher *noun.* carnicero
butcher *verb.* **1.** matar **2.** masacrar
butter *noun.* mantequilla
butter *verb.* untar con mantequilla
butterfly *noun.* mariposa
button *noun.* botón
button *verb.* abrocharse
buy *verb.* comprar
buzz *noun.* zumbido
buzz *verb.* zumbar
by *prep.* **1.** al lado de, junto a **2.** por, en **3.** por delante **4.** para **5.** de **6.** según
by *adv.* **1.** al lado, cerca **2.** por ahí **3.** aparte
bypass *noun.* variante, circunvalación
bypass *verb.* evitar

C

C *abbr.* centígrado
cab *noun.* **1.** taxi **2.** cabina
cabbage *noun.* repollo
cabin *noun.* **1.** cabaña **2.** camarote **3.** cabina
cabinet *noun.* **1.** armario, vitrina **2.** gabinete
cable *noun.* **1.** cable **2.** cablegrama, telegrama
—**cable television** televisión por cable
cable *verb.* cablegrafiar
cage *noun.* jaula
cage *verb.* enjaular
cake *noun.* **1.** torta, pastel, tarta **2.** pastilla
cake *verb.* formar costra
calcium *noun.* calcio
calculate *verb.* calcular
calculation *noun.* cálculo
calculator *noun.* calculadora
calendar *noun.* calendario, agenda
calf *noun.* **1.** pantorrilla, canilla **2.** ternero **3.** piel de becerro
call *noun.* **1.** llamada, grito **2.** canto **3.** visita **4.** demanda **5.** necesidad, motivo
call *verb.* **1.** llamar, gritar **2.** convocar **3.** hacer una visita **4.** marcar, declarar
—**call for** requerir, necesitar
—**call off** cancelar, suspender
caller *noun.* visita, visitante
calling *noun.* vocación, profesión
calm *noun.* calma, tranquilidad
calm *verb.* calmar, tranquilizar
calm *adj.* en calma, tranquilo, apacible
calmly *adv.* con calma, tranquilamente
calorie *noun.* caloría
camera *noun.* cámara fotográfica, cámara
camp *noun.* **1.** campamento **2.** bando, facción
camp *verb.* acampar
campaign *noun.* campaña
campaign *verb.* hacer campaña
campaigner *noun.* defensor, militante
campus *noun.* recinto universitario, campus
can *noun.* lata, bote
can *verb.* **1.** poder **2.** saber **3.** enlatar
Canada *noun.* Canadá
Canadian *noun. adj.* canadiense
canal *noun.* **1.** canal **2.** tubo
cancel *verb.* **1.** cancelar **2.** matasellar **3.** anular
cancellation, cancelation *noun.* cancelación, anulación
cancer *noun.* cáncer
candidate *noun.* candidato, aspirante
candle *noun.* vela
candy *noun.* caramelo, golosina, dulce
cane *noun.* **1.** caña **2.** bastón

cane *verb.* castigar con la palmeta
cannon *noun.* cañón
cannon *verb.* chocar
canon *noun.* **1.** canon **2.** canónigo **3.** obra básica, clásico, canon
canopy *noun.* dosel
canteen *noun.* **1.** cantina, comedor **2.** cantimplora
canvas *noun. adj.* **1.** lona **2.** lienzo
cap *noun.* **1.** gorra, gorro, cofia **2.** capuchón, tapón, tapa
capability *noun.* capacidad
capable (of) *adj.* **1.** capaz **2.** competente
capacity *noun.* **1.** capacidad **2.** calidad
cape *noun.* **1.** capa **2.** cabo
capital *noun.* **1.** capital **2.** mayúscula **3.** principal **4.** capitel
capital *adj.* **1.** capital **2.** principal **3.** mayúsculo
capitalism *noun.* capitalismo
capitalist *noun.* capitalista
capitalistic *adj.* capitalista
captain *noun.* capitán
captain *verb.* capitanear
caption *noun.* leyenda
captive *noun. adj.* cautivo
capture *noun.* captura, apresamiento
capture *verb.* **1.** capturar **2.** cautivar
car *noun.* **1.** carro, automóvil, coche **2.** vagón, coche-restaurante
caravan *noun.* caravana
carbohydrate *noun.* carbohidrato
carbon *noun.* carbono
carbon dioxide *noun.* dióxido de carbono
card *noun.* **1.** carta **2.** cartulina **3.** tarjeta —**cards** cartas
cardboard *noun. adj.* cartón
cardinal *noun.* cardenal
cardinal *adj.* cardinal
care *noun.* **1.** cuidado, atención **2.** preocupación **3.** tratamiento
care *verb.* **1.** preocuparse **2.** querer, gustar
career *noun.* carrera
career *verb.* ir a toda velocidad
careful *adj.* **1.** cuidadoso **2.** minucioso
carefully *adv.* cuidadosamente
careless *adj.* descuidado, despreocupado
cargo *noun.* carga, cargamento
carnival *noun.* carnaval
carol *noun.* villancico
carp *noun.* carpa
carpet *noun.* alfombra
carpet *verb.* cubrir con una alfombra
carriage *noun.* **1.** coche, carruaje **2.** carro **3.** porte
carrot *noun.* zanahoria
carry *verb.* **1.** llevar, transportar **2.** transmitir, ser portador **3.** soportar **4.** comportar, conllevar **5.** aprobar **6.** comportarse
cart *noun.* carro, carrito, cochecito
cart *verb.* llevar, acarrear
cartoon *noun.* **1.** tira cómica, viñeta, caricatura **2.** dibujos animados
carve *verb.* **1.** tallar, grabar, esculpir **2.** cortar, trinchar
carving *noun.* escultura, talla
case *noun.* **1.** caso **2.** proceso **3.** razón **4.** maleta, estuche, funda, vitrina
cash *noun.* **1.** efectivo, metálico **2.** dinero
cash *verb.* **1.** cobrar, **2.** pagar, hacer efectivo
casino *noun.* casino
casket *noun.* **1.** ataúd **2.** estuche, cofre
cassette *noun.* casete
cast *noun.* **1.** molde **2.** escayola, yeso **3.** reparto **4.** desecho, excremento
cast *verb.* **1.** lanzar, arrojar, tirar **2.** moldear, fundir **3.** dar el papel **4.** mudar (skin) **5.** dar (el voto)
caste *noun.* casta
castle *noun.* **1.** castillo **2.** torre (chess)
casual *adj.* **1.** despreocupado, rápido **2.** informal **3.** ocasional, fortuito **4.** eventual
casually *adv.* casualmente
casualty *noun.* baja, víctima
cat *noun.* **1.** gato **2.** felino
catalog *noun.* catálogo
catalog *verb.* catalogar
catastrophe *noun.* catástrofe
catch *noun.* **1.** presa, captura, redada **2.** pestillo **3.** trampa

catch *verb.* **1.** agarrar, coger, asir, tomar **2.** pillar, sorprender, pescar **3.** contagiarse de, contraer **4.** engancharse **5.** dar con, darse con **6.** oír, entender, captar **7.** prender (fuego)
catching *adj.* contagioso
category *noun.* categoría
cater *verb.* **1.** proveer comida, abastecer **2.** atender las necesidades
catering *noun.* servicio de comidas
cathedral *noun.* catedral
catholic *adj.* amplio, variado
Catholic *noun. adj.* católico
cattle *noun plural.* ganado (vacuno)
cause *noun.* **1.** causa **2.** razón, motivo
cause *verb.* causar
caution *noun.* **1.** cautela, precaución, prudencia **2.** advertencia
caution *verb.* advertir
cautious *adj.* cauteloso, prudente, cauto
cautiously *adv.* prudentemente
cavalry *noun.* caballería
cave *noun.* cueva, caverna
CD *noun.* CD, disco compacto
cease *verb.* cesar
ceasefire *noun.* alto al fuego
ceiling *noun.* techo
celebrate *verb.* celebrar
celebrated *adj.* célebre, famoso
celebration *noun.* fiesta, festejo, celebración
celebrity *noun.* celebridad
cell *noun.* **1.** celda **2.** célula
cellar *noun.* sótano, bodega
cellular *adj.* celular
Celsius *adj.* Celsius
Celtic *adj.* celta
cement *noun.* **1.** cemento **2.** adhesivo **3.** empaste
cement *verb.* cementar
cemetery *noun.* cementerio
censorship *noun.* censura
census *noun.* censo
cent *noun.* céntimo
centennial *noun. adj.* centenario
center *noun.* centro
center *verb.* centrar
—**center on** concentrarse en
centigrade *adj.* centígrado
centimeter *noun.* centímetro
central *adj.* **1.** central **2.** principal
centrally *adv.* céntrico
century *noun.* siglo
ceramic *adj.* de cerámica
ceramics *noun.* cerámica
cereal *noun.* cereal
cerebral *adj.* cerebral
ceremony *noun.* ceremonia
certain *adj.* **1.** cierto **2.** seguro
certainly *interj.* por supuesto
certainly *adv.* **1.** seguro **2.** desde luego, por supuesto
certainty *noun.* certeza, seguridad
certificate *noun.* certificado
chain *noun.* cadena
chain *verb.* encadenar, atar
chair *noun.* **1.** silla **2.** presidencia **3.** cátedra
chair *verb.* presidir
chairman, chairperson, chairwoman *noun.* presidente
chalk *noun.* **1.** creta, roca caliza **2.** tiza
challenge *noun.* **1.** desafío, reto **2.** recusación
challenge *verb.* **1.** desafiar, retar **2.** recusar **3.** poner en duda, cuestionar
challenger *noun.* desafiador, contrincante, aspirante
challenging *adj.* desafiante, estimulante, que supone un reto
chamber *noun.* **1.** cuarto **2.** cámara
champagne *noun.* champán, champaña
champion *noun.* **1.** campeón **2.** defensor
champion *verb.* defender
championship *noun.* **1.** campeonato **2.** defensa
chance *noun.* **1.** azar, casualidad **2.** oportunidad, ocasión **3.** posibilidad **4.** riesgo
—**by chance** por casualidad
chance *verb.* **1.** arriesgar **2.** suceder algo por casualidad
—**chance on/upon** encontrarse por casualidad, dar con
chance *adj.* fortuito, casual
chancellor *noun.* **1.** canciller **2.** rector

change *noun.* **1.** cambio **2.** transformación, modificación
change *verb.* **1.** cambiar, cambiarse **2.** transformar, modificar
channel *noun.* **1.** canal, cauce, vía **2.** estrecho
channel *verb.* canalizar, dirigir, encauzar
chant *noun.* **1.** canto litúrgico, cántico **2.** eslogan, consigna
chant *verb.* **1.** cantar **2.** corear, gritar
chaos *noun.* caos
chap *noun.* tío, tipo
chapel *noun.* capilla
chapter *noun.* capítulo
character *noun.* **1.** carácter, naturaleza, personalidad **2.** personaje **3.** tipo, figura
characteristic *noun.* característica
characteristic *adj.* característico
characterize *verb.* **1.** caracterizar **2.** describir
charcoal *noun.* carbón vegetal
charge *noun.* **1.** precio, honorarios **2.** acusación **3.** carga **4.** cargo, cuidado
charge *verb.* **1.** cobrar **2.** poner en la cuenta **3.** cargar contra, atacar **4.** irrumpir **5.** cargar **6.** encargar
—**charge with** acusar
charitable *adj.* **1.** caritativo, comprensivo **2.** benéfico
charity *noun.* **1.** caridad **2.** institución benéfica
charm *noun.* **1.** encanto, simpatía **2.** hechizo **3.** amuleto
charm *verb.* encantar
charming *adj.* encantador
chart *noun.* **1.** carta, mapa **2.** gráfico
chart *verb.* **1.** trazar **2.** representar en un gráfico
charter *noun.* fuero, estatutos
charter *verb.* fletar, alquilar
charter *adj.* chárter
chase *noun.* **1.** persecución **2.** caza
chase *verb.* **1.** perseguir **2.** cazar
—**chase away/off** ahuyentar
chat *noun.* charla, conversación
chat *verb.* charlar, conversar
cheap *adj.* **1.** barato **2.** ordinario
cheat *noun.* **1.** tramposo **2.** trampa, estafa
cheat *verb.* engañar, estafar, timar
check *noun.* **1.** control, revisión, inspección **2.** impedimento, freno **3.** jaque **4.** cuadro **5.** ticket, comprobante, papeleta, resguardo **6.** cuenta, nota **7.** cheque
check *verb.* **1.** controlar, revisar **2.** comprobar, verificar **3.** detener, frenar **4.** marcar, señalar **5.** chequear, facturar
checked *adj.* a cuadros
cheek *noun.* **1.** mejilla **2.** descaro, frescura
cheer *noun.* **1.** ovación, aclamación **2.** alegría, regocijo
cheer *verb.* vitorear, aclamar
cheerful *adj.* alegre, animado, risueño
cheerfully *adv.* alegremente
cheese *noun.* queso
chef *noun.* cocinero, jefe de cocina
chemical *noun.* producto químico
chemical *adj.* químico
chemist *noun.* químico
chemistry *noun.* química
chicken *noun.* **1.** pollo **2.** cobarde
child *noun.* **1.** niño/a **2.** hijo/a
Chile *noun.* Chile
Chilean *noun. adj.* chileno
chili *noun.* chile
chill *noun.* **1.** frío **2.** resfriado
chill *verb.* enfriar
chill *adj.* frío
chimney *noun.* chimenea
chin *noun.* barbilla, mentón
china *noun.* porcelana
China *noun.* China
Chinese *noun. adj.* chino
chip *noun.* **1.** astilla, lasca **2.** desportilladura **3.** ficha **4.** chip
chip *verb.* desportillar, desconchar
chocolate *noun.* chocolate
chocolate *adj.* de chocolate
choice *noun.* elección
choir *noun.* coro
choke *noun.* estrangulador
choke *verb.* **1.** ahogar, asfixiar **2.** ahogarse, asfixiarse **3.** obstruir, atascar
choose *verb.* **1.** escoger, elegir, seleccionar **2.** optar
chop *noun.* **1.** golpe cortante **2.** chuleta

chop (up) *verb.* cortar, picar
chops *noun plural.* mandíbulas
chord *noun.* acorde
chorus *noun.* **1.** coro **2.** estribillo
chorus *verb.* corear
Christ *noun.* Cristo
Christian *noun. adj.* cristiano
Christianity *noun.* cristianismo
Christmas *noun.* Navidad
chronic *adj.* crónico
chronicle *noun.* crónica
chronicle *verb.* hacer la crónica de
chuck *verb.* tirar, botar
chunk *noun.* trozo
church *noun.* iglesia
churchyard *noun.* cementerio
CIA *abbr.* CIA
cider *noun.* sidra
cigarette *noun.* cigarro
cinema *noun.* cine
circle *noun.* círculo
circle *verb.* **1.** rodear, cercar **2.** trazar un círculo
circuit *noun.* **1.** recorrido **2.** circuito **3.** vuelta
circular *noun. adj.* circular
circulate *verb.* **1.** circular **2.** hacer circular
circulation *noun.* circulación
circumstance *noun.* circunstancia
circus *noun.* circo
citizen *noun.* ciudadano, vecino, habitante
citizenship *noun.* ciudadanía
city *noun.* ciudad
civic *adj.* **1.** municipal, cívico **2.** cortés, educado **3.** civil
civil servant *noun.* funcionario
civilian *noun.* civil
civilization *noun.* civilización
claim *noun.* **1.** reivindicación, demanda, reclamación **2.** derecho **3.** afirmación
claim *verb.* **1.** reivindicar, reclamar **2.** afirmar **3.** requerir, exigir
clamp *noun.* **1.** grapa, clip **2.** abrazadera
clamp *verb.* sujetar
clan *noun.* clan
clarification *noun.* aclaración
clarify *verb.* aclarar
clarity *noun.* claridad, lucidez
clash *noun.* **1.** choque, conflicto **2.** ruido, estruendo, fragor **3.** coincidencia
clash *verb.* **1.** oponerse, chocar, enfrentarse **2.** sonar, entrechocar **3.** coincidir **4.** desentonar
class *noun.* **1.** clase **2.** categoría
class *verb.* clasificar
classic *noun. adj.* clásico
classical *adj.* clásico
classification *noun.* clasificación
classified *adj.* secreto, confidencial
classify *verb.* clasificar
clause *noun.* **1.** oración **2.** cláusula
clay *noun.* arcilla, barro
clean *verb.* limpiar, lavar
clean *adj.* **1.** limpio **2.** nuevo, en blanco **3.** puro **4.** neto, bien definido, preciso
clean *adv.* por completo
cleaner *noun.* **1.** encargado de la limpieza **2.** producto de limpieza
cleanse *verb.* limpiar
clear *verb.* **1.** quitar, despejar, aclarar, desalojar **2.** despejarse **3.** salvar
—**clear (of)** absolver
clear *adj.* **1.** claro **2.** despejado, sereno **3.** transparente, nítido **4.** tranquilo **5.** explícito **6.** amplio, absoluto
—**clear (of)** libre (de)
clearance *noun.* **1.** despeje **2.** margen **3.** autorización
clearing *noun.* claro
clearly *adv.* **1.** claramente, con claridad **2.** obviamente
clergy *noun.* clero
clerical *adj.* **1.** clerical, eclesiástico **2.** de oficina, administrativo
clerk *noun.* **1.** oficinista, empleado **2.** funcionario, secretario **3.** dependiente, vendedor
clever *adj.* **1.** inteligente **2.** hábil **3.** ingenioso
click *noun.* clic
click *verb.* hacer clic
client *noun.* cliente
cliff *noun.* acantilado
climate *noun.* **1.** clima **2.** ambiente
climax *noun.* clímax

climb *noun.* escalada, ascenso, subida
climb *verb.* escalar, ascender, subir
climber *noun.* **1.** alpinista, andinista, escalador **2.** enredadera **3.** arribista, trepador
clinch *verb.* cerrar, firmar
cling (to) *verb.* pegarse, agarrarse, aferrarse
clinic *noun.* clínica
clinical *adj.* clínico
clip *noun.* **1.** clip, pasador, grapa, horquilla **2.** tijeretada **3.** cachete, golpe **4.** secuencia
clip *verb.* **1.** sujetar **2.** cortar, podar **3.** dar un cachete
cloak *noun.* capa, manto
cloak *verb.* ocultar
clock *noun.* reloj
clock *verb.* cronometrar
—**clock in/out/on/off** fichar, entrar a trabajar
close *noun.* fin, final
close *verb.* **1.** cerrar **2.** terminar, concluir
close *adj.* **1.** cercano, próximo **2.** íntimo **3.** parecido, igualado **4.** detallado **5.** ajustado, reñido **6.** bochornoso **7.** tacaño **8.** reservado
close *adv.* cerca (de)
closely *adv.* **1.** detenidamente **2.** de cerca **3.** con atención
closet *noun.* armario
closure *noun.* **1.** cierre **2.** clausura
cloth *noun.* tela, paño
clothes *noun plural.* **1.** ropa, vestidos **2.** ropa de cama
clothespin *noun.* pinza
clothing *noun.* ropa, vestimenta
cloud *noun.* nube
cloud *verb.* **1.** nublar, enturbiar, empañar **2.** nublarse
club *noun.* **1.** porra **2.** palo **3.** club
—**clubs** *noun plural.* tréboles, palos
club *verb.* aporrear
clue *noun.* pista, indicio
cluster *noun.* grupo, racimo
cluster *verb.* agruparse
clutch *noun.* **1.** dominio **2.** embrague, cloche
clutch (at) *verb.* **1.** agarrar, asir **2.** apretar
—**clutch (at)** *verb.* tratar de agarrar, aferrarse a
cm *abbr.* centímetro
Co *abbr.* compañía
coach *noun.* **1.** entrenador **2.** profesor particular **3.** vagón, coche
coach *verb.* preparar, entrenar, enseñar
coal *noun.* carbón
coalition *noun.* coalición
coarse *adj.* **1.** áspero, grueso **2.** grosero, ordinario
coast *noun.* costa, litoral
coast *verb.* ir en punto muerto
coastal *adj.* costero
coat *noun.* **1.** abrigo **2.** chaqueta, saco **3.** pelo, pelaje **4.** capa
coat *verb.* cubrir, revestir, bañar
cocaine *noun.* cocaína
cock *noun.* **1.** gallo, macho **2.** grifo, espita **3.** polla, pinga
cock *verb.* **1.** erguir, enderezar **2.** amartillar **3.** ladear
cockpit *noun.* cabina
cocktail *noun.* **1.** cóctel **2.** macedonia
cocoa *noun.* **1.** cacao **2.** chocolate
code *noun.* código
code *verb.* codificar
coffee *noun.* café
coherent *adj.* coherente
coin *noun.* moneda
coin *verb.* **1.** acuñar **2.** inventar
coincide *verb.* coincidir
coincidence *noun.* coincidencia
coke *noun.* coque
cold *noun.* **1.** frío **2.** resfriado, resfrío, catarro
cold *adj.* frío
cold war *noun.* guerra fría
coldly *adv.* fríamente
collaboration *noun.* colaboración
collapse *noun.* **1.** caída, derrumbamiento, hundimiento **2.** colapso **3.** fracaso
collapse *verb.* **1.** caer, derrumbarse, hundirse **2.** sufrir un colapso **3.** fracasar **4.** plegarse
collar *noun.* **1.** cuello **2.** collar **3.** collarín
collar *verb.* **1.** abordar, acorralar **2.** agarrar, apropiarse
colleague *noun.* colega

collect *verb.* **1.** reunir, juntar **2.** coleccionar **3.** cobrar, recaudar **4.** recoger
collected *adj.* **1.** completo **2.** seguro de sí
collection *noun.* **1.** recogida, recaudación, colecta **2.** colección
collective *noun. adj.* colectivo
collector *noun.* **1.** recaudador **2.** coleccionista
college *noun.* facultad
collision *noun.* choque, colisión
Colombia *noun.* Colombia
Colombian *noun. adj.* colombiano
colon *noun.* **1.** dos puntos **2.** colon
colonel *noun.* coronel
colonial *adj.* colonial
colony *noun.* colonia
color *noun.* color
—**colors** bandera, enseña
color *verb.* **1.** pintar, colorear **2.** ponerse colorado, ruborizarse
color *adj.* en color
colored *noun.* persona de color, negro
colored *adj.* **1.** de colores **2.** de color, negro
colorful *adj.* lleno de color, vistoso
coloring *noun.* **1.** colorante **2.** tez
column *noun.* **1.** columna **2.** fila
columnist *noun.* columnista
comb *noun.* peine
comb *verb.* **1.** peinar **2.** peinarse
combat *noun.* combate
combat *verb.* combatir
combination *noun.* combinación
combine *noun.* asociación
combine *verb.* combinar, compaginar
come *interj.* ¡vamos!
come *verb.* **1.** venir **2.** llegar **3.** acercarse
—**come across** toparse con
—**come back** **1.** volver **2.** contestar, replicar
—**come in** entrar
—**come out** aparecer, salir
—**come through** pasar por
—**come to terms** llegar a un acuerdo
comeback *noun.* vuelta, retorno
comedian *noun.* cómico
comedy *noun.* comedia
comet *noun.* cometa
comfort *noun.* **1.** comodidad, confort **2.** consuelo
comfort *verb.* consolar, confortar
comfortable *adj.* **1.** cómodo **2.** tranquilo, relajado **3.** amplio, suficiente, holgado
comfortably *adv.* **1.** cómodamente **2.** sin problemas, holgadamente
comforting *adj.* reconfortante
comic *noun. adj.* cómico
command *noun.* **1.** orden **2.** control, mando
command *verb.* **1.** ordenar, mandar **2.** estar al mando de **3.** imponer, infundir, inspirar
commander *noun.* **1.** comandante **2.** capitán de fragata
commanding *adj.* **1.** dominante **2.** autoritario
commemorate *verb.* conmemorar
commence *verb.* comenzar
comment *noun.* comentario
comment on *verb.* comentar
commentary *noun.* comentario, crítica
commentator *noun.* comentarista
commerce *noun.* comercio
commercial *noun.* anuncio
commercial *adj.* **1.** comercial **2.** rentable
commission *noun.* **1.** comisión **2.** encargo **3.** nombramiento
commission *verb.* **1.** encargar **2.** nombrar
commissioner *noun.* comisario
commit *verb.* **1.** cometer **2.** enviar, destinar, internar **3.** comprometer, comprometerse
commitment *noun.* compromiso, obligación
committed *adj.* comprometido, entregado
committee *noun.* comité, comisión
commodity *noun.* producto, artículo, mercadería, mercancía
common *noun.* tierras comunales
common *adj.* **1.** común, corriente **2.** público **3.** ordinario, vulgar
—**common sense** *noun.* sentido común
commonplace *adj.* común, corriente
commonwealth *noun.* commonwealth

communal *adj.* comunal, común
communicate *verb.* **1.** comunicar **2.** comunicarse
communication *noun.* **1.** comunicación **2.** comunicado, mensaje
—**communications** *noun plural.* comunicaciones
communicative *adj.* comunicativo
communion *noun.* comunión
communism *noun.* comunismo
communist *noun. adj.* comunista
community *noun.* comunidad
commute *verb.* **1.** desplazarse diariamente al lugar de trabajo **2.** conmutar
compact *noun.* **1.** pacto, acuerdo, convenio **2.** polvera
compact *adj.* compacto, sólido
—**compact disc** disco compacto, compact disc
companion *noun.* **1.** compañero **2.** guía, manual
company *noun.* **1.** compañía **2.** visita **3.** compañía
comparable *adj.* comparable
comparative *adj.* **1.** relativo **2.** comparativo
comparatively *adv.* relativamente
compare *verb.* **1.** comparar **2.** compararse
comparison *noun.* comparación
compartment *noun.* compartimiento
compass *noun.* **1.** brújula **2.** compás **3.** alcance
compassion *noun.* compasión
compatibility *noun.* compatibilidad
compatible *adj.* compatible
compel *verb.* obligar, forzar
compensate *verb.* **1.** indemnizar, compensar **2.** recompensar
compensation *noun.* indemnización
compete *verb.* competir
competence *noun.* competencia
competent *adj.* competente
competition *noun.* **1.** competición **2.** competencia
competitive *adj.* competitivo
competitor *noun.* competidor
compile *verb.* compilar
complain *verb.* quejarse
complaint *noun.* **1.** queja, reclamación, denuncia **2.** enfermedad, achaque, dolencia
complement *noun.* complemento
complement *verb.* complementar
complementary *adj.* complementario
complete *verb.* **1.** completar **2.** terminar, acabar, cumplir **3.** rellenar
complete *adj.* **1.** completo, entero **2.** acabado
completely *adv.* completamente, totalmente
completion *noun.* finalización
complex *noun. adj.* complejo
complexity *noun.* complejidad
compliance *noun.* conformidad
complicate *verb.* complicar
complicated *adj.* complicado
complication *noun.* complicación
compliment *noun.* cumplido, halago
compliment *verb.* elogiar
comply *verb.* obedecer
component *noun.* pieza, componente
compose *verb.* **1.** componer **2.** calmarse, serenarse
composed *adj.* sereno, tranquilo
composer *noun.* compositor
composition *noun.* **1.** composición **2.** redacción
compost *noun.* abono orgánico
compound *noun.* **1.** compuesto **2.** recinto
compound *adj.* compuesto, múltiple
comprehension *noun.* comprensión
comprehensive *adj.* completo, exhaustivo, integral
compression *noun.* compresión
comprise *verb.* comprender, incluir, constar de
compromise *noun.* acuerdo mutuo, término medio
compulsory *adj.* obligatorio
compute *verb.* computar, calcular
computer *noun.* ordenador
computerize *verb.* computarizar, informatizar
con *noun.* estafa, timo
con *verb.* estafar, timar
conceal *verb.* ocultar, disimular
concede *verb.* **1.** reconocer, admitir **2.** ceder, darse por vencido

conceive *verb.* **1.** concebir **2.** entender
concentrate *verb.* **1.** concentrar **2.** concentrarse
concentrated *adj.* concentrado
concentration *noun.* concentración
concept *noun.* concepto
conception *noun.* **1.** concepción **2.** noción
concern *noun.* **1.** asunto **2.** preocupación, inquietud **3.** interés **4.** negocio
concern *verb.* concernir, afectar
—**concern about/for** preocuparse
—**concern in/with** interesarse en
concerning *prep.* con respecto a, en lo que se refiere a
concert *noun.* concierto
concession *noun.* concesión
conclude *verb.* **1.** concluir, terminar **2.** concertar, pactar, cerrar
conclusion *noun.* conclusión
concrete *noun.* hormigón
concrete *verb.* revestir de hormigón
concrete *adj.* **1.** concreto **2.** de hormigón
condemn *verb.* **1.** condenar **2.** declarar en ruina (a building)
condemnation *noun.* condena
condition *noun.* **1.** condición **2.** estado
condition *verb.* **1.** condicionar **2.** acondicionar
conditional *adj.* condicional
conduct *noun.* comportamiento, conducta
conduct *verb.* **1.** conducir, guiar **2.** dirigir, llevar **3.** comportarse
conductor *noun.* **1.** conductor **2.** director de orquesta **3.** revisor
confederation *noun.* confederación
confer (with) *verb.* consultar (con), deliberar
—**confer on** conceder, conferir
conference *noun.* conferencia
confess *verb.* confesar
confession *noun.* confesión
confidence *noun.* **1.** confianza **2.** seguridad
confident *adj.* seguro, seguro de sí mismo
confidential *adj.* **1.** confidencial **2.** de confianza
confidentiality *noun.* confidencialidad, reserva
confine *verb.* **1.** confinar, recluir **2.** limitar
confined (to) *adj.* **1.** recluido **2.** reducido, limitado
confirm *verb.* confirmar
confirmation *noun.* confirmación
confirmed *adj.* **1.** empedernido, inveterado **2.** confirmado
conflict *noun.* conflicto
conflict *verb.* estar en conflicto, entrar en desacuerdo
conform *verb.* ajustarse, someterse
—**conform to** adaptarse a
conformity *noun.* conformidad
confront *verb.* hacer frente, plantar cara
confrontation *noun.* enfrentamiento
confuse *verb.* **1.** confundir, desconcertar **2.** complicar, enredar
confused *adj.* confuso, desconcertado
confusion *noun.* confusión
congratulate (on) *verb.* felicitar
congregation *noun.* **1.** congregación, feligresía **2.** reunión
congress *noun.* congreso
congressional *adj.* del Congreso
congressman *noun.* congresista
conjunction *noun.* conjunción
connect *verb.* **1.** conectar, unir, enlazar **2.** asociar
connection *noun.* **1.** conexión, enlace **2.** relación **3.** contacto
—**connections** parientes
conquer *verb.* conquistar, vencer
conquest *noun.* conquista
conscience *noun.* conciencia
conscious *adj.* consciente
consciously *adv.* conscientemente
consciousness *noun.* conciencia
consecutive *adj.* consecutivo
consensus *noun.* consenso
consent *noun.* consentimiento
consent *verb.* consentir
consequence *noun.* **1.** consecuencia **2.** importancia, trascendencia
consequently *adv.* por consiguiente
conservation *noun.* conservación
conservatism *noun.* conservadurismo

conservative *adj.* conservador
consider *verb.* **1.** considerar **2.** tener en cuenta
considerable *adj.* considerable
considerably *adv.* considerablemente
consideration *noun.* **1.** consideración **2.** factor
considering *prep.* teniendo en cuenta, en vista de
consist (of) *verb.* componerse de, constar de
consistency *noun.* **1.** coherencia **2.** consistencia
consistent (with) *adj.* **1.** consecuente **2.** coherente
consistently *adv.* **1.** consecuentemente **2.** sistemáticamente
consolation *noun.* **1.** consolación **2.** consuelo
console *verb.* consolar
consolidate *verb.* consolidar
consolidation *noun.* consolidación
consortium *noun.* consorcio
conspicuous *adj.* llamativo, manifiesto
conspiracy *noun.* conspiración
constant *adj.* **1.** constante, continuo **2.** leal, fiel
constantly *adv.* constantemente
constituency *noun.* distrito electoral
constituent *noun.* **1.** componente **2.** elector
constituent *adj.* constitutivo, integrante
constitute *verb.* constituir
constitution *noun.* constitución
constitutional *adj.* constitucional
construct *verb.* construir
construction *noun.* construcción
constructive *adj.* constructivo
consult *verb.* **1.** consultar **2.** pasar visita
consultant *noun.* asesor, consultor
consultation *noun.* consulta
consume *verb.* consumir
consumer *noun.* consumidor
consumption *noun.* consumo, gasto
contact *noun.* contacto
contact *verb.* contactar
contain *verb.* **1.** contener **2.** contenerse
container *noun.* **1.** recipiente, envase **2.** contenedor
contaminate *verb.* contaminar
contamination *noun.* contaminación
contemplate *verb.* **1.** considerar **2.** contemplar
contemporary *noun.* contemporáneo
contemporary *adj.* contemporáneo
contempt *noun.* desprecio, desdén
contend (with) *verb.* competir
—**contend that** sostener, afirmar
contender *noun.* contendiente
content *noun.* **1.** contenido **2.** satisfacción
—**contents** índice
content *verb.* contentar, satisfacer
content *adj.* satisfecho, contento
contention *noun.* **1.** opinión, argumento **2.** discusión, disensión
contentious *adj.* contencioso, polémico
contest *noun.* competencia, competición, concurso, combate
context *noun.* contexto
continent *noun.* continente
continent *adj.* continente
continental *adj.* continental
contingency *noun.* contingencia
contingent *noun.* contingente
continual *adj.* continuo, constante
continually *adv.* continuamente, constantemente
continuation *noun.* continuación
continue *verb.* continuar, seguir
continuity *noun.* continuidad
continuous *adj.* continuo
continuously *adv.* continuamente
contract *noun.* contrato
contract *verb.* **1.** contraer **2.** contraerse **3.** contratar **4.** comprometerse por contrato
contraction *noun.* contracción
contractor *noun.* contratista
contradiction *noun.* contradicción
contradictory *adj.* contradictorio
contrary *noun.* contrario
contrary *adj.* **1.** contrario **2.** terco, obstinado
contrast *noun.* contraste
contrast *verb.* **1.** contrastar **2.** comparar
contribute *verb.* **1.** contribuir, aportar **2.** escribir, colaborar

contribution *noun.* **1.** contribución, aporte **2.** colaboración, artículo **3.** intervención, aportación
contributor *noun.* **1.** contribuyente **2.** contribuidor **3.** colaborador
control *noun.* **1.** control, dominio **2.** restricción
—**controls** mandos
control *verb.* controlar, dominar, dirigir, regular
controller *noun.* controlador, interventor
controversial *adj.* controvertido, polémico
controversy *noun.* controversia
convene *verb.* **1.** convocar **2.** reunirse
convenience *noun.* comodidad, conveniencia, ventaja
convenient *adj.* **1.** conveniente, cómodo, idóneo **2.** bien situado, accesible
conveniently *adv.* convenientemente, oportunamente
convent *noun.* convento
convention *noun.* **1.** convención **2.** congreso
conventional *adj.* convencional, tradicional
convergence *noun.* convergencia
conversation *noun.* conversación
conversely *adv.* a la inversa
conversion *noun.* **1.** conversión **2.** reforma, remodelación
convert *noun.* converso
convert *verb.* **1.** convertir **2.** convertirse **3.** reformar
convertible *noun.* descapotable
convertible *adj.* convertible
convey *verb.* **1.** transportar, llevar, conducir **2.** comunicar, expresar **3.** traspasar
convict *noun.* presidiario
convict *verb.* declarar culpable, condenar
conviction *noun.* **1.** condena **2.** antecedentes penales **3.** convicción
convince *verb.* convencer
convincing *adj.* convincente
convoy *noun.* convoy
cook *noun.* cocinero
cook *verb.* cocinar, guisar, preparar (la comida), cocer
cookery *noun.* cocina
cookie *noun.* galleta
cool *noun.* frescor
cool *verb.* **1.** refrescar, enfriar **2.** calmarse
cool *adj.* **1.** fresco **2.** tranquilo, sereno **3.** frío, seco **4.** enrollado, macanudo **5.** guay, ¡qué pasada!
coop *noun.* gallinero
co-operation *noun.* cooperación, colaboración
co-operative *adj.* colaborador, servicial, cooperativo
coordinate *verb.* coordinar
coordination *noun.* coordinación
cop *noun.* policía
cope *verb.* arreglárselas, poder con, solucionar
copper *noun.* cobre
copper *adj.* de cobre, cobrizo
copy *noun.* **1.** copia **2.** ejemplar, número **3.** manuscrito
copy *verb.* copiar, imitar
copyright *noun.* derechos de autor
coral *noun.* coral
coral *adj.* de coral
cord *noun.* **1.** cuerda, cordón, cable **2.** pana
—**spinal cord** médula espinal
core *noun.* **1.** corazón (fruit) **2.** centro, núcleo **3.** esencia, meollo
core *verb.* deshuesar
cork *noun.* **1.** corcho **2.** tapón
cork *verb.* tapar con corcho, taponar
corn *noun.* **1.** maíz **2.** callo
corner *noun.* **1.** esquina, ángulo **2.** rincón **3.** córner, saque de esquina
corner *verb.* **1.** arrinconar, acorralar **2.** tomar las curvas
coronary *noun.* infarto de miocardio, trombosis coronaria
coronary *adj.* coronario
coronation *noun.* coronación
coroner *noun.* juez de instrucción
corporal *noun.* cabo
corporal *adj.* corporal
corporate *adj.* conjunto, colectivo
corporation *noun.* **1.** corporación **2.** sociedad limitada

corps *noun.* cuerpo
corpse *noun.* cadáver
correct *verb.* corregir
correct *adj.* correcto
—**to be correct** tener razón
correction *noun.* corrección
correctly *adv.* correctamente
correspond *verb.* mantener correspondencia, escribir
—**correspond to** equivaler a
—**correspond with** corresponder con
correspondence *noun.* correspondencia, conexión
correspondent *noun.* **1.** correspondiente **2.** corresponsal
corresponding *adj.* correspondiente
corridor *noun.* pasillo, corredor
corrupt *verb.* corromper
corrupt *adj.* **1.** corrupto, corrompido **2.** degenerado, depravado
corruption *noun.* **1.** corrupción **2.** degeneración
cosmetic *noun. adj.* cosmético
cost *noun.* precio, coste
—**costs** costas
cost *verb.* **1.** costar, valer **2.** calcular el coste de
costly *adj.* costoso, suntuoso
costume *noun.* **1.** traje **2.** disfraz
cot *noun.* cama plegable
cottage *noun.* casa de campo
cotton *noun.* algodón
couch *noun.* sofá, camilla, diván
couch *verb.* expresar
cough *noun.* tos
cough *verb.* toser
could *verb.* **1.** pasado del verbo **can** **2.** (se usa para expresar posibilidad)
council *noun.* **1.** consejo, junta, concilio **2.** ayuntamiento
councilor *noun.* concejal, miembro de junta
counsel *noun.* **1.** consejo **2.** abogado
counsel *verb.* aconsejar
counselor *noun.* consejero, asesor
count *noun.* **1.** recuento, cuenta, escrutinio **2.** cargo, acusación **3.** conde
count *verb.* **1.** contar **2.** considerar
counter *noun.* **1.** ficha **2.** mostrador, ventanilla **3.** contador
counter *verb.* responder a, contestar a
counter to *adv.* al contrario de, al revés de
counterpart *noun.* homólogo, equivalente
countess *noun.* condesa
countless *adj.* incontable, innumerable
country *noun.* **1.** país, pueblo **2.** patria **3.** terreno, tierra
—**the country** el campo
countryside *noun.* campo, zona rural
county *noun.* **1.** comarca **2.** condado
coup *noun.* **1.** logro, éxito **2.** golpe de estado
couple *noun.* **1.** par **2.** pareja, matrimonio
couple *verb.* acoplar, enganchar, unir
coupon *noun.* **1.** cupón **2.** boleto
courage *noun.* coraje, valor
courier *noun.* **1.** guía de turismo **2.** mensajero
course *noun.* **1.** curso **2.** plato **3.** campo, pista **4.** camino, modo de proceder **5.** rumbo, órbita, ruta
—**of course** por supuesto, cómo no
court *noun.* **1.** juzgado, corte, tribunal **2.** pista, cancha **3.** palacio **4.** patio
court *verb.* **1.** cortejar **2.** buscar **3.** exponerse a
courtesy *noun.* cortesía
courtyard *noun.* patio
cousin *noun.* primo
covenant *noun.* pacto, convenio, alianza
cover *noun.* **1.** tapa, tapadera, funda **2.** cubrecama, colcha **3.** portada **4.** refugio, cobijo, cobertura, amparo
cover *verb.* **1.** cubrir, tapar, forrar **2.** recorrer **3.** abarcar, tratar **4.** suplir
coverage *noun.* **1.** cobertura **2.** reportaje
covering *noun.* capa, envoltura
cow *noun.* **1.** vaca **2.** hembra (de algunos animales)
cow *verb.* intimidar
cowboy *noun.* vaquero, cowboy
coxswain, cox *noun.* timonel
cozy *adj.* acogedor, íntimo
crack *noun.* **1.** grieta, hendidura, raja **2.**

rendija **3.** chasquido, crujido **4.** golpe **5.** chiste, chanza **6.** crack, cocaína dura
crack *verb.* **1.** rajarse, resquebrajarse **2.** abrir, romper, cascar **3.** crujir, chasquear **4.** contar chistes **5.** forzar **6.** resolver, descifrar **7.** rendirse, sucumbir, caer
crack *adj.* de primera
crackdown *noun.* medidas enérgicas, campaña
cracked *adj.* **1.** rajado, agrietado **2.** tarado, chiflado
craft *noun.* **1.** arte, oficio **2.** artesanía **3.** barco, embarcación **4.** astucia, destreza
craftsman *noun.* artesano
crafty *adj.* astuto
crane *noun.* grúa
crane *verb.* estirar (el cuello)
crash *noun.* **1.** estruendo, estrépito **2.** colisión, choque, accidente **3.** quiebra
crash *verb.* **1.** caer con estrépito **2.** chocar contra, colisionar **3.** estrellar(se) **4.** derrumbarse, sufrir una crisis **5.** abrirse camino/paso
crash *adj.* acelerado, intensivo
crawl *noun.* **1.** paso lento **2.** crol
crawl *verb.* **1.** avanzar lentamente **2.** gatear, arrastrarse **3.** estar plagado
crazy *adj.* **1.** loco **2.** entusiasmado
cream *noun.* **1.** nata **2.** crema
—**the cream of society** la flor y nata de la sociedad
cream *verb.* batir
create *verb.* **1.** crear **2.** nombrar
creation *noun.* creación
creative *adj.* creativo
creativity *noun.* creatividad
creator *noun.* creador
creature *noun.* criatura
credibility *noun.* credibilidad
credible *adj.* creíble
credit *noun.* **1.** crédito **2.** solvencia **3.** saldo **4.** mérito **5.** reputación, honor
—**credit card** tarjeta de crédito
—**credits** títulos de crédito
credit *verb.* **1.** abonar, ingresar **2.** creer
—**credit with** atribuir
creditor *noun.* acreedor
creed *noun.* credo
creep *noun.* adulador, lameculos
creep *verb.* **1.** deslizarse, arrastrarse **2.** avanzar sigilosamente **3.** trepar
crescent *noun.* media luna
crescent *adj.* en forma de media luna, creciente
crest *noun.* **1.** cresta **2.** pico, cumbre **3.** penacho **4.** blasón
crew *noun.* **1.** tripulación, dotación **2.** pandilla, equipo
crew *verb.* tripular
cricket *noun.* **1.** cricket **2.** grillo
crime *noun.* **1.** crimen, delito **2.** delincuencia
criminal *noun.* criminal, delincuente
criminal *adj.* criminal, delictivo
cripple *noun.* inválido, lisiado, mutilado
cripple *verb.* **1.** lisiar, mutilar **2.** inutilizar, paralizar
crisis *noun.* crisis, momento crítico
crisp *adj.* **1.** crujiente **2.** fresco **3.** seco, tajante
criterion *noun.* criterio
critic *noun.* crítico
critical *adj.* **1.** crítico **2.** grave, serio
critically *adv.* **1.** críticamente, de manera crítica **2.** gravemente, de gravedad
criticism *noun.* crítica
criticize *verb.* **1.** criticar **2.** censurar
crook *noun.* **1.** cayado, báculo **2.** criminal, maleante **3.** pliegue del codo
crook *verb.* doblar, encorvar
crop *noun.* **1.** cultivo, cosecha **2.** fusta, látigo **3.** corte a lo garçon **4.** buche
crop *verb.* **1.** pacer **2.** cortar
cross *noun.* **1.** cruz **2.** cruce, híbrido
cross *verb.* **1.** cruzar, atravesar **2.** cruzarse **3.** santiguarse **4.** contrariar
cross *adj.* enojado, enfadado
cross-country *adj.* a campo traviesa
crossing *noun.* **1.** cruce **2.** travesía
crossroads *noun singular.* encrucijada, cruce
cross-section *noun.* **1.** corte transversal **2.** sección representativa, muestra
crouch *verb.* **1.** agacharse, ponerse en cuclillas **2.** agazaparse
crowd *noun.* **1.** multitud, muchedumbre **2.** público, espectadores **3.** gente

crowd *verb.* **1.** agolparse, congregarse, reunirse **2.** atestar, llenar
crowded *adj.* **1.** abarrotado, atestado, concurrido **2.** lleno de actividad
crown *noun.* **1.** corona **2.** coronilla **3.** cima, cumbre
crown *verb.* **1.** coronar **2.** rematar **3.** poner una corona **4.** golpear en la cabeza, dar un coscorrón
—**crown prince** príncipe heredero
crucial *adj.* crucial
crude *adj.* **1.** crudo **2.** rudimentario, primitivo
cruel *adj.* cruel
cruelty *noun.* crueldad
cruise *noun.* crucero
cruise *verb.* **1.** hacer un crucero **2.** navegar, volar
crumble *verb.* desmigajar, desmenuzar
crunch *noun.* crujido
crunch *verb.* mascar, ronzar, hacer crujir
crusade *noun.* **1.** cruzada **2.** campaña, cruzada
crusade *verb.* hacer una campaña en pro/contra de algo
crush *noun.* aglomeración, multitud
crush *verb.* **1.** aplastar **2.** estrujar, exprimir, prensar **3.** doblegar, aniquilar, eliminar **4.** comprimir
crust *noun.* **1.** corteza, cuscurro, costra **2.** pasta
cry *noun.* **1.** grito **2.** lloro **3.** aullido
cry *verb.* **1.** llorar **2.** (*often with* out) gritar
crystal *noun.* cristal
Cuba *noun.* Cuba
Cuban *noun. adj.* cubano
cube *noun.* cubo, dado, terrón
cube *verb.* **1.** elevar al cubo **2.** cortar en dados
cue *noun.* **1.** pie (theater) **2.** taco
cuisine *noun.* cocina
cult *noun.* culto
cultivate *verb.* cultivar
cultivated *adj.* **1.** cultivado **2.** culto, refinado
cultivation *noun.* cultivo
cultural *adj.* cultural
culture *noun.* **1.** cultura **2.** cultivo
cumulative *adj.* acumulativo
cup *noun.* **1.** taza **2.** copa
cup *verb.* **1.** ahuecar las manos, hacer bocina con las manos **2.** envolver con las manos
curator *noun.* **1.** conservador **2.** director de museo
curb *noun.* **1.** freno **2.** bordillo
curb *verb.* refrenar, dominar
cure *noun.* cura, remedio
cure *verb.* **1.** curar, remediar **2.** salar
curfew *noun.* toque de queda
curiosity *noun.* curiosidad
curious *adj.* curioso
curiously *adv.* curiosamente
curl *noun.* **1.** rizo **2.** bucle
curl *verb.* **1.** rizar **2.** rizarse
curly *adj.* rizado
currency *noun.* moneda
current *noun.* **1.** corriente **2.** aceptación
current *adj.* actual
currently *adv.* actualmente
curriculum *noun.* currículum, plan de estudios
curry *noun.* curry
curry *verb.* **1.** almohazar **2.** guisar con curry
curse *noun.* **1.** maldición **2.** desgracia
curse *verb.* **1.** maldecir **2.** blasfemar, decir palabrotas
curtain *noun.* cortina
curve *noun.* curva
curve *verb.* torcerse, hacer curva
curved *adj.* curvo, encorvado
cushion *noun.* **1.** cojín **2.** amortiguador
cushion *verb.* suavizar, amortiguar
custody *noun.* **1.** custodia **2.** detención
custom *noun.* **1.** costumbre **2.** clientela
—**customs** (derechos de) aduana
customary *adj.* habitual, de costumbre
customer *noun.* cliente
cut *noun.* **1.** corte **2.** trozo **3.** tajada **4.** rebaja, reducción
cut *verb.* **1.** cortar **2.** recortar, acortar **3.** suprimir **4.** tallar, abrir **5.** ignorar, hacer como si no viera
—**cut down** reducir
cute *adj.* **1.** lindo, precioso **2.** listo, vivo
cutting *noun.* **1.** esqueje **2.** recorte
cutting *adj.* cortante
cutting board *noun.* tabla de cortar

cycle *noun.* **1.** bicicleta **2.** ciclo
cycle *verb.* ir en bicicleta
cylinder *noun.* cilindro
cynical *adj.* cínico
Cypriot *noun.* chipriota
Cypriot *adj.* chipriota
Cyprus *noun.* Chipre
Czech *noun. adj.* checo

D

dad, daddy *noun.* papá
daily *noun.* diario, periódico
daily *adj.* diario
daily *adv.* diariamente, a diario
dairy *noun.* **1.** lechería **2.** vaquería
daisy *noun.* margarita
dam *noun.* **1.** dique **2.** presa, embalse
dam (up) *verb.* embalsar
damage *noun.* daño
—**damages** daños y perjuicios
damage *verb.* dañar, averiar, perjudicar
damaged *adj.* deteriorado, averiado
dame *noun.* **1.** dama **2.** mujer, tía (informal)
damn *noun.* nada de nada
damn *verb.* **1.** maldecir **2.** condenar
damn *interj.* ¡vaya!, ¡carajo!, ¡mecachis!
damned *adj.* **1.** puñetero, fregado **2.** maldito, condenado
damp *noun.* humedad
damp *adj.* húmedo
dance *noun.* baile, danza
dance *verb.* bailar, danzar
dancer *noun.* bailarín, bailaor
dancing *noun.* danza
dandelion *noun.* diente de león
danger *noun.* peligro
dangerous *adj.* peligroso, arriesgado
Danish *noun. adj.* danés
dare *noun.* desafío, reto
dare *verb.* **1.** atreverse, osar **2.** desafiar
daring *noun.* osadía, audacia
daring *adj.* arriesgado, audaz
dark *noun.* oscuridad
dark *adj.* **1.** oscuro **2.** misterioso, siniestro
darkness *noun.* oscuridad
darling *noun.* **1.** cariño **2.** encanto
darling *adj.* **1.** querido **2.** encantador
dart *noun.* **1.** dardo, flecha **2.** movimiento rápido
dart *verb.* lanzarse, precipitarse
dash *noun.* **1.** carrera **2.** poco, gota, chorrito, pizca **3.** raya, guión **4.** viveza
dash *verb.* **1.** correr, ir de prisa **2.** estrellar **3.** frustrar, defraudar
data *noun plural.* datos
database *noun.* base de datos
date *noun.* **1.** fecha **2.** compromiso, cita **3.** pareja, acompañante **4.** dátil
date *verb.* **1.** fechar, datar, poner fecha **2.** pasar de moda **3.** salir con
—**date from/back** datar de, remontarse a
dated *adj.* pasado de moda, anticuado
daughter *noun.* hija
daunting *adj.* desalentador, abrumador
dawn *noun.* **1.** alba, amanecer **2.** albores
dawn *verb.* amanecer
day *noun.* **1.** día **2.** jornada
—**in those days** en aquellos tiempos
daylight *noun.* **1.** luz (del día) **2.** amanecer
daytime *noun.* día
dazzling *adj.* deslumbrante
dead *adj.* **1.** muerto **2.** marchito, seco **3.** desconectado, cortado, apagado **4.** total, completo
dead *adv.* completamente
deadline *noun.* fecha límite
deadly *adj.* **1.** mortal, mortífero **2.** absoluto **3.** aburridísimo
deadly *adv.* completamente
deaf *adj.* sordo
deal *noun.* **1.** trato, acuerdo, pacto **2.** ganga **3.** reparto
deal *verb.* **1.** comerciar **2.** repartir

dealer *noun.* **1.** comerciante, tratante **2.** repartidor
dealings *noun plural.* relaciones, transacciones, negocios
dean *noun.* **1.** deán **2.** decano
dear *noun.* encanto, amor, cariño
—dear, dear!/oh dear! ¡Dios mío!, ¡ay, Dios!, ¡vaya!
dear *adj.* **1.** querido **2.** encantador
death *noun.* muerte
debate *noun.* debate
debate *verb.* **1.** debatir **2.** considerar, dar vueltas
debris *noun.* **1.** escombros **2.** restos
debt *noun.* deuda
debtor *noun.* deudor
debut, début *noun.* presentación, debut
Dec. *abbr.* diciembre
decade *noun.* década
decadence *noun.* decadencia
decay *noun.* **1.** descomposición, caries, deterioro **2.** decadencia
decay *verb.* **1.** pudrirse, cariarse, deteriorarse **2.** decaer
deceased *adj.* difunto
December *noun.* diciembre
decent *adj.* **1.** decente **2.** amable **3.** adecuado
deception *noun.* engaño, falsedad
decide *verb.* **1.** decidir **2.** decidirse
decision *noun.* decisión
decisive *adj.* **1.** decisivo **2.** decidido
deck *noun.* **1.** cubierta **2.** piso **3.** baraja
declaration *noun.* declaración
declare *verb.* **1.** declarar, anunciar **2.** pronunciarse
decline *noun.* **1.** descenso, disminución **2.** decadencia, declive
decline *verb.* **1.** declinar, rehusar, rechazar **2.** disminuir **3.** decaer
decorate *verb.* **1.** decorar **2.** pintar, empapelar **3.** condecorar
decoration *noun.* decoración
decorative *adj.* decorativo
decrease *noun.* disminución, bajada, reducción
decrease *verb.* disminuir, reducir
decree *noun.* **1.** decreto **2.** sentencia
decree *verb.* decretar
dedicate *verb.* **1.** dedicar, consagrar **2.** inaugurar oficialmente
dedicated *adj.* dedicado, entregado
dedication *noun.* **1.** dedicación, consagración **2.** dedicatoria
deduct *verb.* restar, descontar, deducir
deduction *noun.* deducción, descuento, desgravación
deed *noun.* **1.** acción, hecho, hazaña **2.** escritura
deem *verb.* juzgar, considerar
deep *adj.* **1.** profundo **2.** hondo **3.** absorbido **4.** profundo, intenso **5.** grave
deep *adv.* profundamente
deepen *verb.* **1.** profundizar **2.** aumentar, agudizarse, intensificarse
deeply *adv.* profundamente
deer *noun.* ciervo, venado
defeat *noun.* derrota, fracaso, rechazo
defeat *verb.* vencer, derrotar, frustrar
defect *noun.* defecto
defect *verb.* desertar
defective *adj.* defectuoso
defend *verb.* defender
defendant *noun.* demandado, acusado
defender *noun.* defensor
defense *noun.* defensa
defensive *adj.* defensivo
defiance *noun.* desafío
defiant *adj.* insolente, desafiante
deficiency *noun.* deficiencia
deficit *noun.* déficit
define *verb.* definir, delimitar
definite *adj.* definitivo
definitely *adv.* definitivamente
definition *noun.* definición
defy *verb.* **1.** desafiar **2.** desobedecer, contravenir
degree *noun.* **1.** grado **2.** título
delay *noun.* retraso
delay *verb.* **1.** demorar, retrasar, aplazar **2.** tardar, demorarse
delegate *noun.* delegado
delegate *verb.* delegar
delegation *noun.* delegación
delete *verb.* suprimir, tachar
deliberate *verb.* deliberar, reflexionar

deliberate *adj.* **1.** deliberado, intencionado **2.** pausado, lento
deliberately *adv.* **1.** deliberadamente, a propósito **2.** pausadamente, lentamente
delicate *adj.* **1.** delicado, suave **2.** frágil **3.** difícil
delicious *adj.* delicioso, rico
delight *noun.* **1.** placer, gusto, deleite **2.** encanto
delight *verb.* **1.** deleitar, encantar **2.** deleitarse, disfrutar
delightful *adj.* encantador, delicioso
deliver *verb.* **1.** entregar, dar, repartir **2.** pronunciar **3.** asestar **4.** traer al mundo, asistir en el parto
delivery *noun.* **1.** entrega, reparto **2.** presentación oral, declamación **3.** parto, alumbramiento
delta *noun.* delta
demand *noun.* **1.** petición, solicitud **2.** exigencia **3.** demanda
demand *verb.* **1.** exigir, requerir **2.** reclamar
demanding *adj.* exigente, difícil
democracy *noun.* democracia
democrat *noun.* demócrata
democratic *adj.* democrático
demolish *verb.* demoler
demolition *noun.* demolición
demonstrate *verb.* **1.** demostrar **2.** hacer una demostración **3.** manifestarse
demonstration *noun.* **1.** manifestación **2.** demostración
demonstrator *noun.* manifestante
den *noun.* **1.** guarida **2.** cuarto, estudio
denial *noun.* **1.** negación, desmentido **2.** denegación, rechazo
Denmark *noun.* Dinamarca
denounce *verb.* denunciar
dense *adj.* **1.** denso, nutrido **2.** corto, torpe, estúpido
density *noun.* densidad
dental *adj.* dental
dentist *noun.* dentista, odontólogo
deny *verb.* **1.** negar, rechazar, desmentir **2.** denegar
depart *verb.* partir, salir, irse
—**depart from** apartarse de, desviarse de
department *noun.* departamento, sección
—**department store** grandes almacenes
departmental *adj.* departamental
departure *noun.* **1.** partida, marcha, salida **2.** desviación, novedad
depend (on) *verb.* **1.** contar con, fiarse de **2.** depender de
dependent *adj.* dependiente
depict *verb.* **1.** pintar, representar **2.** describir
deplete *verb.* reducir, mermar, agotar
deport *verb.* deportar
deposit *noun.* **1.** depósito **2.** señal, fianza **3.** poso, sedimento **4.** yacimiento
deposit *verb.* depositar, ingresar
depot *noun.* **1.** almacén, depósito **2.** cochera, parque **3.** terminal, estación
depress *verb.* **1.** deprimir, abatir, desalentar **2.** reducir
depressed *adj.* **1.** deprimido **2.** abatido
depressing *adj.* deprimente
depression *noun.* **1.** depresión **2.** recesión, crisis **3.** depresión atmosférica
deprivation *noun.* privación
deprive (of) *verb.* privar de
deprived *adj.* necesitado, marginado
depth *noun.* **1.** profundidad, fondo **2.** intensidad
deputy *noun.* **1.** suplente, lugarteniente **2.** diputado, representante
derelict *adj.* abandonado, en ruinas
derive (from) *verb.* **1.** proceder, venir de **2.** sacar, obtener, encontrar
descend *verb.* **1.** descender, bajar **2.** rebajarse
—**descend on** atacar, caer sobre
descent *noun.* **1.** descenso, bajada **2.** pendiente, cuesta **3.** ascendencia
describe *verb.* **1.** describir **2.** calificar, definir
description *noun.* **1.** descripción **2.** clase, tipo
desert *noun.* desierto
desert *verb.* **1.** abandonar **2.** desertar
deserted *adj.* desierto, abandonado
deserve *verb.* merecer
design *noun.* **1.** diseño, dibujo **2.** plan, proyecto, intención, propósito

design *verb.* diseñar, concebir, proyectar, planear
designate *verb.* designar, nombrar
designer *noun.* diseñador
desirable *adj.* deseable, apetecible, conveniente
desire *noun.* deseo
desire *verb.* desear
desk *noun.* **1.** escritorio, pupitre **2.** mostrador
despair *noun.* desesperación
despair *verb.* desesperarse, perder la esperanza
desperate *adj.* **1.** desesperado **2.** atroz, pésimo
desperately *adv.* **1.** desesperadamente **2.** terriblemente
desperation *noun.* desesperación
despite *prep.* a pesar de
dessert *noun.* postre
destination *noun.* destino
destined *adj.* **1.** destinado **2.** con destino a
destiny *noun.* destino, sino
destroy *verb.* **1.** destruir **2.** matar, sacrificar, exterminar
destruction *noun.* destrucción
destructive *adj.* destructivo, destructor
detached *adj.* **1.** independiente, separado, suelto **2.** objetivo, imparcial
detachment *noun.* **1.** objetividad, imparcialidad **2.** indiferencia **3.** destacamento
detail *noun.* detalle, pormenor
detailed *adj.* detallado, minucioso, pormenorizado
detain *verb.* **1.** demorar, retener **2.** detener, arrestar
detect *verb.* detectar, descubrir
detective *noun.* detective
detention *noun.* detención
deter *verb.* **1.** disuadir **2.** impedir
deteriorate *verb.* empeorar, deteriorarse
deterioration *noun.* deterioro
determination *noun.* determinación
determine *verb.* **1.** determinar, decidir **2.** fijar, definir
determined *adj.* determinado, resuelto, decidido
deterrent *noun.* elemento disuasivo, elemento disuasorio
deterrent *adj.* disuasivo, disuasorio
devaluation *noun.* devaluación
devalue *verb.* devaluar
devastating *adj.* devastador, demoledor, tremendo
develop *verb.* **1.** desarrollar, desarrollarse **2.** elaborar, perfeccionar **3.** contraer, adquirir **4.** aparecer, mostrarse **5.** revelar **6.** surgir
development *noun.* **1.** desarrollo, evolución **2.** novedad, cambio, acontecimiento **3.** explotación
deviation *noun.* desviación
device *noun.* **1.** mecanismo, aparato, artefacto **2.** estratagema, recurso
devil *noun.* **1.** demonio, diablo **2.** pobre diablo, pobrecito
devise *verb.* **1.** concebir, inventar **2.** elaborar, encontrar
devote (to) *verb.* **1.** dedicar **2.** dedicarse
devoted *adj.* leal, fiel
devotion *noun.* **1.** devoción, lealtad **2.** dedicación
diabetes *noun.* diabetes
diabetic *noun. adj.* diabético
diagnose *verb.* diagnosticar
diagnosis *noun.* diagnóstico
diagram *noun.* diagrama, gráfica
dial *noun.* **1.** esfera, carátula **2.** dial
dial *verb.* marcar, discar
dialect *noun.* dialecto
dialog, dialogue *noun.* diálogo
diameter *noun.* diámetro
diamond *noun.* **1.** diamante **2.** rombo
diaper *noun.* pañal
diarrhea *noun.* diarrea
diary *noun.* diario
dice *noun plural.* dado
dictate *verb.* **1.** dictar **2.** mandar
dictator *noun.* dictador
dictatorship *noun.* dictadura
dictionary *noun.* diccionario
die *noun.* troquel
die *verb.* **1.** morir **2.** apagarse, desaparecer **3.** pararse **4.** morirse de ganas de hacer algo

diet *noun.* dieta, régimen
diet *verb.* estar a régimen
differ *verb.* discrepar, no estar de acuerdo
—**differ from** ser distinto
difference *noun.* diferencia
different *adj.* diferente
differentiate *verb.* diferenciar, distinguir
differentiation *noun.* diferenciación
difficult *adj.* **1.** difícil, complicado **2.** problemático
difficulty *noun.* dificultad, problemas
dig *noun.* **1.** excavación **2.** empujón, codazo, golpe
dig *verb.* **1.** cavar, excavar, escarbar **2.** empujar, dar un codazo
digest *noun.* resumen
digest *verb.* digerir, asimilar
digestion *noun.* digestión
digital *adj.* digital
dignity *noun.* dignidad
dilemma *noun.* dilema
dilute *verb.* diluir
dilute *adj.* diluido
dim *verb.* **1.** apagar, atenuar **2.** borrar
dim *adj.* **1.** débil, tenue **2.** borroso, vago
dimension *noun.* dimensión
diminish *verb.* disminuir
diminished *adj.* reducido
dine *verb.* cenar
dining-room *noun.* comedor
dinner *noun.* **1.** comida, cena **2.** banquete
dinosaur *noun.* dinosaurio
diocese *noun.* diócesis
dip *noun.* **1.** depresión, hondonada **2.** salsa **3.** chapuzón, zambullida
dip *verb.* **1.** mojar, sumergir **2.** descender, bajar **3.** meter
diploma *noun.* diploma
diplomacy *noun.* diplomacia
diplomat *noun.* diplomático
diplomatic *adj.* diplomático
dire *adj.* **1.** pésimo, espantoso, atroz **2.** nefasto, funesto **3.** extremo
direct *verb.* **1.** dirigir **2.** indicar el camino **3.** mandar
direct *adj.* **1.** directo **2.** claro, franco, sincero
direction *noun.* **1.** dirección **2.** orientación
—**directions** instrucciones
directive *noun.* orden, directiva
directly *adv.* **1.** directamente **2.** con franqueza **3.** inmediatamente **4.** justo
director *noun.* **1.** director **2.** directivo
directory *noun.* guía telefónica, listín
dirt *noun.* suciedad
dirty *verb.* **1.** ensuciar **2.** ensuciarse
dirty *adj.* **1.** sucio **2.** obsceno, porno, cochino, indecente **3.** malo
disability *noun.* invalidez, discapacidad, minusvalía
disabled *adj.* minusválido, discapacitado
disadvantage *noun.* desventaja, inconveniente
disagree *verb.* **1.** no estar de acuerdo, estar en desacuerdo **2.** discutir, reñir **3.** diferir, no cuadrar **4.** sentar mal
disagreement *noun.* **1.** desacuerdo, disconformidad **2.** discusión, riña, altercado **3.** discrepancia
disappear *verb.* desaparecer
disappearance *noun.* desaparición
disappoint *verb.* decepcionar, defraudar
disappointed *adj.* decepcionado, defraudado
disappointing *adj.* decepcionante
disappointment *noun.* decepción, desilusión
disapproval *noun.* desaprobación
disaster *noun.* desastre
disastrous *adj.* desastroso
disbelief *noun.* incredulidad
disc, disk *noun.* disco
—**disc jockey, DJ** *noun.* discjockey, pinchadiscos
discard *verb.* desechar, deshacerse de
discharge *noun.* **1.** descarga, disparo **2.** alta, liberación **3.** despido **4.** emisión, vertido, supuración **5.** ejercicio, cumplimiento
discharge *verb.* **1.** descargar, disparar **2.** dar de alta, poner en libertad **3.** despedir **4.** verter, emitir **5.** desempeñar, cumplir

disciplinary *adj.* disciplinario
discipline *noun.* disciplina
discipline *verb.* **1.** disciplinar **2.** castigar, sancionar
disclose *verb.* revelar
disclosure *noun.* revelación
disco *noun.* discoteca
discomfort *noun.* incomodidad, malestar, molestia
discontent *noun.* descontento, malestar
discotheque *noun.* discoteca
discount *noun.* descuento, rebaja
discount *verb.* **1.** descontar, rebajar **2.** descartar
discourage *verb.* **1.** desanimar, desalentar **2.** oponerse
—**discourage from** disuadir
discover *verb.* **1.** descubrir, hallar, encontrar **2.** darse cuenta
discovery *noun.* descubrimiento, hallazgo
discredit *noun.* descrédito, deshonor, desprestigio
discredit *verb.* **1.** desacreditar, deshonrar **2.** rebatir, refutar
discreet *adj.* discreto
discretion *noun.* **1.** discreción **2.** criterio, juicio
discrimination *noun.* discriminación
discuss *verb.* **1.** hablar de, discutir **2.** tratar, analizar
discussion *noun.* discusión
disease *noun.* enfermedad, mal
disembark *verb.* desembarcar
disgrace *noun.* **1.** desgracia **2.** deshonra **3.** vergüenza
disgrace *verb.* **1.** caer en desgracia **2.** deshonrar
disguise *noun.* disfraz
—**in disguise** disfrazado
disguise *verb.* **1.** disfrazar **2.** disimular, ocultar
disgust *noun.* **1.** asco, repugnancia **2.** indignación
disgust *verb.* dar asco, repugnar
disgusting *adj.* asqueroso, repugnante
dish *noun.* **1.** plato **2.** fuente
disintegrate *verb.* desintegrar
disk, disc *noun.* disco
dislike *noun.* aversión, antipatía
dislike *verb.* tener antipatía, caer mal, no gustar
dismantle *verb.* desmontar, desarmar, desmantelar
dismay *noun.* consternación
dismay *verb.* consternar
dismiss *verb.* **1.** despedir, destituir **2.** despachar **3.** descartar, rechazar **4.** desestimar
dismissal *noun.* **1.** despido, destitución **2.** rechazo
disorder *noun.* **1.** desorden **2.** disturbio, motín **3.** trastorno, dolencia
dispatch *noun.* **1.** despacho, informe, reportaje **2.** envío, expedición **3.** prontitud, presteza
dispatch *verb.* **1.** enviar, remitir **2.** despachar
disperse *verb.* **1.** dispersar, diseminar **2.** dispersarse
displace *verb.* **1.** desplazar **2.** destituir, quitar el puesto
display *noun.* **1.** exhibición, demostración **2.** exposición **3.** muestrario, surtido **4.** visualizador
display *verb.* **1.** exhibir **2.** exponer **3.** mostrar, manifestar
disposal *noun.* **1.** disposición **2.** venta, traspaso **3.** eliminación
dispose *verb.* predisponer, inclinar
—**dispose of** *verb.* **1.** vender, traspasar **2.** deshacerse de, tirar, botar
disposition *noun.* **1.** carácter, temperamento **2.** predisposición
dispute *noun.* **1.** disputa, discusión **2.** polémica **3.** contencioso
dispute *verb.* **1.** disputar **2.** poner en duda
disrupt *verb.* interrumpir, trastocar, alterar
disruption *noun.* interrupción, alteración
dissatisfaction *noun.* insatisfacción, descontento
dissent *noun.* disentimiento, disconformidad, disidencia
dissent *verb.* disentir, estar disconforme, disidir

dissident *noun. adj.* disidente
dissolution *noun.* disolución
dissolve *verb.* **1.** disolver **2.** disolverse
distance *noun.* distancia
—from a distance desde lejos
—in the distance a lo lejos
distant *adj.* **1.** distante, lejano, remoto **2.** frío **3.** ausente
distinct *adj.* **1.** diferente, distinto **2.** claro, definido, nítido, evidente
distinction *noun.* **1.** distinción **2.** sobresaliente
distinctive *adj.* distintivo, característico
distinctly *adv.* claramente, definitivamente
distinguish *verb.* **1.** distinguir **2.** caracterizar **3.** destacarse
distinguished *adj.* distinguido, eminente
distort *verb.* **1.** deformar **2.** distorsionar **3.** tergiversar
distortion *noun.* **1.** deformación **2.** distorsión
distract *verb.* distraer
distracted *adj.* **1.** distraído **2.** demente, trastornado
distress *noun.* **1.** aflicción, dolor **2.** preocupación, angustia **3.** desdicha, apuro
distress *verb.* afligir, doler
distribute *verb.* repartir, distribuir
distribution *noun.* distribución
district *noun.* distrito
disturb *verb.* **1.** molestar **2.** alterar, interrumpir **3.** preocupar **4.** agitar, desordenar
disturbance *noun.* **1.** disturbio, alboroto, bronca **2.** interrupción
ditch *noun.* zanja, foso, cuneta
ditch *verb.* deshacerse de, dejar plantado
dive *noun.* zambullida, salto de cabeza
dive *verb.* **1.** zambullirse, tirarse de cabeza **2.** precipitarse hacia, abalanzarse **3.** caer en picado
diverse *adj.* diverso, variado
diversify *verb.* diversificar
diversion *noun.* **1.** distracción **2.** diversión
diversity *noun.* diversidad
divert *verb.* entretener
divide *verb.* **1.** dividir **2.** separar, cortar
—divide between/among repartir
dividend *noun.* dividendo
divine *verb.* adivinar
divine *adj.* divino, precioso
division *noun.* **1.** división **2.** separación **3.** desacuerdo, diferencia
divorce *noun.* divorcio
divorce *verb.* **1.** divorciarse **2.** separar
dizzy *adj.* **1.** mareado **2.** vertiginoso
DJ *abbr.* pinchadiscos
do *noun.* fiesta, evento
do *verb.* **1.** hacer **2.** servir, ir bien, ser suficiente **3.** dedicarse, estudiar **4.** ir, estar **5.** arreglar
—do away with abolir, suprimir
—do without prescindir
dock *noun.* **1.** muelle **2.** banquillo de los acusados
dock *verb.* **1.** atracar **2.** descontar dinero
doctor *noun.* **1.** médico **2.** doctor
doctor *verb.* **1.** adulterar, manipular **2.** tratar, curar
doctrine *noun.* doctrina
document *noun.* documento
documentary *noun.* documental
documentary *adj.* documental
dodge *verb.* esquivar, evadir
doe *noun.* gama, liebre, coneja
dog *noun.* perro
dog *verb.* seguir (de cerca)
dole (out) *verb.* repartir
doll *noun.* muñeca
dollar *noun.* dólar
dolly *noun.* muñeca
dolphin *noun.* delfín
domain *noun.* dominio, propiedad
dome *noun.* cúpula
domestic *adj.* **1.** doméstico **2.** familiar **3.** nacional
dominance *noun.* dominio, control, preponderancia
dominant *adj.* dominante
dominate *verb.* dominar
domination *noun.* dominación, dominio
donate *verb.* donar, hacer una donación
donation *noun.* donación
done *adj.* **1.** hecho **2.** cocido, asado (food) **3.** rendido

donkey *noun.* **1.** burro **2.** tonto, imbécil, idiota
donor *noun.* donante
door *noun.* puerta
doorstep *noun.* peldaño, umbral
doorway *noun.* entrada, puerta, portal
dose *noun.* **1.** dosis **2.** ataque
dose *verb.* medicinar
dot *noun.* punto
double *noun.* doble
double *verb.* **1.** duplicar, doblar **2.** hacer las veces de, usarse de
double *adj.* doble
double *adv.* **1.** dos veces, el doble **2.** en dos, por la mitad
doubt *noun.* duda
doubt *verb.* dudar
doubtful *adj.* **1.** dudoso **2.** incierto **3.** poco probable **4.** sospechoso
doubtless *adv.* sin duda, seguramente
down *noun.* plumón
down *verb.* **1.** tragarse, devorar **2.** derribar, vencer
down *prep.* **1.** abajo, hacia abajo **2.** en la dirección de **3.** por
down *adv.* **1.** abajo, hacia abajo **2.** por tierra, en tierra **3.** a través de los tiempos
downstairs *adj. adv.* abajo
downtown *adj.* céntrico
downtown *adv.* en el centro
downward *adj.* descendente
dozen *noun.* docena
Dr *abbr.* Dr, doctor
draft *noun.* **1.** borrador, esbozo **2.** destacamento **3.** letra de cambio, giro **4.** leva, conscripción **5.** corriente de aire **6.** trago **7.** calado
draft *verb.* **1.** esbozar, redactar **2.** reclutar
drag *noun.* **1.** estorbo, freno **2.** calada **3.** lata, plomo, rollo **4.** vestido de travesti
drag *verb.* **1.** arrastrar, llevar a rastras **2.** dragar **3.** hacerse largo/pesado
dragon *noun.* dragón
drain *noun.* **1.** desagüe, sumidero **2.** desgaste, sangría
drain *verb.* **1.** vaciar, drenar, desaguar **2.** escurrir, escurrirse **3.** apurar, vaciar **4.** agotar, consumir
drainage *noun.* drenaje
drama *noun.* **1.** drama **2.** obra de teatro, obra dramática **3.** arte dramático
dramatic *adj.* **1.** dramático **2.** teatral **3.** impresionante, espectacular
dramatically *adv.* dramáticamente
drastic *adj.* drástico, radical
draw *noun.* **1.** atracción **2.** sorteo, lotería **3.** acción de sacar/desenvainar **4.** empate, tablas
draw *verb.* **1.** dibujar, trazar **2.** extraer, sacar, cobrar **3.** acercarse **4.** empatar, entablar **5.** causar, provocar, motivar **6.** correr, descorrer, tirar **7.** atraer
—draw near acercarse
drawer *noun.* cajón
drawing *noun.* dibujo
drawn *adj.* **1.** desenvainado, sacado **2.** ojeroso, demacrado **3.** empatado
dread *noun.* terror, pavor
dread *verb.* temer, tener miedo
dreadful *adj.* terrible, espantoso
dream *noun.* **1.** sueño **2.** maravilla **3.** ensueño
dream *verb.* **1.** soñar **2.** imaginar, imaginarse
dress *noun.* **1.** ropa **2.** vestido
dress *verb.* **1.** vestir, vestirse **2.** preparar, aliñar, aderezar **3.** vendar
dressed *adj.* vestido
dressing *noun.* **1.** aliño **2.** apósito, vendaje **3.** abono
dried *adj.* seco
drift *noun.* **1.** montón **2.** sentido, tendencia **3.** significado
drift *verb.* **1.** amontonarse **2.** vagar, ir sin rumbo, ir a la deriva, dejarse llevar
drill *noun.* **1.** taladro, barrena, perforador **2.** instrucción, ejercicios
drill *verb.* **1.** taladrar, perforar **2.** entrenarse
drink *noun.* **1.** bebida **2.** trago, copa
drink *verb.* beber, tomar
drip *noun.* **1.** gota **2.** goteo **3.** gota a gota
drip *verb.* gotear
dripping *noun.* pringue, grasa de carne asada
drive *noun.* **1.** paseo en coche, viaje **2.** camino de entrada **3.** ímpetu, empuje, dinamismo **4.** campaña **5.** drive, golpe directo **6.** unidad de disco

drive *verb.* **1.** conducir, manejar, pilotar **2.** llevar (en coche) **3.** hincar, clavar **4.** hacer funcionar, mover, impulsar **5.** conducirse, manejarse
driver *noun.* conductor
drop *noun.* **1.** gota **2.** lágrima **3.** caída, descenso, disminución **4.** desnivel, pendiente
drop *verb.* **1.** dejar, abandonar **2.** dejar caer, soltar, lanzar, echar **3.** bajar **4.** suprimir **5.** escribir
drought *noun.* sequía
drown *verb.* **1.** ahogar **2.** ahogarse
drug *noun.* **1.** medicamento **2.** droga, estupefaciente
drug *verb.* drogar
drum *noun.* **1.** tambor **2.** bidón **3.** tímpano
drum *verb.* **1.** tocar el tambor **2.** tamborilear **3.** repiquetear
drummer *noun.* batería
drunk *noun. adj.* borracho
drunken *adj.* **1.** borracho **2.** causado por embriaguez
dry *verb.* **1.** secar **2.** secarse
dry *adj.* **1.** seco, árido **2.** aburrido **3.** sardónico, mordaz
dual *adj.* doble
dub *verb.* **1.** doblar **2.** apodar
dubious *adj.* **1.** dudoso, sospechoso **2.** indeciso
duchess *noun.* duquesa
duck *noun.* pato
duck *verb.* **1.** hundir, zambullir **2.** agachar **3.** eludir, esquivar
due *noun.* merecido
—**dues** cuota, derechos
due *adj.* **1.** debido, merecido, justo **2.** pagadero, pendiente **3.** esperado
due *adv.* hacia
duke *noun.* duque
dull *adj.* **1.** lento, torpe **2.** apagado, sin brillo **3.** monótono, aburrido
duly *adv.* **1.** debidamente **2.** puntualmente
dumb *adj.* **1.** mudo **2.** callado **3.** tonto, estúpido
dump *noun.* **1.** basural, vertedero, basurero **2.** depósito
dump *verb.* **1.** dejar, soltar **2.** verter, descargar
durable *adj.* duradero
duration *noun.* duración
during *prep.* durante
dusk *noun.* crepúsculo
dust *noun.* polvo
dust *verb.* quitar el polvo
dusty *adj.* polvoriento
Dutch *noun.* holandés
Dutch *adj.* holandés, neerlandés
duty *noun.* **1.** deber, obligación **2.** función, responsabilidad **3.** derecho, impuesto
dwarf *noun.* enano
dwarf *verb.* empequeñecer, eclipsar
dwelling *noun.* morada, vivienda
dye *noun.* tinte
dye *verb.* teñir
dynamic *adj.* dinámico
dynamics *noun singular.* dinámica
dynasty *noun.* dinastía

E

each *adj.* cada
each *adv. pron.* cada uno
—**each other** el uno al otro, mutuamente
eager *adj.* ávido, ansioso, entusiasta, ilusionado
eagerly *adv.* con avidez, ansiosamente, con entusiasmo, con ilusión
eagle *noun.* águila
ear *noun.* **1.** oído **2.** oreja **3.** espiga
early *adj.* **1.** temprano **2.** prematuro **3.** antiguo, primitivo **4.** pronto
early *adv.* **1.** temprano **2.** pronto **3.** en los inicios, al principio
—**early riser** madrugador
earn *verb.* **1.** ganar, obtener **2.** merecer
earnest *adj.* serio

earnings *noun plural.* ingresos
earth *noun.* **1.** tierra **2.** suelo **3.** madriguera
—**the Earth** la Tierra
earthquake *noun.* terremoto
ease *noun.* **1.** facilidad **2.** alivio, bienestar **3.** soltura
ease *verb.* **1.** facilitar **2.** aliviar, aligerar, aflojar **3.** mover con cuidado
—**ease off** disminuir, amainar
easily *adv.* **1.** fácilmente **2.** con diferencia, con mucho
east *noun.* este
east *adj.* **1.** este, oriental **2.** del este
east *adv.* hacia el este, en dirección este
Easter *noun.* Pascua, Semana Santa
eastern *adj.* del este, oriental
easy *interj.* ¡despacio!
easy *adj.* **1.** fácil **2.** tranquilo, relajado **3.** natural
eat *verb.* comer
eccentric *noun. adj.* excéntrico
ecclesiastical *adj.* eclesiástico
echo *noun.* eco
echo *verb.* **1.** hacer eco, resonar **2.** repetir
ecological *adj.* ecológico
ecology *noun.* ecología
economic *adj.* **1.** económico **2.** rentable
economical *adj.* económico, ahorrador
economically *adv.* económicamente
economics *noun singular.* economía
economist *noun.* economista
economy *noun.* economía
ecstasy *noun.* éxtasis
edge *noun.* **1.** borde **2.** filo, canto, arista **3.** orilla **4.** ventaja
edge *verb.* **1.** ribetear, bordear **2.** moverse con cautela, moverse poco a poco
edit *verb.* **1.** editar **2.** dirigir **3.** corregir
edition *noun.* edición
editor *noun.* **1.** editor, redactor **2.** director
editorial *noun. adj.* editorial
educate *verb.* educar, formar
education *noun.* educación
educational *adj.* **1.** educativo, docente **2.** pedagógico
eel *noun.* anguila
effect *noun.* **1.** efecto, consecuencia, resultado **2.** sentido
—**effects 1.** bienes **2.** efectos
effect *verb.* efectuar, lograr
effective *adj.* **1.** efectivo **2.** eficaz **3.** logrado, llamativo, impresionante **4.** en vigor, vigente **5.** real
effectively *adv.* **1.** eficazmente **2.** realmente
efficacy *noun.* eficacia
efficiency *noun.* eficiencia, eficacia
efficient *adj.* **1.** eficiente, competente **2.** eficaz, de buen rendimiento
efficiently *adv.* eficientemente, eficazmente
effort *noun.* **1.** esfuerzo **2.** intento
e.g. *abbr.* por ejemplo
egg *noun.* **1.** huevo **2.** óvulo
egg on *verb.* animar, incitar
ego *noun.* ego, amor propio, orgullo
Egypt *noun.* Egipto
Egyptian *noun. adj.* egipcio
eight *noun. adj.* ocho
eighteen *noun. adj.* dieciocho
eighteenth *noun.* decimoctavo
eighth *noun.* octavo
eighties *noun plural.* **1.** entre ochenta y noventa **2.** los años ochenta
eightieth *noun.* octogésimo
eighty *noun. adj.* ochenta
either *adj.* **1.** cualquiera de los dos, ambos (positive) **2.** ninguno de los dos (negative) **3.** cada
either *adv.* tampoco
either *pron.* **1.** cualquiera de los dos (positive) **2.** ninguno de los dos (negative)
either...or *conj.* **1.** o...o (positive) **2.** ni ...ni (negative)
elaborate *verb.* **1.** desarrollar, elaborar **2.** explicar detalladamente
elaborate *adj.* **1.** elaborado **2.** complicado, rebuscado **3.** detallado
elastic *noun.* elástico
elastic *adj.* **1.** elástico **2.** flexible
elbow *noun.* codo
elbow *verb.* dar un codazo
elder *noun.* **1.** mayor **2.** anciano **3.** saúco

elder *adj.* mayor
elderly *adj.* mayor, anciano
eldest *adj.* mayor
elect *verb.* **1.** elegir **2.** decidir
elect *adj.* electo
election *noun.* elección
—**general election** elecciones generales
electoral *adj.* electoral
electorate *noun.* electorado
electric *adj.* **1.** eléctrico **2.** electrizante
electrical *adj.* eléctrico
electricity *noun.* electricidad
electron *noun.* electrón
electronic *adj.* electrónico
electronics *noun singular.* electrónica
elegance *noun.* elegancia
elegant *adj.* elegante
element *noun.* **1.** elemento **2.** factor **3.** parte, ingrediente **4.** resistencia
—**elements** rudimentos
—**the elements** los elementos, las fuerzas de la naturaleza
elementary *adj.* elemental, básico
elephant *noun.* elefante
elevate *verb.* **1.** elevar **2.** ascender
elevator *noun.* **1.** ascensor, elevador **2.** montacargas **3.** elevador de granos
eleven *noun. adj.* once
eleventh *noun.* **1.** undécimo **2.** onceavo
eligible *adj.* **1.** idóneo, apto **2.** elegible
eliminate *verb.* eliminar
elimination *noun.* eliminación
elite *noun.* elite
elitist *noun. adj.* elitista
eloquence *noun.* elocuencia
else *adj. adv.* **1.** más **2.** otra cosa, otro
elsewhere *adv.* **1.** en otro sitio, en otra parte **2.** a otro sitio, a otra parte
elude *verb.* eludir, evitar
elusive *adj.* esquivo
emancipation *noun.* emancipación
embargo *noun.* embargo
embark *verb.* embarcar
embarrassed *adj.* turbado
embarrassing *adj.* embarazoso
embarrassment *noun.* vergüenza, pena
embassy *noun.* embajada
embody *verb.* **1.** encarnar, personificar **2.** plasmar
embrace *noun.* abrazo
embrace *verb.* **1.** abrazar **2.** abarcar
embryo *noun.* embrión
emerge *verb.* **1.** emerger, salir, surgir **2.** resultar
emergence *noun.* aparición
emergency *noun.* emergencia
emigrate *verb.* emigrar
eminent *adj.* eminente
emission *noun.* emisión
emotion *noun.* **1.** emoción **2.** sentimiento
emotional *adj.* **1.** emocional, afectivo **2.** emotivo **3.** sentimental
emotionally *adv.* **1.** emocionalmente **2.** emotivamente
emperor *noun.* emperador
emphasis *noun.* **1.** acento **2.** énfasis
emphasize *verb.* enfatizar, hacer hincapié
empire *noun.* imperio
employ *verb.* **1.** emplear **2.** ocupar
employed *adj.* empleado
employee *noun.* empleado
employer *noun.* empresario, patrón
employment *noun.* empleo
empty *noun.* envase vacío, casco vacío
empty *verb.* **1.** vaciar **2.** vaciarse
empty *adj.* **1.** vacío **2.** desierto **3.** desocupado **4.** vano, hueco
enable *verb.* **1.** permitir, autorizar **2.** posibilitar
enact *verb.* **1.** representar **2.** promulgar
enclose *verb.* **1.** adjuntar **2.** cercar, vallar
enclosure *noun.* **1.** anexo, carta adjunta **2.** cercado **3.** recinto reservado
encounter *noun.* encuentro
encounter *verb.* **1.** encontrar, encontrarse con **2.** tropezar con
encourage *verb.* animar, alentar
encouragement *noun.* ánimo
encouraging *adj.* **1.** alentador **2.** halagüeño
end *noun.* **1.** final, extremo, cabo, punta **2.** conclusión, fin **3.** muerte **4.** objetivo, finalidad, propósito **5.** resto
end *verb.* **1.** terminar, acabar con **2.** terminarse
endanger *verb.* poner en peligro

endeavor *noun.* tentativa, intento, esfuerzo
endeavor *verb.* esforzarse
ending *noun.* final, desenlace
endless *adj.* **1.** interminable, inagotable **2.** continuo, sin fin
endorse *verb.* **1.** endosar **2.** aprobar, respaldar
endorsement *noun.* aprobación, respaldo
endowment *noun.* **1.** dotación **2.** fundación, creación **3.** donación **4.** dote
endure *verb.* **1.** soportar, resistir, aguantar **2.** durar
enemy *noun.* enemigo
energetic *adj.* **1.** activo **2.** enérgico **3.** vigoroso
energy *noun.* **1.** energía **2.** vigor
enforce *verb.* **1.** imponer **2.** hacer cumplir **3.** aplicar, ejecutar
enforcement *noun.* aplicación, ejecución
engage *verb.* **1.** contratar **2.** ocupar, captar **3.** entablar **4.** meterse en, tomar parte en **5.** engranar
engaged *adj.* **1.** prometido **2.** ocupado
engagement *noun.* **1.** compromiso, noviazgo **2.** cita **3.** batalla **4.** contrato
engaging *adj.* atractivo
engine *noun.* **1.** motor **2.** máquina, locomotora
engineer *noun.* **1.** ingeniero **2.** maquinista
engineer *verb.* maquinar, organizar
engineering *noun.* ingeniería
England *noun.* Inglaterra
English *noun. adj.* inglés
Englishman, Englishwoman *noun.* inglés, inglesa
enhance *verb.* realzar, acrecentar, aumentar
enjoy *verb.* **1.** disfrutar, gozar de **2.** poseer, tener
enjoyable *adj.* **1.** agradable **2.** divertido
enjoyment *noun.* placer
enlarge *verb.* **1.** aumentar **2.** ampliar
enlightened *adj.* bien informado, culto
enlightenment *noun.* aclaración
—**the Enlightenment** la Ilustración
enormous *adj.* enorme
enough *adj. pron.* bastante, suficiente
enough *adv.* bastante, suficientemente
ensure *verb.* asegurar
entail *verb.* suponer, implicar, acarrear, traer consigo
enter *verb.* **1.** entrar, entrar en **2.** presentarse **3.** inscribirse, participar **4.** registrar, anotar, escribir **5.** comenzar
enterprise *noun.* **1.** empresa **2.** iniciativa
entertain *verb.* **1.** recibir **2.** divertir, entretener **3.** considerar, abrigar, albergar
entertaining *adj.* divertido, entretenido
entertainment *noun.* **1.** espectáculo **2.** entretenimiento **3.** diversión
enthusiasm *noun.* entusiasmo
enthusiast *noun.* entusiasta
enthusiastic *adj.* entusiasta
entire *adj.* **1.** entero **2.** completo
entirely *adv.* **1.** enteramente, exclusivamente **2.** completamente
entitle *verb.* **1.** dar derecho, tener derecho **2.** titular
entitlement *noun.* derecho
entrance *noun.* **1.** entrada **2.** admisión **3.** ingreso
entrance *verb.* encantar
entrepreneur *noun.* empresario
entry *noun.* **1.** entrada, ingreso **2.** participante **3.** registro, anotación, partida
envelope *noun.* sobre
environment *noun.* entorno, medio ambiente
environmental *adj.* ambiental
environmentalist *noun.* ecologista
envisage *verb.* **1.** prever **2.** imaginar
envoy *noun.* enviado, mensajero
envy *noun.* envidia
envy *verb.* envidiar
epic *noun.* epopeya, poema épico
epidemic *noun.* epidemia
epilog *noun.* epílogo
episcopal *adj.* episcopal
episode *noun.* episodio
epoch *noun.* época
equal *verb.* **1.** igualar **2.** equivaler
equal *noun. adj.* igual

equality *noun.* igualdad
equally *adv.* **1.** igualmente **2.** equitativamente, por igual
equation *noun.* ecuación
equilibrium *noun.* equilibrio
equip *verb.* equipar
equipment *noun.* **1.** equipo **2.** material, herramienta, pertrechos
equitable *adj.* equitativo, justo
equity *noun.* equidad
equivalent *noun. adj.* equivalente
era *noun.* era
eradicate *verb.* erradicar
erase *verb.* borrar
erect *verb.* **1.** erigir **2.** levantar, edificar **3.** montar
erect *adj.* erecto, erguido, parado
erode *verb.* **1.** erosionar, corroer, desgastar **2.** mermar, reducir
erosion *noun.* erosión
erotic *adj.* erótico
error *noun.* error
erupt *verb.* entrar en erupción, estallar
eruption *noun.* erupción
escalate *verb.* **1.** subir vertiginosamente **2.** intensificarse
escape *noun.* fuga, evasión
escape *verb.* **1.** escapar, escaparse **2.** fugarse, huir **3.** librarse de, evitar **4.** salirse
escort *noun.* **1.** escolta **2.** acompañamiento **3.** acompañante, prostituto
escort *verb.* **1.** escoltar **2.** acompañar
especially *adv.* especialmente
essay *noun.* **1.** ensayo **2.** trabajo
essence *noun.* **1.** esencia **2.** extracto
essential *noun.* necesidad, elemento necesario
essential *adj.* **1.** esencial, imprescindible **2.** fundamental
essentially *adv.* **1.** básicamente, en esencia **2.** en lo fundamental, en lo esencial
establish *verb.* **1.** establecer **2.** fundar **3.** afirmar **4.** comprobar, demostrar, verificar **5.** averiguar, determinar
established *adj.* **1.** establecido **2.** oficial **3.** consolidado, arraigado **4.** probado
establishment *noun.* **1.** establecimiento **2.** institución **3.** residencia
—the Establishment la clase dirigente
estate *noun.* **1.** finca, hacienda **2.** urbanización **3.** patrimonio, propiedad **4.** herencia **5.** estado
esteem *noun.* aprecio, estima
esteem *verb.* apreciar, estimar
estimate *noun.* cálculo, estimación, presupuesto
estimate *verb.* estimar, calcular
estuary *noun.* estuario
eternal *adj.* **1.** eterno **2.** constante
ethical *adj.* ético
ethics *noun.* ética
ethnic *adj.* étnico
euro *noun.* euro
Europe *noun.* Europa
European *noun. adj.* europeo
evacuate *verb.* evacuar
evaluate *verb.* **1.** valorar, evaluar **2.** calcular, hallar el valor numérico
evaluation *noun.* **1.** valoración **2.** cálculo
eve *noun.* **1.** víspera **2.** tarde
even *verb.* **1.** igualar **2.** allanar, nivelar
even *adj.* **1.** uniforme, constante, regular **2.** liso, llano **3.** igual **4.** par **5.** constante, tranquilo
even *adv.* **1.** hasta, incluso **2.** ni siquiera **3.** todavía, aún
evening *noun.* **1.** tarde **2.** atardecer **3.** noche
evenly *adv.* **1.** uniformemente **2.** por igual, equitativamente **3.** con calma
event *noun.* **1.** acontecimiento, suceso **2.** prueba, evento
eventual *adj.* final
eventually *adv.* **1.** finalmente **2.** con el tiempo
ever *adv.* **1.** siempre **2.** jamás, nunca **3.** alguna vez
every *adj.* **1.** cada **2.** todo
everybody, everyone *pron.* todos, todo el mundo
everyday *adj.* **1.** cotidiano, diario **2.** habitual
everything *pron.* todo
everywhere *adv.* en todas partes, por todas partes

evidence *noun.* **1.** prueba **2.** indicio, señal **3.** testimonio
evident *adj.* evidente
evidently *adv.* **1.** por lo visto **2.** claramente, evidentemente
evil *noun.* **1.** mal, maldad **2.** desgracia, plaga
evil *adj.* **1.** malo, malvado **2.** diabólico, funesto
evocative *adj.* evocador
evoke *verb.* **1.** provocar, suscitar **2.** evocar
evolution *noun.* evolución, desarrollo
evolutionary *adj.* evolutivo
evolve *verb.* **1.** evolucionar **2.** desarrollar
exact *verb.* **1.** exigir **2.** obtener, conseguir **3.** arrancar
exact *adj.* **1.** exacto **2.** preciso, meticuloso
exactly *adv.* exactamente
exaggerate *verb.* exagerar
examination *noun.* **1.** inspección **2.** examen **3.** interrogatorio **4.** reconocimiento
examine *verb.* **1.** inspeccionar **2.** examinar **3.** interrogar
example *noun.* ejemplo
—**for example** por ejemplo
excavation *noun.* excavación
exceed *verb.* exceder, sobrepasar, rebasar
excellence *noun.* excelencia
excellent *adj.* excelente
except *prep.* excepto, salvo
except *verb.* excluir, exceptuar
exception *noun.* excepción
exceptional *adj.* excepcional
exceptionally *adv.* excepcionalmente
excerpt *noun.* extracto
excess *noun.* **1.** exceso **2.** excedente
excess *adj.* exceso
excessive *adj.* excesivo
exchange *noun.* **1.** intercambio, canje **2.** cambio **3.** bolsa **4.** central telefónica, conmutador
exchange *verb.* **1.** cambiar **2.** intercambiar, canjear
excise *noun.* impuestos indirectos
excise *verb.* extirpar, cortar
excite *verb.* **1.** emocionar, entusiasmar **2.** despertar, suscitar, provocar
excited *adj.* **1.** emocionado, entusiasmado **2.** excitado, nervioso
excitement *noun.* excitación, emoción
exciting *adj.* emocionante, apasionante
exclaim *verb.* exclamar
exclude *verb.* **1.** excluir, expulsar **2.** exceptuar
excluding *prep.* excepto, con excepción de
exclusion *noun.* exclusión, expulsión
exclusive *adj.* **1.** exclusivo **2.** selecto
exclusively *adv.* exclusivamente
excuse *noun.* excusa
excuse *verb.* **1.** perdonar, excusar **2.** justificar **3.** dispensar
execute *verb.* **1.** ejecutar, realizar, llevar a cabo **2.** fusilar
execution *noun.* **1.** ejecución **2.** fusilamiento
executive *noun.* **1.** poder ejecutivo **2.** ejecutivo
executive *adj.* ejecutivo, directivo
exempt *verb.* eximir, dispensar
exempt *adj.* exento
exemption *noun.* exención
exercise *noun.* ejercicio
exercise *verb.* **1.** hacer ejercicio **2.** ejercitar, ejercer
exert *verb.* **1.** ejercer, emplear **2.** esforzarse
exhaust *noun.* tubo de escape
exhaust *verb.* agotar
exhausted *adj.* agotado
exhaustion *noun.* agotamiento
exhibit *noun.* **1.** objeto expuesto **2.** exposición **3.** prueba instrumental
exhibit *verb.* **1.** exponer **2.** manifestar, mostrar
exhibition *noun.* **1.** exposición **2.** demostración
exile *noun.* **1.** exiliado, desterrado **2.** exilio, destierro
exile *verb.* exiliar, desterrar
exist *verb.* **1.** existir **2.** vivir, subsistir
existence *noun.* existencia
exit *noun.* salida
exit *verb.* **1.** salir, salir de **2.** hacer mutis
exotic *adj.* exótico

expand *verb.* **1.** ampliar, aumentar **2.** extender **3.** desplegar
expansion *noun.* **1.** ampliación **2.** desarrollo **3.** dilatación
expect *verb.* **1.** esperar **2.** suponer, creer **3.** imaginarse **4.** exigir
expectancy *noun.* expectativa
expectation *noun.* **1.** expectativa **2.** esperanza
expedition *noun.* expedición
expel *verb.* **1.** expulsar, expeler **2.** despedir
expenditure *noun.* gasto
expense *noun.* gasto, costo
expensive *adj.* caro
experience *noun.* experiencia
experience *verb.* experimentar
experienced *adj.* experimentado
experiment *noun.* experimento
experiment (on/with) *verb.* experimentar con
experimental *adj.* experimental
expert *noun.* experto, especialista
expert *adj.* experto
expire *verb.* **1.** terminar **2.** caducar, vencer **3.** expirar, morir
explain *verb.* **1.** explicar **2.** justificar, defender
explanation *noun.* explicación, aclaración
explanatory *adj.* explicativo
explicit *adj.* explícito
explicitly *adv.* explícitamente
explode *verb.* **1.** explotar, estallar **2.** hacer explotar, hacer estallar **3.** refutar, echar por tierra
exploit *noun.* hazaña
exploit *verb.* **1.** explotar **2.** aprovechar
exploitation *noun.* explotación
exploration *noun.* exploración
explore *verb.* **1.** explorar **2.** examinar
explosion *noun.* **1.** explosión **2.** ataque, arrebato **3.** aumento rápido
explosive *noun. adj.* explosivo
export *noun.* **1.** exportación **2.** artículo de exportación
export *verb.* exportar
expose *verb.* **1.** exponer **2.** descubrir **3.** revelar
exposure *noun.* **1.** exposición **2.** riesgo **3.** fotografía
express *noun.* **1.** expreso **2.** urgente, rápido
express *verb.* **1.** expresar **2.** enviar por correo urgente
express *adj.* **1.** expreso, explícito **2.** rápido, urgente, exprés
express *adv.* urgente
expression *noun.* expresión
expressive *adj.* expresivo
expressly *adv.* expresamente
expulsion *noun.* expulsión
exquisite *adj.* **1.** exquisito **2.** excelente
extend *verb.* **1.** extender, extenderse **2.** ampliar, prolongar **3.** tender, alargar **4.** ofrecer, dar
extension *noun.* **1.** extensión, ampliación, prolongación **2.** prorroga
extensive *adj.* **1.** extenso, vasto, amplio **2.** comprensivo
extent *noun.* **1.** extensión **2.** amplitud, alcance **3.** punto, grado
—**to a certain extent** hasta cierto punto
—**to a large extent** en gran parte
—**to what extent?** ¿hasta qué punto?
exterior *noun. adj.* exterior
external *adj.* externo
extinction *noun.* extinción
extra *noun.* **1.** extra **2.** suplemento **3.** edición especial
extra *adj.* **1.** extra **2.** adicional **3.** de más **4.** de sobra
extra *adv.* **1.** más **2.** extraordinariamente
extract *noun.* **1.** extracto **2.** fragmento
extract *verb.* extraer, sacar
extraction *noun.* **1.** extracción **2.** origen
extradite *verb.* extraditar
extraordinarily *adv.* extraordinariamente
extraordinary *adj.* extraordinario
extreme *noun. adj.* extremo
extremely *adv.* extremadamente
extremist *noun. adj.* extremista
eye *noun.* **1.** ojo **2.** vista, buen ojo **3.** opinión, juicio
eye *verb.* mirar, observar
eyebrow *noun.* ceja

F

F *abbr.* Fahrenheit
fabric *noun.* **1.** tela, tejido **2.** estructura
fabulous *adj.* fabuloso
face *noun.* **1.** cara, rostro **2.** semblante, expresión **3.** superficie **4.** aspecto, faceta **5.** descaro
face *verb.* **1.** estar enfrente de, dar a **2.** mirar, mirar hacia **3.** afrontar, hacer cara
facial *adj.* facial
facility *noun.* **1.** facilidad **2.** habilidad
—**facilities** instalaciones, servicios
facing *prep.* de cara a, frente a
fact *noun.* **1.** hecho **2.** dato **3.** realidad
faction *noun.* facción
factor *noun.* factor
factory *noun.* fábrica
factual *adj.* objetivo, basado en hechos
faculty *noun.* **1.** facultad **2.** habilidad **3.** claustro, profesorado
fade *verb.* **1.** marchitarse **2.** apagarse, descolorarse
Fahrenheit *adj.* Fahrenheit
fail *verb.* **1.** fracasar **2.** fallar **3.** faltar **4.** suspender, reprobar **5.** decepcionar
failing *prep.* a falta de
failing *noun.* defecto, falta
failure *noun.* **1.** fracaso, suspenso **2.** fracasado **3.** omisión, descuido **4.** avería, corte **5.** quiebra
faint *noun.* desmayo, desvanecimiento
faint *verb.* desmayarse, perder el sentido
faint *adj.* **1.** débil, tenue, borroso **2.** desfallecido, lánguido
faintly *adv.* **1.** débilmente **2.** ligeramente
fair *noun.* **1.** feria **2.** mercado
fair *adj.* **1.** justo, imparcial, recto, limpio **2.** considerable **3.** bueno, despejado, sereno **4.** regular, pasable **5.** rubio (hair), blanco (skin) **6.** hermoso, lindo, bello
fairly *adv.* **1.** justamente, equitativamente **2.** bastante
fairness *noun.* justicia, imparcialidad
fairy *noun.* hada
faith *noun.* **1.** fe **2.** religión, doctrina **3.** confianza **4.** palabra
faithful *adj.* fiel, leal
faithfully *adv.* fielmente
fake *noun.* **1.** falsificación **2.** impostor, farsante
fake *verb.* falsificar
fake *adj.* **1.** falso **2.** fingido
fall *noun.* **1.** caída, disminución, bajada **2.** rendición **3.** otoño
—**falls** catarata
fall *verb.* **1.** caer **2.** caerse **3.** disminuir, bajar, descender **4.** incumbir, corresponder, tocar **5.** rendirse, ser tomado **6.** morir
false *adj.* **1.** falso **2.** postizo **3.** desleal, infiel
fame *noun.* fama
familiar *adj.* **1.** conocido, familiar **2.** íntimo
—**familiar with** familiarizado con
familiarity *noun.* familiaridad
family *noun.* familia
famine *noun.* hambre, hambruna
famous *adj.* famoso
fan *noun.* **1.** abanico **2.** ventilador
fan *noun.* aficionado, admirador
fan *verb.* **1.** abanicar **2.** abanicarse **3.** atizar, avivar
fancy *noun.* **1.** capricho, antojo **2.** fantasía **3.** imaginación
fancy *verb.* **1.** gustar, apetecer **2.** imaginarse, figurarse
fancy *adj.* **1.** elegante **2.** elaborado
fantastic *adj.* fantástico
fantasy *noun.* **1.** fantasía **2.** imaginación
far *adj.* **1.** lejano, distante **2.** extremo
far *adv.* **1.** lejos **2.** muy, mucho
fare *noun.* **1.** tarifa, precio del billete **2.** pasajero
farewell *noun.* despedida
farewell *interj.* adiós
farm *noun.* granja, chacra, hacienda
farm *verb.* **1.** cultivar, labrar **2.** ser granjero
farmer *noun.* granjero, agricultor, chacarero

farmhouse *noun.* granja, alquería, casa de labranza
farming *noun.* **1.** agricultura **2.** ganadería, cría
fascinate *verb.* fascinar
fascinating *adj.* fascinante
fascination *noun.* fascinación
Fascism *noun.* fascismo
fascist *noun. adj.* fascista
fashion *noun.* **1.** modo, manera **2.** moda
fashionable *adj.* de moda, a la moda
fast *noun.* ayuno
fast *verb.* ayunar
fast *adj.* **1.** rápido **2.** firme, seguro **3.** adelantado
fast *adv.* **1.** rápidamente **2.** firmemente, seguramente **3.** profundamente
fat *noun.* **1.** grasa **2.** manteca, grasa
fat *adj.* **1.** gordo, relleno **2.** sustancioso, grande
fatal *adj.* **1.** mortal **2.** fatal
fate *noun.* **1.** destino **2.** suerte
father *noun.* **1.** padre **2.** sacerdote
father *verb.* engendrar
fatigue *noun.* fatiga, cansancio
fatty *adj.* graso
faucet *noun.* grifo, llave
fault *noun.* **1.** culpa **2.** defecto, tara **3.** falla
fault *verb.* criticar, encontrar defectos
faulty *adj.* defectuoso
favor *noun.* **1.** favor **2.** aprobación **3.** preferencia, favoritismo
favor *verb.* **1.** apoyar, preferir **2.** preferir
favorable *adj.* **1.** favorable **2.** propicio
favorite *noun. adj.* favorito, preferido
fax *noun.* **1.** fax **2.** telefax
fax *verb.* mandar por fax, faxear
FBI *abbr.* FBI
fear *noun.* temor, miedo
fear *verb.* temer, tener miedo
fearful *adj.* **1.** temeroso **2.** terrible, espantoso **3.** horrible
feasibility *noun.* factibilidad
feasible *adj.* factible
feast *noun.* **1.** banquete, festín **2.** fiesta
feast *verb.* banquetear, festejar
feat *noun.* hazaña, proeza
feather *noun.* pluma
feather *verb.* emplumar
feature *noun.* **1.** característica **2.** rasgo **3.** crónica, artículo de fondo **4.** largometraje
feature *verb.* presentar
Feb. *abbr.* febrero
February *noun.* febrero
fed up *adj.* harto
federal *adj.* federal
federation *noun.* federación
fee *noun.* **1.** honorarios **2.** matrícula
feed *noun.* comida, alimento
feed *verb.* dar de comer, alimentar —**feed on** alimentarse, nutrirse
feel *verb.* **1.** sentir **2.** tocar, palpar **3.** sentirse, encontrarse **4.** creer
feeling *noun.* **1.** sensación **2.** sentimiento **3.** impresión **4.** opinión **5.** sensibilidad, percepción
fell *verb.* talar, derribar
fellow *noun.* **1.** tipo **2.** compañero, camarada **3.** socio, miembro
fellow *adj.* compañero
fellowship *noun.* **1.** asociación **2.** compañerismo **3.** beca
felt *noun. adj.* fieltro
female *noun.* hembra
female *adj.* femenino
feminine *adj.* femenino
feminism *noun.* feminismo
feminist *noun. adj.* feminista
fen *noun.* pantano
fence *noun.* valla, cerca
fence *verb.* **1.** cercar **2.** practicar la esgrima **3.** defenderse con evasivas
ferry *noun.* transbordador, ferry
ferry *verb.* transportar
fertile *adj.* fértil
fertility *noun.* fertilidad
fertilizer *noun.* fertilizante, abono
festival *noun.* **1.** fiesta **2.** festival
fetch *verb.* **1.** traer, ir por, ir a buscar **2.** venderse por
feudal *adj.* feudal
fever *noun.* fiebre
few *adj. pron.* **1.** pocos **2.** algunos
fiber *noun.* **1.** fibra **2.** nervio, carácter
fiction *noun.* **1.** ficción **2.** literatura de ficción, narrativa

fictional *adj.* ficticio
field *noun.* **1.** campo **2.** cancha **3.** yacimiento **4.** terreno **5.** campo de batalla
fierce *adj.* **1.** feroz, salvaje **2.** intenso, fuerte
fiercely *adv.* **1.** ferozmente, violentamente **2.** intensamente
fiery *adj.* **1.** ardiente, llameante **2.** violento, colérico
fifteen *noun. adj.* quince
fifteenth *noun.* decimoquinto
fifth *noun.* quinto
fifties *noun plural.* **1.** entre cincuenta y sesenta **2.** los años cincuenta
fiftieth *noun.* quincuagésimo
fifty *noun. adj.* cincuenta
fig *noun.* higo
fight *noun.* **1.** pelea **2.** lucha **3.** combatividad, ánimo de lucha **4.** resistencia
fight *verb.* **1.** pelear, pelearse **2.** luchar, combatir **3.** discutir
fighter *noun.* **1.** combatiente, luchador **2.** avión de caza
figure *noun.* **1.** figura **2.** talle **3.** cifra, número **4.** diagrama
figure *verb.* **1.** aparecer **2.** figurar, calcular
file *noun.* **1.** carpeta **2.** archivo **3.** fila, hilera **4.** lima
file *verb.* **1.** archivar, clasificar **2.** presentar **3.** desfilar **4.** limar
fill *verb.* **1.** llenar, ocupar **2.** llenarse **3.** satisfacer, cubrir, cumplir **4.** rellenar, tapar, empastar
filling *noun.* **1.** empaste **2.** relleno
film *noun.* **1.** carrete **2.** película **3.** capa
film *verb.* **1.** filmar **2.** cubrirse, nublarse
filter *noun.* filtro
filter *verb.* **1.** filtrar **2.** filtrarse
filthy *adj.* **1.** sucio, asqueroso **2.** obsceno
fin *noun.* aleta
final *noun.* final
final *adj.* **1.** final, último **2.** definitivo
finally *adv.* **1.** finalmente **2.** al final
finals *noun plural.* finales
finance *noun.* **1.** finanzas **2.** fondos
finance *verb.* financiar
financial *adj.* financiero
financially *adv.* económicamente
find *noun.* hallazgo
find *verb.* **1.** encontrar, hallar **2.** descubrir, inventar **3.** fallar, dar sentencia **—find out** descubrir, averiguar
fine *noun.* multa
fine *interj.* muy bien, bien hecho
fine *verb.* multar
fine *adj.* **1.** excelente **2.** bueno, magnífico **3.** bien **4.** fino, delgado **5.** delicado **6.** sutil
fine *adv.* muy bien, a la perfección
finely *adv.* **1.** delicadamente **2.** elegantemente **3.** muy fino **4.** con precisión
finger *noun.* dedo
finger *verb.* manosear
finish *noun.* **1.** final **2.** acabado
finish *verb.* **1.** acabar **2.** terminar
finished *adj.* **1.** acabado, completo **2.** pulido, perfecto **3.** rendido, hecho polvo
finite *adj.* **1.** finito, limitado **2.** conjugado
Finland *noun.* Finlandia
Finn *noun.* finlandés
Finnish *noun. adj.* finlandés, finés
fire *noun.* **1.** fuego **2.** lumbre, chimenea **3.** incendio **4.** ardor, pasión
fire *verb.* **1.** incendiar, prender fuego **2.** enardecer, excitar **3.** disparar **4.** despedir, echar **—fire at/on** disparar
fireplace *noun.* chimenea
firm *noun.* empresa, firma
firm *adj.* **1.** firme, sólido **2.** severo **3.** tenaz
firmly *adv.* firmemente
first *noun. adj. adv.* primero
first-class *adj.* **1.** de primera clase **2.** de primera calidad, excelente
firstly *adv.* en primer lugar, primero
fish *noun.* **1.** pez **2.** pescado
fish *verb.* **1.** pescar **2.** buscar
fisherman *noun.* pescador
fist *noun.* puño
fit *noun.* **1.** ataque **2.** acceso, arrebato **3.** corte (de un traje)
fit *verb.* **1.** quedar bien, encajar, entrar

en **2.** adecuarse a **3.** instalar, poner, colocar **4.** equipar **5.** concordar, corresponderse
fit *adj.* **1.** sano, en forma **2.** adecuado, conveniente
fitness *noun.* **1.** buena forma **2.** aptitud, capacidad
fitting *noun.* **1.** mobiliario, accesorios **2.** prueba
fitting *adj.* adecuado, propio, digno
five *noun. adj.* cinco
fiver *noun.* billete de cinco dólares
fix *noun.* apuro, aprieto
fix *verb.* **1.** fijar **2.** asegurar **3.** clavar, atar, amarrar, sujetar **4.** arreglar **5.** convenir
fixed *adj.* **1.** fijo **2.** amañado
fixture *noun.* instalación fija
flag *noun.* bandera
flag *verb.* decaer, flaquear
flame *noun.* llama
flame *verb.* **1.** arder **2.** encenderse, llamear, brillar
flank *noun.* **1.** costado **2.** flanco
flank *verb.* flanquear
flap *noun.* **1.** solapa, faldón **2.** aleteo
flap *verb.* ondear, agitar, aletear, batir
flare *verb.* **1.** llamear **2.** acampanarse, ensancharse
flash *noun.* **1.** destello **2.** arrebato **3.** instante **4.** flash **5.** noticia de última hora
flash *verb.* **1.** brillar, centellear, relampaguear **2.** mostrar **3.** lanzar, dirigir **—flash by/past** pasar como un rayo
flashing *adj.* relampagueante, intermitente
flash-light *noun.* **1.** linterna **2.** antorcha
flat *noun.* **1.** llanura **2.** palma **3.** hoja (of a sword) **4.** bemol
flat *adj.* **1.** llano, plano, liso **2.** monótono, aburrido, soso **3.** rotundo, terminante **4.** desinflado **5.** sin gas **6.** desafinado **7.** fijo
flat *adv.* **1.** horizontalmente **2.** rotundamente, terminantemente
flavor *noun.* **1.** sabor **2.** aire
flavor *verb.* sazonar, condimentar
flee *verb.* huir
fleet *noun.* **1.** flota **2.** armada
flesh *noun.* **1.** carne **2.** pulpa
flexibility *noun.* flexibilidad
flexible *adj.* flexible
flick *noun.* movimiento rápido
flick *verb.* hacer un movimiento rápido
flight *noun.* **1.** vuelo **2.** huida, fuga **3.** tramo **4.** bandada
fling *verb.* **1.** arrojar, lanzar **2.** arrojarse
flint *noun. adj.* **1.** sílex **2.** pedernal
flip *noun.* tirada, echada, coletazo
flip *verb.* **1.** tirar al aire **2.** hojear
float *noun.* boya, flotador
float *verb.* **1.** flotar, poner a flote, hacer flotar **2.** emitir, poner en circulación
flock *noun.* **1.** rebaño, bandada **2.** tropel, multitud
flock (to/into) *verb.* congregarse, reunirse
flood *noun.* **1.** inundación **2.** torrente, avalancha
flood *verb.* inundar
floor *noun.* **1.** suelo **2.** piso, planta
floor *verb.* **1.** solar, entarimar **2.** derribar, tumbar
flop *noun.* fracaso, fiasco
flop *verb.* **1.** tumbarse, dejarse caer **2.** caer **3.** fracasar
floppy *adj.* **1.** blando, que se cae **2.** flexible
flora *noun.* flora
flounder *verb.* revolcarse, andar dificultosamente
flour *noun.* harina
flourish *noun.* **1.** floritura **2.** ademán, movimiento ostentoso **3.** floreo
flourish *verb.* **1.** florecer **2.** prosperar **3.** agitar, blandir
flow *noun.* corriente, flujo, circulación
flow *verb.* **1.** fluir **2.** subir **3.** circular
flower *noun.* flor
flower *verb.* florecer
flu *noun.* gripe
fluid *noun.* **1.** fluido **2.** líquido
fluid *adj.* **1.** fluido, líquido **2.** flexible
flush *noun.* **1.** rubor **2.** arrebato **3.** cisterna
flush *verb.* **1.** ruborizar, sonrojar **2.** tirar de la cadena **3.** hacer salir, desalojar

flushed *adj.* sonrojado
flux *noun.* inestabilidad, cambio constante
fly *noun.* **1.** mosca **2.** mosca artificial
fly *verb.* **1.** volar **2.** pilotar, ir en avión **3.** huir, salir de, abandonar **4.** pasar volando
foam *noun.* espuma
foam *verb.* hacer espuma
focal *adj.* focal
focus *noun.* **1.** foco **2.** centro
—**in/out of focus** enfocado/desenfocado
focus *verb.* **1.** enfocar **2.** centrar, concentrar
fog *noun.* niebla
fog *verb.* empañarse
foil *noun.* **1.** papel de aluminio **2.** florete
foil *verb.* frustrar, desbaratar los planes
fold *noun.* **1.** pliegue **2.** redil
fold *verb.* **1.** doblar, plegar **2.** cruzar
folded *adj.* doblado, plegado, cruzado
folding *adj.* plegable
foliage *noun.* follaje
folk *adj.* popular, folclórico, tradicional
folks *noun plural.* gente
follow *verb.* **1.** seguir **2.** entender **3.** deducirse
follower *noun.* seguidor
following *prep.* después de
following *noun.* seguidores
following *adj.* siguiente
following *pron.* lo siguiente
follow-up *noun.* **1.** seguimiento **2.** continuación
folly *noun.* locura
fond *adj.* **1.** cariñoso, afectuoso **2.** ilusorio, vano
food *noun.* comida, alimento
fool *noun.* tonto, imbécil
fool *verb.* engañar
—**fool about/around** hacer el tonto, bromear
foolish *adj.* **1.** tonto, imprudente **2.** ridículo
foot *noun.* **1.** pie **2.** pata
football *noun.* **1.** fútbol americano **2.** balón de fútbol
footstep *noun.* paso, pisada
for *prep.* **1.** para **2.** hacia, en dirección a **3.** durante **4.** por **5.** a favor de **6.** a causa de **7.** a pesar de **8.** de
for *conj.* ya que, puesto que
for example por ejemplo
forbid *verb.* prohibir
forbidden *adj.* prohibido
force *noun.* **1.** fuerza **2.** cuerpo, personal
—**in force** vigente, en vigor
—**forces** fuerzas armadas
force *verb.* **1.** forzar **2.** obligar **3.** imponer
forced *adj.* forzado, forzoso
ford *noun.* vado
ford *verb.* vadear
forecast *noun.* pronóstico, previsión
forecast *verb.* pronosticar
forefront *noun.* vanguardia
forehead *noun.* frente
foreign *adj.* **1.** extranjero **2.** ajeno **3.** exterior **4.** de asuntos exteriores
foreigner *noun.* **1.** extranjero **2.** extraño
foreman, forewoman *noun.* **1.** capataz, maestro de obras **2.** presidente del jurado
foremost *adj.* principal, más destacado
forensic *adj.* forense
foresee *verb.* prever
forest *noun.* **1.** bosque **2.** reserva
forestry *noun.* silvicultura
forestry *adj.* forestal
forge *noun.* forja
forge *verb.* **1.** forjar **2.** falsificar
—**forge ahead** abrirse camino, avanzar
forget *verb.* **1.** olvidar **2.** olvidarse **3.** perder los estribos
forgive *verb.* perdonar
fork *noun.* **1.** tenedor **2.** bifurcación **3.** horca, horquilla
fork *verb.* **1.** bifurcarse, ramificarse **2.** torcer, girar **3.** cargar con la horca
form *noun.* **1.** forma **2.** clase, tipo **3.** formulario **4.** formalidad **5.** banco
form *verb.* **1.** formar, constituir **2.** formarse **3.** construir, hacer, elaborar, formular
formal *adj.* **1.** formal **2.** oficial **3.** de eti-

queta, de ceremonia, solemne **4.** regular **5.** correcto
formally *adv.* formalmente
format *noun.* formato
format *verb.* formatear
formation *noun.* formación
former *adj.* antiguo, anterior
—**the former** el primero
formerly *adv.* antiguamente, anteriormente
formidable *adj.* **1.** temible, imponente **2.** formidable
formula *noun.* fórmula
fort *noun.* fortaleza, fuerte
forth *adv.* adelante
forthcoming *adj.* **1.** próximo, venidero **2.** abierto, comunicativo
forties *noun plural.* **1.** entre cuarenta y cincuenta **2.** los años cuarenta
fortieth *noun.* cuadragésimo
fortnight *noun.* quincena
fortress *noun.* fortaleza, fuerte
fortunate *adj.* afortunado
fortunately *adv.* afortunadamente
fortune *noun.* fortuna, suerte
forty *noun. adj.* cuarenta
forum *noun.* foro
forward, forwards *adv.* **1.** adelante, hacia adelante **2.** en adelante
forward *noun.* delantero
forward *verb.* remitir, expedir, enviar
forward *adj.* **1.** hacia delante **2.** delantero **3.** precoz, adelantado **4.** atrevido, insolente
fossil *noun.* fósil
foster *verb.* **1.** acoger, criar **2.** fomentar, promover, favorecer
foul *noun.* falta
foul *verb.* **1.** cometer una falta **2.** ensuciar, contaminar
foul *adj.* **1.** asqueroso, fétido **2.** vil, terrible **3.** ordinario, grosero **4.** antirreglamentario, sucio
found *verb.* fundar
—**found on/upon** basar
foundation *noun.* **1.** fundación **2.** fundamento, base **3.** cimientos
founder *noun.* fundador
founding *noun.* fundación
fountain *noun.* fuente
four *noun. adj.* cuatro
fourteen *noun. adj.* catorce
fourteenth *noun.* **1.** catorceavo **2.** decimocuarto
fourth *noun.* cuarto
fox *noun.* zorro
fox *verb.* confundir, despistar, dejar perplejo
fraction *noun.* **1.** fracción **2.** poquito, parte
fracture *noun.* fractura
fracture *verb.* fracturar
fragile *adj.* frágil
fragment *noun.* fragmento, pedazo, trozo
fragment *verb.* fragmentarse, hacerse añicos
fragrance *noun.* fragancia, perfume
frail *adj.* débil, delicado
frame *noun.* **1.** armazón, estructura, montura **2.** marco **3.** cuerpo, constitución
frame *verb.* **1.** enmarcar **2.** encuadrar **3.** incriminar, culpar
framework *noun.* estructura, marco
franc *noun.* franco
France *noun.* Francia
franchise *noun.* **1.** sufragio **2.** licencia, concesión, franquicia
frank *verb.* franquear
frank *adj.* franco
frankly *adv.* francamente
frantic *adj.* **1.** desesperado **2.** frenético
fraud *noun.* **1.** fraude, estafa **2.** impostor
freak *noun.* **1.** fenómeno, monstruo, anomalía **2.** fanático
free *verb.* **1.** liberar, poner en libertad **2.** deshacerse de, librarse de **3.** desatar, soltar
free *adj.* **1.** libre **2.** abierto **3.** vacante, desocupado **4.** gratuito, gratis
—**free with** generoso
freedom *noun.* libertad
freely *adv.* **1.** libremente **2.** voluntariamente **3.** generosamente
freeway *noun.* autopista
freeze *noun.* helada

freeze *verb.* **1.** congelar **2.** helar **3.** helarse, congelarse **4.** quedarse inmóvil
freezing *adj.* helado, glacial
freight *noun.* **1.** carga, mercancías **2.** flete
French *noun. adj.* francés
French fries *noun plural.* papas fritas, patatas fritas
Frenchman, Frenchwoman *noun.* francés
frequency *noun.* frecuencia
frequent *verb.* frecuentar
frequent *adj.* frecuente
frequently *adv.* frecuentemente
fresh *adj.* **1.** fresco **2.** recién hecho **3.** lozano, saludable **4.** nuevo, reciente **5.** dulce
freshly *adv.* recién
friction *noun.* fricción
Friday *noun.* viernes
fridge *noun.* frigorífico, refrigeradora, nevera
friend *noun.* **1.** amigo **2.** conocido
friendly *adj.* simpático, amigable
friendship *noun.* amistad
frighten *verb.* asustar
frightened *adj.* asustado
frightening *adj.* espantoso, aterrador
fringe *noun.* **1.** fleco, franja **2.** linde, periferia, borde
fringe *verb.* bordear, circundar
frog *noun.* rana
from *prep.* **1.** de **2.** desde **3.** por
front *noun.* **1.** parte delantera **2.** fachada **3.** portada **4.** frente
frontier *noun.* frontera
frost *noun.* **1.** helada **2.** escarcha
frost (over/up) *verb.* **1.** helarse **2.** escarchar
frown *noun.* ceño
frown *verb.* fruncir el ceño
fruit *noun.* **1.** fruta **2.** fruto
fruit *verb.* dar fruto
frustrate *verb.* frustrar
frustrated *adj.* frustrado
frustration *noun.* frustración
fry *verb.* **1.** freír **2.** freírse
ft. *abbr.* pie
fuel *noun.* combustible, carburante
fuel *verb.* abastecer de combustible
fulfill *verb.* **1.** cumplir, desempeñar **2.** satisfacer **3.** realizar, alcanzar
fulfillment *noun.* **1.** cumplimiento **2.** satisfacción **3.** realización
full *adj.* **1.** lleno **2.** completo, entero, íntegro **3.** detallado, extenso **4.** holgado, amplio **5.** de mucho vuelo **6.** ocupado
full *adv.* **1.** completamente, al máximo **2.** totalmente **3.** de cuerpo entero **4.** justo, de lleno
full-time *adj. adv.* a tiempo completo
fully *adv.* **1.** completamente, enteramente, plenamente **2.** por lo menos, como mínimo
fun *noun.* diversión
function *noun.* **1.** función **2.** recepción, acto
function *verb.* funcionar, marchar
functional *adj.* funcional
fund *noun.* **1.** fondo **2.** reserva
fundamental *noun.* fundamento, piedra angular, aspecto básico
fundamental *adj.* fundamental
fundamentally *adv.* fundamentalmente, básicamente, en esencia
funeral *noun.* funeral
funny *adj.* **1.** divertido, gracioso **2.** extraño, raro, curioso
fur *noun.* **1.** pelo, pelaje **2.** piel
furious *adj.* **1.** furioso **2.** violento
furnish *verb.* **1.** amueblar **2.** proporcionar, proveer, suministrar
furnished *adj.* amueblado
furniture *noun.* mobiliario, muebles
further *verb.* fomentar, promover, favorecer
further *adj.* **1.** más **2.** adicional **3.** ulterior, más distante
further *adv.* **1.** lejos, a lo lejos **2.** mucho **3.** más **4.** más lejos **5.** más allá
furthermore *adv.* además
fury *noun.* furia, furor
fusion *noun.* **1.** fusión **2.** fundición
fuss *noun.* **1.** jaleo, alboroto, ruido **2.** conmoción, bulla
fuss *verb.* preocuparse por cosas sin importancia
future *noun. adj.* futuro

G

g. *abbr.* gramo
gain *noun.* **1.** aumento **2.** beneficio, ganancia
gain *verb.* **1.** ganar, adquirir **2.** obtener, conseguir **3.** aumentar **4.** adelantarse, ir adelantado
galaxy *noun.* **1.** galaxia **2.** constelación
gall *noun.* **1.** bilis, hiel **2.** atrevimiento, caradura
gall *verb.* fastidiar, molestar
gallery *noun.* **1.** galería **2.** tribuna, gallinero
gallery *adj.* de galería, de gallinero
gallon *noun.* galón
gamble *noun.* riesgo, apuesta
gamble *verb.* apostar, jugar dinero
gambling *noun.* juego
game *noun.* **1.** juego **2.** partido, partida **3.** caza mayor, caza menor
game *adj.* valiente, animoso, bien dispuesto
gang *noun.* **1.** grupo, cuadrilla, equipo **2.** banda
gap *noun.* **1.** hueco, espacio, vacío **2.** brecha
garage *noun.* **1.** garaje, cochera **2.** taller, gasolinera, estación de servicio
garbage *noun.* basura
garbage-can *noun.* cubo de la basura
garden *noun.* jardín, huerto
—gardens parque, jardines
garden *verb.* trabajar en el jardín/huerto
gardener *noun.* jardinero
gardening *noun.* jardinería
garlic *noun.* ajo
garment *noun.* prenda de vestir
garrison *noun.* guarnición
garrison *verb.* guarnecer
garrison *adj.* fortificado
gas *noun.* **1.** gas **2.** anestesia **3.** gasolina
gas *verb.* asfixiar con gas, gasear
gasoline *noun.* gasolina
gasp *noun.* boqueada, jadeo, grito ahogado
gasp *verb.* **1.** jadear, respirar con dificultad **2.** gritar
gastric *adj.* gástrico
gate *noun.* **1.** puerta, entrada **2.** verja
gateway *noun.* **1.** puerta de acceso **2.** portal
gather *noun.* pliegue, fruncido
gather *verb.* **1.** coger, recoger, recopilar **2.** reunir, juntar **3.** reunirse, juntarse, congregarse **4.** enterarse, tener entendido **5.** acumularse, amontonarse **6.** recolectar **7.** fruncir
gathering *noun.* **1.** reunión, asamblea **2.** concurrencia, muchedumbre
gauge *noun.* **1.** calibrador, indicador **2.** calibre **3.** ancho de vía
gauge *verb.* **1.** medir, calibrar **2.** juzgar, estimar
gay *noun.* gay, homosexual
gay *adj.* **1.** gay, homosexual **2.** vivo, vistoso, alegre
gaze *noun.* mirada fija
gaze *verb.* mirar fijamente, clavar la vista
gear *noun.* **1.** engranaje **2.** marcha **3.** mecanismo **4.** equipo, bártulos, trastos, herramientas
gender *noun.* género
gene *noun.* gen
general *noun.* general
general *adj.* **1.** general **2.** común
generally *adv.* generalmente, en general, por lo general
generate *verb.* generar, producir, causar, suscitar
generation *noun.* generación
generator *noun.* generador
generic *adj.* genérico
generosity *noun.* generosidad
generous *adj.* **1.** generoso **2.** abundante
genetic *adj.* genético
genetics *noun singular.* genética
genius *noun.* genio
gentle *adj.* **1.** amable, dulce, tierno **2.** suave, ligero, moderado
gentleman *noun.* caballero
gently *adv.* **1.** amablemente, dulcemente, tiernamente **2.** suavemente, ligeramente, moderadamente

genuine *adj.* **1.** genuino, auténtico, verdadero **2.** sincero
genuinely *adv.* **1.** realmente, verdaderamente **2.** sinceramente
geography *noun.* geografía
geological *adj.* geológico
geology *noun.* geología
German *noun. adj.* alemán
Germany *noun.* Alemania
gesture *noun.* gesto
gesture *verb.* hacer un gestos
get *verb.* **1.** conseguir **2.** obtener **3.** tomar **4.** recibir, ganar, cobrar **5.** traer, ir a buscar, procurar **6.** llevar **7.** encontrar **8.** coger, recoger, agarrar, atrapar **9.** adquirir, comprar **10.** entender, comprender **11.** poner, ponerse **12.** hacer **13.** hacerse, volverse, convertirse **14.** convencer, persuadir **15.** llegar **16.** lograr, llegar a **17.** tener **18.** acertar, dar en
—**get along** llevarse bien
—**get down** bajar, descender
—**get off** apearse de, bajar de
—**get out** salir
—**get over 1.** superar **2.** atravesar
—**get up** levantarse
ghetto *noun.* gueto
ghost *noun.* fantasma
giant *noun.* **1.** gigante **2.** as, coloso
giant *adj.* gigante, gigantesco, descomunal
gift *noun.* **1.** regalo, presente, obsequio **2.** don, talento
gift *verb.* regalar, obsequiar
gifted *adj.* talentoso
giggle *noun.* risa tonta, risa nerviosa
giggle *verb.* reírse tontamente, dar la risa tonta
gill *noun.* branquia, agalla
gilt *noun.* dorado
gin *noun.* ginebra
ginger *noun.* jengibre
ginger *adj.* **1.** de jengibre **2.** rojo, pelirrojo, bermejo
girl *noun.* niña, chica, muchacha
—**Girl Scout** exploradora
give *noun.* elasticidad, resistencia
give *verb.* **1.** dar **2.** regalar, entregar, otorgar, conceder **3.** proporcionar, proveer, servir, suministrar **4.** provocar, causar **5.** ceder, dar de sí **6.** lanzar, proferir
—**give in** darse por vencido
—**give out** acabarse, agotarse
—**give up 1.** renunciar, dejar de **2.** rendirse, entregarse
given *adj.* **1.** dado **2.** determinado
—**given to** dado a, propenso a
glad *adj.* feliz, alegre, contento
glamour, glamor *noun.* glamour, encanto, atractivo
glamorous *adj.* glamuroso, atractivo
glance *noun.* mirada, vistazo, ojeada
glance *verb.* echar un vistazo, dar una mirada
glancing *adj.* oblicuo
gland *noun.* glándula
glare *noun.* **1.** mirada feroz **2.** deslumbramiento
glare *verb.* **1.** mirar ferozmente, fulminar con la mirada **2.** deslumbrar
glass *noun.* **1.** vidrio, cristal **2.** vaso, copa **3.** espejo **4.** barómetro
glasses *noun plural.* gafas, anteojos
gleam *noun.* **1.** brillo, destello **2.** rayo, resquicio
gleam *verb.* relucir, brillar, destellar
glimpse *noun.* vislumbre, destello
glimpse *verb.* vislumbrar, entrever
glitter *noun.* brillo, resplandor
glitter *verb.* brillar, relucir
glittering *adj.* brillante, reluciente
global *adj.* global, mundial, universal
globe *noun.* **1.** globo, esfera **2.** globo terráqueo
gloom *noun.* **1.** penumbra, oscuridad **2.** pesimismo, tristeza, melancolía
gloomy *adj.* **1.** sombrío, lóbrego **2.** triste, pesimista
glorious *adj.* **1.** glorioso **2.** magnífico, espléndido
glory *noun.* gloria, esplendor
glory *verb.* enorgullecerse, jactarse
glossy *adj.* lustroso, brillante, reluciente
glove *noun.* guante
glow *noun.* brillo, resplandor, incandescencia

glow *verb*. brillar, resplandecer, estar al rojo vivo
glowing *adj*. brillante, resplandeciente, incandescente
glucose *noun*. glucosa
glue *noun*. cola, pegamento
glue *verb*. colar, pegar
go *noun*. **1.** intento **2.** turno **3.** energía, empuje
go *verb*. **1.** ir **2.** irse, marcharse, salir, partir **3.** acudir **4.** conducir a, ir a **5.** enviarse, tramitar, pasar **6.** venderse, darse **7.** desarrollarse, marchar **8.** desaparecer, gastarse, pasar, esfumarse, transcurrir **9.** averiarse, fallar, desgastarse, romperse, ceder **10.** funcionar **11.** volverse, ponerse **12.** valer, estar permitido, ser aceptable **13.** hacer **14.** pasar **15.** extenderse, llegar **16.** hacer juego, pegar, armonizar **17.** caber
—**go by** pasar por, pasar junto a
—**go off 1.** marcharse, irse **2.** estallar
—**go on** seguir, proseguir
—**go out** salir
—**go through 1.** pasar por **2.** padecer, sufrir
—**go with 1.** acompañar **2.** armonizar, hacer juego
go-ahead *noun*. luz verde, visto bueno
goal *noun*. **1.** gol **2.** objetivo, finalidad, meta
goalkeeper *noun*. portero, arquero
goat *noun*. cabra
God *noun*. Dios
goddess *noun*. diosa
going *noun*. **1.** salida, partida, ida **2.** estado
going *adj*. **1.** próspero, que funciona bien **2.** actual, del momento
gold *noun*. oro
golden *adj*. dorado, de oro
golf *noun*. golf
golf *verb*. jugar al golf
golfer *noun*. golfista, jugador de golf
good *interj*. bueno, bien
good *noun*. **1.** bien, provecho, beneficio **2.** bondad, lado bueno
—**goods** artículos, bienes, mercancías
good *adj*. **1.** buen, bueno **2.** correcto **3.** competente **4.** amable, bondadoso **5.** útil, beneficioso **6.** agradable **7.** apropiado, adecuado, oportuno **8.** apto, cualificado **9.** sano, saludable **10.** positivo **11.** profundo **12.** virtuoso
goodbye *interj. noun*. adiós
good-looking *adj*. guapo, bien parecido
goodness *interj*. ¡Dios mío!
goodness *noun*. bondad
goodwill, good will *noun*. **1.** clientela, renombre comercial **2.** buena voluntad
goose *noun*. ganso
gore *noun*. sangre derramada, sangre coagulada
gore *verb*. cornear, dar una cornada
gorgeous *adj*. **1.** hermoso, precioso, guapísimo **2.** magnífico, espléndido
gosh *interj*. ¡cielos!
gospel *noun*. evangelio
gossip *noun*. **1.** chisme, chismorreo, cotilleo **2.** charla, conversación **3.** chismoso, cotilla
gossip *verb*. **1.** chismorrear, cotillear **2.** charlar, conversar
govern *verb*. **1.** gobernar **2.** dominar **3.** regir **4.** guiar
government *noun*. **1.** gobierno **2.** dirección
governmental *adj*. gubernamental, gubernativo
governor *noun*. gobernador
gown *noun*. **1.** vestido largo **2.** toga
grab *noun*. asimiento, acto de agarrar
grab *verb*. **1.** asir, agarrar, coger **2.** apropiarse de, arrebatar, echar mano a
grace *noun*. **1.** gracia, elegancia **2.** delicadeza, cortesía, gentileza **3.** bendición **4.** plazo, demora **5.** Ilustrísima, Excelencia
grade *noun*. **1.** nivel, clase, categoría, calidad, grado **2.** curso, año **3.** nota **4.** pendiente
grade *verb*. **1.** clasificar **2.** calificar
gradient *noun*. pendiente
gradual *adj*. gradual
gradually *adv*. gradualmente
graduate *noun*. licenciado, graduado, egresado

graduate *verb.* **1.** licenciarse, graduarse **2.** graduar
grain *noun.* **1.** grano **2.** cereal **3.** veta, fibra **4.** pizca, ápice
grammar *noun.* gramática
grammatical *adj.* gramatical
grand *noun.* mil dólares
grand *adj.* **1.** grandioso, magnífico, espléndido, imponente **2.** ambicioso **3.** distinguido, respetable
grandchild *noun.* nieto, nieta
granddad *noun.* abuelo
granddaughter *noun.* nieta
grandfather *noun.* abuelo
grandmother *noun.* abuela
grandparent *noun.* abuelo, abuela
grandson *noun.* nieto
granite *noun.* granito
granny, grannie *noun.* abuelita
grant *noun.* otorgamiento, concesión
grant *verb.* **1.** conceder, otorgar **2.** reconocer, admitir
grape *noun.* uva
graph *noun.* gráfica, gráfico
graphic *adj.* gráfico
grasp *noun.* **1.** apretón **2.** control, dominio **3.** alcance **4.** comprensión, conocimientos
grasp *verb.* **1.** asir, agarrar, sujetar, empuñar **2.** comprender, entender
grass *noun.* **1.** hierba, césped **2.** marihuana, mota
grate *noun.* parrilla
grate *verb.* **1.** rallar **2.** crispar, irritar, poner nervioso
grateful *adj.* agradecido
gratitude *noun.* gratitud
grave *noun.* tumba
grave *adj.* grave, serio
gravel *noun.* grava
gravity *noun.* **1.** gravedad **2.** seriedad
gray, grey *noun.* gris
gray, grey *verb.* encanecer
gray, grey *adj.* **1.** gris **2.** canoso
graze *noun.* rasguño, roce
graze *verb.* **1.** pastar, pacer **2.** raspar **3.** rozar
great *adj.* **1.** gran, grande **2.** importante **3.** enorme, vasto **4.** mucho **5.** maravilloso, espléndido, fantástico **6.** excelente, buenísimo
Great Britain *noun.* Gran Bretaña
greatly *adv.* muy, mucho
Greece *noun.* Grecia
greed *noun.* **1.** avaricia, codicia **2.** gula
greedy *adj.* **1.** avaricioso, codicioso **2.** glotón
Greek *noun. adj.* griego
green *noun.* **1.** verde, verdor **2.** césped, prado **3.** green (golf)
—**greens** verduras
green *adj.* **1.** verde **2.** inexperto, bisoño **3.** inocente **4.** ecologista
greenhouse *noun.* invernadero
greet *verb.* saludar
greeting *noun.* saludo
grid *noun.* **1.** cuadrícula **2.** reja
grief *noun.* dolor, pesar, aflicción
grill *noun.* **1.** parrilla, grill **2.** parrillada
grill *verb.* **1.** asar a la parrillar, hacer al grill **2.** interrogar
grim *adj.* **1.** desalentador **2.** horrible, macabro, espantoso **3.** ceñudo, austero, severo **4.** inflexible, inexorable
grimly *adv.* **1.** severamente **2.** horriblemente, espantosamente **3.** inflexiblemente
grin *noun.* sonrisa de oreja a oreja
grin *verb.* sonreír de oreja a oreja
grind *noun.* trabajo pesado
grind *verb.* **1.** moler, triturar, picar **2.** rechinar **3.** afilar
grip *noun.* **1.** apretón **2.** asidero, asa, empuñadura **3.** saco de mano, bolsa **4.** conocimiento, comprensión
grip *verb.* empuñar, agarrar, aferrar, asir
groan *noun.* **1.** gemido **2.** gruñido
groan *verb.* **1.** gemir **2.** gruñir
groove *noun.* surco, ranura, estría
gross *noun.* totalidad
gross *adj.* **1.** flagrante, grande, craso **2.** grosero, ordinario **3.** muy gordo, obeso **4.** bruto
ground *noun.* **1.** suelo, tierra **2.** terreno, campo
—**grounds** **1.** jardines **2.** razones, motivos **3.** poso, sedimento
ground *verb.* **1.** basarse, fundarse **2.**

encallar **3.** obligar a quedarse en tierra
group *noun.* grupo, conjunto
group *verb.* **1.** agrupar **2.** agruparse
grow *verb.* **1.** crecer **2.** aumentar **3.** desarrollarse **4.** dejarse **5.** hacerse, ponerse, volverse **6.** cultivar
grower *noun.* cultivador
grown *adj.* adulto
growth *noun.* **1.** crecimiento, desarrollo **2.** aumento **3.** tumor
guarantee *noun.* garantía
guarantee *verb.* garantizar
guard *noun.* **1.** guardia, centinela **2.** carcelero **3.** vigilancia, protección
guard *verb.* **1.** guardar **2.** vigilar, proteger, defender
guarded *adj.* cauteloso, prudente
guardian *noun.* **1.** tutor **2.** guardián, protector
guess *noun.* suposición, conjetura, estimación
guess *verb.* **1.** adivinar, acertar **2.** suponer, creer
guest *noun.* invitado, huésped
guidance *noun.* orientación, consejo
guide *noun.* **1.** guía **2.** modelo, pauta
guide *verb.* guiar, dirigir
guideline *noun.* directriz, pauta
guilt *noun.* culpa, culpabilidad
guilty *adj.* culpable
guitar *noun.* guitarra
guitarist *noun.* guitarrista
gulf *noun.* golfo
gum *noun.* **1.** goma **2.** pegamento **3.** chicle, goma de mascar **4.** encía
gum *verb.* pegar
gun *noun.* **1.** arma de fuego **2.** fusil **3.** escopeta **4.** pistola
gunman *noun.* pistolero
gut *noun.* **1.** intestino, tripa **2.** cuerda de tripa
—**guts** agallas, coraje
gut *verb.* **1.** destripar **2.** destruir el interior
guy *noun.* tipo, tío, individuo
gym *noun.* **1.** gimnasio **2.** gimnasia
gypsy *noun. adj.* gitano

H

habit *noun.* **1.** costumbre **2.** hábito
habitat *noun.* hábitat
hack *noun.* **1.** corte, tajo, machetazo, hachazo **2.** taxi
hack *verb.* cortar, tajar
hail *interj.* salve
hail *noun.* **1.** granizo **2.** lluvia **3.** grito
hail *verb.* **1.** granizar **2.** llamar **3.** aclamar
hair *noun.* pelo, cabello, vello
half *noun.* mitad
half *adj.* **1.** medio **2.** mitad
half *adv.* **1.** medio **2.** a medias **3.** casi
half-time *noun.* descanso, intervalo
hall *noun.* **1.** vestíbulo, entrada **2.** sala **3.** ayuntamiento **4.** pasillo, corredor **5.** residencia, colegio mayor
hallo *interj. noun.* hola
halt *noun.* **1.** alto, interrupción **2.** parada **3.** apeadero
halt *verb.* **1.** parar, detener **2.** pararse, detenerse
halve *verb.* **1.** partir en dos **2.** reducir a la mitad
ham *noun.* jamón
hammer *noun.* **1.** martillo **2.** macillo
hammer *verb.* **1.** martillar, martillear, clavar, batir **2.** hacer entender algo a alguien a fuerza de repetirlo
hamper *noun.* cesta, canasta
hamper *verb.* estorbar, impedir, obstaculizar
hand *noun.* **1.** mano **2.** manecilla, aguja **3.** trabajador, operario **4.** habilidad **5.** influencia **6.** ayuda **7.** partida **8.** palmo **9.** caligrafía, escritura
hand *verb.* **1.** dar, entregar **2.** devolver, pasar
handbag *noun.* bolso
handbook *noun.* manual
handful *noun.* puñado
handicap *noun.* **1.** obstáculo, impedimento **2.** desventaja **3.** handicap **4.** discapacidad, minusvalía

handicap *verb*. obstaculizar, impedir, perjudicar
handicapped *adj*. **1.** discapacitado **2.** deficiente mental
handkerchief *noun*. pañuelo
handle *noun*. **1.** mango, asa, manilla, pomo **2.** asa **3.** manilla **4.** pomo
handle *verb*. **1.** manejar **2.** tocar, manipular **3.** tratar **4.** comerciar con
handsome *adj*. **1.** guapo, hermoso, bien parecido **2.** generoso, considerable
handwriting *noun*. caligrafía
handy *adj*. **1.** a mano, cerca **2.** práctico, útil **3.** hábil, diestro
hang *verb*. **1.** colgar **2.** tender **3.** ahorcar **4.** caer **5.** inclinar, bajar
hanging *noun*. ahorcamiento
happen *verb*. **1.** ocurrir, pasar, acontecer, suceder **2.** dar la casualidad, resultar que
happening *noun*. acontecimiento, suceso
happily *adv*. felizmente, por suerte
happiness *noun*. felicidad, alegría, dicha
happy *adj*. **1.** feliz, alegre, dichoso **2.** contento
harassment *noun*. acoso
harbor *noun*. puerto
hard *adj*. **1.** duro **2.** firme **3.** difícil **4.** agotador **5.** severo **6.** riguroso **7.** irrefutable **8.** fuerte
hard *adv*. **1.** duro, duramente **2.** con ahínco **3.** fuerte, fuertemente **4.** fijamente **5.** severamente **6.** completamente, totalmente
harden *verb*. **1.** endurecer **2.** endurecerse
hardly *adv*. **1.** apenas **2.** casi **3.** difícilmente
hardship *noun*. **1.** infortunio **2.** privación **3.** sufrimiento
hardware *noun*. **1.** ferretería **2.** hardware, soporte físico
hardy *adj*. fuerte, resistente, robusto
harm *noun*. daño, mal, perjuicio
harm *verb*. hacer daño, perjudicar
harmful *adj*. nocivo, perjudicial, dañino
harmless *adj*. inofensivo, inocuo
harmony *noun*. armonía
harness *noun*. arneses, guarniciones, arreos
harness *verb*. **1.** enjaezar, poner los arreos **2.** aprovechar, utilizar
harry *verb*. acosar, hostigar, atormentar
harsh *adj*. **1.** severo, duro, cruel **2.** fuerte, chillón **3.** áspero
harvest *noun*. cosecha
harvest *verb*. cosechar
hastily *adv*. apresuradamente, precipitadamente
hasty *adj*. **1.** apresurado, precipitado **2.** irritable, con genio
hat *noun*. sombrero
hatch *noun*. **1.** ventanilla **2.** escotilla
hatch *verb*. **1.** empollar, incubar **2.** romper el cascarón **3.** tramar, urdir, madurar
hate *noun*. odio, aversión
hate *verb*. odiar, detestar, aborrecer
hatred *noun*. odio, aversión
haul *noun*. **1.** tirón, estirón **2.** redada, botín
haul *verb*. tirar, arrastrar
haunt *noun*. **1.** guarida, lugar frecuentado **2.** lugar predilecto
haunt *verb*. **1.** aparecer, rondar **2.** perseguir, obsesionar **3.** frecuentar
haunted *adj*. encantado, embrujado
have *verb*. **1.** tener **2.** haber (auxiliary) **3.** tomar **4.** poseer **5.** pasar **6.** tolerar, sufrir **7.** recibir **8.** hacer **9.** lograr, conseguir **10.** dar **11.** hacer que alguien haga algo, mandar hacer algo **12.** tomar el pelo, engañar
—**have to** deber, tener que
haven *noun*. puerto, refugio
hawk *noun*. halcón
hawk *verb*. vender de puerta en puerta
hay *noun*. heno
hazard *noun*. riesgo, peligro
hazard *verb*. arriesgar, aventurar
hazardous *adj*. arriesgado, peligroso
hazel *noun*. avellano
hazel *adj*. color de avellana
he *noun*. **1.** macho **2.** varón
he *pron*. **1.** él **2.** el que, aquel que
head *noun*. **1.** cabeza **2.** mente **3.** direc-

tor, jefe **4.** fuente, nacimiento, origen **5.** cabecera, principio **6.** parte superior **7.** cara **8.** cabo, punta **9.** espuma

head *verb.* **1.** encabezar **2.** estar al frente de, dirigir, capitanear **3.** titular **4.** cabecear, rematar con la cabeza

—**head for** dirigirse, encaminarse

headache *noun.* **1.** dolor de cabeza **2.** quebradero de cabeza

heading *noun.* encabezamiento, título

headline *noun.* titular, cabecera

head-on *adv. adj.* de frente, frontal

headquarters *noun.* **1.** cuartel general **2.** sede, oficina central

heal *verb.* curar, sanar

health *noun.* salud

healthy *adj.* **1.** sano **2.** saludable **3.** próspero, sustancioso

heap *noun.* montón, pila

heap *verb.* **1.** amontonar, apilar **2.** colmar, llenar

hear *verb.* **1.** oír **2.** escuchar **3.** ver **4.** enterarse, tener noticias

hearing *noun.* **1.** oído **2.** oportunidad de hablar **3.** audiencia, vista

—**within hearing** al alcance del oído

heart *noun.* **1.** corazón **2.** entrañas **3.** centro, meollo **4.** valor

—**hearts** corazones, copas (cards)

—**lose heart** descorazonarse

heart attack *noun.* infarto, ataque al corazón

heat *noun.* **1.** calor **2.** pasión, ardor, vehemencia **3.** furia, ira **4.** eliminatoria

heat (up) *verb.* **1.** calentar **2.** calentarse

heated *adj.* **1.** caliente **2.** climatizado **3.** acalorado

heater *noun.* **1.** calentador **2.** estufa

heather *noun.* brezo

heating *noun.* calefacción

heaven *noun.* **1.** cielo **2.** paraíso, gloria

heavily *adv.* **1.** muy, mucho **2.** fuertemente **3.** profundamente **4.** pesadamente

heavy *adj.* **1.** pesado **2.** fuerte, abundante **3.** empedernido **4.** profundo **5.** considerable, cuantioso **6.** grueso, tosco **7.** cargado, encapotado **8.** denso **9.** difícil

heavyweight *noun. adj.* peso pesado

hectare *noun.* hectárea

hedge *noun.* seto

hedge *verb.* **1.** contestar con evasivas **2.** cercar (con un seto)

heel *noun.* **1.** talón **2.** tacón

heel *verb.* poner un tacón

height *noun.* **1.** altura, estatura **2.** cúspide, apogeo, punto culminante **3.** cumbre, cima **4.** colmo

heighten *verb.* **1.** elevar, realzar **2.** aumentar, intensificar

heir *noun.* heredero

helicopter *noun.* helicóptero

hell *noun.* infierno

hello *interj. noun.* **1.** hola **2.** ¡vaya!, ¡ándale!

helmet *noun.* casco

help *noun.* **1.** ayuda **2.** criado, asistente, empleado, ayudante **3.** remedio

help *verb.* **1.** ayudar **2.** socorrer, auxiliar **3.** contribuir **4.** aliviar **5.** servir

—**cannot help** no poder evitar

helpful *adj.* **1.** servicial **2.** útil

helping *noun.* ración, porción

helpless *adj.* indefenso, desvalido

hemisphere *noun.* hemisferio

hen *noun.* **1.** gallina **2.** hembra (de ave)

hence *adv.* **1.** por lo tanto, por consiguiente **2.** de aquí a

her *adj.* su, sus (de ella)

her *pron.* **1.** la (direct object) **2.** le, se (indirect object) **3.** ella (after prep)

herald *noun.* **1.** heraldo **2.** precursor

herald *verb.* anunciar, proclamar

herb *noun.* hierba

herd *noun.* **1.** rebaño, manada, piara **2.** multitud, tropel

herd *verb.* **1.** llevar en rebaño **2.** reunirse

here *interj.* **1.** ¡oye!, ¡eh! **2.** ¡presente!

—**here, there and everywhere** por todas partes, en todas partes

here *adv.* **1.** aquí, acá **2.** entonces, llegado a ese punto **3.** aquí presente

hereditary *adj.* hereditario

heritage *noun.* herencia, patrimonio

hero *noun.* **1.** héroe **2.** protagonista, personaje principal

heroic *adj.* heroico
heroin *noun.* heroína
hers *pron.* **1.** (el) suyo, (la) suya, (los) suyos, (las) suyas (de ella) **2.** de ella
herself *pron.* **1.** se **2.** sí misma **3.** ella misma **4.** ella sola
hesitate *verb.* vacilar, titubear, dudar
hesitation *noun.* indecisión, vacilación, duda
hey *interj.* ¡eh!, ¡oye!
hi *interj.* ¡hola!
hidden *adj.* escondido, oculto
hide *noun.* **1.** cuero **2.** piel, pellejo
hide *verb.* **1.** esconder, ocultar **2.** esconderse, ocultarse
hiding *noun.* **1.** escondrijo **2.** paliza
hierarchical *adj.* jerárquico
hierarchy *noun.* jerarquía
high *adj.* **1.** alto **2.** elevado **3.** grande **4.** superior **5.** excelente **6.** bueno **7.** noble **8.** fuerte **9.** agudo **10.** pasado **11.** importante
high *adv.* **1.** alto **2.** arriba, hacia arriba
high school *noun.* instituto, escuela de secundaria
higher education *noun.* enseñanza superior
highlight *noun.* punto culminante, guinda
highlight *verb.* destacar, dar relieve
highly *adv.* **1.** muy **2.** mucho **3.** sumamente **4.** extremadamente
high-tech, hi-tech, high technology *noun.* alta tecnología
highway *noun.* **1.** carretera **2.** autopista
hike *noun.* caminata, excursión a pie
hike *verb.* dar una caminata, ir de excursión
hill *noun.* **1.** colina, loma **2.** cuesta
hillside *noun.* ladera
him *pron.* **1.** lo, le (direct object) **2.** le, se (indirect object) **3.** él (after prep)
himself *pron.* **1.** se **2.** sí mismo **3.** él mismo **4.** él solo
Hindu *noun. adj.* hindú
hint *noun.* **1.** insinuación, indirecta **2.** indicación, sugerencia **3.** indicio
hint *verb.* **1.** insinuar, dar a entender **2.** soltar indirectas
hip *noun.* cadera
hip *adj.* a la última
hire *noun.* alquiler
hire *verb.* **1.** alquilar **2.** contratar
his *adj. pron.* **1.** su, sus (de él) **2.** (el) suyo, (la) suya, (los) suyos, (las) suyas (de él) **3.** de él
historian *noun.* historiador
historic, historical *adj.* histórico
historically *adv.* históricamente
history *noun.* historia
hit *noun.* **1.** golpe, tiro **2.** acierto **3.** éxito
hit *verb.* **1.** golpear, lanzar **2.** pegar, chocar **3.** dar con, dar contra **4.** afectar, dañar **5.** dar en, alcanzar
hitherto *adv.* hasta la fecha, hasta ahora
HIV *abbr.* VIH, virus del sida
hobby *noun.* pasatiempo
hockey *noun.* hockey
hold *noun.* **1.** agarre, asimiento **2.** dominio, influencia **3.** llave **4.** bodega
hold *verb.* **1.** tener en las manos, agarrar, sujetar, coger, asir **2.** sostener **3.** mantener, mantenerse **4.** creer, opinar **5.** tener **6.** retener **7.** guardar **8.** defender **9.** resistir **10.** ser válido, regir **11.** contener **12.** tener capacidad, tener cabida **13.** aguantar **14.** soportar **15.** ocupar, desempeñar, ejercer **16.** tener lugar, celebrarse **17.** deparar **18.** atenerse
—**hold on** **1.** seguir, persistir **2.** aguantar, resistir
—**hold together** **1.** unir, juntar **2.** mantenerse juntos
hole *noun.* **1.** agujero **2.** cavidad, hueco **3.** hoyo **4.** bache
hole *verb.* **1.** agujerear **2.** meter en el hoyo
holiday *noun.* **1.** fiesta, día festivo **2.** vacaciones
Holland *noun.* Holanda
hollow *noun.* **1.** hueco **2.** hondonada
hollow *adj.* **1.** hueco, hundido **2.** falso, vacío
holly *noun.* acebo
holy *adj.* **1.** sagrado **2.** santo
home *noun.* **1.** casa **2.** domicilio **3.** cuna, patria **4.** asilo, orfanato **5.** hogar

home *adj.* **1.** casero, del hogar **2.** local, nacional **3.** en casa, de casa
home *adv.* **1.** a casa, en casa **2.** de vuelta
homeland *noun.* patria, tierra natal
homeless *noun.* sin techo
homeless *adj.* sin hogar, sin vivienda
homework *noun.* deberes
homogeneous *adj.* homogéneo
homosexual *noun. adj.* homosexual
homosexuality *noun.* homosexualidad
honest *adj.* honesto
honestly *interj.* ¡hay que ver!, ¡vamos!
honestly *adv.* **1.** honestamente **2.** francamente, sinceramente
honesty *noun.* honestidad
honey *noun.* **1.** miel **2.** querido, cariño
honeymoon *noun.* luna de miel
honor *noun.* **1.** honor **2.** condecoración
honor *verb.* **1.** honrar **2.** condecorar **3.** cumplir
—**Your/His/Her Honor** Su Señoría
honorable *adj.* **1.** honrado **2.** honorable
honorary *adj.* **1.** honorario, honorífico **2.** no remunerado
hood *noun.* **1.** capucha, caperuza **2.** capó **3.** muceta
hook *noun.* **1.** anzuelo **2.** gancho **3.** alcayata **4.** croché
hook *verb.* **1.** pescar **2.** enganchar
hooked *adj.* ganchudo
—**hooked on** enganchado, adicto
hop *noun.* **1.** lúpulo **2.** salto, brinco
hop *verb.* dar saltos, brincar
hope *noun.* **1.** esperanza **2.** sueño, ilusión **3.** posibilidad
hope *verb.* esperar
hopeful *adj.* **1.** optimista, esperanzado **2.** prometedor
hopefully *adv.* **1.** con esperanza **2.** con suerte
hopeless *adj.* **1.** inútil **2.** desesperado, imposible
—**hopeless at** negado, desastre
horizon *noun.* horizonte
horizontal *adj.* horizontal
hormone *noun.* hormona
horn *noun.* **1.** cacho, cuerno, asta **2.** trompa **3.** bocina, claxon
horrible *adj.* horrible, horroroso
horrify *verb.* **1.** horrorizar **2.** escandalizar
horror *noun.* horror
horse *noun.* **1.** caballo **2.** potro
hospital *noun.* hospital
hospitality *noun.* hospitalidad
host, hostess *noun.* **1.** anfitrión, anfitriona **2.** huésped **3.** multitud
hostage *noun.* rehén
hostel *noun.* **1.** albergue **2.** residencia
hostile *adj.* **1.** hostil, contrario **2.** adverso, desfavorable
hostility *noun.* hostilidad
hot *adj.* **1.** caliente **2.** caluroso, cálido **3.** picante **4.** acalorado, impetuoso, violento **5.** reciente, de última hora
hotel *noun.* hotel
hound *noun.* perro de caza
hound *verb.* perseguir, acosar
hour *noun.* hora
house *noun.* **1.** casa **2.** hogar **3.** sala **4.** cámara
house *verb.* **1.** alojar **2.** guardar, poner
household *noun.* casa, familia
housekeeper *noun.* gobernanta, ama de llaves
housewife *noun.* ama de casa
housework *noun.* quehaceres domésticos, faenas de la casa
housing *noun.* alojamiento, vivienda
hover *verb.* **1.** planear, flotar en el aire **2.** revolotear, rondar
—**hover between** dudar, vacilar
how *adv. conj.* **1.** cómo **2.** qué **3.** cuánto, cómo de, a qué
however *conj.* de todas formas, de cualquier modo
however *adv.* **1.** sin embargo, no obstante **2.** cómo **3.** por más que
howl *noun.* rugido, aullido, gemido, alarido
howl *verb.* rugir, aullar, gemir, dar alaridos
hug *noun.* abrazo
hug *verb.* **1.** abrazar **2.** arrimarse, pegarse
huge *adj.* enorme
hull *noun.* casco
hum *noun.* murmullo, zumbido

hum *verb.* **1.** tararear, canturrear **2.** zumbar **3.** bullir
human, human being *noun.* ser humano
human *adj.* humano
humanity *noun.* humanidad
humble *verb.* humillar
humble *adj.* humilde, modesto
humiliation *noun.* humillación
humor *noun.* **1.** humor **2.** comicidad, gracia
humor *verb.* complacer, consentir
hundred *noun.* ciento, centenar, centena
hundred *adj.* cien, ciento
Hungarian *noun. adj.* húngaro
Hungary *noun.* Hungría
hunger *noun.* **1.** hambre, apetito **2.** deseo
hunger (for) *verb.* ansiar, anhelar
hungry *adj.* hambriento
hunt *noun.* **1.** caza **2.** busca, búsqueda, persecución
hunt *verb.* **1.** cazar **2.** buscar, perseguir
hunter *noun.* cazador
hunting *noun.* caza, cacería
hurdle *noun.* **1.** valla **2.** obstáculo
hurl *verb.* arrojar, tirar, lanzar
hurricane *noun.* huracán
hurried *adj.* **1.** apresurado, precipitado **2.** apremiado
hurry *noun.* **1.** prisa **2.** apuro
hurry *verb.* **1.** meter prisa, apurar **2.** darse prisa, apurarse **3.** hacer deprisa **4.** llevar deprisa, marchar deprisa
hurt *verb.* **1.** herir, hacer daño, lastimar **2.** doler **3.** perjudicar **4.** ofender
hurt *adj.* **1.** herido, lastimado **2.** dolido
husband *noun.* marido, esposo
husband *verb.* administrar bien, dosificar
hut *noun.* cabaña, choza
hydrogen *noun.* hidrógeno
hygiene *noun.* higiene
hypothesis *noun.* hipótesis
hypothetical *adj.* hipotético

I

I *pron.* yo
ice *noun.* **1.** hielo **2.** helado
ice *verb.* glasear
Icelandic *noun. adj.* islandés
icing *noun.* alcorza, glaseado
icy *adj.* **1.** helado, glacial **2.** frío, seco, desabrido
ID *noun.* **1.** identidad **2.** cédula de identidad, carné de identidad
idea *noun.* **1.** idea **2.** concepto, juicio **3.** impresión
ideal *noun. adj.* ideal
ideally *adv.* idealmente, perfectamente
identical *adj.* idéntico
identification *noun.* identificación
identify *verb.* identificar
identity *noun.* identidad
idiot *noun.* idiota
idle *verb.* **1.** holgazanear, estar ocioso, haraganear **2.** funcionar en vacío
idle *adj.* **1.** parado, inactivo, desocupado **2.** flojo, perezoso, holgazán **3.** inútil, vano **4.** infundado
i.e. *abbr.* es decir, esto es
if *conj.* **1.** si **2.** en caso de que **3.** cuando **4.** a pesar de, aunque
ignorance *noun.* ignorancia
ignorant *adj.* ignorante
ignore *verb.* desatender, no hacer caso, hacer caso omiso
ill *noun.* **1.** mal **2.** padecimiento, dolencia
ill *adj.* **1.** adverso, dañino **2.** malo **3.** enfermo, delicado
ill *adv.* mal, a duras penas
illegal *adj.* ilegal
illegally *adv.* ilegalmente
illness *noun.* enfermedad, mal, dolencia
illuminate *verb.* iluminar
illuminated *adj.* ilustrado
illusion *noun.* ilusión
illustrate *verb.* **1.** ilustrar **2.** demostrar **3.** aclarar, explicar

illustration *noun.* **1.** ejemplo **2.** ilustración **3.** aclaración
image *noun.* **1.** imagen **2.** efigie **3.** retrato **4.** reflejo
imaginary *adj.* imaginario
imagination *noun.* imaginación
imaginative *adj.* imaginativo
imagine *verb.* **1.** imaginar **2.** imaginarse **3.** suponer, creer
imitation *noun.* **1.** imitación **2.** copia, reproducción
imitation *adj.* de imitación
immaculate *adj.* inmaculado, impecable
immediate *adj.* **1.** inmediato **2.** directo **3.** urgente
immediately *adv.* **1.** inmediatamente **2.** directamente
immense *adj.* inmenso
immensely *adv.* inmensamente
immigrant *noun. adj.* inmigrante
immigration *noun.* inmigración
imminent *adj.* inminente
immune (to/from) *adj.* inmune
immunity *noun.* inmunidad
impact *noun.* impacto
impatient *adj.* impaciente
impatiently *adv.* impacientemente
imperative *noun. adj.* imperativo
imperial *adj.* imperial
impetus *noun.* ímpetu
implement *noun.* instrumento, herramienta
implication *noun.* **1.** consecuencia, implicación **2.** complicidad
implicit *adj.* implícito
implicitly *adv.* implícitamente
imply *verb.* insinuar, dar a entender
import *noun.* importación
import *verb.* importar
importance *noun.* importancia
important *adj.* importante
importantly *adv.* importantemente, con importancia
impose *verb.* imponer
—**impose on** abusar de
imposing *adj.* imponente, impresionante
imposition *noun.* imposición
impossible *adj.* imposible
impress *verb.* **1.** impresionar **2.** grabar **3.** imprimir **4.** subrayar, recalcar
impression *noun.* **1.** impresión **2.** huella, marca **3.** edición, tirada
impressive *adj.* impresionante
imprison *verb.* encarcelar
imprisonment *noun.* encarcelamiento, prisión
improve *verb.* **1.** mejorar, perfeccionar **2.** aumentar
improvement *noun.* **1.** mejora **2.** aumento
impulse *noun.* impulso
in *prep.* **1.** en **2.** dentro **3.** por **4.** con **5.** de
in *adv. adj.* **1.** dentro, adentro **2.** en **3.** de moda
inability *noun.* incapacidad
inadequate *adj.* insuficiente, inadecuado, inepto
inappropriate *adj.* inadecuado, impropio, inoportuno
incapable (of) *adj.* incapaz
incentive *noun.* incentivo
inch *noun.* **1.** pulgada **2.** pizca, poco
inch *verb.* avanzar poco a poco
incident *noun.* incidente, suceso
incidentally *adv.* por cierto, a propósito
inclination *noun.* **1.** inclinación **2.** propensión **3.** afición, deseo
include *verb.* incluir
including *prep.* inclusive, incluido
inclusion *noun.* inclusión
income *noun.* renta, ingreso
—**income tax** impuesto sobre la renta
incoming *adj.* que llega, entrante
incompatible *adj.* incompatible
incomplete *adj.* incompleto
inconsistent (with) *adj.* **1.** inconsecuente, contradictorio **2.** irregular, desigual
incorporate *verb.* incorporar
incorporated, Inc. *adj.* sociedad anónima
incorrect *adj.* incorrecto
increase *noun.* aumento
increase *verb.* aumentar
increasingly *adv.* cada vez más
incredible *adj.* increíble

incredibly *adv.* increíblemente
incur *verb.* **1.** incurrir en, provocar **2.** contraer, sufrir
indeed *interj.* ¿de verdad?, ¡no me digas!
indeed *adv.* **1.** de hecho **2.** realmente
indefinitely *adv.* indefinidamente
independence *noun.* independencia
independent *adj.* independiente
independently *adv.* independientemente
index *noun.* índice
India *noun.* India
Indian *noun. adj.* **1.** indio, indígena **2.** hindú
indicate *verb.* indicar
indication *noun.* indicación
indicative *noun. adj.* indicativo
indicator *noun.* indicador
indifference *noun.* indiferencia
indifferent (to) *adj.* **1.** indiferente **2.** mediocre
indirect *adj.* indirecto
individual *noun.* **1.** individuo **2.** persona
individual *adj.* **1.** individual **2.** personal, propio
individually *adv.* individualmente
Indonesia *noun.* Indonesia
Indonesian *noun. adj.* indonesio
indoor *adj.* **1.** de interior **2.** cubierto
indoors *adv.* **1.** dentro **2.** bajo techo
indulge *verb.* **1.** consentir **2.** satisfacer **3.** darse el gusto
industrial *adj.* industrial
industrialized *adj.* industrializado
industry *noun.* **1.** industria **2.** diligencia
ineffective *adj.* ineficaz
inefficient *adj.* ineficaz
inequality *noun.* desigualdad
inevitable *adj.* inevitable
inevitably *adv.* inevitablemente
inexperienced *adj.* inexperto
infant *noun.* menor, párvulo
infantry *noun.* infantería
infect *verb.* infectar
infection *noun.* infección
infectious *adj.* infeccioso
inference *noun.* inferencia, deducción
inferior (to) *adj.* inferior, peor
infinite *adj.* infinito
infinitely *adv.* infinitamente
infinitive *noun.* infinitivo
infirmary *noun.* hospital, enfermería
inflation *noun.* **1.** inflación **2.** hinchazón
inflict (on) *verb.* infligir, imponer
influence *noun.* influencia
influence *verb.* influir, influenciar
influential *adj.* influyente
inform *verb.* informar
—**inform against/on** denunciar, delatar
informal *adj.* **1.** informal **2.** familiar, coloquial
information *noun.* información
informative *adj.* informativo
ingredient *noun.* ingrediente
inhabit *verb.* habitar, ocupar, vivir en
inhabitant *noun.* habitante
inherent *adj.* inherente
inherit *verb.* heredar
inheritance *noun.* herencia
inhibit *verb.* impedir, inhibir
inhibited *adj.* inhibido
inhibition *noun.* inhibición
initial *noun. adj.* inicial
initial *verb.* firmar con las iniciales
initially *adv.* al principio
initiate *noun.* iniciado
initiate *verb.* **1.** iniciar, poner en marcha, empezar **2.** admitir
initiative *noun.* iniciativa
inject *verb.* inyectar
injection *noun.* inyección
injure *verb.* herir, lastimar, dañar, perjudicar
injured *adj.* herido, lesionado, dolido
injury *noun.* herida, lesión
injustice *noun.* injusticia
ink *noun.* tinta
inland *adj.* interior
inland *adv.* tierra adentro
inmate *noun.* **1.** interno, paciente **2.** recluso
inn *noun.* **1.** albergue **2.** posada, venta
inner *adj.* **1.** interior **2.** íntimo, profundo
—**inner tube** cámara, llanta
innocence *noun.* inocencia
innocent *adj.* **1.** inocente **2.** ingenuo
innovation *noun.* innovación

input *noun.* **1.** input **2.** entrada **3.** insumo, inversión
inquest *noun.* investigación, pesquisa
inquire, enquire *verb.* preguntar
—**inquire into** investigar, indagar
inquiry, enquiry *noun.* **1.** interrogación, pregunta **2.** investigación, pesquisa
insect *noun.* insecto
insecure *adj.* **1.** inseguro **2.** inestable, precario
insert *verb.* insertar
inset *noun.* recuadro
inside *prep.* dentro de, en el interior de
—**inside of** en menos de
inside *noun.* **1.** interior, parte interior **2.** entrañas, tripas
inside *adj.* interior
inside *adv.* dentro, adentro
insight *noun.* **1.** perspicacia **2.** comprensión
insignificant *adj.* insignificante
insist (on/that) *verb.* **1.** insistir **2.** exigir
insistence *noun.* insistencia
inspect *verb.* **1.** inspeccionar, examinar, revisar **2.** pasar revista
inspection *noun.* inspección
inspector *noun.* inspector
inspiration *noun.* inspiración
inspire *verb.* **1.** inspirar **2.** animar, alentar
instability *noun.* inestabilidad
install *verb.* instalar
installation *noun.* instalación
instance *noun.* ejemplo, caso
instant *noun.* instante, momento
instant *adj.* instantáneo, inmediato
instantly *adv.* instantáneamente, inmediatamente
instead *adv.* en cambio
—**instead of** en vez de, en lugar de
instinct *noun.* instinto
instinctive *adj.* instintivo
instinctively *adv.* instintivamente
institute *noun.* instituto
institute *verb.* fundar, establecer
institution *noun.* institución
institutional *adj.* institucional
instruct *verb.* **1.** instruir, enseñar **2.** ordenar, mandar
instruction *noun.* **1.** instrucción, enseñanza **2.** orden
—**instructions** instrucciones
instructor *noun.* **1.** instructor, monitor **2.** profesor auxiliar
instrument *noun.* instrumento
instrumental *adj.* instrumental
—**to be instrumental in** contribuir decisivamente a
insufficient *adj.* insuficiente
insulation *noun.* aislamiento
insulin *noun.* insulina
insult *noun.* insulto
insult *verb.* insultar
insurance *noun.* seguro
insure *verb.* asegurar
intact *adj.* intacto
intake *noun.* **1.** admisión **2.** entrada, toma **3.** consumo
integrate *verb.* **1.** integrar **2.** integrarse
integration *noun.* integración
integrity *noun.* integridad
intellectual *adj.* intelectual
intelligence *noun.* **1.** inteligencia **2.** información **3.** servicio de inteligencia
intelligent *adj.* inteligente
intend *verb.* **1.** proponerse, tener la intención **2.** pretender, querer decir **3.** ir dirigido, destinar
intense *adj.* intenso
intensely *adv.* intensamente
intensity *noun.* intensidad
intensive *adj.* intensivo
intent *noun.* intención, propósito
intent *adj.* decidido, resuelto
—**intent on** absorto
intention *noun.* intención
inter *verb.* enterrar
interact *verb.* **1.** influirse mutuamente **2.** relacionarse
interaction *noun.* interacción, interrelación
interactive *adj.* interactivo
intercourse *noun.* **1.** relaciones, trato **2.** relación sexual
interest *noun.* **1.** interés **2.** provecho **3.** participación **4.** grupo de intereses
interest (in) *verb.* interesar
interested *adj.* interesado

interesting *adj.* interesante
interestingly *adv.* **1.** curiosamente **2.** de manera interesante
interfere (in/with) *verb.* **1.** interferir, entrometerse **2.** afectar
interference *noun.* interferencia, intromisión
interior *noun.* interior
interior *adj.* interior
intermediate *adj.* intermedio
internal *adj.* **1.** interno **2.** interior
internally *adv.* internamente
international *noun. adj.* internacional
internationally *adv.* internacionalmente
interpret *verb.* **1.** interpretar **2.** explicar
interpretation *noun.* interpretación
interpreter *noun.* intérprete
interrupt *verb.* **1.** interrumpir **2.** obstruir
interruption *noun.* interrupción
interval *noun.* **1.** intervalo **2.** descanso
intervene *verb.* **1.** intervenir **2.** interponerse **3.** transcurrir
intervention *noun.* intervención
interview *noun.* entrevista
interview *verb.* entrevistar
interviewer *noun.* entrevistador
intestinal *adj.* intestinal
intimacy *noun.* **1.** intimidad **2.** familiaridad
intimate *noun.* amigo íntimo
intimate *verb.* insinuar
intimate *adj.* **1.** íntimo **2.** privado, personal **3.** profundo
intimidate *verb.* intimidar
into *prep.* **1.** en, dentro de **2.** contra **3.** entre
intolerable *adj.* intolerable
intricate *adj.* intrincado, complejo
intriguing *adj.* intrigante
introduce (to/into) *verb.* **1.** presentar **2.** introducir **3.** iniciar en
introduction *noun.* **1.** presentación **2.** introducción **3.** prólogo, prefacio
introductory *adj.* introductorio, preliminar
invade *verb.* invadir
invalid *noun.* inválido, disminuido
invalid *verb.* **1.** licenciar por invalidez **2.** quedarse inválido
invalid *adj.* **1.** inválido **2.** nulo
—**to became invalid** caducar
invaluable *adj.* inestimable
invariably *adv.* invariablemente
invasion *noun.* invasión
invent *verb.* **1.** inventar **2.** inventarse
invention *noun.* **1.** invención, invento **2.** mentira
inventory *noun.* inventario
invest *verb.* investir
—**invest in** invertir
investigate *verb.* **1.** investigar **2.** examinar, estudiar
investigation *noun.* investigación
investigator *noun.* investigador
investment *noun.* inversión
investor *noun.* inversor
invisible *adj.* invisible
invitation *noun.* invitación
invite *verb.* **1.** invitar **2.** pedir, solicitar **3.** provocar
inviting *adj.* tentador, atractivo
invoke *verb.* invocar
involve *verb.* **1.** implicar, suponer, traer consigo **2.** involucrar
involved *adj.* complicado
involvement *noun.* **1.** implicación, participación **2.** enredo, complicación
inward, inwards *adv.* hacia dentro
inward *adj.* **1.** interior **2.** hacia dentro
Iran *noun.* Irán
Iranian *noun. adj.* iraní
Iraq *noun.* Irak, Iraq
Iraqi *noun. adj.* iraquí
Ireland *noun.* Irlanda
iris *noun.* **1.** iris **2.** lirio
Irish *noun. adj.* irlandés
iron *noun. adj.* **1.** hierro, fierro **2.** plancha
iron *verb.* planchar
ironically *adv.* irónicamente
irony *noun.* ironía
irregular *adj.* irregular
irrelevant *adj.* irrelevante
irresistible *adj.* irresistible
irrespective (of) *adj.* sin tomar en cuenta
irritate *verb.* irritar, molestar
irritation *noun.* irritación
Islam *noun.* Islam
Islamic *adj.* Islámico
island *noun.* isla
isle *noun.* isla
isolated *adj.* aislado

isolation *noun.* aislamiento
Israel *noun.* Israel
Israeli *noun. adj.* israelí
issue *noun.* **1.** tema, asunto **2.** emisión **3.** ejemplar, número
issue *verb.* **1.** emitir **2.** hacer público **3.** expedir **4.** distribuir **5.** salir
it *pron.* **1.** él, ella, ello **2.** lo, la (direct object) **3.** le (indirect object) **4.** (often not translated)
Italian *noun. adj.* italiano
Italy *noun.* Italia
item *noun.* artículo
its *adj.* su, sus
itself *pron.* **1.** se **2.** sí mismo, sí misma **3.** él mismo, ella misma **4.** él solo, ella sola
ivory *noun.* marfil
ivory *adj.* de marfil, de color marfil
ivy *noun.* hiedra

J

jack *noun.* **1.** gato, gata **2.** jota, sota
jacket *noun.* **1.** chaqueta, saco **2.** sobrecubierta, funda
jaguar *noun.* jaguar, tigre
jail *noun.* cárcel, prisión
jail *verb.* encarcelar
jam *noun.* **1.** atasco, embotellamiento **2.** apuro, aprieto **3.** mermelada, confitura
jam *verb.* **1.** abarrotar, apiñar **2.** atascar, atascarse **3.** causar interferencia
Jamaica *noun.* Jamaica
Jamaican *noun. adj.* jamaicano
Jan. *abbr.* enero
January *noun.* enero
Japan *noun.* Japón
Japanese *noun. adj.* japonés
jar *noun.* **1.** tarro, bote, jarra **2.** sacudida, choque
jar (on) *verb.* **1.** chirriar, discordar **2.** sacudir, afectar
jargon *noun.* jerga
jaw *noun.* maxilar
—jaws 1. mandíbula **2.** fauces
jazz *noun.* jazz
jealous (of) *adj.* **1.** celoso **2.** envidioso
jealousy *noun.* **1.** celos **2.** envidia
jeans *noun plural.* vaqueros, tejanos, bluejeans
jelly *noun.* mermelada
jerk *noun.* sacudida
jerk *verb.* sacudir
jersey *noun.* jersey, suéter
jet *noun. adj.* azabache
jet *noun.* **1.** chorro **2.** boquilla **3.** avión a reacción, reactor
Jew *noun.* judío
jewel *noun.* joya, alhaja, piedra preciosa
jewelry *noun.* joyas
Jewish *adj.* judío
jingle *noun.* **1.** tintineo **2.** tonadilla publicitaria
jingle *verb.* tintinear
job *noun.* **1.** trabajo, empleo **2.** tarea
jockey *noun.* jockey
join *noun.* juntura, unión
join *verb.* **1.** juntar, unir **2.** hacerse socio, afiliarse, ingresar **3.** juntarse, confluir **4.** acompañar
joint *noun.* **1.** junta, juntura, unión, bisagra **2.** articulación, nudillo, coyuntura
joint *adj.* **1.** mutuo **2.** compartido
jointly *adv.* conjuntamente
joke *noun.* **1.** chiste **2.** broma
joke *verb.* **1.** contar chistes **2.** bromear
jolly *adj.* alegre, divertido, gracioso
journal *noun.* **1.** periódico **2.** revista **3.** diario
journalism *noun.* periodismo
journalist *noun.* periodista, reportero
journey *noun.* **1.** viaje **2.** tramo, trayecto **3.** expedición
journey *verb.* viajar
joy *noun.* **1.** alegría, júbilo **2.** deleite
Jr. *abbr.* hijo, junior
jubilee *noun.* jubileo, aniversario
judge *noun.* **1.** juez **2.** jurado **3.** conocedor, entendido
judge *verb.* **1.** juzgar **2.** calcular

judicial *adj.* judicial
jug *noun.* jarro, jarra
juice *noun.* **1.** zumo **2.** jugo
July *noun.* julio
jump *noun.* **1.** salto **2.** brinco **3.** obstáculo **4.** aumento, subida
jump *verb.* **1.** saltar **2.** sobresaltarse **3.** subir, aumentar
jumper *noun.* pichi
junction *noun.* empalme, cruce, crucero
June *noun.* junio
jungle *noun.* jungla, selva
junior *noun.* menor
junior *adj.* **1.** menor **2.** subordinado, auxiliar **3.** juvenil **4.** hijo
junk *noun.* **1.** trastos, baratijas **2.** junco
jurisdiction *noun.* jurisdicción
jury *noun.* jurado
just *adj.* **1.** justo **2.** merecido **3.** correcto **4.** apropiado
just *adv.* **1.** justamente, justo **2.** exactamente **3.** precisamente **4.** sencillamente **5.** ahora mismo **6.** recién **7.** a penas **8.** sólo, nomás **9.** absolutamente **10.** por poco
justice *noun.* **1.** justicia **2.** juez
justification *noun.* justificación
justify *verb.* justificar
juvenile *noun. adj.* **1.** juvenil **2.** infantil

K

keen *adj.* **1.** entusiasta, aplicado **2.** vivo, grande **3.** cortante, afilado, agudo, fino
keep *noun.* sustento
keep *verb.* **1.** guardar **2.** mantener, conservar **3.** mantenerse **4.** quedarse con **5.** continuar, seguir **6.** cuidar **7.** criar **8.** tener **9.** llevar al día **10.** retener, entretener **11.** cumplir, observar **12.** celebrar **13.** dirigir
—**keep from** abstenerse, guardarse de
—**keep on** continuar, seguir
keeper *noun.* guarda, guardián
keeping *noun.* cuidado
Kenya *noun.* Kenia
Kenyan *noun. adj.* keniata
kettle *noun.* hervidor, caldero
key *noun.* **1.** llave **2.** tecla **3.** clave **4.** leyenda
key *adj.* clave
keyboard *noun.* **1.** teclado **2.** instrumento de teclado
kg *abbr.* kilogramo
kick *noun.* **1.** puntapié, patada, coz **2.** culetazo **3.** diversión, emoción
kick *verb.* **1.** dar un puntapié, dar una patada, cocear **2.** recular
kid *noun.* **1.** niño, crío, chaval, chamaco **2.** cabrito, chivo
kid *verb.* engañar, tomar el pelo
kidnap *verb.* secuestrar, raptar
kidney *noun.* riñón
kill *verb.* matar, asesinar
killer *noun.* asesino
kilo *noun.* kilo
kilogram *noun.* kilogramo
kilometer *noun.* kilómetro
kin *noun plural.* familiares, parientes
kin *adj.* de la familia
kind *noun.* tipo, género, clase
kind *adj.* amable, atento
kindly *adj.* bondadoso, amable
kindly *adv.* **1.** amablemente **2.** favorablemente
kindness *noun.* bondad, amabilidad
king *noun.* rey
kingdom *noun.* reino
kiss *noun.* beso
kiss *verb.* besar
kit *noun.* **1.** equipo, kit **2.** herramientas, avíos
kitchen *noun.* cocina
kite *noun.* cometa
km *abbr.* kilómetro
knee *noun.* **1.** rodilla **2.** rodillera
kneel *verb.* arrodillarse

knife *noun.* **1.** cuchillo **2.** puñal, navaja
knife *verb.* acuchillar, apuñalar
knight *noun.* **1.** caballero **2.** caballo (chess)
knit *verb.* **1.** tejer, hacer punto, tricotar **2.** soldarse
knitting *noun.* **1.** labor de punto **2.** prenda de punto
knock *noun.* **1.** golpe **2.** choque **3.** llamada
knock *verb.* **1.** golpear **2.** chocar **3.** llamar **4.** tirar, hacer caer
knot *noun.* nudo
knot *verb.* anudar, atar
know *verb.* **1.** saber **2.** conocer **3.** comprender **4.** reconocer
know-how *noun.* conocimientos, experiencia
knowing *adj.* de complicidad
knowledge *noun.* **1.** conocimiento **2.** conocimientos **3.** saber
Korea *noun.* Corea
Korean *noun. adj.* coreano
Kuwait *noun.* Kuwait
Kuwaiti *noun. adj.* kuwaití
lab *abbr.* laboratorio

L

label *noun.* **1.** etiqueta **2.** marca
label *verb.* etiquetar
labor *noun.* **1.** trabajo **2.** obreros, mano de obra **3.** parto, dolores de parto
labor *verb.* **1.** trabajar duro **2.** esforzarse, afanarse **3.** avanzar penosamente, funcionar con dificultad
laboratory *noun.* laboratorio
lace *noun.* **1.** cordón **2.** cinta **3.** encaje
lace *verb.* atar, amarrar
lack *noun.* falta, carencia, escasez
lack *verb.* **1.** carecer de **2.** hacer falta
lad *noun.* muchacho, chico, chaval, pibe
ladder *noun.* escalera (de mano)
lady *noun.* **1.** señora **2.** dama **3.** lady
lag *noun.* retraso
lag *verb.* retrasarse, quedarse atrás
lake *noun.* lago
lamb *noun.* cordero
lamp *noun.* lámpara
land *noun.* **1.** tierra **2.** terreno **3.** tierras, fincas **4.** país **5.** territorio, región
land *verb.* **1.** aterrizar **2.** desembarcar **3.** caer **4.** ir a parar
landing *noun.* **1.** aterrizaje **2.** desembarco **3.** desembarcadero **4.** descansillo, rellano
landlord *noun.* **1.** dueño, propietario **2.** patrón
landmark *noun.* **1.** punto de referencia **2.** hito
landowner *noun.* terrateniente, hacendado
landscape *noun.* paisaje
landscape *verb.* ajardinar, diseñar
lane *noun.* **1.** callejuela, callejón **2.** calle **3.** carril, vía **4.** ruta
language *noun.* **1.** lenguaje **2.** lengua, idioma
lap *noun.* **1.** regazo, rodillas **2.** vuelta **3.** etapa
lap *verb.* **1.** lamer **2.** chapalear
large *adj.* **1.** grande **2.** corpulento **3.** extenso **4.** numeroso
largely *adv.* en gran parte, en gran medida
laser *noun.* láser
lash *noun.* **1.** pestaña **2.** latigazo, azote **3.** látigo
lash *verb.* **1.** azotar **2.** atar, amarrar **3.** agitar, mover
last *verb.* durar
last *adj.* **1.** último **2.** pasado
last *adv.* **1.** en último lugar **2.** por último **3.** la última vez
lasting *adj.* **1.** duradero **2.** permanente
late *adj.* **1.** tarde, atrasado, tardío **2.** difunto **3.** anterior
—**late riser** dormilón

late *adv.* tarde
lately *adv.* **1.** últimamente **2.** recientemente
latent *adj.* latente
lateral *adj.* lateral
Latin *noun.* **1.** latín **2.** latino
Latin *adj.* latino
Latin American *noun. adj.* latinoamericano
latter *adj.* último
laugh *noun.* risa, carcajada
laugh *verb.* **1.** reír **2.** reírse
laughter *noun.* **1.** risa **2.** risas
launch *noun.* **1.** lancha **2.** lanzamiento **3.** botadura **4.** estreno **5.** fundación **6.** emisión
launch *verb.* **1.** lanzar **2.** botar, echar al mar **3.** estrenar **4.** fundar **5.** emitir
laundry *noun.* **1.** lavandería **2.** ropa sucia, colada
lavatory *noun.* lavabo, baño, aseos
lavender *noun.* espliego, lavanda
lavish *verb.* prodigar
lavish *adj.* **1.** pródigo, generoso **2.** suntuoso **3.** abundante
law *noun.* ley
lawful *adj.* **1.** legal, lícito **2.** legítimo
lawn *noun.* césped, pasto
lawsuit *noun.* pleito, proceso
lawyer *noun.* abogado
lay *noun.* romance, trova
lay *verb.* **1.** poner **2.** colocar **3.** tender **4.** depositar **5.** preparar, hacer **6.** calmar, aquietar **7.** apostar
—lay down **1.** establecer, sentar **2.** entregar **3.** trazar, dibujar
—lay out **1.** presentar, exponer **2.** planear, diseñar
lay *adj.* **1.** laico, lego, seglar **2.** profano
layer *noun.* **1.** capa, estrato **2.** ponedora
layer *verb.* poner en capas
layout *noun.* plan, disposición, trazado
lazy *adj.* perezoso, vago
lb. *abbr.* libra
lead *noun.* **1.** delantera **2.** ejemplo **3.** liderazgo **4.** ventaja **5.** pista **6.** papel principal **7.** protagonista **8.** plomo **9.** mina **10.** correa
lead *verb.* **1.** llevar **2.** conducir **3.** liderar, dirigir **4.** encabezar **5.** aventajar **6.** ser mano
—lead to ocasionar, causar
lead *adj.* de plomo
leader *noun.* **1.** líder **2.** cabecilla, jefe **3.** reportaje principal
leadership *noun.* **1.** liderazgo **2.** dirección, jefatura
leaf *noun.* **1.** hoja **2.** página
leaflet *noun.* folleto, octavilla
league *noun.* **1.** legua **2.** liga
leak *noun.* **1.** fuga, escape **2.** rotura, gotera, grieta **3.** filtración
leak *verb.* **1.** perder, gotear, salir **2.** filtrar, divulgar
lean *verb.* **1.** inclinarse **2.** apoyarse
lean *adj.* **1.** delgado, flaco **2.** magro **3.** malo, escaso, pobre
leaning *noun.* inclinación, tendencia
leap *noun.* **1.** salto, brinco **2.** subida
leap *verb.* **1.** saltar, brincar **2.** incrementarse, aumentar
learn *verb.* **1.** aprender **2.** enterarse, saber
learned *adj.* **1.** docto, erudito **2.** liberal
learner *noun.* principiante, estudiante
learning *noun.* **1.** conocimientos **2.** aprendizaje
lease *noun.* contrato de arrendamiento
lease *verb.* arrendar
least *adj. pron.* lo menos, lo mínimo
least *adv.* menos
leather *noun.* piel, cuero
leather *adj.* de piel, de cuero
leave *noun.* permiso
leave *verb.* **1.** dejar **2.** salir **3.** marcharse **4.** legar
—to be left quedar
—leave behind dejar atrás, olvidar
—leave out omitir, excluir
Lebanese *noun. adj.* libanés
Lebanon *noun.* Líbano
lecture *noun.* **1.** conferencia, clase **2.** reprimenda, sermón
lecture *verb.* **1.** dar clase **2.** sermonear
lecturer *noun.* conferenciante, profesor
lee *noun.* sotavento
leek *noun.* puerro
left *noun.* izquierda
left *adj.* **1.** izquierdo **2.** de izquierda
left *adv.* a la izquierda

left-hand *adj.* a la izquierda
left-wing *adj.* de izquierda
leg *noun.* **1.** pierna **2.** pernera **3.** pata, muslo **4.** etapa
legacy *noun.* herencia
legal *adj.* **1.** legal **2.** jurídico
legally *adv.* legalmente, por ley
legend *noun.* leyenda
legendary *adj.* legendario
legion *noun.* legión
legislation *noun.* legislación
legislative *adj.* legislativo
legislature *noun.* cuerpo legislativo
legitimacy *noun.* legitimidad
legitimate *adj.* legítimo, justificado
leisure *noun.* ocio
lemon *noun. adj.* limón
lemonade *noun.* limonada, gaseosa
lend *verb.* prestar
length *noun.* **1.** longitud, largo **2.** extensión **3.** duración **4.** pedazo, trozo
lengthy *adj.* largo
lens *noun.* **1.** lente, objetivo **2.** cristalino
Lent *noun.* Cuaresma
less *adj. adv. prep. pron.* menos
lesser *adj. adv.* menor
lesson *noun.* **1.** lección **2.** clase **3.** lectura
let *verb.* **1.** dejar, permitir **2.** alquilar **3.** (as an expression of imperative is rendered in Spanish by the subjunctive or the imperative)
—**let down** fallar
lethal *adj.* letal, mortal
letter *noun.* **1.** letra **2.** carta
leukemia *noun.* leucemia
level *noun.* **1.** nivel **2.** piso **3.** llano, llanura
level *verb.* **1.** nivelar, aplanar **2.** igualar **3.** arrasar
—**level at** apuntar
level *adj.* **1.** llano, plano **2.** a nivel, nivelado **3.** uniforme
lever *noun.* palanca
lever *verb.* sopalancar
leverage *noun.* **1.** acción de palanca **2.** influencia, poder
levy *noun.* impuesto
levy *verb.* **1.** recaudar, imponer **2.** reclutar
lexicon *noun.* léxico
liability *noun.* **1.** responsabilidad **2.** carga
liable *adj.* **1.** propenso **2.** responsable **3.** expuesto, sujeto
liaison *noun.* **1.** enlace, coordinación **2.** relación
libel *noun.* libelo, difamación
libel *verb.* difamar
liberal *adj.* **1.** liberal **2.** abundante, generoso
liberate *verb.* liberar, poner en libertad
liberation *noun.* liberación
liberty *noun.* **1.** libertad **2.** atrevimiento
—**liberties** privilegios, derechos
librarian *noun.* bibliotecario
library *noun.* biblioteca
Libya *noun.* Libia
Libyan *noun. adj.* libio
license *noun.* licencia, permiso
license *verb.* autorizar, dar permiso
licensed *adj.* con licencia
lick *noun.* **1.** lamedura, lengüetada **2.** mano
lick *verb.* lamer
lid *noun.* **1.** tapa **2.** párpado
lie *noun.* mentira
lie *verb.* **1.** echarse, tumbarse **2.** ubicarse, estar situado **3.** quedarse **4.** mentir
lieutenant *noun.* **1.** teniente **2.** alférez de navío
life *noun.* **1.** vida **2.** vitalidad
—**life imprisonment** cadena perpetua
lifeboat *noun.* bote salvavidas, lancha de salvamento
lifetime *noun.* vida
lift *noun.* **1.** acción de levantar **2.** ascensor, montacargas **3.** estímulo
lift *verb.* **1.** levantar **2.** alzar **3.** levantarse, alzarse **4.** coger **5.** descolgar **6.** elevarse **7.** disiparse
light *noun.* **1.** luz **2.** lámpara **3.** fuego **4.** perspectiva, punto de vista
light *verb.* **1.** encender **2.** iluminar **3.** encenderse, iluminarse
light *adj.* **1.** claro **2.** luminoso **3.** ligero **4.** leve
lighter *noun.* encendedor, mechero
lighting *noun.* iluminación, alumbrado
lightly *adv.* **1.** ligeramente **2.** suavemente
lightning *noun.* rayo, relámpago

lightweight *adj.* ligero
like *conj.* como
like *prep.* como
like *noun.* semejante, igual
like *verb.* **1.** gustar **2.** querer
like *adj.* parecido, igual
likelihood *noun.* probabilidad
likely *adj.* **1.** probable **2.** apropiado
likewise *adv.* igualmente, asimismo, también
liking *noun.* gusto, simpatía, aprecio
lily *noun.* lirio, azucena
limb *noun.* **1.** miembro, extremidad **2.** rama
lime *noun.* **1.** cal **2.** lima **3.** tilo
limestone *noun.* piedra caliza
limit *noun.* límite
limit *verb.* limitar, restringir
limitation *noun.* limitación, restricción
limited *adj.* **1.** limitado, restringido **2.** escaso
limp *noun.* cojera
limp *verb.* cojear
limp *adj.* **1.** débil **2.** flojo, fláccido **3.** mustio
line *noun.* **1.** línea **2.** renglón **3.** arruga, surco **4.** fila, hilera **5.** cola **6.** linaje **7.** vía **8.** profesión, ramo **9.** especialidad **10.** gama **11.** cuerda, cordel, sedal
line *verb.* **1.** alinear, poner en fila **2.** forrar, revestir **3.** surcar
linear *adj.* lineal
lined *adj.* **1.** forrado, revestido **2.** arrugado **3.** rayado, pautado
linen *noun.* **1.** lino, hilo **2.** ropa blanca
liner *noun.* transatlántico
lines *noun plural.* texto, papel
linger *verb.* **1.** rezagarse **2.** persistir, perdurar, quedarse
linguistic *adj.* lingüístico
linguistics *noun singular.* lingüística
lining *noun.* **1.** revestimiento **2.** forro
link *noun.* **1.** enlace **2.** conexión, relación **3.** vínculo, lazo **4.** eslabón
link *verb.* unir, conectar
lion *noun.* león
lip *noun.* **1.** labio **2.** borde
lipstick *noun.* lápiz de labios
liquid *noun. adj.* líquido
liquor *noun.* licor, bebida alcohólica
list *noun.* lista, catálogo
list *verb.* **1.** hacer una lista **2.** enumerar
listen *verb.* escuchar
liter *noun.* litro
literacy *noun.* capacidad de leer y escribir
literal *adj.* literal
literally *adv.* literalmente
literary *adj.* literario, de literatura
literature *noun.* literatura
Lithuania *noun.* Lituania
Lithuanian *noun. adj.* lituano
litigation *noun.* litigio
litter *noun.* **1.** basura, papeles **2.** cama, lecho **3.** camada
litter *verb.* poner en desorden
little *adj.* **1.** pequeño, chico **2.** poco, escaso **3.** insignificante
little *adv.* **1.** poco **2.** ni la menor idea
little *pron.* poco
live *verb.* **1.** vivir **2.** sobrevivir
live *adj.* **1.** vivo **2.** en directo **3.** cargado **4.** conectado
live *adv.* en directo
lively *adj.* alegre, vivo, vivaz
liver *noun.* hígado
livestock *noun.* ganado
living *noun.* **1.** medio de vida, sustento **2.** vida
living *adj.* vivo
load *noun.* **1.** carga **2.** peso, cantidad **3.** montón, montones
load *verb.* cargar
loaded *adj.* cargado
loan *noun.* **1.** préstamo **2.** empréstito
loan *verb.* prestar
lobby *noun.* **1.** vestíbulo, pasillo **2.** grupo de presión
lobby *verb.* presionar, cabildear
local *adj.* local, del barrio, municipal, regional
locality *noun.* localidad
locally *adv.* en la localidad, en la zona
locate *verb.* **1.** situar, ubicar **2.** localizar
location *noun.* **1.** lugar **2.** situación, ubicación
lock *noun.* **1.** cerradura, chapa **2.** esclusa **3.** llave **4.** mecha, mechón

lock *verb.* **1.** cerrar con llave **2.** inmovilizar, bloquear
locks *noun.* cabellos
locomotive *noun.* locomotora
lodge *noun.* **1.** garita **2.** logia
lodge *verb.* **1.** alojar, hospedar **2.** alojarse, hospedarse **3.** presentar, interponer
loft *noun.* desván
log *noun.* tronco, leño
logic *noun.* lógica
logical *adj.* lógico
logically *adv.* lógicamente
lone *adj.* solitario
loneliness *noun.* soledad
lonely *adj.* **1.** solo **2.** aislado, solitario
long *adj.* **1.** largo **2.** de largo **3.** prolongado
long *adv.* mucho, mucho tiempo
long (for) *verb.* anhelar, desear
longing *noun.* anhelo, añoranza
long-range *adj.* **1.** de largo alcance **2.** a largo plazo
look *noun.* **1.** ojeada **2.** mirada **3.** aspecto, apariencia **4.** moda, estilo
look *verb.* **1.** mirar **2.** parecer **3.** dar (a)
—**look after** cuidar
—**look for 1.** buscar **2.** esperar
—**look forward to** desear, esperar con ilusión
loom *noun.* telar
loom (up) *verb.* surgir, asomar
loop *noun.* **1.** lazo **2.** recodo, curva
loop *verb.* atar con un lazo
loose *adj.* **1.** suelto **2.** flojo **3.** descosido **4.** flexible, libre, aproximado **5.** a granel
loosely *adv.* **1.** aproximadamente **2.** ligeramente **3.** vagamente
loosen *verb.* **1.** desatar **2.** aflojar
loot *noun.* botín
loot *verb.* saquear
lord *noun.* **1.** señor **2.** lord
—**Our Lord** Nuestro Señor, Dios
lose *verb.* **1.** perder **2.** atrasarse
loser *noun.* perdedor
loss *noun.* pérdida
lost *adj.* **1.** perdido **2.** desaparecido
lot *noun.* **1.** suerte, destino **2.** lote **3.** parte, porción **4.** solar
—**a lot** mucho
—**lots** mucho
lottery *noun.* lotería
lotus *noun.* loto
loud *adj.* **1.** alto, fuerte **2.** chillón
loudly *adv.* fuertemente, ruidosamente
lounge *noun.* sala, salón
lounge *verb.* **1.** apoltronarse **2.** holgazanear
love *noun.* **1.** amor **2.** afición **3.** cero (tennis)
love *verb.* **1.** amar, querer **2.** gustar, encantar
lovely *adj.* **1.** lindo, bello, hermoso **2.** encantador, amoroso
lover *noun.* **1.** aficionado **2.** amante, enamorado
loving *adj.* cariñoso, tierno
low *verb.* mugir
low *adj.* **1.** bajo **2.** grave **3.** deprimido, triste **4.** inferior **5.** humilde
low *adv.* bajo
lower *verb.* **1.** bajar **2.** rebajar **3.** encapotarse
loyal *adj.* leal, fiel
loyalty *noun.* lealtad, fidelidad
luck *noun.* suerte
luckily *adv.* afortunadamente
lucky *adj.* **1.** afortunado **2.** de la suerte
lucrative *adj.* lucrativo
luggage *noun.* equipaje
lump *noun.* **1.** terrón **2.** trozo, pedazo **3.** bulto, chichón
lump (together) *verb.* amontonar, agrupar
lunch *noun.* almuerzo, comida
lunch *verb.* almorzar, comer
lunchtime *noun.* hora del almuerzo, hora de comer
lung *noun.* pulmón
lure *noun.* aliciente, reclamo
lure *verb.* atraer, tentar
lust *noun.* codicia, lujuria
luxurious *adj.* lujoso
luxury *noun.* **1.** lujo **2.** artículo de lujo
lyric *noun.* poema lírico
—**lyrics** letra
lyric *adj.* lírico

M

MA *abbr.* máster en letras
machine *noun.* **1.** máquina, aparato **2.** organización
machine *verb.* **1.** elaborar a máquina **2.** coser a máquina
machinery *noun.* **1.** maquinaria **2.** mecanismo
mad *adj.* **1.** loco **2.** furioso
madam *noun.* señora
madness *noun.* locura
Madonna *noun.* la Virgen
magazine *noun.* **1.** revista **2.** recámara
maggot *noun.* gusano, cresa
magic *noun.* magia
magic *adj.* mágico
magical *adj.* **1.** mágico **2.** fascinante
magistrate *noun.* magistrado
magnetic *adj.* magnético
magnificent *adj.* magnífico
magnitude *noun.* magnitud
mahogany *noun.* caoba
maid *noun.* criada, sirvienta
maiden *noun.* doncella
mail *noun.* **1.** correo **2.** correspondencia
mail *verb.* mandar por correo
main *noun.* conducto principal, tubería principal, cañería principal
main *adj.* principal
mainland *noun.* continente, tierra firme
mainly *adv.* **1.** principalmente **2.** en su mayoría
mainstream *noun.* corriente principal
maintain *verb.* **1.** mantener **2.** guardar, conservar **3.** sostener
maintenance *noun.* mantenimiento, cuidado
majesty *noun.* majestad
major *noun.* **1.** comandante, mayor **2.** especialidad
major *adj.* **1.** mayor **2.** principal **3.** muy importante **4.** serio, grave
major (in) *verb.* especializarse (en)
majority *noun.* mayoría
make *noun.* marca
make *verb.* **1.** hacer **2.** crear, producir, construir, fabricar, confeccionar **3.** rodar, grabar **4.** preparar **5.** cometer **6.** obligar **7.** ganar **8.** calcular
—make for encaminarse a, dirigirse a
—make out 1. distinguir, divisar **2.** comprender **3.** arreglárselas, ir
—make up 1. inventar **2.** pintarse, maquillarse **3.** reconciliarse
—make up for compensar
—make up one's mind decidirse
maker *noun.* fabricante, creador
make-up *noun.* **1.** maquillaje **2.** carácter **3.** composición
making *noun.* fabricación, preparación
Malaysia *noun.* Malasia
Malaysian *noun. adj.* malasio
male *noun. adj.* macho, varón
Malta *noun.* Malta
Maltese *noun. adj.* maltés
mamma, mama *noun.* mamá
mammal *noun.* mamífero
man *noun.* **1.** hombre **2.** persona **3.** el hombre, la humanidad **4.** pieza, ficha
man *verb.* **1.** tripular, dirigir **2.** guarnecer, armar
manage *verb.* **1.** dirigir, llevar, administrar **2.** manejar, poder **3.** arreglárselas (para), conseguir
management *noun.* **1.** dirección, administración, gestión **2.** gerencia, cuerpo directivo
manager *noun.* **1.** director, gerente, administrador **2.** representante, mánager
maneuver *noun.* maniobra
maneuver *verb.* **1.** maniobrar **2.** manipular
manifest *verb.* manifestar, hacer patente
manifest *adj.* manifiesto, patente
manifestation *noun.* **1.** manifestación **2.** demostración
manifesto *noun.* manifiesto
manipulate *verb.* **1.** manipular **2.** manejar
manipulation *noun.* **1.** manipulación **2.** manejo

mankind *noun.* género humano, humanidad
manner *noun.* **1.** manera, modo **2.** porte, aire **3.** clase
—**manners** modales, educación
manpower *noun.* mano de obra
mansion *noun.* mansión
manslaughter *noun.* homicidio sin premeditación
manual *noun. adj.* manual
manufacture *noun.* **1.** manufactura **2.** fabricación
manufacture *verb.* fabricar, manufacturar
manufacturer *noun.* fabricante
manuscript *noun.* manuscrito
many *adj. pron.* muchos, muchas
—**how many?** ¿cuántos?, ¿cuántas?
—**too many** demasiados, demasiadas
map *noun.* **1.** mapa **2.** plano **3.** carta
map *verb.* hacer un mapa
mar *verb.* estropear, aguar
Mar. *abbr.* marzo
marathon *noun.* maratón
marble *noun.* **1.** mármol **2.** canica
march *noun.* marcha
march *verb.* **1.** marchar **2.** manifestarse
March *noun.* marzo
mare *noun.* yegua
margin *noun.* margen
marginal *adj.* **1.** marginal **2.** mínimo
marine *noun.* infante de marina
marine *adj.* marino, marítimo
marital *adj.* conyugal
maritime *adj.* marítimo
mark *noun.* **1.** marca **2.** calificación **3.** mancha **4.** señal **5.** blanco **6.** marco
mark *verb.* **1.** marcar **2.** señalar, indicar **3.** calificar, poner nota **4.** poner precio
marked *adj.* marcado, notable
markedly *adv.* notablemente, visiblemente
marker *noun.* **1.** marcador **2.** marca **3.** rotulador
market *noun.* mercado
market *verb.* vender, comercializar
marketing *noun.* marketing, mercadotecnia
marriage *noun.* **1.** boda **2.** matrimonio **3.** unión
married *adj.* casado
marry *verb.* **1.** casar **2.** casarse
marsh *noun.* ciénaga, pantano
marshal *noun.* **1.** maestro de ceremonias, organizador **2.** oficial de justicia **3.** jefe de policía/bomberos **4.** mariscal
marshal *verb.* **1.** poner en orden, arreglar **2.** dirigir
martial *adj.* marcial
marvelous *adj.* **1.** maravilloso **2.** excelente
masculine *adj.* masculino
mask *noun.* máscara, careta, mascarilla
mask *verb.* enmascarar
mason *noun.* **1.** albañil **2.** masón
mass *noun.* **1.** masa **2.** montón **3.** misa **4.** muchedumbre
mass *verb.* congregarse, concentrarse
mass *adj.* multitudinario, de masas
massacre *noun.* masacre
massacre *verb.* masacrar
massage *noun.* masaje
massage *verb.* dar masajes, masajear
massive *adj.* **1.** enorme **2.** macizo, sólido **3.** cuantioso
master *noun.* **1.** señor, dueño, amo **2.** máster **3.** maestro, profesor **4.** capitán, patrón
master *verb.* dominar
master *adj.* maestro, experto
masterpiece *noun.* obra maestra
mat *noun.* estera, felpudo
match *noun.* **1.** cerilla, fósforo **2.** partido, encuentro, juego **3.** igual **4.** casamiento, matrimonio
match *verb.* **1.** hacer juego, combinar **2.** emparejar **3.** igualar **4.** enfrentar
mate *noun.* **1.** pareja **2.** compañero **3.** colega **4.** ayudante **5.** segundo de a bordo **6.** mate
mate *verb.* **1.** aparear **2.** dar jaque mate
material *noun.* **1.** material, materia **2.** tela, tejido
material *adj.* **1.** material **2.** esencial, primordial
maternal *adj.* **1.** maternal **2.** materno
maternity *noun.* maternidad
mathematical *adj.* matemático
mathematics, math *noun singular.* matemáticas

matter *noun.* **1.** materia, sustancia **2.** asunto, cuestión **3.** pus
matter *verb.* importar
mature *verb.* **1.** madurar **2.** vencer
mature *adj.* **1.** maduro **2.** añejo, curado
maturity *noun.* madurez
maxim *noun.* máxima
maximum *noun. adj.* máximo
may *verb.* **1.** poder **2.** ser posible **3.** ojalá que (expressing wish, hope)
May *noun.* mayo
maybe *adv.* quizás, tal vez
mayor *noun.* alcalde
me *pron.* **1.** me **2.** mí, conmigo (after prep) **3.** yo
meadow, meadows *noun.* prado
meal *noun.* **1.** comida **2.** harina
mean *noun.* término medio, medio, promedio
mean *verb.* **1.** significar, querer decir **2.** pretender, tener la intención **3.** destinar
mean *adj.* **1.** malo, ruin **2.** mediano **3.** medio **4.** mezquino, tacaño **5.** humilde, pobre
meaning *noun.* **1.** significado, sentido **2.** propósito
meaningful *adj.* **1.** significativo **2.** valioso
meaningless *adj.* sin sentido
means *noun plural.* **1.** recursos, medios de vida **2.** medio, manera
meantime *noun. adv.* entretanto, mientras tanto
meanwhile *adv.* entretanto, mientras tanto
measure *noun.* **1.** medida **2.** grado, cantidad **3.** compás, ritmo
measure *verb.* medir
measurement *noun.* **1.** medida **2.** medición
meat *noun.* carne
mechanic *noun.* mecánico
mechanical *adj.* mecánico
mechanics *noun plural.* mecanismo
mechanics *noun singular.* mecánica
mechanism *noun.* mecanismo
medal *noun.* medalla
mediate *verb.* mediar, arbitrar
medical *noun.* reconocimiento médico
medical *adj.* médico
medicine *noun.* medicina
medieval, mediaeval *adj.* medieval
meditation *noun.* meditación
medium *noun.* **1.** medio **2.** médium
medium *adj.* medio, mediano
meet *noun.* encuentro
meet *verb.* **1.** encontrar **2.** encontrarse con **3.** quedar con **4.** ir/venir a buscar **5.** conocer **6.** juntarse **7.** satisfacer **8.** enfrentarse con **9.** reunirse **10.** confluir
meeting *noun.* **1.** encuentro **2.** reunión **3.** cita **4.** confluencia
melody *noun.* melodía
melt *verb.* **1.** derretir, fundir **2.** derretirse, fundirse
member *noun.* miembro, socio, afiliado
membership *noun.* **1.** calidad de miembro/socio **2.** afiliación **3.** cuota
membrane *noun.* membrana
memo *noun.* memorándum
memoirs *noun plural.* memorias, autobiografía
memorable *adj.* memorable
memorandum *noun.* memorándum
memorial *noun.* monumento conmemorativo
memory *noun.* **1.** memoria **2.** recuerdo
menace *noun.* amenaza, peligro
menace *verb.* amenazar
mental *adj.* **1.** mental **2.** psiquiátrico
mentally *adv.* mentalmente
mention *noun.* mención, alusión
mention *verb.* mencionar, hablar de
menu *noun.* **1.** menú **2.** carta
merchandise *noun.* mercancía
merchant *noun.* comerciante
mercury *noun.* mercurio
mercy *noun.* **1.** misericordia, clemencia **2.** suerte
mere *adj.* mero, simple
merely *adv.* meramente, solamente
merge *verb.* **1.** fusionar, unir **2.** fusionarse, fundirse
merger *noun.* fusión
merit *noun.* mérito
merit *verb.* merecer
merry *adj.* alegre

mess *noun.* desastre, enredo, lío
mess (with) *verb.* interferir
message *noun.* **1.** mensaje **2.** recado
messenger *noun.* mensajero
messy *adj.* **1.** sucio **2.** desordenado
metal *noun.* metal
metal *adj.* metálico, de metal
metaphor *noun.* metáfora
meter *noun.* **1.** metro **2.** contador, medidor
meter *verb.* medir
method *noun.* **1.** método, forma **2.** procedimiento **3.** técnica
metropolitan *adj.* metropolitano
Mexican *noun. adj.* mexicano
Mexico *noun.* México
mg. *abbr.* miligramo
microcomputer *noun.* microordenador, microcomputador
microphone, mike *noun.* micrófono
microscope *noun.* microscopio
microwave (oven) *noun.* microondas
mid *adj.* a mediados de
midday *noun.* mediodía
middle *noun.* **1.** medio, centro **2.** cintura
middle *adj.* medio, central
Middle East *noun.* Oriente Medio
middle-aged *adj.* de mediana edad
midnight *noun.* medianoche
might *noun.* fuerza, poder
might *verb.* poder, ser posible
mighty *adj.* poderoso, potente, enorme
migrant *noun.* emigrante
migrate *verb.* emigrar
migration *noun.* migración
mild *adj.* **1.** apacible, afable **2.** ligero, leve **3.** suave, moderado
mildly *adv.* **1.** ligeramente **2.** suavemente
mile *noun.* milla
militant *adj.* militante
military *adj.* militar
milk *noun.* leche
milk *verb.* ordeñar
mill *noun.* **1.** molinillo **2.** molino **3.** fábrica
mill *verb.* moler
—**mill about/around** arremolinarse, apiñarse
miller *noun.* molinero
milliliter *noun.* mililitro
millimeter *noun.* milímetro
million *noun. adj.* millón
millionaire *noun.* millonario
millionth *noun.* millonésimo
mind *interj.* ¡cuidado!
mind *noun.* mente, cabeza, cerebro
mind *verb.* **1.** cuidar **2.** importar, molestar **3.** tener cuidado **4.** hacer caso de
mine *noun.* mina
mine *verb.* **1.** extraer **2.** minar **3.** sembrar minas
mine *pron.* (el) mío, (la) mía, (los) míos, (las) mías
miner *noun.* minero
mineral *noun.* mineral
mini *noun.* minifalda
mini *adj.* mini-
miniature *noun. adj.* miniatura
minimal *adj.* mínimo
minimize *verb.* minimizar
minimum *noun. adj.* mínimo
mining *noun.* minería, explotación de minas
miniskirt *noun.* minifalda
minister *noun.* **1.** ministro **2.** pastor, clérigo
minister *verb.* atender, servir
ministerial *adj.* ministerial
ministry *noun.* **1.** ministerio **2.** sacerdocio, clerecía
minor *noun.* menor
minor *verb.* estudiar como asignatura secundaria
minor *adj.* **1.** menor, de poca importancia **2.** secundario
minority *noun.* minoría
mint *noun.* **1.** casa de la moneda **2.** menta **3.** caramelo de menta
mint *verb.* acuñar
minus *noun. prep.* menos
minus *adj.* negativo
minute *noun.* **1.** minuto **2.** momento, instante
minute *adj.* **1.** diminuto, minúsculo **2.** minucioso, detallado
minutes *noun plural.* acta

miracle *noun.* milagro
mirror *noun.* espejo
mirror *verb.* reflejar
miscarriage *noun.* **1.** aborto **2.** error
miserable *adj.* **1.** abatido, triste, infeliz **2.** miserable
misery *noun.* **1.** miseria **2.** tristeza, pena **3.** dolor
misleading *adj.* engañoso
miss *noun.* fallo, tiro errado
miss *verb.* **1.** fallar, errar **2.** perder **3.** lamentar, sentir **4.** echar de menos, extrañar **5.** no asistir, faltar **6.** no entender
Miss *noun.* señorita
missile *noun.* misil
missing *adj.* **1.** perdido, extraviado, desaparecido **2.** que falta
mission *noun.* misión
missionary *noun.* misionero
mist *noun.* neblina
mistake *noun.* error, equivocación
mistake (for) *verb.* **1.** confundir **2.** equivocarse, entender mal
mistaken *adj.* equivocado
Mister, Mr. *noun.* señor
mistress *noun.* **1.** señora, ama **2.** amante
misunderstanding *noun.* malentendido
mix *noun.* mezcla, preparado
mix *verb.* **1.** mezclar **2.** mezclarse **3.** combinar **4.** juntarse, alternar
mixed *adj.* **1.** variado **2.** diverso **3.** mixto
mixture *noun.* **1.** mezcla **2.** preparado
ml. *abbr.* mililitro
mm. *abbr.* milímetro
moan *noun.* **1.** gemido **2.** queja
moan *verb.* **1.** gemir **2.** quejarse
mob *noun.* banda, chusma
mob *verb.* **1.** acosar **2.** atacar
mobile *adj.* **1.** móvil **2.** ambulante
mobility *noun.* movilidad
mobilize *verb.* movilizar
mock *verb.* burlarse
mock *adj.* fingido, falso
mode *noun.* **1.** modo **2.** medio **3.** moda
model *noun.* modelo
model *verb.* **1.** modelar **2.** hacer de modelo, posar
moderate *noun.* moderado
moderate *verb.* moderar
moderate *adj.* **1.** moderado **2.** regular
modern *adj.* moderno
modernize *verb.* modernizar
modest *adj.* **1.** modesto **2.** recatado **3.** pequeño
modification *noun.* modificación
modify *verb.* modificar
module *noun.* módulo
moist *adj.* húmedo
moisture *noun.* humedad
mold *noun.* **1.** molde **2.** moho
mold *verb.* moldear
mole *noun.* **1.** lunar **2.** topo
molecular *adj.* molecular
molecule *noun.* molécula
mom, momma, mommy *noun.* mamá
moment *noun.* momento, instante
momentarily *adv.* momentáneamente
momentum *noun.* impulso, ímpetu
monarch *noun.* monarca
monarchy *noun.* monarquía
monastery *noun.* monasterio
Monday *noun.* lunes
monetary *adj.* monetario
money *noun.* dinero, plata
monitor *noun.* **1.** responsable, encargado **2.** monitor
monitor *verb.* controlar, observar
monk *noun.* monje
monkey *noun.* **1.** mono **2.** diablillo, pillo
monkey *verb.* juguetear
monopoly *noun.* monopolio
monster *noun.* monstruo
month *noun.* mes
monthly *adj.* mensual
monthly *adv.* mensualmente
monument *noun.* monumento
mood *noun.* humor
moody *adj.* malhumorado
moon *noun.* luna
moonlight *noun.* luz de la luna
moonlight *verb.* estar pluriempleado
moor *noun.* páramo
moor *verb.* amarrar
moral *noun.* moraleja
moral *adj.* moral
morale *noun.* moral

morality *noun.* moral, moralidad
morally *adv.* moralmente
more *adj. adv. pron.* más
moreover *adv.* además
morning *noun.* mañana
Morse *noun.* morse
mortal *noun. adj.* mortal
mortality *noun.* mortalidad
mortar *noun.* **1.** argamasa **2.** mortero
mortgage *noun.* hipoteca
mortgage *verb.* hipotecar
mosaic *noun.* mosaico
Moslem, Muslim *noun. adj.* musulmán
mosque *noun.* mezquita
moss *noun.* musgo
most *adj.* **1.** más **2.** la mayoría de, la mayor parte de
most *adv.* **1.** más **2.** muy **3.** sumamente
most *pron.* la mayor parte
—**at (the) most** como máximo
mostly *adv.* principalmente, en su mayor parte
mother *noun.* madre
mother *verb.* **1.** cuidar como una madre **2.** consentir
motion *noun.* **1.** movimiento **2.** gesto **3.** moción
motion *verb.* hacer señas
motivate *verb.* motivar
motivation *noun.* motivación
motive *noun.* motivo
motor *noun.* motor
motor *verb.* ir en coche
motorist *noun.* automovilista, conductor
mound *noun.* montículo
mount *noun.* **1.** monte **2.** montura **3.** soporte, base
mount *verb.* **1.** montar **2.** subir, aumentar, crecer **3.** fijar, engastar **4.** preparar
mountain *noun.* montaña
mouse *noun.* ratón
mouth *noun.* **1.** boca **2.** desembocadura **3.** entrada
mouth *verb.* decir con los labios
move *noun.* **1.** movimiento **2.** jugada, turno **3.** mudanza, traslado
move *verb.* **1.** mover **2.** trasladar **3.** inducir **4.** conmover
—**move back** retroceder
movement *noun.* **1.** movimiento **2.** expresión corporal **3.** tendencia
movie *noun.* película
—**the movies** el cine
moving *adj.* conmovedor
Mrs. *noun.* señora
Ms. *noun.* señora
M.S. *abbr.* doctorado en ciencias
much *adj. adv. pron.* mucho
mud *noun.* barro, lodo
muddy *verb.* ensuciar de barro, llenar de barro
muddy *adj.* fangoso, lleno de barro
mug *noun.* **1.** tazón **2.** jeta
mug *verb.* asaltar, atracar
multiple *noun.* múltiplo
multiple *adj.* múltiple
multiply *verb.* **1.** multiplicar **2.** multiplicarse
multitude *noun.* multitud, muchedumbre
municipal *adj.* municipal
murder *noun.* asesinato, homicidio
murder *verb.* asesinar, matar
murderer *noun.* asesino
murmur *noun.* murmullo, susurro
murmur *verb.* murmurar, susurrar
muscle *noun.* músculo
muscular *adj.* **1.** muscular **2.** musculoso
muse *verb.* reflexionar, meditar
museum *noun.* museo
mushroom *noun.* seta, champiñón
mushroom *verb.* crecer de la noche a la mañana
music *noun.* música
musical *noun.* musical
musical *adj.* **1.** musical **2.** dotado para la música
musician *noun.* músico
Muslim, Moslem *noun. adj.* musulmán
must *noun.* algo imprescindible
must *verb.* **1.** deber, tener que (obligation) **2.** deber de (probability)
mustache *noun.* bigote
mustard *noun.* mostaza
mute *adj.* mudo
mutter *noun.* murmullo
mutter *verb.* hablar entre dientes, murmurar

mutual *adj.* mutuo, recíproco
mutually *adv.* mutuamente, recíprocamente
my *interj.* ¡Dios mío!
my *adj.* mi, mis
myself *pron.* **1.** me **2.** mi (after prep) **3.** yo mismo/a **4.** yo solo/a
mysterious *adj.* misterioso
mystery *noun.* misterio
myth *noun.* mito

N

nail *noun.* **1.** uña **2.** clavo
nail *verb.* clavar
naked *adj.* **1.** desnudo **2.** patente, manifiesto
name *noun.* **1.** nombre **2.** fama, reputación
name *verb.* **1.** llamar **2.** mencionar **3.** nombrar
namely *adv.* a saber
nanny *noun.* niñera
narrative *noun.* narrativa, narración
narrow *verb.* estrechar
narrow *adj.* **1.** estrecho **2.** escaso **3.** reducido
narrowly *adv.* por poco
nasty *adj.* **1.** asqueroso, desagradable, repugnante **2.** malo **3.** feo, grave **4.** peligroso, difícil
nation *noun.* **1.** nación **2.** pueblo
national *adj.* nacional
nationalism *noun.* nacionalismo
nationalist *noun.* nacionalista
nationality *noun.* nacionalidad
nationally *adv.* nacionalmente
native *noun.* **1.** nativo **2.** indígena
native *adj.* **1.** natal **2.** indígena **3.** autóctono **4.** natural, innato
natural *noun.* natural
natural *adj.* **1.** natural **2.** innato **3.** normal **4.** biológico
naturally *adv.* **1.** naturalmente **2.** por naturaleza **3.** con naturalidad
nature *noun.* **1.** naturaleza **2.** carácter **3.** tipo
naught, nought *noun.* **1.** nada **2.** cero
naughty *adj.* travieso
naval *adj.* naval
naïve, naive *adj.* **1.** naif **2.** ingenuo
navigation *noun.* navegación
navy *noun.* marina
navy *adj.* azul marino
near *prep.* **1.** cerca de **2.** casi
near *verb.* acercarse a
near *adj.* **1.** cercano **2.** próximo
near *adv.* cerca
nearby *adv.* cerca
nearly *adv.* casi
neat *adj.* **1.** pulcro, ordenado **2.** bien hecho
neatly *adv.* con esmero, hábilmente
necessarily *adv.* necesariamente
necessary *adj.* necesario
necessity *noun.* necesidad
neck *noun.* cuello
neck *verb.* besuquearse
need *noun.* **1.** necesidad **2.** motivo, razón
need *verb.* **1.** necesitar **2.** hacer falta
needle *noun.* aguja
needless *adj.* innecesario
negative *noun.* **1.** negativa **2.** negativo
negative *adj.* negativo
neglect *noun.* descuido, dejadez
neglect *verb.* **1.** descuidar, desatender, no cumplir con **2.** omitir
negligence *noun.* descuido, negligencia
negotiate *verb.* **1.** negociar **2.** salvar
negotiation *noun.* negociación
negotiator *noun.* negociador
neighbor *noun.* vecino
neighborhood *noun.* **1.** barrio, vecindario **2.** alrededores, cercanías
neighboring *adj.* vecino
neither *adj. pron.* ninguno de los dos
nephew *noun.* sobrino
nerve *noun.* **1.** nervio **2.** valor **3.** descaro

nerve *verb.* hacer de tripas corazón
nervous *adj.* nervioso
nervously *adv.* nerviosamente, con inquietud
nest *noun.* nido
nest *verb.* anidar
net *noun.* red, malla
net *verb.* coger (con red)
net *adj.* neto
Netherlands *noun.* Países Bajos
network *noun.* red
neutral *noun.* **1.** neutral **2.** punto muerto
neutral *adj.* **1.** neutral **2.** neutro
neutrality *noun.* neutralidad
never *adv.* nunca, jamás
nevertheless *adv.* sin embargo, no obstante
new *adj.* nuevo
new *adv.* recién
newcomer *noun.* recién llegado
newly *adv.* recién
news *noun singular.* noticias
newscaster *noun.* locutor, presentador
newsletter *noun.* boletín informativo
newspaper *noun.* periódico, diario
next *adj.* próximo, siguiente
next *adv.* luego, a continuación, después
next *pron.* el siguiente
next door *adv.* al lado
nice *adj.* **1.** amable, simpático, agradable **2.** bonito, lindo **3.** preciso
nicely *adv.* **1.** bien **2.** agradablemente
nick *noun.* muesca, hendidura
nick *verb.* cortar
nickname *noun.* apodo
nickname *verb.* apodar
Nigeria *noun.* Nigeria
Nigerian *noun. adj.* nigeriano
night *noun.* noche
nightmare *noun.* pesadilla
nil *noun.* cero
nine *noun. adj.* nueve
nineteen *noun. adj.* diecinueve
nineteenth *noun.* decimonono
nineties *noun plural.* **1.** entre noventa y cien **2.** los años noventa, los noventa
ninetieth *noun.* nonagésimo
ninety *noun. adj.* noventa
ninth *noun.* nono, noveno
nitrogen *noun.* nitrógeno
no *interj.* ¡no!
no *noun.* no
no *adj.* **1.** ningún **2.** ninguno/a
no *adv.* no
nobility *noun.* nobleza
noble *noun. adj.* noble
nobody *noun.* don nadie
nobody *pron.* nadie
nod *noun.* señal de asentimiento
nod *verb.* **1.** saludar con la cabeza, asentir **2.** dar cabezadas
node *noun.* nudo
noise *noun.* ruido, sonido
noisy *adj.* ruidoso
nominal *adj.* **1.** nominal **2.** simbólico
nominate *verb.* nombrar
nomination *noun.* **1.** nombramiento **2.** nominación, propuesta
nominee *noun.* candidato
none *adv.* de ningún modo
none *pron.* **1.** ninguno **2.** nada
nonetheless *adv.* no obstante, sin embargo
nonsense *noun.* tontería, disparate, bobada
noon *noun.* mediodía
no-one *pron.* nadie
nor *conj.* ni, tampoco
normal *adj.* normal
normally *adv.* normalmente
north *noun.* norte
north *adj.* **1.** norte **2.** del norte
north *adv.* al norte, hacia el norte
northern *adj.* del norte
Norway *noun.* Noruega
Norwegian *noun. adj.* noruego
nose *noun.* **1.** nariz **2.** hocico **3.** olfato **4.** morro, parte delantera
nose *verb.* **1.** avanzar con cuidado **2.** fisgonear, husmear
nostalgia *noun.* nostalgia
not *adv.* no
notable *adj.* notable, distinguido
notably *adv.* **1.** especialmente **2.** notablemente
notation *noun.* notación

note *noun.* **1.** nota **2.** billete
—**notes** *noun plural.* apuntes
note (down) *verb.* **1.** apuntar, anotar **2.** observar
notebook *noun.* cuaderno, libreta
noted *adj.* famoso, célebre
nothing *noun. pron.* **1.** nada **2.** cero
nothing *adv.* de ningún modo, de ninguna manera
notice *noun.* **1.** anuncio **2.** letrero, cartel **3.** atención **4.** aviso
notice *verb.* notar, fijarse en, darse cuenta de
noticeable *adj.* **1.** evidente **2.** notable, digno de atención
notify *verb.* notificar, avisar
notion *noun.* **1.** noción **2.** idea, concepto
notorious *adj.* notorio
notoriously *adv.* notoriamente
notwithstanding *prep.* a pesar de, no obstante
noun *noun.* nombre, sustantivo
Nov, *abbr.* noviembre
novel *noun.* novela
novel *adj.* novedoso, original
novelist *noun.* novelista
novelty *noun.* novedad
November *noun.* noviembre
novice *noun.* **1.** novato, principiante **2.** novicio
now *conj.* ahora que, ya que
—**now, now!** vale, basta
now *adv.* **1.** ahora **2.** ya, ahora mismo **3.** entonces
nowadays *adv.* hoy en día, en la actualidad
nowhere *adv.* en ninguna parte
nuclear *adj.* nuclear
nucleus *noun.* núcleo
nuisance *noun.* molestia, fastidio
number *noun.* **1.** número **2.** cantidad, multitud **3.** ejemplar
number *verb.* **1.** numerar **2.** contar
numerical *adj.* numérico
numerous *adj.* numeroso
nun *noun.* monja, religiosa
nurse *noun.* **1.** enfermero **2.** niñera, nodriza
nurse *verb.* **1.** cuidar **2.** amamantar **3.** acunar, mecer **4.** abrigar, alimentar
nursery *noun.* **1.** cuarto de los niños **2.** vivero
nursing *noun.* **1.** enfermería **2.** asistencia, cuidado **3.** lactancia
nurture *noun.* crianza, educación
nurture *verb.* criar, educar
nut *noun.* **1.** fruto seco **2.** tuerca
nutrient *noun.* nutriente
nutrition *noun.* nutrición, alimentación
nutty *adj.* **1.** con nueces **2.** chalado
nylon *noun.* nilón, nailon
nylon *adj.* de nilón, de nailon

O

o *interj.* ¡oh!
oak *noun.* roble
oak *adj.* de roble
oath *noun.* **1.** juramento **2.** palabrota
obedience *noun.* obediencia
obey *verb.* obedecer
obituary *noun.* necrología, obituario
object *noun.* **1.** objeto **2.** objetivo, fin **3.** complemento
object (to) *verb.* objetar
objection *noun.* objeción
objective *noun.* objetivo, fin
objective *adj.* objetivo
obligation *noun.* obligación
oblige *verb.* **1.** obligar **2.** hacer un favor, ayudar
obscene *adj.* obsceno
obscure *verb.* obscurecer, ocultar
obscure *adj.* **1.** oscuro, poco claro **2.** desconocido **3.** borroso
observation *noun.* **1.** observación **2.** comentario
observe *verb.* **1.** observar **2.** ver **3.** cumplir, guardar **4.** señalar

observer *noun.* observador
obsess *verb.* obsesionar
obsession *noun.* obsesión
obstacle *noun.* obstáculo
obstruction *noun.* obstrucción
obtain *verb.* obtener, conseguir
obvious *adj.* evidente, obvio
obviously *adv.* evidentemente
occasion *noun.* **1.** ocasión **2.** acontecimiento
occasional *adj.* ocasional, poco frecuente
occasionally *adv.* de vez en cuando, a veces
occupation *noun.* ocupación, profesión
occupational *adj.* profesional
occupy *verb.* **1.** ocupar **2.** habitar, vivir en
occur *verb.* **1.** ocurrir, suceder, tener lugar **2.** darse, encontrarse **3.** ocurrirse
occurrence *noun.* suceso
ocean *noun.* océano
Oct. *abbr.* octubre
October *noun.* octubre
odd *adj.* **1.** extraño, raro **2.** impar **3.** suelto, desparejado **4.** ocasional
oddly *adv.* de manera extraña
odds *noun plural.* **1.** probabilidades **2.** ventaja
odor *noun.* olor
of *prep.* **1.** de **2.** por
of course por supuesto, claro, naturalmente
off *prep.* **1.** de **2.** sin **3.** fuera de
off *adv.* **1.** fuera **2.** apagado, cerrado **3.** libre **4.** completamente **5.** malo, mediocre **6.** pasado, caducado **7.** anulado
offend *verb.* **1.** ofender **2.** desagradar
offender *noun.* delincuente, infractor
offense, offence *noun.* **1.** ofensa **2.** delito, infracción
offensive *noun.* ofensiva
offensive *adj.* **1.** ofensivo, insultante **2.** repugnante, desagradable
offer *noun.* oferta, ofrecimiento
offer *verb.* **1.** ofrecer **2.** ofrecerse
offering *noun.* **1.** regalo **2.** ofrenda
office *noun.* **1.** despacho, oficina **2.** cargo
officer *noun.* **1.** oficial **2.** funcionario
official *noun.* **1.** oficial **2.** funcionario
official *adj.* oficial
officially *adv.* oficialmente
offshore *adj.* de la costa
often *adv.* a menudo, con frecuencia
oh *interj.* ¡ah!, ¡oh!
oil *noun.* **1.** aceite **2.** óleo **3.** petróleo
oil *verb.* engrasar, lubricar
O.K., okay *noun.* aprobación, visto bueno
O.K., okay *adj. adv.* bien
O.K., okay *interj.* ¡vale!, ¡okey!
old *adj.* **1.** viejo, mayor **2.** de edad **3.** antiguo
old-fashioned *adj.* anticuado, pasado de moda
olive *noun.* **1.** aceituna, oliva **2.** olivo **3.** verde oliva
Olympic Games, the Olympics *noun plural.* Juegos Olímpicos
omission *noun.* omisión
omit *verb.* **1.** omitir **2.** olvidarse de **3.** suprimir
on *prep.* **1.** encima de, en **2.** sobre **3.** acerca de **4.** de **5.** a, al **6.** por, mediante **7.** tras
on *adj.* **1.** en curso, funcionando, en marcha **2.** en pie
on *adv.* **1.** puesto **2.** adelante, hacia adelante **3.** en marcha, en funcionamiento **4.** en exhibición, en cartelera **5.** a bordo
on the spot en el acto
once *conj.* una vez que, en cuanto
once *adv.* **1.** una vez **2.** antes, en otro tiempo
 —at once inmediatamente
 —all at once **1.** de repente **2.** simultáneamente, a la vez
one *noun.* **1.** uno **2.** un año
 —one another el uno al otro
one *adj.* **1.** un **2.** cierto **3.** único
one *pron.* **1.** el, la **2.** uno, una
one-off *noun. adj.* único, aislado
oneself *pron.* **1.** se **2.** sí mismo/a **3.** uno mismo/a
ongoing *adj.* en curso
onion *noun.* cebolla

on-line, online *adj.* conectado, en línea
only *conj.* pero, sólo que
only *adj.* único
only *adv.* sólo, solamente
onset *noun.* inicio, comienzo
open *verb.* **1.** abrir **2.** abrirse **3.** empezar
open *adj.* **1.** abierto **2.** destapado, desabrochado, descubierto **3.** franco
opening *noun.* **1.** abertura, brecha **2.** comienzo **3.** apertura, inauguración **4.** oportunidad
openly *adv.* abiertamente
opera *noun.* ópera
operate *verb.* **1.** funcionar **2.** operar, intervenir
operation *noun.* **1.** operación **2.** funcionamiento
operational *adj.* operativo
operative *adj.* en vigor
operator *noun.* **1.** operario **2.** telefonista
opinion *noun.* opinión
opponent *noun.* adversario, oponente
opportunity *noun.* oportunidad, ocasión
oppose *verb.* **1.** oponerse, estar en contra **2.** luchar contra
opposite *prep. adv.* en frente de, frente a
opposite *noun.* lo contrario
opposite *adj.* **1.** opuesto, contrario **2.** de enfrente
opposition *noun.* oposición
oppression *noun.* opresión
opt *verb.* optar, escoger
—**opt out (of)** abandonar, dejar de participar
optical *adj.* óptico
optimism *noun.* optimismo
optimistic *adj.* optimista
option *noun.* opción
optional *adj.* opcional
or *conj.* o
oracle *noun.* oráculo
oral *noun.* examen oral
oral *adj.* oral
orange *noun.* **1.** naranja **2.** naranjo
orange *adj.* **1.** naranja **2.** de naranja
orbit *noun.* órbita
orbit *verb.* orbitar, estar en órbita
orchard *noun.* huerto
orchestra *noun.* orquesta
ordeal *noun.* experiencia dura
order *noun.* **1.** orden **2.** pedido
order *verb.* **1.** ordenar, mandar **2.** pedir, encargar
orderly *noun.* **1.** celador **2.** ordenanza
orderly *adj.* formal, ordenado
ordinary *adj.* **1.** ordinario, común, normal **2.** mediocre, vulgar
ore *noun.* mineral, mena
organ *noun.* órgano
organic *adj.* orgánico
organism *noun.* organismo
organization *noun.* organización
organize *verb.* organizar
organized *adj.* organizado
organizer *noun.* organizador
oriental *noun. adj.* oriental
orientation *noun.* orientación
origin *noun.* origen
original *noun. adj.* original
originally *adv.* originalmente
originate *verb.* **1.** originar, crear, suscitar **2.** originarse
orthodox *adj.* ortodoxo
other *adj. pron.* otro
otherwise *conj.* si no, de lo contrario
otherwise *adv.* **1.** aparte de eso, por lo demás **2.** de otra manera
ought (to) *verb.* deber
ounce, oz. *noun.* onza
our *adj.* nuestro/a, nuestros/as
ours *pron.* el (nuestro), la (nuestra), (los) nuestros, (las) nuestras
ourselves *pron.* **1.** nos **2.** nosotros mismos, nosotras mismas **3.** nosotros solos, nosotras solas
oust *verb.* desbancar, expulsar
out *adv.* **1.** fuera, afuera **2.** apagado **3.** en voz alta **4.** eliminado **5.** en huelga **6.** pasado de moda **7.** expirado, vencido **8.** equivocado **9.** publicado **10.** conocido **11.** completamente
—**out of 1.** fuera de **2.** de cada **3.** sin **4.** por **5.** de
outbreak *noun.* estallido
outcome *noun.* resultado

outdoor *adj.* al aire libre
outer *adj.* exterior, externo
outfit *noun.* traje
outgoing *adj.* **1.** extrovertido, sociable **2.** saliente
outing *noun.* excursión, paseo
outlaw *noun.* prófugo, fugitivo
outlaw *verb.* proscribir
outlet *noun.* salida
outline *noun.* **1.** contorno, silueta **2.** resumen, esbozo
outline *verb.* perfilar, resumir
outlook *noun.* **1.** vista **2.** actitud, punto de vista **3.** perspectivas
output *noun.* producción
outrage *noun.* atrocidad, escándalo, ultraje
outrage *verb.* ultrajar
outrageous *adj.* escandaloso, ofensivo
outright *adj.* absoluto
outright *adv.* **1.** francamente **2.** de inmediato, en el acto
outset *noun.* principio, comienzo
outside *prep.* fuera
outside *noun.* exterior
outside *adj.* **1.** exterior **2.** externo **3.** ínfimo, remoto
outside *adv.* **1.** fuera, afuera **2.** por fuera
outsider *noun.* **1.** forastero, desconocido **2.** competidor con pocas posibilidades de ganar
outskirts *noun plural.* afueras, alrededores
outstanding *adj.* **1.** excepcional, extraordinario, excelente **2.** pendiente, atrasado
outward *adj.* **1.** exterior, externo **2.** de ida
oval *noun.* óvalo
oval *adj.* oval, ovalado
oven *noun.* horno
over *prep.* **1.** sobre **2.** encima de, arriba de **3.** al otro lado, enfrente **4.** más de **5.** por **6.** durante **7.** superior a
over *adv.* **1.** por encima, por arriba **2.** al otro lado, enfrente **3.** de un lado al otro **4.** otra vez **5.** hacia abajo **6.** más **7.** de sobra, en exceso **8.** acabado, terminado **9.** arruinado, perdido
overall *noun.* mono, overol
overall *adj.* total
overall *adv.* en total
overcome *verb.* superar, vencer
overcome *adj.* turbado, confundido
overhead *adv.* por lo alto, en alto
overlap *noun.* superposición
overlap *verb.* superponerse, solaparse
overlook *verb.* **1.** tener vistas a, dar a **2.** hacer la vista gorda, pasar por alto
overnight *adj.* **1.** nocturno **2.** repentino
overnight *adv.* **1.** de noche **2.** repentinamente
overseas *adj.* **1.** extranjero **2.** exterior
overseas *adv.* en el extranjero
oversee *verb.* supervisar
overt *adj.* abierto, manifiesto, público
overtake *verb.* adelantar
overthrow *verb.* derrocar, derribar
overtime *noun.* horas extras
overturn *verb.* volcar
overwhelm *verb.* **1.** vencer, aplastar **2.** agobiar, abrumar
overwhelming *adj.* **1.** aplastante **2.** abrumador **3.** irresistible
owe *verb.* deber
owing *adj.* debido
owl *noun.* búho, lechuza
own *verb.* **1.** poseer, tener, ser dueño de **2.** confesar, admitir
own *adj. pron.* propio
owner *noun.* propietario, dueño
ownership *noun.* propiedad
oxygen *noun.* oxígeno
oz *abbr.* onza
ozone *noun.* ozono

P

p. *abbr.* página
pace *noun.* paso
pace *verb.* ir de un lado a otro
pack *noun.* **1.** paquete **2.** cajetilla **3.** fardo, bulto **4.** manada, jauría **5.** hatajo, cuadrilla, pelotón
pack *verb.* **1.** empaquetar, embalar **2.** hacer la maleta **3.** envasar **4.** amontonarse, hacinarse, apiñarse
package *noun.* **1.** paquete **2.** oferta
package *verb.* **1.** empaquetar, embalar **2.** envasar
packet *noun.* **1.** paquete **2.** cajetilla
packing *noun.* **1.** preparación de las maletas **2.** embalaje
pact *noun.* pacto
pad *noun.* **1.** almohadilla **2.** taco, bloc **3.** plataforma
pad *verb.* **1.** almohadillar, acolchar **2.** caminar sin hacer ruido
pagan *noun. adj.* pagano
page *noun.* **1.** página **2.** mensajero **3.** paje
page *verb.* llamar por megafonía/altavoz
pain *noun.* dolor
pain *verb.* doler, afligir, apenar
painful *adj.* doloroso
painfully *adv.* dolorosamente
paint *noun.* pintura
paint *verb.* pintar
painter *noun.* pintor
painting *noun.* **1.** pintura **2.** cuadro
pair *noun.* **1.** par **2.** pareja
pair *verb.* emparejar
Pakistan *noun.* Pakistán
Pakistani *noun. adj.* paquistaní
pal *noun.* amigo, colega
palace *noun.* palacio
pale *verb.* palidecer
pale *adj.* pálido, claro
Palestine *noun.* Palestina
Palestinian *noun. adj.* palestino
palm (tree) *noun.* palma, palmera
pan *noun.* cazuela, cazo, sartén, olla
panama (hat) *noun.* panamá
panel *noun.* **1.** panel, entrepaño **2.** tablero **3.** jurado
panic *noun.* pánico
panic *verb.* **1.** entrarle a alguien el pánico **2.** provocar pánico
pants *noun plural.* **1.** calzoncillos **2.** bragas, calzones **3.** pantalones
papal *adj.* papal
paper *noun.* **1.** papel **2.** periódico **3.** revista **4.** examen
—**papers** *noun plural.* documentación, papeles
paperback *noun.* libro en rústica
paperback *adj.* en rústica
paperwork *noun.* trabajo de oficina
par *noun.* par
parachute *noun.* paracaídas
parachute *verb.* **1.** lanzar en paracaídas **2.** lanzarse en paracaídas
parade *noun.* **1.** desfile **2.** revista
parade *verb.* **1.** desfilar **2.** formar, pasar revista **3.** lucir, hacer alarde de
paradise *noun.* paraíso
paradox *noun.* paradoja
paragraph *noun.* párrafo
parallel *noun.* **1.** paralela **2.** paralelismo, semejanza, analogía **3.** paralelo
parallel *verb.* equiparar, igualar, comparar
parallel *adj.* **1.** paralelo **2.** análogo
parallel *adv.* paralelamente
parcel *noun.* paquete
pardon *interj.* ¡perdón!, ¿cómo?
pardon *noun.* **1.** perdón **2.** indulto
pardon *verb.* **1.** perdonar, disculpar **2.** indultar
parent *noun.* padre, madre
parental *adj.* de los padres, paterno
parish *noun.* parroquia
park *noun.* **1.** parque **2.** jardín
park *verb.* aparcar, estacionar
parking lot *noun.* parking, aparcamiento
parliament *noun.* parlamento
parliamentary *adj.* parlamentario
parlor *noun.* salón

parsley *noun.* perejil
parson *noun.* **1.** párroco, cura **2.** clérigo
part *noun.* **1.** parte **2.** papel **3.** función
part *verb.* **1.** partir **2.** dividir **3.** separar, separarse **4.** abrir, correr **5.** apartarse
partial *adj.* parcial
participant, participator *noun.* participante
participate *verb.* participar
participation *noun.* participación
particle *noun.* partícula
particular *adj.* **1.** particular, especial **2.** exigente
particularly *adv.* especialmente
particulars *noun plural.* detalles, pormenores
parting *noun.* **1.** partida, separación, despedida **2.** raya (del pelo)
partly *adv.* en parte
partner *noun.* **1.** socio **2.** pareja
partner *verb.* acompañar
partnership *noun.* **1.** sociedad **2.** asociación **3.** relación de pareja
part-time *adj. adv.* a tiempo parcial, media jornada
party *noun.* **1.** fiesta, reunión **2.** grupo **3.** partido
pass *noun.* **1.** pase **2.** permiso **3.** desfiladero, paso, puerto
pass *verb.* **1.** pasar **2.** traspasar, ceder **3.** superar **4.** adelantar **5.** transcurrir **6.** aprobar **7.** juzgar, dictar sentencia **8.** desaparecer **9.** morir **10.** aprobar **11.** sufrir, tolerar
passage *noun.* **1.** pasaje **2.** pasillo, pasadizo **3.** paso **4.** viaje, travesía
passenger *noun.* pasajero
passing *adj.* transitorio, pasajero, temporal
passion *noun.* pasión
passionate *adj.* apasionado
passive *adj.* pasivo
passport *noun.* pasaporte
past *prep.* **1.** por delante de **2.** más allá de
past *noun.* **1.** pasado **2.** historia
past *adj.* **1.** anterior **2.** antiguo **3.** último **4.** pasado
pasta *noun.* pasta
pastoral *adj.* **1.** pastoril **2.** pastoral
pastry *noun.* **1.** masa **2.** pastel
pasture *noun.* pasto
pat, off pat *adj.* preparado
pat *noun.* **1.** palmadita, caricia **2.** porción pequeña
pat *verb.* acariciar, dar palmaditas, tocar
pat *adv.* de memoria, al dedillo
patch *noun.* **1.** remiendo, parche **2.** parcela, terreno
patch *verb.* remendar
patent *noun.* patente
patent *verb.* patentar
path *noun.* **1.** camino, sendero **2.** trayectoria, recorrido
pathetic *adj.* **1.** lastimoso, patético **2.** inútil
patience *noun.* paciencia
patient *noun.* paciente
patient *adj.* paciente, sufrido
patiently *adv.* pacientemente
patriot *noun.* patriota
patriotic *adj.* patriótico
patrol *noun.* patrulla
patrol *verb.* patrullar
patron *noun.* **1.** mecenas **2.** cliente habitual, parroquiano
patronage *noun.* mecenazgo, patrocinio, apoyo
pattern *noun.* **1.** patrón, molde **2.** modelo
pause *noun.* pausa, silencio
pause *verb.* hacer una pausa, parar
pave *verb.* pavimentar, empedrar, adoquinar
pavement *noun.* pavimento, acera
pavilion *noun.* pabellón
pay *noun.* salario, sueldo, paga
pay *verb.* **1.** pagar, retribuir, remunerar **2.** saldar, liquidar **3.** compensar, sacar provecho **4.** prestar, rendir, ofrecer
payable *adj.* pagadero
payment *noun.* pago, recompensa
PC *abbr.* **1.** ordenador, computadora **2.** políticamente correcto
pea *noun.* guisante
peace *noun.* paz
peaceful *adj.* tranquilo, sosegado, relajado

peach *noun.* melocotón
peak *noun.* **1.** pico, cumbre **2.** cumbre, cúspide, apogeo **3.** visera
peak *verb.* alcanzar el punto más alto
pear *noun.* pera
pearl *noun.* perla
peasant *noun.* campesino, labrador
peasantry *noun.* campesinado
peculiar *adj.* **1.** curioso, extraño **2.** peculiar, propio, característico
pedestrian *noun.* peatón
pedestrian *adj.* pedestre
peel *noun.* piel, corteza
peel *verb.* **1.** pelar **2.** pelarse, desconcharse
peer *noun.* par, noble
peer *verb.* escudriñar
peg *noun.* **1.** clavija, estaca **2.** percha, colgador
peg *verb.* sujetar
pen *noun.* **1.** pluma **2.** corral
penalty *noun.* pena, castigo, multa
pencil *noun.* lápiz
pencil *verb.* escribir con lápiz
penetrate *verb.* penetrar
penetration *noun.* penetración
penguin *noun.* pingüino
peninsula *noun.* península
penis *noun.* pene
penny *noun.* centavo
pension *noun.* pensión
pensioner *noun.* pensionista
pentagon *noun.* pentágono
people *noun plural.* **1.** gente **2.** personas **3.** pueblo
pepper *noun.* **1.** pimienta **2.** pimentero **3.** pimiento
pepper *verb.* sazonar con pimienta —**pepper with** acribillar
per *prep.* por
per cent *adv.* por ciento
perceive *verb.* percibir, comprender
percentage *noun.* porcentaje
perception *noun.* **1.** percepción **2.** perspicacia, agudeza
perch *noun.* **1.** perca **2.** percha
perch *verb.* **1.** posarse, sentarse **2.** encaramar
perennial *adj.* perenne, eterno, perpetuo
perfect *verb.* perfeccionar
perfect *adj.* **1.** perfecto **2.** completo
perfection *noun.* perfección
perfectly *adv.* **1.** perfectamente **2.** completamente, totalmente
perform *verb.* **1.** realizar, efectuar, ejecutar **2.** actuar **3.** representar, interpretar **4.** rendir
performance *noun.* **1.** realización, ejecución **2.** resultado, desempeño **3.** representación, actuación **4.** rendimiento
performer *noun.* artista, intérprete, músico, actor
perfume *noun.* perfume
perfume *verb.* **1.** perfumar **2.** perfumarse
perhaps *adv.* quizás, tal vez
period *noun.* **1.** período **2.** era, fase, etapa **3.** punto
period *adj.* de época
periodic *adj.* periódico
peripheral *adj.* periférico
permanent *adj.* permanente
permanently *adv.* permanentemente
permission *noun.* permiso, autorización
permit *noun.* permiso, pase, licencia
permit *verb.* permitir
perpetual *adj.* perpetuo, eterno, continuo
persist *verb.* **1.** persistir, continuar **2.** insistir, empeñarse
persistence *noun.* persistencia, insistencia
persistent *adj.* persistente, insistente
person *noun.* persona
personal *adj.* **1.** personal **2.** en persona —**personal computer, PC** ordenador personal, computadora personal
personality *noun.* personalidad
personally *adv.* personalmente, en persona
personnel *noun.* personal
perspective *noun.* perspectiva
persuade *verb.* **1.** persuadir, convencer **2.** disuadir
persuasion *noun.* persuasión
persuasive *adj.* persuasivo
Peru *noun.* Perú

Peruvian *noun. adj.* peruano
pest *noun.* **1.** plaga, animal/insecto nocivo **2.** pelma, fregón **3.** lata, rollo
pesticide *noun.* pesticida
pet *noun.* animal doméstico, mascota
pet *verb.* **1.** acariciar **2.** acariciarse, sobarse
pet *adj.* favorito, predilecto
petition *noun.* petición, instancia
petition *verb.* **1.** presentar una petición **2.** dirigir una instancia
petroleum *noun.* petróleo
petty *adj.* **1.** insignificante, nimio, de poca monta **2.** mezquino
pharmaceutical *adj.* farmacéutico
phase *noun.* fase
phenomenon *noun.* fenómeno
Philippines *noun.* Filipinas
philosopher *noun.* filósofo
philosophical, philosophic *adj.* filosófico
philosophy *noun.* filosofía
phoenix *noun.* fénix
phone *noun.* teléfono
phone *verb.* telefonear, llamar por teléfono
phone call *noun.* llamada de teléfono
photo *noun.* foto, fotografía
photograph *verb.* fotografiar
photographer *noun.* fotógrafo
photographic *adj.* fotográfico
photography *noun.* fotografía
phrase *noun.* frase
phrase *verb.* expresar
physical *adj.* **1.** físico **2.** material
physically *adv.* físicamente
physician *noun.* médico
physicist *noun.* físico
physics *noun singular.* física
piano *noun.* piano
pick, pickax *noun.* pico, piqueta
pick *noun.* **1.** elección, selección **2.** lo mejor
pick *verb.* **1.** elegir, escoger **2.** coger, recoger **3.** levantar **4.** forzar
picnic *noun.* picnic, jira, merienda campestre
picnic *verb.* ir de picnic, hacer un picnic
picture *noun.* **1.** pintura, cuadro, retrato **2.** fotografía **3.** película **4.** imagen **5.** descripción
picture *verb.* **1.** representar, describir **2.** imaginar, figurarse
picturesque *adj.* pintoresco
pie *noun.* tarta, empanada, pastel
piece *noun.* **1.** trozo, pedazo **2.** pieza **3.** moneda
pier *noun.* muelle, embarcadero
pierce *verb.* **1.** atravesar, traspasar **2.** perforar, agujerear
pig *noun.* cerdo, puerco
pigeon *noun.* paloma
pike *noun.* lucio
pile *noun.* **1.** montón, pila **2.** poste, pilar **3.** pelo
pile *verb.* amontonar, apilar
pilgrim *noun.* peregrino
pilgrimage *noun.* peregrinación
pill *noun.* píldora, pastilla
pillar *noun.* pilar, columna
pillow *noun.* almohada
pillow *verb.* apoyar
pilot *noun.* **1.** piloto **2.** práctico
pilot *verb.* pilotar, pilotear
pilot *adj.* piloto, experimental
pin *noun.* **1.** alfiler **2.** insignia, pin
pin *verb.* **1.** prender, sujetar **2.** inmovilizar
pinch *noun.* **1.** pellizco **2.** pizca
pinch *verb.* **1.** pellizcar **2.** apretar
pine *noun.* pino
pine (away) *verb.* languidecer, consumirse
pine (for) *verb.* suspirar por, anhelar
pink *noun. adj.* rosa, rosado
pint *noun.* pinta
pioneer *noun.* pionero, precursor
pioneer *verb.* se el primero en, marcar un nuevo rumbo
pipe *noun.* **1.** tubería, tubo, cañería **2.** pipa, cachimbo **3.** flauta **4.** gaita
pipe *verb.* **1.** canalizar, llevar por tubería/gaseoducto/oleoducto **2.** tocar
pipeline *noun.* **1.** tubería, cañería **2.** oleoducto **3.** gaseoducto
piper *noun.* **1.** flautista **2.** gaitero
pipes *noun plural.* **1.** gaita **2.** flauta
pirate *noun.* pirata

pirate *verb.* piratear
pistol *noun.* pistola
pit *noun.* **1.** hoyo, foso, fosa **2.** mina, pozo **3.** boxes **4.** hueso, pepita, pepa
pit *verb.* deshuesar, quitar las pepitas
pitch *noun.* brea
pitch *noun.* **1.** tono **2.** grado, punto, extremo **3.** puesto **4.** lanzamiento, tiro **5.** alquitrán, brea
pitch *verb.* **1.** armar, montar **2.** tirar, lanzar, arrojar **3.** caer **4.** cabecear **5.** graduar el tono
pity *noun.* **1.** piedad, compasión **2.** pena, lástima
pity *verb.* **1.** compadecer **2.** compadecerse de, tener lástima
pizza *noun.* pizza
place *noun.* **1.** sitio, lugar **2.** asiento **3.** posición **4.** lugar **5.** pasaje, página **6.** función, deber, obligación **7.** puesto, trabajo **8.** casa **9.** plaza
place *verb.* **1.** colocar, poner **2.** situar, ubicar **3.** echar, achacar, dar **4.** invertir **5.** recordar, identificar, reconocer
plague *noun.* **1.** peste **2.** plaga
plague *verb.* importunar
plain *noun.* **1.** llanura **2.** punto del derecho
plain *adj.* **1.** sencillo, liso, sin ornamentos **2.** claro, evidente **3.** franco **4.** común, ordinario, poco atractivo
plainly *adv.* **1.** sencillamente **2.** claramente **3.** francamente
plaintiff *noun.* demandante, querellante
plan *noun.* **1.** plan, proyecto **2.** plano
plan *verb.* **1.** planear **2.** planificar, proyectar **3.** diseñar
plane *noun.* **1.** avión **2.** plano **3.** nivel **4.** cepillo **5.** plátano
plane *verb.* cepillar, alisar
planet *noun.* planeta
planner *noun.* planificador
planning *noun.* planificación
plant *noun.* **1.** planta **2.** instalaciones, maquinaria **3.** fábrica
plant *verb.* **1.** plantar, sembrar **2.** plantarse **3.** colocar, poner, infiltrar
plantation *noun.* plantación
plasma *noun.* plasma
plaster *noun.* **1.** revoque, enlucido **2.** yeso **3.** esparadrapo, curita
plaster *verb.* **1.** enyesar, enlucir **2.** embadurnar, untar
plastic *noun.* plástico
plastic *adj.* plástico, moldeable
plate *noun.* **1.** plato **2.** quemador, fuego **3.** vajilla **4.** placa **5.** lámina, grabado **6.** dentadura (postiza)
plateau *noun.* meseta, altiplano
platform *noun.* **1.** plataforma **2.** andén
plausible *adj.* **1.** plausible **2.** convincente
play *noun.* **1.** juego **2.** diversión **3.** obra, pieza dramática **4.** función, representación
play *verb.* **1.** jugar (a), mover **2.** representar, actuar **3.** ser representado **4.** tocar, interpretar **5.** dirigir
player *noun.* jugador
playground *noun.* patio de recreo
playwright *noun.* dramaturgo
plea *noun.* **1.** súplica, petición **2.** alegato, defensa
plead *verb.* **1.** declarar, alegar **2.** defender, hablar por alguien
—**plead with** suplicar
pleasant *adj.* agradable, amable, simpático
please *verb.* **1.** complacer, agradar **2.** querer, dar la gana
please *adv.* por favor
pleased *adj.* contento, satisfecho
pleasing *adj.* agradable
pleasure *noun.* placer
pledge *noun.* **1.** promesa **2.** empeño, prenda
pledge *verb.* **1.** prometer **2.** empeñar
plenty *adj.* suficiente
plenty *pron.* **1.** bastante, suficiente **2.** mucho
plight *noun.* apuro, situación grave
plot *noun.* **1.** complot **2.** trama, argumento **3.** terreno, solar
plot *verb.* **1.** maquinar, urdir **2.** trazar
plow *noun.* arado
plow *verb.* **1.** arar **2.** abrirse camino
plug *noun.* **1.** enchufe **2.** tapón
plug *verb.* tapar
—**plug in** enchufar

plump *adj.* regordete, rechoncho
—**plump for** optar por, decidirse por
plunge *noun.* zambullida, chapuzón
plunge *verb.* **1.** lanzarse, zambullirse **2.** caer, hundirse
plus, plus sign *noun.* (signo) más
plus *prep.* más
plus *adj.* positivo
pm, p.m., P.M. *abbr.* de la tarde/noche
pocket *noun.* **1.** bolsillo **2.** tronera **3.** bolsa
pocket *verb.* **1.** meterse/guardar en el bolsillo **2.** embolsar, quedarse con
poem *noun.* poema
poet *noun.* poeta
poetic *adj.* poético
poetry *noun.* poesía
point *noun.* **1.** punto **2.** punta **3.** cabo **4.** momento preciso **5.** cuestión **6.** finalidad, motivo **7.** cualidad
point *verb.* **1.** apuntar **2.** señalar, indicar **3.** rejuntar
pointed *adj.* puntiagudo
pointless *adj.* sin sentido, inútil
poised *adj.* **1.** equilibrado, ecuánime **2.** listo, preparado
poison *noun.* veneno
poison *verb.* envenenar
Poland *noun.* Polonia
polar *adj.* polar
pole *noun.* **1.** polo **2.** palo, poste
police *noun plural.* policía
police *verb.* vigilar, mantener el orden
police station *noun.* comisaría
policeman, policewoman *noun.* policía, agente de policía
policy *noun.* **1.** política **2.** póliza
polish *noun.* **1.** brillo, lustre **2.** cera, betún **3.** abrillantador
polish *verb.* **1.** lustrar, abrillantar, limpiar **2.** perfeccionar, mejorar
Polish *noun. adj.* polaco
polished *adj.* pulido
polite *adj.* educado
politely *adv.* educadamente
political *adj.* político
politically *adv.* políticamente
politically correct *adj.* políticamente correcto
politician *noun.* político
politics *noun.* política
poll *noun.* **1.** votación, elecciones **2.** índice de participación **3.** encuesta, sondeo
poll *verb.* obtener, recibir
pollute *verb.* contaminar
pollution *noun.* contaminación
polo *noun.* polo
polytechnic *noun.* politécnico
pond *noun.* estanque
ponder *verb.* ponderar, considerar
pony *noun.* poni, póney
pool *noun.* **1.** charca, alberca, piscina **2.** charco **3.** reserva **4.** fondo común
pool *verb.* juntar, poner en común
poor *adj.* **1.** pobre **2.** malo **3.** escaso
poorly *adj.* pachucho, indispuesto
poorly *adv.* mal
pop *noun.* pequeño estallido
pop *verb.* **1.** reventar, estallar **2.** saltar, salir disparado
pop *adj.* pop
Pope *noun.* Papa
popular *adj.* **1.** popular **2.** generalizado, extendido **3.** de moda
popularity *noun.* popularidad
population *noun.* población
porch *noun.* **1.** pórtico **2.** terraza, porche
pork *noun.* cerdo
port *noun.* **1.** puerto **2.** ciudad portuaria **3.** babor **4.** vino de Oporto
portable *adj.* portátil
porter *noun.* **1.** mozo de equipajes, maletero **2.** cargador
portfolio *noun.* **1.** carpeta **2.** cartera
portion *noun.* **1.** parte, porción **2.** ración
portrait *noun.* retrato
portray *verb.* **1.** retratar, pintar, describir **2.** representar
Portugal *noun.* Portugal
Portuguese *noun. adj.* portugués
pose *noun.* **1.** postura, pose **2.** afectación
pose *verb.* **1.** posar **2.** plantear, presentar
—**pose as** hacerse pasar por
position *noun.* **1.** posición **2.** postura **3.** situación **4.** puesto

position *verb.* colocar, situar
positive *noun.* positivo
positive *adj.* **1.** positivo **2.** constructivo **3.** seguro
positively *adv.* **1.** categóricamente **2.** positivamente **3.** con seguridad
possess *verb.* poseer, tener
possession *noun.* **1.** posesión **2.** tenencia
possibility *noun.* posibilidad
possible *adj.* posible
possibly *adv.* **1.** posiblemente **2.** quizás
post *noun.* **1.** correo **2.** poste **3.** empleo, cargo **4.** puesto
—**post office** oficina de correos
post *verb.* **1.** poner **2.** hacer público, anunciar **3.** destinar **4.** mandar por correo
postal *adj.* postal
postcard *noun.* postal
poster *noun.* póster, cartel
postpone *verb.* posponer, aplazar
posture *noun.* **1.** postura **2.** posición
pot *noun.* **1.** pote, cacerola, puchero **2.** tarro **3.** maceta, tiesto
pot *verb.* plantar en una maceta, plantar en un tiesto
potato *noun.* papa, patata
potent *adj.* potente
potential *noun. adj.* potencial
potentially *adv.* potencialmente
potter *noun.* alfarero; ceramista
pottery *noun.* **1.** cerámica, loza **2.** alfarería
pound *noun.* **1.** libra **2.** corral **3.** libra esterlina
pound *verb.* **1.** aporrear, golpear **2.** machacar, triturar
pour *verb.* **1.** verter, derramar, echar **2.** chorrear, manar **3.** servir **4.** llover a cántaros
poverty *noun.* pobreza
powder *noun.* **1.** polvo **2.** polvos **3.** pólvora
powder *verb.* empolvar
power *noun.* **1.** poder **2.** potencia, fuerza, poderío **3.** energía **4.** capacidad, facultad **5.** autoridad
power station *noun.* central eléctrica
powered *adj.* accionado, movido por
powerful *adj.* **1.** potente, poderoso **2.** convincente
PR *abbr.* relaciones públicas
practicable *adj.* practicable, factible
practical *adj.* práctico
practically *adv.* **1.** prácticamente, casi **2.** en la práctica
practice *noun.* **1.** práctica **2.** costumbre **3.** entrenamiento, ejercicio **4.** profesión **5.** clientela
practice *verb.* **1.** entrenarse, ejercitarse **2.** practicar, ejercer
practiced *adj.* experto
praise *noun.* elogio, alabanza
praise *verb.* **1.** elogiar **2.** alabar
pray *verb.* **1.** rezar, orar **2.** rogar
prayer *noun.* oración, rezo
preach *verb.* **1.** predicar **2.** sermonear, dar un sermón **3.** aconsejar
precaution *noun.* precaución
precede *verb.* preceder, anteceder
precedent *noun.* precedente
preceding *adj.* precedente, anterior
precious *adj.* precioso
precise *adj.* preciso, exacto
precisely *adv.* **1.** precisamente **2.** exactamente
precision *noun.* precisión
predator *noun.* depredador, predador
predecessor *noun.* **1.** predecesor **2.** antepasado, antecesor
predict *verb.* predecir, pronosticar
predictable *adj.* predecible, previsible
prediction *noun.* predicción, pronóstico
predominantly *adv.* predominantemente
prefer *verb.* preferir
preferable *adj.* preferible
preferably *adv.* preferiblemente
preference *noun.* preferencia
pregnancy *noun.* embarazo
pregnant *adj.* embarazada, encinta
prejudice *noun.* prejuicio
prejudice *verb.* **1.** predisponer, prevenir **2.** perjudicar
preliminary *adj.* preliminar
premature *adj.* prematuro
premier *noun.* primer ministro

premier *adj.* primero, principal
premises *noun plural.* local, establecimiento, propiedad
preoccupation *noun.* preocupación
preparation *noun.* **1.** preparación **2.** preparativo
prepare *verb.* **1.** preparar **2.** prepararse
prepared *adj.* preparado
prescribe *verb.* **1.** recetar **2.** prescribir
prescription *noun.* **1.** receta **2.** prescripción
presence *noun.* presencia
present *noun.* **1.** presente **2.** regalo
present *verb.* **1.** entregar, hacer entrega de **2.** presentar **3.** ofrecer
present *adj.* **1.** presente **2.** actual
presentation *noun.* presentación
presently *adv.* **1.** en breve, dentro de poco **2.** en este momento, actualmente
preservation *noun.* conservación
preserve *noun.* **1.** dominio, terreno **2.** coto, reserva **3.** confitura
preserve *verb.* **1.** proteger, guardar **2.** conservar
preside *verb.* presidir
presidency *noun.* presidencia
president *noun.* presidente
presidential *adj.* presidencial
press *noun.* **1.** apretón **2.** imprenta **3.** prensa
press *verb.* **1.** apretar, pulsar **2.** exprimir, estrujar **3.** prensar **4.** presionar **5.** apremiar, instar **6.** insistir **7.** planchar
press conference *noun.* conferencia de prensa
pressing *adj.* urgente, apremiante
pressure *noun.* presión
prestige *noun.* prestigio
presumably *adv.* se supone que, es de suponer
presume *verb.* **1.** presumir, suponer **2.** atreverse
presumption *noun.* presunción, suposición
pretend *verb.* **1.** fingir, simular **2.** pretender
pretty *adj.* **1.** bonito, lindo **2.** buen
pretty *adv.* bastante
prevail (against/over) *verb.* **1.** prevalecer, imponerse **2.** predominar
prevailing *adj.* **1.** predominante, imperante **2.** común
prevalence *noun.* **1.** predominio **2.** frecuencia
prevalent *adj.* prevaleciente, común
prevent *verb.* **1.** impedir **2.** evitar
prevention *noun.* prevención
preview *noun.* preestreno
previous *adj.* anterior, previo
previously *adv.* anteriormente, previamente
prey *noun.* presa
price *noun.* precio
price *verb.* **1.** poner/marcar el precio **2.** valorar
pride *noun.* **1.** orgullo, arrogancia **2.** manada
priest *noun.* **1.** cura **2.** sacerdote
priestess *noun.* sacerdotisa
primarily *adv.* principalmente, en primer lugar
primary *adj.* **1.** principal **2.** primario
prime *noun.* flor de la vida, plenitud
prime *verb.* **1.** preparar **2.** cebar
prime *adj.* **1.** principal **2.** primer, primero **3.** óptimo, perfecto
primitive *adj.* primitivo, rudimentario
prince *noun.* príncipe
princess *noun.* princesa
principal *noun.* **1.** director, rector **2.** capital
principal *adj.* principal
principally *adv.* principalmente
principle *noun.* principio
print *noun.* **1.** huella, marca **2.** copia **3.** grabado **4.** estampado **5.** letra
print *verb.* **1.** imprimir **2.** publicar, editar **3.** sacar una copia **4.** estampar **5.** escribir con letra de imprenta
printer *noun.* **1.** impresor **2.** impresora
printing *noun.* impresión, tipografía
prior *noun.* prior
prior *adj.* **1.** previo, anterior **2.** prioritario
priority *noun.* prioridad
prison *noun.* prisión, cárcel
prisoner *noun.* preso, recluso, prisionero

privacy *noun.* intimidad, privacidad
private *noun.* soldado raso
private *adj.* **1.** privado **2.** particular
privately *adv.* privadamente, en privado
privilege *noun.* privilegio
privileged *adj.* privilegiado
prize *noun.* premio
prize *verb.* apreciar, valorar
probability *noun.* probabilidad
probable *adj.* probable
probably *adv.* probablemente
probation *noun.* libertad provisional
probe *noun.* **1.** sonda **2.** investigación
probe *verb.* **1.** investigar **2.** explorar **3.** sondar
problem *noun.* problema
procedural *adj.* procesal
procedure *noun.* procedimiento
proceed *verb.* **1.** proseguir, continuar **2.** proceder, actuar **3.** empezar
proceedings *noun plural.* **1.** actas **2.** proceso
proceeds *noun plural.* ganancias
process *noun.* **1.** proceso **2.** procedimiento
process *verb.* **1.** procesar, tratar **2.** revelar
procession *noun.* desfile
proclaim *verb.* proclamar
produce *noun.* productos agrícolas
produce *verb.* **1.** producir **2.** sacar, presentar **3.** tener, dar a luz **4.** provocar **5.** fabricar **6.** escribir, componer **7.** poner en escena
producer *noun.* productor
product *noun.* producto
production *noun.* **1.** producción **2.** montaje, puesta en escena
productive *adj.* productivo
productivity *noun.* productividad
profession *noun.* **1.** profesión **2.** cuerpo **3.** declaración, afirmación
professional *noun.* profesional
professional *adj.* **1.** profesional **2.** muy bueno
professionally *adv.* profesionalmente, con profesionalidad
professor, Prof. *noun.* profesor universitario
profile *noun.* perfil
profit *noun.* **1.** beneficio, ganancia **2.** provecho
profit (by/from) *verb.* **1.** ganar, sacar ganancia **2.** aprovechar
profitable *adj.* **1.** lucrativo, rentable **2.** provechoso, ventajoso
profound *adj.* profundo
profoundly *adv.* profundamente
program *noun.* programa
program *verb.* programar
progress *noun.* progreso
progress *verb.* **1.** avanzar **2.** progresar, mejorar
progressive *adj.* progresivo
progressive (tense) *noun.* continuo
progressively *adv.* progresivamente
prohibit *verb.* prohibir
prohibition *noun.* prohibición
project *noun.* **1.** proyecto **2.** estudio, trabajo
project *verb.* **1.** proyectar, planear **2.** sobresalir **3.** lanzar
projection *noun.* proyección
prolonged *adj.* prolongado
prominence *noun.* prominencia, importancia
prominent *adj.* **1.** prominente **2.** saliente **3.** destacado, notable
promise *noun.* **1.** promesa **2.** futuro
promise *verb.* prometer
promising *adj.* prometedor
promote *verb.* **1.** promover, fomentar **2.** ascender **3.** promocionar
promoter *noun.* promotor
promotion *noun.* **1.** promoción **2.** ascenso
prompt *verb.* **1.** mover, incitar, provocar **2.** apuntar
prompt *adj.* **1.** pronto, inmediato **2.** puntual
promptly *adv.* **1.** con prontitud, inmediatamente **2.** puntualmente
prone *adj.* postrado
—**prone to** propenso a
pronounce *verb.* pronunciar
pronounced *adj.* pronunciado
pronunciation *noun.* pronunciación
proof *noun.* prueba

prop *noun.* puntal
prop *verb.* apoyar
propaganda *noun.* propaganda
proper *adj.* **1.** apropiado, adecuado **2.** correcto
proper name *noun.* nombre propio
properly *adv.* **1.** apropiadamente, adecuadamente **2.** correctamente
property *noun.* **1.** propiedad **2.** accesorio
proportion *noun.* proporción
proportional *adj.* proporcional
proposal *noun.* **1.** propuesta **2.** proposición
propose *verb.* **1.** proponer **2.** presentar **3.** proponer matrimonio, pedir la mano
proposition *noun.* proposición
proposition *verb.* hacer proposiciones deshonestas
proprietor *noun.* propietario
pros *noun.* pro
—**pros and cons** pros y contras
prose *noun.* prosa
prosecute *verb.* procesar, enjuiciar
prosecution *noun.* **1.** proceso, juicio **2.** acusación
prospect *noun.* **1.** porvenir, futuro **2.** perspectiva
prospect *verb.* prospectar, explorar
prosperity *noun.* prosperidad
prosperous *adj.* próspero
prostitute *noun.* prostituta
protect *verb.* proteger, amparar
protected *adj.* protegido
protection *noun.* protección
protective *adj.* protector, de protección
protein *noun.* proteína
protest *noun.* **1.** protesta, queja **2.** manifestación
protest *verb.* protestar
Protestant *noun. adj.* protestante
protester *noun.* manifestante
proud *adj.* **1.** orgulloso, soberbio **2.** magnífico, espléndido
proudly *adv.* orgullosamente
prove *verb.* **1.** probar **2.** resultar
proven *adj.* probado
provide *verb.* **1.** proporcionar, **2.** proveer, suministrar, facilitar
provided, providing *conj.* siempre que, a condición de que
province *noun.* provincia
provincial *adj.* provincial
provision *noun.* **1.** provisión, abastecimiento **2.** cláusula, disposición, estipulación **3.** condición
provision *verb.* aprovisionar, abastecer
provisional *adj.* provisional
provoke *verb.* provocar
proximity *noun.* proximidad
prudent *adj.* prudente
prune *noun.* ciruela pasa
prune *verb.* podar
psychiatric *adj.* psiquiátrico
psychiatrist *noun.* psiquiatra
psychological *adj.* psicológico
psychologist *noun.* psicólogo
psychology *noun.* psicología
public *adj.* público
—**public relations** relaciones públicas
publication *noun.* publicación
publicity *noun.* publicidad
publicize *verb.* **1.** publicar **2.** anunciar
publicly *adv.* públicamente
publish *verb.* **1.** publicar **2.** anunciar, hacer público
publisher *noun.* **1.** editor **2.** editorial
publishing *noun.* edición
Puerto Rico *noun.* Puerto Rico
Puerto Rican *noun. adj.* puertorriqueño
pudding *noun.* budín,
pull *noun.* **1.** tirón, jalón **2.** calada, chupada **3.** sorbo **4.** atracción **5.** enchufe
pull *verb.* **1.** tirar, jalar, arrastrar **2.** remar **3.** sacar, arrancar
—**pull at/on** chupar
pulse *noun.* pulso
pulse *verb.* latir, palpitar
pump *noun.* bomba
pump *verb.* **1.** bombear **2.** sonsacar, sacar información de alguien
punch *noun.* **1.** perforadora, taladro **2.** ponche **3.** puñetazo **4.** fuerza, garra
—**Punch** Polichinela
punch *verb.* **1.** perforar, taladrar **2.** dar un puñetazo
punish *verb.* castigar
punishment *noun.* **1.** castigo **2.** pena

pup, puppy *noun.* cachorro
pupil *noun.* **1.** alumno **2.** pupila
purchase *noun.* compra, adquisición
purchase *verb.* comprar, adquirir
purchaser *noun.* comprador
pure *adj.* puro
purely *adv.* puramente
purity *noun.* pureza
purple *noun. adj.* púrpura, morado
purpose *noun.* **1.** propósito, fin **2.** función, uso, utilidad **3.** determinación
purse *noun.* **1.** monedero **2.** bolso
purse *verb.* fruncir
pursue *verb.* **1.** perseguir **2.** dedicarse a **3.** seguir
pursuit *noun.* **1.** persecución **2.** desempeño, ocupación
push *noun.* **1.** empujón **2.** empuje, dinamismo, ímpetu
push *verb.* **1.** empujar **2.** apretar, pulsar **3.** promover **4.** pasar, traficar
put *verb.* **1.** poner **2.** colocar **3.** presentar **4.** expresar, exponer **5.** escribir
—put aside **1.** dejar a un lado **2.** omitir, pasar por alto
—put down **1.** aplastar, suprimir **2.** atribuir
—put in **1.** introducir **2.** dedicar **3.** presentar
—put off **1.** desechar **2.** diferir, aplazar
—put on **1.** ponerse **2.** encender, prender **3.** afectar, adoptar
—put out **1.** tender la mano **2.** echar **3.** apagar **4.** emitir, lanzar **5.** molestarse
—put up with transigir
putt *verb.* patear
puzzle *noun.* **1.** enigma **2.** rompecabezas
puzzle *verb.* **1.** dejar perplejo, confundir **2.** devanarse los sesos, romperse la cabeza
pyramid *noun.* pirámide

Q

qualification *noun.* **1.** aptitud, capacidad **2.** diploma, título **3.** reserva, salvedad
qualified *adj.* cualificado, capacitado
qualify *verb.* **1.** capacitar, reunir las condiciones **2.** calificar
—qualify as obtener el título, obtener la licencia para ejercer una profesión
—qualify for clasificarse
qualifying *adj.* eliminatorio
quality *noun.* **1.** calidad **2.** cualidad
quantity *noun.* cantidad
quarrel *noun.* pelea, riña
quarrel *verb.* pelearse, reñir
quarry *noun.* **1.** cantera **2.** presa, víctima
quarry *verb.* sacar, extraer
quarter *noun.* **1.** cuarto **2.** veinticinco centavos **3.** barrio **4.** gracia **5.** trimestre
—from all quarters de todas partes
quarter *verb.* **1.** dividir en cuatro, cuartear **2.** acuartelar, alojar
quarter-final(s) *noun.* cuartos de final
quarterly *noun.* publicación trimestral
quarterly *adj.* trimestral
quarterly *adv.* trimestralmente
quarters *noun plural.* **1.** dependencias **2.** cuartel
quartet *noun.* cuarteto
queen *noun.* **1.** reina **2.** dama **3.** marica
query *noun.* **1.** pregunta **2.** signo de interrogación
query *verb.* **1.** poner en duda, cuestionar **2.** preguntar
quest *noun.* busca, búsqueda
question *noun.* **1.** pregunta **2.** cuestión **3.** problema **4.** duda **5.** posibilidad
question *verb.* **1.** hacer preguntas, interrogar **2.** cuestionar, poner en duda
questionable *adj.* **1.** cuestionable, discutible **2.** dudoso
questionnaire *noun.* cuestionario
queue *noun.* fila

queue *verb.* hacer cola
quick *adj.* **1.** rápido **2.** listo, agudo **3.** ágil
quick *adv.* de prisa, rápido, rápidamente
quickly *adv.* deprisa, rápidamente
quiet *noun.* tranquilidad, calma
quiet *adj.* **1.** tranquilo **2.** silencioso **3.** suave **4.** callado **5.** relajado, calmado **6.** discreto
quiet (down) *verb.* **1.** tranquilizar, calmar **2.** tranquilizarse, calmarse
quietly *adv.* **1.** tranquilamente **2.** silenciosamente
quit *verb.* abandonar, dejar
quite *interj.* pues sí, así es
quite *adv.* **1.** totalmente **2.** bastante
quiz *noun.* **1.** concurso **2.** prueba
quota *noun.* cuota
quotation *noun.* **1.** cotización **2.** cita **3.** citación
quote *verb.* **1.** cotizar, estimar **2.** citar

R

rabbit *noun.* conejo
race *noun.* carrera
race *noun.* raza
race *verb.* **1.** correr **2.** competir en una carrera **3.** hacer una carrera
racial *adj.* racial
racism *noun.* racismo
racist *noun. adj.* racista
rack *noun.* anaquel
radar *noun.* radar
radiation *noun.* radiación
radiator *noun.* radiador
radical *noun.* radical
radical *adj.* radical, fundamental
radically *adv.* radicalmente
radio *noun.* radio
radio *verb.* **1.** radiar **2.** comunicarse por radio
radioactive *adj.* radioactivo
radius *noun.* radio
raffle *noun.* rifa
raffle *verb.* rifar
rag *noun.* trapo
rage *noun.* rabia, ira, furia
rage *verb.* **1.** estar furioso **2.** enfurecerse, rabiar **3.** bramar, embravecerse **4.** arrasar, hacer estragos
ragged *adj.* **1.** harapiento, andrajoso **2.** roto, deshilachado **3.** irregular, accidentado
raid *noun.* **1.** incursión, ataque **2.** redada
raid *verb.* **1.** asaltar, atracar **2.** invadir **3.** hacer una redada
rail *noun.* **1.** barra, pasamanos, riel **2.** carril, raíl
rail (in/off) *verb.* cercar
railroad *noun.* **1.** ferrocarril **2.** vía férrea
rain *noun.* lluvia
rain *verb.* llover
rainbow *noun.* arco iris
raise *noun.* aumento
raise *verb.* **1.** levantar **2.** subir, aumentar **3.** cultivar **4.** criar **5.** plantear, sacar **6.** provocar, suscitar **7.** recaudar, movilizar, reunir **8.** reclutar **9.** erigir
rally *noun.* **1.** reunión, mitin **2.** rally **3.** recuperación **4.** peloteo
rally *verb.* **1.** reunir **2.** concentrar **3.** recuperarse
ram *noun.* **1.** carnero **2.** ariete, espolón, pisón
ram *verb.* **1.** apisonar, apretar **2.** chocar, embestir
random *adj.* aleatorio, al azar
range *noun.* **1.** gama, variedad, surtido **2.** alcance, autonomía **3.** escala, rango **4.** cadena, cordillera **5.** dehesa, terreno de pasto **6.** campo de tiro **7.** cocina
range *verb.* **1.** alinear **2.** ordenar, clasificar **3.** variar, fluctuar **4.** extenderse, cubrir
rank *noun.* **1.** fila, hilera **2.** rango, categoría **3.** clase
rank *verb.* **1.** clasificar **2.** ocupar un puesto

rank *adj.* **1.** absoluto, total **2.** fétido
rap *noun.* golpe seco
rap *verb.* dar un golpe seco
rape *noun.* violación
rape *verb.* violar
rapid *adj.* rápido
rapidly *adv.* rápidamente
rare *adj.* **1.** raro, poco común **2.** poco hecho
rarely *adv.* raramente
rash *noun.* erupción, sarpullido
rash *adj.* imprudente
rat *noun.* **1.** rata **2.** canalla
rat *verb.* **1.** rajarse, volverse atrás **2.** chivarse
rate *noun.* **1.** tasa, índice **2.** porcentaje **3.** velocidad, ritmo **4.** tarifa
rate *verb.* estimar, valorar, considerar
rather *adv.* **1.** bastante **2.** algo, un poco **3.** antes que, en lugar de **4.** más bien, para ser más precisos
ratify *verb.* ratificar
rating *noun.* **1.** clasificación, posición **2.** índice de audiencia
ratio *noun.* proporción
rational *adj.* racional
rationality *noun.* racionalidad
rattle *noun.* **1.** ruido, golpeteo, tintineo **2.** sonajero
rattle *verb.* **1.** hacer ruido, sonar **2.** desconcertar, confundir
rave *verb.* **1.** delirar **2.** hablar con entusiasmo
raw *adj.* **1.** crudo **2.** bruto, sin refinar, en rama **3.** en carne viva **4.** verde, inexperto
ray *noun.* **1.** rayo **2.** brizna, resquicio
Rd *abbr.* **1.** calle **2.** carretera
reach *noun.* alcance
reach *verb.* **1.** llegar (a) **2.** alcanzar **3.** alargar la mano **4.** contactar **5.** extenderse
react *verb.* reaccionar
reaction *noun.* reacción
reactor *noun.* reactor
read *noun.* lectura
read *verb.* **1.** leer **2.** adivinar, descifrar **3.** decir **4.** estar escrito **5.** indicar, marcar
reader *noun.* **1.** lector **2.** libro de lectura
readily *adv.* **1.** de buena gana **2.** fácilmente
readiness *noun.* **1.** prontitud **2.** buena disposición
reading *noun.* **1.** lectura **2.** interpretación
ready *adj.* **1.** preparado, listo **2.** dispuesto **3.** pronto **4.** a punto de
real *adj.* **1.** verdadero, real **2.** auténtico
real *adv.* muy
real estate *noun.* bienes raíces
realism *noun.* realismo
realistic *adj.* realista
reality *noun.* realidad
realization *noun.* **1.** comprensión **2.** realización
realize *verb.* **1.** comprender, darse cuenta **2.** llevar a cabo **3.** reportar
really *interj.* ¿de verdad?
really *adv.* **1.** en realidad **2.** realmente, muy
realm *noun.* **1.** reino **2.** dominio, sector
rear *noun.* **1.** parte trasera **2.** trasero
rear *verb.* **1.** criar **2.** encabritarse **3.** levantar, alzar
rear *adj.* trasero, de detrás
reason *noun.* razón
reason *verb.* razonar
reasonable *adj.* **1.** razonable **2.** sensato, juicioso
reasonably *adv.* razonablemente
reasoning *noun.* razonamiento
reassurance *noun.* tranquilidad, consuelo
reassure *verb.* tranquilizar
reassuring *adj.* tranquilizador
rebel *noun.* rebelde
rebel *verb.* rebelarse
rebellion *noun.* rebelión
recall *noun.* **1.** retirada, destitución **2.** memoria, recuerdo
recall *verb.* **1.** hacer volver **2.** recordar
receipt *noun.* **1.** recibo **2.** recepción
receive *verb.* recibir
receiver *noun.* **1.** auricular **2.** receptor **3.** síndico (de quiebras)
recent *adj.* reciente
recently *adv.* recientemente
reception *noun.* **1.** recepción **2.** acogida

recession *noun.* recesión
recipe *noun.* receta
recipient *noun.* receptor
reckless *adj.* temerario
reckon *verb.* **1.** calcular **2.** considerar **3.** pensar, creer
recognition *noun.* reconocimiento
recognize *verb.* reconocer
recommend *verb.* recomendar
recommendation *noun.* recomendación
reconcile *verb.* **1.** reconciliar **2.** conciliar **3.** resignarse
reconciliation *noun.* reconciliación
reconstruction *noun.* reconstrucción
record *noun.* **1.** documento, constancia (escrita) **2.** registro **3.** datos **4.** disco **5.** récord, plusmarca **6.** historial, antecedentes
record *verb.* **1.** registrar **2.** dejar constancia escrita **3.** grabar **4.** consignar
recorder *noun.* **1.** flauta **2.** grabadora, magnetófono
recording *noun.* grabación
recover *verb.* **1.** recuperar **2.** recuperarse
recovery *noun.* recuperación
recreation *noun.* recreación
recreational *adj.* recreativo
recruit *noun.* **1.** recluta **2.** nuevo miembro
recruit *verb.* **1.** reclutar **2.** contratar
recruitment *noun.* **1.** reclutamiento **2.** contratación
rectangular *adj.* rectangular
recurrence *noun.* recurrencia
recurrent *adj.* recurrente
recycle *verb.* reciclar
red *noun. adj.* **1.** rojo **2.** tinto **3.** comunista
redemption *noun.* redención
reduce *verb.* **1.** reducir **2.** rebajar **3.** disminuir **4.** adelgazar, perder peso
reduction *noun.* **1.** reducción **2.** rebaja
reed *noun.* **1.** junco, caña **2.** lengüeta
reef *noun.* arrecife
reel *noun.* **1.** carrete, bobina **2.** baile escocés
reel *verb.* **1.** tambalear **2.** tambalearse
re-elect *verb.* reelegir
refer (to) *verb.* **1.** referirse (a) **2.** enviar, remitir **3.** consultar
referee *noun.* árbitro
referee *verb.* arbitrar
reference *noun.* **1.** referencia **2.** consulta
referendum *noun.* referéndum
refined *adj.* refinado
reflect *verb.* **1.** reflejar **2.** reflexionar
reflecting *adj.* reflector
reflection *noun.* **1.** reflejo **2.** reflexión
reform *noun.* reforma
reform *verb.* **1.** reformar **2.** reformarse
reformed *adj.* reformado
reformer *noun.* reformador
refreshing *adj.* **1.** refrescante **2.** reconfortante
refrigerator *noun.* frigorífico, refrigeradora
refuge *noun.* refugio
refugee *noun.* refugiado
refund *noun.* reembolso
refund *verb.* reembolsar
refusal *noun.* negativa
refuse *noun.* basura, desperdicios
refuse *verb.* **1.** negarse **2.** rechazar **3.** negar, denegar
regain *verb.* **1.** recobrar, recuperar **2.** volver a alcanzar
regard *noun.* **1.** consideración **2.** respeto **3.** estima
regard (as) *verb.* **1.** considerar **2.** estimar **3.** mirar **4.** prestar atención, tener en cuenta
regarding *prep.* con respecto a, en cuanto a
regardless *adj. adv.* **1.** a pesar de **2.** sin hacer caso de
regards *noun plural.* saludos, recuerdos
regime, régime *noun.* régimen
regiment *noun.* regimiento
regiment *verb.* disciplinar, reglamentar
region *noun.* región
regional *adj.* regional
register *noun.* **1.** registro **2.** lista
register *verb.* **1.** registrar **2.** registrarse, inscribirse, matricularse **3.** certificar **4.** marcar
registered *adj.* certificado

registrar *noun.* registrador
registry *noun.* registro
regret *noun.* **1.** pesar **2.** remordimiento
regret *verb.* **1.** lamentar **2.** arrepentirse (de)
regular *noun.* **1.** soldado profesional **2.** habitual
regular *adj.* **1.** regular **2.** habitual **3.** normal, común **4.** frecuente **5.** profesional
regularly *adv.* regularmente
regulate *verb.* regular
regulation *noun.* **1.** regla **2.** regulación
regulator *noun.* regulador
rehabilitate *verb.* rehabilitar
rehabilitation *noun.* rehabilitación
rehearsal *noun.* ensayo
reign *noun.* reinado
reign *verb.* reinar
rein *noun.* rienda
reinforce *verb.* reforzar
reject *noun.* artículo defectuoso
reject *verb.* rechazar
rejection *noun.* rechazo
relate *verb.* **1.** relatar **2.** relacionar, asociar —**relate to** relacionarse con
related *adj.* **1.** emparentado **2.** relacionado
relation *noun.* **1.** relación **2.** pariente
relationship *noun.* **1.** relación **2.** parentesco
relative *noun.* pariente
relative *adj.* relativo
relatively *adv.* relativamente
relax *verb.* **1.** relajar, suavizar **2.** relajarse
relaxation *noun.* **1.** relajación **2.** diversión
relay *noun.* retransmisión
relay *verb.* retransmitir
release *noun.* **1.** liberación, puesta en libertad **2.** lanzamiento, estreno **3.** anuncio, comunicado
release *verb.* **1.** liberar **2.** soltar **3.** hacer público, dar a conocer **4.** sacar **5.** estrenar
relegate *verb.* relegar
relegation *noun.* relegación
relentless *adj.* implacable
relevance *noun.* **1.** pertinencia **2.** relevancia
relevant *adj.* **1.** pertinente **2.** relevante
reliability *noun.* fiabilidad
reliable *adj.* fiable, de confianza
reliance *noun.* dependencia
relief *noun.* **1.** alivio **2.** auxilio, socorro **3.** beneficencia **4.** suplente **5.** liberación **6.** relieve
relieve *verb.* **1.** aliviar **2.** relevar, sustituir **3.** destituir **4.** librar **5.** socorrer, auxiliar
religion *noun.* religión
religious *adj.* religioso
relish *noun.* **1.** placer, gusto, deleite **2.** condimento
relish *verb.* saborear
reluctance *noun.* renuencia
reluctant *adj.* renuente, reacio
reluctantly *adv.* de mala gana
remain *verb.* **1.** quedar **2.** quedarse **3.** permanecer, continuar
remainder *noun.* resto
remains *noun plural.* sobras, restos
remark *noun.* observación, comentario
remark *verb.* observar, comentar, hacer comentarios
remarkable *adj.* **1.** notable **2.** singular
remarkably *adv.* **1.** notablemente **2.** singularmente
remedy *noun.* remedio
remedy *verb.* remediar
remember *verb.* **1.** recordar **2.** acordarse de
remind *verb.* **1.** recordar a **2.** recordar algo a alguien
reminder *noun.* recordatorio
remote *adj.* **1.** remoto **2.** lejano
removal *noun.* extirpación, eliminación
remove *verb.* **1.** quitar, llevarse **2.** quitarse
remuneration *noun.* remuneración
render *verb.* **1.** dejar, volver **2.** prestar, dar **3.** interpretar
renew *verb.* renovar
renewal *noun.* renovación
renowned *adj.* renombrado, famoso
rent *noun.* **1.** alquiler **2.** rasgadura
rent *verb.* alquilar
rental *noun.* alquiler
reorganization *noun.* reorganización
reorganize *verb.* reorganizar

repair *noun.* **1.** reparación, arreglo **2.** estado
repair *verb.* reparar, arreglar
repay *verb.* devolver, pagar, liquidar
repayment *noun.* reembolso
repeat *noun.* **1.** repetición **2.** reposición
repeat *verb.* **1.** repetir **2.** recitar
repeated *adj.* repetido
repeatedly *adv.* repetidamente
repetition *noun.* repetición
replace *verb.* **1.** sustituir, reponer **2.** volver a colocar
replacement *noun.* sustituto
replay *noun.* partido de desempate
reply *noun.* respuesta
reply *verb.* responder
report *noun.* **1.** informe **2.** rumor **3.** detonación
report *verb.* **1.** relatar, informar, dar parte de **2.** acusar, denunciar **3.** presentar informe **4.** presentarse, personarse
reporter *noun.* reportero
represent *verb.* representar
representation *noun.* representación
representative *noun.* representante
representative *adj.* representativo
repression *noun.* represión
reproduce *verb.* **1.** reproducir **2.** reproducirse
reproduction *noun.* reproducción
reproductive *adj.* reproductor
republic *noun.* república
republican *adj.* republicano
reputation *noun.* reputación
request *noun.* petición, solicitud
request *verb.* pedir
require *verb.* **1.** necesitar, precisar **2.** exigir
requirement *noun.* **1.** necesidad **2.** requisito
rescue *noun.* rescate
rescue *verb.* rescatar, socorrer
research *noun.* investigación
research *verb.* investigar
researcher *noun.* investigador
resemblance *noun.* semejanza, parecido
resemble *verb.* parecerse (a)
resent *verb.* ofenderse, tomarse a mal
resentment *noun.* resentimiento
reservation *noun.* reserva
reserve *noun.* reserva
reserve *verb.* reservar
reserved *adj.* reservado
reservoir *noun.* embalse, depósito, represa
residence *noun.* **1.** residencia **2.** estancia
resident *noun.* habitante
resident *adj.* **1.** residente **2.** interno, que duerme en casa
residential *adj.* **1.** residencial **2.** interno
residual *adj.* residual
residue *noun.* residuo
resign *verb.* dimitir
—**resign to** resignarse
resignation *noun.* **1.** dimisión **2.** resignación
resigned *adj.* resignado
resist *verb.* **1.** resistir **2.** resistirse
resistance *noun.* resistencia
resistant *adj.* resistente
resolution *noun.* **1.** resolución **2.** propósito **3.** definición
resolve *noun.* resolución
resolve *verb.* resolver
resolved *adj.* resuelto, decidido
resort *noun.* centro turístico, lugar de veraneo
resort (to) *verb.* recurrir (a)
resource *noun.* **1.** recurso **2.** inventiva, ideas
respect *noun.* **1.** respeto **2.** aspecto
respect *verb.* **1.** respetar **2.** acatar
respectable *adj.* **1.** respetable **2.** adecuado, decente **3.** considerable
respective *adj.* respectivo
respectively *adv.* respectivamente
respects *noun plural.* saludos, recuerdos
respiratory *adj.* respiratorio
respond (to) *verb.* **1.** responder **2.** reaccionar
response *noun.* **1.** respuesta **2.** reacción **3.** responsorio
responsibility *noun.* responsabilidad
responsible *adj.* **1.** responsable **2.** de responsabilidad

responsive *adj.* sensible
rest *noun.* **1.** descanso **2.** reposo **3.** apoyo, soporte **4.** resto
rest *verb.* **1.** descansar **2.** reposar **3.** apoyar, apoyarse **4.** relajarse, estar tranquilo **5.** depender **6.** basarse
restaurant *noun.* restaurante
restless *adj.* inquieto, agitado
restoration *noun.* restauración
restore *verb.* **1.** restaurar **2.** restablecer 3. devolver
restrain *verb.* **1.** sujetar **2.** refrenar
restrained *adj.* moderado, comedido, refrenado
restrict *verb.* **1.** restringir **2.** limitar
restricted *adj.* **1.** restringido, limitado 2. vedado, prohibido
restriction *noun.* restricción, limitación
restrictive *adj.* restrictivo
result *noun.* resultado
result *verb.* resultar
—**result in** acabar en
resume *verb.* reanudar
resurrection *noun.* resurrección
retail *verb.* vender al por menor
retail *adj.* al por menor
retailer *noun.* detallista, comerciante al por menor
retain *verb.* **1.** retener **2.** conservar
retaliate *verb.* desquitarse, tomar represalias
retention *noun.* retención
retire *verb.* **1.** retirarse **2.** jubilarse
retired *adj.* **1.** retirado **2.** jubilado
retirement *noun.* **1.** retiro **2.** jubilación
retiring *adj.* **1.** saliente **2.** retraído, reservado
retort *noun.* réplica
retort *verb.* replicar
retreat *noun.* **1.** retirada **2.** retiro
retreat *verb.* retirarse
retrieval *noun.* recuperación
retrieve *verb.* **1.** recuperar, recobrar **2.** reparar, subsanar
return *noun.* **1.** vuelta, regreso **2.** reaparición **3.** devolución **4.** ganancia, rendimiento
return *verb.* **1.** volver, regresar **2.** devolver **3.** reaparecer **4.** fallar, declarar
reunion *noun.* reunión
rev (up) *verb.* acelerar, girar
reveal *verb.* **1.** revelar **2.** poner de manifiesto
revealing *adj.* revelador
revelation *noun.* revelación
revenge *noun.* venganza
revenge (on) *verb.* vengarse (de)
revenue *noun.* ingresos
reverend *noun.* reverendo
reversal *noun.* **1.** inversión **2.** revocación
reverse *noun.* **1.** contrario **2.** revés **3.** marcha atrás **4.** reverso, dorso
reverse *verb.* **1.** invertir, poner del revés **2.** cambiar **3.** dar marcha atrás **4.** revocar
reverse *adj.* **1.** contrario **2.** inverso **3.** marcha atrás
revert *verb.* volver
review *noun.* **1.** examen, análisis **2.** crítica **3.** revista **4.** revisión, repaso
review *verb.* **1.** examinar, analizar **2.** hacer una crítica **3.** revisar, repasar
revise *verb.* revisar
revision *noun.* revisión
revival *noun.* **1.** renacimiento, recuperación, vuelta **2.** reestreno, reposición **3.** reanimación
revive *verb.* **1.** recuperar, resurgir **2.** reponer **3.** reanimar
revolt *noun.* rebelión
revolt *verb.* **1.** rebelarse, sublevarse **2.** repugnar, dar asco
revolution *noun.* **1.** revolución **2.** vuelta
revolutionary *noun. adj.* revolucionario
reward *noun.* recompensa
reward *verb.* recompensar
rewarding *adj.* gratificante
rhythm *noun.* ritmo
rhythmic, rhythmical *adj.* rítmico
rib *noun.* **1.** costilla **2.** cuaderna **3.** nervadura
ribbon *noun.* cinta
rice *noun.* arroz
rich *adj.* **1.** rico **2.** abundante **3.** fértil **4.** exquisito, suculento **5.** suntuoso, lujoso
rid (of) *verb.* librar (de)

—**get rid of** librarse de
ride *noun.* **1.** paseo, vuelta **2.** viaje
ride *verb.* **1.** montar (a/en) **2.** recorrer **3.** montar a caballo
rider *noun.* **1.** jinete **2.** ciclista, motorista **3.** viajero, pasajero
ridge *noun.* **1.** cresta **2.** cadena **3.** caballete
ridiculous *adj.* ridículo
rifle *noun.* rifle
rifle *verb.* **1.** rebuscar, revolver **2.** desvalijar
rig *noun.* **1.** torre de perforación **2.** plataforma petrolífera **3.** aparejos
rig *verb.* aparejar
right *interj.* de acuerdo, bien
right *noun.* **1.** derecho **2.** bien **3.** razón, justicia **4.** derecha
right *verb.* **1.** enderezar **2.** corregir
right *adj.* **1.** derecho **2.** correcto **3.** bien **4.** verdadero **5.** adecuado, apropiado **6.** justo **7.** recto
right *adv.* **1.** exactamente **2.** inmediatamente **3.** justo **4.** totalmente, completamente **5.** a la derecha **6.** bien, correctamente
right-hand *adj.* **1.** derecho **2.** a la derecha, a mano derecha
rightly *adv.* **1.** justificadamente **2.** debidamente **3.** con razón
rights *noun plural.* derechos
rigid *adj.* **1.** rígido **2.** estricto, severo
rigorous *adj.* riguroso
rim *noun.* **1.** llanta **2.** borde, canto
ring *noun.* **1.** anillo **2.** aro **3.** argolla **4.** círculo **5.** ring, cuadrilátero **6.** red, banda **7.** toque **8.** llamada de teléfono
ring *verb.* **1.** rodear, cercar **2.** anillar **3.** sonar **4.** llamar **5.** tintinear
—**ring up** llamar por teléfono
riot *noun.* disturbio, motín
riot *verb.* amotinarse
rip *noun.* rasgadura, desgarro
rip *verb.* rasgar, desgarrar
ripe *adj.* maduro
rise *noun.* **1.** ascenso, subida **2.** aumento
rise *verb.* **1.** subir **2.** aumentar **3.** elevarse **4.** levantarse **5.** sublevarse, rebelarse **6.** ascender **7.** nacer **8.** alzarse, erigirse **9.** resucitar
rising *noun.* **1.** sublevación, rebelión **2.** salida
rising *adj.* **1.** en aumento, en alza **2.** naciente
risk *noun.* riesgo
risk *verb.* **1.** arriesgar **2.** arriesgarse
risky *adv.* arriesgado
rite *noun.* rito
ritual *noun. adj.* ritual
rival *noun.* rival
rival *verb.* rivalizar
rivalry *noun.* rivalidad
river *noun.* río
road *noun.* **1.** camino **2.** carretera **3.** calle
roar *noun.* **1.** rugido, bramido **2.** grito **3.** carcajada **4.** estruendo, fragor
roar *verb.* **1.** rugir, bramar **2.** decir a gritos **3.** reírse a carcajadas **4.** retumbar
roast *noun. adj.* asado
roast *verb.* **1.** asar **2.** tostar
rob *verb.* robar
—**rob of** quitar
robbery *noun.* robo
robin *noun.* petirrojo
robust *adj.* robusto
rock *noun.* **1.** roca **2.** peñasco **3.** rock
rock *verb.* **1.** acunar, mecer **2.** balancearse **3.** sacudir
rocket *noun.* cohete
rocket *verb.* dispararse
rocky *adj.* **1.** inestable, poco firme **2.** rocoso
rod *noun.* vara, barra
role *noun.* papel
roll *noun.* **1.** rollo, fajo **2.** lista **3.** panecillo **4.** revolcón **5.** balanceo **6.** retumbo, fragor **7.** michelín **8.** redoble
roll *verb.* **1.** (hacer) rodar **2.** enrollar, liar **3.** dar(se) la vuelta **4.** moldear **5.** estirar **6.** balancearse, mecerse **7.** retumbar **8.** redoblar **9.** ondular, fluir **10.** pasar, sucederse
roller *noun.* **1.** rodillo **2.** rulo **3.** ola grande
rolling *adj.* ondulante
Roman *noun. adj.* romano

Roman Catholic *noun.* católico romano
romance *noun.* **1.** romance **2.** amorío, idilio **3.** novela sentimental
Romania *noun.* Rumania
Romanian *noun. adj.* rumano
romantic *adj.* romántico
roof *noun.* techo
roof *verb.* techar
room *noun.* **1.** habitación, cuarto, pieza **2.** espacio, sitio
—**rooms** alojamiento, habitaciones de alquiler
root *noun.* **1.** raíz **2.** origen
root *verb.* **1.** arraigarse, echar raíces **2.** escarbar, revolver
rope *noun.* cuerda, soga
rope *verb.* amarrar, atar
rose *noun.* rosa
rot *noun.* **1.** putrefacción, podredumbre **2.** tonterías, bobadas
rot *verb.* pudrir, corromper, descomponer
rotate *verb.* **1.** rotar, girar **2.** hacer girar
rotation *noun.* rotación
rotor *noun.* rotor
rotten *adj.* **1.** podrido **2.** malo, vil
rough *noun.* **1.** bruto, gamberro **2.** rough, zona de matojos (golf)
rough *adj.* **1.** áspero, basto **2.** accidentado **3.** rudo, bruto, violento **4.** turbulento, embravecido **5.** aproximado, esbozado, preliminar
roughly *adv.* **1.** aproximadamente **2.** bruscamente, toscamente
round *noun.* **1.** círculo **2.** ronda **3.** recorrido **4.** salva, tiro **5.** cartucho **6.** vuelta, asalto **7.** canon
round *verb.* girar, virar
round *prep.* **1.** alrededor de, en torno a **2.** por
round *adj.* redondo
round *adv.* **1.** en sentido contrario **2.** en círculo **3.** de persona en persona **4.** de un sitio a otro, por ahí **5.** de circunferencia **6.** a casa
roundabout *adj.* indirecto
rounded *adj.* redondeado, curvado
route *noun.* camino, itinerario
route *verb.* encaminar
routine *noun.* rutina
routine *adj.* rutinario, de rutina, habitual
rover *noun.* vagabundo
row *noun.* **1.** bronca, pelea **2.** barullo, escándalo **3.** hilera, fila **4.** paseo en bote de remos
row *verb.* remar
royal *adj.* **1.** real **2.** espléndido, magnífico, suntuoso
royalty *noun.* **1.** derechos de autor **2.** realeza, miembro de la familia real
rub *noun.* friega
rub *verb.* restregar, frotar
rubber *noun. adj.* **1.** caucho **2.** goma **3.** condón
rubbish *noun.* **1.** basura, desperdicios **2.** tonterías, chorradas
ruble *noun.* rublo
rude *adj.* **1.** grosero, maleducado **2.** indecente
rug *noun.* **1.** tapete, alfombrilla **2.** manta de viaje
rugby *noun.* rugby
ruin *noun.* **1.** ruina **2.** perdición
ruin *verb.* **1.** arruinar **2.** estropear
ruined *adj.* **1.** en ruinas **2.** destrozado
rule *noun.* **1.** gobierno **2.** norma, reglamento **3.** regla
rule *verb.* **1.** reinar, gobernar **2.** decidir, fallar **3.** trazar
ruled *adj.* pautado
ruler *noun.* **1.** gobernante, dirigente **2.** regla
ruling *noun.* fallo, decisión
ruling *adj.* gobernante, reinante, dirigente, en el poder
rumor *noun.* rumor
run *noun.* **1.** carrera **2.** viaje, excursión, paseo, vuelta **3.** racha, período, etapa **4.** corral
run *verb.* **1.** correr **2.** circular, moverse **3.** funcionar, estar en marcha **4.** dirigir, gobernar, organizar **5.** seguir vigente, durar **6.** permanecer en cartel **7.** tener **8.** desteñir, correrse **9.** llevar **10.** pasar **11.** estar
rung *noun.* escalón
runner *noun.* **1.** corredor **2.** patín
runner-up *noun.* segundo, subcampeón
running *adj.* continuo, en directo

running *adv.* seguido, consecutivo
runway *noun.* pista de aterrizaje
rural *adj.* rural
rush *noun.* **1.** abalanzamiento, ímpetu **2.** prisa, urgencia **3.** junco
rush *verb.* **1.** precipitarse **2.** meter prisa
Russia *noun.* Rusia
Russian *noun. adj.* ruso
ruthless *adj.* despiadado, implacable
rye *noun.* centeno

S

sack *noun.* saco
sack *verb.* despedir
sacred *adj.* sagrado
sacrifice *noun.* sacrificio
sacrifice *verb.* sacrificar
sad *adj.* triste, melancólico
saddle *noun.* silla (de montar), sillín
saddle *verb.* ensillar
sadly *adv.* tristemente
sadness *noun.* tristeza, melancolía
safari *noun.* safari
safe *noun.* caja de caudales
safe *adj.* **1.** seguro **2.** digno de confianza
safeguard *noun.* salvaguardia, protección, garantía
safeguard *verb.* proteger
safely *adv.* **1.** seguramente **2.** sin percance
safety *noun.* seguridad
sail *noun.* **1.** vela **2.** paseo en barco **3.** aspa
sail *verb.* **1.** navegar **2.** pilotar **3.** zarpar
sailing *noun.* navegación a vela
sailor *noun.* marinero
saint. St. *noun.* santo/a
salad *noun.* ensalada
salary *noun.* salario
sale *noun.* **1.** venta **2.** rebaja
salesman *noun.* vendedor
sally *noun.* salida
salmon *noun.* salmón
salon *noun.* salón
saloon *noun.* taberna, bar, cantina
salt *noun.* sal
salt *verb.* salar
salt *adj.* salado
salute *noun.* **1.** saludo **2.** salva
salute *verb.* saludar
salvation *noun.* salvación
same *adj.* **1.** mismo **2.** igual
same *adv.* del mismo modo, de la misma manera
same *pron.* lo mismo
sample *noun.* muestra
sample *verb.* **1.** probar, degustar **2.** catar
sanction *noun.* **1.** sanción **2.** autorización, permiso
sanction *verb.* **1.** sancionar **2.** autorizar, permitir
sanctuary *noun.* **1.** santuario **2.** asilo **3.** reserva
sand *noun.* **1.** arena **2.** playa arenosa
sand *verb.* lijar
sandwich *noun.* bocadillo, sándwich
sandwich *verb.* **1.** encajonar, apretujar entre dos objetos **2.** intercalar
sandy *adj.* **1.** arenoso, de arena **2.** rubio oscuro
satellite *noun.* satélite
satisfaction *noun.* satisfacción
satisfactorily *adv.* satisfactoriamente
satisfactory *adj.* satisfactorio
satisfied *adj.* satisfecho
satisfy *verb.* satisfacer
satisfying *adj.* satisfactorio
Saturday *noun.* sábado
sauce *noun.* salsa
Saudi (Arabian) *noun. adj.* saudí, saudita
sausage *noun.* salchicha
savage *noun.* salvaje
savage *verb.* atacar ferozmente, embestir
savage *adj.* **1.** salvaje **2.** feroz, violento
save *prep. conj.* excepto
save *noun.* parada

save *verb.* **1.** salvar, rescatar **2.** ahorrar, guardar, economizar **3.** parar **4.** guardar, archivar
savings *noun plural.* ahorros
saw *noun.* sierra
saw *verb.* serrar
say *noun.* opinión, voz y voto
say *verb.* decir
saying *noun.* dicho
scale *noun.* **1.** escala **2.** balanza **3.** escama
scale *verb.* escalar
scan *noun.* exploración con un escáner
scan *verb.* **1.** escudriñar **2.** dar un vistazo, recorrer con la vista **3.** explorar **4.** escanear
scandal *noun.* **1.** escándalo **2.** chisme, chismorreo, habladuría
scar *noun.* cicatriz
scar *verb.* dejar una cicatriz
scarce *adj.* escaso
scarcely *adv.* apenas
scare *noun.* **1.** susto **2.** pánico
scare *verb.* asustar
scared *adj.* asustado, atemorizado
scarf *noun.* bufanda
scarlet *noun. adj.* escarlata
scatter *verb.* **1.** dispersar **2.** dispersarse **3.** esparcir, desparramar
scattered *adj.* disperso
scene *noun.* **1.** escena **2.** episodio, incidente **3.** cuadro, paisaje, panorama **4.** escenario, decorado
scenery *noun.* **1.** escenario, decorado **2.** paisaje
scent *noun.* **1.** perfume, aroma **2.** rastro, pista
scent *verb.* **1.** oler, olfatear **2.** olerse algo, sospechar **3.** perfumar
schedule *noun.* **1.** horario **2.** programa
schedule *verb.* programar, fijar
scheme *noun.* **1.** plan, programa, proyecto **2.** estratagema
scheme *verb.* conspirar
scholar *noun.* **1.** erudito **2.** becario
scholarly *adj.* erudito, estudioso
scholarship *noun.* **1.** erudición **2.** beca
school *noun.* **1.** escuela **2.** colegio **3.** curso **4.** facultad **5.** universidad
school *verb.* enseñar, educar
schoolboy, schoolgirl *noun.* alumno/a
science *noun.* ciencia
scientific *adj.* científico
scientist *noun.* científico
scissors *noun plural.* tijeras
scoop *noun.* **1.** pala, cucharón **2.** palada, cucharada **3.** primicia
scoop *verb.* cavar
scope *noun.* **1.** oportunidad **2.** alcance
score *noun.* **1.** tanteo, resultado, puntuación **2.** cuenta **3.** partitura **4.** veinte, veintena
score *verb.* **1.** marcar, hacer, meter **2.** llevar el marcador
—**score off/out** eliminar
scorer *noun.* **1.** encargado del marcador, persona que lleva el marcador **2.** goleador
Scot *noun.* escocés
scotch *verb.* poner fin
Scotch, Scots *adj.* escocés
Scotland *noun.* Escocia
Scottish *adj.* escocés
scramble *noun.* lucha, pelea, confusión, barullo
scramble *verb.* **1.** trepar, escalar **2.** revolver **3.** cifrar, codificar
—**scramble for** pelearse por
scrap *noun.* **1.** pedacito, retazo **2.** recorte **3.** chatarra **4.** pelea
—**scraps** *noun plural.* restos, sobras
scrap *verb.* desechar
scrap *verb.* pelear
scrape *noun.* **1.** rasguño, arañazo, roce **2.** chirrido **3.** lío
scrape *verb.* **1.** rasguñarse, arañarse **2.** raspar, rascar **3.** rozar, pasar rozando
scratch *noun.* **1.** arañazo, rasguño, raspadura **2.** línea de salida **3.** cero
scratch *verb.* **1.** arañar, rasguñar, rayar **2.** rascarse **3.** retirarse
scream *noun.* grito, chillido
scream *verb.* gritar, chillar
screen *noun.* **1.** biombo **2.** pantalla
screen *verb.* **1.** ocultar, proteger **2.** proyectar, emitir **3.** investigar **4.** examinar
screw *noun.* **1.** tornillo **2.** vuelta

screw *verb.* **1.** atornillar **2.** enroscar, apretar **3.** echar un polvo, joder, follar **4.** timar, clavar
script *noun.* **1.** guión **2.** escritura **3.** texto
scrub *noun.* fregado, lavado
scrub *verb.* **1.** fregar **2.** restregar **3.** cancelar
scrutiny *noun.* escrutinio, recuento
sculpture *noun.* escultura
scum *noun.* **1.** espuma **2.** escoria
sea *noun.* mar
seal *noun.* **1.** foca **2.** sello **3.** lacre **4.** cierre hermético
seal *verb.* **1.** sellar **2.** cerrar herméticamente **3.** cerrar, concluir
search *noun.* búsqueda, registro, cacheo
search (for) *verb.* **1.** buscar **2.** cachear, registrar
searching *adj.* penetrante
seaside *noun.* orilla del mar
season *noun.* **1.** estación **2.** temporada
season *verb.* sazonar, aliñar
seasonal *adj.* de temporada
seat *noun.* **1.** asiento **2.** culo, trasero **3.** plaza **4.** sede, centro
seat *verb.* **1.** sentar **2.** tener cabida para
second *noun.* segundo
second *verb.* apoyar, secundar
second *adj. adv.* segundo
secondary *noun.* escuela de secundaria
secondary *adj.* secundario
second-hand *adj.* de segunda mano
secondly *adv.* en segundo lugar
secrecy *noun.* secreto, reserva
secret *noun.* secreto
secret *adj.* secreto
secretary *noun.* **1.** secretario **2.** ministro
secretion *noun.* secreción
secretly *adv.* en secreto
section *noun.* sección
sector *noun.* sector
secular *adj.* secular, seglar
secure *verb.* **1.** proteger **2.** sujetar, atar, amarrar
secure *adj.* **1.** seguro **2.** firme
security *noun.* seguridad
sediment *noun.* sedimento
seduce *verb.* seducir
see *noun.* sede
see *verb.* **1.** ver **2.** imaginarse **3.** comprender, entender **4.** acompañar **5.** visitar
seed *noun.* **1.** semilla **2.** pizca, punta **3.** cabeza de serie
seed *verb.* **1.** sembrar **2.** granar **3.** preseleccionar
seek (for) *verb.* **1.** buscar **2.** tratar de, intentar **3.** pedir, solicitar
seem *verb.* parecer
seeming *adj.* aparente
seemingly *adv.* aparentemente
segment *noun.* segmento
seize *verb.* **1.** asir, agarrar, coger **2.** incautar, embargar
seldom *adv.* raramente
select *verb.* escoger, elegir, seleccionar
select *adj.* selecto, escogido
selection *noun.* **1.** elección **2.** selección
selective *adj.* selectivo
self- *prefix* **1.** propio, a/de/por sí mismo **2.** auto- **3.** ego-
self *noun.* **1.** uno mismo **2.** sí mismo
self-esteem *noun.* amor propio
selfish *adj.* egoísta
sell *verb.* **1.** vender **2.** venderse
semi-final *noun.* semifinal
senate *noun.* senado
senator *noun.* senador
send *verb.* enviar, mandar
senior, Sr. *adj.* padre
senior *noun. adj.* **1.** estudiante del último curso **2.** mayor
sensation *noun.* sensación
sense *noun.* **1.** sentido **2.** sensación **3.** sentido común, juicio, sensatez **4.** significado
sense *verb.* **1.** sentir, percibir **2.** presentir
sensible *adj.* **1.** sensato **2.** práctico
sensitive (about/to) *adj.* sensible, delicado
sensitivity *noun.* sensibilidad
sentence *noun.* **1.** frase **2.** sentencia
sentence (to) *verb.* condenar
sentiment *noun.* sentimiento
sentimental *adj.* sentimental
separate *verb.* **1.** separar **2.** separarse

separate *adj.* **1.** separado **2.** distinto, diferente
separately *adv.* por separado
separation *noun.* separación
separatist *noun.* separatista
September, Sept. *noun.* septiembre
sequence *noun.* serie, secuencia
sergeant, Sgt. *noun.* sargento
serial *noun.* novela por entregas, radionovela, telenovela
serial *adj.* **1.** en serie, consecutivo **2.** seriado, en capítulos
series *noun.* serie
serious *adj.* serio
seriously *adv.* en serio
seriousness *noun.* seriedad
serum *noun.* suero
servant *noun.* **1.** criado, sirviente **2.** funcionario
serve *noun.* servicio
serve *verb.* **1.** servir **2.** atender **3.** cumplir **4.** entregar **5.** sacar
server *noun.* **1.** servidor **2.** acólito
service *noun.* **1.** servicio **2.** entrega **3.** revisión, mantenimiento **4.** oficio **5.** misa **6.** vajilla **7.** servicio militar
—**services** fuerzas armadas
service *verb.* **1.** dar servicio **2.** hacer la revisión
serviceman *noun.* militar
serving *noun.* porción, ración
session *noun.* **1.** sesión **2.** período
set *noun.* **1.** juego, colección, equipo, conjunto **2.** aparato **3.** grupo, pandilla **4.** decorado, plató **5.** set
set *verb.* **1.** poner **2.** colocar **3.** fijar, acordar **4.** dar, asignar **5.** establecer **6.** montar, engastar **7.** componer, encajar **8.** provocar **9.** ponerse **10.** endurecerse **11.** cuajarse
—**set about** empezar
—**set aside** apartar, poner a un lado, desechar
—**set down** **1.** depositar **2.** anotar, apuntar, poner por escrito
—**set out** **1.** partir, salir **2.** exponer, manifestar
—**set up** **1.** fijar **2.** levantar, erigir **3.** establecerse
set *adj.* **1.** fijo **2.** inflexible, rígido **3.** resuelto, decidido **4.** listo
setback *noun.* revés
setting *noun.* **1.** escenario **2.** montura, engaste **3.** arreglo, adaptación musical
settle *verb.* **1.** resolver, acordar, decidir, fijar **2.** instalar, colocar **3.** asentarse **4.** calmar **5.** instalarse, establecerse **6.** pagar, saldar la cuenta
settlement *noun.* **1.** acuerdo, convenio **2.** liquidación **3.** poblado, colonia **4.** establecimiento
settler *noun.* colono, colonizador
set-up *noun.* sistema
seven *noun. adj.* siete
seventeen *noun. adj.* diecisiete
seventeenth *noun.* decimoséptimo
seventh *noun.* séptimo
seventies *noun plural.* **1.** entre setenta y ochenta **2.** los años setenta
seventieth *noun.* septuagésimo
seventy *noun. adj.* setenta
several *adj.* varios
several *pron.* varios
severe *adj.* **1.** grave, serio **2.** severo **3.** austero
severely *adv.* severamente
severity *noun.* severidad
sewage *noun.* aguas residuales
sewing *noun.* costura
sex *noun.* sexo
sexual *adj.* sexual
sexually *adv.* sexualmente
sexy *adj.* seductor
shade *noun.* **1.** sombra **2.** pantalla, visera **3.** tono, matiz **4.** poquito, tantito
shade *verb.* **1.** proteger, resguardar **2.** sombrear
—**shade into** convertirse
shadow *noun.* **1.** sombra **2.** ojera
shadow *verb.* **1.** hacer sombra **2.** seguir la pista
shaft *noun.* **1.** mango **2.** vara **3.** eje **4.** hueco, pozo **5.** rayo
shake *noun.* **1.** sacudida **2.** batido
shake *verb.* **1.** agitar, sacudir **2.** debilitar
shaking *noun.* sacudida
shall *verb.* **1.** (se usa para expresar el futuro) **2.** (se usa para expresar

obligación) **3.** (se usa para expresar el condicional)
shallow *adj.* **1.** poco profundo **2.** superficial
shame *noun.* **1.** vergüenza **2.** deshonra **3.** pena, lástima
shame *verb.* **1.** avergonzar **2.** deshonrar
shape *noun.* **1.** forma **2.** figura **3.** bulto
shape *verb.* **1.** modelar, dar forma **2.** decidir, determinar
shaped *adj.* en forma de
share *noun.* **1.** parte **2.** acción, participación
share (among/between/with) *verb.* **1.** repartir, dividir **2.** compartir
shareholder *noun.* accionista
sharp *noun.* sostenido
sharp *adj.* **1.** afilado, puntiagudo **2.** definido, nítido, marcado **3.** brusco, repentino **4.** agudo, fuerte **5.** severo **6.** agudo **7.** repentino, súbito **8.** desafinado
sharp *adv.* **1.** en punto **2.** bruscamente **3.** demasiado alto
sharply *adv.* bruscamente, repentinamente
shatter *verb.* **1.** romper, quebrantar **2.** destrozar
shattered *adj.* hecho polvo, trastornado
shave *noun.* afeitado
shave *verb.* **1.** afeitarse **2.** pasar rozando
—shave off cepillar
she *noun.* **1.** hembra **2.** niña
she *pron.* **1.** ella **2.** la que, aquella que
shed *noun.* cobertizo, nave
shed *verb.* **1.** arrojar **2.** mudar **3.** derramar
sheep *noun.* oveja
sheer *adj.* **1.** puro, absoluto **2.** vertical, escarpado **3.** fino, ligero
sheer *adv.* verticalmente, en picado
—sheer off/away desviarse
sheet *noun.* **1.** sábana **2.** hoja
shelf *noun.* **1.** estante **2.** plataforma
shell *noun.* **1.** concha, caracol **2.** armazón **3.** cartucho
shell *verb.* **1.** desvainar, quitar la concha **2.** bombardear
shelter *noun.* **1.** abrigo **2.** albergue
shelter *verb.* **1.** abrigar, proteger **2.** abrigarse, protegerse
sheltered *adj.* protegido
shepherd *noun.* pastor
shepherd *verb.* guiar, conducir
sheriff *noun.* sheriff, alguacil
sherry *noun.* jerez
shield *noun.* **1.** escudo **2.** placa
shield (from) *verb.* proteger
shift *noun.* **1.** cambio **2.** turno
shift *verb.* **1.** mover, desplazar **2.** traspasar, transferir **3.** quitar
shilling *noun.* chelín
shine *noun.* **1.** brillo **2.** lustre
shine *verb.* **1.** brillar **2.** relucir **3.** sacar brillo, limpiar
—shine at sobresalir, destacar
shining *adj.* brillante
shiny *adj.* brillante
ship *noun.* barco, nave, buque, navío
ship *verb.* enviar, consignar
shipment *noun.* **1.** envío, consignación **2.** embarque, transporte
shipping *noun.* flota
shirt *noun.* camisa
shiver *noun.* escalofrío, tiritón, estremecimiento
shiver *verb.* temblar, tiritar, estremecerse
shock *noun.* **1.** conmoción, golpe **2.** choque, impacto **3.** shock **4.** mata de pelo
—electric shock *noun.* descarga
shock *verb.* **1.** conmocionar, conmover, afectar **2.** escandalizar
shocking *adj.* **1.** terrible, espantoso **2.** escandaloso
shoe *noun.* **1.** zapato **2.** herradura
shoe *verb.* herrar
shoot *noun.* brote, retoño
shoot (at) *verb.* **1.** disparar **2.** lanzar **3.** fusilar, matar de un tiro **4.** salir disparado **5.** rodar, filmar **6.** tirar, chutar **7.** cazar
shop *noun.* **1.** tienda, comercio **2.** taller
shop *verb.* comprar, hacer compras
shopping *noun.* compra
shore *noun.* costa, playa
short *adj.* **1.** corto **2.** bajo **3.** breve **4.** de menos **5.** escaso **6.** quebradizo

short *adv.* bruscamente, en seco
shortage *noun.* falta, escasez
short-lived *adj.* efímero
shortly *adv.* dentro de poco, en breve
shorts *noun plural.* pantalones cortos
short-term *adj.* a corto plazo
shot *noun.* **1.** tiro **2.** disparo **3.** jugada **4.** tentativa, intento **5.** bala, proyectil **6.** foto, toma **7.** inyección, pinchazo **8.** tirador
should *verb.* **1.** deber (expressing obligation) **2.** deber de (expressing probability) **3.** gustar (expressing future/conditional) **4.** (expressing subjunctive)
shoulder *noun.* **1.** hombro **2.** hombrera **3.** ladera, falda **4.** paletilla
shoulder *verb.* **1.** ponerse al hombro, echarse al hombro **2.** cargar (con) **3.** abrir paso a codazos
shout *noun.* grito
shout *verb.* gritar
shove *noun.* empujón
shove *verb.* empujar
show *noun.* **1.** exposición, espectáculo **2.** exhibición, demostración, alarde **3.** ostentación, apariencia **4.** actuación
show *verb.* **1.** enseñar **2.** mostrar **3.** notarse, verse **4.** exhibir **5.** indicar **6.** demostrar
—**show (a)round** conducir, acompañar
shower *noun.* **1.** ducha **2.** chubasco, chaparrón **3.** lluvia
shower *verb.* **1.** ducharse **2.** tirar, rociar
shred *noun.* triza, jirón
shred *verb.* hacer trizas, cortar en tiras
shrine *noun.* **1.** santuario **2.** relicario
shrink *noun.* psiquiatra, loquero
shrink *verb.* **1.** encoger **2.** retroceder, echarse atrás **3.** esquivar
shrub *noun.* arbusto
shrug *noun.* encogimiento de hombros
shrug *verb.* encogerse de hombros
shuffle *noun.* baraje, barajadura
shuffle *verb.* **1.** caminar arrastrando los pies **2.** barajar
shut *verb.* **1.** cerrar **2.** cerrarse
—**shut up** hacer callar
shut *adj.* cerrado
shuttle *noun.* **1.** lanzadera **2.** servicio regular
shy *verb.* espantarse
shy *adj.* **1.** tímido, vergonzoso, reservado **2.** asustadizo, huraño
sick *adj.* **1.** enfermo **2.** mareado **3.** harto, cansado **4.** morboso, de muy mal gusto
sickness *noun.* **1.** enfermedad **2.** mareo
side *noun.* **1.** lado **2.** cara **3.** costado **4.** ijada **5.** parte **6.** ladera, falda **7.** aspecto, punto de vista **8.** bando
side *adj.* lateral, secundario
sidewalk *noun.* calzada, pavimento
sideways *adj. adv.* lateral, de lado, de reojo
siege *noun.* asedio, cerco, sitio
sigh *noun.* suspiro
sigh *verb.* **1.** suspirar **2.** susurrar
sight *noun.* **1.** vista **2.** visión **3.** espectáculo, atracción turística **4.** figura **5.** mira
sight *verb.* **1.** observar, ver, divisar **2.** apuntar
sign *noun.* **1.** signo, símbolo **2.** señal **3.** panel, letrero **4.** gesto, seña
sign *verb.* **1.** firmar **2.** hacer señas
signal *noun.* señal
signal *verb.* **1.** indicar, señalar **2.** comunicar por señas
signature *noun.* firma
significance *noun.* **1.** significado **2.** importancia
significant *adj.* **1.** significativo **2.** importante **3.** elocuente, expresivo
significantly *adv.* **1.** significativamente **2.** considerablemente
silence *interj.* ¡silencio!
silence *noun.* silencio
silence *verb.* hacer callar, acallar, silenciar
silent *adj.* silencioso
silently *adv.* silenciosamente
silk *noun.* seda
silly *adj.* tonto, bobo
silver *noun.* plata
silver *adj.* de plata
similar *adj.* similar, semejante, parecido
similarity *noun.* similitud
similarly *adv.* **1.** igualmente **2.** de manera similar

simmer *verb.* hervir a fuego lento
simple *adj.* **1.** simple **2.** fácil, sencillo **3.** mero **4.** ingenuo, cándido
simplicity *noun.* sencillez
simplified *adj.* simplificado
simply *adv.* **1.** simplemente **2.** sencillamente
simulation *noun.* **1.** simulación, simulacro **2.** imitación
simultaneous *adj.* simultáneo
simultaneously *adv.* simultáneamente
sin *noun.* pecado
sin *verb.* pecar
since *conj.* **1.** desde que **2.** después que **3.** ya que, puesto que
since *prep.* desde
since *adv.* desde entonces
sincere *adj.* sincero
sincerely *adv.* sinceramente
sing *verb.* cantar
singer *noun.* cantante
singing *noun.* canto, cantar
single *noun.* **1.** (disco) sencillo, single **2.** billete/boleto de ida
—**singles** individuales (sport)
single *adj.* **1.** solo, único **2.** individual **3.** soltero
singular *noun. adj.* singular
sinister *adj.* siniestro
sink *noun.* **1.** fregadero, pila **2.** lavabo
sink *verb.* **1.** hundir **2.** hundirse, irse a pique **3.** caer **4.** bajar, descender **5.** hundir, hincar **6.** perforar, excavar **7.** venirse abajo, desanimarse **8.** invertir
sip *noun.* sorbo
sip *verb.* sorber, beber a sorbos
sir *noun.* **1.** señor, caballero **2.** sir
sister *noun.* **1.** hermana **2.** monja
sister *adj.* similar, parecido
sit *verb.* **1.** estar sentado **2.** sentar **3.** sentarse **4.** posar **5.** estar, encontrarse **6.** posarse **7.** posar **8.** reunirse
—**sit on** ser miembro de, formar parte de
site *noun.* **1.** sitio **2.** lugar **3.** web site
sit-in *noun.* huelga, encierro
sitting *noun.* sesión
situated *adj.* situado
situation *noun.* **1.** situación **2.** ubicación **3.** empleo, vacante
six *noun. adj.* seis
sixteen *noun. adj.* dieciséis
sixteenth *noun.* decimosexto
sixth *noun.* sexto
sixties *noun plural.* **1.** entre sesenta y setenta **2.** los años sesenta
sixtieth *noun.* **1.** sexagésima parte **2.** sexagésimo
sixty *noun. adj.* sesenta
size *noun.* **1.** tamaño, magnitud, estatura **2.** talla, número
sizeable *adj.* considerable, importante
skate *noun.* **1.** patín **2.** raya
skate *verb.* **1.** patinar **2.** deslizarse
skeleton *noun.* **1.** esqueleto **2.** armazón
skeptical *adj.* escéptico
skepticism *noun.* escepticismo
sketch *noun.* **1.** esbozo, croquis **2.** borrador, esquema **3.** sainete
sketch *verb.* **1.** dibujar **2.** esbozar
ski *noun.* esquí
ski *verb.* esquiar
skiing *noun.* esquí
skill *noun.* **1.** destreza, habilidad **2.** técnica, arte
skilled *adj.* **1.** experto, cualificado, calificado **2.** especializado
skin *noun.* **1.** piel **2.** cáscara **3.** película
skin *verb.* despellejar, desollar
skinny *adj.* flaco, enjuto
skip *noun.* salto, brinco
skip *verb.* **1.** saltar **2.** saltarse
skipper *noun.* capitán
skipper *verb.* capitanear
skirt *noun.* falda
skull *noun.* calavera
sky *noun.* cielo
slab *noun.* losa
slam *noun.* golpe, portazo
slam *verb.* **1.** cerrar de golpe **2.** estamparse
slap *noun.* palmada, cachete, bofetada, bofetón
slap *verb.* abofetear, dar una bofetada
slash *noun.* **1.** tajo, cuchillada **2.** golpe
slash *verb.* **1.** dar un tajo, rajar **2.** rebajar, reducir
—**slash at** golpear

slate *noun.* pizarra
slate *verb.* criticar duramente
slaughter *noun.* **1.** masacre **2.** matanza
slaughter *verb.* **1.** sacrificar **2.** matar **3.** dar una paliza
slave *noun.* esclavo
slave *verb.* trabajar como una bestia, trabajar como un negro
sleek *adj.* **1.** liso, lustroso **2.** impecable
sleep *noun.* sueño
sleep *verb.* dormir
sleeve *noun.* **1.** manga **2.** funda **3.** manguito
slender *adj.* **1.** delgado, esbelto, fino **2.** escaso
slice *noun.* **1.** porción, trozo **2.** parte
slice *verb.* **1.** cortar **2.** cortar a rodajas, cortar a lonchas
sliced *adj.* rebanado, en rodajas
slick, oil-slick *noun.* marea negra
slick *adj.* mañoso
slide *noun.* **1.** deslizamiento, desliz **2.** tobogán **3.** diapositiva **4.** platina, portaobjetos **5.** pasador
slide *verb.* **1.** deslizar **2.** deslizarse
slight *adj.* **1.** pequeño, ligero **2.** delicado
slightest *adj.* mínimo
slightly *adv.* **1.** ligeramente **2.** frágilmente
slim *verb.* adelgazar, hacer régimen
slim *adj.* **1.** delgado, esbelto, fino **2.** escaso
slip *noun.* **1.** error, equivocación, desliz **2.** resbalón, traspiés, tropezón **3.** combinación **4.** papelito, trocito de papel
slip *verb.* **1.** resbalar, tropezar **2.** deslizar **3.** escabullirse, escurrirse **4.** soltarse, escaparse **5.** pasar
slogan *noun.* eslogan, lema
slope *noun.* **1.** cuesta, pendiente **2.** inclinación, vertiente
slope *verb.* inclinarse
slot *noun.* **1.** ranura **2.** hueco, cuña
slot (in/into) *verb.* insertar, introducir
slow *verb.* retrasar, ralentizar, retardar
slow *adj.* **1.** lento **2.** atrasado **3.** torpe, estúpido
slowly *adv.* lentamente
slump *noun.* **1.** bajón, bajada repentina **2.** crisis económica, recesión económica
slump *verb.* bajar/caer en picado, caer de repente, desplomarse
smack *noun.* **1.** palmada, bofetada **2.** toque, sabor, olor
smack *verb.* dar una palmada
—**smack of** *verb.* presentir, oler
smack *adv.* de lleno, directamente
small *adj.* **1.** pequeño **2.** chico **3.** poco **4.** minúsculo
smart *noun.* dolor, resentimiento
smart *verb.* **1.** escocer, picar, arder **2.** sentirse ofendido
smart *adj.* **1.** elegante **2.** listo, despierto **3.** rápido
smash *noun.* **1.** quiebra **2.** golpe **3.** smash, mate
smash (up) *verb.* **1.** romper, quebrar **2.** romperse, quebrarse **3.** pulverizar, hacer pedazos
smell *noun.* **1.** olfato **2.** olor
smell *verb.* **1.** oler **2.** oler, olfatear
smile *noun.* sonrisa
smile *verb.* sonreír
smiling *adj.* sonriente
smith *noun.* **1.** herrero **2.** orfebre, artesano
smoke *noun.* humo
smoke *verb.* **1.** fumar **2.** ahumar
smoked *adj.* ahumado
smoking *noun.* fumar
smooth *adj.* **1.** liso **2.** homogéneo **3.** tranquilo, en calma **4.** suave, parejo **5.** sin problemas **6.** zalamero, meloso
smooth (down/out) *verb.* alisar
smooth (into/over) *verb.* esparcir
smoothly *adv.* suavemente
smuggle *verb.* pasar de contrabando
snack *noun.* tentempié
snake *noun.* serpiente
snake *verb.* serpentear
snap *noun.* ruido seco
snap *adj.* precipitado, repentino
snap (at) *verb.* **1.** partir **2.** chasquear **3.** regañar, hablar con brusquedad **4.** intentar morder

snatch *noun.* **1.** arrebatamiento **2.** fragmento
snatch *verb.* **1.** arrebatar, arrancar, coger **2.** aprovechar
sneak *noun.* acusica, chivato, soplón
sneak *verb.* **1.** moverse sigilosamente **2.** sacar a escondidas **3.** acusar, delatar
sniff *noun.* aspiración
sniff *verb.* **1.** resollar **2.** olfatear, husmear
snooker *noun.* snooker, billar ruso
snow *noun.* nieve
snow *verb.* nevar
so *conj.* **1.** así que, por lo tanto, de manera que **2.** para
so *adv.* **1.** tan, tanto **2.** así **3.** eso **4.** también **5.** así es, en efecto
soak *verb.* **1.** remojar **2.** empaparse **3.** remojarse, empaparse
—**soak in/into/through** penetrar
—**soaked through** empapado, hecho una sopa
soap *noun.* jabón
soap *verb.* enjabonar
soar *verb.* remontar el vuelo, elevarse
sober *adj.* **1.** sobrio **2.** formal **3.** serio
so-called *adj.* supuesto, presunto
soccer *noun.* fútbol
social *adj.* social
socialism *noun.* socialismo
socialist *noun. adj.* socialista
socialize *verb.* relacionarse, mezclarse con la gente
socially *adv.* socialmente
society *noun.* **1.** sociedad **2.** asociación **3.** alta sociedad **4.** compañía
sock *noun.* **1.** calcetín, media **2.** puñetazo
sock *verb.* pegar un puñetazo
socket *noun.* enchufe
sodium *noun.* sodio
sofa *noun.* sofá
soft *adj.* **1.** blando **2.** suave **3.** no alcohólico **4.** tonto, bobo
soften *verb.* suavizar
softly *adv.* suavemente
software *noun.* software
soil *noun.* tierra, suelo
soil *verb.* ensuciar, manchar
solar *adj.* solar
soldier *noun.* soldado
sole *noun.* **1.** planta **2.** suela **3.** lenguado
sole *adj.* **1.** único **2.** exclusivo
solely *adv.* únicamente, sólo
solemn *adj.* **1.** solemne **2.** serio
solicitor *noun.* **1.** representante, agente **2.** abogado municipal
solid *noun.* sólido
solid *adj.* **1.** sólido **2.** macizo **3.** de una sola pieza **4.** seguido, ininterrumpido
solid *adv.* ininterrumpidamente
solidarity *noun.* solidaridad
solitary *adj.* **1.** solitario **2.** único
solo *noun.* solo
solo *adj.* en solitario
solution *noun.* solución
solve *verb.* resolver
solvent *noun. adj.* solvente
some *adj.* **1.** bastante **2.** algo de **3.** cerca de, alrededor de
some *adv.* un poco, algo
some *pron. adj.* **1.** algún, alguno/a, algunos/as **2.** unos/as **3.** un poco, unos pocos, unas pocas **4.** cierto
somebody *pron.* alguien
somehow *adv.* de algún modo, de alguna manera
someone *pron.* alguien
someplace *adv.* en algún lugar
something *pron.* algo
sometime *adv.* **1.** en alguna ocasión **2.** en algún momento
sometimes *adv.* a veces
somewhat *adv.* algo, un tanto
somewhere *adv.* en algún lugar
son *noun.* hijo
song *noun.* **1.** canción **2.** canto
soon *adv.* **1.** pronto, en breve, dentro de poco **2.** temprano
soothe *verb.* calmar, tranquilizar, aliviar
sophisticated *adj.* **1.** sofisticado **2.** sutil, complejo
sophistication *noun.* sofisticación
sore *noun.* llaga, herida, úlcera
sore *adj.* **1.** doloroso **2.** dolorido **3.** resentido, enojado
sorrow *noun.* pena, pesar, dolor

sorry *interj.* ¡perdón!, ¡disculpe!
sorry *adj.* **1.** lo siento **2.** triste, arrepentido, desolado **3.** lamentable
sort *noun.* clase, tipo, género
sort *verb.* clasificar
soul *noun.* **1.** alma, espíritu **2.** persona
—**soul music** música soul
sound *noun.* **1.** sonido **2.** ruido **3.** volumen
sound *verb.* **1.** tocar, hacer sonar **2.** sonar, resonar **3.** parecer **4.** pronunciarse **5.** auscultar **6.** sondear
sound *adj.* **1.** sano, sólido, firme **2.** juicioso, sensato, acertado **3.** completo, severo **4.** bueno **5.** profundo
soup *noun.* sopa
soup up *verb.* trucar
sour *verb.* **1.** agriar **2.** agriarse
sour *adj.* **1.** agrio, ácido, amargo **2.** rancio **3.** amargado, áspero
source *noun.* **1.** fuente, origen **2.** nacimiento
south *noun.* sur
south *adj.* **1.** sur, meridional **2.** del sur
south *adv.* hacia el sur
southern *adj.* **1.** sur, meridional **2.** del sur
sovereign *noun. adj.* soberano
soviet *noun. adj.* soviético
sow *noun.* puerca, marrana
sow *verb.* sembrar
space *noun.* **1.** espacio, hueco **2.** sitio, lugar
—**outer space** espacio exterior
space (out) *verb.* espaciar, separar
spacious *adj.* espacioso
Spain *noun.* España
span *noun.* **1.** luz, tramo **2.** envergadura **3.** espacio, período, lapso
span *verb.* **1.** atravesar, cruzar **2.** abarcar
Spanish *noun. adj.* español
spare *verb.* **1.** prescindir, pasar sin **2.** disponer de **3.** perdonar **4.** evitar **5.** escatimar
spare *adj.* **1.** de repuesto, **2.** de sobra **3.** libre
spark *noun.* chispa
spark *verb.* echar chispas, chispear
—**spark off** hacer estallar, provocar
sparkle *noun.* **1.** centelleo, destello **2.** viveza
sparkle *verb.* **1.** centellear, destellar **2.** brillar, lucirse
sparkling *adj.* **1.** espumoso **2.** con gas **3.** brillante, chispeante
speak *verb.* **1.** hablar **2.** conversar **3.** decir **4.** pronunciar
speaker *noun.* persona que habla, interlocutor, conferenciante
speaking *adj.* hablante, parlante
special *noun.* especial
special *adj.* **1.** especial **2.** extraordinario **3.** específico, particular
specialist *noun.* especialista
specialize (in) *verb.* especializarse
specialized *adj.* especializado
specially *adv.* **1.** especialmente **2.** particularmente
specialty *noun.* especialidad
species *noun.* especie
specific *adj.* **1.** preciso **2.** específico
specifically *adv.* específicamente
specify *verb.* **1.** especificar **2.** precisar
specimen *noun.* espécimen, muestra
spectacle *noun.* espectáculo
spectacles *noun plural.* gafas, anteojos
spectacular *adj.* **1.** espectacular **2.** impresionante
spectator *noun.* espectador
spectrum *noun.* **1.** espectro **2.** gama
speculate *verb.* especular
speculation *noun.* especulación
speech *noun.* **1.** habla **2.** palabras **3.** lenguaje, forma de hablar **4.** discurso
speed *noun.* **1.** velocidad **2.** rapidez
speed *verb.* **1.** ir corriendo, ir a toda prisa **2.** ir con exceso de velocidad
speeding *noun.* exceso de velocidad
speedy *adj.* rápido
spell *noun.* **1.** hechizo **2.** encanto **3.** turno **4.** temporada **5.** período
spell *verb.* **1.** deletrear **2.** formar **3.** escribir correctamente **4.** significar, representar
spelling *noun.* ortografía
spend *verb.* **1.** gastar **2.** pasar
spent *adj.* **1.** usado, gastado **2.** agotado
sperm *noun.* esperma

sphere *noun.* esfera
spice *noun.* **1.** especia **2.** salsa, sabor
spice *verb.* sazonar, condimentar
spider *noun.* araña
spike *noun.* **1.** punta, pincho **2.** clavo
spill *verb.* derramar, verter
spin *noun.* **1.** vuelta, giro **2.** paseo
spin *verb.* **1.** hacer girar **2.** hilar
spine *noun.* **1.** columna vertebral **2.** espina dorsal **3.** lomo **4.** espina
spiral *noun.* espiral
spiral *verb.* moverse en espiral
spiral *adj.* **1.** espiral **2.** en espiral
spirit *noun.* **1.** espíritu **2.** valor
spirits *noun plural.* **1.** humor, ánimo **2.** licor
spiritual *adj.* espiritual
spit, spittle *noun.* saliva
spit *noun.* asador
spit *verb.* escupir
spite *noun.* rencor
—**in spite of** a pesar de
spite *verb.* fastidiar
splash *noun.* **1.** salpicadura **2.** mancha **3.** chapoteo
splash *verb.* **1.** salpicar **2.** esparcirse **3.** chapotear
splendid *adj.* **1.** maravilloso **2.** espléndido
split *noun.* **1.** grieta, raja **2.** división
split *verb.* **1.** rajar **2.** dividir
spoil *verb.* **1.** estropear **2.** mimar
spoke *noun.* radio, rayo
spoken *adj.* hablado, oral
spokesman *noun.* portavoz
sponge *noun.* **1.** esponja **2.** bizcocho
sponge *verb.* **1.** lavar con esponja **2.** vivir de gorra
sponsor *noun.* patrocinador
sponsor *verb.* patrocinar
sponsorship *noun.* patrocinio
spontaneous *adj.* espontáneo
spoon *noun.* **1.** cuchara **2.** cucharada
spoon *verb.* dar de comer
sport, sports *adj.* deportivo
sport *noun.* **1.** deporte **2.** buena persona, buena gente **3.** diversión
sport *verb.* lucir
sporting *adj.* **1.** deportivo **2.** caballeroso
spot *noun.* **1.** mancha **2.** punto **3.** grano **4.** sitio, lugar
—**on the spot** en el acto
spot *verb.* **1.** ver **2.** reconocer **3.** darse cuenta
spotted *adj.* moteado, con puntos
spread *verb.* **1.** untar **2.** extenderse **3.** difundirse
spring *noun.* **1.** primavera **2.** fuente, manantial **3.** origen
spring *verb* **1.** saltar **2.** accionar
—**spring from** surgir de
stick *noun.* **1.** ramita **2.** bastón **3.** palo, vara
stiff *adj.* **1.** rígido, tieso **2.** duro **3.** espeso **4.** difícil **5.** fuerte **6.** frío, formal, estirado
still *noun.* fotograma
still *adj.* **1.** quieto, inmóvil, parado **2.** sin gas
still *adv.* **1.** aún, todavía **2.** a pesar de todo, no obstante, sin embargo
stimulate *verb.* estimular
stimulating *adj.* estimulante
stimulation *noun.* estimulación
stimulus *noun.* estímulo
sting *noun.* **1.** aguijón **2.** picadura
sting *verb.* **1.** picar **2.** escocer, arder
stink *noun.* peste, hedor
stink *verb.* apestar
stir *noun.* agitación, conmoción
stir *verb.* **1.** remover, revolver **2.** moverse, agitarse **3.** conmover, provocar, estimular
stirring *adj.* emocionante, conmovedor
stitch *noun.* **1.** puntada **2.** punto **3.** flato
stitch *verb.* coser, suturar
stock *noun.* **1.** existencias, stock **2.** reserva, provisión **3.** ganado **4.** caldo **5.** culata
stock *verb.* **1.** tener en stock, vender **2.** abastecer, surtir
stock *adj.* corriente, típico
stock exchange, stock market *noun.* bolsa
stocking *noun.* media
stocks *noun plural.* **1.** acciones, valores **2.** cepo
stoke *verb.* atizar
stomach *noun.* **1.** estómago **2.** barriga

stone *noun. adj.* **1.** piedra **2.** unidad de peso que equivale a 6.4 kg **3.** cálculo
stone *verb.* apedrear, lapidar
stool *noun.* taburete
stop *noun.* **1.** parada **2.** alto, interrupción **3.** descanso, pausa **4.** punto **5.** registro, llave **6.** tope
stop *verb.* **1.** parar **2.** pararse **3.** detener **4.** suspender, cortar, interrumpir **5.** impedir, evitar **6.** tapar **7.** obstruir, atascar **8.** quedarse
stopping *noun.* empaste
storage *noun.* almacenamiento
store *noun.* **1.** provisión **2.** reserva **3.** almacén, depósito **4.** tienda
store *verb.* **1.** almacenar, guardar, acumular **2.** proveer
storm *noun.* **1.** tormenta **2.** bronca
storm *verb.* **1.** vociferar, bramar **2.** marcharse hecho una furia **3.** asaltar, tomar por asalto
story *noun.* **1.** historia **2.** cuento
stout *adj.* **1.** sólido, fuerte **2.** firme, resuelto **3.** corpulento, robusto
stove *noun.* estufa, cocina, horno
straight *noun.* heterosexual
straight *adj.* **1.** recto, liso **2.** derecho, recto **3.** honrado, directo, sincero, franco **4.** arreglado, ordenado **5.** claro **6.** consecutivo **7.** serio, dramático
straight *adv.* **1.** recto, en línea recta **2.** directamente **3.** con franqueza
straighten *verb.* **1.** enderezar, poner derecho **2.** arreglar, ordenar
straightforward *adj.* **1.** sencillo **2.** honrado, sincero
strain *noun.* **1.** tensión **2.** presión **3.** carga **4.** esfuerzo **5.** estrés **6.** torcedura, esguince **7.** raza, tipo **8.** vena **9.** son, compás
strain *verb.* **1.** estirar, tensar, forzar **2.** torcerse, hacerse un esguince, dañarse **3.** poner a prueba, abusar **4.** colar, escurrir
strained *adj.* tenso, forzado
strand *noun.* hebra, hilo
strange *adj.* extraño
strangely *adv.* extrañamente
stranger *noun.* **1.** extraño, desconocido **2.** forastero
strap *noun.* **1.** correa **2.** asa
strap *verb.* **1.** azotar a alguien con correa **2.** atar con correa
strategic *adj.* estratégico
strategy *noun.* estrategia
straw *noun. adj.* **1.** paja **2.** pajita
strawberry *noun.* fresa
stray *noun.* animal extraviado
stray *verb.* extraviarse, perderse
stray *adj.* **1.** perdido, extraviado, callejero **2.** aislado
streak *noun.* **1.** raya, veta, filón **2.** vena
streak *verb.* **1.** rayar, surcar **2.** pasar como un rayo
stream *noun.* **1.** riachuelo, arroyo **2.** flujo, chorro **3.** corriente **4.** clase, grupo, nivel
stream *verb.* **1.** manar, correr, chorrear **2.** separar por niveles
street, St. *noun.* calle
strength *noun.* **1.** fuerza **2.** intensidad **3.** número, efectivos
strengthen *verb.* **1.** fortalecer **2.** fortalecerse
stress *noun.* **1.** estrés **2.** tensión **3.** énfasis, acento
stress *verb.* enfatizar
stretch *noun.* **1.** estiramiento **2.** extensión, tramo, trecho
stretch *verb.* **1.** estirar, extender **2.** extenderse
strict *adj.* **1.** estricto, severo **2.** riguroso
strictly *adv.* rigurosamente
stride *noun.* zancada
stride *verb.* andar a zancadas
strike *noun.* **1.** huelga **2.** hallazgo, descubrimiento **3.** golpe, strike (sports)
strike *verb.* **1.** pegar, golpear **2.** atacar **3.** encender, prender **4.** hacer huelga, declararse en huelga **5.** encontrar **6.** chocar contra **7.** parecer, dar la impresión **8.** acuñar **9.** desmontar
striker *noun.* **1.** huelguista **2.** delantero
striking *adj.* **1.** llamativo **2.** impresionante, sorprendente
string *noun.* **1.** cuerda, cordel, cabuya **2.** fibra, hebra **3.** sarta, collar, ristra **4.** hilera, fila
string *verb.* **1.** ensartar **2.** encordar **3.** desfibrar, quitar la hebra **4.** colgar

stringent *adj.* riguroso, severo
strip *noun.* **1.** tira, franja **2.** tira cómica, historieta
strip *verb.* **1.** quitar, despojar **2.** desnudar, desnudarse
stripe *noun.* **1.** raya, lista **2.** galón
striped *adj.* a rayas
strive *verb.* esforzarse
stroke *noun.* **1.** caricia **2.** golpe **3.** ocurrencia **4.** campanada **5.** trazo, pincelada **6.** brazada **7.** apoplejía
stroke *verb.* acariciar
stroll *noun.* paseo, vuelta
stroll *verb.* pasearse
strong *adj.* **1.** fuerte **2.** sano **3.** firme **4.** que cuenta con un número de
strongly *adv.* firmemente, rotundamente
structural *adj.* estructural
structure *noun.* **1.** estructura **2.** construcción
struggle *noun.* lucha
struggle *verb.* **1.** luchar **2.** forcejear **3.** tener problemas
stubborn *adj.* cabezota
student *noun.* **1.** estudiante **2.** alumno
studio *noun.* **1.** estudio **2.** taller
study *noun.* **1.** estudio **2.** biblioteca, despacho
study *verb.* **1.** estudiar **2.** examinar, mirar detenidamente
stuff *noun.* **1.** cosa, cosas **2.** sustancia, materia **3.** chismes, cachivaches, trastos **4.** paño, tela, género
stuff *verb.* **1.** llenar, rellenar **2.** meter, atestar **3.** atiborrarse **4.** disecar
stumble *verb.* **1.** tropezar **2.** avanzar dando tropezones/traspiés **3.** balbucir
stump *noun.* **1.** tocón, cepa **2.** palo, poste **3.** muñón **4.** raigón
stump *verb.* **1.** andar pisando muy fuerte **2.** dejar perflejo, desconcertar **3.** eliminar, dejar fuera de juego
stun *verb.* **1.** dejar inconsciente, aturdir **2.** pasmar, asombrar
stunning *adj.* alucinante, estupendo, maravilloso
stupid *adj.* **1.** estúpido **2.** atontado
style *noun.* **1.** estilo **2.** moda **3.** clase, elegancia
style *verb.* **1.** marcar, peinar **2.** diseñar
stylish *adj.* **1.** con estilo, elegante **2.** a la moda
sub *noun.* sub
subdued *adj.* **1.** suave **2.** apagado
subject *noun.* **1.** súbdito **2.** tema, asunto **3.** asignatura **4.** motivo **5.** sujeto
subject *verb.* **1.** dominar, subyugar **2.** someter
subject *adj.* dominado, subyugado
—**subject to** **1.** sujeto a **2.** expuesto a **3.** propenso a
subjective *adj.* subjetivo
submarine *noun. adj.* submarino
submission *noun.* sumisión
submit *verb.* **1.** presentar **2.** someter **3.** someterse, rendirse
subordinate *noun. adj.* subordinado
subscription *noun.* **1.** suscripción **2.** abono, cuota
subsequent *adj.* subsiguiente, posterior
subsequently *adv.* posteriormente
subsidiary *noun.* filial
subsidiary *adj.* **1.** secundario **2.** filial
subsidize *verb.* subvencionar
subsidy *noun.* subsidio, subvención
substance *noun.* sustancia
substantial *adj.* **1.** sustancial **2.** importante
substantially *adv.* sustancialmente
substitute *noun.* sustituto
substitute *verb.* sustituir
substitution *noun.* sustitución
subtle *adj.* **1.** sutil **2.** agudo, perspicaz
suburb, suburbs *noun plural.* afueras
suburban *adj.* de las afueras, de cercanías
succeed *verb.* **1.** conseguir, triunfar, tener éxito **2.** suceder
success *noun.* éxito
successful *adj.* afortunado, exitoso
successfully *adv.* con éxito
succession *noun.* sucesión
successive *adj.* sucesivo
successor *noun.* sucesor
such *adj.* **1.** tal **2.** parecido, semejante **3.** así **4.** tan, tanto
such *pron.* **1.** el que, la que, lo que, los que, las que **2.** tal

suck *verb.* **1.** mamar, chupar **2.** sorber **3.** aspirar **4.** ser una mierda
sudden *adj.* súbito, repentino
suddenly *adv.* súbitamente, de repente, de golpe
sue *verb.* demandar
—**sue for divorce** solicitar el divorcio
suffer *verb.* **1.** sufrir, padecer **2.** soportar **3.** resentirse, verse afectado
suffering *noun.* sufrimiento
suffice *verb.* bastar, ser suficiente
sufficient *adj.* suficiente, bastante
sufficiently *adv.* suficientemente
sugar *noun.* azúcar
sugar *verb.* azucarar, endulzar
suggest *verb.* **1.** sugerir **2.** proponer **3.** insinuar
suggestion *noun.* **1.** sugerencia **2.** propuesta **3.** insinuación **4.** indicio, asomo
suicide *noun.* **1.** suicidio **2.** suicida
suit *noun.* **1.** traje **2.** pleito, juicio **3.** petición de mano, oferta de matrimonio **4.** palo
suit *verb.* **1.** convenir, venir bien **2.** quedar bien, favorecer **3.** adaptar
suitable *adj.* adecuado, conveniente, apropiado
suitably *adv.* convenientemente, adecuadamente, apropiadamente
suitcase *noun.* maleta
suite *noun.* **1.** juego **2.** suite
sulfur *noun.* azufre
sum *noun.* **1.** suma **2.** cantidad **3.** total **4.** problema de aritmética
summarize *verb.* resumir
summary *noun.* resumen
summer *noun.* verano
summit *noun.* **1.** cumbre, cima, cúspide **2.** punto álgido
summit *adj.* cumbre
summon *verb.* convocar
sun *noun.* sol
sun *verb.* tomar el sol
Sunday *noun.* domingo
sunlight *noun.* luz del sol
sunny *adj.* **1.** soleado **2.** alegre
sunset *noun.* puesta de sol, crepúsculo
sunshine *noun.* **1.** luz del sol **2.** alegría, jovialidad
super *adj.* estupendo, tremendo
superb *adj.* magnífico, excelente
superficial *adj.* superficial
superintendent *noun.* superintendente, director, inspector
superior *noun.* superior
superior *adj.* superior
superiority *noun.* superioridad
supermarket *noun.* supermercado
supervise *verb.* supervisar, controlar
supervision *noun.* supervisión
supervisor *noun.* supervisor
supper *noun.* cena
supplement *noun.* suplemento
supplement *verb.* complementar
supplementary *adj.* suplementario
supply *noun.* suministro, provisión, abastecimiento
—**supplies** *noun plural.* **1.** provisiones **2.** existencias
supply *verb.* proporcionar, abastecer
support *noun.* **1.** apoyo **2.** soporte
support *verb.* **1.** aguantar, sostener **2.** apoyar, respaldar **3.** corroborar, confirmar **4.** mantener
supporter *noun.* **1.** defensor, partidario **2.** seguidor
supporting *adj.* secundario
suppose *verb.* **1.** suponer **2.** creer
—**supposing** suponiendo que, en el caso de que
suppress *verb.* **1.** suprimir **2.** reprimir **3.** contener, sofocar **4.** censurar **5.** ocultar
suppression *noun.* **1.** supresión **2.** represión **3.** ocultación
supreme *adj.* supremo
sure *adj.* **1.** seguro **2.** cierto
sure *adv.* claro, por supuesto
surely *adv.* **1.** seguramente **2.** sin duda
surface *noun.* **1.** superficie, cara **2.** apariencia
surface *verb.* **1.** revestir, asfaltar **2.** salir, aflorar
surge *noun.* **1.** oleada, arranque **2.** oleaje, marejada
surge *verb.* levantarse, agitarse
surgeon *noun.* **1.** cirujano **2.** oficial médico
surgery *noun.* **1.** cirugía **2.** quirófano

surgical *adj.* quirúrgico
surplus *noun.* excedente
surprise *noun.* sorpresa
surprise *verb.* sorprender
surprised *adj.* sorprendido
surprising *adj.* sorprendente
surprisingly *adv.* sorprendentemente
surrender *noun.* rendición
surrender *verb.* **1.** rendirse **2.** rendir **3.** renunciar (a) **4.** devolver
surround *verb.* **1.** rodear **2.** cercar, sitiar
surrounding *adj.* circundante
surroundings *noun plural.* **1.** alrededores, cercanías **2.** entorno, ambiente
survey *noun.* **1.** examen, estudio **2.** encuesta **3.** reconocimiento, inspección **4.** medición
survey *verb.* **1.** mirar, contemplar **2.** estudiar, examinar **3.** encuestar **4.** reconocer, inspeccionar **5.** medir, levantar el plano
surveyor *noun.* **1.** agrimensor **2.** topógrafo **3.** perito
survival *noun.* supervivencia
survive *verb.* sobrevivir
surviving *adj.* superviviente
survivor *noun.* superviviente
suspect *noun.* sospechoso
suspect *verb.* **1.** sospechar **2.** desconfiar **3.** creer
suspect *adj.* **1.** sospechoso **2.** dudoso
suspend *verb.* **1.** suspender **2.** colgar, pender **3.** aplazar, posponer
suspension *noun.* suspensión
suspicion *noun.* **1.** sospecha **2.** pizca, atisbo
suspicious *adj.* **1.** desconfiado **2.** sospechoso
sustain *verb.* **1.** sostener, aguantar **2.** mantener, dar fuerzas
swallow *noun.* **1.** golondrina **2.** trago
swallow *verb.* **1.** tragar, engullir **2.** tragarse
swamp *noun.* pantano, ciénaga
swamp *verb.* empantanar, inundar, anegar
swan *noun.* cisne
sway *noun.* **1.** balanceo, bamboleo **2.** dominio, influencia
sway *verb.* **1.** balancear, mecer **2.** balancearse, mecerse **3.** influir, influenciar
swear *verb.* **1.** jurar **2.** blasfemar
sweat *noun.* sudor
sweat *verb.* **1.** sudar **2.** sudar la gota gorda, matarse a trabajar
sweater *noun.* suéter, jersey
Sweden *noun.* Suecia
Swedish *noun. adj.* sueco
sweep *noun.* **1.** barrido **2.** gesto/movimiento amplio **3.** batida, rastreo
sweep *verb.* **1.** barrer **2.** limpiar, recoger **3.** arrasar **4.** arrastrar, llevarse **5.** azotar, asolar **6.** deslizarse, pasar rápidamente **7.** extenderse, recorrer
sweeping *adj.* **1.** amplio **2.** aplastante, arrollador **3.** radical
sweet *noun.* caramelo, golosina
sweet *adj.* **1.** dulce **2.** fresco, sano **3.** melodioso **4.** encantador **5.** agradable **6.** mono, lindo
swell *noun.* marejada, oleaje
swell *verb.* **1.** hinchar **2.** hincharse **3.** aumentar
swell *adj.* estupendo, bárbaro, formidable
swift *noun.* vencejo
swift *adj.* rápido, veloz
swiftly *adv.* rápidamente
swim *noun.* baño
swim *verb.* **1.** nadar, flotar **2.** dar vueltas
swimming *noun.* natación
swimming *adj.* nadando, flotando
swing *noun.* **1.** balanceo, vaivén, oscilación **2.** swing (golf) **3.** swing (music) **4.** giro, viraje, cambio **5.** columpio
swing *verb.* **1.** balancearse, oscilar **2.** girar, doblar **3.** cambiar, decidir **4.** columpiarse
swinging *adj.* con mucha marcha
Swiss *noun. adj.* suizo
switch *noun.* **1.** interruptor, conmutador **2.** cambio, viraje **3.** vara, varilla
switch *verb.* **1.** cambiar **2.** desviar, trasladar
—**switch off** apagar
—**switch on** encender

Switzerland *noun.* Suiza
swollen *adj.* hinchado
swop, swap *noun.* intercambio, canje, trueque
swop, swap *verb.* intercambiar
sword *noun.* espada
sworn *adj.* **1.** declarado **2.** jurado, bajo juramento
syllable *noun.* sílaba
symbol *noun.* símbolo
symbolic *adj.* simbólico
symmetry *noun.* simetría
sympathetic *adj.* **1.** compasivo **2.** comprensivo
sympathy *noun.* **1.** compasión, lástima **2.** simpatía **3.** solidaridad, comprensión
symphony *noun.* sinfonía
symptom *noun.* síntoma
syndicate *noun.* **1.** corporación, sindicato **2.** agencia de prensa
syntax *noun.* sintaxis
synthesis *noun.* síntesis
synthetic *noun. adj.* sintético
Syria *noun.* Siria
Syrian *noun. adj.* sirio
system *noun.* **1.** sistema **2.** organismo **3.** método
systematic *adj.* sistemático
systematically *adv.* sistemáticamente

T

table *noun.* **1.** mesa **2.** tabla, cuadro
tablespoon *noun.* **1.** cuchara sopera **2.** cucharada grande
tablet *noun.* **1.** pastilla **2.** comprimido **3.** lápida
tabloid *noun.* tabloide
tack *noun.* **1.** tachuela **2.** hilván **3.** bordada, viraje **4.** rumbo, dirección
tack *verb.* **1.** clavar con tachuelas **2.** dar bordadas, virar
tackle *noun.* **1.** placaje **2.** equipo, aparejos **3.** jarcia, cordaje
tackle *verb.* **1.** agarrar, asir **2.** abordar **3.** emprender **4.** encararse con **5.** entrar (a), placar
tactical *adj.* táctico
tactics *noun plural.* táctica
tag *noun.* **1.** etiqueta, marbete **2.** cita **3.** cabo
tag *verb.* etiquetar
tail *noun.* **1.** cola **2.** cruz (coin)
tail *verb.* seguir de cerca
tailor *noun.* sastre
tailor *verb.* **1.** confeccionar, hacer a medida **2.** adaptar
take *noun.* **1.** caja, ventas, recaudación **2.** toma
take *verb.* **1.** tomar **2.** coger **3.** agarrar **4.** sacar **5.** extraer **6.** llevar **7.** llevarse **8.** anotar, apuntar **9.** aguantar, tolerar **10.** necesitar, requerir **11.** tener cabida **12.** aceptar **13.** obtener, ganar **14.** dar, estudiar **15.** medir **16.** asumir **17.** tomar a cargo de uno, encargarse de **18.** tomarse, reaccionar ante **19.** robar
—take a turn for the better/worse mejorar or empeorar, volverse mejor or peor
—take away quitar, llevarse
—take for granted dar por supuesto, dar por sentado
—take in 1. engañar **2.** acortar, achicar
—take off 1. despegar **2.** quitar, quitarse **3.** descontar
—take on 1. abordar, emprender **2.** contratar **3.** asumir
—take over tomar el poder, asumir el mando
—take up 1. llevar, ocupar **2.** subir, levantar **3.** volver, retomar
tale *noun.* **1.** historia, relato **2.** mentira, trola
talent *noun.* talento
talented *adj.* talentoso

talk *noun.* **1.** conversación, plática **2.** conferencia, charla **3.** comentario, chismorreo, cotilleo **4.** palabrería, charlatanería
—**talks** conversaciones, negociaciones
talk *verb.* **1.** hablar **2.** chismorrear
tall *adj.* alto
tan *noun.* bronceado
tan *noun. adj.* marrón claro
tan *verb.* **1.** curtir **2.** broncearse
tangible *adj.* tangible
tangle *noun.* desorden, maraña, enredo
tangle *verb.* enredar, enmarañar
tank *noun.* **1.** tanque, depósito **2.** tanque de guerra
tanker *noun.* **1.** petrolero **2.** avión cisterna
tap *noun.* **1.** golpecito, palmadita **2.** grifo
tap *verb.* **1.** explotar, utilizar **2.** pinchar, intervenir
—**tap at/on/with** *verb.* golpear ligeramente, dar una palmadita
tape *noun.* **1.** cinta **2.** cinta métrica **3.** meta
tape *verb.* **1.** grabar **2.** cerrar con una cinta, pegar con cinta adhesiva
target *noun.* blanco
tariff *noun.* **1.** lista de precios **2.** arancel
task *noun.* tarea
task force *noun.* destacamento especial
taste *noun.* **1.** gusto **2.** sabor **3.** prueba, degustación **4.** afición
taste *verb.* **1.** probar, degustar, catar **2.** saber (a) **3.** saborear **4.** experimentar, probar
tax *noun.* **1.** impuesto **2.** carga
tax *verb.* **1.** gravar, imponer contribuciones **2.** cargar, abrumar
taxation *noun.* impuestos, sistema tributario
taxi, taxi-cab *noun.* taxi
taxi *verb.* rodar por la pista
taximeter *noun.* taxímetro
taxpayer *noun.* contribuyente
tbsp *abbr.* cucharada sopera
tea *noun.* té
teacart *noun.* mesita de ruedas
teach *verb.* enseñar, dar clases
teacher *noun.* maestro, profesor
teaching *noun.* **1.** enseñanza **2.** lección **3.** doctrina
team *noun.* equipo
tear *noun.* **1.** lágrima **2.** rasgón, desgarrón, rotura
tear *verb.* **1.** romper, rasgar, despedazar **2.** romperse, rasgarse, hacerse pedazos/trizas **3.** ir/correr a toda velocidad
tease *noun.* provocador, bromista
tease *verb.* **1.** molestar, irritar **2.** provocar, picar **3.** tomar el pelo, reírse de alguien
teaspoon *noun.* **1.** cucharilla **2.** cucharadita
technical *adj.* técnico
technically *adv.* **1.** técnicamente **2.** desde el punto de vista técnico **3.** en teoría
technician *noun.* técnico
technique *noun.* técnica
technological *adj.* tecnológico
technology *noun.* tecnología
teddy (bear) *noun.* oso de peluche
tedious *adj.* tedioso, aburrido
teenage *adj.* adolescente
teenager *noun.* adolescente
tel. *abbr.* número de teléfono
telecommunications *noun plural.* telecomunicaciones
telegraph *noun.* telégrafo
telegraph *verb.* telegrafiar
telephone *noun.* teléfono
telephone *verb.* telefonear, llamar por teléfono
telescope *noun.* telescopio
telescope *verb.* encajar, meter
televise *verb.* televisar
television, TV *noun.* televisión
tell *verb.* **1.** contar **2.** decir **3.** mandar **4.** distinguir **5.** divulgar, revelar **6.** notarse, hacerse notar
telling *adj.* eficaz
temper *noun.* **1.** humor **2.** genio **3.** furia
temper *verb.* **1.** templar **2.** suavizar
temperament *noun.* temperamento
temperature *noun.* **1.** temperatura **2.** fiebre
temple *noun.* **1.** templo **2.** sien
temporarily *adv.* temporalmente

temporary *adj.* temporal
tempt *verb.* tentar
temptation *noun.* tentación
tempting *adj.* tentador
ten *noun. adj.* diez
tenant *noun.* inquilino, arrendatario
tend *verb.* **1.** tender, inclinarse, tener tendencia **2.** atender, cuidar
tendency *noun.* tendencia
tender *noun.* **1.** guardián **2.** oferta **3.** gabarra
tender *adj.* **1.** tierno **2.** sensible, delicado **3.** afectuoso
tennis *noun.* tenis
tense *noun.* tiempo
tense *verb.* tensar
tense *adj.* **1.** tenso **2.** tirante
tension *noun.* tensión
tent *noun.* tienda (de campaña)
tentative *adj.* **1.** provisorio, de prueba, provisional **2.** vacilante, tímido
tenth *noun.* décimo
term *noun.* **1.** período, etapa **2.** mandato **3.** trimestre **4.** plazo **5.** término —**terms** condiciones
term *verb.* llamar, calificar
terminal *noun. adj.* terminal
terminate *verb.* **1.** terminar, concluir **2.** terminarse
termination *noun.* fin, conclusión
terminology *noun.* terminología
terrace *noun.* terraza, bancal
terrible *adj.* terrible, espantoso
terribly *adv.* muy, extremadamente
terrific *adj.* **1.** estupendo, fabuloso **2.** tremendo, enorme
terrified *adj.* aterrorizado
terrify *verb.* aterrorizar
terrifying *adj.* aterrador, espantoso
territorial *adj.* territorial
territory *noun.* **1.** territorio **2.** especialidad, campo
terror *noun.* **1.** terror **2.** diablillo
terrorism *noun.* terrorismo
terrorist *noun.* terrorista
test *noun.* **1.** examen, test **2.** ensayo, prueba
test *verb.* **1.** probar, examinar **2.** hacer un análisis
testament *noun.* testamento
testify *verb.* **1.** declarar, atestiguar **2.** testificar
testimony *noun.* testimonio
text *noun.* texto
textbook *noun.* libro de texto
textile *noun.* textil
texture *noun.* textura
Thai *noun. adj.* tailandés
Thailand *noun.* Tailandia
than *conj. prep.* **1.** que **2.** de
thank *verb.* agradecer
thank you *interj.* ¡gracias!
thankfully *adv.* agradecidamente
thanks *interj.* ¡gracias!
thanks *noun plural.* agradecimiento
that *conj.* **1.** que **2.** para que **3.** ¡y pensar que!, ¡ojalá!
that *relative pron.* que
that *adj.* **1.** ese, esa **2.** aquel, aquella
that *adv.* tan
that *pron.* **1.** ése, ésa, eso **2.** aquél, aquélla, aquello **3.** el, la, lo
the *def. art.* el, la, los, las —**the more the better** cuanto más mejor
theater *noun.* teatro
theatrical *adj.* **1.** teatral **2.** dramático
thee *pron.* **1.** te **2.** ti
theft *noun.* robo, hurto
their *adj.* su, sus
theirs *pron.* **1.** (el) suyo, (la) suya, (los) suyos, (las) suyas **2.** de ellos, de ellas
them *pron.* **1.** los, las (direct object) **2.** les (indirect object) **3.** ellos, ellas (after prep) **4.** le, la
theme *noun.* **1.** tema **2.** asunto
themselves *pron.* **1.** se **2.** sí mismos, sí mismas **3.** ellos mismos, ellas mismas **4.** ellos solos, ellas solas
then *conj.* entonces, en ese caso
then *adj.* entonces
then *adv.* **1.** entonces **2.** en aquel momento **3.** luego, después **4.** además
theological *adj.* teológico
theology *noun.* teología
theoretical *adj.* teórico
theoretically *adj.* teóricamente
theorist *noun.* teórico

theory *noun.* teoría
therapeutic *adj.* terapéutico
therapist *noun.* terapeuta
therapy *noun.* terapia
there *interj.* **1.** venga, bueno **2.** ¿ves?
there *adv.* **1.** allí, allá, ahí **2.** en eso, en ese punto
there *pron.* haber (there is/are)
therefore *adv.* por tanto, por consiguiente
thermal *adj.* **1.** termal **2.** térmico
these *adj.* estos, estas
these *pron.* éstos, éstas
thesis *noun.* tesis
they *pron.* ellos, ellas
thick *noun.* **1.** espesor **2.** centro
thick *adj.* **1.** grueso **2.** espeso, denso **3.** numeroso **4.** cargado
thickness *noun.* densidad, espesor
thief *noun.* ladrón
thigh *noun.* muslo
thin *verb.* **1.** disminuir **2.** disiparse **3.** diluir, aclarar
thin *adj.* **1.** fino **2.** delgado **3.** aguado, poco espeso, claro **4.** ralo, escaso **5.** poco convincente, pobre
thing *noun.* **1.** cosa **2.** asunto, cuestión **3.** criatura, ser
things *noun plural.* **1.** cosas, bártulos **2.** ropa
think *noun.* reflexión, pensamiento
think *verb.* **1.** pensar, reflexionar **2.** creer **3.** opinar **4.** imaginar **5.** esperar
third *noun.* **1.** tercio **2.** tercero **3.** tres
third *adv.* en tercer lugar
thirdly *adv.* en tercer lugar
thirsty *adj.* sediento
thirteen *noun. adj.* trece
thirteenth *noun.* **1.** decimotercera parte **2.** decimotercero
thirties *noun plural.* **1.** entre los treinta y treinta y nueve **2.** años treinta
thirtieth *noun.* trigésimo
thirty *noun. adj.* treinta
this *adj.* este, esta
this *adv.* tan, así de
this *pron.* éste, ésta, esto
thorn *noun.* espina
thorough *adj.* **1.** cuidadoso, minucioso, concienzudo **2.** completo, absoluto
thoroughly *adv.* **1.** cuidadosamente, minuciosamente, concienzudamente **2.** completamente
those *adj.* **1.** esos, esas **2.** aquellos, aquellas
those *pron.* **1.** ésos, ésas **2.** aquéllos, aquéllas **3.** los, las
thou *pron.* vos, tú
though *conj.* aunque
though *adv.* sin embargo, a pesar de todo
thought *noun.* **1.** pensamiento **2.** reflexión
thoughtful *adj.* **1.** pensativo **2.** considerado, atento
thoughtfully *adv.* **1.** pensativamente **2.** con consideración
thousand *noun. adj.* mil
thread *noun.* **1.** hilo, hebra **2.** rosca
thread *verb.* **1.** enhebrar **2.** ensartar **3.** abrirse camino
threat *noun.* amenaza
threaten *verb.* amenazar
three *noun. adj.* tres
three-dimensional, 3-D *adj.* tridimensional
threshold *noun.* **1.** umbral **2.** puertas
thrift *noun.* economía, frugalidad
thrill *noun.* emoción
thrill *verb.* emocionar, conmover
thriller *noun.* obra de suspense/o
thrive *verb.* **1.** crecer **2.** prosperar
thriving *adj.* próspero, floreciente
throat *noun.* **1.** garganta **2.** cuello
throne *noun.* trono
through *prep.* **1.** por, a través de **2.** de cabo a rabo, de principio a fin, entero **3.** a causa de
through *adj.* directo
through *adv.* **1.** directamente **2.** entero, todo **3.** de un lado a otro
throughout *prep.* **1.** por todas partes **2.** durante todo
throughout *adv.* enteramente, por completo
throw *noun.* lanzamiento, tirada
throw *verb.* **1.** lanzar, tirar, echar **2.** desarzonar, desmontar **3.** confundir, desconcertar **4.** derribar

thrust *noun.* **1.** ataque, asalto **2.** empuje **3.** empujón
thrust *verb.* **1.** acometer, atacar **2.** empujar **3.** meter, hincar
thumb *noun.* pulgar
thumb (through) *verb.* **1.** hojear **2.** manosear
thunder *noun.* **1.** trueno **2.** estruendo
thunder *verb.* tronar
Thursday *noun.* jueves
thus *adv.* así
tick *noun.* **1.** garrapata **2.** tictac **3.** instante, segundo
tick *verb.* hacer tictac
ticket *noun.* **1.** billete, boleto **2.** multa **3.** etiqueta **4.** candidatura, planilla
—**one-way ticket** billete/boleto sencillo
—**round-trip ticket** billete/boleto de ida y vuelta
tide *noun.* marea
tidy *verb.* ordenar
tidy *adj.* **1.** ordenado **2.** considerable
tie *noun.* **1.** corbata **2.** lazo, vínculo **3.** empate
tie *verb.* **1.** amarrar, atar **2.** atar, anudar **3.** atarse, anudarse **4.** relacionar **5.** empatar
tiger *noun.* tigre
tight, tightly *adv.* **1.** bien cerrado **2.** apretado
tight *adj.* **1.** apretado, estrecho **2.** riguroso, estricto
tighten *verb.* **1.** apretar, tensar **2.** hacer más severo
tights *noun plural.* medias
tile *noun.* **1.** teja **2.** baldosa **3.** azulejo
tile *verb.* **1.** tejar **2.** embaldosar **3.** alicatar, revestir de azulejos
till *prep. conj.* hasta (que)
till *noun.* cajón
tilt *noun.* inclinación, ladeo
tilt *verb.* inclinar, ladear
timber *noun.* **1.** madera de construcción **2.** árboles maderables **3.** viga
time *noun.* **1.** tiempo **2.** hora **3.** momento **4.** vez **5.** época, período
time *verb.* **1.** cronometrar **2.** escoger el momento de/para **3.** planear, calcular
times *noun plural.* **1.** tiempos **2.** veces
timetable *noun.* horario
timing *noun.* **1.** cronometraje **2.** coordinación, sentido del tiempo
tin *noun.* **1.** estaño, hojalata **2.** lata
tin *adj.* de lata
tiny *adj.* minúsculo, pequeñísimo, diminuto
tip *noun.* **1.** consejo, sugerencia **2.** propina **3.** punta, cabo, extremidad
tip *verb.* **1.** inclinar **2.** ladearse, inclinarse **3.** volcar **4.** dar una propina
tire *noun.* neumático
tired *adj.* cansado
tissue *noun.* **1.** tejido **2.** pañuelo de papel
title *noun.* título
to *prep.* **1.** a **2.** hacia **3.** hasta **4.** según **5.** en **6.** contra **7.** por **8.** de
to *adv.* cerrado
toast *noun.* **1.** brindis **2.** tostada
toast *verb.* **1.** brindar por **2.** tostar
tobacco *noun.* tabaco
today *noun. adv.* hoy
toe *noun.* **1.** dedo del pie **2.** punta
together *adv.* **1.** juntos **2.** al mismo tiempo
toilet *noun.* lavabo, servicios
token *noun.* **1.** señal, prueba **2.** ficha
tolerance *noun.* tolerancia
tolerate *verb.* tolerar
toll *noun.* **1.** peaje **2.** número de víctimas, pérdidas
toll *verb.* tañer, doblar
tomato *noun.* **1.** tomate **2.** tomatera
tomb *noun.* tumba
tomorrow *noun. adv.* **1.** mañana **2.** futuro
ton *noun.* tonelada
tone *noun.* tono
tongue *noun.* **1.** lengua **2.** idioma
tonic *noun.* **1.** tónico **2.** tónica
tonight *noun. adv.* esta noche
tons *noun plural.* montones
too *adv.* **1.** demasiado, muy **2.** también
tool *noun.* instrumento
tooth *noun.* diente
top *noun.* **1.** cumbre **2.** cima **3.** copa **4.** parte superior **5.** cabeza, primer lugar

6. lo alto de 7. tapadera 8. tapón 9. blusa (corta), camiseta, top 10. peonza, trompo
top *verb.* 1. encabezar 2. cubrir, recubrir 3. coronar 4. superar, sobrepasar 5. desmochar, descabezar
top *adj.* 1. mejor, primero 2. superior, de arriba 3. máximo
topic *noun.* asunto, tema
topical *adj.* 1. actual, de actualidad 2. local
topple *verb.* 1. volcar 2. volcarse 3. derribar, derrocar
torch *noun.* 1. linterna 2. antorcha
torture *noun.* tortura
torture *verb.* torturar
toss *noun.* 1. sacudida 2. tirada, lanzamiento
toss *verb.* 1. arrojar, tirar, lanzar 2. sacudir 3. echar a cara o cruz
total *noun. adj.* total
total *verb.* sumar, ascender a
totally *adv.* totalmente
touch *noun.* 1. toque 2. roce 3. tacto 4. contacto 5. retoque 6. sello, estilo
touch *verb.* 1. tocar 2. tocarse 3. rozar 4. conmover
touching *adj.* conmovedor
tough *noun.* chulo, matón
tough *adj.* 1. fuerte 2. duro 3. resistente 4. violento, conflictivo 5. difícil, espinoso
tour *noun.* 1. viaje, excursión 2. visita 3. gira
tour *verb.* viajar
tourism *noun.* turismo
tourist *noun.* turista
tournament *noun.* torneo
tow *noun.* remolque
tow *verb.* remolcar
toward, towards *prep.* 1. hacia 2. para 3. con respecto a, para con 4. alrededor de, sobre
towel *noun.* toalla
towel *verb.* secar con toalla
tower *noun.* torre
tower *verb.* descollar, sobresalir
town *noun.* ciudad, población
toxic *adj.* tóxico
toy *noun.* juguete
toy (with) *verb.* jugar con
trace *noun.* 1. rastro, huella, vestigio 2. pizca
trace *verb.* 1. localizar, averiguar el paradero 2. trazar 3. calcar
track *noun.* 1. rastro, huella 2. camino, senda 3. pista 4. vía
track *verb.* seguir la pista, rastrear
tract *noun.* 1. extensión 2. tracto 3. folleto
tractor *noun.* tractor
trade *noun.* 1. comercio 2. negocio 3. oficio 4. industria
trade *verb.* 1. comerciar 2. cambiar, intercambiar
trader *noun.* comerciante
tradition *noun.* tradición
traditional *adj.* tradicional
traditionally *adv.* tradicionalmente
traffic *noun.* tráfico
traffic *verb.* traficar
tragedy *noun.* tragedia
tragic *adj.* trágico
trail *noun.* 1. pista, rastro 2. camino, sendero 3. reguero, estela
trail *verb.* 1. arrastrar 2. ir arrastrando los pies 3. seguir la pista (de)
trailer *noun.* 1. remolque 2. caravana 3. tráiler, avance
train *noun.* 1. tren 2. cola 3. serie, sucesión 4. séquito, comitiva 5. recua, fila, convoy
train *verb.* 1. formar, enseñar, instruir, entrenar, adiestrar 2. apuntar 3. enfocar 4. guiar 5. entrenarse
trained *adj.* cualificado, capacitado, educado, adiestrado
trainee *noun.* 1. aprendiz 2. recluta
trainer *noun.* entrenador, preparador
training *noun.* 1. entrenamiento 2. formación, instrucción, adiestramiento
trait *noun.* rasgo, característica
transaction *noun.* transacción
transcript *noun.* 1. transcripción 2. expediente
transfer *noun.* 1. traspaso, traslado 2. transferencia 3. calcomanía
transfer *verb.* 1. traspasar, trasladar 2.

trasladarse **3.** transferir **4.** pasar **5.** transmitir
transform *verb.* transformar
transformation *noun.* transformación
transit *noun.* tránsito, paso
transition *noun.* transición
transitional *adj.* transitorio
translate *verb.* traducir
translation *noun.* traducción
translator *noun.* traductor
transmission *noun.* transmisión
transmit *verb.* transmitir
transparent *adj.* transparente
transplant *noun.* trasplante, injerto
transplant *verb.* **1.** trasplantar **2.** injertar
transport *noun.* transporte
transport *verb.* transportar
transportation *noun.* transporte
trap *noun.* trampa
trap *verb.* **1.** atrapar, cazar, agarrar **2.** tender una trampa
trash *noun.* basura
—**trash can** cubo de la basura
travel *noun.* viaje, viajar
travel *verb.* **1.** viajar **2.** ir **3.** recorrer
traveler *noun.* **1.** viajero **2.** viajante
tray *noun.* bandeja
tread *noun.* **1.** paso **2.** pisada, huella **3.** escalón **4.** llanta de neumático
tread *verb.* **1.** pisar, hollar **2.** caminar, andar
treasure *noun.* tesoro
treasure *verb.* **1.** valorar **2.** guardar, atesorar
treasurer *noun.* tesorero
treat *noun.* regalo
treat *verb.* **1.** tratar **2.** invitar, convidar
treatment *noun.* **1.** trato **2.** tratamiento
treaty *noun.* tratado
tree *noun.* árbol
trek *noun.* **1.** expedición **2.** caminata
trek *verb.* caminar
tremble *noun.* temblor
tremble *verb.* temblar
tremendous *adj.* tremendo, enorme
trench *noun.* trinchera
trend *noun.* tendencia
trial *noun.* **1.** prueba, ensayo **2.** proceso, juicio **3.** aflicción, sufrimiento, desgracia
triangle *noun.* triángulo
tribal *adj.* tribal
tribe *noun.* tribu
tribunal *noun.* tribunal
tribute *noun.* tributo, homenaje
trick *noun.* truco, trampa, engaño
trick *adj.* trucado
tricky *adj.* difícil, complicado, espinoso
trigger *noun.* **1.** gatillo **2.** disparador **3.** desencadenante
trigger (off) *verb.* **1.** desencadenar, provocar **2.** hacer estallar
trillion *noun. adj.* billón
trim *noun.* corte
trim *verb.* **1.** cortar, recortar **2.** podar **3.** adornar, decorar
trim *adj.* arreglado, aseado, cuidado
trio *noun.* trío
trip *noun.* viaje, excursión, salida
trip (over/up) *verb.* **1.** tropezar **2.** ir con paso ligero
triple *noun. adj.* triple
triple *verb.* triplicar
triumph *noun.* triunfo
triumph *verb.* triunfar
triumphant *adj.* triunfante
trivial *adj.* **1.** trivial, insignificante, banal **2.** superficial, frívolo
trolley *noun.* carrito
troop *noun.* **1.** tropa **2.** grupo
troop *verb.* ir en tropel
troops *noun plural.* tropas
trophy *noun.* trofeo
tropical *adj.* tropical
trouble *noun.* **1.** problema, apuro, dificultad **2.** disturbio, conflicto, altercado **3.** enfermedad
trouble *verb.* **1.** preocupar **2.** molestar **3.** molestarse
troubled *adj.* **1.** preocupado, inquieto **2.** conflictivo
trousers *noun plural.* pantalones
trout *noun.* trucha
truce *noun.* tregua
truck *noun.* camión
true *adj.* **1.** verdadero, verídico **2.** cierto, exacto **3.** fiel, leal **4.** auténtico, real
truly *adv.* **1.** verdaderamente, realmente **2.** de verdad

trumpet *noun.* **1.** trompeta **2.** barrito
trumpet *verb.* **1.** tocar la trompeta **2.** barritar
trunk *noun.* **1.** tronco **2.** baúl **3.** trompa **4.** maletero
trust *noun.* **1.** confianza **2.** carga, cuidado **3.** responsabilidad **4.** fundación **5.** fideicomiso **6.** fondo de inversión **7.** trust, cartel
trust *verb.* **1.** confiar **2.** esperar
trustee *noun.* **1.** fideicomisario **2.** administrador
truth *noun.* verdad
try *noun.* **1.** tentativa, intento **2.** ensayo
try *verb.* **1.** intentar **2.** probar **3.** juzgar, procesar **4.** poner a prueba
trying *adj.* **1.** difícil; molesto, latoso **2.** pesado
T-shirt, tee shirt *noun.* camiseta
tube *noun.* **1.** tubo **2.** trompa **3.** metro, ferrocarril subterráneo
tuck *noun.* pliegue
tuck *verb.* **1.** meter **2.** plegar
Tuesday *noun.* martes
tug *noun.* **1.** tirón, estirón **2.** remolcador
tug *verb.* tirar (de), dar un estirón
tumble *noun.* **1.** caída, tumbo **2.** voltereta
tumble *verb.* caerse, tropezar
tumor *noun.* tumor
tune *noun.* melodía
tune *verb.* **1.** afinar **2.** sintonizar **3.** poner a punto
Tunisian *noun. adj.* tunecino
tunnel *noun.* túnel
tunnel *verb.* excavar un túnel
turbulent *adj.* turbulento
turf *noun.* césped
Turk *noun.* turco
turkey *noun.* pavo
Turkey *noun.* Turquía
Turkish *noun. adj.* turco
turmoil *noun.* caos, confusión
turn *noun.* **1.** giro **2.** vuelta **3.** curva, recodo **4.** turno **5.** número **6.** cambio
turn *verb.* **1.** girar **2.** dar media vuelta, girarse **3.** torcer **4.** doblar **5.** dirigir **6.** volver **7.** volverse **8.** convertirse **9.** enroscar, atornillar **10.** cambiar, meterse a
—turn down **1.** rechazar, rehusar **2.** bajar (el volumen)
—turn inside out volver del revés
—turn off apagar
—turn on encender, prender
—turn out **1.** producir **2.** expulsar, echar **3.** resultar **4.** concurrir, presentarse
—turn over voltear, dar la vuelta
turnover *noun.* facturación, volumen de ventas
tutor *noun.* **1.** profesor, profesor particular **2.** método
tutor *verb.* **1.** enseñar, instruir **2.** dar clases particulares
TV *abbr.* televisión
tweed *noun. adj.* tela inglesa de lana de Escocia
twelfth *noun.* duodécimo
twelve *noun. adj.* doce
twenties *noun plural.* **1.** entre veinte y treinta **2.** los años veinte
twentieth *noun.* vigésimo
twenty *noun. adj.* veinte
twice *adv.* dos veces
twin *noun.* **1.** gemelo **2.** copia
twist *noun.* **1.** torsión, giro, vuelta **2.** trenza
twist *verb.* **1.** torcer, retorcer, dar vueltas, serpentear **2.** trenzar, entrelazar **3.** enrollar
twisted *adj.* **1.** torcido **2.** deformado, contrahecho
two *noun. adj.* dos
type *noun.* **1.** tipo **2.** carácter **3.** letra
type *verb.* mecanografiar
typical *adj.* típico
typically *adv.* típicamente
typing, typewriting *noun.* mecanografía

U

ugly *adj.* **1.** feo **2.** desagradable
ulcer *noun.* úlcera
ultimate *adj.* último, final, postrero
ultimately *adv.* al final, finalmente
umbrella *noun.* paraguas
umpire *noun.* árbitro
umpire *verb.* arbitrar
unable *adj.* incapaz
unaffected *adj.* **1.** sencillo, natural **2.** inalterado, no afectado
unanimous *adj.* unánime
unanimously *adv.* unánimemente
unaware *adj.* ignorante, inconsciente
unbelievable *adj.* increíble
uncertain *adj.* incierto
uncle *noun.* tío
uncomfortable *adj.* incómodo, molesto
uncommon *adj.* raro, poco común
unconditional *adj.* incondicional
unconscious *noun.* inconsciente
unconscious *adj.* inconsciente
uncover *verb.* descubrir
under *prep.* **1.** debajo de **2.** bajo **3.** menor de, de menos de **4.** a las órdenes de **5.** de acuerdo con, según
under *adv.* por debajo
underestimate *verb.* subestimar
undergo *verb.* sufrir, padecer, pasar por
undergraduate *noun.* estudiante universitario no licenciado
underground *noun. adj.* subterráneo
underground *adv.* **1.** bajo tierra **2.** clandestinamente
underline *verb.* **1.** subrayar **2.** destacar
undermine *verb.* minar, socavar
underneath *prep. adv.* bajo, debajo de
underneath *noun.* parte inferior
understand *verb.* **1.** comprender, entender **2.** tener entendido
understandable *adj.* comprensible
understanding *noun.* **1.** inteligencia **2.** comprensión **3.** entendimiento **4.** acuerdo
understanding *adj.* comprensivo
undertake *verb.* **1.** emprender, acometer **2.** asumir, comprometerse a
undertaking *noun.* **1.** empresa, tarea **2.** promesa, garantía
undesirable *adj.* indeseable
undoubted *adj.* indudable
undoubtedly *adv.* indudablemente
undue *adj.* **1.** indebido **2.** excesivo
unduly *adv.* **1.** indebidamente **2.** excesivamente
uneasy *adj.* **1.** inquieto **2.** molesto
unemployed *noun plural.* desempleados, parados
unemployed *adj.* desempleado, parado, en paro
unemployment *noun.* desempleo, paro
uneven *adj.* desigual, irregular
unexpected *adj.* inesperado
unfair *adj.* injusto
unfamiliar *adj.* **1.** desconocido **2.** no familiarizado
unfold *verb.* **1.** desplegar, desdoblar **2.** revelar
unfortunate *adj.* **1.** desafortunado, desgraciado, desventurado **2.** infeliz, inoportuno
unfortunately *adv.* por desgracia, desgraciadamente, desafortunadamente
unhappy *adj.* **1.** infeliz **2.** inoportuno
unidentified *adj.* no identificado
unification *noun.* unificación
uniform *noun. adj.* uniforme
unify *verb.* unificar
union *noun.* **1.** unión **2.** sindicato
unique *adj.* único
unit *noun.* unidad
unite *verb.* **1.** unir, unificar **2.** unirse
united *adj.* unido
unity *noun.* unidad
universal *adj.* universal
universally *adv.* universalmente
universe *noun.* universo
university *noun.* universidad
unknown *adj.* desconocido
unless *conj.* a menos que, excepto
unlike *prep.* a diferencia de
unlike *adj.* diferente
unlikely *adj.* **1.** improbable **2.** insólito **3.** inverosímil

unlucky *adj.* **1.** desafortunado **2.** nefasto
unnatural *adj.* **1.** poco normal **2.** antinatural
unnecessary *adj.* innecesario
unpleasant *adj.* desagradable
unpopular *adj.* impopular
unprecedented *adj.* sin precedente
unreasonable *adj.* **1.** irrazonable, poco razonable **2.** excesivo
unrest *noun.* agitación
unsatisfactory *adj.* insatisfactorio
until *prep. conj.* hasta (que)
unusual *adj.* **1.** raro, poco común, extraño **2.** excepcional
unusually *adv.* excepcionalmente
unveil *verb.* descubrir, destapar
unwilling *adj.* reacio, reluctante
up *prep.* **1.** arriba de, en lo alto de **2.** a lo largo de **3.** hacia arriba
up *verb.* aumentar, elevar, subir
up *adv. adj.* **1.** arriba **2.** hacia arriba, para arriba **3.** de pie **4.** levantado **5.** erguido **6.** concluido, terminado **7.** agitado, sublevado
update *verb.* actualizar, poner al día
upgrade *noun.* mejora
upgrade *verb.* mejorar
uphold *verb.* **1.** apoyar **2.** confirmar **3.** mantener
upon *prep.* **1.** sobre **2.** al
upper *noun.* pala
upper *adj.* **1.** superior **2.** alto
upright *adj. adv.* **1.** derecho, vertical **2.** honrado
uprising *noun.* sublevación
upset *verb.* **1.** volcar **2.** desbaratar, dar al traste **3.** afectar, trastornar
upset *adj.* **1.** molesto, disgustado **2.** afligido
upstairs *noun.* piso de arriba
upstairs *adv.* arriba
up-to-date *adj.* **1.** actualizado, al día **2.** actual, moderno
upward *adj.* hacia arriba, ascendente
uranium *noun.* uranio
urban *adj.* urbano
urge *noun.* impulso, deseo
urge *verb.* **1.** instar, animar **2.** insistir, recomendar
urgency *noun.* urgencia
urgent *adj.* urgente
urgently *adv.* urgentemente
urine *noun.* orina
us *pron.* **1.** nos (direct/indirect object) **2.** nosotros, nosotras (after prep)
use *noun.* **1.** uso, utilización, empleo **2.** modo de empleo **3.** utilidad
use *verb.* **1.** usar, utilizar, emplear **2.** consumir, gastar
used *adj.* **1.** utilizado, gastado **2.** usado, de segunda mano
useful *adj.* útil
usefulness *noun.* utilidad
useless *adj.* inútil
user *noun.* usuario
usual *adj.* habitual, acostumbrado, común
usually *adv.* por lo general, normalmente
utility *noun.* **1.** utilidad **2.** servicio público
utilize *verb.* utilizar
utmost *adj.* extremo, mayor
utter *verb.* pronunciar, articular
utter *adj.* absoluto, total
utterly *adv.* completamente, totalmente
U-turn *noun.* cambio de sentido

V

v., vs. *abbr.* contra, versus
vacancy *noun.* **1.** vacante **2.** vacío
vacant *adj.* **1.** libre **2.** vacío
vacation *noun.* vacaciones
vaccine *noun.* vacuna
vacuum *noun.* **1.** vacío **2.** aspiradora
vacuum *verb.* pasar la aspiradora
vague *adj.* vago
vaguely *adv.* vagamente, un poco
vain *adj.* **1.** vanidoso, presumido **2.** vano, inútil
vale *noun.* valle
valid *adj.* válido
valley *noun.* valle
valuable *adj.* valioso
value *noun.* **1.** valor, importancia **2.** precio
value *verb.* **1.** valorar **2.** tasar
valued *adj.* valioso, precioso
values *noun plural.* valores
valve *noun.* **1.** válvula **2.** lámpara
van *noun.* camioneta
vanish *verb.* desvanecerse, desaparecer
vapor *noun.* vapor
variable *noun.* variable
variable *adj.* variable, inestable
variation *noun.* variación
varied *adj.* variado
variety *noun.* **1.** variedad **2.** surtido **3.** (espectáculo de) variedades
various *adj.* **1.** diverso, vario **2.** diferente
vary *verb.* variar
vase *noun.* jarrón, florero
vast *adj.* vasto, inmenso
vat *noun.* tinaja, cuba
vegetable *noun.* **1.** verdura, hortaliza **2.** vegetal
vegetarian *noun.* vegetariano
vegetation *noun.* vegetación
vehicle *noun.* vehículo
veil *noun.* velo
veil *verb.* velar, cubrir con un velo
vein *noun.* vena, nervio
velocity *noun.* velocidad
velvet *noun. adj.* terciopelo
vendor *noun.* vendedor, tendero
Venezuela *noun.* Venezuela
Venezuelan *noun. adj.* Venezuela
ventilation *noun.* ventilación
venture *noun.* empresa arriesgada, aventura
venture *verb.* **1.** aventurar **2.** atreverse **3.** arriesgar
veranda(h) *noun.* porche
verb *noun.* verbo
verbal *adj.* verbal
verdict *noun.* veredicto
verge *noun.* margen, borde
verge on *verb.* rayar en
versatile *adj.* **1.** versátil, polifacético **2.** flexible
verse *noun.* **1.** estrofa **2.** versículo **3.** verso
version *noun.* versión
versus *prep.* contra
vertical *adj.* vertical
very *adj.* **1.** justo, mismo **2.** extremo, final **3.** sólo, mero
very *adv.* **1.** muy **2.** completamente **3.** exactamente
vessel *noun.* **1.** recipiente, vasija **2.** nave, buque
vest *noun.* **1.** camiseta **2.** chaleco
veteran *noun. adj.* veterano
veterinary *adj.* veterinario
veto *noun.* veto
veto *verb.* **1.** vetar **2.** prohibir
via *prep.* vía, por
vicar *noun.* **1.** párroco **2.** vicario
vice *noun.* vicio
vicinity *noun.* vecindad, proximidad, inmediaciones
vicious *adj.* **1.** vicioso **2.** cruel, malintencionado
victim *noun.* víctima
victor *noun.* vencedor, ganador
Victorian *noun. adj.* victoriano
victory *noun.* victoria
video *noun.* vídeo
video *verb.* grabar en vídeo
videotape *noun.* cinta de vídeo
videotape *verb.* grabar en vídeo

view *noun.* **1.** vista **2.** opinión, parecer
view *verb.* ver, examinar
viewer *noun.* **1.** espectador **2.** visor
viewpoint *noun.* punto de vista
vigor *noun.* vigor
vigorous *adj.* vigoroso
vigorously *adv.* vigorosamente
villa *noun.* chalet, casa de campo, villa, quinta
village *noun.* pueblo
villager *noun.* habitante del pueblo, aldeano
vine *noun.* **1.** vid **2.** parra **3.** trepadora
vinegar *noun.* vinagre
vineyard *noun.* viña, viñedo
vintage *noun.* **1.** cosecha **2.** añada
violence *noun.* violencia
violent *adj.* violento
violently *adv.* violentamente
violet *noun.* violeta
violin *noun.* violín
virgin *noun.* virgen
virtual *adj.* virtual
virtually *adv.* prácticamente
virtue *noun.* virtud
virus *noun.* virus
virus *adj.* vírico
visa *noun.* visado
vise, vice *noun.* torno de banco
visibility *noun.* visibilidad
visible *adj.* visible
vision *noun.* **1.** visión **2.** visión (de futuro) **3.** vista
visit *noun.* visita
visit *verb.* visitar, ir a
visitor *noun.* **1.** visita **2.** turista, visitante
visual *adj.* visual
visually *adv.* visualmente
vital *adj.* vital
vitamin *noun.* vitamina
vivid *adj.* **1.** vivo, intenso **2.** despierto, activo
vividly *adv.* intensamente, vivamente
vocabulary *noun.* **1.** vocabulario **2.** léxico
vocal *adj.* **1.** vocal **2.** hablador, locuaz **3.** ruidoso
vogue *noun.* moda
voice *noun.* voz
voice *verb.* **1.** expresar **2.** sonorizar
voiced *adj.* sonoro
void *noun.* vacío
void *adj.* nulo, inválido
—void of vacío, carente
volcanic *adj.* volcánico
volcano *noun.* volcán
volt *noun.* voltio
voltage *noun.* voltaje
volume *noun.* volumen
voluntarily *adv.* voluntariamente
voluntary *adj.* **1.** voluntario **2.** benéfico
volunteer *noun.* voluntario
volunteer *verb.* **1.** ofrecerse voluntario **2.** ofrecer, expresar
vote *noun.* **1.** voto **2.** derecho de voto
vote *verb.* votar
voter *noun.* votante, elector
voucher *noun.* vale, bono
vow *noun.* voto, promesa
vow *verb.* jurar, prometer
voyage *noun.* viaje, travesía
voyage *verb.* viajar
vulnerability *noun.* vulnerabilidad
vulnerable *adj.* vulnerable

W

W *abbr.* vatio
wage *verb.* hacer, emprender, llevar a cabo
wage(s) *noun plural.* salario, sueldo
wagon *noun.* **1.** carro **2.** furgoneta
waist *noun.* **1.** cintura, talle **2.** parte estrecha
wait *noun.* espera
wait (for) *verb.* esperar, aguardar —**wait on** servir
waiter *noun.* camarero
wake *noun.* estela
wake *verb.* **1.** despertar **2.** despertarse
Wales *noun.* Gales
walk *noun.* **1.** paseo, caminata **2.** andares, modo de andar **3.** itinerario, ruta
walk *verb.* **1.** andar, caminar **2.** pasear, sacar a paseo **3.** ir a pie, ir caminando
walker *noun.* paseante, peatón, excursionista
wall *noun.* **1.** pared **2.** muro, tapia, muralla
wall *verb.* amurallar
wallet *noun.* cartera, billetera
wallpaper *noun.* **1.** papel pintado **2.** fondo de escritorio
wallpaper *verb.* empapelar
wander *noun.* paseo
wander *verb.* **1.** pasear **2.** errar, vagar
want *noun.* **1.** deseo **2.** pobreza, miseria **3.** falta, ausencia, escasez
want *verb.* **1.** querer **2.** desear **3.** necesitar, precisar, requerir **4.** carecer de **5.** faltar
wanted *adj.* se busca
war *noun.* guerra
war *verb.* guerrear
ward *noun.* **1.** sala, pabellón **2.** pupilo
warden *noun.* **1.** director **2.** alcaide
wardrobe *noun.* **1.** guardarropa, ropero **2.** vestuario
warehouse *noun.* almacén, depósito
warfare *noun.* guerra, arte militar
warm *verb.* **1.** calentar **2.** entusiasmarse (con)
warm *adj.* **1.** caliente **2.** tibio, templado, cálido **3.** de abrigo, abrigado **4.** simpático, afable
warmly *adv.* **1.** calurosamente, efusivamente **2.** acaloradamente **3.** bien abrigado
warmth *noun.* calor
warn *verb.* advertir, avisar, prevenir
warning *noun.* **1.** advertencia **2.** aviso
warning *adj.* de aviso
warrant *noun.* orden judicial
warrant *verb.* justificar
warren *noun.* madriguera, conejera
warrior *noun.* guerrero
wartime *noun.* tiempo de guerra
wary *adj.* cauteloso, cauto, prudente
wash *noun.* **1.** lavado **2.** baño **3.** colada, ropa sucia **4.** chapoteo **5.** capa **6.** estela
wash *verb.* **1.** lavar, fregar, bañar **2.** lavarse **3.** chapotear **4.** arrastrar, llevarse
washing *noun.* **1.** lavado **2.** colada, ropa sucia
waste *noun.* **1.** residuos **2.** desperdicio, derroche **3.** terreno baldío, yermo
waste *verb.* desperdiciar, malgastar, derrochar, perder
watch *noun.* **1.** reloj (de pulsera) **2.** vigilancia **3.** guardia, vigía, centinela
watch *verb.* **1.** mirar, ver **2.** observar **3.** vigilar, cuidar **4.** esperar **5.** acechar
water *noun.* agua
water *verb.* **1.** regar **2.** abrevar, dar de beber **3.** hacerse la boca agua **4.** llorar
waters *noun plural.* aguas
watt *noun.* vatio
wave *noun.* **1.** ola **2.** onda **3.** gesto con la mano
wave *verb.* **1.** ondear, agitar, blandir **2.** saludar (con la mano)
wax *noun.* **1.** cera **2.** lacre
wax *verb.* **1.** encerar **2.** crecer (moon)
way *noun.* **1.** camino **2.** dirección **3.** viaje, travesía **4.** ruta, vía **5.** distancia **6.** manera, modo, forma **7.** costumbre **8.** sentido

—**way of life** modo de vida
way *adv.* muy, mucho
we *pron.* nosotros, nosotras
weak *adj.* **1.** débil **2.** endeble, frágil **3.** aguado, diluido **4.** pobre, poco convincente **5.** sin gracia, soso
weaken *verb.* **1.** debilitar **2.** debilitarse **3.** flaquear
weakness *noun.* debilidad
wealth *noun.* **1.** fortuna, riqueza **2.** abundancia
wealthy *adj.* rico
weapon *noun.* arma
wear *noun.* **1.** ropa **2.** uso **3.** desgaste, deterioro
wear *verb.* **1.** vestir **2.** llevar, llevar puesto **3.** tener, lucir **4.** desgastarse **5.** durar, aguantar
wearily *adv.* con cansancio
wearing *adj.* agotador, cansado, pesado
weary *verb.* **1.** cansar **2.** cansarse
weary *adj.* cansado, agotado
weather *noun.* tiempo, clima
weather *verb.* **1.** erosionar, desgastar **2.** resistir, aguantar, soportar
weave *verb.* **1.** tejer, trenzar **2.** tramar, crear, inventar **3.** zigzaguear, serpentear
web *noun.* **1.** tela **2.** tejido **3.** membrana interdigital
wed *verb.* casarse (con)
wedding *noun.* boda
wedge *noun.* **1.** cuña **2.** calza **3.** porción, pedazo
wedge *verb.* **1.** acuñar, meter cuñas **2.** calzar
Wednesday *noun.* miércoles
weed *noun.* mala hierba
weed *verb.* escardar, desherbar
week *noun.* semana
weekend *noun.* fin de semana
weekly *noun.* semanario
weekly *adj.* semanal
weekly *adv.* semanalmente, cada semana
weep *verb.* llorar
weigh *verb.* **1.** pesar **2.** sopesar
weight *noun.* **1.** peso **2.** pesa
weight *verb.* cargar
weird *adj.* extraño, raro
welcome *noun.* bienvenida, acogida, recepción
welcome *verb.* dar la bienvenida, recibir con gusto
welcome *adj. interj.* bienvenido
welcoming *adj.* acogedor
welfare *noun.* **1.** bienestar **2.** asistencia social
well *interj.* **1.** bueno **2.** bien, pues **3.** ¡vaya!, ¡anda!
well *noun.* **1.** pozo **2.** hueco
well *verb.* brotar
well *adj.* **1.** bien **2.** bien de salud
well *adv.* **1.** bien **2.** adecuadamente
—**as well** también
well-being *noun.* bienestar
well-known *adj.* conocido, famoso
Welsh *noun. adj.* galés
west *noun.* oeste
west *adj.* **1.** oeste **2.** del oeste
west *adv.* al oeste
West Indian *noun. adj.* antillano
western *noun.* western
western *adj.* del oeste
wet *noun.* **1.** humedad **2.** lluvia
wet *verb.* mojarse
wet *adj.* **1.** mojado **2.** lluvioso
whale *noun.* ballena
wharf *noun.* muelle
what *relative pron.* **1.** lo que **2.** el que, la que, los que, las que
what *pron. adj.* **1.** qué **2.** cuánto
whatever *relative adj. relative pron.* todo lo que
whatever *adj. pron.* **1.** cualquier, cualquiera **2.** cuanto
whatever *adj.* en absoluto
whatever *pron.* qué
whatsoever *adj.* en absoluto, para nada
wheat *noun.* trigo
wheel *noun.* **1.** rueda **2.** volante
wheel *verb.* **1.** conducir **2.** girar **3.** revolotear
wheelchair *noun.* silla de ruedas
when *conj.* **1.** cuando **2.** si
when *adv.* cuando
whenever *adv. conj.* cuando, siempre que

where *adv. relative pron.* dónde
whereabouts *noun.* paradero
whereabouts *adv.* dónde
whereas *conj.* mientras
whereby *relative pron.* por lo cual
wherever *relative pron.* **1.** dondequiera que **2.** donde
wherever *adv.* donde sea
whether *conj.* si
which *relative adj. relative pron.* que
which *adj. pron.* cuál
whichever *relative adj. relative pron.* **1.** cualquier **2.** el que, la que
while, whilst *conj.* **1.** mientras **2.** aunque
while *noun.* rato, momento
whip *noun.* **1.** látigo **2.** azote
whip *verb.* **1.** azotar, fustigar **2.** batir, montar **3.** moverse rápidamente
whisk *noun.* **1.** sacudida, movimiento rápido **2.** batidora
whisk *verb.* **1.** llevar rápidamente **2.** batir
whiskey *noun.* whisky
whisper *noun.* susurro
whisper *verb.* **1.** susurrar, cuchichear, hablar en voz baja **2.** murmurar
whistle *noun.* **1.** silbido, pitido **2.** silbato, pito
whistle *verb.* **1.** silbar **2.** pitar **3.** pasar silbando
white *noun.* **1.** blanco **2.** clara (de huevo) **3.** blanco de los ojos
white *adj.* **1.** blanco **2.** con leche
who *relative pron.* **1.** que **2.** el que, la que, los que, las que
who *pron.* quién, quiénes
whoever *relative pron.* quien, quienquiera que, el que
whoever *pron.* **1.** quienquiera que, cualquiera que **2.** quién
whole *noun.* **1.** todo **2.** totalidad
whole *adj.* entero, íntegro, todo
wholesale *adj. adv.* **1.** al por mayor **2.** en masa, indiscriminado
wholly *adv.* completamente
whom *relative pron.* **1.** que, quien, quienes **2.** a quien, a quienes **3.** al que, a la que, a los que, a las que **4.** de que
whom *pron.* a quién, a quiénes
whose *relative adj. relative pron.* cuyo, cuya, cuyos, cuyas
whose *adj. pron.* de quién, de quiénes
why *adv. relative pron.* por qué
wicked *adj.* malvado, cruel
wicket *noun.* **1.** terreno **2.** entrada, turno
wide *adj.* **1.** ancho, grande **2.** de largo **3.** amplio, extenso **4.** variado, diverso
wide *adv.* completamente
widely *adv.* ampliamente
widen *verb.* ensanchar, ampliar, extender
widespread *adj.* extendido, generalizado
widow *noun.* viuda
widow *verb.* enviudar
width *noun.* anchura
wife *noun.* esposa, mujer
wig *noun.* peluca
wild *adj.* **1.** salvaje **2.** bravío **3.** agreste **4.** furioso, borrascoso **5.** loco, alocado **6.** disparatado, descabellado, desorbitado **7.** precipitado, impetuoso **8.** colérico, frenético
wilderness *noun.* **1.** desierto **2.** monte **3.** tierra virgen
wildlife *noun.* fauna
wildly *adv.* salvajemente, furiosamente, locamente
will *noun.* **1.** voluntad, albedrío **2.** testamento
will *verb.* **1.** (expressing future) **2.** querer, desear **3.** (expressing willingness) **4.** soler, acostumbrar (expressing habits)
willing *adj.* complaciente, dispuesto
willingness *noun.* buena voluntad
win *noun.* victoria
win *verb.* **1.** ganar **2.** ganarse
wind *noun.* **1.** viento, aire **2.** aliento **3.** gases, flato
wind *verb.* **1.** dejar sin aliento, cortar la respiración **2.** enrollar **3.** ovillar **4.** serpentear, zigzaguear **5.** dar cuerda
wind *adj.* de viento
winding *adj.* tortuoso
window *noun.* ventana, ventanilla
windy *adj.* de mucho viento, ventoso
wine *noun.* vino
wing *noun.* **1.** ala **2.** aleta **3.** extremo, banda **4.** escuadrón

winger *noun.* extremo
wings *noun plural.* bastidores
winner *noun.* ganador, vencedor
winning *adj.* **1.** ganador, vencedor, premiado **2.** encantador, cautivador, irresistible
winter *noun.* invierno
wipe *noun.* lavado, fregado
wipe *verb.* **1.** limpiar **2.** secar, enjugar
wire *noun. adj.* **1.** alambre, cable **2.** hilo **3.** telégrafo **4.** telegrama
wire *verb.* **1.** atar con alambre **2.** enviar un telegrama **3.** telegrafiar
wireless *noun.* radio
wisdom *noun.* sabiduría
wise *adj.* **1.** sabio **2.** sensato, juicioso
wish *noun.* deseo
—**wishes** *noun plural.* saludos, recuerdos
wish *verb.* **1.** desear **2.** querer
wit *noun.* **1.** agudeza, ingenio, chispa, gracia **2.** persona salada, chistoso, ingenioso **3.** juicio, inteligencia
witch *noun.* bruja
with *prep.* **1.** con **2.** junto con **3.** de **4.** a
withdraw *verb.* **1.** retirar **2.** retirarse
withdrawal *noun.* retirada
withdrawn *adj.* reservado, introvertido
withhold *verb.* negar, rehusar
within *prep.* dentro de
within *adv.* dentro, en el interior
without *prep.* sin
witness *noun.* testigo
witness *verb.* **1.** presenciar, ver **2.** firmar como testigo
witty *adj.* ingenioso, agudo, salado, gracioso
wolf *noun.* lobo
wolf *verb.* zampar
woman *noun.* mujer
wonder *noun.* **1.** admiración, asombro **2.** maravilla, milagro
wonder *verb.* **1.** sorprenderse, extrañarse **2.** preguntarse
wonderful *adj.* maravilloso
wonderfully *adv.* maravillosamente
woo *verb.* cortejar
wood *noun. adj.* **1.** madera **2.** palo de madera
wooden *adj.* de madera
woodland *noun.* bosque
woods *noun.* bosque
wool *noun. adj.* lana
woolen, woollen *adj.* de lana
word *noun.* **1.** palabra **2.** noticia
word *verb.* expresar
wording *noun.* redacción, expresión
work *noun.* **1.** trabajo **2.** obra
work *verb.* **1.** trabajar **2.** tener empleo **3.** funcionar **4.** dar resultados **5.** progresar, desarrollar **6.** volverse **7.** fabricar
worker *noun.* **1.** trabajador **2.** obrero
workforce *noun.* mano de obra
working class *noun.* proletariado
works *noun plural.* **1.** mecanismo **2.** obras, acciones **3.** fábrica
workshop *noun.* taller
world *noun.* **1.** mundo **2.** inmenso
worldwide *adj.* mundial, universal
worldwide *adv.* mundialmente, universalmente
worm *noun.* gusano, lombriz
worm *verb.* **1.** deslizarse, insinuarse **2.** sacar, sonsacar, ganarse la confianza de alguien
worn *adj.* desgastado, deteriorado
worried *adj.* preocupado
worry *noun.* preocupación
worry *verb.* **1.** preocupar **2.** preocuparse **3.** molestar, estorbar **4.** acosar, perseguir, atacar
worse *adj. adv.* peor
worse *pron.* lo peor
worsen *verb.* empeorar
worship *noun.* adoración, veneración
worship *verb.* **1.** adorar **2.** rendir culto
worst *adj. adv.* peor
worst *pron.* lo peor
worth *noun.* valor
worth *adj.* **1.** que vale, que tiene un valor de **2.** digno de, merecedor de, que merece la pena
worthwhile *adj.* que vale/merece la pena
worthy *noun.* prócer, dignitario
worthy *adj.* **1.** noble **2.** digno, merecedor
—**worthy of** merecedor/digno de
would *verb.* **1.** (past tense of will) **2.** (speaking of something that will, may or might happen) **3.** (politely expressing

an opinion) **4.** (expressing annoyance)
would-be *adj.* **1.** aspirante **2.** frustrado
wound *noun.* herida
wound *verb.* herir
wounded *noun plural.* heridos
wounded *adj.* herido
wrap *noun.* chal
wrap *verb.* **1.** enrollar **2.** envolver
wreck *noun.* **1.** restos **2.** ruina, cacharro **3.** naufragio
wreck *verb.* destruir, hacer pedazos, hundir
wretched *adj.* **1.** miserable **2.** maldito
wrist *noun.* muñeca
write *verb.* escribir
writer *noun.* escritor
writing *noun.* escritura
writings *noun plural.* escrito, obra escrita
written *adj.* escrito
wrong *noun.* mal
wrong *verb.* ser injusto con, juzgar, agraviar
wrong *adj.* **1.** equivocado, erróneo, incorrecto **2.** malo **3.** inadecuado, impropio, inoportuno **4.** que no va bien, que no funciona
wrong *adv.* mal, incorrectamente
wrongly *adv.* **1.** incorrectamente **2.** injustamente

X, Y, Z

xenophobe *noun.* xenófobo
xenophobia *noun.* xenofobia
xenophobic *adj.* xenófobo
X-ray *noun.* radiografía
X-ray *verb.* hacer una radiografía
yacht *noun.* yate
yard *noun.* **1.** yarda **2.** patio **3.** recinto
yarn *noun.* **1.** hilo **2.** cuento
year *noun.* año
yell *noun.* grito, alarido
yell *verb.* gritar, dar alaridos
yellow *verb.* amarillear
yellow *noun. adj.* amarillo
yen *noun.* yen
yes *interj.* sí
yesterday *noun. adv.* ayer
yet *conj.* pero, aunque
yet *adv.* todavía, aún
yield *noun.* cosecha, rendimiento
yield *verb.* **1.** ceder **2.** producir
you *pron.* **1.** tú, vosotros, vosotras, usted, ustedes (subject) **2.** se, uno (impersonal subject) **3.** te, ti, os (object) **4.** la, le, lo, los, las (direct object) **5.** le, les (indirect object)
young *noun plural.* crías
young *adj.* joven
youngster *noun.* joven
your *adj.* **1.** tu, tus **2.** vuestro, vuestra, vuestros, vuestras **3.** su, sus
yours *pron.* **1.** (el) tuyo, (la) tuya, (los) tuyos, (las) tuyas **2.** (el) suyo, (la) suya, (los) suyos, (las) suyas **3.** (el) vuestro, (la) vuestra, (los) vuestros, (las) vuestras —**yours faithfully/sincerely/truly** le saluda atentamente (letters)
yourself *pron.* **1.** te, se **2.** tú mismo, usted mismo, tú misma, usted misma
yourselves *pron.* **1.** os, se **2.** vosotros mismos, ustedes mismos, vosotras mismas, ustedes mismas
youth *noun.* **1.** juventud **2.** joven
youthful *adj.* **1.** joven **2.** juvenil
yuan *noun.* yuan
Zambia *noun.* Zambia
zero *noun.* **1.** cero **2.** hora cero
Zimbabwe *noun.* Zimbabue
zinc *noun.* cinc
zipper *noun.* bragueta
zone *noun.* zona
zoo *noun.* zoo, parque zoológico
zoom *noun.* zumbido
zoom *verb.* pasar volando